MEDIA
RESEARCH
METHODS

D1078027

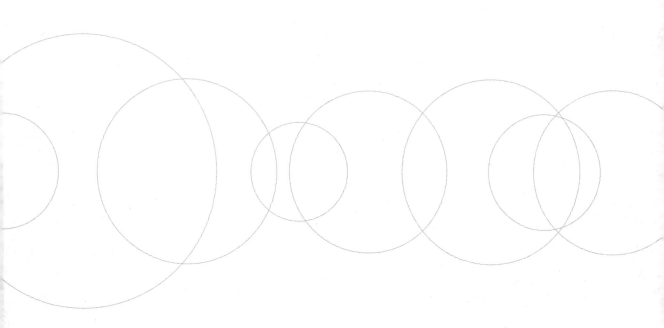

MEDIA
RESEARCH
METHODS

Understanding Metric and Interpretive Approaches

JAMES A. ANDERSON

UNIVERSITY OF UTAH

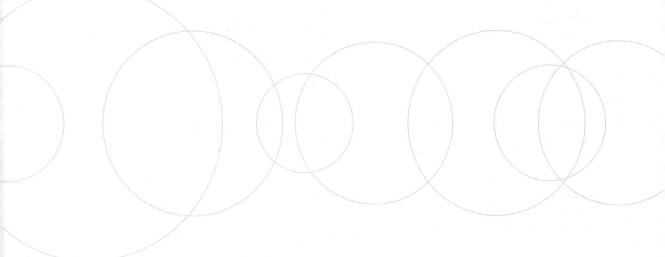

Los Angeles | London | New Delhi
Singapore | Washington DC

Los Angeles | London | New Delhi
Singapore | Washington DC

FOR INFORMATION:

SAGE Publications, Inc.
2455 Teller Road
Thousand Oaks, California 91320
E-mail: order@sagepub.com

SAGE Publications Ltd.
1 Oliver's Yard
55 City Road
London EC1Y 1SP
United Kingdom

SAGE Publications India Pvt. Ltd.
B 1/I 1 Mohan Cooperative Industrial Area
Mathura Road, New Delhi 110 044
India

SAGE Publications Asia-Pacific Pte. Ltd.
33 Pekin Street #02-01
Far East Square
Singapore 048763

Acquisitions Editor: Matthew Byrnie
Associate Editor: Nathan Davidson
Editorial Assistant: Elizabeth J. Borders
Copy Editor: Melinda Masson
Typesetter: C&M Digitals (P) Ltd.
Proofreader: Annette R. Van Deusen
Indexer: Diggs Publication Services
Cover Designer: Janet Kiesel
Marketing Manager: Liz Thornton
Permissions: Karen Ehrmann

Copyright © 2012 by SAGE Publications, Inc.

Printed in the United States of America

Library of Congress Cataloging-in-Publication Data

Anderson, James A.

Media research methods : understanding metric and interpretive approaches / James A. Anderson.

p. cm.
Includes bibliographical references and indexes.

ISBN 978-1-4129-9956-4 (pbk.)

1. Mass media—Research—Methodology. I. Title.

P91.3.A58 2012
302.2301—dc22   2011011487

This book is printed on acid-free paper.

11 12 13 14 15 10 9 8 7 6 5 4 3 2 1

Brief Contents

Contents

2 Mapping the Mediascape 23

3 Methods of Exploration: Asking Questions 37

4 Methods of Exploration: Finding Answers   63

SECTION II: FOUNDATIONS OF RESEARCH PRACTICE   81

5 From Concepts to Data   83

6 Research Questions and Hypotheses — 106

7 Literatures and Databases — 133

SECTION III: DESIGNING PROTOCOLS IN METRIC RESEARCH — 157

8 Sampling — 159

9 Statistics and Statistical Analysis   181

10 Designing Surveys   218

11 Protocols for Experiments 239

14 Critical Interpretive Methods: Social Meanings and Media Texts   323

15 Ethnographic Methods   351

16 An Excursion Into Writing   374

Preface

This book is a coming-of-age story about managing a career conducting and teaching research in an era of radical changes in methodology. Each change seems to be ushered in with great promise, and although there are some benefits gained by the discipline, the basic questions remain unanswered. Each new method presents itself as a solution to the ills that plagued the previous one, and yet upon close examination, the glosses, contradictions, and improbabilities begin to appear. Ideologues from every side attempt to advance their own agenda by pointing out the weaknesses of others.

Nonetheless, this is not the story we tell our students. In the classroom, we are typically the wizards of science and scholarship; our discipline is really the best; and the answers, if not in hand, are there for the next study that comes along. Our textbooks consistently present this picture, often directly but certainly in the silences, in what authors choose to praise and refuse to criticize. I wrote this book because I thought it was time to grow up.

This is neither a neutral nor a dogmatic text. It adopts a critical point of view that is both postmodern and constructionist and does not shy away from noting the glosses, compromises, and contradictions that allow research and scholarship to move forward, even as they are imperfectly developed and executed. Consequently, this text is not a "Yellow Brick Road" book where all problems will be solved if one just follows the directed path. At the same time, it attempts to identify the moments when that positional voice is explicitly speaking in order that students may decide on its value and instructors can point out alternative points of view. It offers no more comfort or distress to either side of the metric-interpretive boundary. I use both methodologies extensively and have an experienced practitioner's understanding of the strengths and weaknesses of each.

I also believe the text is grounded in a realist view of the effectiveness of communication research. That view is that our approaches have a low level of instrumentality, which is a central reason why there are so many different methodological approaches available. No single method or set of methods has been able to provide compelling answers to the issues that have been before us from ancient thought to the present. This is a book neither of myths nor of method advocacy. It is a book for grown-ups.

READERS AND COURSES

This book is designed for the reader who has had some instruction and, perhaps, some experience in doing research and is now ready to put together both the methods and the issues of research and scholarship. Its presumed reader may be an upper-division undergraduate about to go into a corporate world under the influence of Six Sigma data-based management that has also become more and more dependent on the interpretive analysis of its customers and clients. Or that reader might be the entering graduate student struggling with the great variations of research methodologies available to the academic researcher today. In either case, this book provides the reader with an exploration of what is available in sufficient detail that actual research can be produced from either a metric (quantitative) or an interpretive (qualitative) perspective.

The book begins with an overview of the study of media, is filled with examples from media, and reviews considerable research in media. It is most at home in journalism, media studies, mediated communication, and all the other disciplinary forms that house the study of media. It works in methods courses that are beyond the introduction to research or as a more sophisticated introduction to research and scholarship for the graduate student.

FEATURES AND ORGANIZATION

I've attempted a conversational style throughout, pulling the reader in with comments and stories that present the process of scholarship as a human endeavor in which, for the most part, we struggle to do our best but are continually faced with the limitations of time and money. The compromises we make are real and have consequences for the quality of the work but are necessary nonetheless. The message is that this is what we have, and it may be as good as it gets.

Each chapter begins with a preview that consists of an overview paragraph, a list of the major topics, and a set of terms that are in use and may be unfamiliar to the readers. Each chapter ends with a "So what?" paragraph ("Why Does It Matter?"), a list of the points to remember, additional points for discussion, and a reference or two for further reading. In each of these sections, I have attempted to offer a little different slant—an expansion, if you will, of the main text. It's not throwaway writing. The issues for further discussion are deliberately provocative. They often challenge typical practice or even the position taken in the main text of the chapter. This reflexivity is a postmodern strategy to leave things that are fundamentally unsettled unresolved. The push is always toward complexity and nuance.

The book is divided into four parts: overview, foundational practices, metric protocols, and interpretive scholarship. The overview section starts with two discussions. The first takes up the disciplinary differences that exist within the research and scholarship directed toward media; the second focuses on the methodological differences and their epistemological foundations. The section then takes up the process of research, moving through the classes of problems to the processes that develop an actual problem for study. The last chapter of this section works through metric, interpretive, critical-empirical hybrids, and the mixed methods of qualitative-quantitative combinations.

The foundational practices section, as one might expect, works through the activities that any research has to take up: making the move from theory to analysis; dealing with issues of validity and trustworthiness; developing the research focus or topic; developing the research question or hypothesis; and, in the third chapter of this section, describing practices appropriate to contemporary literatures and databases.

The metric section deals with the practices of quantitative research. Its four chapter topics are sampling, statistical analysis, surveys, and experimental protocols. In this section, I have adopted a Monte Carlo approach assuming that every student will be able to put together the resources to connect to useful websites and to have a basic data handling application such as Excel or Calc available. This approach is based on the assumption that media students do not always have sufficient mathematical background to address the issues in metric research, but they can see those issues in action with constructed data sets.

The interpretive section starts with traditional content analysis in order to provide a side-by-side comparison of metric coding and interpretive coding. The purpose is to lower the rhetoric and to raise the clarity of understanding of the differences between them. These twin chapters also adopt the position that a text is a text. It does not matter if the text is industrially produced content or the responses of participants in interviews or narrative constructions. Coding has to address the same issues throughout. The second set of two chapters steps clearly over the metric-interpretive boundary into the critical-empirical hybrid of textual analysis for the first and then to the domain of ethnography for the second.

The last chapter of the book returns to a foundational practice: writing and its deep preparation in foundational reading. The approach is not toward the one-off writer or sometime scholar, but to the person who sees her or his career filled with processes of writing and scholarship.

AUXILIARY FEATURES

The website developed for this text provides both instructor and student support materials. Professor Janet Colvin at Utah Valley University has developed lecture notes in the form of detailed chapter outlines, along with PowerPoint presentations, for each chapter. Professor Nancy Tobler, also of Utah Valley, has written a set of test questions in both multiple choice and short-answer essay forms.

The development of student support materials was based on strong evidence that most students have access to the Internet in the locations where they study. Consequently, the student materials are designed to provide demonstrations of the concepts and techniques presented in the text. My experience is that students learn much more and have a deeper understanding of what they learn by reading *and* doing rather than just one or the other. These exercises build on one another so the student can prepare a substantial portfolio of work that can be evaluated as a demonstration of learning achievements and outcomes.

Visit **www.sagepub.com/andersonmrm** to access the online resources for instructors and students.

Acknowledgments

N o book finds its way without a lot of help. My thanks go to Professor Janet Colvin, who read multiple drafts and offered support throughout the project. I wish to thank my graduate students and colleagues at Utah: James Bunker, Autumn Garrison, and Keith Massie, along with Professors Glen Feighery and Jim Fisher. Each read drafts and gave the gift of insightful criticism. Thanks too are due to the students of the undergraduate and graduate research classes who helped refine the demonstrations and Monte Carlo exercises. I offer my deep appreciation to the reviewers, Barbara L. Baker (University of Central Missouri), Brad J. Bushman (University of Michigan), Georgina Grosenick (Carleton University), Sharon Kleinman (Quinnipiac University), Thomas R. Lindlof (University of Kentucky), Timothy P. Meyer (University of Wisconsin–Green Bay), David W. Park (Lake Forest College), Norma Pecora (Ohio University), and Christopher F. White (Sam Houston State University), whose collective efforts greatly advanced the revisions of the work. While all acknowledged are responsible for much of what is good, whatever that remains that is not is solely of my own doing. Thanks again to Janet Colvin, as well as Nancy Tobler, both of Utah Valley University, for their work on the instructor materials. Finally, my thanks to the fine folks at SAGE. Their support and professionalism are outstanding.

Section I

Overview

Section I is a set of four introductory chapters that intends to provide an overview of the empirical study of mediated communication. Chapter 1 starts to explore the "lay of the land" by considering the disciplines that are currently home to the study of media. Chapter 2 picks out the properties that make the mediascape a unique territory of analysis. Chapters 3 and 4 show how the research process comes together in the conceptual forms of the mediascape.

Exploring the Mediascape

CHAPTER PREVIEW

What's It All About?

Chapter 1 is an introductory chapter. Introductory chapters do the work of positioning the reader inside the playing field of the writer. I am striving to provide you with an understanding of the overall approach as well as an overview of the targets, methods, and foundations of the methodologies we will study in this book.

What Are the Major Topics?

This chapter first takes up the negotiation of what we will mean when we talk about communication and media. The alternative terms *mass communication* and *media studies* are considered and gently set aside in favor of the more inclusive *mediated communication*. Mediated communication includes all media, modes of presentation, audiences, technologies, and texts past, present, and to come and is contrasted with in-person, face-to-face communication. This contrast is drawn out by considering the unique characteristics of face-to-face communication.

Next, readers are quickly reminded that communication is a diverse field, and what counts as a field of study at one institution may not count as such at another. Further, there are divisions across what is believed to be science, good scholarship, and good research. I argue that good research can and should happen anywhere and that the arguments about science and scholarship are often more ideological (heat) than instrumental (light). You don't have to accept this position, but I will try to hold it throughout.

The next section takes up the center of the work by looking at methodological differences. A number (and a growing one at that) of scientific and scholarly methods are widely practiced in communication. Primarily concerned with two methodologies residing inside the empirical domain, metric and interpretive, Chapter 1 also takes notice of emerging hybrid forms as well as the critical-analytical.

The chapter ends by guiding the reader through the epistemological foundations of each of these methodologies. These foundations are the belief systems that underlie the justified application of a methodology. For the individual researcher, these belief systems might be all-encompassing—that is, accepting one requires the rejection of all others. For other researchers, the belief systems form the standards under which one approach is selected over another. It is hard for the professional to be that flexible because real, expert knowledge is required for any given approach. The chapter mostly follows a given approach and tries to be on speaking terms with everything else. Students of methods have an advantage here because they do not have the overburden of extensive invested effort. Now's the time to try stuff out.

What Special Terms Are Used?[1]

Analytical methods	Frankfurt School	Technological determinism
Atomism	Hermeneutics	Transcendental
Critical rhetorical theory	Interpretive empiricism	Universalism
Critical theory	Metric empiricism	Variable
Epistemology	Synthetic variable	

[1]These are terms that might not be in ordinary usage. Definitions can be found in the glossary.

INTRODUCTION

Communication is a particularly demanding field of study, and communication scholars are just beginning to learn how to explore it. This book is about the methods of exploration, and the mediascape will be the territory of that exploration. The methods examined come from the careful practices of science and scholarship. Science is the systematic exploration of the world around us. And scholarship is the crafting of well-constructed arguments that meet the tests of good evidence and justified conclusions.

COMMUNICATION DOMAINS

To begin an exploration of the mediascape, we first need to know who we are. Scholars and scientists have divided up the world of communication into different domains. These domains carry such familiar names as *interpersonal, intercultural, organizational,* and, in our case, *mediated communication.* Communication itself is not really different in one domain or the other, but the focal points of interest and sometimes the methods of study are different. And, certainly, those differences make a difference to those who study communication. In mediated communication, we don't even have to cross the border to encounter some dispute. We, who explore this territory, are in the process of a name change. Our field is called by many "mass communication" (or "mass communications"), by others "media studies," and by this book "mediated communication." Like my own name, if you call me James, Jim, or Jimmy, it makes a difference.

Mass Communication

Mass communication is the oldest term for our field of study.[2] It developed prominence in the decade just prior to World War II when U.S. and European scholars were concerned with totalitarian governments, propaganda, revolutionary social movements, and the presumed decline of culture represented by the popular media. It supported a strong, objective press that would contain the excesses of government and promoted a message-based analysis. In the tradition of mass communication, the mediascape was described by industrially produced messages that were delivered to large, heterogeneous audiences. For 50 years the concept of mass communication made a lot of sense. Motion pictures, popular magazines, radio, and then television were industries with relatively few sources of production that had huge audiences. The concept of one-to-many or a few-to-millions seemed to describe what was going on.

Starting in the early 1950s, the large audience part of these conditions began to erode, and by the early 1980s, the landscape was radically restructured. The motion picture industry was broken apart by antitrust action, and its traditional forms disintegrated under the onslaught of television. Radio networks withered, and with the advent of FM broadcasting, dozens of independent stations were competing in every market of size. Changes in regulations have allowed reconcentration of ownership, but programming can still be quite local. We have yet to see what satellite radio will bring and may not get the chance, given the state of its financial health.

Magazine circulations declined, and magazines themselves returned to more specialized content. Newspaper circulations declined, the independent paper became a part of a chain, and bankruptcy has claimed more than a few. The monolith of television was fractured first by cable and then by satellite distribution of subscription services. TV has gone from three channels that controlled nearly all of the audience to an audience distributed across hundreds of channels, and it is now moving toward liberating content from channels altogether as well as seeing the end of free (broadcast) television.

It is the Internet that causes the most problems for the term *mass communication*. Mass communication is built on the premise that a few outlets control most of the available content. In mass communication, content is scarce and access limited. The Internet, however, is built on the premise that everything is available to everybody and anybody can

---

[2]The plural—*mass communications*—appeared in schools particularly interested in the content of the media and, perhaps initially, less interested in the process of media. The battle over the *s* seems to be waning as more surrender to the argument that the study of communication versus the study of communications is like the study of medicine versus the study of medicines. There are fine schools, nonetheless, that uphold the tradition of the *s*.

produce the content. The technology that supports all this is less than 20 years old, but it essentially writes the end of the mass communication story.

That doesn't mean that there will not be a lot of people watching a particular show or listening to a kind of music. It does mean that a population can no longer be characterized by its media content. For example, one can extrapolate from ratings data that close to 30 million U.S. citizens have watched something from the reality show genre. That is a lot of people, but it is also (depending on when you are reading this) less or substantially less than 10% of the U.S. population. The phrase *everybody's watching* has always been false, and is even more so now.

Throughout its history *mass* has always meant something more than size (though size counts). *Mass* has also meant less: less able to understand, resist, manage, and control the forces and influence of the media. And in that sentence media became *the* media—some entity working purposefully toward some end. Remember that *mass communication* comes from an era when social activists were concerned about the susceptibility of the undereducated and poor to communist (Stalinist) and fascist propaganda. The masses were those people.

As *mass audience* has meant less capable, so *media* has always meant something more than various delivery systems. *Media* has referenced an institution under the governance of the state (in so-called socialist countries) or of a market ideology (in so-called capitalist countries) that promoted particular social, political, and economic goals. Media were the conspiratorial forces that would deceive and misdirect those people.

The term *mass communication* became linked to the scientific study of media messages when it was appropriated from the social critics (of the Frankfurt School and elsewhere) in the late 1930s by the social scientists funded by the Rockefeller Foundation. The Rockefeller Foundation, at that time the premier source of social science funding, was committed to an antipropaganda agenda and was funding studies that promised control of mass media effects. Those scientists then migrated to the Office of War Information and other U.S. government agencies during World War II. By the end of that war, mass communication was firmly established in the United States as a scientific rather than critical enterprise, although the legacy of audiences for popular media was less and the media as a coherent, conspiratorial entity remained.

Media Studies

Media studies was first popularized in Great Britain where a strong, and mostly successful, program in media literacy has developed in primary and secondary education (U.S. terms). There, *media studies* "involves the close analysis of the images, sounds and text that we experience via the media."[3] Exported to the United States, it has become the catchall term that manages the difficult alliances that constitute the contemporary academic interests in media, texts, and audiences (see, for example, *The SAGE Handbook of Media Studies*, 2004). *Media studies* recovers the critical in the study of media while providing a mostly unhappy home for the mass communication scientist.

---

[3]http://www.mediaknowall.com/index.html. Accessed January 6, 2010; now an archived site.

Depending on where you study media studies, it can take an outsider or insider perspective. The outsider perspective views media and their texts as at least potentially corrosive if not always so. This is the perspective typical of (but not necessary for) critical rhetorical theory, cultural studies, and media effects. In most of this scholarship whether analytical or empirical, the emphasis is on the potential for harm across issues of class, race, ethnicity (colonization), gender, economic justice, bias, aggression, sexuality, and the like. This perspective elevates the scholar above the audience and considers the media to be under a common set of influences. It is a continuation of the Frankfurt School legacy.

The insider position takes a more neutral stance vis-à-vis the audience as evidenced in uses and gratifications or social action theory and works a more celebratory critique. It often adapts an industry perspective in regard to the media, considering questions of message effectiveness (instead of effects), audience behavior, and return on investment. Its view of the media as an industry is generally much more complex, recognizing the ecology of writers, actors, producers, craft unions, narrative forms, technologies, distribution channels, competitions, and collusions that are behind what an audience sees and hears.

Mediated Communication

Mediated communication (or sometimes the more ambiguous *media communication*)[4] is yet another take on our domain of study and is the perspective of this book. The term began to appear in the early 1980s when it became apparent that *mass* was no longer going to be an adequate descriptor of the communication processes of interest. The term presumes that face-to-face communication is the alternate form and that all other forms of communication involve some intermediary of technology that constitutes real differences. Old media, new media, emerging media, and converging media, static or interactive, are all included. If it is not just face-to-face, then it is part of the purview of mediated communication. Our first task, then, is to understand how mediated communication is different from face-to-face communication.

Comparing Mediated and Face-to-Face Communication

We can get to that understanding by looking at the unique requirements of face-to-face communication. Those are usually listed as (a) the copresence of communicators, (b) the necessity of an intercommunicant relationship based on a set of mutual obligations, (c) the consequential management of that relationship, (d) the reciprocal production of the text, and (e) the mutual supervision of the interpretation of that text.

Copresence. Copresence means that the communication activity is occurring at the same time and place for all communicators. The issue is not so much togetherness but that the totality of message information is in play (vocal articulation, tonality, other sounds, facial

---

[4]Both terms are not without their critics. Some point out that all communication is mediated in some way—sound requires some medium to be transmitted. To this *media communication* supporters reply, "Yeah, right." *Media communication* is criticized for actually pointing to communication between media. To this its supporters reply, "Whatever."

expression, body position and action, and the possibility of odors, pheromones, and touch). Those rules mean that not all copresence is equal. A lecturer talking to 400 students may approach copresence with some of her class, but the student scrunched down in the back-most row clearly isn't copresent. Consequently, not all interpersonal communication is face-to-face communication. Mediated communication to date, however, always involves some reduction in these cues, but also the addition of others. For example, you can mis-pronounce a word in speaking, but not in writing, and you cannot "mystpell" a word in ordinary talk.

In writing to you, I can use different fonts and colors and pictures that are not available to me in ordinary conversation, but I have lost all the physical aspects of myself with which

Photo 1.1   Reverberations

to communicate. Further, in this writing I do not know who you are or even if there will be a "who" out there to do the reading.

Intercommunicant relationship. The intercommunicant relationship component is built on the notion that face-to-face communication always involves a relationship between the individuals producing the communication event. That relationship may be one between friends, intimate partners, or even strangers at a bus stop. Whatever the relationship, it is present to the communicants and necessarily affects the event itself.

The industrial act of producing a textbook—which I am participating in by writing at my computer at this moment—does not offer me that context of performance. Certainly, there are many relationships that impinge on the writing, including with my reviewers, my editor, my coauthor, and my colleagues, but none of those relationships is at risk in the writing of this sentence, if for no other reason than that none of those people consider this sentence directed toward them.

There are mediated communication practices encoded in the relationship. E-mail is an excellent example. I'm betting that all of us have written an e-mail that has gotten us in trouble, relationally. A hasty message composed while emotionally upset, a carelessly worded sentence, the thoughtless composition that forgets just to whom you are writing—or, perhaps, a misdirected twitpic—all can do relational damage at work, home, or play. The potential for damage can be heightened because of the lack of consequential management that is typical of mediated communication.

Consequential management. Consequential management recognizes that in face-to-face communication each turn has to manage both its content and the relational consequences of that content because both the performance of the relationship and the production of the content are fully integrated in the speech act in immediate and ongoing reciprocity. Certainly, individuals consider their relationships in what they write, include in a message, or say—or at least ought to—in mediated communication, but, as you have seen, (a) there is often no necessity of a relationship to produce the content, (b) the content can freely move across relationships, and (c) there is usually no immediate feedback loop. Consider these examples: a blog that no one reads (a); the playful excess of a social network posting that leads to unintended consequences at the job site (b); or any case where content intended for one sort of presentation of self is appropriated for other ends completely without permission, supervision, or the ability to manage the consequences (c). This disconnection is the reason for the Miranda warning that whatever you say may be used against you. It should be posted on every social networking site.

Reciprocal production. Reciprocal production means that each action of all participants in face-to-face communication contributes to the text that is produced. Even silence by one is telling. Here, your action in reading will not affect my action of writing, although it may affect the economic success of the book itself. (The reading by the reviewers and my copy editor, however, will make a big difference in the final text.) Industry estimates suggest that about 50% of all books bought (not just textbooks) are not read by the buyer.

Mutual supervision. Last, mutual supervision of interpretation means that each participant will strive to produce an internal coherence to the performance by engaging and responding to the actions of the other as the conversational text is produced. Only the telephone conversation (not machine tag) or the chat room allows this mutual supervision with any facility. Certainly I anticipate a reader's response—you might be thinking, "Why we are going through all this face-to-face stuff?" (Because you need it; trust me.) But you are not here to help me say it better or to stop me from continuing on.

The Mediascape of Mediated Communication

Mediated communication, then, becomes any communicative process (a term yet to be defined) that not only meets but also adds something to the requirements of face-to-face communication. In mediated communication, picking up the telephone, doing an instant chat, or text messaging is each within the domain of study, as are 25 million people watching *American Idol*. Mediated communication enlarges the mediascape beyond the boundaries of mass communication or media studies, although it includes both. No longer are researchers limited to the industrial productions that were the primary territory of mass communication and media studies—the texts of individually produced blogs can be of interest. No longer are communicants limited by the requirement of a large, heterogeneous audience—in fact no audience at all is needed if we look at the auto-communication properties of those blogs, for example. And it is those blogs and the other products of the Internet that require researchers—and us—to look wider, in order not to miss the most important aspect of contemporary communication processes.

But, clearly, not all instances of mediated communication are equally interesting. Most people probably are not interested in your latest tweet (although the government might be, and so might others, if you become famous). Researchers, are however, interested in the consequences of the elevated connectivity provided by text messaging on, say, intimate relationships (Yin & Tong, 2007). Do you still have a text message treasure from a long-departed partner? Have you used text messaging to manage a relationship because you didn't want to do it in person? In the techno-slang of the early 21st century, are you a "CrackBerry" flirt?

Media researchers are also interested in how organizational members use text messaging as a backstage management of, say, a meeting in progress, or how corporations use national advertising campaigns to define the organization for its members. It is these practices of mediated communication that require us to look wider and will take us further than either mass communication or media studies. We would miss the most important aspect of contemporary communication processes if we didn't follow its lead.

New Media and Old Media

Communication scholars are now watching another mitotic division within the field, splitting it between new media and old. Old media are the media of mass communication. New media are the media of interactive networking. Old media are message-oriented, vertically organized, one-directional, cyclical, and fixed in time and often material. New media are flowing, horizontally distributed, self-organizing, performance-oriented, multidirectional, and virtual. New media invoke new theories and will require and may well provide new methods of study. Such theories and methods will have to be much more focused on process and performance than on content and effects. Methodologies may be able to take advantage of both the networked and the interactive properties of new media to develop an emergent form of data that has depth instead of being a cross-sectional slice taken in a moment of time.

Convergence is the concept that marks the intersection between new and old media. The basic idea is that all information and entertainment becomes distributable to any display form from the wide-screen to the Kindle to the smart phone via wireless networking. The technology appears to be inevitable; what is taking longer is the business model, where technologists, content providers, and distributors all make money.

Convergence is an example of technological determinism where the force of the technology produces change in society. Those changes are not welcomed by all or good for all.

In many markets, the physical newspaper is disappearing with attendant loss of jobs and the practices that surrounded the "reading of the newspaper" as a communal and sharing activity. ("You done with the comics yet?") We have very little information on the flip side issues of how families manage computer access and other screen resources. Our typical visions are very much on the upscale side of the digital divide and well within the digital enclosure.

Scholarly Communities of the Mediascape

Communication scholars manage the scope of this great landscape of study through communities of interest. There are communities of interest attached to all aspects of mediated communication—its practitioners, audiences, technologies, industries, textual and symbolic forms, narrative structures, social consequences—everything. Where I work, there are feminist scholars interested in body image, cultural studies scholars working on the representation of the Arab world, journalists studying bias within the pictorial narrative, cognitivists looking at the processing of information, and social action scholars investigating families' changing media use. These folks work at the same institution, but their scholarly communities are well beyond its walls. (In fact, the virtual community of scholarship is a mediated study all its own.) The folks at your institution are each the local node of some community-of-interest network. They will gravitate toward some questions and lack interest in others, as will you. The result is that the book will offer you more than you want and will reach beyond my expertise as its author. But that is what explorations are all about.

Science and Scholarship

The problem of what is science and what is not is called the demarcation problem in the philosophy of science. Philosophers haven't been able to solve the problem, and we won't either. At this point in most methods books there is a list of the characteristics of scientific work (see Keyton, 2006, pp. 10–11, for a list of 12 characteristics). It is testable, empirical, systematic, public, replicable, parsimonious, and the like. The problem with these lists is that a lot of what is considered science doesn't meet the criteria and, like much of theoretical physics, may never meet the criteria. In the methodology wars, science has been used as a club to beat down one's rivals, a flag to wrap one's smug self in, and an unreachable talisman to demonstrate one's quixotic commitment. I'd like to dial down the rhetoric on whether something is scientific or not and put the emphasis on doing careful, mindful work based on a foundation of empirical evidence, being open to review and the possibility of error, producing results of instrumental value, and maintaining a modesty of claim. If we can do that, whether it is science or not won't matter.

Good science or good scholarship of any sort meets the nine-*I* test. It is inquisitive, intelligent, investigative, informed, insightful, and implicative and not imitative, idiosyncratic, or ideological. Good work from any domain of inquiry asks questions that present the world and ideas to us in interesting ways. It investigates the answers to those questions inside a framework of evidence to provide new knowledge that is trustworthy, entailing, and socially significant. It's heady work.

Scientific, Proprietary, and Personal Research

Scientific research and academic scholarship are part of the public knowledge production apparatuses and are often considered top-of-the-line as far as practices and credibility are concerned. (There are issues, of course, that we take up in our various ethics discussions.) We will use the criteria of scientific practice as the basis of our descriptions, while recognizing that most likely few using this book will become communication scientists. Nonetheless, at some time or another, each of us will have questions we want to answer and that would benefit from the good practices of science and scholarship.

Business has a great demand for the skills that produce reliable and useful information. A company may want to test out the ease of navigation on its website, or the effectiveness of a training program or, perhaps, of an advertising campaign. Companies have to make all sorts of decisions concerning the cost-effectiveness of cell phone usage, Internet services, software adoptions, and even the number and size of computer monitors to put on employees' desks. And, of course, people trained in communication research methods can provide those answers. This research is usually proprietary, which means that it is to be used by those conducting (or paying for) it and no one else.

Our personal lives can be affected as well. The characteristics that generate good research—curiosity, skepticism, systematic investigation, recognizing the possibility of error—can serve each of us well in meeting the challenges of daily life (properly applied and in moderation, of course).

Consequently, academic, business, and personal examples will be used throughout this book to illustrate the conduct of research. It is important to understand the differences. Scientific scholarship intends to produce information with the widest application or generalizability. It is a public activity, subject to peer review.[5] Proprietary research might aim at high generalizability but often is focused on problems that are particular to the company, and rarely is it open to review or independent of the political processes of organizational decision making. Personal research, of course, is very local in its purview, the value of which depends on the particular people for which it is developed. But the academy, the corporation, and the individual are all part of the mediascape, and each needs to know about it. That process starts now with a review of the different ways to gain knowledge about the mediascape.

UNDERSTANDING METHODOLOGICAL DIFFERENCES

There are four methodological communities within the field of communication that come within the scope of this book: metric empiricism, interpretive (or hermeneutic) empiricism, critical-cultural hybrids, and analytical criticism. This book has a primary interest in the first two, a secondary interest in the third, and an instrumental acquaintance with the fourth.

---

[5]It is important to separate scientific research from university research. One is a standard; the other is a practice. Good proprietary research is often better funded, better designed, and better executed than much of the research from the academy, where the economics of tenure, the needs of the discipline, and the absence of adequate funding, time, and other resources distort the process.

Metric empiricism is what is commonly called quantitative methods; interpretive empiricism is typically called qualitative research; critical-cultural hybrids form a newly and rapidly developing area that couples (as you might guess) critical advocacy arguments with empirical methodologies (usually interpretive); and analytical criticism methods are the sort that make up film criticism, rhetorical criticism, and literary criticism. Let's take the time to put some definitions in order before beginning to explore these different methodologies.

Methodologies

A methodology is a set of more or less standardized practices for producing knowledge. A methodology includes an epistemological foundation and associated rules of evidence for making a claim as well as a set of practices for generating that evidence. The word *methods* is sometimes a synonym for *methodology* but more often used to describe a subset of activities within a methodology. Communication scholars talk both of quantitative methods as the whole class of metric methodology and of statistical methods as a subset of practices residing in metric methodology. A method, such as analysis of variance, is a set of procedures within a set of methods within a methodology. All the nesting and terminology can be a bit confusing, but the basic rule is that if it describes a set of practices, it is a method; if it describes a global process of constructing knowledge, it is a methodology. Most of what appears in the journals are methods even if the author grandly claims them as methodologies.

Standardization means that the designated authorities of a scholarly community have operated individually and jointly to establish the requirements of good practice. These authorities are the methodologists—people who study, test, and report on methods; the methods and ethics committees of professional organizations (of which communication associations have none); journal editors (of which communication associations have lots); journal reviewers; and even textbook authors. The sum of this social process establishes the standards of competent work, the boundaries of what belongs and what does not, and takes up the policing of those borders.

In our methodologies of interest, metric empiricism is the most standardized, critical-cultural hybrids is the least, and methods that mix those are still in discussion. As they move down the level of standardization, the practitioners of these methods are not in agreement as to what constitutes the methods, let alone their good practice. Consequently, as an author I am most secure in telling you what the methods of metric empiricism are, reasonably secure in interpretive approaches, least secure in what the hybrid methods are, and can only speculate what the latest mash-ups—which at present are an analytic strategy, not a methodology—might turn out to be. Reader take notice.

The Empirical

The empirical has to do with our experience and the things and conditions that we experience. Our experience is the result of our interaction with the material and ideational world. The concept of empirical looks like it might be hard-edged, but it gets fuzzy in communication because so many of the things and conditions in which individuals have interest take their final form inside some cognitive and/or social-interpretive process. For example, the words you are reading off this page are deposits of carbon—that is their material reality—but they become words in a semiotic process that involves both the cognitive processes of semiosis and the social action of language. The words gain their meaning in some interpretation. Interpretation puts the words into the service of some instrumental action. If you are reading these words as a copy editor, you have a fistful of blue pencils at the ready. If you are reading these words for a class, you may be thinking, "Will this be on the test?" The way we will make use of the words in our subsequent behavior—their meaningfulness—is responsive to the cognitive and action processes, not to the carbon deposits. Consequently, communication processes may start with material conditions and facts, but they quickly move into the ideational and constituted worlds of social action where the empirical is much less secure.

One very important thing to note about the empirical is that its definition says nothing about numbers. Empirical research is about our interaction with the material and ideational world of which we are a part, but do not contain. Numbers play a central part in a particular form of empirical research, popularly called quantitative research, that depends on the logic of metrics and utilizes the characteristics of numerical scales in its analysis. This book takes up that form next.

The Metric

Metric methods involve the systematic identification of variables and the procedures of assigning quantitative values to the states or conditions of those variables. The variables themselves are either discovered or constituted. To be discovered, a variable has to preexist theoretical interest in it and be directly addressable. It is very controversial (in some quarters) as to whether this preexistence or direct addressability is possible. Most of the variables studied are not naturally occurring but rather are synthetic. They are created in some interaction between the action and its measurement. For example, say we were counting hits to a blog site. The variable is a "hit." But what is a "hit"? Is it the simple connection between a browser and a server? Does it have to include the completion of a file-sending action by the server? Does it count if the browser is a robot rather than a person? All of these issues have to be reconciled in the definition of a "hit," and those definitions will constitute the synthetic variable, even though there is an independent activity going on.

Quantification adopts the characteristics and logical entailments of number systems and applies them to variables and variable states (all of these topics are discussed in greater detail in Chapter 5). Because variables don't show up with numbers attached to them, some translation method is required. In the example on blog hits, we could attach a hit counter to the home page. A "hit" then becomes defined as an action of the hit counter, and whatever the counter counts equals one hit. The number of hits we get is the number reported by this quantification device.

The Hermeneutic

The major alternative to metric research, popularly called qualitative research, falls in the branch of scholarship called the hermeneutic. Hermeneutics is the systematic application of interpretation, and in empirical research, it depends on the logic of narrative and the characteristics of action to make its claims. Interpretation is the understanding that develops out of the analysis of our experience. Interpretation makes sense of that experience. Sense making locates experience in the matrix of our knowledge. For example, one hears a sharp sound while watching television. Was it something from the television or something that signals a problem in the house? The interpretation of the sound (the story of the sound) will depend on one's analysis of what is on television and what a subsequent search of the house might reveal.

This interpretation is done pretty much unproblematically in the above example. In research, this interpretation is systematically guided by the conventions of the research community. For example, an analyst might be interested in the values expressed in celebrity advertising in Chinese, European, and U.S. magazines. Current interpretive methods would suggest two or more coders for each cultural group who would first code separately through grounded methods and then reconcile differences in discussion, arriving at a consensus of understanding.

The Critical

Edward Said (1983) has said that the critical takes what appears to be and reveals what it is. Present-day critical analyses are mostly interested in revealing the underlying power relationships and mechanisms of control that media texts and social action practices encode. For example, consumerism is a social practice that not only drives the economy but also structures society into a hierarchy of haves and have-nots. For the critic this creates a condition of social injustice and a power imbalance. The critical-empirical, in this example, then, would focus on the material practices of consumerism for the empirical side and the social justice consequences of materialism for the critical side. It is amped-up interpretation with an advocacy edge.

Epistemological Foundations

Methodologies are public processes that develop out of our fundamental understandings of the world, ourselves, and what we can know about them. These are called the epistemological foundations of method. Epistemology is the study of knowledge. There are a number of things that distinguish one methodological field from another. People take on memberships in different communities, and the emblematic or signature practices of these communities are different (even with poaching and cooption), the character of the argument (e.g., the journal article) is different, but most important the methods encode a different understanding of the world and one's knowledge of it. I'm going to spend a little time talking about these differences because they are the best way to understand why people do the things they do. In drawing these differences, I will approach the center of each of a set of overlapping communities. So, can a metric empiricist and an interpretive empiricist stand in exactly the same methodological space? Yes, but both would be a good distance from the center of their governing epistemology.

Metric Empiricism

At its center metric empiricism is based on a belief in an independent, objective, material reality that has direct consequences in people's interaction with it. The qualifying effort of metric methods is to describe that material reality. That reality is tangible, durable, stable, and reliable. The accurate descriptions produced will have similar characteristics. They will reach across time and place. They are called transcendental and context-free. Those descriptions are true because of what is, and they are independent of what ought to be.

The surface of that reality—the action and objects that one can see and encounter—is not composed of a single piece, but rather is a composite of causally related components. There are many layers of these composites. As we drill down, we will find structures that are composed of molecules that are composed of atoms that are composed of particles that are composed of . . . until we reach some finite number of elemental building blocks upon which the whole structure of reality stands. This is the principle of atomism: that the world is built up from a set of components operating in causal relationships. What one sees as the presented product is not really where the action is.

For example, if an analyst was studying those people who have established a blog on the Internet, he or she would not start with the assumption that each person has a unique set of reasons for establishing a blog. Rather, the analyst would argue that there are characteristics held in common by these individuals that predict or explain their action. The scientific interest is not in the people (it doesn't matter who the people are) but in the characteristics. The general term for these characteristics and all such components is *variable*, which is why metric empiricism is also known as variable-analytic—metricians analyze things through variables.

A variable is simply a characteristic that can take different values across different circumstances. The reason for interest in studying variables is the assumption that everything is connected in causal chains. Each variable is the result of some other variable(s) and is the cause or partial cause of yet another variable. The more one learns about variables, the more one will know about the world. Consequently, metric methods are designed to collect information about variables—to identify their appearance, to measure their values, to investigate their relationships, and to determine their function in some causal structure.

Interpretive Empiricism

The foundational shift that occurs when one crosses the boundary from metric empiricism to interpretive empiricism has to do with the change from metric empiricism's interest in the objective characteristics of the world to an effort to represent the multiple meanings held for these characteristics. For the hermeneut (love that funny name), the objective characteristics are part of the analysis but not the whole of it.

The other part—the part that has caused all this struggle—develops out of the antiuniversalist movement that has characterized the social, political, philosophical, and scientific activities of the last half of the 20th century (sometimes called the "interpretive turn"). Universalism holds to a final truth of the matter—a transcendental claim is possible. The response to universalism most interesting for purposes of this book is social constructionism. In its opening development (Berger & Luckmann, 1967), social constructionism had to do with the development of human knowledge. The argument was that all knowledge is developed and sustained through human practices. There might be an independent objective reality out there, but it is engaged only through the material practices of human beings. Consequently, what we know depends not on reality alone but also on the material practices of knowledge production. Knowledge is relative to what we do to produce it; a claim lasts only as long as the practices that sustain it.

That basic idea has been escalated to the principle that whatever is known (or whatever is true) requires a community of knowers to produce it, sustain it, and implement it. Consequently, knowledge changes from one community to another.[6] When knowledge about entities, processes, consequences, and values changes, human action toward and within these entities, processes, consequences, and values changes as well. Therefore if we are to understand human action, we need to understand the knowledge system under which it is produced. This principle has been applied from the most global cultural distinctions (even extraterrestrial) down to the very local knowledge practices of the group. The amulet of achieving this understanding is member knowledge. To achieve member knowledge one must participate and become competent in the material practices by which this knowledge is produced, maintained, and implemented.

What I am demonstrating (or attempting to demonstrate) here is the difference between the principle of an objective knowledge set and a socially constructed one. Metric empiricism depends on an objective knowledge set. It makes little sense to do a survey of television usage unless the prior concept of television is the same for everyone. Interpretive empiricism presumes a socially constructed knowledge set and would approach the concept of television as a variable concept. The question that remains is "When does that difference make a difference? When can the analyst say, 'Well, television is television, and it's television for everyone'?"

You might think that the hard-core hermeneut's answer would be "Never; the difference always makes a difference." But that can't be true, or individuals would all be walled off from each other by their particular memberships. The key to the application of metric and hermeneutic methods is to know when the difference makes a difference.

Interpretive empiricism's rejection of the universal has created some movement of interpretation toward critical goals and some openings in empirical methods that defy some of the traditional criteria of science. This rejection of universalism has encouraged the reformulation of one criterion that is nearly axiomatic in the physical sciences and that is the separation of what is from what ought to be. This principle, known as Hume's gap (after 18th-century British empiricist David Hume), has been taken to claim that the business of science is to describe what is and not to take sides on what ought to be. Working from the principle of the social construction of knowledge, however, Hume's gap closes with a snap as all knowledge requires social processes with their attendant political underpinnings to exist. Any claim of what is is also a claim of what ought to be, given whatever social processes of knowledge construction are in place. That shift introduces a critical component into interpretive-empirical work.

Just as the antiuniversalist and social constructionist characteristics of the interpretive move analysts away from the true and transcendental of the metric, the critical component in this set moves them away from their independence of what ought to be and jams their feet directly in

---

[6]This is sometimes called the social construction of reality, which unfortunately leads to all sorts of silly arguments—for example, if the table is socially constructed, why can't one walk through it? The material character of the table is not socially constructed; what is known as a table and what characteristics constitute a table are socially constructed.

the moral morass. The critical holds that every study advances some political purpose and that social science practitioners need to come clean and explicitly examine their social agenda.

OK, the gloves are off now. You see, Hume's gap provides a protection for the traditional social scientist: As long as there is a separation between what is true and what is right, the scientist is not responsible for the consequences of a claim achieved through competent scientific methods. The scientist can make a claim (in fact must make the claim) because it is true; it doesn't matter if it is morally right. This principle collapses in social constructionism because what is true depends on the community of knowers that makes it so. So, the European American scientists who make claims about African American respondents within a racist society must be concerned about their potential contribution to racism. For the radical critic, if a claim gives comfort to racist practices, it is racist. The critical makes researchers responsible for the consequences of their work—both intended and unintended—in ways rarely accepted by the traditional scientist. When this critical impulse becomes the primary activity within interpretive empiricism, it becomes a hybrid methodology.

Hybrid Methodologies

Consequently, the parsing of empirical methodologies does not end with only metric and interpretive. Just as the interpretive has entered the critical, so has the critical entered the empirical. During the past decade a family of critical-empirical methodologies has appeared. These are hybrid methodologies that apply cultural-critical-interpretive methods to empirical texts. The parentage of these hybrids is multiple. They are influenced by the social commentary heritage of rhetorical analysis now mostly known as critical rhetoric; they show and often embrace the postmodern rejection of the universal narrative (aka the True); they accept the requirement of some empirical grounding, but are less interested in telling the what or how of text than in understanding the cultural force of a class of texts or in promoting what ought to be the cultural consequences of their engagement; and they associate mostly with the hermeneutic side of empiricism although some metric applications are present as well. These hybrid methodologies go by a number of different names—discourse analysis, dialogic analysis, rhetorical field studies, critical studies, colonial and race studies, cultural studies, interpretive studies, and the like—and it is all very much in flux. Empirical methodologies, both metric and interpretive, have been around for over 100 years. A pretty good agreement exists among practitioners as to how these methodologies should be conducted (at least in comparison with the hybrid forms). A couple more decades are needed to reach a level of conventionalization in the hybrid forms, which by their nature resist conventionalization.

Critical-Analytical

Critical-analytical methods are in use in this text in the service and toward the betterment of the empirical. Let me spend just a few paragraphs talking about the difference between empirical and critical-analytical methods because this difference can be a source of a lot of confusion.[7] This difference hinges first on whether the ascendant

---

[7]Admittedly, this may be more of a cautionary tale for an instructor than any source of confusion for a student.

evidence is formal or empirical—whether it is derived through reason or discovered in observation.[8] For example, I could argue analytically that the color of that swan you have in a box (I have no idea why you would have a swan in a box) must be white. I would say all swans are white; you have a swan in the box; therefore, its color is white. I would not need to look in the box to know the color of your swan. I could logically declare the color of your swan with no need for empirical evidence. It's a big advantage as long as my first premise is true. Alas, in the history of this famous syllogism, black swans were discovered in Australia.

Consequently, I can no longer say that your swan is white, but there is still a great deal I can say. For example, I can say with certainty that it is not red.

Empiricist distrust of the analytical stems from the possibility that red swans may be discovered in the back jungles of Indonesia (where several new species—none of them swans—were recently found). In fact, most first premises of the analytical—statements that are held to be axiomatically true—can be questioned for their empirical content. Any statement that starts with "audiences for reality programming," "children," "media programmers," or "voters" or that makes use of similar, constructed aggregates (such as "any statement") is invariably an analytical statement that can be challenged for its empirical foundation (as can this statement).

Photo 1.2   White Swan

Photo 1.3   Black Swan

When we add the critical on top of this foundation, we can see that it is akin to advocating a social policy on the basis of universal principles. This might work fine for the constitutions of nation-states, but it does not work at all to claim that all children are at risk from, say, digital games because of some analytically derived universal principle.

---

[8]The language of "discovery" is as contested as that of exploration. As the example that follows this note suggests, the issue is whether you open the box and look at the swan to determine its color.

On the other hand, if the empiricists gave up everything except that which was empirically demonstrated, they would be reduced to a pretty banal field of knowledge[9] with no implications for the future and little understanding of the past. In fact, as we will see, even the plainest of empiricists depend on analytical methods to achieve any consequential results for their research. As you read the literature, you will find that empiricists celebrate their objective experience while quietly practicing analytical interpretations, and hybridists celebrate their critical intentions while quietly grounding them in the objective characteristics of the text. We will, therefore, find the analytical firmly on the table in Chapter 3. We need to know these methods.

Assaying the Differences

Learning a methodology means taking up both the epistemology of its foundation and the ideology of its social practice. Methodologies are designed to produce evidence for a particular class of claims and to fit inside arguments of a certain kind that are themselves grounded in ways of knowing. Metric empiricists base their arguments on the logic of mathematics. Interpretive empiricists base theirs on the logic of the narrative. Metric empiricists quantify their observations; interpretive empiricists narrativize them.

When researchers quantify an observation, they first unitize it by constructing secure boundaries around it. It starts at some point and ends at another. Researchers can then count each observation, put it in some order with other observations, space these observations along some dimension, or put them in some relationship. They can then use the tools of arithmetic and mathematical logic to make the observations sensible: It all adds up. When analysts narrativize an observation, they create a discursive line that brings in character, action, agency, and scene.[10] The observation becomes sensible within the logic of a narrative form: It tells a credible story.

You can pretend that it doesn't matter and use methodologies outside their proper domain or poach from one domain into another. It's done all the time, but it is not careful, mindful work. When a methodology is transported from its "natural" domain, such as using surveys in an interpretative approach or participant observation in an experiment, the recognition of its transformation has to be carefully described and justified.

Over the years, there has been a lot of argument over which of these approaches is better. Much of that argument had to do with the business of researchers and scholars creating and preserving space and resources to conduct their research. These professionals are now in a kind of uneasy coexistence with excursions and border patrols and even some ostensible cooperation, which still is considered suspiciously by many (including me) as cooption. Practitioners do tend to be of one sort or another. And you can sort that out for yourself as you develop experience in the approaches.

---

[9]Consider opening the box and declaring, "Your swan is not red!"

[10]This is a cultural studies update of Burke's pentad, placing more emphasis on cultural subjectivity than individual identity.

MOVING ON

This chapter started out by looking at the communities of scholars and researchers who generate the research published in the journals and textbooks of communication, psychology, sociology, and other social sciences as well as those of critical and social scholarship. The three distinct communities usually called mass communication, media studies, and mediated communication were described, and while the present advice is to be a good citizen of all three, the affinities of this writing would tend toward mediated communication because it is the most inclusive of the three. It was acknowledged that a good deal of research goes on in the proprietary halls of corporations, regulatory agencies, nonprofits, and nongovernmental agencies, and you could benefit from adopting the systematic investigation for your personal mediascape. The most intensive discussion focused on detailing the epistemological differences among metric, interpretive, and hybrid methodologies, hoping to demonstrate that it is these foundational differences in epistemologies that result in the different methodological practices that occur. As I close this summary, I think all the ramping-up to the topic is finally done, and we are ready to get on with it. The next chapter will begin by considering the properties, processes, consequences, and character of the mediascape.

REFLECTIONS

What Are Some Points to Remember?

- There are multiple perspectives on what is variously called mass or mediated communication. These perspectives make a difference on what is considered important to study and how those important things should be studied.
- A good understanding of mediated communication can be gained by comparing it with face-to-face communication.
- The lines between science, scholarship, and proprietary research have more to do with ideology and membership than with good practices of inquiry.
- A methodology is a class of inquiry practices. Empirical methodologies require a connection to experience. Metric empirical methodologies depend on a logic of quantities and rates; interpretive empiricism depends on the logic of narrative. Hybrids mix the critical-rhetorical with the empirical.
- Any methodology depends on a set of "truth-making" rules that govern the relationship between evidence and claim. Across methodologies, practices may seem the same or may be appropriated, but the epistemological foundations are not.

Why Does It Matter?

Introductions of the sort that you just read matter because both the discipline of communication and the methods of its science and scholarship are not under any consensus of agreement. Consequently, for me to write honestly to you and for you to successfully use this book, we need to co-orient to common positions. There are controversies in the positions I adopt, but that is because there are controversies in the field—not, I would hope, because of any idiosyncrasies of mine. In some way or another, you will have to resolve those for yourself. This is a book for grown-ups.

What Else Could We Talk About?

Higher education is notoriously nonreflexive. In classrooms and textbooks, there is a move to gloss contradictions and explanatory absences. Part of the motive for this nonreflexivity is the demand for answers and the shared belief that practitioners of the field are supposed to have them.

What Else Might Be Interesting to Read?

Park, D. W., & Pooley, J. (Eds.). (2008). *The history of media and communication research: Contested memories*. New York: Peter Lang.

Mapping the Mediascape

CHAPTER PREVIEW

What's It All About?

Chapter 2 continues our introduction to this field of study, turning to the topics of what we study and how we study them. We are introduced to properties, processes, consequences, and character as the targets of analysis and to surveys, sequential measurement, and experimental design as well as close reading, participant observation, and hybrid critical analysis as the methods appropriate to those targets. An extended example using social networking sites is presented to show the types of research questions that could be generated over the properties, processes, consequences, and character of such sites.

What Are the Major Topics?

Properties are the elements and entities that characterize the mediascape. They are usually measured by surveys to describe what is there for metric research and by close reading in interpretive analysis.

Processes focus on the practices that appear within the mediascape across production, reception, participation, social impact, and so on. The proper metric measurement of processes requires sequential measurement methodologies that involve repeated measurements over time. Interpretive approaches would be centered on participant observation.

Consequences are generally known as the effects that occur within the mediascape. Consequences appear as the result of some action by an agent inside a causal relationship. The best metric approach is through experimental methods, but often the logically weaker survey methods have to be used. There is no experimental analogue in interpretive research, but consequences are studied and done best in participant observation.

The character of the mediascape is the value we attach to its various elements, processes, and effects. Metric research treats character as a variable attribute in survey and experimental methods. The interpretive analysis of value generally requires some type of critical analysis, which, when coupled with empirical methods, constitutes a hybrid research form. These are our newest, least conventionalized, and (therefore) most controversial methodologies.

The last section of the chapter takes us through an example using social networking sites. The example compares and contrasts the similarities and differences across properties, processes, consequences, and character. It develops research questions appropriate to each of these and provides some insight on ways answers to those questions might be generated.

What Special Terms Are Used?

Agency	Consequences	Properties
Attribute	Mediascape	Social construction
Character	Processes	

INTRODUCTION

As I trudge up the trail in the Deep Creek Mountains to the west of Salt Lake City, I will be passing through five different ecoscapes generated by climatic changes associated with altitude and physical structure. I enter the trail from a Sonoran desert subject to high heat and little moisture. At the top of the trail, I will be in alpine meadows. Each ecozone has its characteristic geology, plants, and animals that form an ecology quite unlike the next.

The research methods of this book are the tools and techniques of exploration, and the territory of our exploration is called the mediascape. Like the mountains in western Utah, the mediascape is a complex and changing communication ecology. Depending on where we are, we will find different media industries, technologies, audiences, texts, symbolic values, and cultural understandings (to name just a few elements)—all interacting and interdependent. We will also find ourselves, as we are an integral part of the mediascape as individuals, as aggregates of type and kind, and as members of communities, including those that practice research.

FOUR CORNERS OF ANALYSIS

We will likely end up exploring only some small part of what is possible, but it is good to start with something of the larger picture. As the number of elements is overwhelming, we need some organizing principles to explore the mediascape. Let's start with a four-corner compass.

The compass points to the properties, processes, consequences, and character of the mediascape, and each is analogous to the same elements one would find in any landscape.

Properties

The properties of any domain are the elements and entities that characterize that domain. The elements and entities of our mediascape are not rocks, plants, and animals but such items as industries, technologies, texts, rules and regulations, ratings, jobs, and even media[1] themselves. They are also audiences, producers, stockholders, managers, artists, and craft

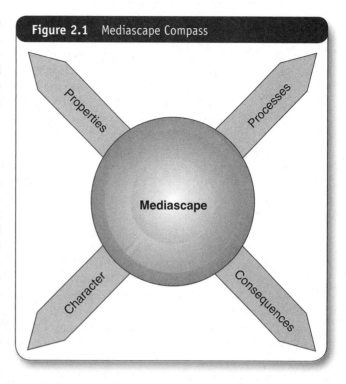

Figure 2.1 Mediascape Compass

unions as well as the individuals who belong to each category. In increasing levels of abstraction, they are domains of activity, interactive ecologies, and economic niches. All of the items listed and more are objects and entities that we can poke at, classify, and describe in a classic scientific manner.

For example, I was interested in finding out something about reality television. It was being presented in the literature as if it were a unitary classification—that we could think about reality TV as a single thing in the same way we might think about local evening news as a single entity. One answer to this question might come from a careful examination of content to see if the forms, structures, and narratives show the same consistency across programs as the evening news does across markets—it is, after all, news, weather, and sports from Fargo to Miami. But I was more interested in audiences, so the question I asked was whether the audience showed the same constitution across different reality programs.

Our primary information about television audiences comes from the ratings industry (not academic scholarship), and Nielsen Media Research is, perhaps, the premier member of that industry. As a professional courtesy, I asked the firm to prepare a special report on the average audiences for a set of 12 programs (listed here in order of popularity): *American Idol, Extreme Makeover, The Apprentice, The Amazing Race, American Inventor, Cops, Blind Date, Starting Over, Girls Behaving Badly, American Chopper, Date My Mom,* and *Unsolved Mysteries.* To my delight, the fine folks there did.

---

[1]Most complex objects can be approached as processes, as consequences, and according to their character as well.

As you look at that list, I presume you have all sorts of questions: Why those programs and not others? What makes those programs reality television? And whoever heard of *Girls Behaving Badly?* As a scholar writing a research report, I would be expected to answer those questions in such a manner that would establish the credence of the research. And of course I will, but right now I want to get to the juicy bits.

In order to test the composition of the audience, I looked at three ratios: (a) the ratio of people to households to get a measure of the amount of coviewing in a given household, (b) the ratio of women to men, and (c) the ratio of adults to children. *American Idol* had the highest proportion of coviewing (3 viewers for every 2 households) and the highest percentage of children (ages 2–17) in the audience (17%). *Starting Over,* a daytime reality program about six women starting over with the aid of a life coach, on the other hand, was mostly solitarily viewed, by more women than men (2.7:1) and with less than 10% of the audience being children. Finally, *American Chopper*—Discovery Channel's coverage of a father-and-son team of custom motorcycle builders—flipped the male-female ratio to 2:1 with nonetheless a reasonably healthy coviewing of 4 viewers, 11% of whom were children, for every 3 households (which was also the overall average).

Two interesting findings: (a) The ratio of women to men across all reality programming was 3:2. Only *Cops* and *American Chopper* shifted the balance to men. (b) The average percentage of children across these programs was 13.5%; the lowest percentage of children (7%) was for *The Apprentice*—Donald Trump's intoning of "You're fired"; the highest percentage of children (48%) appeared for *Date My Mom*—an MTV program in which an 18- to 24-year-old dates the mother of an eligible son or daughter to decide whether to date the son or daughter (hey, it must work for somebody)—and the 12- to 17-year-old group was the largest audience segment.

The consistency of the ratio of women to men (with only two exceptions) suggests that there is a communality of some sort in the content (that it is really about relationships, perhaps). On the other hand, we know that young men are migrating from television to the Net.[2] Consequently, the ratio may just be a function of more women watching television than men generally. I certainly have more work to do to understand the audiences of reality programs. Nonetheless, I would conclude that reality television is more complex than singular and that the classification can be only loosely used.

Metric Methodologies for Properties

The study of properties is a study of characteristics and quantities. Survey methodologies—questionnaires, diaries, and even automated data collections such as Internet cookies, credit card sales, and grocery store value cards—are the primary methodologies of the study of properties. They all reveal the properties of the mediascape according to the lens of the survey instrument. Properties may exist independently, but they appear in the measurement in use. In our example on reality programming, the 18- to 24-year-old audience appears because the A. C. Nielsen measurement process classifies people that way. There is a 19- to 23-year-old audience as well, but we cannot access it, because the measurement does not report it. We are very early in this discussion, but how you ask a question (or take any measurement) matters to your understanding of what is out there. Suffice it to say at

---

[2]http://www.wired.com/news/business/0,1367,64439,00.html. Accessed December 27, 2006.

this point that a survey is not just a survey. It also defines into existence the characteristics that will fill our reports. In a very real way, if we don't measure it, it doesn't exist for us.

Interpretive Methodologies for Properties

Interpretive methodologies are primarily immersive methods that require an extensive engagement with the object, group, or practice of interest—methods such as close reading for texts and participant observation for groups and practices. The properties of interest to the analyst are those that are somehow meaningful. To use a very simple example, that a light hanging over a road is green is of no importance except that it grants legal passage. The interpretive analyst starts with material properties but as a foundation for understanding the meaningful properties of an object or entity.

That statement is not to say that the metric scholar has no interest in such meaning, but there is a shift in analytic obligation. It might be sufficient for the metric analyst to report that the 2010 premiere of *Dancing with the Stars* had an audience of nearly 21 million viewers as the highest-rated program of the week. That report, however, would not be sufficient for the interpretive scholar, who would carry the responsibility for outlining the attractiveness (meaningfulness) of the program. That attractiveness and meaningfulness could be claimed by analyzing the content, but the better work would be to find them in the audience.

Processes

The study of properties is necessary and important. It fills about 60% of the research archive. But such study is a static enterprise, and communication is much more a dynamic process. One lesson that we can learn from the analysis of reality programs is that as we explore the entities that occupy, inhabit, and constitute the mediascape, we become more sophisticated in understanding how the mediascape is a set of processes, which themselves are more or less integrated systems of practice. We could, for example, be interested in describing the vertical integration characteristics of media industries in contrast to the horizontal, leveling characteristics of technology. That might lead us to question how these processes function.

Peer-to-peer file downloading is a good example of a process that demonstrates technology's leveling effect. Sony's much criticized music copy protection encoding scheme demonstrated an industry response to this leveling effect in an effort to maintain vertical control. From a strictly technological point of view, neither the artist nor the consumer needs Sony anymore. And that should scare Sony a lot. Sony and all content distributors survive by producing artificial scarcities through the manipulation of supply and demand. (That claim would make a fine research question for an excellent study.)

Metric Process Methods

Processes require sequential measurement methodologies that are measurement dense. Measurement density is achieved through the number of different measures taken, the number of times those measurements are repeated, and the time span between repetitions. Because processes involve real-time interactions in which significant change can happen at any moment, true process methodologies require something that approaches continuous measurement. We are not even close to this ability in measuring mediated communication processes. As in the case of our example on copy protection, we often can simply describe different sets of circumstances as Step A and Step B without knowing the intervening steps that connect them.

Processes and the properties involved in them combine with other processes to create systems. Program production, for example, is a system that involves the processes of writing, scripting, scene construction, prop work, costuming, makeup, camera and actor blocking, acting, directing, and editing. And then there are systems of systems such as the advertising system that generates the money that provides for much of the program production itself. Systems at this level quickly overwhelm our ability to collect empirical data on their functioning. We are often left with formal analysis that constructs logical connections according to reasonable speculations but not real data.

Interpretive Process Methods

The difficulty of process study means that we do not know a lot about the processes that attend to mediated communication. For example, 90% of us live in multiperson households (single-person householders tend to be either in their 20s or past the decade of their 60s). That necessarily means that media use is an ongoing accommodation among household members. We know very little about what those accommodation processes are, however, because the best method to find out about them is to actually observe and in some way participate in them, to carefully detail both the observation and the participation, and finally to interpret the meaningful interconnections that fuse acts into action. There are metric and hybrid alternatives—extensive survey instruments, long-form interviews, placement of diaries, protocol analysis or sequential data collections (that now use cell phones and could use Twitter)—but generally these are less successful in capturing the continuities and discontinuities that populate actual practice.

Consequences

The consequences of the media for 21st-century life are enormous. The economic value of the global media industry is approaching a trillion dollars. Every other industry has to account for the media in some way. The character of global and local politics is inalterably changed from campaigns to methods of governance. Many of the ways we earn our living and conduct our work depend on media and the technologies of communication. And certainly our recreation and entertainment are marked by media.

We also know there are consequences (or effects as they are often called) that result from each individual's participation in mediated communication. If nothing else, participation in mediated communication leads to a reduced ability to participate in face-to-face communication (leading to the new rule of etiquette of taking out at least one earpiece—even if grudgingly—when addressed). But certainly there is more. We attribute the increasing obesity of U.S. citizens to the choice of media over exercise. We insist that media violence increases social aggression even in the face of falling violent crime rates. We claim addictions to pornography, to the Internet, to materialism, to playing games. We claim that our version of the world around us is shaped by media—our sense of race, ethnicity, gender, and even self-worth. (Generally, scholars find all that media influence off-putting, as if there was some better way—some *real* way—in which our sense making could be accomplished.)

Metric Methods for Studying Consequences

Consequences and the causal relationships that invoke them are the gold standard of science and of our exploration. The best method we have for demonstrating consequence is the controlled experiment. The design of a controlled experiment attempts to hold all the active elements constant except the one we are interested in. The challenge of experimental design is twofold: One must know what the active elements in the causal chain are in order to apply the proper controls, and the protocol of the design (what one does in the experiment) must approximate what people actually do with media in real life (have ecological validity). We have an uneven track record in meeting these two challenges.

In fact, many of the consequences in which we are very interested do not appear to be amenable to testing in an experiment. The effect of media on presidential campaigns is an example, because we cannot construct a presidential campaign without media. In those cases, we are often reduced to using survey methods and attributing the conditions described to an effect of the media. Logically this is very weak evidence, but it is a common research practice and often may be the best information available.

Interpretive Methods for Studying Consequences

There is no interpretive analogue for the metric experiment. This absence has more to do with the underlying and different theories of knowledge that support each approach than with any methodological insufficiency. The problem focuses on the differences between a socially constructed reality and an objective one and whether personal agency is allowed or dismissed. We discussed a little of this problem in Chapter 1, and we will revisit it in Chapter 5. For an interpretive scholar the question of the experimental protocol is similar to asking, "Can the analyst set up a set of conditions in which certain actions are more likely than others?" The answer is invariably "Yes!" because that is exactly what a socially constructed reality means.

The problem with agency is a bit subtler. Agency is the ability to do otherwise. In any experiment, there are typically respondents who show no effect of, say, the message. Those data fall into the error component of the metric analysis and receive no further attention. For the interpretive scholar (who also sustains agency), those may be the people who say, "No way." They may become the very focus of the analysis because they allow a comparison with those who say, "Yes way."

While there is no interpretive experiment (see Chapter 5 for further evidence), there certainly are consequences and the study of them in interpretive research. Most often, these consequences and their study happen in the cultural analysis of texts or, as would be my preference, in the analysis of audiences using long-form interviews, protocol analysis, or (gold standard) participant observation.

Character

Character refers to the quality or value that is inherent in or attributed to some element, process, or relationship of or within the mediascape. In a natural landscape, character develops in the relationship between humans and the terrain. We value the products of upthrust and erosion more than those of sedimentation and entropy, which means we generally like mountains and canyons more than marshes and swamps. The character of a landscape is, of course, all us; it's entirely an attribution. Nature doesn't care; it's not showing off when it pushes a fracture 20,000 feet above sea level. The value we attach to the height plays no part in how high it will go.

The mediascape, however, is entirely a human endeavor. That means that the values that we attach to the elements, processes, and relationships do play a part in determining how high it will go. There are, then, inherent values in the mediascape (albeit constructed through social processes). And they are a significant element in understanding not only the terrain but also the exploration. In understanding the terrain, for example, Apple, by most accounts, produced a superior computer well before the introduction of the IBM personal computer, but Apple's failure to understand the values of the business community led to its current 4% market share. On the other hand, the Apple iPod holds between 75% and 80% of the media player market. Most agree that as an MP3 player, it has fewer features and the same technology as most, but it also presented a "startlingly original" design, which allowed it to sell its limitations at a premium price.[3] A different set of values was obviously in play.

The issue of character comes into sharp focus when we turn to issues of policy. We have debated the effects of media violence on society for over 100 years with no fundamental resolution of the science or the significance. There are those who say that the evidence of harm is patently clear and irrefutable and those who reply that obviously most of us watch at least some media violence with no harmful effects at all. There are those who say that we should ban violence and those who reply that censorship does more damage to a society than the content. These are issues of value and a legitimate part of our scholarship.

A further example continues to develop: In 1999 the American Academy of Pediatrics issued a recommendation of "No TV Under 2." Recently, *Sesame Street*, that bastion of quality children's television, approved the licensing of its characters for programming for the 0–3 audience. Supporters of the "No TV Under 2" rule sharply criticized that decision as promoting television use for those for whom all screen media are deemed unsuitable. The argument in reply was that children under 2 will watch television despite the recommendation; they may benefit or at least encounter less harm if they watch something designed for them.

Scholars have a love-hate relationship with the concept of character. It's OK to consider as long as it's an attribute "out there" that we can objectively describe. We get more than a little touchy when we bring it "in here" to consider the process of scholarship. Scholars and researchers, nonetheless, are part of the mediascape. Their footprints are everywhere—in the design of products, programs, and content as well as in legislative action, regulation, and social response. The current character of children's programming in the United States is unarguably marked by the activity of scholars and researchers. The V-chips in our television sets and the warning labels on music and games come from research initiatives and scholarly testimony, and programs themselves are designed in response to research findings.

We scholars also extract value from the mediascape. Those of us who study and teach media make a living within it. Our research (and here I am advancing a most contentious principle) has to reflect the values that justify that livelihood. It is not by chance that we see a nearly 300:1 ratio of studies on the negative effects of media compared to studies on

---

[3]http://www.pcmag.com/article2/0,1895,1622992,00.asp. Accessed March 27, 2006.

the prosocial effects of media, although the clear evidence is that there are both (based on the analysis of 966 studies in Anderson, 2008b). Why so many more negative studies? There are any number of answers, but they all come down to choices the research community makes in what scholarship to conduct and to support. What we know about the media and how we know it depend on both us and the values we represent.

Issues of character, quality, and value express themselves most directly in scholarship on policy, social change, political action, cultural impact, and critical analysis, but they appear everywhere in both the significance of the problem and the "So what?" or implications sections that are part of most research. The effects scholar who justifies a study because it represents the analysis of a "social problem" or who concludes that parents should monitor their children's screen media use introduces an argument of value in what otherwise might appear to be objective science. Indeed, science in media has a long history of following the sharp cries of danger that social critics have issued as each new medium or technology has arrived on the scene. Such science, seemingly, loves the smell of moral decay because it signals the availability of funding, disciplinary legitimation, and personal prominence.

Metric Methods for the Analysis of Character

For the mainstream metric analyst, character is an attribute or property of an entity or an attribute attached to an entity by some segment of a population. We might find that older, White males value the news more highly than any other age/race/sex segment of the audience. As an attribute, character is amenable to survey research or could be used as a control or covariate variable in an experiment.

Interpretive Methods for the Analysis of Character

Interpretive scholars are turning more and more to the critical approaches of rhetorical theory, cultural studies, and the sociology and rhetoric of science to study character. Historically, these methods have been more formal (following the canons of rational argument, e.g., mathematics) than empirical. Contemporary methods of those approaches now include the formal and the empirical in hybrid methods that combine the "hard data" of measurement, the "interpretive data" of observation, and the critical evaluation of cultural analysis. These hybrid methods investigate the cultural practices of race and gender, the presentation of the self in form and action, the decoration of our homes and offices, and the role of media in them all. Of course, they are also in play in the study of us. These hybrid methods are developing observational analysis of our research practices and protocols as well as content analysis and critical analysis of the research texts that result.

PUTTING IT TOGETHER: FRIENDS IN SOCIAL NETWORKING SITES

In beginning any new study, it is always a good idea to think through each of the four component sets that will constitute the problem. Certainly any particular publication or report might focus mainly on one portion (say, properties or consequences), but having the big picture beforehand is always a plus. We can work an extended example by taking up the issue of friends in social networking sites (SNS). There are any number of ways that we can focus this issue: an interest or concern for the changing definition of friends; the risks/costs/losses/gains of such friendships; the role of technology in interpersonal relationships; the utilities of SNS friends; and so forth. Again, however, we want to think the whole thing through before adopting a particular focus. There is amazingly little in the literature (as of this writing) concerning SNS friends, which is even more reason to do our own careful analysis. Consequently, we need to go round the compass. We start with properties.

Properties

Properties answer the questions of what and who make up the phenomenon under study. There are some elements that are obvious—the what of a social networking site, membership on a site, and an SNS friend—but there are important things that you would not know unless you joined. To begin, the concept of a social networking site is not in itself simple. The open web itself is a giant social network. I connect with people and their ideas nearly every time I use it, but it is rarely considered as such in SNS studies. Beyond the behemoth of Facebook (more than 500 million active members claimed), there are dozens of specialized SNSs such as PeopleAggregator, Moxie Moms, MuslimSpace, Tribe, and Stardoll (claiming 14 million tween doll fans) just to offer five examples. (These change daily.)

Even ostensibly similar networking sites can have important differences. Observations posted by danah boyd (lowercase is apparently her preference) suggest strong class differences between the teen members of Myspace and the teen members of Facebook.[4] While boyd's piece is not a vetted academic article, it appears to be based on careful observations and is worth noticing; plus she is a known, published author. Why would the chosen SNS matter? It matters because all the other entities, friends, memberships, profiles, and so on very likely change with it. Any knowledgeable reviewer is going to challenge the unmarked selection of a site.

I joined both Myspace and Facebook for the purpose of writing this section. In Facebook, there was a request-and-confirm process to get friends. In Myspace, Tom was a friend before I got my profile up. (Tom—the avatar of Tom Anderson, founder of Myspace—is everybody's friend.) That friendship did not last very long, however, in the turmoil of technology as Myspace morphed into a music and entertainment site in the presence of Facebook's overwhelming success as the global social networking site.[5]

Processes

Membership in Facebook is a status that constitutes me as a countable entity, one of the more than 500 million. Being a member, however, is a process that involves all the steps required to maintain an active profile. Blog sites on the web critical of SNS membership claims suggest that fewer than 40% of those who join bother to maintain an active profile.[6]

[4]http://www.danah.org/papers/essays/ClassDivisions.html. Accessed February 10, 2008.

[5]Alas, Myspace apparently will not survive my membership. Today's *Salt Lake Tribune* (June 29, 2011, p. E4) reported that Myspace was about to be sold for a fire sale price of $20–30 million—a bit down from the $580 million News Corp. paid for it. There are two cautionary tales here, one about using real-life examples in books and the other about the longevity of research claims (like boyd's). On the facing page (E5), however, the *Trib* reported Google's second try at social networking. Facebook may have competition yet.

[6]http://www.web-strategist.com/blog/2010/01/19/a-collection-of-social-network-stats-for-2010/. Accessed April 11, 2011.

Most social networking sites encourage activity by pushing messages to one's e-mail address. Traffic, of course, is their lifeblood for their advertising income.

For the member, the process of being a member can be quite demanding, entailing regular check-ins, joining and contributing to groups, responding to messages from friends real and erstwhile, maintaining a blog, writing comments on the wall, and all the other demands that the sites create both to provide services and to keep one coming back.

Why does the difference between membership as an entity status and membership as a process matter? Consider that you were writing a questionnaire investigating SNSs and you asked the simple question, "Do you belong to a social networking site?" Perhaps the purpose of your question is to discover the differences that might exist across a set of criteria between people who belong and people who do not. If the critics are right, then the majority of those who answer "Yes" are members in name only. That may be enough distinction to generate differences across the criteria, but more than likely those who actively participate will show even greater differences or perhaps different data profiles.

Process is an important and oft-neglected domain of study. Many of the demographic variables that are treated as categorical states may be more profitably considered as processes. Race, age, gender (aka sex), ethnicity, and even income are more about the processes of being White, 52, male, euro-mongrel, and six-figured than they are about set membership. The difference between sex as a category and gender as an enactment (process) is instructive. Sex refers to the conclusion of a genetic process; gender refers to the performance of the cultural roles of male and female. Unless our theory is based on genitalia and hormones, our real interest is in the consequences of those cultural roles. Noted interpersonal scholar Anita Vangelisti commented to me that the differences within a gender are greater than the differences across the averages for gender. In other words, the enactment variations within a process (the many ways of being female or male) can be much greater than the difference across categories.

Because I work in a cultural studies shop, my bias is toward processes rather than properties, but both have their place. The key is to recognize the difference in what one's theory requires for doing competent research work. In the example we are working here, the process of membership—the enactment of belonging—would seem to offer a far richer understanding than the simple categorical value of member. Clearly, such concepts as commitment, activity and time costs, performance expertise, and technological demands can all be derived from an examination of the process of membership rather than the state of membership. On the other hand, a count of the different categories of friends (say, preexisting, self-selecting, trolled-for, etc.) might be very useful for exploring the complexity of SNS friendship.

In the end, however, the answer to the question of what it means to be a friend on a social networking site is answered by examination of the things one does in the name of being a friend. This examination might help us better understand the differences between the strong-tie connections of face-to-face networking and the weak-tie connections of the social networking sites. If the entire transaction is completed by two clicks of the mouse with no further obligation entailed, then the issue shifts from a concern about friendship to the meaning of SNS friends as ornaments of a profile. When Jon Stewart on *The Daily Show* (the fake news program on Comedy Central) teasingly (and incorrectly) begged his audience to "friend" the show on Facebook (*The Daily Show* became a member on January 28, 2008), one may have suspected that his effort at a friend surge was an entirely commercial move that had nothing to do with the traditional performances of friendship.[7] Facebook seems to consider the difference, because despite Stewart's plea, one cannot befriend the show; one can only become a fan.

Consequences

The study of consequences has a long history and a very central position in mediated communication studies. The study of consequences runs from the very weak relationship of a "compare and contrast" or correspondence analysis to the very strong relationship of a "cause and effect" analysis. In a correspondence analysis, a researcher might collect information on the characteristics noted by respondents for face-to-face (FtF) friendships and those noted for SNS friendships to see if in some sort of essential way they are the same or different. In that analysis, one can discover whether SNSs provide an alternative way for constituting friendship or whether SNSs have provided a new form of relationship that corresponds to "friend" in name only. We might also be interested in following up boyd's observation of differences across SNSs themselves: Are LinkedIn *colleagues* different from Facebook *friends* in the actual practices of networking? (The consequence here is in the effect of technology and its application.)

Moving on from that analysis, we might be interested in whether SNS friendships complement or compete with FtF friendships across time and activity demands or in terms of uses served and gratifications fulfilled or whether SNS friends are merely popularity indices with no implications for FtF friends. (The consequence here is the effect of new forms of relationship on old forms.) Finally, we might arrive at questions concerning the effects on individuals. Do individuals with a large number of SNS friends have different attitudes toward friendship? Are people with more SNS friends less cognitively complex than those with more FtF friends? (The argument here would take off from Aristotle's claim that true friends are to develop the mind and spirit of each other.) Both of these questions come from a particular theoretical position called cognitivism, which is the dominant theoretical position of effects studies. But there are more than "effects" going in this question, because there is an implication of damage being done. That implication calls on us to consider the character of this domain.

Character

Readers are reminded that the study of character is an oft-disputed activity in science. Be that as it may, most of the current concern with SNSs has been with the naïveté of users who think that whatever is posted in this domain of play will not be used against them in the domains of work, adjudication, and finance.

Studies of friends on social networking sites are just now moving from academic conventions to publication. The issues raised in these convention papers include time wasted, false friends, dishonest representation, and the like, all of which are exacerbated by the Internet. One such report concludes, "While online social networks are very unlikely to

---

[7]It is, nonetheless, an outstanding example of intertextuality or the interaction of one textual form with another.

ever replace real-life social networks, it is possible that their ability to aid communication may bring about a change in the size and structure of real-life social networks in the future" (British Association for the Advancement of Science, 2007). This language offers both comfort and a warning. The comfort is that the old will remain; the warning is that it will not be the same, and (implicitly) you better prepare for it (although the older among us may take comfort in Dunbar's estimate that 150 relationships is our neocortical limit).[8]

As a postmodernist, I have no problem with creating studies that argue for a world that ought to be. Personally, I think that is more honest than a modernist pretense of simply describing the world that is while at the same time trading off of the values of social concern and offering gratuitous advice at the end. I am a long way from creating such a study about friends and friending on social networking sites. Not only do I not know enough to argue either effectiveness or harm (although there are clearly things I do not like); I also do not know any worthwhile alternative. Yet in the area of character, those are my responsibility: First, what is the contribution to the quality of life of the properties, processes, and consequences under study? And second, what is the contribution that my study can offer?

Some obvious studies come to mind: First I could search for increased effectiveness as Reader (British Association for the Advancement of Science, 2007) did in concluding that SNSs allow individuals to maintain contact with a much larger number of friends than would be possible in FtF relationships. (One of my real-life friends claims to have over 1,100 Facebook friends, but has not friended me.) I could argue harm in that SNS friends are more likely to be faint friends entailing no commitment to safeguard the other. In either of these directions, my ethical responsibility is to play fair. My claims have to be more than self-fulfilling. Showing that the technology allows members to have an unlimited number of friends substitutes a mouse click for the substantial responsibilities of friendship. And claiming that a mouse click is no basis for sharing intimate information presumes there is something inherently wrong with sharing such information. I am gee-whizzing in the first claim and acting as a scold in the second. Neither is the careful, systematic study to which we should aspire.

MOVING ON

We've been doing a lot of hard work developing a sophisticated understanding of our disciplines, our methodologies, and our media world. It may be time to pause for a little fun and to take a look at the technological and media history that traces from whence we came to help us understand why we are here. In training films, this is called the "from the dawn of time" moment—you know, when the narrator sonorously intones, "From the dawn of time, the human spirit has sought to enlarge its expression across time and space." Well, our "from the dawn of time" moment is a 20-page express train through media history, shown in Appendix A. If you simply must get on with the work, take yourself off to Chapter 3.

---

[8]http://en.wikipedia.org/wiki/Dunbar's_number. Accessed April 11, 2011.

REFLECTIONS

What Are Some Points to Remember?

- Media research is not just about content and audiences. Media are fully integrated in contemporary society and culture through multiple industries, technologies, practitioners, and participants.
- The mediascape is a complex ecology that presents properties, processes, consequences, and character.
- Properties, processes, consequences, and character each have varying affinities for metric and interpretive methodologies. Further, within a given methodology, typical methods are associated with each.
- Each of us lives in a different location within the mediascape. We may share some or even much of it, but just as my life in the mountains is not your life on the coasts, the highlands, or the plains, so your media life is not mine.

Why Does It Matter?

The purpose of this chapter is to provide the reader with an understanding of the what and why of research methods before learning how to do them. It provides a basic foundation for the work to be done in the next two chapters. Learning only how to do something develops little or no ability to self-evaluate the performance. Learning the what and why allows the analyst to move beyond the simple recipes of research.

What Else Could We Talk About?

The United States is just one, relatively small part of the global mediascape. Different parts of the world have different industry configurations, different content regulations—some with much more freedom of content; many with much less—different audience practices, different ways of integrating media into political structures. While at one time U.S. footprints were all over the mediascape, now others are more prominent.

What Else Might Be Interesting to Read?

Lievrouw, L. A., & Livingstone, S. (Eds.). (2002). *The handbook of new media*. London: Sage.

CHAPTER 3

Methods of Exploration

Asking Questions

CHAPTER PREVIEW

What's It All About?

The purpose of research is to add to the archive of public knowledge. The findings of that research may be open to all or restricted by government or corporate interests, but all that qualifies as research is open to some independent review. Well-designed research starts out with a well-thought-out problem. Developing research problems is a systematic process that might start with an intellectual itch, but then moves through a step-by-step refinement.

What Are the Major Topics?

All research and scholarship regardless of foundation or method meets the standards of public review, evidence-based argument, and rule-directed practice.

Theory and method are closely interrelated. Theory must have an attached methodology in order to be complete. A method always invokes its justifying theory. The use of a method also introduces the epistemological foundations of the theory into the argument whether appropriate or not.

Successful problems are socially significant, unresolved in the literature, and open to empirical study. Problem development starts with a curiosity about something that leads to a preliminary investigation that outlines the properties and relationships within the problem, ending in a short description. That description is further refined in discussion with knowledgeable others and in analysis of the literature.

Different methodologies develop problems in different ways. The deductive logic of metric approaches calls for a well-developed set of initiating premises and problem boundaries. The grounded approach of interpretive methods calls for this deep understanding of the problem to emerge in contact with the participants, site, and action. Hybrid methods start with a standpoint—a particular perspective—and move to a deeper understanding of that perspective through the analysis of some resonating problem.

The ethical issues in problem selection stand on the public import of the problem and the public value of its analysis.

What Special Terms Are Used?

Analytical methods	Emergent	Provisional claim
Argument	Falsified claim	Public knowledge
Certified claim	Hypothesis	Research question
Critical rationalism	Inductive	Settled science
Deductive	Private knowledge	

INTRODUCTION: PRIMACY OF THE PROBLEM

All research starts with a problem, not with a method. The problem properly stated and analyzed will establish everything else. In fact, good problems are the heartbeat of any discipline. Their quality sets the quality of the discipline's scholarship. In settled sciences, problems are what set the agenda for research by the entire discipline. We are not a settled science with a consensus agenda, but we do have a full set of unsolved problems—problems that have to do with concepts like content, effects, audiences, meaning, interpretation, and nearly any other topic in media.

Researchers are directed by the problems they engage. A successful researcher has a curiosity about the world and adopts a questioning approach: What is that? How does it work? Why does it work that way? What value does it have? While that researcher may have more than the usual amount of natural inquisitiveness, the approach is a learned one, systematically applied. In this chapter, we take up the problem of problems. In the next chapter, we will take up the problem of finding answers.

For right now, however, we need to make sure that we are all on the same page of understanding some foundational principles before we get to the big picture of the process of research. We turn to those preliminaries next; remember that the problem is where it all starts.

PRELIMINARIES

Commonalities

All of the methods we will study have three common characteristics that distinguish them from other claims of knowing such as inspiration, revelation, authority, faith, and opinion. They are public, evidence based, and rule directed. The methods are public because (a) each presents its claim and the process by which that claim was achieved in some public forum (e.g., a journal article) and (b) each is subject to public review that leads to its acceptance or rejection (the claim is engaged by the research community in which it resides).

The second characteristic is that each is based on explicit evidence. That evidence can be formal, such as in a mathematical equation, or empirical, such as a survey, fieldwork, or a textual warrant. What makes that evidence explicit is that it is available to anyone who follows the same set of procedures. That statement does not mean that the evidence will be the same, supporting the same conclusions. It means that the procedures will generate the same kind of evidence in each application, allowing a comparison across instances.

The third common characteristic is that each follows a set of conventions or publicly agreed-upon rules of process that establish both what is to be done and the criteria of competent research. (This characteristic is what textbooks on research methods are all about.) Developing methods, such as the hybrid methods we will briefly encounter, generally present weakly drawn rules of process. That characteristic is part of their attraction as the practitioner has more freedom to mess around. But if the method is to stand the test of time, the community will have to agree on its practices.

Creating Public Knowledge

The goal of these methods and the reason they have these commonalities is, ultimately, the creation of public knowledge—claims that some community of knowers hold to be certified. Public knowledge is contrasted with private knowledge. Private knowledge is the ineffable claims that we each hold to be true from our own life experience and that are particular to the individual. Private knowledge becomes public knowledge through social control (e.g., you get installed as supreme ruler) or by submitting a claim to one of the public methods for testing.

What About the Truth of the Matter?

Note that in all of this discussion I have been careful not to use the word *true* in referencing public knowledge. That word carries a lot of problems with it. My preference is to keep the focus on the sociocultural processes by which knowledge is created rather than debate the truth of the matter. In this preference, I follow Karl Popper's critical rationalism (see the entry in Blackwell's Communication Encyclopedia).[1] His position is that claims

---

[1]http://www.communicationencyclopedia.com/public/tocnode?id = g9781405131995_yr2011_chunk_g9781405131 9958_ss158-1. Accessed April 11, 2011.

are either false or certified as having passed a fair test and survived professional scrutiny,[2] and are, therefore, considered acceptable until they fail or are replaced by something better. A claim is certified by passing a fair test under the governance of an acceptable methodology. We are justified in acting in accordance with certified claims, although we could be in error by doing so.

In Popper's formulation (and the position of this book on both metric and interpretive research), a claim is either untested or tested in an accepted methodology and, if tested, is either falsified or for the moment certified. Falsified claims provide us with no scientific justification to act in accordance with their terms, although we may find justification from some other source (e.g., deep personal belief). Certified claims give us adequate reason to act according to their terms. *Falsified* and *certified* are either/or categories, not probabilities, albeit ones that result from human activity, not some necessary function of the world. Claims do not become more certified or less falsified.

In between these two categories, however, is the great limbo of provisional claims—claims that have not been adequately tested to be considered falsified or certified. It is in this area of provisional claim that most of the work of normal science occurs. Consequently, most of what we read in our journals is provisional in nature. There is very little in communication research that is considered definitively falsified or definitively certified by anything approaching the majority of the communication research community.

Why is this issue important? Because as scholars, corporate managers, and individuals, we need to understand the limits of any claim we support. It is easy to forget those limits after all the hard work of coming up with a hypothesis or research question, devising some evidentiary method to test the hypothesis or to find answers, writing up the report, and getting it accepted for public review. At that point, we are understandably proud of our work and in the most danger of forgetting that we could still be wrong. We want other people to believe in our work. We may want our organization or parents or even all people to follow the recommendations it supports. When we act on those desires, we enter into a political (agenda-pushing) process and leave the epistemological (knowledge-making) process. Claims that are merely provisional suddenly become true. So, should we not advance what we believe in? Ah, a worthy question for an ethics discussion. But there are also clear implications about how we address and present our evidence in the methods we use. Stay tuned.

Theory and Method

The last preliminary in this list has to do with the relationship between theory and method. Methods develop in response to the demands of theory. Attitudinal scales make no sense if there are not such things as attitudes. There were no attitude scales in the epistemology of behaviorism. Attitudes, however, are theoretical constructs. We can see attitude but not an attitude. Most of the scales we see in questionnaires—agree/disagree; like/dislike—depend on some form of cognitive theory to make sense. Similarly, most forms of ethnographic study (reconnaissance, participant, performative, and critical ethnography) depend on some

---

[2]Note that there are several parts to certification that we will discuss in later sections.

form of social action theory. It just wouldn't make a lot of immediate sense to hand out questionnaires and claim you were doing ethnography.

Consequently, when you adopt a particular method, you are also importing the theory that supports it and provides the basis by which the information generated becomes evidence in the service of some claim. Tracing these connections can be complex at times, and they are also often controversial because we may want to use a method off-label, so to speak. I will try to give you a heads-up as to what you are buying in to; at the same time, you need to recognize that as a critic of methodologies, I am probably more severe in my assessment of boundaries.

With this preliminary framing, we can begin to look at an overview of the research process. That process comes in definable steps that appear regardless of problem or approach, but each of those steps poses its own set of challenges that must be met through both systematic and creative effort. I can show you how to be prepared for those moments of insight—the 90% perspiration part of inspiration—but the inspiration counts.

THE PROCESS OF RESEARCH

The process of research looks something like Figure 3.1 (at least in the neat world of methods textbooks). It starts with some curiosity, some disquieting moment that is sufficient to motivate the effort of a preliminary investigation to see if there is an adequate response to that itch of curiosity already out there. Absent that satisfaction, the heavy lifting starts with the analytical process of refining the problem into its testable components and the search process of the literature review. These are connected in the diagram as they feed off one another. But note that problem refinement takes the lead. One needs to think before reading in order to make the reading effort most efficient.

Once the problem is refined so that we know what it is that we actually want to know and we have situated ourselves in the literature, we can start making some decisions about how we are going to find answers. Finding answers is the business of the next chapter, so the rest of the model will have to wait while we more carefully examine the front end.

Nonetheless, we have to recognize at this point that the process is an integrated effort to produce an argument (see box for an explanation of an argument) for some claim or set of claims. We have to go through the whole process to produce that result, and without the argument, the process is incomplete. With that caveat, we are ready to explore the elements of this process.

> ### The Argument
>
> In everyday life we *have* arguments; in scholarship we *produce* arguments. The argument is a presentational form (usually a text) that couples evidence to claim through warrants (Toulmin, 1963). A warrant is an axiomatic principle, belief, or argument segment that justifies the use of the data collected (evidence) to support the claim. For a very good, interactive explanation of the theory of argument, see The Toulmin Project Home Page (http://www.unl.edu/speech/comm109/Toulmin/index.htm. Accessed September 27, 2010).

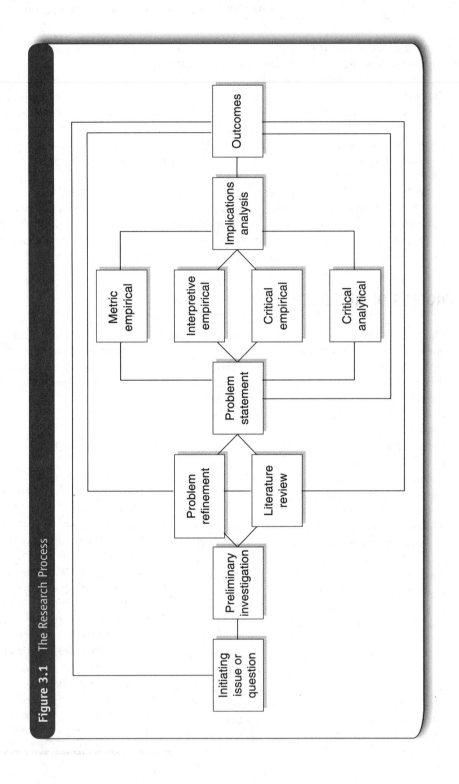

Figure 3.1 The Research Process

Initiating Issues and Preliminary Investigations

If research begins with a problem, where do we find the problem? For the professional researcher, finding problems is an integral part of the profession. We adopt activities that help us articulate and frame problems that will lead to published research. These activities include staying current with the academic and trade literature; training in and learning about media and technology, convergences, and markets; developing connections with media practitioners; and managing our understanding of audiences and audience practices. Doing research itself always generates more questions. And doing all of this on a world-wide, not just U.S., scope forces us to consider old questions under new contexts. There is an authentic professional practice involved that is not something easily adapted to or adopted by the occasional or just-learning researcher. Your instructor might make it look easy, but it is only because she or he works so hard at it.

For the media and corporate practitioner, problems for research usually develop out of the pragmatics of decision making. That too involves its own set of professional practices—practices of production and/or management. Questions routinely arise in those practices: What is the most efficient media mix for my advertising dollar? Can I move employee training to online? Is there a more cost-effective/audience-effective layout for this spread? What policies should we adopt for e-mail and web surfing? Mostly, these problems find their solutions (good and bad) in the authority and experience of managers or consultants. But each of these questions could be the source (or—dare I say it?—ought to be the source) of original research.

Professional practice alone, however, will not generate the problem. One must add that creative moment when one says something like "Huh, I wonder what is happening here?" That question in whatever way it is framed starts the process of the preliminary investigation. The preliminary investigation seeks to determine whether or not there is a real problem—a question for which there is not already a settled answer. Clearly, the professional scholar has a leg up here as she or he should already have a deep understanding of the conversation (as we lovingly call the research literature) that has been going on. Nonetheless, it is fairly easy to get connected with the key issues to see if the question is worth pursuing. Let's take some examples—first one that might be approached by metric methodologies and then one that might be addressed through interpretive methodologies.

Political Talk Radio: A Metric Study

One of the continuing questions in political campaigns has been the effect of media coverage. One of the newer forms of this coverage has been political talk radio. All the talk on this talk radio seems to be from one side of the political spectrum. Perhaps the more or less recent concentration of ownership of radio stations is reducing the diversity of opinion. This reduction of diversity is taking the effect of this coverage in a coordinated direction to the right, which explains (maybe) the political turn of U.S. politics. Or, to put it in conversational style, "Look, talk radio commentators are mainly conservative and ultraconservative at that. They form a unified force that has mobilized a group of voters to push this conservative agenda. That bloc of voters has had an outsized effect on our elections."

This issue seems juicy enough on the face of it. There are questions of fact to be resolved, insights to process, consequences of media exposure, and issues of social policy and broadcast regulation. Let's see if any work has been done by Googling the search term *effect of talk radio*. Google returns over 11 million sites that reference talk radio, but the first screen gives me some idea of what is going on.

Screenshot 3.1 Results of Google Search on "Effect of Talk Radio"

Source: http://www.google.com/

In fact, the first two items seem right on the money. (How does Google do that? Or—framed as a research question—what is the role of content aggregators in the structure of information and public knowledge formation?) The second item is an article by Yanovitzky and Cappella (2001) that reports on the effects of call-in political talk radio (PTR) shows.

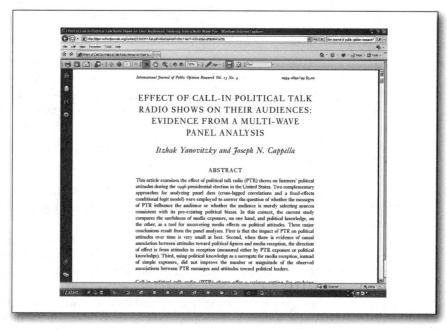

Screenshot 3.2 First Page of Yanovitsky and Cappella (2002)

Source: http://ijpor.oxfordjournals.org/

That site presents the citation to the article in the *International Journal of Public Opinion Research* and its abstract, which concludes:

Three major conclusions result from the panel analyses. First is that the impact of PTR on political attitudes over time is very small at best. Second, when there is evidence of causal association between attitudes toward political figures and media reception, the direction of effect is from attitudes to reception (measured either by PTR exposure or political knowledge). Third, using political knowledge as a surrogate for media reception, instead of simple exposure, did not improve the number or magnitude of the observed associations between PTR messages and attitudes toward political leaders.[3]

Well, that's kind of disappointing. Not only is effect small, but it is in the opposite direction; that is, people match their political ideology with the programs they listen to rather than have their political ideology formed by what they listen to.

At the bottom of that page, there is a notation of another article that has cited Yanovitzky and Cappella (2001) titled "Political Talk Radio, Perceived Fairness, and the Establishment

---

[3]http://ijpor.oxfordjournals.org/content/13/4/377.full.pdf + html?sid = b5710917-9e77-41f0-83bd-0f8b9547a755. Accessed January 16, 2007.

of President George W. Bush's Political Legitimacy" from *The International Journal of Press/ Politics*. Its abstract says,

> Political talk radio use leads to negative perceptions of Gore, which negatively influences perceptions of the perceived fairness of the 2000 election. Conversely, talk radio use generates more positive feelings toward Bush, which positively affects perceptions of fairness. Thus, feelings toward both candidates serve as important mediators that allow the use of this public affairs information source to make citizens feel better about how the fiercely contested 2000 presidential election was decided.[4]

This study suggests that the initial premise of the problem that there is a conservative slant to PTR was correct and that it affects people's judgments, but again it doesn't create their political ideology.

My conclusion from this preliminary investigation is that we have a good problem. It is not the one we started with but better, and its answer will give us a much more sophisticated understanding of how media participate in political attitudes. Mediated content apparently is not a simple hammer that shapes people's political positions. People have political positions prior to listening to talk radio, and they use talk radio to develop other judgments.[5] At this point, while we have a problem to study, we certainly don't have anything like a research question that might help us to decide the approach to an answer. That will be the goal of the twined activities of problem refinement and literature review.

Media Use by the Homeless: An Interpretive Study

For our second example, I am going to take something that is most likely far and away from our normal experiences. My current ethnographic work focuses on the homeless. In looking back from this writing, three things seem to have converged to spark this interest: (a) a conversation with a neighbor who is in a service agency, (b) a conversation with a colleague at a convention, and (c) a turn toward advocacy research (another stop in my own postmodern journey). I had the itch to know more, and I started my preliminary investigation.

At this point, the differences between metric empiricism and interpretive empiricism begin to appear. The epistemological foundation for metric empiricism invokes a process of increasing precision of description of some independent, objective condition. The goal is to arrive at the final statement about something. We want a transcendental law that holds for all conditions within the scope of the law. That still leaves us with a lot of wiggle room for new work, but ultimately a topic can become settled. There is no need to do additional work (and it won't be accepted in the public record anyway). The ethnographic work of interpretive empiricism is built on a different epistemological foundation—one that holds that knowledge is universally expanding, limited only by our interest and enthusiasm for achieving a new narrative on the topic. There is no final answer, only an increasing density of narrative.

---

[4]http://hij.sagepub.com/content/9/3/12.abstract. Accessed January 16, 2007.

[5]This is the language appropriate to uses and gratifications theory, an alternative position to the cognitive formation theory that was the basis of the initial formulation of our problem. It shifts the initiating point of the relationship from the media to the audience.

In practical terms, what this means in the hermeneutic approach is that the importance of the literature recedes particularly at this preliminary stage. What counts is whether I can get sufficiently connected into the community to generate useful insights. Consequently, at this point of problem development, I don't Google the homeless; I don't turn to the literature. I go to the site.

To start this preliminary investigation, then, I went down to an area in town where several of the homeless agencies were located and just started to hang out for about four hours a day. I would listen, watch, and interact when someone approached me. I didn't try to pass (though I don't look that much different), and I did not eat meals or make use of other services available (more issues for a discussion in research ethics). I would go home from those observations and write field notes (I did not take notes on-site). I did that for about a year. At the end of that period, I began to put together a picture of what I knew.

There were some surprising things: Homelessness is both a condition and an identity; homelessness and addiction can be copresent, but neither is a necessary condition of the other (there are plenty of domiciled drunks and druggies); there are different levels of homelessness; the more homeless one is, the more likely he or she will be a member of some homeless community; a homeless community is a system of relationships and reciprocal obligations rather than a place, but time and place are very important for survival on the streets; homelessness is different for men and women and for different ethnicities (homelessness for men is often a loss or failure of masculine identity; for women homelessness is quite often the literal loss of home); agencies can participate in homelessness in their policies and procedures; the domiciled can tell only a very simple story of homelessness; the homeless have both the same and very different media experiences compared to the domiciled. All of these findings deserve their own particular study with the conditions of observation, participation, and performance prioritized to accomplish a particular set of narrative goals. I have to craft the argument in each case. But note the direction here. The work of developing an argument or sets of arguments occurs after intensive fieldwork in the strong ethnographic form. Although common practice in the abbreviated forms of ethnography—6 months or less in the field—the analyst does not embark on fieldwork with an argument in mind in the strong form.

To show how it is done, I'll demonstrate the development of a study around the way members of different homeless communities experience media. After more than two years of fieldwork, I know it is not the trivial issue it might seem. Most media content has to do with appearance, status, power, gender roles, materialism, stability, and security. These are all elements that on the face of it have to be renegotiated from the cultural standard of the domiciled and have to be renegotiated in different ways by those who have a different psychic and physical distance from home. Further, the homeless do not have the opportunity to experience media as the domiciled do (no home, you see) with the apparent exception of personal music and cell phones, both of which are common among the homeless.[6]

I am now ready to find out what is in the literature. Google fails me, but one of my favorite databases, *Communication and Mass Media Complete,* returns 99 entries, among which is an article by Dordick and Rachlin (1997).

---

[6]Consider your reaction to that information.

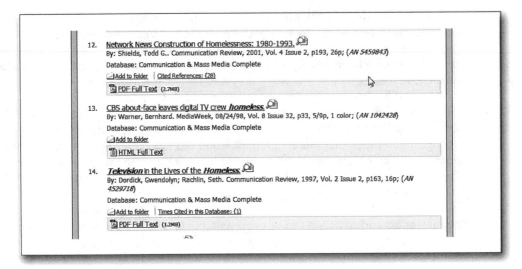

Screenshot 3.3   Results From Communication and Mass Media Complete

Source: http://www.ebsco.com/

Their abstract summarizes their study as showing "that, over and above what is actually on TV, television as a cultural object is used by certain groups of homeless individuals to reflect and reinforce status differences and social boundaries between them [the homeless groups]" (Dordick & Rachlin, 1997, p. 163).

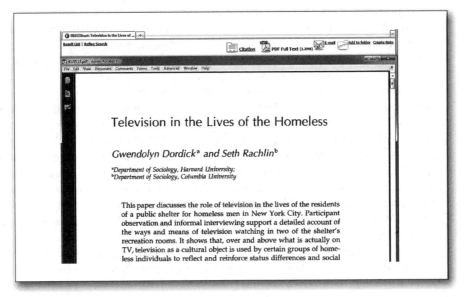

Screenshot 3.4   First Page of Dordick and Rachlin (1997)

Source: http://www.ebsco.com/

As an ethnographer, I am not particularly interested in Dordick and Rachlin's (1997) finding, however. I will not be building my narrative on their results. What they and a handful of other references demonstrate is that there is a narrative field in which I can participate and to which I have a lot to add.

Refining the Problem

Our preliminary investigation has demonstrated that in both examples we have identified a problem worth pursuing. The job now is to refine the problem statement to the specific research questions or hypotheses that we will attempt to answer. We use analytical methods to engage the problem, to determine the problem domain and its components. From there, we can begin to investigate what we need to know and how we can find that knowledge.

An Excursion Into Analytical Methods

As promised in Chapter 1, we will explore the use of analytical methods. Analytical methods are those that help the researcher see the elements of the problem, the interrelationships among those elements, the operation of those elements and relationships, and the implications of elements, relationships, and operations. Analytical methods are based in language, logic, mathematics, and visual mapping as well as their combinations. The method one uses is typically driven by the character of the problem and the propensities of the researcher. In some cases, it involves writing the problem out and letting the demands of the narrative unfold the problem. For others, it is setting up the problem according to logical or mathematical principles. For me, it's often a diagram in combination with a narrative.

But the key is that analysis involves some systematic method that is intentionally directed at understanding the problem. That method is rehearsed and refined, and when executed to guide research, it is done at a high level of performance. All methods in media research, and especially analytical methods, then, presume an active investigator who interrogates the mediascape even as she or he uses it, is connected to its research and practitioner communities through regular reading, observes the media use of others, utilizes media and technology in an observant way, and is open to practices and consequences.[7] One cannot analyze from ignorance. Analytical explorations play three different roles. Analytical approaches are used to develop a position based on established evidence and reason. They are also the primary means of theory development, and in this use they are prior to any data collection. They constitute the map, if you will, of what ought to be out there. Analytical methods establish the requirements by which a hypothesis can be tested or answers to research questions can be found. And, analytical approaches are used after data collection or textual capture to examine the formal and inferential properties of those data and texts.

Research and scholarship use a basic argument form. If we look at the form, we can see where analytical methods come into play. That standard form traditionally addresses the following elements: (a) statement of the problem, (b) review of existing research, (c) method of the current study (hypotheses or research questions and protocol design for testing or finding answers), (d) results, (e) implications and limitations, and (f) summary, conclusions, and recommendations.

---

[7]Finally, a justification for all the time you spend with your favorite technology.

In metric research, these elements will be clearly demarcated, each forming a separate section. In interpretive research, the elements will be integrated into the narrative, but the narrative still has to answer the questions of what we are talking about and why, what others have said, how the author went about the work of her or his scholarship, what the author learned, what makes those learning claims trustworthy, and why we the readers should care. The entirety of these sections is called the scientific or scholarly argument. It is an argument and not a proof because the claim is always in doubt. Analytical methods are the mainstay of sections (a), (b), (c), (e), and (f). At this point in our journey through the research process, we are at points (a) and (b).

The statement of the problem and the review of literature establish the justification for why the current research should be done. They basically make a bid to join the ongoing conversation and give reason why one should pay attention to what we have to say. Proper analysis in these sections lays out the problem domain, its history, certified and falsified claims, missing elements, and the like. (Learning techniques is important but not nearly enough.) Long before you go into the field, you need to know what the research community has been doing in order to establish your credentials for doing more. This is equally true if you are doing proprietary research. There is nothing so embarrassing as presenting in a boardroom to a group of people who know you obviously don't know what is current.

So how do you find out? Read the academic and trade literatures, surf the Internet to get to the most current topics, ask experts and practitioners, write an "elevator speech," discuss the topic with knowledgeable people, develop the map (written, diagrammatic, or mathematic) of the problem domain showing the elements and the relationships, consider the implications for your research, and find yourself in the problem. The first four items listed are directed at becoming knowledgeable about what is accepted as known and what is still being debated. There is little value in going through the work of collecting data only to find that it's already old news or that your idea is so wild-eyed that no one will engage it. One ends this set by writing the elevator speech: Imagine that you are on the elevator with the most knowledgeable person on earth, and you need to capture her interest before the elevator stops at her floor. The elevator speech is a clear, concise description.

The second set of four has to do with gaining a complex understanding of the problem. Discussing the topic with others helps refine that description of the topic. As you talk with others, they will undoubtedly point out things you haven't thought of. You can start to map these out. Let's return to our talk radio example to show how analytical methods work inside the deductive approach of metric empiricism (see box, left).

Deductive Method

The deductive method in logic is a syllogistic form that moves from a set of general principles (provided by theory in research) to a particular instance in which that theory is engaged (the research problem) to a conclusion as to the outcomes that should be reached under the conditions of the particular case. In the well-designed deductive study, those predicted outcomes are the research hypotheses. If the research hypotheses are supported in a study, that support accrues to the reasoning and to the general principles. The purpose of a deductive study is the certification of theory.

Analytical Methods in Deductive Approaches. Our preliminary analysis of political talk radio showed that our original formulation of PTR forming political ideologies was misdirected. What might be going on, however, is that PTR serves to sustain both a personal political identity and the feeling of membership within a like-minded community. Your first map might look something like Figure 3.2.

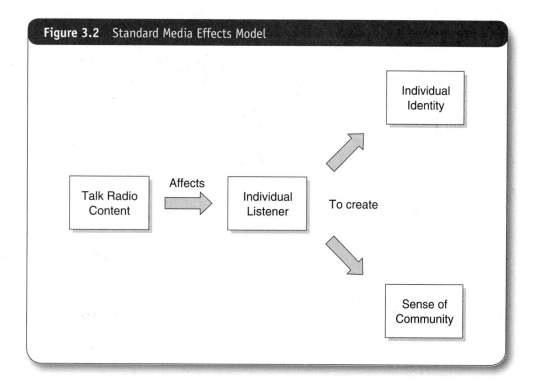

Figure 3.2 Standard Media Effects Model

This is a standard "media effects" model. You can recognize it as such because it begins with content, and works through the individual to produce consequences for that individual. What does this model tell me about talk radio effects and how to measure them? The relationship between content and identity seems pretty straightforward. Working from a cognitivist perspective, I could claim that the themes expressed in the talk radio content are assimilated by the individual to become attitudes about people, objects, and issues. Right away I would know I'd have to do some more reading in cognitivism to figure out how this process happens. Maybe I would find out that it is through repetition from a highly credible source. We can scratch out a to-do list on this first relationship in the diagram, as shown in Figure 3.3.

I show this diagram to one of my colleagues, and after we get over the snide comments about my handwriting (that word is *issues?*), he summarizes what has to be done.

Figure 3.3   Marked Model

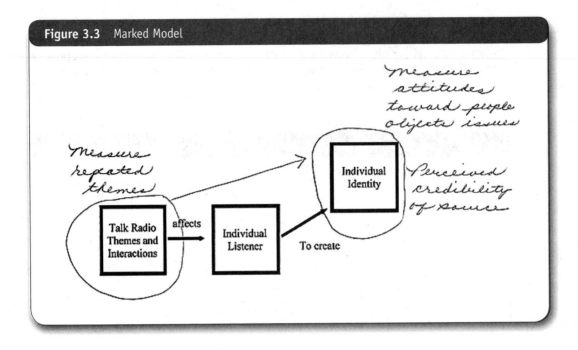

He: OK, you're going to record a whole bunch of talk radio shows; do content analysis to discover the repeated themes; analyze the themes for what they say about people, objects, and issues; construct attitude scales to measure listeners' attitude toward similar people, objects, and issues; and get a measure of how the listener perceives the credibility of the source, right?

Me: Yep.

He: Then listeners who attach high credibility to the source should show attitudes in line with the themes.

Me: Right.

He: What about listeners who attach low credibility to the source? And what about listeners who show high credibility but don't have similar attitudes? Are those possible outcomes? Is there some way you can say something about them?

So more work to do. After that work is done, I can turn to the sense-of-community side of the diagram (Figure 3.4). Now I just don't see how the repeated themes would produce a sense of community. I can see how I would like the commentator, but that is not what we usually consider to be community. More reading, now in the community literature. I learn about membership processes, joint identity, and coordinated action, but I just don't get it.

Figure 3.4 The Community Side of the Diagram

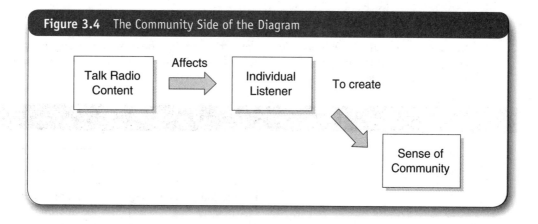

Again I seek out help and present the community side of the diagram to a colleague.

She: For community to happen, you have to have some sort of social process involving multiple people. Do you have that in talk radio?

Me: Hmm, what about the callers? Would they work to produce this social process?

She: I dunno, maybe, but you would have to examine the turns of talk, see if it's interactive, see if they reference one another, see if they reference some community. There has to be some material evidence.

Even more work and a new element in the diagram (see Figure 3.5).

Figure 3.5 Element Added to Diagram

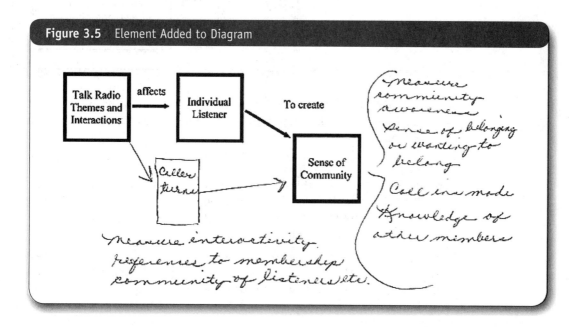

Now my content analysis of the talk radio content is twofold: (a) the themes developed mainly by the commentator and (b) the interactive turns provided by the callers. The themes will provide the evidence for development of attitudes and the interactions for the construct of community. I can now draw a much refined model (Figure 3.6), which I take back to my colleagues.

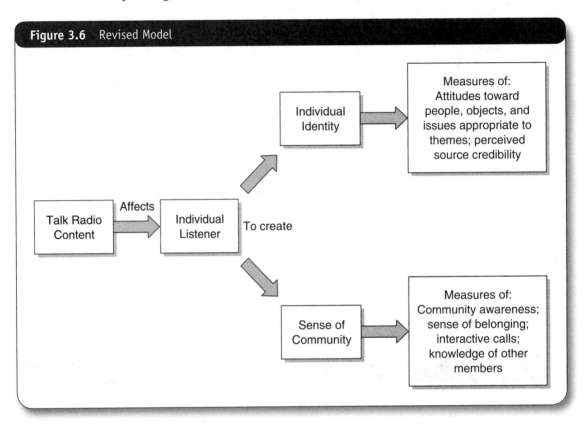

Figure 3.6 Revised Model

He: Not bad. That's a lot better than last time. But look, are you really talking about individual identity here? Is that possibly something else? Maybe you ought to do some reading on identity.

Me: [More work!]

She: Good idea on the reading; I think the concept of identity will work, however, Still, you will need to be able to justify the term. Now here's something: What about the relationship between identity and community? Aren't these going to connect? Won't they reinforce one another?

He: That idea will really help you with the source credibility and attitudes issues we talked about before. [To she:] I was wondering about people who listen but don't believe. Seems like community might solve that.

She: [Turning to me] How would it work for you? Would your sense of community interact with your attitudes?

She has invoked the *find yourself in your theory* criterion. Too often, it seems, we develop theoretical positions and research designs that make sense for *them*—the respondents in the study—but would never apply to *us*. Typically, this is an elitist error. It is of the sort that says, "Talk radio could have no effect on people like me. It works on those people." The correction to this error is to hold to the principle: If the research question doesn't entail the researcher, then the question hasn't been asked correctly. One's position vis-à-vis the focal problem has historically been a big problem for media researchers. As we saw in Chapter 1, our history has been to consider technology, the media, and the popular as something suspect, a threat to society, and a danger to our children. That has led to a literature that until very recently has been about *them*—the ordinary people of much lesser ability than *we*. Whatever we talk about, it has to apply to us as well. In this example, I would start my analysis with the recognition that I have a particular opinion about talk radio, I don't listen to it, and I summarily turn it off if it comes on. Before I can do good research in this area, I have to deal with those issues.

Analytical Methods in Emergent Approaches. We leave *me* with considerable more work to do to refine the model that will direct the research. The PTR example of the application of analytic methods works well (I hope) for research approaches that make use of a lot of front-end theorizing. But even those methods that use a more grounded approach where more theory work follows the data collection than precedes it have to do something like that analysis. It just happens in a different sequence (see box, right).

In the preliminary investigation stage of an interpretive problem, we will actually want to spend some time in the field (or with the texts) without a specific agenda. To do that, the researcher needs to identify an appropriate site (if one is interested in family media use, for example, one could find a family—not one's own—that will allow a visit); literally hang around in that site; create a body of field notes from which to draw preliminary insights; and then select a focal insight for the study. It follows the approach of our homeless example. In that example, the researcher (me) was way out of his comfort zone of experience. As a result, it took an extended period of time to achieve some semblance of member knowledge that would allow the refinement of the research agenda.

Inductive Method?

Most philosophers of science agree that there is no secure logic of induction. Consequently, one cannot unproblematically call hermeneutic methods inductive. Hermeneutic methods depend on a coherent (rather than a rules-based) model of knowledge. The test for success is not that premises analytically implicate one another but that the understanding gained is coherent (makes sense) internally and coheres to the external (resonates with what we already know). Hermeneutic methods are not inductive; they do not depend on some questionable method by which the particular case can prove the general principle. They depend on meeting the demands of a coherent narrative of understanding.

With that foundation, we can now go through the analytical steps. Those steps again are read, surf, inquire, describe, discuss, map, contemplate, and discover. Read the literature; surf the topic; ask others about the problem[8]; describe the problem in succinct terms; present and discuss your elevator speech; map the components and their relationships; contemplate the implications of the elements and their relationships; and find yourself in the problem both as an exemplar and as a researcher.

Once again this analysis directs me to the literature I should be engaging and lays out the sites I should be attending and the conversations I should be having. I can even map it out (see Figure 3.7).

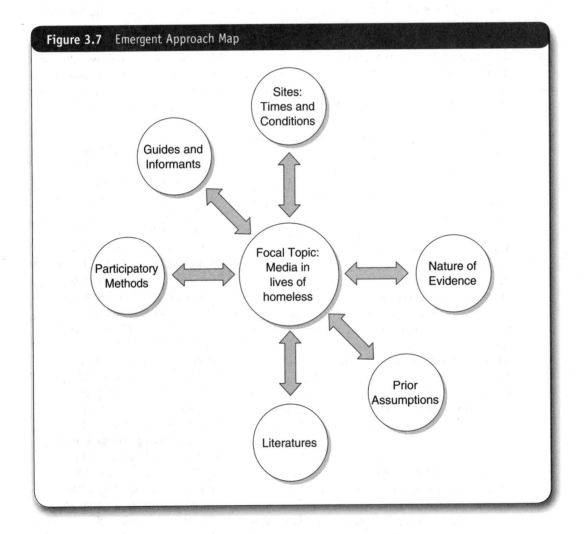

Figure 3.7 Emergent Approach Map

---

[8]Any time you ask others, you should practice active listening techniques (they're on the web; try Mind Tools).

The map looks quite a bit different in grounded approaches than it does in deductive ones. First, the model is a bit misshapen and lumpy because the concepts cannot be unitized. I cannot know on any a priori basis the relative weight of any of the elements. Second, all of the connections are double headed.

The focal topic will affect each of the orbiting decision domains, but each decision I make in those domains will affect how the topic is ultimately delineated. I will not know what the topic actually is until the study is in write-up. Again I take this map to my colleagues:

He: Looks to me like this map could be used for any focal topic with any respondent group.

Me: [Proudly] Well, yes, but the decision fields would change with the topic and group, of course.

He: Mmhmm, but shouldn't your map contain something unique to the focal topic? Have you just flopped a template down and declared your thinking over?

Always more work, and sometimes *he* is not a nice person (actually, colleagues who will authentically engage the critical review process are priceless).

At any rate, I go back to working on the map (see Figure 3.8). A couple of things come to mind immediately: First of all, I think the domain of technology will be framed and engaged in a different way. I am going to have to be responsive to the cues of that difference. I also think that the circumstances of homelessness will generate different methods of using the media. Both of these additions mean that I have to review my own practices of media use and how I frame and engage technology because necessarily my circumstances become baseline (as they do for each ethnographer in every study). I start to fill in some of the other circles. I decide that *sites* is a better term than *locations* as physical place is not the issue—a meeting room becomes a theater when the DVD plays. I note literatures and people to engage. I decide that my most likely participatory methods will be conversations and evoking narratives ("Are you anything of a movie fan?"). I also note that I don't have a clue as to what the evidence will look like. More work to do.

A Note on Proprietary Research

The initiation, preliminary investigation, and refinement of the problem stages of the research process occur in proprietary research in much the same manner as academic research. There is nothing about proprietary research that makes it necessarily less than academic research.[9] It typically uses the same public methods of research, although the claims are commonly held inside the proprietary domain. It will show critical differences, however, in the presentational form, in the political processes of review and acceptance, as well as in the subsequent action steps or consequences attached to the findings. Consultants and industry researchers can do good, often well-funded work. Unfortunately, there

---

[9]I know that we academicians like to wrap ourselves in the grand old flag of science, but more often than that we like to admit our research is underfunded, using solutions of convenience rather than what is called for.

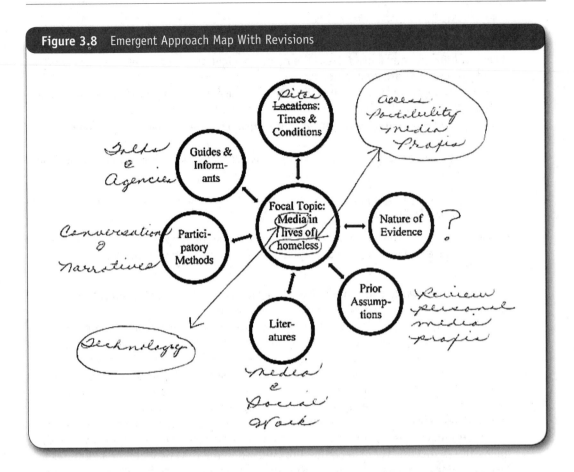

Figure 3.8   Emergent Approach Map With Revisions

is the small percentage of work done for persuasive rather than epistemological purposes, just as there is academic work that does not meet the standard.

Literature Review

The literature review for a study has a set of standard responsibilities and typical procedures regardless of the methodology used, but its application within the argument will vary according to the epistemological foundations that are in place. The reason for this variation is that the warrants—the justifications for claiming something as evidence—change. For example, in metric empiricism, the foundation is a progressively improving approximation of an independent reality. The review of the literature has heightened importance because it establishes the starting point for the work to be done. The literature review is supposed to establish the general theoretical principles from which the research questions and hypotheses can be derived.

In interpretive empiricism with its social constructionist foundation, the issue is more about fit within the narrative field than about standing on some prior work. Further, I have to be wary that a thorough reading of the literature will colonize my experience. Consequently, I will deliberately refrain from reading deeply until I have achieved an understanding from the field. The literature review comes in at the back end of the hermeneutic study rather than at the front (an issue that drives the supervisors of research nuts). We will have a chance to revisit this issue when we work through the writing process.

Notwithstanding this difference, the work is the same. The review of the literature is the connection to the rest of the field. It has to be sufficiently thorough that you, and subsequently your readers, have confidence in your understanding of the major issues that are under discussion. It is this understanding that works in tandem with the process of problem refinement. Note that in the model I have drawn, the review is lagging slightly behind the problem analysis. The analysis has to take the lead because it directs the literature review. Unless you are writing a dissertation or thesis where the rules change somewhat, the literature review is appropriate to the problem in the main and then to requirements of the argument as they emerge.

The literature review is another place where the difference between the professional scholar and the sometime researcher shows up. The active professional is current with the literature and knows the issues. The task of the literature review is reduced to the careful rereading of the key studies that motivate and justify or ground the present work. The sometime researcher has to get connected with the conversation. The analogy is a good one. If you have ever joined or attempted to join an extended conversation, you quickly find that the conversants have already covered whatever you might bring. It takes a lot of listening to catch up. Search strategies, the construction of the review, and its application in the argument are taken up in Chapter 7.

Problem Statement

The outcome of the problem refinement and literature review processes is the problem statement or question for which the researcher will be seeking some resolution. There are four kinds of problem questions we can ask: What is . . . ? How does . . . ? Why does . . . ? What good is . . . ? These questions, of course, relate to the properties, processes, consequence, and character of the mediascape. Chapter 8 investigates a current set of 100 media studies and carefully examines a set of 20 to give you a better idea of how it is done.

Our model would suggest that once the problem is stated and refined, the researcher would select from available methodologies to begin the process of finding answers to the problem now in hand. That, of course, is the lie of linearity in the model. One's chosen methodologies are not an overcoat one puts on lightly. There is a considerable investment of time and commitment to develop the expertise and experience necessary to competently execute a study and to be proficient in a methodology. For most professional researchers, methodology is a resolved choice that suffuses the way we even encounter those disquieting moments that initiate the entire process. In many respects, beginning researchers have an advantage here, because they do not have to carry the burden of the prior investment, although they may be fully colonized by their training process. Problems do direct the choice of methods, but not all problems are equally probable for the different research communities.

In principle, research questions can be taken up by any of these communities. In practice, what and why questions are more prevalent in metric empiricism's survey and experimental methodologies, and how and what questions are more prevalent in interpretive empiricism's participative and critical methodologies. There are good epistemological reasons for this practical difference. As we have seen in Chapter 1 and in the warning labels of this chapter, and as we will explore further in Chapter 5, methods invoke theory, and theory has affinities for particular kinds of problems. As a result, there are different outcomes from the problem analysis stage of research for metric studies and for interpretive studies.

In metric studies, the fully formed research problem is the basis for generating the research questions and hypotheses that will establish both the evidentiary requirements and the relationship between that evidence and subsequent claims. Research questions are the more general form as they allow the researcher considerable room in the formulation of the answer. They usually indicate a more exploratory study. Hypotheses are declarative statements that are to be supported or falsified by the metric research study. They are the norm for confirmatory metric studies. In the best of the metric studies, hypotheses are the necessary conclusion of some line of reasoning based on theory. In our young discipline, the best are also rare.

In the interpretive study, the research problem establishes the terms of engagement of the community, social process, set of texts, and so forth that are the focus of analysis. It also generates a dynamic set of questions that reflect the current interest and knowledge of the researcher. I call them dynamic because they are not fixed in the deductive logic appropriate to metric research that directs the connection between evidence and claim, but rather interpretive research questions are responsive to the emerging insights that are produced through engagement. The write-up will typically fix those questions as prior, but in the process, the researcher does not know precisely what is being asked until the answer is in hand.

THE ETHICS OF THE PROBLEM

Problem selection and development carry a number of ethical burdens that connect to obligations to society at large and to fairness of the process. Scholarship and research are part of the public knowledge production system. Like any public system—health, education, safety—the expectation is that the system will focus on significant topics that will benefit society. Knowledge production is somewhat loosely connected to this criterion because one cannot know where a study or line of research will lead. Nonetheless, it is not a narcissistic process where personal interest is all that counts.

There is an increased burden on academic research because in most cases this research makes use of public and disciplinary resources. Academicians are paid, in part, to do research by tax, corporate, or personal dollars. They have an obligation to make a difference. Consultants, too, have an obligation to do good work. That obligation may even involve persuading clients that a project, while potentially lucrative for the consultant, is inappropriate or fatally flawed.

The academic system of publication—the certification of scholarly value—is a permanently failing system. Authors, editors, and reviewers are paid by one set of institutions to produce content that is donated to corporations who profit from it by selling it back to the authors, editors, reviewers, and funding institutions. This system is on life support given the digital revolution, sustained only by the ultraconservativism of the academy.

The system may be ridiculous on the face of it, but it does mean that the submission of a work engages the volunteer labor of several individuals who represent a commitment of the discipline to certifying good work. Ethically, authors should not waste their time. Further, even in voluntary labor, editors and reviewers have to be competent to evaluate the content in hand—a requirement that is very unevenly met.

The analyst's obligation to the fairness of the process of investigation is basically the assurance that the project can fail to achieve its goals. That may seem to be an odd way of putting it. But, consider that if one is designing a hypothetic-deductive metric study, the design cannot be self-fulfilling. It has to be possible for the research hypothesis to fail and to fail in a meaningful way. It is fairly easy to design instruments and protocols that will push a result. (We will encounter a couple of examples in Chapter 5.) It may be great marketing or vita-building, but it is unethical research.

Similarly, in interpretive research, it has to be possible for the narrative not to cohere. If the analyst starts with the final story in mind prior to any engagement, then it is an easy task to attend to only that evidence that supports the preconceived story and ignore that which confounds it. This use of evidence is called cherry-picking or creaming, and it is nearly undetectable in the final argument except that the narrative works all too well. Cherry-picking, creaming, and poaching (misappropriating evidence) are all unethical practices that are great temptations in critical issue and advocacy research. In our discussion on the treatment of interpretive evidence, we'll identify procedures that will resist these temptations.

MOVING ON

Asking questions in science and scholarship is a refined and systematic process that begins innocently enough with an idea that pops into your head, but then moves quickly into a considerable amount of thinking, reading, writing, talking, analyzing, studying, and reworking effort that must get done before a single methodological technique is employed. A well-constructed problem in metric research clearly identifies the constructs and variables of interest, establishes the definitional and relational requirements that must be met before data can be collected, and sets the parameters of measurement and analysis. In interpretive research, the well-considered problem provides the interest, motivation, and initial directions and a continuing point of reference as the dynamic process of engagement unfolds.

In both forms of research, a good problem statement is a guiding light to the final argument. Truth be told, however, we often work from undeveloped, poorly developed, or incompletely developed problem statements. As a reader of research, one can recognize those cases when the researcher engages in a mighty struggle in the discussion section to make sense of it all. Those cases usually mark a failure to develop an adequate problem statement. Once we have refined the problem to register a question worth asking, however successfully, we are ready to take up the methods of finding a resolution. The next chapter presents an overview of those methods.

REFLECTIONS

What Are Some Points to Remember?

- The methods of both metric and interpretive empirical research are public, evidence based, and rule directed. They are directed toward creating public knowledge, which means that others can review the claim and evidence even if those others are a very few (such as in proprietary or restricted research).
- We generally do not use words like *true* or *proven*. All claims, no matter how well supported or how often falsified, are open to revision, although that revision may face great opposition.
- Every method invokes a particular set of theories. There are no theory-free methods, just naïve researchers.
- The generation of problems and their subsequent refinement is a systematic process that is part of the professional expertise of the researcher or scholar. That process differs across metric and interpretive approaches.
- The researcher or scholar is under an ethical obligation to avoid false claims.

Why Does It Matter?

This chapter seeks to underline the principle that research is really about problems and not about methods. Methods are tools that are used in the resolution or understanding of problems. The quality of the research starts with the quality of the problem. Even the best execution of method will not rescue an unrefined problem.

What Else Could We Talk About?

The problems that appear in our journals are not just things that interest the author or researchers. To reach the light of publication, those problems also have to be seen as important to the discipline and to, at least to some extent, society at large. This rhetorical obligation of publication immerses the research in the political processes by which we determine whether something is important or not. Problems in research can be considered uninteresting, banal, out of date, naïve, and of no importance. On the other hand, problems can also ride an upswing in popularity. The changing social status of problems explains much of the ebb and flow of topics in our journals—more so than the quality of research.

What Else Might Be Interesting to Read?

Keyton, J. (2006). *Communication research: Asking questions, finding answers*. New York: McGraw Hill. (See Chapter 2.)

CHAPTER 4

Methods of Exploration

Finding Answers

CHAPTER PREVIEW

What's It All About?

Chapter 4 catalogues and provides a brief introduction to the methods of metric, interpretive, and hybrid research and scholarship.

What Are the Major Topics?

In metric research, the major methods discussed are observation, different kinds of surveys, and field and laboratory experiments. Content analysis and the case study are presented as bridging over to the interpretive domain.

In interpretive research, the methods of reconnaissance, participant observation, critical ethnography, and performance ethnography as well as the bridge methods of the long-form interview and protocol analysis (aka experience sampling) are described.

The hybrid methods of textual analysis, discourse analysis, cultural/critical analysis, and dialogic analysis are outlined.

The issue of mixed methods—typically those that mix metric and interpretive methodologies—is examined. Three forms are identified: a primary/secondary approach where one method controls the argument, quasi-independent studies that run parallel to one another, and the convergence of triangulation. The major debate on mixed methods that focuses on the possibility of triangulation is detailed.

The chapter concludes with a discussion of the value of research practices for all of us, even those who will not ordinarily make a living in their execution.

What Special Terms Are Used?

The critical	Narrative	Semiotic
Dependent variable	Objective	Triangulation
Experimental controls	Performative	
Independent variable	Semiosis	

INTRODUCTION

As we left Chapter 3, we had a refined problem statement in hand that posed a question or an unresolved issue that we wished to answer or move to resolve or that generated a quest for deeper understanding. Our next consideration then is how to find an answer, a resolution, or understanding. That consideration has two parts: The first focuses on the kind of general question we are asking (What is . . . ? How does . . . ? Why does . . . ? What value is . . . ?), and the second refers to the kind of claim we wish to produce (objective, narrative, critical, performative). We can take a look at the back half of the research process diagram to see how this works (see Figure 4.1).

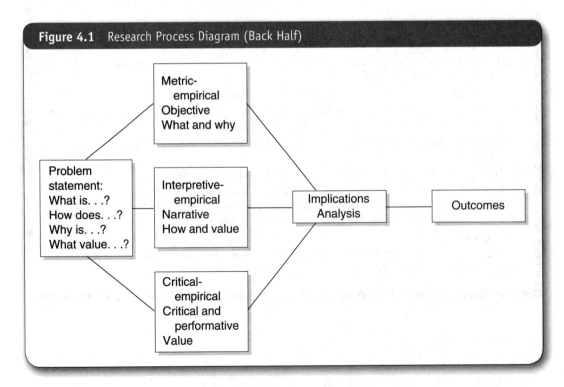

Figure 4.1   Research Process Diagram (Back Half)

In the diagram, we see that metric methods produce objective evidence and have an affinity for what and why questions, interpretive approaches produce narrative arguments and work well with how and value questions, and critical, empirical, or hybrid methods produce critical and performative arguments and are uniquely suited to questions of value. (Critical-analytical has disappeared given our empirical focus in this chapter.)

The purpose of any methodology is to produce the evidence to support the claims of the argument to be produced. Those claims might be in the form of a research hypothesis developed from a deductive approach, or they may be those that will emerge in a descriptive or narrative argument or that will provide the foundation for critical evaluation. The method in use does not answer the question or solve the problem itself. That, of course, is the task of the argument as a whole.[1]

AN INTRODUCTION TO EMPIRICAL METHODS

Empirical explorations involve the original collection of information (data) that is probably best described as factual. At its clearest, *factual* has the quality of the statement "The last word of the first sentence of this paragraph is *factual*." Our agreement runs pretty much downhill from there, however. If, for example, I wrote, "The first sentence of this paragraph is factual," I could bet on an argument from someone (even myself). The slope gets really slippery when we recognize that we are rarely interested in the facts themselves; more often we are interested in what the facts mean. I'll describe the techniques we use to manage the slippage in a later chapter, but for now it's enough to recognize that few facts are simple, and we do a lot of work on those that are not.

If *factual* is the first operative word in this description, then *original* is the second. *Empirical* is derived from the Greek word for experience (and not from any word meaning numerical). An empirical study has the force of the claim "I was there; I experienced it," of firsthand observation. There are only a few forms of empirical research where the researcher is the one actually doing the experiencing, however. Mostly we record through some means or another the experience of others. On the other hand, those observations would not exist without the action of the researcher, and the researcher is responsible for them. There is an evidentiary line that leads back to a particular individual or individuals. She or he was there. Of course, we have just as much problem with the word *there* as we do with *factual*. One can be too *there,* as in personal experience; or too *not there,* as in certain highly contrived experiments; or there may be no *there* to be, as in aggregated locations. (Isn't this fun?)

In the end, we can pretty well claim that empirical studies are the more or less experienced, more or less factual properties of individuals, entities, and activities with the goal of describing what is (more or less) there. And if that isn't a loose enough definition, remember that we divide it again. Plain empiricists come in shades of two sorts: metric and interpretive. The difference, as we have seen, is pretty simple but, as always in scholarship, hotly contested. Metric empiricists, remember, base their arguments on the logic of mathematics. Interpretive empiricists base theirs on the logic of the narrative.

---

[1]Researchers, of course, do not live their lives in diagrammatic boxes. Consequently, in Chapter 6, you will find examples of research that attack any of the questions from any of the domains.

The most common way this distinction has been marked in the past is with the terms *quantitative* and *qualitative*. So why am I suggesting that we use a different pair of terms? (In a very real sense, you could call them Thing 1 and Thing 2.) Very simply, I don't think the terms *quantitative* and *qualitative* are very descriptive (especially *qualitative*) of the actual difference. In quantitative research, we parse the action into metrics—hence the preferred term *metric empiricism*. In qualitative research, we unify the action by interpreting it in a narrative—hence the preferred *interpretive empiricism*. Quantities and qualities can be addressed by either form.

CATALOGUING METHODS

Empirical research of any sort falls into one of three categories: descriptive, field/life-world, and laboratory. These categories are more practical than analytically sound in that they mix kind and location. They are also hegemonic in that they tend to privilege a positivist agenda, but they are the ones we have and they work well enough. They occupy the first three rows of Table 4.1, which lays out the matrix of form and target and fills in the cells with the typical methods.

In the table, I have mixed metric and hermeneutic methods, but I do not mean to imply that they are interchangeable. Remember a method always invokes a foundation in epistemology and theory. I've given the hybrids their own row, recognizing that we have probably crossed some line in the sand—at least at this point in time—reminiscent of the line that was once drawn between metric and interpretive empiricism. The boundary is a line in the sand, because all scholarly boundaries are made to be crossed, as this one is. We'll spend a few sentences describing the content of those cells, sorting them by the metric, hermeneutic, and hybrid affinities.

Metric Methods

Our conclusion of our analysis of the epistemological foundations of metric methods in Chapter 2 was that these methods are designed to collect information about variables—to identify their appearance, to measure their characteristics, to investigate their relationships, and to determine their function in some causal structure. The first three of these purposes are met through observation and survey methodologies, and the last is met through experimental methodologies.

Observation

The observation of metric empiricism is focused on the objective characteristics of human behavior. This behavior can be watched through a one-way mirror or recorded for off-site analysis. The behavior is coded as being of a certain type. The researcher can count the types and occurrences of each type (sometimes called tokens of the type), compare types and occurrences across circumstances, and so on. Observations are usually taken of individual instances or episodes of behavior. (Longer frames of activity fall under the case study

Table 4.1   Methodologies by Research Form and Analytical Target

Form/Target	Properties	Processes	Consequences	Character
Empirical descriptive	Archival and databases[a] Observation[b] Single-point survey[c] Content analysis[c]	Multipoint surveys[c] Interviews[b] Ethnographic reconnaissance[d]	Longitudinal surveys[c] Correlational analysis[c] Ethnographic reconnaissance[d]	Value/attitude surveys[c] Ethnographic reconnaissance[d]
Empirical field/life-world	Case study[c] Ethnographic reconnaissance[d]	Long-form interviews[b] Protocol analysis[b] Participant ethnography[d]	Field experiment[c] Participant ethnography[d]	Performative and critical ethnography[d]
Empirical laboratory	Development stages[c] Cognitive structures[c]	Simulations[c]	Controlled experiments[c]	Game analysis[c]
Rhetorical/critical/empirical hybrids	Textual analysis[e] Critical and cultural analysis[e]	Discourse analysis[e] Dialogic analysis[e]		

Note: Superscripts and font colors mark the principal research community membership:

[a]All (font color black)

[b]Both metric and interpretive (light gray)

[c]Metric (light blue)

[d]Interpretive (darker blue)

[e]Hybrid (darker gray)

discussed below.) The people who produce the behavior are usually anonymous, and their individual intentionality is not part of the analysis.

Survey Methods

If you ever filled out a guest-response card for a hotel or restaurant or a customer-satisfaction form for Internet buying, you have participated in a survey. If I wanted to find out how many of us have taken a survey, I would take a survey. Survey methods are descriptive methods. Strictly speaking, they can tell us only what is there. Survey methods represent the most common methodology in communication and most social sciences as well.

Single-point surveys collect information at one point in time. The value of the information beyond that point in time depends on the rate of change that occurs within the circumstances being surveyed. In most circumstances involving media and technology, the shelf life of a survey is not very long.

Multipoint surveys collect information on the same circumstances over more than one point in time. Although the information is about what is there each time the survey is taken, we typically infer systemic or systematic change from the differences.

Longitudinal surveys collect information from the same respondent panel over multiple points in time. Again they report only what is there each time, but we infer a pattern of change or development or consistency (with those variables that don't change their values) within the panel. Multipoint surveys study the same circumstances but do not preserve the respondent group (they use different people); longitudinal surveys preserve the respondent group (they use the same people) over different life circumstances.

Experimental Methods

Experimental methodologies are intended to test the effects of one set of conditions on another. The two key concepts in experimental research are manipulation and control. In an experiment, a researcher manipulates the values of one set of conditions—called the independent variable(s)—and measures the consequence for another set—called the dependent variable(s). The experiment depends on the ability to specify or to establish the value of the independent variable and to measure the consequent values of the dependent variable.[2] In order to be sure that the dependent variable is being affected only by the independent variable, the researcher has to institute some controls on both the respondents and the conditions. Respondent controls have to do with the capacity of the dependent variable to be affected by the independent across different respondent types. Condition controls are used to ensure that it is the independent variable and only the independent variable that is effecting the change.

The necessity of controls usually means that the experiment has to be conducted in a constructed setting, designed to provide those controls. These are called laboratory experiments. Occasionally, conditions will be such that the research can be conducted in normal settings. These are called field experiments.

A natural manipulation supporting a field experiment might occur, for example, when half of a neighborhood is wired for digital cable and the other half will remain analog for six more months. A researcher could study any effects of the different delivery systems for subscribers on, say, program choices. The problem, of course, comes when trying to control for other sources of influence on the dependent variable. The best one can hope for is

---

[2]My students sometimes complain, "Why do they call it an independent variable when you manipulate it and a dependent variable when you don't do anything to it?" The naming convention has to do with the relationship between the variables—one of which is dependent on the other for its value—not on the relationship between the variable and the researcher.

that these extraneous influences will balance out on both sides of the ledger. It is this lack of control that gives field experiments a reputation for being messier than laboratory experiments, but they are usually less artificial.

Bridge Methods

Surveys and experiments are the central methods of metric empiricism. They correspond nicely with metric empiricism's core belief in an independent reality that contains states and traits that can be objectively measured. There are other methods in use in metric empiricism that bridge the gap between metric empiricism and interpretive empiricism. I would list those as content analysis; the case study; open-ended, long-frame interviews; and protocol analysis. Content analysis and the case study bridge over from metric empiricism, and the long-frame interview and protocol analysis bridge back from interpretive empiricism. We will take up the first two here and the second set after the discussion of interpretive methods.

Content analysis in metric empiricism is directed toward the objective features of some text (written), a graphic, a sound recording, a video program, a website, and the like. It attempts to build an understanding of the meaning of the content by a thorough description of its component properties. Meaning poses some difficulties for metric empiricists. From a philosopher's viewpoint, metric empiricism has no theoretical grounding to attempt to deal with meaning as meaning cannot exist in the object. Researchers, of course, just do what has to be done regardless of philosophical niceties. Metric empiricism claims about the meaning of a text tend to hold meaning as global (literal), whereas interpretive empiricism would be more interested in meanings as activated by individuals or hermeneutic communities.

The corresponding activity in interpretive empiricism is called textual analysis. There is an important difference between content and text. Whereas content is concerned with objective characteristics, text focuses on the cultural and semiotic activity that the objective characteristics invoke in the effort to be meaningful and evoke in their meaningfulness. Content analysis and textual analysis can look a lot alike. Both commonly use some coding procedure and may even come to similar conclusions, but content analysis, as we will see in Chapter 13, is a top-down, variable-analytic process, while textual analysis is a bottom-up, emergent process. My sense of the movement in the field is a melding of these methods.

The case study is another area of merging methods (in interpretive empiricism it is called ethnographic reconnaissance). The case study is observation of some extended activity. It attempts to build an understanding of the activity by describing its components (generally smaller units of behavior). The case study takes plain observation up a few notches in complexity in an attempt to understand process and outcomes that occur within the activity.

The case study in metric empiricism is usually considered pre-science (in traditional terms, only hypothetic deductive approaches—usually experimental approaches—are authentic science). It is the means by which the researcher develops enough information about something to be able to develop good hypotheses for real science. Ethnographic reconnaissance has a similar reputation of being "less than" on the interpretive empiricism side as it eschews any attempt to achieve member knowledge, the hallmark of interpretive empiricism methods.

Interpretive Methods

In the empirical domain, interpretive methods are directed toward the analysis of human action. These methods are designed to produce evidence for narratives that advance our understanding of the meanings of the properties, processes, consequences, and character of that action. These narratives, typically based in social constructionism, depend on their grasp of member knowledge to derive their hermeneutic power. When the critical enters the scene, the narrative intent moves from plain understanding to understanding through advocacy. For the critic, it is advocacy and its performance that achieve the deepest understanding because they are truly implicative and consequential. (I will remind you that we have agreed that these notes are controversial and that as we move up the scale, the descriptions must be less precise.) On the basic hermeneutic side, we have ethnographic reconnaissance and participant observation, and as we cross to the critical, we have critical ethnography and performance ethnography.

Ethnographic Reconnaissance

Against the criterion of member knowledge, ethnographic reconnaissance is at the lowest rung of the hermeneutic ladder. It involves the technical procedures of hanging around, doing static and dynamic analyses of location, noting performance roles, suppressing assumptions of knowledge, and being open to reconceptualization, but it rarely involves any consequential participation. Ethnographic reconnaissance is the level usually reached by methods that use multiple field-workers engaging a common site for a short period of time. Ethnographic reconnaissance is also the typical work of the methods class and is often the necessary precursor to the more complex integrative efforts. It was the approach I used in the preliminary investigation for the homeless study.

Ethnographic reconnaissance is the method of choice, however, when the focal group is a one-off aggregate whose members have no interactive structure. Observing and interviewing television viewers in an airport might be an example where the researcher has no reason to believe that the viewers are connected by any material social practices that would constitute the viewing experience. Ethnographic reconnaissance produces a descriptive rather than hermeneutic narrative—hence its similarities to the case study, in the same way that a Chevy is like a Ford (you decide which is which).

Participant Observation

Participant observation is at the center of interpretive empiricism. The operational word here is *participant,* and one criterion of the quality of the work is determined by the complexity of participation achieved. That participation has to make a difference for the membership and for the researcher. It has to be implicative for both. There are many issues and tensions involved in this requirement, and we will get to them in their own chapter.

The requirement of participation is based on the principle of the social construction of knowledge. Understanding is achieved through action. But, participation is always tempered by observation. Even at the most heated moments of participation, the researcher must withdraw to observe, to be outside him- or herself, watching. Each activity contains the means by which the activity makes sense to those enacting it. It is that sense making that is the goal of the participation, and it is making the sense making explicit that is the goal of the observation.

The goal of participant observation is the production of an ethnographic argument. Ethnography is the writing of a culture—the transformation of cultural practice to the written word. With its social constructionist foundation, participant observation seeks to support the transformation of consequential social practices into their written description at such a depth and complexity that the nonmember can achieve an understanding of what it must mean to be a member.

Critical Ethnography

Critical ethnography is a merging of critical theory and ethnographic methods (see Madison, 2005; or Noblit, Flores, & Murillo, 2004).[3] It has twin responsibilities: to develop a complex understanding of some domain of everyday life and to advocate for the reduction of the social injustices that occur within that domain. Critical ethnography explicitly rejects Hume's gap—that what is true is independent of what is right. The true and right work in tandem; one informs the other. We cannot know what is true until we can advocate for what is right from that foundation.

Critical ethnography intentionally adopts some political purpose. It has shown lesser interest in being responsible for the consequences, both intended and unintended, of this purpose. The dedication to that responsibility needs to be its next achievement. But how, you may ask, is this science? The answer to that question depends on whether you are a universalist or not. If you are, then the method is empirical (of sorts), but it is not science. If you are a social constructionist, then science is merely a set of human practices so designated as scientific, which generate what are considered to be good outcomes. In that case, why can't critical ethnography belong?

Performance Ethnography

Be careful how you answer that question because there are others waiting for membership more radical than the critical. Performance ethnography may well be in that class. Performance ethnography embraces the politics of liberation through public performance (Conquergood, 1985, 1991, 2002). This is the YouTube of science. It is famous ethnographer Norm Denzin (2003) doing a music video on MTV. Now before you throw your hands up in whatever emotion this evokes, consider that the purpose of critical ethnography (from

---

[3]Critical ethnography is being shadowed by the merger of critical rhetoric and ethnography in what is being called rhetorical field methods (Middleton, Senda-Cook, & Endres, in press). Both are part of the larger empirical advocacy movement, the distinctions across which have more to do with the membership, training, and foundational texts of the practitioners than with method or framework of argument.

which performance ethnography follows) is to achieve some political goal. The presentational forms (academic journals) of this ethnography virtually ensure that it will have no political consequences. Performance ethnography takes it to the streets and delivers the message in presentational forms appropriate to its political ends.

This insistence on performance recognizes that the presentational form does more than provide access to the work. It constitutes the work by the structure, relationships, necessities, and force of the form. It is not by chance or simple circumstance that the American Psychological Association, in all its objectivist tradition, has a 400+ page publication manual that controls every element of the typescript (even the number of spaces after a period). It is because the form of the text carries its own intention and logic. When the arguments are in the same textual form, knowledge presumably grows incrementally, like a brick wall. When they are liberated, they have to be engaged on their own terms, like a rock wall. We do not have many examples of performance ethnography as of yet, though the YouTube ethnographic section grows daily (e.g., http://www.youtube.com/watch?v = FLunHw53XZg or http://mediatedcultures.net/youtube.htm). Mostly, however, there is a lot of writing about what it should be, but not much professional output.[4]

Bridge Methods

There are two remaining methods that bridge to metric empiricism, the open-ended, long-frame interview and protocol analysis. The long-frame interview is a directed interview that allows the interviewer to follow the discursive line taken by the respondent but still has particular goals (often expressed in actual questions) to fulfill. Long-frame interviews (LFI) are often 30–60 minutes long and therefore much different from the open-ended questions of surveys. When the interview transcripts are coded and the codes analyzed for their number and rates, the LFI becomes a metric method. When the transcripts are coded to produce the narrative of the topic, it is a hermeneutic method.

The remaining bridge method is protocol analysis. The term protocol analysis (PA) has two different applications in the literature. The first involves collection of verbal descriptions of what is being done by the reporting individual who is involved in some process. In this approach, PA has been used to document human cognitive performance by having the respondent describe the thinking processes used in some cognitive activity (Newell & Simon, 1972). It has also been used to render apparent to an observer the steps in some action (see Myin-Germeys, Oorschot, Collip, Lataster, Delespaul, & van Os, 2009, for an overview). And it has been used over time and distance to discover the integration of media into everyday life (Csikszentmihalyi & Kubey, 1981). In these approaches, PA (also called experience sampling in this application; see Fullagar & Kelloway, 2009) reveals or at least provides some insight into what cannot be seen. I do believe that the term *protocol analysis* will be replaced by the term *experience sampling method* (ESM).

---

[4]The phrase *professional output* would alert the critic to the presence of a discursive gloss or discursive silence. Those are the textual moments where what is not said is more important than what is said.

Protocol analysis is also becoming popular as a term to describe computer-assisted textual analysis that is directed to the purpose of building knowledge base systems that could emulate the expert (Shadbolt, Motta, & Rouge, 1993). The term *protocol analysis* as applied to textual analysis is associated with knowledge structures (coming out of computer information transfer and automated reasoning terminology). One could collect the texts posted by game players on discussion sites and blogs, for example, and then analyze them for their expertise. PCPACK from Epistemics and CatPac II from Galileo are two programs that provide the computer assistance.

Hybrid Methods

Hybrid methodologies bring a distinct focus on texts. This portion of the field has come to use the word *texts* to mean any unit of discourse that has distinct boundaries and a more or less clear beginning, middle, and end. So, a text can be a conversation, a document, a PowerPoint presentation of a lecture, that lecture itself, a motion picture, a television series, a podcast, a text message, or even this book. Texts are the objects of all methodologies but are at the center of hybrid and critical-analytical methods.

Textual Analysis

Textual analysis is the critical-cultural correspondent to content analysis. Old-school content analysis usually involved counting of nonproblematic textual entities (number of nouns, verbs, etc., or even the number of close-ups, establishing shots, etc.), and it still holds an important place in media scholarship (Krippendorff, 2004). New-school content analysis is moving toward a merger with textual analysis techniques as it begins to search out character, motive, action, and themes. Textual analysis would add such cultural elements as interpellation, implication, referentiality, and intertextuality to describe the work texts do to sustain power relationships and cultural order. (Not to worry if you don't recognize any of those terms; you can learn them if you need them for your own work.)

Textual analysis usually starts with close reading. Close reading is the foundational method for critical empiricism. The purpose of the technique is to break through the surface of the texts of language and action that we experience to explore their consequential foundations. The basic principle is that nothing is recognizable among us except through an underlying set of shared understandings that render it recognizable. It is those underlying shared understandings that are the targets of close reading activities. These are not bloodless explorations, however. Most critical approaches that build on close readings are interested in recuperation or reformation.

From there, we move to a more critical domain. In this book, we are interested in the newer critical forms that Hoggart (1970) describes as part philosophical, part sociological, and part critical. This combination creates them as a hybrid of the analytical (philosophical and critical) and the empirical (sociological), but still clearly on the analytical side of the ledger. I've listed three sorts of analysis: discourse, critical, and cultural. These are not highly conventionalized methodologies—there is no approved handbook, but they do have interrogative affinities.

Discourse Analysis

Discourse analysis tends to be interested in questions of how kinds of speaking and writing produce certain cultural results. These results are not the "direct effects" of message analysis but the cultural consequences of a discursive framework. For example, nearly all local television news programs do the same kind of discursive work. Turn on a news program in any market in the United States, and it is immediately recognizable as a news program. The language of the program produces cultural orders of importance of people and events and positions the viewers as observers of others as if we were somehow not in their world. Discourse analysis is interested in demonstrating how that gets done (e.g., Baym, 2000). Discourse analysis tends to be the most closely tied to empirical data of the three and often provides the ramp-up to critical and cultural analysis.

Cultural-Critical Analysis

Critical analysis would take those same news programs and be concerned about the consequences of the social orderings that are produced. It might, for example, look at the distributions of power that are enhanced and maintained by those discursive processes. Finally, cultural analysis would take up the paths of resistance and opposition from both the audience and the media themselves, looking, for example, at the alternative readings that are provided by Comedy Central's *The Daily Show* and *The Colbert Report* (Baym, 2005, 2007).

Dialogic Analysis

Dialogic analysis is one of the latest products to come out of cultural studies (there based on Bakhtin, 1981), but it has a fairly long history in sociology and social movement analysis (there based on Simmel, 1949, and, in the United States, particularly Goffman, 1959). Dialogic analysis is based on the theoretical principle that meaningful texts and action are the results of the collective conversation that is continually ongoing (Steinberg gives a nice overview in the 1993, 1999, and 2002 citations).[5] I may be the agent keyboarding this sentence, but the discourse of this text is the product of the collective work that has preceded it and that it anticipates. Further, what this text will become is based not on its intrinsic merits but on the dialogue between it and the reader, the critics, the marketplace, and so on (see Pinter & Nielsen, 1990, for an example from the cinema). If we were looking for a more objectivist analogue, we could see the connection between dialogic analysis and systems analysis. They achieve a lot of the same results though with different vocabularies and different character of evidence.

Discourse, cultural, and dialogic analyses are often three variations on the same theme. It is quite possible that a particular study would use all three. They are all based on the principles of sodality and collective action. Critical analysis, coming out of critical theory, is more universalist in character. Cultivation analysis—the study of the cumulative effects of a narrative form (e.g., Gerbner & Gross, 1976)—with its strong empirical foundation and equally strong reformist impulse, is a good example.

---

[5]It should not be confused with the dialogic analysis of psychoanalysis.

Hybrid methods are strategies and tactics for engaging texts. These strategies and tactics are uniquely connected to the analyst, the texts, and the purposes of the argument. At this point in their development, we have little foundation for arguing for one strategy over another as some general rule. We will look at a few specific examples in the remainder of this text to consider what others have done and their relative success, but the reader will not find a "how to" chapter.

Mixed Methods

The term *mixed methods* has come to mean any combination of metric and interpretive methods that is used in the service of investigating some problem. In most published uses, one method is secondary to the other. For example, interpretive approaches such as focus groups or long-form interviews can be used to refine a survey questionnaire, or a survey may be used to define the boundaries of a community or membership later targeted for ethnographic study. Benoit and McHale (2003) used this approach in their content analysis of television campaign spots. In this sort of mixture, the primary method remains in control of the argument, and the epistemological foundation is secure.

Another approach to mixed methods is to mount quasi-independent or parallel studies inside a single effort or to use different methodologies for different research questions in a single study. There is a relatively small (but growing) number of examples of either in the mediated communication literature, but one example of the former is given in Liebler, Schwartz, and Harper (2009) and of the latter in Schultz and Sheffer (2008). Liebler et al. used both quantitative content analysis and interpretive textual analysis in the study of the framing of same-sex stories in the press. Schultz and Sheffer surveyed sports bloggers using a questionnaire that included 15 items and an open-ended question (p. 186). The open-ended answers were analyzed for thematic representations. Most of the examples that I saw used relatively low-level qualitative applications in combination with more complex quantitative instruments. The conversation between the two approaches was usually resolved in typical "science" claims.

Multimethod approaches such as these are receiving considerable interest at the moment, perhaps being seen as a way out of the allegedly false quantitative-qualitative dichotomy. Such approaches, however, were commonplace at the introduction of scaling methods in the late 1920s (see, for example, the Payne studies available at http://www .brocku.ca/MeadProject/Blumer/1933/Blumer_1933_toc.html). It was only the suppression of the interpretive during the '40s and '50s along with its subsequent reemergence in the '80s that now gives mixed methods the appearance of something new on the scene.

Critical issues are raised in the mixed methods approach when methods are removed from their epistemological moorings and treated as if they were simple tools. Epistemologically denaturing the tool allows for an application that is unmindful of the worldviews that developed the method. This approach certainly liberates the analyst at the design stage of the study, but it does so by pushing the questions of evidence and warrants to the point where the argument of the study is constructed.

This is the approach used by Caracelli and Greene (1993) who define quantitative methods as those "designed to collect numbers" and qualitative methods as those "designed to collect words" (p. 195). Caracelli and Greene quote their prior work (Greene, Caracelli, & Graham, 1989) to posit five purposes for mixed methods: development and initiation, complementarity and expansion, and triangulation. Development and initiation refer to our first approach (superordinate/subordinate) and complementarity and expansion to our second (parallel studies).

The critical issues are raised in triangulation, which Caracelli and Greene (1993) define as "convergence, corroboration, and correspondence of results" (p. 196). The unanswered question is where the convergence, corroboration, and correspondence of the data reside. They certainly cannot reside *in* the data, because at least part of the data is the result of the researcher's interpretative work. As a consequence, they must be constructed *through* the data. The claim for convergence, therefore, is a claim based on the insight of the author, not on the necessity of the evidence.

My reading of a fairly extensive search of the mixed methods literature is that the use of one method to support another while remaining in the epistemological home of the primary method is the most frequent, but for all the talk still rare. It is also the least controversial. The quasi-independent approach is also rather noncontroversial and may be growing—certainly has grown from no instances to at least some. (In this book, I encourage either approach, but without all the fanfare.) Critics like myself grumble about corroboration arguments as being defective, but at least a few editors appear willing to publish them, although Trumbo found none in eight communication journals in his 2004 review.

A most interesting argument from a methodologist's point of view is that summarized and advanced by Johnson and Onwuegbuzie (2004). These scholars argue that mixed methods represent a "third paradigm" (p. 14) that can be located epistemologically in the American pragmatism of Charles Sanders Peirce, William James, and John Dewey. Further, they argue that the combination of this philosophy and method can provide superior results to those generated by either metric or interpretive purists. Proponents of this position have yet to work out the logical necessity of the evidence produced by mixed methods. As of the moment, the plentitude of evidence is addressed as a text in another layer of authorial interpretation. Pursuit of this argument is well beyond my scope for this section, but this "in your face" claim was one taken by the interpretive turn some 40 years ago. We might keep an eye on where this turn leads.

Mixed methods is in a nascent stage. Scholars are working out what is the proper arrangement of the mixing and how the claims from them should be advanced (for an extensive social science review, see Tashakkori & Teddlie, 2010). At this point, there is considerably more talk about mixed methods in the literature than actual work using such methods. If our history from the interpretive reemergence is any guide, it may be another decade before we see a regular presence in our literature. In any case, mixed methods is a demanding approach requiring more expertise, time, and resources. Such requirements are not always popular.

CONSIDERING PURPOSES BEYOND METHOD

The practice of research is justified by two general purposes: to create a contribution to a body of knowledge and/or to devise a problem solution that offers a better way. The first of these purposes describes theoretical research, and the second describes applied research.

In academic hierarchies, theoretical research is more valued, but elsewhere theoretical research gains its value when it is applied to some further purpose. My guess is that most of you reading this book will not be called on to do theoretical research but are very likely, at least sometime in your career, to be asked to solve a problem in which the systematic methods of research can genuinely contribute. The fact that you can bring those insights and skills to the table should be to your advantage.

The methods, of course, "don't care" whether you are a scientist, a social critic, a service provider, a corporate manager, or even a blogger. Methods are simply designed to establish a reviewable set of procedures, which are thought to exercise some control over possible error and can, therefore, generate good information. (It is still a human enterprise and can be replete with error, nevertheless.)

It is somewhat ironic that theoretical research can maintain any error of its own for decades because there is no immediate confirmation or disconfirmation of the claim. Practical research is a less tolerant regime, though error can persist there as well, as the hosts of permanently failing organizations (Meyer & Zucker, 1989) attest.

I would suggest that we are often involved in practical research though we might not identify it as such. A friend of mine who commutes 15 miles from the south valley has documented average travel times along the available routes for the major sections of the day. Sarah is a mother of two, and she notes, "When family responsibilities call, I have to be able to get there quickly. Like it or not, fair or not, their father cannot leave as I can. So it falls to me." Her decision making, however, is more nuanced than a simple set of travel time probabilities. In choosing a route for a given trip, she factors in immediate, local conditions, often pulling up the transportation CommuterLink site to check the freeways.

For its part, CommuterLink hopes that more people will do what Sarah does, because if commuters adjust their routes or the time of travel by the information they provide, it may provide a safer commute and, in the longer run, delay the need for new roads. The traffic authority wonders how to get more people to visit the site and have taken a poll of visitors to find out how they got there in order to figure out the methods it should use to get more visitors. CommuterLink asked:

What prompted you to visit this website?

And its results[6] were:

12%	A friend or family member recommended it
28%	I heard about it on the radio or TV
2%	I read about it in the newspaper or in a brochure
7%	My employer encourages us to use it
51%	Other

[6]http://commuterlink.utah.gov/ie.htm. Accessed March 10, 2008.

These are not results that I would want to build a lasting theory on, but if I were CommuterLink, I would probably feel pretty good about my radio and TV initiatives and certainly would want to know a lot more about the components of that "Other" category.

This sort of web-based data collection is commonplace across organizations of every sort and is a central feature of data-based cost management. If you work for an organization in the typical positions that communication folks occupy, you will be involved in this sort of stuff as a research practitioner, a corporate analyst, and/or a manager.

The use of the Internet to conduct practical research is also an authentic media effect worthy of scholarly attention. A methodologist might be interested in the quality of information he or she receives, posing questions about the design of the instrument (question) or who the respondents represent. An organizational scholar might want to know how this information is used in decision making within the organization (or whether it is just window dressing for the site). A media scholar might want to know about the credibility or application of this information by seasoned commuters (are there more Sarahs out there?).

But it is not only in the workplace in which we might find our involvement. Research plays an enormous part in the life of a contributing member of our society, a consumer, and even a family member. For the past week or so, my brother and I have been in a discussion about the current hot political issue. To a large extent, we have been quoting opposing websites to one another. (Mine are much better, of course, but then I am a trained professional.) What we both have found is that websites are not independent but are interlocked in ideological networks. As a result, one can build a consistent argument drawing from a number of sites that appear to confirm the claims and facts of another when, in fact, it is simple reproduction, not verification. The effect is one of *truthiness* (the word made famous once again).

Nonetheless, the web is the best information source for the two of us. It brings together government reports, national publications, newspaper articles, public-interest broadsides, and ideological screeds all in one place. It allows us to construct our arguments using all of these resources and to exchange our sources so that we can each see firsthand the basis of our different positions. In our discussion, we are both consumers of empirical and critical-analytical content and at a very local level practitioners of the research craft. And, of course, one can ratchet this up to the workplace where decisions are based on arguments that can be profitably founded on research methodologies.

Both of these practical activities are also grist for the scholar's mill. Clearly, the shifting preferences for information sources and the manner of their use is a prime target for the media scholar, as is the manner in which information is crafted for web presentation. Relational scholars might be interested in how family is enacted over e-mail. And organizational scholars have shown a long-standing interest in the participation of mediated content in decision-making processes.

The moral of this section is that this stuff can be good for you on a number of levels, from discussing with a sibling or friend, to successful coursework, to advancing your career, to your later life as a media scholar should you choose to follow that path.

MOVING ON

This chapter is the last of the overview section. We have now done a brief tour of all the elements of the different methodologies we will study. The next section of three chapters takes up the ideas and processes from which actual studies get produced.

REFLECTIONS

What Are Some Points to Remember?

- The foundation of empiricism is in experience and engagement, not in quantification or interpretation. Methods are either empirical or analytical first before they can be considered metric or interpretive.
- Metric empiricism is the most conventionalized (rule-directed) form of research and scholarship, having over a century of practice across a wide variety of disciplines. Interpretive forms have half that history, and hybrids are writing their history right now. Communication continues to enlarge the field of hybrid methods.
- The foundation of metric empiricism is measurement that produces the quantification of concepts. The various protocols of metric empiricism are designed to locate the objects of measurement.
- The foundation of "traditional" interpretive empiricism is participant observation, a method that requires a substantial commitment of time and personal resources. Alternative methods in interpretive empiricism generally aim at reducing those costs.
- The term *mixed methods* is currently in vogue. The field is uncertain (though individuals clearly are not) as to what mixed methods actually mean and how the epistemological conflicts and contradictions inherent in the mix are to be managed. The excitement of a proselytizing zeal can be read in some sources.
- Empirical research should be an ordinary part of the well-examined life.

Why Does It Matter?

Even a briefly developed understanding of the range of methodologies and their associated methods allows the researcher to participate in a much wider conversation that circulates around important problems and allows a more sophisticated evaluation of the worth of any particular part of that conversation.

What Else Could We Talk About?

Both mainstream media and new media are leading the devolution of expertise. The careful, systematic, and dispassionate examination of evidence and claim seems an impossible burden in the continuing need to produce yet another performance or blog update. Academic research faces many of the same pressures with an increasing number of journals demanding content and an increase in demand for publication by even the most junior of our members. The good news is that more work is seeing the light of publication; the bad news is that more of what is published is of questionable quality.

What Else Might Be Interesting to Read?

Conquergood, D. (1991). Rethinking ethnography: Cultural politics and rhetorical strategies. *Communication Mono-graphs, 58,* 179–194.

Jackson, J. (2005). *Real Black: Adventures in racial sincerity.* Chicago: University of Chicago Press.

Rosengren, K. E. (2002). The distaste of taste: Bourdieu, cultural capital and the Australian postwar elite. *Journal of Consumer Culture, 2,* 219–239.

Section II

Foundations of
Research Practice

T his section of three chapters might be considered a common "toolbox" for the beginning empirical researcher as it considers the fundamental activities that have to be conducted regardless of orientation. The activities that we consider are, first, the line from our assumptions to theory to empirical facts; second, the line from our initiating interest to the questions to which our research intends to make a contribution; and, third, the methods of joining the ongoing conversation.

There is a chapter attached to each of these sets, but the work, most certainly, goes on simultaneously and interactively. Whatever the order or lack thereof, the goal at the end is a rock-solid foundation for designing the protocol that the particular study requires. We start this work by considering the assumptions that allow the research argument to be formed.

CHAPTER 5

From Concepts to Data

CHAPTER PREVIEW

What's It All About?

Chapter 5 takes us from the assumptive and theoretical foundation of a research problem to an overview of the methodological tools that would be available to the analyst in metric or interpretive research and scholarship. It then provides the bases for evaluating the quality of that research and scholarship in a discussion of reliability, accuracy, precision, and validity in metric research as well as coherence, resonance, and vraisemblance in interpretive scholarship.

What Are the Major Topics?

Research practice starts with problems, but problems appear out of the assumptions we make about the domain of media, texts, audiences, culture, society, and the individual. Even as researchers, we are inextricably bound to the ecology of media. How we understand our own experience, particularly our agency to manage our role in that ecology, affects our problem development as well.

Research practitioners also work inside some theoretical framework, level of approach, conceptualization, or overarching epistemology that shapes both problem development and methodological choices.

A distinction is drawn between constructs and concepts. Concepts are the ideas from which we form theory. Constructs are these ideas as located within some location of theory and methodology. Concepts can move across theory domains but don't readily lend themselves to measurement or analysis. Constructs are less flexible but give good specificity for measurement and analysis.

The process of engaging the empirical from either metric or interpretive standpoints requires separate sets of tools and practices. In the metric, the set composes the means of quantification and measurement. In the interpretive, the study of people is conducted through participant observation, and the study of texts is conducted through close reading, coding, and an examination of the textual warrants.

At the end of each of the metric and interpretive methods, the criteria of trustworthy work in those methods are discussed. Metric arguments depend on a level of precision that produces reliable and accurate measurements that are valid representations of the construct under analysis. Trustworthy interpretive arguments require narrative that hangs together in a coherent fashion, resonates with the context of performance, and exhibits vraisemblance as a plausible analysis.

What Special Terms Are Used?

Agency	Axiom	Cognitivism
Critical issue theories	Determinism	False Consciousness

Figure 5.1 Enigmatic Data

3	8	5	7	2	14
2	6	7	7	1	15
1	8	7	7	1	15
6	4	4	9	2	15
2	8	3	6	2	11
2	9	5	6	1	12
2	7	5	5	2	12
3	9	4	8	2	14
6	4	6	9	3	18
5	8	6	5	2	13
5	9	5	5	5	15
5	10	6	4	4	14
4	7	6	4	5	15
5	8	6	5	3	14
2	9	6	3	2	11
6	8	4	2	7	13
4	6	5	4	5	14
5	10	5	2	8	15
8	4	8	6	10	24
2	5	5	5	8	18
5	7	4	2	9	15
4	5	4	1	9	14
6	4	7	5	9	21
6	5	7	4	9	20
3	8	4	3	8	15
6	1	8	9	3	20
9	3	7	9	2	18
7	3	7	9	3	19
9	4	8	8	3	19
8	4	6	9	2	17
8	6	7	7	3	17
10	2	8	9	4	21
5	1	5	9	1	15
10	2	7	10	3	20
8	3	6	7	4	17
7	5	7	6	3	16
5	3	5	3	8	16
8	6	7	6	6	19
7	5	8	7	5	20

THE FOUNDATIONS OF ARGUMENT IN RESEARCH

This chapter is about the materials and tools we use to build arguments. Research would be much easier if we could simply collect the data, run a few summary calculations and some tests for significance, and say, "See, there it is." But just as taking delivery of a load of bricks does not build the wall, so, too, do data have to be used in an argument to reach some conclusion or action step.

We make this claim for two reasons: First, data make sense only when viewed as embedded in some provenance of theory and protocol. It's a silly example, but Figure 5.1 shows what data look like when stripped of this provenance.

While there is some information that can be gleaned by careful inspection, the numbers make little sense until you add in what they are supposed to mean (measure), who (or what) they represent, and how they were collected. The construction of that provenance is the result of human action, not of some objective process.

The second reason for the necessity of an argument is that research is a human practice. Because humans act based on both what they believe to be true and what they believe to be right, data are shot through with uncertainty and necessarily contain error both suspected and unknown.

The result is that when I present data to you, I also have to convince you that the data are trustworthy and appropriate for you to base some subsequent action on. That task is made a lot easier if you and I believe in the same principles. If you believe all numerical measures are junk or that ethnographic field notes are just a fancy diary or that hybrid studies are poaching and preaching, then a study from any of those positions is going to have a difficult time gaining your acceptance. One role of methods textbooks is to show the value of methodology and why it can be trusted in a manner appropriate to its limitations. That work is often done in an "of course it's true" sort of way. I'm hoping to be a bit more cautious, but we'll see, and you'll be the judge.

ASSUMPTIONS PRIOR TO DATA

We have to make some pretty complex assumptions before we can begin to collect data of any sort, and they start well before the first number or field note. We might call these the epistemological foundations of the research problem or, more simply, what has to be believed to be true for a particular problem to be studied. There seem to be three constellations of assumptions that we have to address: The first involves the media-text-audience configuration; the second is the way we configure the relationship among culture, society, and the individual; and the third is the evidence, warrants, and claims configurations—or, more simply, the logic-in-use that supports the research approach. We deal with the third set throughout the book and specifically in the whole of this chapter. Let's complete the triptych by considering a few of the different starting places for media/texts/audiences and culture/society/individuals.

Assumptions About Media/Texts/Audiences

Media

Assumptions about the media play across the devices and the industries. We are certainly aware of assumptions (common in critical theory, for example) about the media as a common conspiracy or under the control of a single set of interests. We may reject that assumption, but we ordinarily think of a medium as a singular entity. Our assumptions about television, for example, often preserve that medium as it was in the 1970s—a limited-production oligarchy, with vertical control of content, and few consumer choices. Thirty years ago, the majority of viewers were limited by their over-the-air service. Now fewer than 15% receive their television off of a broadcast antenna. Yet we still read of calls for regulation (and draconian penalties) that are based only on that small percentage within a much larger system that may soon undergo yet another era of radical change.

How would we better describe television today? Is YouTube television? Is Hulu television? Is the basketball game on my smartphone the same television as the game in my home theater? Am I watching television when I skip the commercials? With a DVR, I can watch a three-hour football game in under an hour. Is that television? Is "television" so diverse that it is no longer a medium? I've used television here, but I think you could plug in any of our contemporary media—newspapers, radio, film (how long do you think motion pictures will actually be physically on film?)[1]—into the analysis.

Texts

Assumptions determine what we consider to be a text. Is the text the same as the content? Or is the text the interpretation that results in the confluence of content, audience, and culture? And we can push the assumptive level down to ask what counts as content. Is the content of this sentence the words on the page (does layout matter)? The words on the page as presented in a textbook? In a textbook used in a course? In a course in which the reader is enrolled? You get the idea. The questions are "Where are the boundaries?" and "What are the differences that occur across those boundaries?" As a researcher, the most accessible boundary is the words on the page, but that might not be the most effective boundary. Certainly, if I am doing a critical or cultural analysis, that can't be the boundary.

Audiences

The third set of assumptions in this constellation deals with the audience. In his interview with Jon Stewart on *The Daily Show*, Bruce Springsteen noted that when he plays before an audience, he is really playing before multiple audiences.[2] Some are there to hear their favorite hits; some are there for his message; some are there for the party. The only thing many have in common is that they are there. If diversity of purpose is the key to understanding an audience of 50,000 in an arena, how much more of a role does it play in an audience of 30 million for a reality TV program?

Nonetheless, we routinely read about *the audience* in the singular for large, heterogeneous groups of people whose singular commonality may be that a television set is tuned to a particular channel. Yes, it is *the* audience in that sense, but the language masks the wide variations across motive, attention, interest, viewing practices, and environment. The classification of audience or not audience may make no other useful distinction.

We have other visions of media audiences dancing in our head: They concern how smart, how vulnerable, how insightful, and how gullible the people are who form them. The elitist legacy of our field looms large in these assumptions. There is a solid assumptive vein that characterizes the audience for popular culture as something less; that glorifies old media over new; and that considers the under-20 group as foolish and vulnerable (rather than celebratory and imaginative), the under-30 group as shallow and vain (rather than altruistic and passionate), and the over-60 group as disconnected and declining (rather than wise and discerning).

The greatest effect of these assumptions about media/texts/audiences occurs when we connect the dots. A vision of a medium connects to an understanding of its content that is delivered to some sort of an audience. One of the most important questions that are answered in the resultant conceptual figure is whether I can look at a text and declare what

---

[1]Developing and distributing a product on a long plastic strip that has to be mechanically driven past a shutter and a light source at 24 frames per second does seem to be a bit costly given the growing ability of the digital alternative.

[2]http://www.thedailyshow.com/watch/thu-march-19-2009/bruce-springsteen—interview. Accessed April 15, 2011.

it means for others. This assumption is basic to all effects research and to research in the design of messages in general. An alternative assumption is that the meaning of a text is a probability rather than a certainty. The text will mean X a certain percentage of the time it is engaged or to a certain percentage of the audience that engages it. The former suggests that meaning X might be governed by the conditions of engagement, and the latter indicates that meaning X is based on the individuals who engage it.

The assumption that meaning is the same for all gets marked by our interpersonal experience of usually achieving a successful communication. Our experience supports the notion that we can be generally successful in accomplishing our communication goals in face-to-face communication. What we fail to track are the processes of message modification, supervision of interpretation, and confirmation of understanding that are part of interpersonal communication. All of those processes are missing in asynchronous, noninteractive, industry-produced texts. (Few know better than an author in a classroom of how often meanings for the same content differ.)

In the research argument, assumptions are necessarily implied and not stated. We have to start the argument somewhere, and everything that supports that starting place is assumed to be true (at least for the argument). The effects scholar who is concerned about children and violence in the media has a particular set of assumptions about children as an audience, about what is violence and its representation, about the literal character of content, about the relationship between the child and the viewing experience, about the properties and character of social aggression, and about the proper way to measure all of it. Those assumptions permit the interpretations of the data. Change the assumptions, and the data change their implications. My argument here is that such is true of all research. And I believe in the assumptions about the world that make that argument possible.

Assumptions About Culture/Society/Individuals

The abstractions of culture, society, and the individual require us to act from a set of assumptions that allow the logic of analysis to proceed. The following sections consider some of those commonly made.

Definitions of Culture

Wikipedia tells me that culture has a variety of definitions, the shadings of which help distinguish different academic disciplines. For example, the entry author claims that in American anthropology, culture "most commonly refers to the universal human capacity to classify and encode their experiences symbolically, and [to] communicate symbolically encoded experiences socially."[3] At a more disciplinary level, Anderson and Englehardt (2001, p. 57) define culture as a set of seven systems: the semiotic (the system of meaning in language and action), the epistemic (the system of truth making), the ethical (the system of right and wrong), the aesthetic (the system of beauty), the economic (the system of value exchange), the political (the system of allocation), and the social (the system of self, other, and relationships). All culture is composed of these systems, and all cultures have some

---

[3]http://en.wikipedia.org/wiki/Culture. Accessed March 26, 2009.

component that connects to each. Anderson and Englehardt would hold that a society is the particular structurations (configurations of actions, structures, and resources) that provide for the expression of those systems in a particular time and place.

Relationship Among Culture, Society, and the Individual

Concepts like culture, society, and the individual have multiple definitions because they are abstractions that are put in the service of some intention. What appears to be important in media studies is not so much the particular definition, but the relationship among the elements. For the critical-cultural scholar and often for the ethnographer, the order is culture, society, and individual in that culture provides for the society and the society provides for the individual. Consequently, one's analysis starts at the cultural level rather than the individual level. The individual is simply the route we have for understanding the cultural.

Psychology in the United States has traditionally taken the opposite view, in that the individual provides for both society and culture and, in turn, is modified by each. We study the individual because the individual is the fundamental building block of culture and society.

How does this difference make a difference? I think we can see the difference by looking at effects research in comparison with cultural analysis. Effects research depends on the assumption of literal referentiality of content (meaning of content is fixed, and we all know what it means) and on the assumption that an individual can be changed from one predictive state to another by exposure to that content. The effect, then, occurs when the probabilities and rates of one performance (rather than another) have changed for that individual. The individual is, in short, one thing before exposure and another after exposure.

A cultural analysis would look at the relationship between media content and the individual and start by saying that both are embedded in a common field of understanding where only the particular arrangement of elements can be new. (Even now, I know what the weather will be on the news tonight; it's just the numbers that change.) Anyone who is culturally competent (see box, left) already knows the story about sex, violence, drug use, AIDS, and so on; the surprise is how you will tell it this time. So content doesn't change things; it lays down another layer on an already existing multilayered platform of understanding. Consequently, watching sexually inflected popular television will not lead one to more sex. There is no position of innocence for any of us. The possibility of more sex is already there. Our cultural values provide both for the program and for the possibility.

Note that the data we collect from individuals about the relationship between watching sexually inflected television programs and participating in more sexual activity might look exactly the same, but the interpretation that we would give them would be substantially different. In the one, content changes a person's beliefs about sexual behavior and leads to greater promiscuity.

> ### The Concept of *Competent*
>
> *Competent* (and *competence*), as used in theory, refers to the quality of being recognizable as being wholly formed, correctly done, capable, and the like. Theorists use the term to exclude the incomplete, the deviations of error, the random, and the unrecognizable from the scope of their explanations.

In the other, sex causes sex, and culture is the basis of understanding both how content can be considered sexually inflected and how a person could be considered more promiscuous.

Agency

There is one other element that is involved in this difference and that entails the issue of agency. Agency is an individual's ability to do otherwise. From a strict cognitivist point of view, an individual has no agency. There is no central faculty of the will that can invent a different set of probabilities from what the existing cognitive structures provide. Our action is not by choice but by the confluence of circumstances that bring one set of probabilities into play over another. If we could analyze the situation well enough, we could see how each action is determined by the particular conditions at the moment of its performance.

Few analysts choose to maintain that strict a position, but the concept of agency remains a problem for much of social science but particularly for the cognitivist and the effects scholar. Understand that if I really can "just say no," then an effect cannot be driven by content. It becomes a choice. There have been two traditional solutions to the problem. One is to focus on respondent groups with supposed diminished capacity of the will (reason) such as children or, sadly, in our history whomever is designated as the Other. The second is to hold that one can "say no," but he or she does not have to "say yes." Media influence can be blocked, but it takes effort to do so. In the absence of that effort, media can effectively influence their audiences. Either or both of these positions form the basis of most media literacy programs and other interventionist strategies.

The early work of critical theory and cultural studies suffered from the same conflict between agency and determinism. Early critical theorists were diviners—people who were inspired to see things that others could not. The critical theorist could see the influence of the dominant interests by their control of media; the masses were under the rule of "false consciousness"—a self-deceiving state of mind that allowed the media to work their influence. This position was pretty much undermined by the appearance of the postmodern critique, which essentially asked, "What makes you so special?" Stuart Hall and the Birmingham School coined the term *cultural dupe* to express the cartoonish figure that inhabited early critical theory and introduced the concept of resistance to the dominant readings, thereby recouping some form of agency for us all (see Edgar & Sedgwick, 2005).

Regardless of epistemological standard, it is difficult for the media scholar and student alike to grant agency or reasoned action to the audience. Part of that resistance comes from the critical impulse that is central to science and scholarship to take things as they seem and reveal what they actually are to an otherwise unknowing reader. We scholars do have advanced technical skills that generate higher-level insights. (If we don't, then we are frauds.) It is easy to look down from that higher ground.

Summary of Assumptions

An assumption is a statement that is necessary for us to believe as true in order to conduct some line of reasoning. In logic we call it an axiom. Any enterprise in scholarship or research has to start with some set of assumptions. (One assumption of the postmodern critique is that there is no solid ground—there is no epistemological standpoint that is not supported by assumptions.) The assumption set is the ultimate vulnerability of any argument; refuse the assumption, and the argument is moot. I believe it is in each of our own self-interests to reveal as much as we can about the assumptions we hold concerning all of the elements in media research. It will help us understand the lines of research we accept and those we don't.

You might consider writing out the answers to a set of questions about assumptions just to clarify your own thinking. For example, consider these question-and-answer sets: What is the starting point for an analysis of the consequences of media engagement? Possible answers might be culture, society, the discursive domain, the individual, content, the content-medium combination, or the interaction between content and the individual. What best describes the conditions under which content is effectively encountered? Simple exposure, attentive presence, or active engagement, as activated in an interpretive process? Are the boundaries of a medium defined in its technology, the combination of technology and the forms and conventions of content, the intentions and narrative forms of the text regardless of delivery system, its constitution in society and culture, or its history because media are indistinguishable in this era of convergence? Do media in their industrial texts produce a consistent set of cultural values, offer a heterogeneous and disconnected set of values, or ignore values except as economically important?

There are dozens of questions like these to be asked (notice that I have asked one question each for consequences, practices, properties, and value), and the answers you develop will guide you toward a particular theoretical and methodological path. It's not a take-out menu, however. The answers have to form a coherent and noncontradictory foundation for research. The pedagogical impulse is, of course, to direct the reader to an appropriate set of selections. This can be effective reproductive teaching, but it does not support critical thinking.

POSTASSUMPTIVE THEORY

All research problems are embedded in some theory whether explicitly stated or not. Theory develops on the foundation of assumptions or irreducible axiomatic beliefs. Theory starts when we assemble a more or less coherent base to consider the implications in some domain. There are a very large number of theories or theory-like claims in mediated communication. In the next sections, we spend some time with the variations.

Theory Types

Given the variety of positions that can form the foundations for theory, it is not surprising that there is not a singular domain of analysis that we could call media theory. Media theory is a much divided territory with border skirmishes throughout. The major states are (a) cognitivism, an inwardly looking set, which houses theories of messages and effects that are adapted to metric methods; (b) social action, an outwardly looking approach in which we find interactionist and interpretivist theories that are adapted to ethnographic methods; (c) psychoanalytical-semiotic theories that are concerned with the mechanisms of understanding and meaning and are drawn to discursive methods; (d) critical issue theories such as Marxism or feminism or race studies with their focus on class, gender, and race or ethnicity as the center of concern in media analysis and a general affinity for any method but metric; and finally (e) critical-cultural theories that are an eclectic membership that borrows extensively from literary and rhetorical criticism as well as critical issue and psychoanalytical-semiotic theories and generally uses discursive methods.

Levels of Approach

But, of course, we are not done because each of these domains can be addressed at the psychological, sociological, and/or cultural level. The psychological is concerned with the formations and behaviors of the individual, the sociological addresses the functions and performances of societies, and the cultural targets the understandings that bind individuals to a society and across nation-states. One could build a tidy table and fill in the cells with particular named theories such as agenda setting at the intersection of the cognitive and the psychological.

Initiating Concepts

Unfortunately, even that complexity is not enough because we can further parse theories according to their starting place in the nexus of media, content, message, audience, and performance. If one starts with media, one goes into McLuhanesque theories of hot and cold media or into technological determinism. If one starts with content, the move is to typologies such as formalism, master contracts, genre theory, and forms and conventions. If message is the starting place, one moves to effects and cultivation theories. Starting with the audience (or auditor or spectator—one audience member) leads to a field called audience studies or to uses and gratifications theories. Finally, starting with performance (the culturally recognizable things that people do) leads to social action theories in which media and their messages are part of a larger ecology in which we act out our lives.

Epistemic Divisions

And finally we have the epistemic divisions of Cartesianism, modernism, and postmodernism. Cartesianism (after Rene Descartes) holds that reason is the foundation of true knowledge, modernism would look to objective science as that foundation, and postmodernism would argue that human performance is the source of human knowledge, discarding both capital-T truth and objectivity. Theories and methods can be distributed along these divisions. Postmodern ethnography, for example, is quite different from modernist (or material) ethnography.

It may be self-serving, but I believe that it is impossible to master this complexity. The result is that just like the communities of methodologists we met in Chapter 1, individual theorists tend to gravitate toward some intersection and hang around with others on the same corner. We are a disparate community, and I'm not willing to say that any group has strong answers to the questions we pursue. Nothing in the theory of 10 years ago would have predicted the appearance of Twitter (nor can we now predict the causes of its inevitable disappearance). Consequently, as scholars, we take up a theory knowing that it has limits, flaws, and many alternatives. That doesn't stop us from a passionate and extended relationship with a set of ideas that would flow from our theory of choice, however.

CONCEPTS AND CONSTRUCTS

Assumptions provide the foundations for theory, and theory provides the concepts and constructs that populate our research problems. The terms *concepts* and *constructs* are often used interchangeably, but there is some value in maintaining a difference. Concepts can be viewed as ideas that populate theories—the "agenda" in agenda-setting theory is a concept of our thinking-speaking-performing menu. Constructs can be seen as ideas that populate methodologies—an agenda as a construct is a predictive cognitive state that can be measured on a scale in metric methods or is an emergent understanding of performance in ethnographic ones. Constructs are concepts encountered in some context of method.

Concepts can travel across theoretical domains. I can take the idea of media producing a common knowledge base (an agenda) on which a social interaction might develop (giving us something to talk about) and leave behind both the negative implications of a lessened ability because of media influence and the need for a cognitive state limiting us to that agenda. Exporting this liberated concept of agenda, I can explore how those of us into ballroom dancing (have I revealed too much?) can use *Dancing with the Stars* as the basis of conversation without constraining our evaluations of the dance or the show.

It is much more difficult to manipulate constructs because they are anchored into a particular location in the complex matrix we described in theory. Take the idea of message effectiveness. Traditionally, this concept is anchored in a transmission model of communication (e.g., who says what to whom with what effect). The transmission model depends on us being able to specify the "who," "what," "whom," and "effect" unproblematically. Traditional message effectiveness depends on the "what" moving from the "who" to the "whom" in a manner that maintains the properties of the message. The analyst wants to be able to specify the properties of the message upon construction and prior to delivery and then observe those same properties in the receiver. Message effectiveness in this example is a construct because it depends on the delivery of a set of sender-developed intentions and properties through a message constructed for that purpose to a receiver capable of reproducing those intentions and properties. It specifies the requirements of its measurement in great detail.

What happens if we pull effectiveness out of the transmission model? Is the construct of effectiveness robust enough to survive as a concept in a different epistemological location? For me, the fundament of effectiveness is consequence. Something happens as a result of something else. I don't have to start the analysis of what happens with the intentions of the sender, however. I could start with the intentions of the receiver (as uses and gratifications theory would direct us to do) or with the culturally influenced interpretations produced under the supervision of an interpretive community (as social action theory might suggest). What would message effectiveness look like under those analytical conditions?

Let's try one more example: the third-person effect. The third-person effect is an interesting amalgam of cognitivism and psychoanalysis. It holds that in an agenda-setting/cultivation analysis/media effects sort of way, we are aware of the consequences of engaging media (increased violence, body image, stereotyping), but instead of attributing those consequences to ourselves or our own, we project those consequences on others and particularly on the Other. What happens when we pull it out of its effects location? What if we do a mash-up with it and the spiral of silence (the idea that the more different we perceive our own opinions to be, the less likely we are to express them)? Or what happens if we see the third-person effect as a coping mechanism to deal with the disconnect between what we are told are the effects of media and what we see are the effects of media?

In finding answers for these questions, the evidence for the third-person effect remains the same, but the argument we can construct—the knowledge that we gain—is quite different. That is the value of concepts over constructs. Concepts can be manipulated without a lot of theory or method baggage. It is also their weakness. We have a number of communication theories that are conceptually exciting—chaos theory (for dealing with the self-organization of new media), systems theory (for dealing with media ecologies), and structuration theory (for understanding media texts as resources) are three that come to mind—but at the same time we have not been able to develop the constructs that will allow a robust program of research to develop. They remain ideas without research practices.

The quantitative-qualitative debates of 30 years ago (with pockets of resistance still) were part of the process by which interpretive empiricism moved itself from an idea to a research practice. We now have conventionalized criteria for what good auto, interpretive, and critical ethnography as well as close textual readings ought to look like (even if there could be far more evidence of the actual practice). Probably the strongest evidence we have for the existence of constructs in a field is the availability of computer software to provide an analytical framework. Metric studies are supported by SPSS, SAS, and SATA as full-featured data analytical schemes, and interpretive studies are supported by ATLAS.ti, Framework, and NVivo 9 as text-based (multimedia) analytical methods. (As a side note, media effects scholars should consider investigating the effect of computer software on the research process.)

ENGAGEMENT, EVIDENCE, CLAIM, AND TRUSTWORTHINESS

We will split the discussion under this heading into metric and interpretive, but I want to point out at the beginning that the problems that are faced in metric and interpretive empiricism are relatively parallel, albeit under different names and procedures. Each has to engage the empirical whether it is considered objectively material or semiotically constituted. Each has to capture that engagement in some form of evidence. Each has to demonstrate the consequential value of that evidence in a claim about the empirical produced in the research argument. And each has to demonstrate the trustworthiness of the claim.

We engage the empirical in our research protocols, which will be the subject of the next two sections and constitute argument in the processes of publication that we will only brush against in this book. Here we look at the formation of evidence and the criteria of trustworthiness.

Metric Evidence

In the metric domain, evidence is generated through the quantitative measurement of variables, which in turn produces the data that move through the statistical analyses of the protocol. In the following sections, we take up variables and their constitution in measurement, quantification, data, and instruments.

Figure 5.2 Netflix Ratings Legend

Ratings Legend

Loved It

Really Liked It

Liked It

Didn't Like It

Hated It

⊘ Not Interested

Not interested in this movie

No Opinion

I don't know enough about this movie to have an opinion

Source: http://www.netflix.com/

Variables

A construct is an idea that has been positioned at some point in the theory-method matrix, and a variable is a construct that can take different values in the measurement processes of a particular study. (Constructs that don't vary within a study are either ignored or called constants.) Variables become visible in the measurement process. The fact that a variable can be measured is evidence of its existence, and the reliable differences in the variations of values are used as evidence of the performance of the variable under the conditions of the study.

Measurement

Variables exist as ideas; measurements exist as processes or operations. The connection between the two is managed by the operational definition. The operational definition is a philosophically contentious but common practice used to complete the connection between theory and data. Again, it is easy to think of it as a line that starts with a concept, which then is located in the matrix as a research construct and more specifically as a problem variable, and then makes its operationally defined appearance in some measurement device and practice. Netflix, for example, asks you to rate the movie you just watched. It gives you a 5-point rating scale with two "disliked it" choices and three "liked it" choices ranging from "Hated it" to "Loved it" (see Figure 5.2).

That is their operational definition of some like-dislike construct. Of course, it is marketing and not research, but the practice is the same.

Professional researchers would criticize this operational definition because it does not appear to make a good connection to the like-dislike construct. It is a single-item scale evaluating a complex text. It appears to deliberately bias the answers toward liking, and the distances between intervals do not appear to be evenly spaced. We would say that it lacks construct validity. It does not make a good connection to what we expect to be the idea of liking a movie. Netflix may be just delighted with it as a marketing tool, however.

Quantification

Measurement processes connect to theory through operationalism, produce data as their product, and, in metric studies, produce those data in numerical form through quantification. Quantification is the process by which we attach the properties of the object or individual under study to the properties of numbers. Numbers have four characteristics: uniqueness, order, distance, and relative value. These characteristics get used to produce different kinds of data. We call the four types of data nominal, ordinal, interval, and ratio data.

Nominal Scales. Nominal data make use of the uniqueness of each number. Each number is its own set, and its set does not overlap with any other set. Figure 5.3 shows five circles, each representing the boundaries of a set and each with a separate number inside. They are floating in figure space in no particular arrangement because we have no information as to arrangement. The utility they have for us is that each one is unique. If the number is of one value, it cannot be of another. These are called nominal data. We use nominal scales when the properties being measured fall into unique categories: true or false, yes or no, male or female. More technically, we use the unique name of each number (hence *nominal*) to identify a unique property of a class of entities.

We use it improperly when, say, that yes or no could also mean maybe. In that case, both the yes and no choices might also contain some instances of maybe. As a result, they are not truly independent of one another. We would say that this circumstance is a source of measurement error. To correct this error, we could add a third unique category called maybe. Does the researcher know when he or she makes this kind of error? Generally not, and most ordinarily not until after the fact of data collection when it is discovered that the variable doesn't "act" as predicted.

Nominal scales allow us to count things—give the number of things classified as, say, 9—and to know that the count of 9s does not affect the count of, say, 7s. They are independent

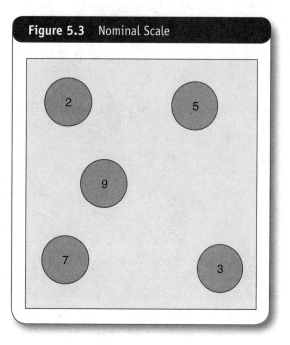

Figure 5.3   Nominal Scale

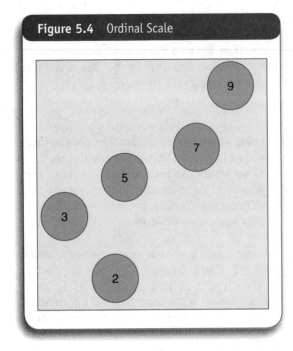

Figure 5.4   Ordinal Scale

categories. The average that reflects the most common value in a set of categories is the mode (the largest class), and the inferential statistics in use are chi-square and tests of proportion.

Ordinal Scales. The second property of numbers is that they can be arranged in order of greater and lesser as I have done in Figure 5.4. When used in measurement, this *ordinal scale* indicates more or less of something. Each point on the scale represents a unique value of whatever is being measured, and that value is ordered in relation to the other values on the scale. The way we identify the ordinal value is different from the cardinal number terms. In the figure, we would call the number 9 first, 7 second, and 2 fifth or last. An ordinal scale makes no claim about the distance between the points on the scale; it claims only that they increase or decrease.

In the case of the Netflix scale, the dimension in play is the more or less "likability" of a film. The Netflix scale is a good example of what should be treated as an ordinal scale. No attempt (in my reading of it) has been made to make the descriptors of the points equally spaced in the cognitive state of liking the film, but clearly the values move up.

Ordinal values allow for all the analysis that nominal values do—one can always move down in the assumptions of properties. In addition, there are tests of the median (the halfway point of occurrences) and of ordinal relationships.

Interval Scales. The third property of numbers takes up the distance (the interval) between the numbers. In not-so-simple terms, the principle holds that one can unitize a scale of numbers such that the relationship between any contiguous pair of points on the scale is the same. If one has a scale of integers ranging from 1 to 10, then the distance from 1 to 2 is the same as the distance between 9 and 10. Figure 5.5 shows a scale in which the points are two units

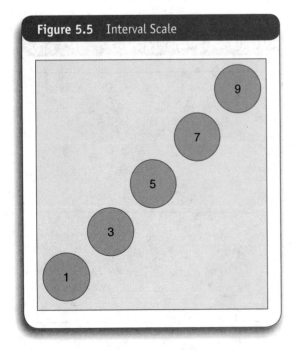

Figure 5.5   Interval Scale

apart, but the relationship between 1 and 3 is the same as the relationship between 7 and 9. This sort of scale is called an *interval scale*. Each point on the scale represents a unique value, the values are ordered along some dimension of more or less, and when the points are displayed in equal intervals, the distance between the points is the same. If we were to consider the Netflix scale an interval scale, it certainly would not be an equal interval scale. I think it would look like Figure 5.6 with discontinuities on the dislike side. I would much prefer a 7-point scale as in Figure 5.7 with missing units (in dark blue) added in.[4]

YouTube, by the way, has a similar problem with its Poor/Nothing Special/Worth Watching/Pretty Cool/Awesome! scale. Again there are two negatives to three positives, and how does one go from Nothing Special to Worth Watching in one step?

Why does all this matter anyway? Good measurement is the foundation of good results. The goal of quantification is to use the properties of numbers to represent the properties of the object under study. Both Netflix and YouTube inflate their ratings (which may the source of multiple disappointments), perhaps because getting people to watch something is how they make their money. If a similar error is accepted into the scholarly archive, it tends to reproduce itself. If it becomes authoritative, it cements the error in as others repeat it. In consulting, the consequences are often much more immediate when recommendations fail to produce the results expected.

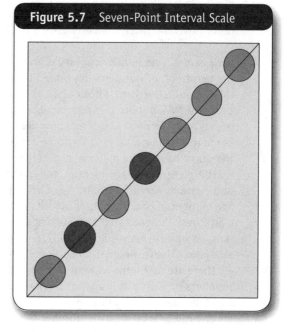

Figure 5.6   Interval Scale With Discontinuities

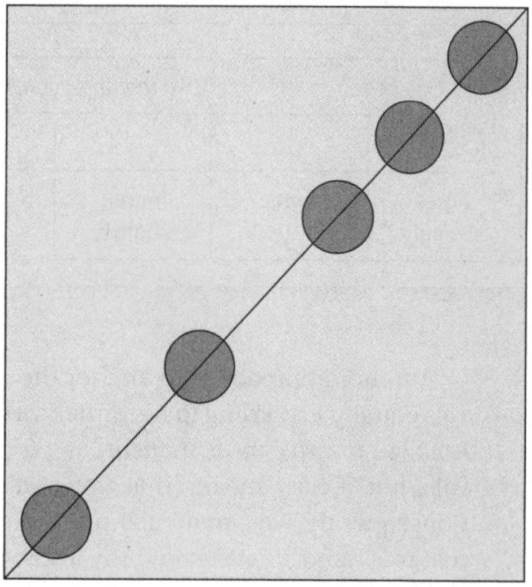

Figure 5.7   Seven-Point Interval Scale

---

[4]Or perhaps, better yet, a slider across the values from 1 to 10.

Equal (appearing) interval scales have been more or less standardized in metric research. Quite often the scale is composed of a declarative sentence followed by an agree or disagree response element. For example:

I like reading about the properties of numbers.						
—	—	—	—	—	—	—
Agree strongly	Agree	Agree slightly	Neither	Disagree slightly	Disagree	Disagree strongly

Another approach is to anchor the endpoints and let each respondent divide the intervals equally according to his or her own evaluation of the relative distances. This approach is called *ipsative measurement,* and it avoids the semantic problems of labeling the intervals, but it also means that your value of 5 may not be the same as my value of 5. Consequently, we cannot claim that a movie that was rated a 4 is twice as good as a movie that was rated a 2. We could say it was two units better, however, without any notion of the size of the units.

Despite the uncertainties and the high potential for error in using interval scaling, it is the measurement of choice. It is preferred because this form of quantification not only allows us to count and order entities, but we can also apply nearly the whole range of descriptive and inferential analyses. More than enough will be said about that later.

Ratio Scales. The fourth property of numbers is the zero. Zero is a relatively late arrival in the pantheon of numbers developed by Hindu mathematicians in the second century of the Common Era. Zero is both a placeholder and the representation of the absence of some property. When there is a natural absence of a property, we can take ratios. A *ratio scale* depends on the presence of a natural zero value. Age, height, weight, income, and the number of magazines received in a home are measures with natural zeros. Note that all of these measures have some material character about them. They exist in front of the eyes.

The great advantage of ratio scales is that measurements can be referenced to some known value. According to the Association of Magazine Media (www.magazine.org), the average number of issues read per month (subscription multiplied by appearance per month) is a little over 11. I read 16 (3 weekly magazines and 4 monthlies), not counting academic journals. My issue index would be 1.45 (16 divided by 11), indicating that I read 45% more magazine issues than average. That sort of claim would not be justified with an interval scale.

There are problems with ratio scales, of course. Most of them have to do with very small numbers or with a shifting base. There was a time when my daughter was .04 times my age. Now she is 0.65 times my age. (If we plot those points out, she will be older than I in a short while.) Of course, the number of years between us has remained the same, but our relative rates of change have not been the same. Her age doubled 5 times during the time it took for mine to double once. (If you remember your algebra, you can figure our respective ages.) Growth rates, relative growth rates, and changes in probabilities are all susceptible to these errors in interpretation because with small numbers, small changes can make large differences in reported values. There are other issues such as the question of scale: If you take 4 magazines and I take 2, you have twice as many. If you take 400 magazines and I take 200, you have twice as many, and we both have a serious problem. Consequently, we have to exercise some care.

Measurements that have a natural zero allow us to use all the properties of numbers to represent the properties of the objects measured. We can count them, order them, space them, and consider the values relative to one another. I'm a big fan.

Instruments

The last element in our list is (instruments). I've put the term in parentheses because it is most often left out of the discussion. Like servants in a 19th-century British household, instrumentation is the invisible but necessary element that makes the whole enterprise possible.

As little as three decades ago, we might have been excused this oversight because the majority of instrumentation was "paper and pencil." Such is no longer the case, and in fact there is little reason to use such primitive methods. True to form, there will be little discussion here because it would overwhelm this section (more later on, however). Nonetheless, instrumentation is not transparent. It is face-to-face or mediated communication with all the complications that communication entails.

Metric Trustworthiness: Reliability, Precision, Accuracy, and Validity

Because the common assumptions of metric measurement include the notion that whatever is being measured has something of the characteristics of a material object, the questions of the reliability, precision, accuracy, and validity of the measurement come into play. A few definitions: Reliability is the ability to repeatedly get the same values from the measurement of the same thing. If my desk measures 72 inches at Time 1, it should measure 72 inches at Time 2. If it doesn't, there are two theoretical possibilities: Either one of my measurements is in error, or the object has changed in dimension. More on this later.

Precision is the level at which a measurement is both reliable and accurate. U.S. government standards hold that a tape measure has to be accurate to plus or minus one sixteenth of an inch over 6 feet (72 inches). That means that any measurement between 71 and fifteen sixteenths of an inch and 72 and one sixteenth of an inch is the same within the tolerance standards, but don't try to build furniture at that level of precision (use the same tape measure throughout).

Accuracy is the ability of a measurement to reproduce some standard. If I build a 72-inch desk consistently using a tape measure that is one inch short, my measurements will be reliable and very precise (I'm bragging), but inaccurate. And validity is measuring what you claim you are measuring. If I measure the top of my desk by pulling a calibrated tape measure over the top of the books and papers piled upon it, my measurements will be reliable, precise, and accurate, but they will not be of the top of my desk.

Now we need to walk these ideas over to a 7-point Likert scale measuring a socially constructed, nonmaterial, composite variable that resides in some communication context held in place by human enactment. As the sentence implies, this is a difficult task. People do, however, behave in consistent ways, that behavior reaches some standard of performance, and the performance is often what we expected. Consequently, human behavior can be reliable, accurate, and valid within some level of precision. If we claim to be measuring that behavior, then our measurements should show the same characteristics.

Reliability is the starting place. If the analyst cannot repeat a set of measurements, either the measurement device or the behavior is unreliable, and in either case we do not know what is being measured. Game over. If the two measurements approximate one another, we will say they are reliable within some level of precision. The approximation device is usually the correlation between the two sets of measures—called a reliability coefficient. Reliability coefficients in the .70 range are routinely reported in the literature. That value means that a little less than half of the variability between the two sets of scores is shared. This is not a very high level of precision, but it is what we work with.

If the measure we are working with correlates with another accepted measure ostensibly of the same behavior, we can claim some level of accuracy. We call that concurrent validity. From here it gets a little murky. We attribute face validity to any measurement that looks like it should be measuring what we hope it is measuring to both the analyst and the respondent. Content validity is the level of test specification that is achieved in the measurement—the measurement covers all known aspects of the intended construct. Content validity can be only as good as what current knowledge of and consensus about the construct will allow. Predictive validity appears when the measurement predicts what it intends to predict. This form is also known as instrumental validity—the measurement does what it says it will do. Finally, a measurement achieves construct validity when the preponderance of the evidence supports its use as a measurement of the construct. This is the process known as consilience, and it is a form of probabilistic epistemology. It essentially says that if it works in all these cases, there must be something more than chance involved. It cannot, however, unproblematically specify what that "something" is.

There are three other forms of validity that enter into the research process. These are the levels of validity that are reached by the research protocol—the entire set of procedures in data generation. They make the most sense for experimental protocols but are used elsewhere as well. The first of these is internal validity. Internal validity is achieved when the protocol meets the standards of causal inference. External validity extends that success to other situations. Ecological validity means that the causal relationship will hold in the ecology of natural performance. We will deal with these issues in Chapter 12.

In the final analysis, we can provide good evidence of reliability but only indirect and often unsatisfactory evidence of validity. Because of this conundrum, we worship at the altar, but don't spend a lot time on the issues.

Interpretive (and Hybrid) Evidence

Interpretive and hybrid arguments depend on the skillful insights of the researcher or scholar responsible for the interpretation. The principle is that the researcher is the instrument. That instrument is not some Cartesian individual—a right mind thinking well—but rather a culturally located and informed agent engaged in somewhat conventionalized practices that are intended to provide the resources of the interpretation. In the end, the argument will stand or fall on the ability of the researcher to produce a coherent and resonant narrative. In the in-between, there will be plenty of evidence for that success or failure. We start this discussion with the observation and participation of ethnography and then move to the engagement of texts.

Observation and Participation

All ethnography is based on a systematic observation of the practices and performances of some congregation of individuals who share common (but often conflicted) understandings of those practices and performances. The gold standard of that observation is, perhaps surprisingly, participation.

A definitional note here: The term *congregation* and its forms refer to a group of individuals that are semiotically connected in meaningful practices and performances that the members cocreate. They are bound together in commonly understood beliefs, norms, and actions. A congregation would contrast with an aggregation.

The congregate group may be composed of a few to a very large and unknown number of individuals. The observational work that can be done depends on the number of different memberships that run through the group, the access that is granted to those memberships, and the ability of the ethnographer to grasp the significance of the differences that define the memberships.

For example, let's say I wanted to study the use of e-mail and networking sites across a large university in some Midwestern state. Would I expect the use of these communication technologies to be the same in the department of communication as in the department of mechanical engineering? Would I expect these departments to grant me the same access to their e-mail and sites? Finally, would I expect to understand the differences that might appear across these departments? I don't know the answers to those questions, but I better not start with any of those expectations.

Once admitted to any congregate group, then, the analyst is faced with the tasks of identifying the significant memberships, gaining access to those memberships, and developing a deep understanding of the practices that are emblematic of each of those memberships. Ethnographers, particularly academic ethnographers constrained by time, typically have to settle for a less-than-perfect accomplishment.

One measure of success of the observation, however, is the complexity of participation that can be achieved within the group memberships by the ethnographer. Observation and participation function as a duality in full-fledged ethnography. Observation is the foundation of competent participation, and participation opens the field of understanding that allows competent observation.

In the range of the ethnographic form, ethnographic reconnaissance is short on participation as this form has the analyst in the field for a few days or even hours. Consequently, its observations are much closer to the one-way mirror. At the other end, auto-ethnography (sometimes disparagingly called reminiscent ethnography, attic ethnography, or even narcissistic ethnography) is long on participation but suspect in any claim of systematic observation.[5]

---

[5]The emancipatory impulse of critical ethnography speaks for the group rather than about the group. Performance ethnography is an alternative form of participant observation.

Participant-observation ethnography alternates sessions of field participation with the writing of observations to create matched sets of participation and observation. Chapter 15 takes up that relationship is some detail. Here, it is enough to say that, once past that initial phase of hanging around, participation happens at the site when the ethnographer has achieved sufficient competence to actually do something that is both meaningful and instrumental to the membership, but observation happens in the writing of the field notes back at the office or its equivalent. This observation is obviously not photographic; it is a written analysis of experience. Participation takes its first step toward public knowledge in this systematic exploration of one's experience through the process of writing.

The set of field notes produced in an ethnography is a text, and it needs to be approached within the demands of good textual analysis. That text would be augmented by the artifacts, photographs, documents, and the like collected at the site, and these too are texts that must be analyzed. That analysis generally starts with the facts of the text.

Facts of the Text

Studies based on hermeneutic empiricism create a strong foundation for their contribution by starting with a systematic inventory of the facts of the text. The facts of the text are the properties of the text that might be the object of content analysis. These are called facts because they generally are not in dispute. A critic cannot argue a case against the existence of a researcher's field note or whether there are DVD chapters, scenes, or shots in a visual narrative or sentences (paragraphs, sections, whatever the unit) or this word and not that word in a written text. Those are the facts of the case. The first level of evidence resides within them. Whether in ethnography or textual analysis, there has to be factual evidence of the resources available in the action or texts for the interpretation proposed.

An Intimate Familiarity

As the researcher is the instrument, we expect the analyst to gain an intimate familiarity with those facts. In ethnography, this expectation might appear to be met in an extended schedule of multiple engagements in the action and the timely, dedicated production of field notes. But in a lengthy ethnographic effort, that familiarity fades, and the field notes and collected texts become the text of engagement, carrying the additional burden of textual analysis.

In textual analysis for whatever is the text, the expectation of intimate familiarity is met in the process called close reading. For most scholars, that means multiple "readings" of the whole text designed to get a deep understanding of what it achieves—its coherences, references, discontinuities, glosses, and the like. We have not systematized what counts as evidence of this effort as of this writing. Mostly, as we will see in Chapter 13, we just declare it as accomplished. I would argue for a deliberately systematic and publicly accessible approach in which the proximal insights gained in the close reading are archived in some written form. That written form is the second level of evidence.

Coding

For many literary scholars, the analysis ends with the close reading, and the understanding achieved is presented as the critical analysis. I would argue for a firmer empirical foundation, and that involves systematic, perhaps computer-assisted, but certainly grounded coding. Grounded coding is the process of working through a text, unit by unit, and attaching interpretations as to the topic, significance, rhetorical force, cultural location, and the like of each unit. Not only does coding rub one's nose in the text so to speak, but the codes (and the coding software) allow the texts to be manipulated and investigated in ways nearly impossible through the simple strength of one's memory. Coding is powerful evidence of effective engagement.

Warrants

The final step is to reveal the warrants. A warrant is a justification for some action. When a judge issues a search warrant, it means that there is legal justification for the search. A logical warrant means there is a basis for constructing a valid argument. In argumentation, a warrant means there is some foundation in common understanding (those "of course it's true" assumptions) for connecting evidence to claim. In interpretive research, a warrant is the basis for constructing a competent text.

Like a variable, a warrant exists in the evidence of its existence (where there's smoke, there's fire). For example, consider a film in which a White male, a White female, and a Black male are all thrashing about in the water with both rescue ship and shark in sight. What happens? Our White male and Black male are rescuing children from invading Japanese. Who dies?

We start with the facts of the case: There are a fair number of U.S. films spanning decades of time in which a White character and a character of color are in mortal danger. The situation is resolved with the death of one and the survival of the other. And it is mostly true in these cinematic choices that the White character survives and the person of color dies. (In fact, in at least one film, the Black character makes a joke about his impending death.) Exceptions are noted as exceptional.

If we presume that these narratives are competent—that they are believable—what is the cultural warrant that justifies our belief in them? In current cultural theory, we would probably frame that warrant in terms of the construction of Whiteness. In that theory, the warrant might be called the White privilege of survival. Films that resolve the threat of danger by killing off the Black character depend on this warrant for the emotional satisfaction of the solution, affirm the right of this privilege, and instruct us all in the way that it works.[6]

Once we arrive at this understanding, we might want to investigate how the warrant works in other circumstances where the outcomes seem otherwise equally likely for characters of color. We might investigate scenes of competition, romance, and the fates. We might want to see if the principle is apparent naïvely, ironically, or oppositionally in films produced by and for persons of color. Note that in the examination of warrants we have created a program of research, which will now reach well beyond our original interest.

---

[6]The insight of "depends, affirms, and instructs" comes from my colleague, Professor Ronald B. Scott.

Interpretive Trustworthiness: Coherence, Resonance, and Vraisemblance

Coherence, resonance, and vraisemblance are the interpretive equivalents to metric's reliability and validity. Interpretive empiricism is not based on any set of assumptions that places the meaningfulness of human action within the realm of the material. Human action is firmly semiotic and socially constructed. Any suggestion of reliability or validity as external to the narrative would be sadly in error. But there are standards of acceptability and of good work.

Coherence requires that the narrative hangs together and has a recognizable arc of performance. This concept might correspond to the idea of internal validity. Resonance means that the narrative has to make sense within its context and would be recognizable within the domain of the performance that it describes. In some texts, this requirement leads to a recommendation that the narrative be "checked by the members of the community of members." That position requires beliefs in the uncomplicated representation and referentiality of language and discourse. These are modernist beliefs that would pose difficulties for a postmodernist. Nonetheless, resonance might be considered as the correspondence to external validity—the narrative is more than just itself. Vraisemblance is the recognition of the narrative as plausible, without fatal defect. The reader has a sense of what it means to be a member, and enactment is considered possible. Vraisemblance might correspond to ecological validity.

There are no conventionalized measures of these standards. They are particular to the context of the study. And conventionalization is an unlikely event at any rate, given the antiestablishment impulses of interpretation. That absence does not mean that we cannot ask for the evidence of coherence, resonance, and vraisemblance as readers of the work or that we do not have an obligation to provide that evidence as analysts. We can ask and have those responsibilities in all cases.

MOVING ON

This chapter is the first of this "toolbox" section that is intended to provide you with the activities that are found in all research so that we can carry on our conversation in more specialized topics without too many disconnections. In this chapter, we have been discussing the practical foundations of these common activities. Each of us comes to this practice out of some axiomatic framework that provides the warrants for our actions. Textbooks (like all narratives) depend on those warrants, affirm their necessity, and instruct the reader on their right practice. This textbook is mediated communication just like that television show.[7] It speaks from inside the epistemological edifice that these warrants can construct. It is not really a house of cards, but it is one of human endeavor that has to be subject to critical evaluation. The next chapter takes up the specifics of research questions and hypotheses and starts our investigation of the literature.

---

[7]Of course, my intention is not to entertain (nailed it!) or to sell you something else.

REFLECTIONS

What Are Some Points to Remember?

- All research and scholarship is based on some assumptions about the properties, processes, consequences, and character of what we study. In media research, those focus on the media themselves and their texts and audiences. The key is not the suppression of those assumptions but the recognition of their presence, influence, and consequences.
- Just as we have assumptions about the world, so too we have affinities for particular theoretical approaches. A belief in a theory entails the likelihood of a methodology. Theory determines what counts as evidence. It is not by chance that cognitive theorists gravitate toward measurement scales and social action theorists move toward ethnography.
- A methodology is a means of producing evidence. The form of that evidence depends on the theory in use.
- Different methodologies have different criteria for judging the quality of that evidence. Importing criteria from one methodology to another is a political action, not an epistemological one.

Why Does It Matter?

What the analyst does and how well it is done establishes the quality of the contribution that can be made. The better we understand what we are doing and why we are doing it, the better we can achieve the quality we seek.

What Else Could We Talk About?

Media scholars have a conflicted relationship with media. Media researchers and scholars reflect elitist and class-based attitudes toward content and audiences and often hold industries as vast conspiracies. Media are seen as an overlay or a distraction from a true culture or an authentic society. Media are rarely seen as a force for good in society or even as a neutral element in our cultural environment. Scholars focus on one kind of content and attribute high levels of effectiveness to it. Many see audience members as victims or unwitting dupes. Our research mirrors those beliefs.

What Else Might Be Interesting to Read?

Jensen, K. B., & Rosengren, K. E. (1990). Five traditions in search of the audience. *European Journal of Communication, 5,* 411–420.

Mastro, D., Lapinski, M. K., Kopacz, M. A., & Behm-Morawitz, E. (2009). The influence of exposure to depictions of race and crime in TV news on viewer's social judgments. *Journal of Broadcasting & Electronic Media, 53,* 615–635.

CHAPTER 6

Research Questions
and Hypotheses

CHAPTER PREVIEW

What's It All About?

Chapter 6 completes our investigation of research problems by showing how an interest in a research problem is transformed into a research study, tracing the different routes to be taken by metric and interpretive research. It offers a review of contemporary examples from the literature and ends with the role to be played by institutional review boards in academic research.

What Are the Major Topics?

Disciplines form around constellations of problems. Problems can be divided into questions of what, how, why, and value.

In metric research, problems are translated into research studies through the research question or the research hypothesis. The difference between these two devices is explained.

In interpretive research, the translation device is the construction of a coherent narrative that encompasses the systematic experience of the analyst.

In hybrid research, the problem is diagnosed for its rhetorical force—the call for transformation.

Community-based research translates the research problem into a return of value to the community in which the study is located.

One hundred contemporary research studies are sorted into their focus on properties, practices, consequences, or value. Fifteen studies drawn proportionately from these categories are analyzed in detail. The implications of contemporary practice for how research is actually done are discussed.

The chapter ends with a discussion of the role of the institutional review board, a committee mandated by federal regulation to ensure the protection of human participants in research. That protection focuses on two concerns: the competence of the research design and the adequacy of the process and documents of informed consent.

What Special Terms Are Used?

Axiology

Etiology

Ontology

Praxeology

CREATING A RESEARCH STUDY

In this chapter, we consider how one goes from a problem to a research study. The route takes us through research questions and hypotheses. Along the way, we will mind the differences between metric and interpretive research and introduce the special conditions of action research and community-engaged scholarship.

Good, engaging, complex problems can be the bases of entire research programs, not just a single study. Further, disciplinary fields are formed around constellations of problems, and research methods develop within disciplines that are appropriate to the constellation of problems. (Students of mediated communication do not ordinarily take the advanced engineering mathematics necessary to calculate the stress on steel girders, because that is not one of our problems.)

Finally, there is a symbiotic relationship between what is possible in methodology and the theories by which we make sense of the findings of our research methods. For example, the great failure of early animal behaviorism to explain motivation in human action led to cognitivist theories. And the great failure of both structuration and systems theories to develop effective methodologies has left those theories in the "more promise than performance" category of ideas.

Human problems are complex and messy. Research typically aims at being systematic and tidy. The two very different sets of characteristics can lead to research that looks great but fails the criterion of ecological validity—a laboratory creation that can never happen in natural performances. Even the strongest of research can ordinarily address only some small part of the problem that motivates it. As a result, we are not very good at resolving the problems that invigorate our scholarship. Consequently, we have a traditional set of research problems or problem categories that we have been studying for a century or more (millennia if you include philosophical analysis). Not surprisingly (given who is doing the writing here), the questions fall along the four compass points of ontology, praxeology, etiology, and axiology. The "ologies" translate into questions about things and their properties (ontology), methods and practices (praxeology), causes and consequences (etiology), and character and value (axiology).

Things and Properties: Questions of "What?"

The things can be content, audiences, technologies, industries, managers, editors, reporters, race, ethnicity, gender, class, and the like, and the properties might be called characteristics, structures, types, compositions, frames, forms, logics, conventions, expressions, representations, portrayals, perceptions, preferences, views, nature, and the like. Ontological methods include content analysis and surveys, and their results might be used to demonstrate the conceptualizations in play; the state of something; associations, comparisons, and relationships among elements; and the like.

Methods and Practices: Questions of "How?"

Questions about methods and practices seem to distribute according to differences in scholarly communities. Questions on the methods of design, production, best practices, message strategies and tactics, and industry and regulatory practices tend to appear in the professionally oriented literature. Questions about cultural practices such as gender, race, ethnicity, memory, dominance and oppression, myths, rituals, and the performances associated with them tend toward the critical rhetorical literature. So a question about how to best frame an antismoking campaign might appear in the *Journal of Communication*, but a question on how the framing of antismoking campaigns leads to the reification of class structures would most likely appear in *Critical Studies in Media Communication*. Both questions, however, might start with content analysis methods as the foundation for an answer.

A word here about the correspondence between things and practices. We see that gender appears both in the *thing* list and in the *practice* list. Gender, as well as race, ethnicity, and nearly any other social construction, is treated by the literatures as both a thing and a practice. Metric literatures tend to treat all social constructions as things or states of existence. Gender, in this literature, is reported as male or female rather than masculine or feminine, confounding gender with physiology. Interpretive literatures will work to separate gender from sex by describing the social practices through which gender appears (generally, body image, decoration, grooming practices, clothing styles, and ways of being in the world). But this approach too confuses gender with physiology in its arguments concerning the association of gender roles with persons of a given sex. One of the subtext intentions of such arguments may be the disappearance of gender, as the differences—no matter what they are—that are required for gender to appear are considered inherently unjust.

You can imagine the methodological headaches if we actually treated gender as independent of sex. No longer could we make simple divisions of males and females—unless, of course, we had some theoretical justification based on sexual physiology. Instead we would have to take measures of the gender practices in play at the time associated choices were made. It is no wonder such little effort has been made to sort this out.

Causes and Consequences: Questions of "Why?"

Traditional etiology views the world as organized in an unending series of causal relations. Each "What?" has a "Why?" attached to its prior conditions and its consequential outcomes, such that each entity is the consequent of some antecedent and is subsequently the antecedent of some result. Etiological questions could theoretically start anywhere and go in either direction—toward the antecedents or toward the consequences. Most etiological questions, however, start with a suspected cause and consequence in hand with the intent of demonstrating the relationship. But there are certainly some times when we have a variable in hand whose place we want to sort out in the fabric of causation.

Typical causation studies, then, look at "known" forms of content, technologies and the practices within them, industries, industrial practices, the economics of media, and similar sorts of priors as the causes (or at least antecedents) for "known" states and/or conditions in individuals, families, groups, audiences, organizations, societies, and cultures (depending on the unit of analysis and the level of explanatory attack). Most effects studies start this way: There is violence, sexual promiscuity, race/gender/class injustice, eating disorders, smoking by youth, and so on in the world, and there is content that appears to promote these conditions. Could media be part of the cause?

In the realm of metric analysis, this search for the causal relationship typically makes use of the logic of straight-line causation, where we have some well-conventionalized methodologies (experimental, correlational, and linear modeling) for studying causal relationships. It is important to remember that in the metric world only experimental methods, which contain proper controls for alternative explanations, can provide *direct* evidence for causation. (Correlational and modeling methods as well as interpretive approaches cannot put these necessary controls in place and, therefore, can provide only *indirect* evidence.) The experimental methods that are available to us, however, suffer from weaknesses in operational definitions and the failure to achieve ecological validity in the protocol. The difficulty of tracing causation is not an excuse for doing nothing. It is good reason for lowering expectations and being cautious about the claims we make. A modesty of claim still is best.

Interpretive studies have an uneasy relationship with causation but, nonetheless, regularly invoke its presence, albeit indirectly. The interpretive argument hangs on claims about discursive practices constituting social practices, showing how media-wide presentations and representations produce certain cultural outcomes. Here, too, at least the foundational methodology—content analysis—is well conventionalized. It then moves to the analyst as interpretative agent, which is subjective but not idiosyncratic.

Character and Value: Questions of "So What?"

Questions of character and value include analysis of policy, regulation, and legislation; power relations in race, ethnicity, class, gender, and similar critical-issue approaches; hegemony of the dominant and the oppressed along with acts of resistance; and the cultural constitutions of the true, the good, and the beautiful (there being no objective standard of any of these).[1]

---

[1]This claim follows the argument of Berger and Luckmann (1967) on the sociology of knowledge in which the true is a social construction.

If metric philosophy organizes the world into a causal fabric of deterministic relationships, interpretive philosophy organizes the social world into a fabric of power relationships in which value is attached to material characteristics and values (concepts of the good, the true, and the beautiful) are attached to cultural success. Metric scholars have an uneasy relationship with character and value because of a presumed lack of objectivity and because they operate outside the domain of the individual. Nonetheless, issues of character arise directly in cognitivist studies of attitudes and value formation, and we certainly see values appearing in the justifications for the "importance of the problem" and implications of the research sections of the metric report. Fowers and Richardson (1993) provide an excellent example of an analysis of the values inherent in such research, and I with my coauthor Janet Colvin (Anderson & Colvin, 2008a) have argued that ideology, not epistemology, drives much of the violence- and promiscuity-in-the-media research.

The richness of character and value, however, appears in interpretive analyses, cultural studies, action research, and community-engaged scholarship where (the pretense of)[2] disassociated objectivity is abandoned in favor of lively argument about how things ought to be in the world.

RESEARCH QUESTIONS AND HYPOTHESES

Metric Studies

Problem statements as they appear in the literature usually end in some form of research questions or hypotheses. Actual questions are the exit form of the problem statement when the issue is in a more general, less precise state or when, as is common in interpretive empiricism, the full character of the problem is to emerge from the subsequent research process. In our political talk radio (PTR) example, we might write the research question as RQ1: What is the relationship between PTR content themes and respondent political identities?

In this typical research question form, any finding—even one of no relationship—counts as an answer. Philosophers of science would say that it is an undisciplined question, one that provides no method for validating the answer. Research questions are used precisely because of that characteristic. They allow research to go forward without jeopardizing the development of further research, because no subsequent avenue is closed. Used in conjunction with hypotheses, research questions can allow the search for alternative hypotheses to be coupled with a test of actual hypothesis, but metric studies that pose only research questions and not hypotheses are in a preliminary stage of development.

Hypotheses, on the other hand, are a form of conditional statement that is the conclusion of a deductive analysis that starts with some generalized theoretical principle and moves through what that principle entails to reach what has to occur in the specific case of the study at hand if the general principle is true. The study is then designed to produce the conditions of the specific case to see if the circumstances required by the theory indeed appear. In authentic hypotheses, this analysis is explicitly stated. We don't often see authentic hypotheses in communication research because our theory typically is not

---

[2]As such scholars would likely argue.

adequately developed to provide effective general principles. Most often, our hypotheses are educated guesses as to what should be true or, more simply, are research questions written as declarative statements.

This masquerade might not be a big deal—good research can still be done, but the appearance of hypotheses in a study is often something of a game of dress-up. In our PTR study again, a hypothesis of the latter kind would be

H1: Liberal-conservative valence scores of PTR themes will be positively related to liberal-conservative valence scores of respondent identity.

There is more specificity in this hypothesis form (direction of the relationship, for example), but the reason why this should be true is entirely implicit. Consequently, our example is more of a research question in a declarative disguise.

There are some costs to the disguise. The foremost of these is that there is no clear path as to what theory a confirming result would support or a disconfirming finding would falsify. Given that lack of connection, we have no way of knowing where the contribution falls except in some form of general theory (cognitive theory in our example). That opens the researcher up to all sorts of temptations to advance well beyond a modesty of claim or the equally noxious practice of claiming success if even a small subset of hypotheses is supported (partial support is like almost significance—neither can logically occur).

Interpretive Studies

On the other hand, hypotheses rarely appear in interpretive studies (I would say they never appear in good ones). Interpretive studies do not follow the deductive form. They follow a narrative coherence model. In the simplest terms in the homeless study, my starting point is the questions of whether and how I can put the two ideas of homelessness and community together in a coherent narrative that is responsive to my experiences of both. At this starting point, I have no idea of how (or even if) they might come together. And, as noted, I have to be careful about a colonizing literature.

At the end of my initial sojourn in the field, I came up with a number of understandings about what I was looking at. One such claim was that homelessness for the White male—who constitutes the majority of the homeless—is mostly about the loss of masculine identity. That claim now becomes a target for further work and can seem something like a hypothesis. In fact, metric research might take it on as a hypothesis for its own activity. For the interpretive researcher, further study involves the way the concept works to make sense of what is being experienced. It certainly doesn't work for the psychiatrically diagnosed or in the one-time homeless episode. Consequently, the subsequent narrative will work the boundaries of the concept's frame of understanding.

Hybrid Studies

Hybrid studies (critical-empirical mergers) work from an initiating analysis that establishes the rhetorical force of a set of conditions. Rhetorical force is what justifies the rhetorical action of the research study and its implications for social reform. As Eadie (1985) puts it, rhetorical force is "the necessity for talk, resolution, invention, transformation, and change in identification."[3] The work to establish this necessity can be extensive (see the examples under "Questions of Character" below), taking up a third to a half of the total argument.

The importance of this section lies in the fact that it establishes both the terms of the empirical analysis and the conclusions to be drawn. The entire study succeeds or fails on the basis of the resonance and coherence of the analysis. As a result, the study has a very different look and feel from either metric or interpretive studies.

Community-Based Research

Community-based research was placed firmly in the academic consciousness by the 1990 Boyer report on scholarship in higher education. Boyer identified four types of scholarship: discovery, integration, application, and teaching. In speaking of the scholarship of application, he asked the question "How can knowledge be responsibly applied to consequential problems?" (Boyer, 1990, p. 22). For Boyer, application was one of the ways that the scholarship of discovery (the top of Boyer's hierarchy) was made manifest (see also Boyer, 1996).

Boyer did not satisfy the growing number of critics of traditional research that was appearing at the turn of the last century. They saw Boyer as presenting a top-down model in which the expert researcher brings the fruits of science to the citizen within problem frameworks deemed consequential by the researcher. The problem and the solution were entirely under his or her ownership. It did not change the character of research but changed only its venue. Researchers used communities to enliven the journals with real people but returned little of value to the people's real problems. Oftentimes, the consequential problem addressed was the traditional problem of the success of the professoriat at the expense of the community.

Community-engaged scholarship (aka community-based research)[4] is a movement that both struggles with and seeks to resolve the difficulties with the scholarship of Boyer's model. The movement is fueled by a generalized discontent with how things are currently done in the academy without any clear consensus of how to do them differently. If the details of the practice are yet to be ironed out, what does seem to be clear and unifying is the call for action.

The call for action is simple in its statement but complex in its execution. The call is to locate a substantial amount of the research activity of the academy—particularly public health and social science research but also research in engineering and the biological sciences—physically, culturally, and intellectually in the communities that both support and are to benefit from that research. Further, the research undertaken needs to be participatory, collaborative, and inclusive of the members of those communities, taking into account their interests and goals as well as their insights and knowledge (see, for example,

---

[3]http://www.eric.ed.gov/ERICWebPortal/custom/portlets/recordDetails/detailmini.jsp?_nfpb=true&_&ERICExtSearch_SearchValue_0=ED258306&ERICExtSearch_SearchType_0=no&accno=ED258306. Accessed April 15, 2011.

[4]Generally speaking, civic engagement is a particular form of community-based research that encourages citizen activity in political processes.

the 2008 white paper "Global Alliance on Community-Engaged Research"[5]). Community-based research, consequently, starts in the needs of the community as articulated and advanced by the community members. They own the research question, and it is up to the researcher to find the means of an answer that will return value to the community.

Let's take a deliberately provocative example that will set all the issues in motion. Both the American Medical Association and the American Psychological Association have been moving to declare an average of more than two hours a day per week of video game use a symptom of an addiction. (From what I hear from my gamer friends—mostly in their 20s and 30s—15 hours might be a slow Saturday.) The AMA and the APA represent an authorized voice speaking the truth of a community to which it does not belong. How different would it be if the research had started in the gaming community, aiming to develop the physical and psychological resources a hard-core gamer needs to achieve the highest level of performance? I can hear the not-too-distant cries of "enabler" and "codependency," yet this approach is exactly what we do with professional sports. It wouldn't be the money, would it?

Proprietary Research

Proprietary research will follow the requirements of the type of research being conducted for the role of research questions and hypotheses. Questions and/or hypotheses will typically be expressed in the more locally relevant terms of the sponsoring organization as the research is directed toward those particular issues rather than a more generalized frame.

CONTEMPORARY EXAMPLES

In doing the research for this chapter, I built an archive of empirical studies taken from the most recently available issues[6] of *Critical Studies in Media Communication, Journal of Broadcasting and Electronic Media, Journal of Communication,* and *Journalism and Mass Communication Quarterly*. I took 25 articles from each.[7] Each article was coded into one of the four compass point categories according to its overarching argument and where apropos according to such secondary questions that were engaged. From that initial sorting, I extracted the characteristics that appear here in the opening paragraphs of the preceding sections.

From a methodological theory standpoint, I am mixing metric and interpretive approaches using an a priori, theory-based set of categories but creating the descriptions of those categories in a grounded analysis (based on the elements themselves) of the sample. It is a hybrid method that offers both containment and flexibility. There are a number of methodological issues that we can explore, but for the moment let's look at the results as presented in Table 6.1.

---

[5]http://www.scienceshops.org/. Accessed April 15, 2011.

[6]*Critical Studies in Media Communication* has a one-year embargo on its online content, an ironic bit of capitalism.

[7]The list of articles is in Appendix B.

Table 6.1   Distribution of 100 Articles Across Question Type

Journal/Category	CSMC	JOBEM	JOC	J&MCQ	Total
Properties	6	9	5	13	33
Praxis	9	0	0	0	9
Consequences	0	15	18	11	44
Character	10	1	2	1	14

Note: CSMC = *Critical Studies in Media Communication;* JOBEM = *Journal of Broadcasting and Electronic Media;* JOC = *Journal of Communication;* J&MCQ = *Journalism and Mass Communication Quarterly.*

To anyone familiar with these journals, there are no surprises in the results either in the distribution of questions or in the way the questions distribute over the journals. As a field, we are very much interested in questions of why and what and seemingly much less interested in character and praxis, although all appear in the literature.

We can examine the prototypical questions for each of these categories by drawing on the statement of the problem from five "categorically centered" articles. In the sections that follow, I first offer the author description of the study and then my interpretation of the research questions as contextualized in research practice.

Questions of Properties

The 33 properties studies in our set of 100 investigated types of content; differences across portrayals of gender, ethnicity, and nationality; the representation of violence; the activity of witnessing; types of beauty; the character of news viewing and viewership; conceptualizations of web portals; media choices; comparison of content across media; comparison of viewer traits across media; content analysis studies; attitudes of reporters; qualities of news and the news viewer; the transnational nature of contemporary news; visual framing of the Iraq War; characteristics of mash-up culture; cigarette advertising; decision-making styles; issue agendas; characteristics of news browsing; perception of media influence; environmental reporting; conceptual underpinnings of the people's right to know; characteristics of NASCAR dads; food marketing; coverage and ethnicity of newspaper staffs; and the concept of "eyewitnessing." Protocols for the study of properties include surveys, long-form interviews, focus groups, ethnographic reconnaissance, and the examination of texts via content-critical-cultural analysis. The following are the five studies I selected for their pedagogical value.

Tsfati and Livio (J&MCQ, 2008)

How journalists perceive media influence was explored by comparing results from a survey of Israeli journalists ($n = 200$) and a survey of the Israeli adult population ($n = 1,203$). As predicted, journalists demonstrated significant third-person perceptions (TPPs), but these were actually smaller than those of the public. Journalists tended more than the public to perceive media influence as positive. Journalists perceiving a stronger media influence were relatively new journalists and worked for local media, but had some formal education in journalism. (Abstract, p. 113)

This study approaches an archetypal example of this question type. A survey instrument is prepared to measure the presence of certain characteristics, and the results are presented. There is not much interpretation, and the study is not strongly theory driven. The longevity of the findings would be rather short.

Behm-Morawitz and Mastro (J&MCQ, 2008)

This two-part exploratory study utilized a social cognitive theory framework in documenting gender portrayals in teen movies and investigating the influence of exposure to these images on gender-based beliefs about friendships, social aggression, and roles of women in society. First, a content analysis of gender portrayals in teen movies was conducted, revealing that female characters are more likely to be portrayed as socially aggressive than male characters. Second, college students were surveyed about their teen movie-viewing habits, gender-related beliefs, and attitudes. Findings suggest that viewing teen movies is associated with negative stereotypes about female friendships and gender roles. (Abstract, p. 131)

This study is a "backdoor" effects study. It is basically two surveys, one concerning the characteristics of a genre of content and the other about audience behavior and beliefs. The connection between the two in a causal relationship is made through social cognitive theory (p. 136). Certain characteristics were found in the content and certain attitudes in a segment of the audience, allowing the authors to conclude, "It is a reasonable argument that one very important outcome of viewing teen films may be the impact on individuals' actual relationship behaviors" (p. 142). That may be a reasonable argument, but the conversion of ontological studies into etiological claims doesn't add much to the reasonableness of the argument.

Glascock (JOBEM, 2008)

The objective of this study was to examine the prevalence of verbal, physical, and indirect aggression on network prime-time programming. Given the theoretical implications, such an analysis would serve as a starting point for understanding the breadth and potential impact of aggression on primetime network television. (p. 272)

Glascock pulls a similar switch from ontology to etiology with even less evidence in that only content is surveyed. Once again, the connection is made through theory. In this case, the theory includes notions of a passive, "defenseless" audience. The author concludes by stating that audience members "will, on average, be exposed to substantial amounts of aggressive behavior, and subject to the inevitable, ensuing social learning and cultivation processes" (p. 279). There are, of course, alternative constitutions of the audience that included terms such as *actively interpreting, evaluating, resisting*, and the like. These descriptions, however, lessen the etiological value of content studies as cause and consequence are generally considered the highest level of explanation. Making the move to consequences enhances the study.

Carlyle, Slater, and Chakroff (JOC, 2008)

The study presented here content analyzes a nationally representative sample of newspaper coverage of IPV [intimate partner violence] over a 2-year period and compares this coverage to epidemiological data, examining implications of discrepancies between coverage and social reality. (pp. 168–169)

While ostensibly a study of content characteristics, Carlyle, Slater, and Chakroff also produce an implicit study of value in making judgments as to the quality of the newspaper reportage of intimate partner violence by comparing the nonscientific content of the newspaper with the science-based content of the Centers for Disease Control and Prevention. Because of the apples-and-oranges comparison, there is little basis to make sense of the similarities and differences found. The comparison makes sense only if it is based on the assumption that newspaper reporting ought to be the same as science-based data collection—an obvious assumption of character.

In the end, the authors also move to consequence, claiming "that how media portray a particular health issue has important implications for how it is perceived by the public" (p. 180). Indeed it does, but I don't need this study to draw that conclusion, and this study tells me nothing about how IPV is perceived by the public. One cannot legitimately draw conclusions about audience behavior based on content characteristics. But clearly folks do it anyway.

Shiga (CSMC, 2007)

This essay traces the logic of mash-up culture, an online music scene in which practitioners use audio-editing software to splice and combine pop songs encoded in MP3 format to produce hybrid or "mashed-up" recordings. The study focuses on the logic that guides the development of works, styles and reputations in mash-up culture. Several fields of practice shape this cultural logic, including "virtual studios," online message boards, dance clubs, and the market for "underground" and "unofficial" remixes. This cultural logic generates a new kind of amateur musicianship based on pluralistic listening and the reorganization of the relations that constitute musical recordings. (Abstract, p. 93)

Shiga's work presents a good representation of the rhetorical-analytical side of hybrid methods. He seems to be very knowledgeable of the people and performances of the members of the mash-up culture (or at least he is brave about it). Where we might expect a detailed description of participation and artifacts analyzed in an ethnographic study,

Shiga's bona fide membership appears in a single line (p. 94). What makes the argument work is not systematic empiricism, but the resonance of the argument.

As with most hybrid arguments, this argument is a pastiche of "what is" along with an analysis of what it means to be that way. The critical underpinning of hybrid approaches nearly always forces the issue of character.

Arguments of both properties and character are typically grand and could be considered undisciplined by any empirical foundation. It is much easier to draw the critical conclusion if the what-it-is issue can be settled with an essentializing description (such as this one).

Questions of Praxis

Nine of the 100 studies concerned questions of praxis. They covered the practices of surveillance, constructing narratives of heroism, agency in sexualized content, selling, political transformation, academic publishing, cultural memory, and family political discussion. Two studies are presented in extended discussion.

Andrejevic (CSMC, 2006)

After considering how surveillance practices discipline the objects of the monitoring gaze, I argue for a focus on the discipline of watching. An era of reflexive skepticism and generalized risk puts a premium on the ability to see through public façades by relying on strategies of detection and verification facilitated by interactive communication technologies that allow users to monitor one another. Interactive communication technologies allow for peer-to-peer surveillance of friends, significant others, and family members. If, in commercial and state contexts, the promise of interactivity serves as a ruse for asymmetrical and nontransparent forms of monitoring, this model of interactivity has also infiltrated the deployment of interactive technologies in personal relationships. (Abstract, p. 391)

Andrejevic performs a critical analysis of interactive technologies and the practice of interactivities that involve "asymmetric, nontransparent forms of information gathering" (p. 395)—such as surreptitiously looking at your partner's cell phone call list—without ever looking at actual practices but rather by examining the practices that appear in reality show texts. The empirical investigative object is content; the implication is drawn to the Internet Generation and in that practice is not much different from Glascock. The question the author asks concerns the unintended consequences of participating in interactive technologies and the heightened exposure to surveillance and detection that such practices present.

Good question, but why study texts of practices instead of actual practices? Probably for the same reason we study content to make statements about consequences in audiences—time, money, accessibility, and the like. We can consider this method a clever way to get around these problems or an interesting analysis of content that really doesn't answer the question. I believe the method was clever 50 years ago, but no longer is. Nonetheless, Andrejevic's argument resonates. Perhaps, most of us have Googled someone (or ourselves) or checked out social networking site entries or blogs or websites or cell phones to gather information that can be used in a relationship with another person. Understanding that others do the same to us can be a revelation.

Rodino-Colocino (CSMC, 2006)

Drawing on an array of promotional texts, including news articles, press releases, promotional Web sites, and ads appearing in newspapers and magazines, this paper tells the story of how the computer industry aimed to sell smaller, faster computing devices to women while promising to mediate and thus reproduce women's overwork as paid and familial laborers. After experimenting with the PDA as a sexy fashionable gadget for working women, marketers approached women as mothers with "Audrey," an Internet appliance designed for the kitchen. (Abstract, p. 375)

Audrey as an Internet appliance had a very short life even for technology, lasting only from October 2000 to March 2001 according to CNET News.[8,9] In its short market life span, however, it apparently accomplished great things. It became a "significant cultural product/object" (pp. 376, 383) that "symbolized the struggle to envision the geographical contours of the domestic sphere in an age of proliferating mobile information and communication technologies" (p. 385). The language used here reveals some of the work that an author (all authors) has to do to situate that work as worthy of the archive. Certainly, that would be more difficult if Audrey were an insignificant cultural object. (Perhaps, Audrey is the most significant cultural object that no one ever heard of, but see the DigiBarn Computer Museum[10] to make your own decision.)

It is, however, the phrase "she [sic] symbolized the struggle to envision" that is most interesting, because it is a factual claim entirely devoid of evidence. It did not come to symbolize; it was not used to symbolize; but right out of the box (and it would have had to have been that quick) it symbolized the struggle to envision. What is going on here?

This study is ostensibly a study of marketing practices and how those practices approached a gendered subject. But the author uses only about half the space allocated to the article for that purpose. That analysis forms a platform for commentary about gender and social justice that ranges far from the data. And it is this ringing rhetoric that Audrey comes to symbolize. I see this as a move from analysis to preaching. And while it is common in hybrid studies with their rhetorical tradition, it is not at all uncommon in even the "most scientific" of effects studies. Simple questions become grand statements.

---

[8]http://news.cnet.com/2100-1040-254497.html. Accessed April 18, 2011.

[9]But wait, it came back (sort of). Verizon marketed The Hub in the same way with an upscale woman preparing a paella recipe from a foodie site and then texting her teenage son for approval. Dolt that he is, he videos back that he is not pleased. She calls for pizza (http://www.splendad.com/ads/show/3018-Verizon-Wireless-Hub-Paella). The other commercial that I have seen was of an upscale Black man checking traffic reports and texting a route to his wife on her way to work, while drinking from the orange juice carton (http://www.splendad.com/ads/show/3019-Verizon-Wireless-Hub-Umbrella). Both clearly stereotype the masculine. Announced in 2009, marketing for The Hub has since disappeared. It appears to have lasted about as long as Audrey.

[10]http://www.digibarn.com/collections/movies/audrey.html. Accessed April 18, 2011.

For the reader, then, the issue becomes "What was the original question the analyst was addressing?" In this case, we may wonder if there was a question at all, or was it that Audrey was simply a convenient event on which to mount an argument? Audrey was, after all, a complete marketing failure.

Questions of Consequence

There were 44 studies in this set that addressed questions of consequence. The topics covered included the long-term consequences of a sun safety campaign, the cognitive effort in viewing men's and women's sports, fictional narratives and world beliefs, coverage effects on public safety, values held and media use, transportive experiences and cultivation, body image and the third-person effect, framing and the effectiveness of public health messages, cable television news and partisanship, favorite television characters and national pride, a meta-analysis of campaign messages, crime news and racialized beliefs, economic framing, exposure and political cynicism, effects of exposure to sexualized content, perceived influence of newspaper editors, effects of selective exposure, decline of network news, socialization to work values, viewing habits and risk behaviors, entertainment and information acquisition, emotional appeals and health, gender stereotyping and computers, plagiarism, parody and inoculation, eating disorders, modeling behavior, personality traits and cultivation, affective states and entertainment, adolescents and antismoking, support for censorship, influence of war images, Internet dependency, meta-analysis of the third-person effect, credibility and blogs, 24/7 news, tailored communication effectiveness, newscaster credibility, cognitive processing of online news, channel changing and editing, and TV and quality of life. I have selected five articles that represent many of the issues in these sorts of studies.

Eyal and Kunkel (JOBEM, 2008)

The current study extends previous research by examining the effects of exposure to a specific contextual variable associated with the portrayal of sex on television on sexual attitudes and moral judgments. Specifically, the study tests the effects of exposure to differentially valenced consequences of premarital sexual intercourse. It tests effects immediately after exposure to two episodes of 1-hour dramas and the persistence of effects 2 weeks later. The study examines sexual media effects during the important development period of emerging adulthood, between the ages of 18 and 25 (Arnett & Tanner, 2006). (p. 162)

This study makes use of a conventional (normal science) study protocol (paper-and-pencil measurement, pretest, exposure to content, posttest, delayed posttest) to investigate the standard "effects" question of "What is the effect of X content on Y behavior?" where Y behavior is some socially problematic activity (social aggression, premarital sex, body image symptomatology, issues of race or gender) and X content has been the subject of social criticism (violence, sexuality, ideal body image, racial and gender portrayals).[11]

---

[11]Sexual conduct seems to be the concern du jour of the early 21st century, replacing violence, perhaps influenced by the political and funding climate.

The delivery medium can be television as it is here, video games, film, radio, comic books, or newspapers—typically whatever is the dominant popular medium of the time. The protocol has demonstrated itself as quite dependable in delivering reportable results.

Graf and Aday (JOBEM, 2008)

This paper is a report about a series of experiments that used unobtrusive measures of attention to news stories on a Web page, a computer program that determines which Web page a subject chooses and then records how long each subject is exposed to the page. Such measurement techniques have not yet been widely used (one example is Knobloch, Carpentier, & Zillman [sic],[12] 2003). The current authors believe that in contrast to many prior studies, this operationalization of media attention has greater internal validity because it does not rely on self-reports, and the experiments have greater external validity because the protocol uses ordinary news stories in their typical context of an online publication. (pp. 86–87)

The topic of this study concerns selective attention—the notion that we seek out agreeable information and avoid disagreeable information. Selective attention is well believed but poorly evidenced. Consequently, these authors are at least equally interested in the question of method as they are in the substantive findings. As they say, "Like most ideas in communication research, selective attention is repeatedly studied in the same way" (p. 86). They believe their "new" methodology reduces the conflict in evidence for selective attention (see pp. 96–97).

Appel (JOC, 2008)

A huge part of our daily media fare consists of fictional narratives that portray the world as a more predictable and just place than it really is. Cultivation theory claims that media content diffuses into our real-world belief system, leading to a linear correlation between television exposure and corresponding beliefs. Hence, those who watch a lot of fiction should have a stronger belief in the world as a just place. (p. 67)

Questions that arise out of cultivation theory begin with an assumption that the content (or, more sophisticatedly, particular content forms) of a medium presents consistent value structures that are gradually reproduced in the audiences for them.

Cultivation theory hovers at the intersection of methodological individualism (where explanations must reside in the individual) and methodological holism (where explanations reside in social practices in which individuals are dependent elements). Cultivation theorists typically opt for a lower standard of causation or perhaps a more subtle causal effect where values infiltrate or are adopted over time (see Belsey, 2008, for a different take).

---

[12]Dolf Zillmann's last name is spelled with a double *n*, a fact routinely missed by authors and copy editors.

Cultivation studies that make use of gross exposure measures (this one does not) have been criticized for naïvely ignoring selective processes within viewing. This study, for example, found no effect across a gross measure of viewing time but a significant effect for particular narrative forms. The evidence for a cultivation effect must necessarily be correlational as it is the force of regular viewing, not that of a single program (as in Eyal & Kunkel), that produces the effect, a requirement present methodologies cannot reproduce in an experiment.

Cultivation theory is a legacy of the "mass communication" perspective. We are concerned about cultivation effects because the masses are being duped into false beliefs about the world. The theory elevates the analyst (one of its appeals) because he or she gets to declare what the world really is like (see the opening sentence in the quote). In this regard, it is a partner to critical theory that resides in cultural studies, perhaps as the social science expression.

Moriarty and Harrison (JOC, 2008)

We argue that selective exposure based on interest in body-relevant programming like fitness and dieting shows may explain some portion of the relationship between television exposure and disordered eating but not all of it. Even in the absence of interest in ideal-body television content, eating disorder symptomatology should be more pronounced among individuals reporting higher levels of television exposure. (p. 364)

Moriarty and Harrison have given us a good example of an "at risk" study. Researchers who adopt this position basically argue that any exposure to certain types of content is toxic to some degree.

Lim and Ki (J&MCQ, 2007)

To test the proposed hypotheses and answer the research question, a Web-based experiment was administered. Participants were drawn from the same pool and randomly assigned. In a pretest-posttest control group design, the experimental group received the inoculation pretreatment, while the control group participants did not. Participants in both groups were then exposed to a parody video. A third group of participants assigned to the post-hoc refutation group also did not receive pretreatment, but they were provided a post-hoc refutation message following their exposure to the parody video. Finally, their resistance to the intended persuasion was measured to test the effectiveness of inoculation strategy in conferring resistance to the parody video induced persuasion. (p. 717)

This is another study that appears to adopt a protectionistic stance, but instead of the masses, the entities to be protected are organizations under attack by counter-messages. The inoculation approach has always interested me because such studies routinely demonstrate that simple counter-messages have great effect in mitigating other substantive effects including violence, sexuality, and, here, opinion formation that results from other message exposure. What does that mean for us as media scholars studying certain kinds of content when the audience has spent an evening ranging across fields of content and perhaps media as well? Are the consequences of media contained in the last message received? I don't know the answers to those questions, and our current research methods are not yet up to finding those answers (IMHO).

Questions of Character

There were 14 studies that specifically addressed questions of value. Topics included political cynicism, construction of Whiteness, feminism, globalization, hegemonic masculinity, regulatory responses to sex and violence, memory construction, the sins of communication research, pulp fiction and identity, media policy, technology design, and narratives from mothers of soldiers. I have selected three topics for extended comment.

Butterworth (CSMC, 2007)

News media in the United States often present sports figures as ideal representations of heroism. In the U.S., heroism has long been linked to frontier mythology, which celebrates the rugged individualist. This figure privileges a construction of heroism based on strength, masculinity, and a white ideal associated with American exceptionalism. Accordingly, in affirming the promise of the American dream, sports media often devalue racial inclusion. To show how heroism in contemporary American culture is a mythological enactment of whiteness, I analyze news media accounts of the 1998 home run race between Mark McGwire and Sammy Sosa. (Abstract, p. 228)

Butterworth and Shiga are similar studies in that both start from a set of texts (sports articles and online message boards, respectively) and move to their critical interpretation of those texts. What moves Butterworth to the category of character is that the first premise of the study is the character of the representation of race in the sporting news. That representation, he states, holds "McGwire as the archetypal American hero, his racial identity never mentioned, the fact of his whiteness taken for granted; and Sosa as the grateful, dark-skinned buddy just happy to be along for the ride" (p. 238). Shiga's somewhat muted critical observations arrive late, but Butterworth's are never in doubt.

Pinchevski and Brand (CSMC, 2007)

The Stalags, an Israeli pulp fiction series whose advent coincided with the 1961 trial of Adolf Eichmann in Jerusalem, portrayed sadomasochistic scenarios between SS female guards and Allied soldiers in POW camps. Written in Hebrew by native Israelis, these cheap pocketbooks were enormously popular with Israeli teenagers, many of whom were children of Holocaust survivors. We posit the Stalags (a) as a fictional counterpart of the trial, complementing the legal procedure with feats of the imagination, and (b) as a text upon which the Israeli young generation negotiated issues of power and identity. (Abstract, p. 387)

Pinchevski and Brand are no less guilty of constituting the audience in their complete absence than Behm-Morawitz and Mastro; Glascock; or Carlyle, Slater, and Chakroff, but they give us a very different view of an audience from that promoted by those metric scholars. In Pinchevski and Brand, the audience is far from passive and defenseless against inevitable consequences. Rather, this audience is active in appropriating content to accomplish its members' goals. The authors state that this pulp fiction series "can be read as a cultural text upon which the young generation negotiated issues of power, identity, and sexuality" (p. 388).

This conceptualization of the audience changes the questions that can be asked of textual analysis. The question is no longer what the text does to the audience. It is now how the text is negotiated and interpreted into the cultural necessities of identity, pleasure, and desire. It would be difficult to imagine a typical effects study admitting that people at the height of their sexual development have a legitimate interest in the texts that permit the negotiation of that development.

Hennessy, Bleakley, Busse, and Fishbein (JOBEM, 2008)

The Annenberg National Health Communication Survey (ANHCS) [was] analyzed to answer the following research questions:

RQ1:   What is the perception of the amount of sex and violence on television?

RQ2:   What are the beliefs of survey respondents about the effects of television sex and violence on adolescent behavior?

RQ3:   How do exposure to television, perceptions of TV sex and violence, and beliefs about the effects of TV sex and violence on adolescent behavior affect a specific regulatory response: fining television stations for broadcasting sex and violence? (p. 390)

This study provides an effective comparison between metric approaches to character and hybrid approaches to character. This study starts with the analysis of survey items that were designed to answer the three quoted research questions. In that approach, it is a "properties" study. It moves to the character category in its interest in the support for regulatory action in the fining of broadcast stations for the presentation of sexual and violent content. Notice, however, that it is a step removed. It is not the authors' claim as to what ought to be done, but the respondents' claim.

The authors presume that respondents who perceive greater amounts of sex and violence on television and believe in strong effects of sexual and violent content on adolescent behavior will favor punishing broadcast stations. It didn't turn out that way; rather they found "unexplained diversity" (p. 403) in respondents' regulatory choices. They did find that all three choices were connected to both religious and political ideology. Their conclusion is that regulation is more likely to be driven by ideological processes than empirical ones.

We might wonder why we care about the questions addressed in this study. The authors seek to establish the social significance by attaching the article to the notorious "wardrobe malfunction" of the 2004 Super Bowl halftime show with Justin Timberlake and

Janet Jackson[13] and the $500,000 fine levied against CBS by the Federal Communications Commission for the display of Ms. Jackson's right breast. The data themselves, however, have no relevance to the event, so we learn nothing new about that incident. Nonetheless, it may not have been published without it.

IMPLICATIONS FOR DEVELOPING RESEARCH QUESTIONS

In the perfect world of metric methods textbooks, scientific research questions are supposed to be all about theory predicting the empirical. A developing theory makes some claim about the world, and the researcher devises a study protocol to determine if what happens in the world matches what is claimed by the theory. The reason it is supposed to happen this way is that it results in a fully supported (though never proven) theory that allows us to know what is going on in the world without always having to take its temperature.

In the actual world of metric research practice, the direction is more likely to be reversed. The researcher has some interest in what is happening in our life-world, devises a study to find out, and then fits a theory into the explanation of why things are the way they are. The difficulty with this approach is that it provides only correspondence evidence (rather than predictive evidence) in support of the theory—sort of support by coincidence, weak evidence indeed. The method is weak, but probably appropriate to the state of development of our science and our theories. We have far too many theories in the field, none of which has been without its failures and many of which are contradictory (sometimes with themselves).

In the very imperfect (and relatively small) world of interpretive research methods textbooks, empirical study of the real world serves to enlarge our theoretical understanding of it. There is no closure in interpretive research; a new narrative for the body of theory can always be crafted. Further, in the social construction of reality, human practice does not stand still. It is a dynamic process, and the researcher is always behind the curve.

In the actual world of interpretive research practice, narratives are more likely to be recycled rather than made more sophisticated or complex. The reader can quickly become adept at recognizing the narrative form even before the evidence is presented. We have seen some of these typical arguments—the deficit audience, the audience as victim, the media as conspiracy, the critical-issue narratives of race, gender, and class. In the recycled narrative, the demands of the narrative drive both the evidence and the conclusions.

Consequently, it is good practice to locate one's research question both in the life-world and in the world of theory. For example, I may notice that many of the programs on Comedy Central (the cable channel that is home to *The Daily Show* and *South Park*) are iconoclastic, at least mildly disrespectful of authority, cynical about the powerful, and generally critical (if comedically so) about the actions of others. Taking this interest into the research process, I would first want to systematize my impressions through some form of content analysis.

If I do this analysis carefully, I will be able to regale you with many facts (e.g., the number of bodily function jokes on *South Park* or the number of bleeps on *The Daily Show*).

---

[13]http://www.youtube.com/watch?v=gOLbERWVR30. Accessed April 18, 2011.

If, however, I also engage the theory of comedy, I will have a much deeper understanding of those facts. I will learn how comedy works to uphold the very values and principles it seems to undercut, how it sustains the taboos it violates (the bleep reminds us that something is wrong), and how it allows us to feel better about ourselves through comparison (I may be a lowly middle-class schmuck, but at least I am not a pretentious blowhard) or through vicarious expression (I'm glad somebody said/did that). Even slapstick humor works only in the presence of standards of proper behavior. Comedy cannot destroy those standards except to destroy itself.

At the same time, I am likely to discover some facts that are not explained in the theory of comedy. I now have two choices: Either the characteristics are not comedic (but they make me laugh), or human invention has exceeded human explanation. I would generally trust my laughing response and go with the latter.

Proprietary research works in much the same way in developing its questions and in the way that the questions relate to theory. Both questions and theory, however, develop in relation to practices. This advertising message is supposed to have this sort of effect (theory). Does it (research question)?

Community-based research takes the direct interest in outcomes of proprietary research and the longer view of the academy. I not only want to deliver the books of the Imagination Library to every child in Salt Lake, I also want to know what happens to those books in those homes and the long-term consequences of the opportunity.

One of the truisms of research methods books is that the question one asks establishes the methods one uses. What this analysis has shown is that there is some truth to that aphorism. Not every method maps well on every category of question. For example, current metric methods do not map well on questions of praxis (performance). Such questions require continuous measurements over time from multiple viewpoints. Further, the measurements have to be adaptive to the changes that occur as the performance emerges. It is easier to accommodate these requirements from an ethnographic approach than from a metric one.

Nonetheless, questions of what, how, why, and so what can be addressed from any methodological standpoint, although some are more likely than others. What is more true of the relationship between question and method is that questions become research questions when they engage theory, and every effective theory has its method. It is the theory that drives the choice of method—not so much the question. The reasoning works just as well in the opposite direction. If one learns a method, one implicitly engages the theory that makes the method sensible; that theory, in turn, has an affinity for certain kinds of research questions. That is why this book addresses so many different sorts of methods. It allows the learner to address the widest range of questions.

ANTICIPATING INSTITUTIONAL REVIEW

The design of any academic study has to anticipate review by the local institutional review board (IRB). (The design of proprietary research may also require IRB review and certainly will go by legal.) The institutional review board is a committee mandated by the National Research Act of 1974 and required of any institution receiving research funding or otherwise subject to regulation by any federal department. Nearly all universities and hospitals as well as many other research organizations are required to constitute a review board that is charged with the protection of the participants (human subjects) in research.

Local boards are governed by what is called the "common rule" contained in Title 45 CFR (Code of Federal Regulations) Part 46.[14] Local boards, however, have substantial latitude in determining their institutional mission, what their practices will be, and even their name. Some boards are nationally accredited; others have no interest in accreditation. Consequently, practices and decisions vary widely across these boards. There is no singular IRB.

All boards, however, are charged with the protection of the participants of research. I have served on an IRB for nearly 20 years, reviewing some 10,000 research proposals during that time. That gives me some insight for offering advice, recognizing that local conditions will prevail. Protection concerns usually take two parts: concerns focusing on the competency of the research design and concerns focusing on adequacy of informed consent.

Competent Scholarship

In the review focusing on research design, the question is asked whether the science or scholarship justifies the proposed involvement of its participants. This part of the review investigates the likelihood that what the study claims to want to accomplish can actually be accomplished within its design. The intent is to provide some protection against researcher incompetence. Incompetence in communication research designs usually poses little danger, but not always. If the study targets culturally marginalized groups, poor practices can expose those individuals to societal harm.

Second, research design concerns also involve the equitable selection of respondents. The benefits of science and scholarship are intended to extend to all. According to the regulations, the analyst cannot deliberately exclude groups that would be covered by the findings of the study. This concern surfaces when convenience samples are in play that clearly systematically exclude important groups or when critical-issue studies exclude respondents based on gender, race, or ethnicity despite studying a problem that would transcend those categories.

Finally, research design is the basis for determining the risk-benefit ratio. Studies are allowed to pose risks to respondents only if the benefits that accrue from the study outweigh the risks that are posed. The reviewer has to determine that ratio, but it is up to the researcher to provide the evidence both of the benefits and of the risks. If no benefits can be seen or, more sinisterly, the risks appear to be unanalyzed or even trivialized, the study should not be approved. It is important that the analyst present the careful work of detailing the benefits and the risks inherent in the study design. Studies that pose greater risks can be approved given appropriate benefits and given the thoroughness of informed consent.

---

[14]http://ohsr.od.nih.gov/guidelines/45cfr46.html. Accessed April 18, 2011.

Informed Consent

Because most of our studies involve little risk beyond the waste of time or minor embarrassment, most of the focus of the review is directed toward the process and documents of informed consent. Informed consent works from the model of the rational person thinking well. Any circumstance that moves from that model (e.g., the use of children, research in coercive environments, research with vulnerable populations) puts a greater burden on informed consent. Research that contains high risk and targets vulnerable populations carries a substantial burden to demonstrate that both the process and the informed consent document (ICD) do indeed appropriately inform the respondent and allow for freely given consent.

More and more, the conversation among IRBs on the issue of consent is focusing on the process of consent, not just the consent document. Internal research on our board shows that many (most) respondents do not read the consent document, but rather depend on an oral interpretation usually from the analyst as to what the document contains. In a typical study, the researcher will hand the ICD to the respondent and then wait expectantly. This approach makes it very difficult for the respondent to take the time to read carefully or even to say no. Consequently, more emphasis is being placed on early and researcher-independent delivery of the ICD, private time to consider the terms of the study, and time to consult with others and/or the research team. The feeling is that the researcher has a vested interest in getting the respondent to participate and should not, therefore, be involved in the consent process. Many universities (including mine[15]) provide templates for what an ICD should contain.

Informed Consent and Interpretive Studies

Interpretive studies, and in particular ethnographies, pose real challenges to the principles of informed consent. In the fluid designs of such studies, it is very difficult to establish the terms of what "informed" means. In most cases, the analyst cannot predict the twists and turns that a conversational interview or protocol analysis might take, much less what would happen over the many months of an ethnography. Informed consent documents are nearly useless in extended ethnographies because the participants change or are unknown. Where possible, of course, they should be used as they give protection to the respondent and analyst alike. But where they cannot be used, the analyst has to become the agent of informed consent by the means of conducting the contact.

Let me give an example from my own research. When I started my research in the homeless community, I had a great deal of difficulty getting IRB approval (and I was a board member). The hang-up was twofold: First the board was inexperienced in reviewing ethnographic research (the initial effort was a decade ago) and kept applying the power relationships that would be in place in a typical laboratory setting. Second, the reviewers were not convinced that I had sufficiently safeguarded my contacts, particularly if children were involved or around. The first problem was fairly easily handled by providing the evidence that the respondent was actually in the superior power position. The second issue was

---

[15]http://www.research.utah.edu/irb/forms/campus/index.html. Accessed April 18, 2011.

solved when the reviewers and I developed a set of conversational strategies that would alert or remind contacts that I was a university professor conducting research. In essence, the board charged me with ensuring at least a minimal level of informed consent with the participants in every episode. They also charged me with walking away if I could not attain the consent of a parent and the assent of the child when a child came into the frame of the episode.

But what harm could I do? What harm could any of us do in an unpredictable situation involving a vulnerable group? Set up improbable expectations for relief? Inappropriately "out" a member? Inadvertently trigger a psychotic episode? I would not knowingly do any of those, but the board's responsibilities cannot be discharged by my good intentions. Some protection had to be put in place. The conversational strategies embodied that protection. The process of that review certainly heightened my sensitivities to the risks involved.

Tensions

Institutional review boards have been in the communication literature lately. The database *Communication and Mass Media Complete* returned 19 references on that search term, with dates ranging from 2002 to 2009. The largest number was in the special issue on the topic in the *Journal of Applied Communication Research* (2005, Vol. 33, No. 3). The greatest difficulty in interpreting these studies is that they treat IRBs as if they shared a great number of common elements. Institutional review boards can range from very large, accredited, multipanel boards with budgets in seven figures, professional staff, and weekly meetings to very small boards that have neither budgets nor assigned staff and meet once or twice a year. Further, boards may be charged with an enlarged mission by the institution that makes comparison even more difficult. None of the studies that I have read controlled for these variations. To expect some communality of experience across that range is inappropriate.

Nonetheless, there are fundamental tensions that exist in the relationship between researcher and board. The researcher has a primary dedication to the research practice and its completion while the board's primary charge is the protection of the participants. These goals often come in conflict, sometimes in ludicrous ways such as a board requiring focus groups to be anonymous or a researcher promising confidentiality of focus group responses. Neither can be done unless anonymity means no names and confidentiality means a request for participants to forget what they heard (maybe one of those flashy things from *Men in Black*). The most tension occurs when the board attempts to design the research or when the researcher attempts to derail the board's interest in the well-being of the respondent. Both should step aside and let the other do its job.

Something in excess of 90% of the social research and scholarship that passes through our IRB does so without problem or with minor negotiation between researcher and reviewer. In that something less than 10%, however, I have seen researchers advance thoughtless insensitivities, designed coercions, deliberate exposures to risk, unintelligible study descriptions, deceptive consent documents, assent documents for children who have not yet learned to read or that are written in unreadable disciplinary language, the premeditated exclusion of otherwise qualified respondents, and outrage when called on these practices. Boards are not perfect; neither are researchers. Both are needed.

COMMENTARY ON METHODS AND IMPLICATIONS

Let's talk about the method used to develop this data set and its subsequent use in this chapter. The question addressed was "What are the conversations occurring in the empirical research literature now?" The idea that a research literature is a conversation rather than independent entries into a ledger of factual discoveries comes out of the perspective of the social construction of knowledge. That perspective encourages us to recognize that one has to know the *what, how, why,* and *so what* aspects of a conversation before one can competently join that conversation. This chapter has focused on the topics—the *what* aspect—being currently addressed with somewhat gratuitous excursions into how, why, and so what. That focus would seem to meet the requirements of the "what are the conversations" part of the questions.

There are two other elements that have to be operationally defined—"research literature" and "now." The research literature is generally understood as everything published and/or presented as research in a topical domain. Like "all the stars in the sky," that definition references a population so large as to be unknowable. I defined it as four journals, a considerably smaller universe—not four randomly selected journals, but four journals intentionally selected for their known characteristics—flagship publications of communication associations that are associated with types of research. Will that selection provide me with a valid representation of the conversations?[16] It could, as long as there are no major topics being discussed that do not appear in these four. The path for falsifying my claim for validity is pretty clear. Go find a major topic that is not covered in the 100 articles listed in the reference list.[17] If you criticize without the evidence, however, you are just being dismissive.

Now what about "now"? Now, in physiological terms, is about seven tenths of a second, the time it takes to process a sensation. Now in the research literature seems to be about 5 years from the current date. Work older than 5 years becomes work done then. In this very young field, work done 10 years or more ago is history. Consequently, taking the most recently available publications meets the "now" of now but not the "then" of now. The interval is current but not wide enough. Upon publication of the book, however, which might take a year from this data collection, I will have lost the "now" and be moving toward the "then." It's all clear, right? (Well, as TV comic Craig Ferguson would say, "I made myself laugh.") The serious part of this discussion is that different operational definitions will return different findings. The definition one chooses to use is an epistemological matter, not simply a practical one.

There is one last word to be defined in my question, and that word is *empirical*. I hope we no longer think of *empirical* as numbers. When we talk about an empirical study, we are talking about one that addresses a field of information (often called data) that exists independently of the analyst. With this definition, the study by Rodino-Colocino (2006)

---

[16]It will necessarily be a reliable representation because the method does not allow any sampling error to occur. Reliability is not validity.

[17]For example, none of the four journals has any record of publishing community-based research.

qualifies, even though it is hard on the rhetorical side of its hybridization. She does address an independent set of texts. The definition also allows me to distinguish what I did in this data collection with a "Review of the Literature" section in the typical article. A review is a construction by the analyst to advance an argument. It does not exist independently of the analyst. If you think you know a topic because of reading the literature review of an article, you are mistaken. You know what the author wants you to know framed in the way that best advances what the author wants to achieve. (And who says science is not rhetorical? More on this issue in a bit.)

To this point, I have created a rationale for the choices I have made (an operational definition if you will) that, while not bulletproof, reasonably justifies those choices as not being systematically biased toward some outcome. My next step is more problematic. That step involves the coding of the articles into one of the four categories of questions. The issues here include whether or not the codes are adequately defined to provide good identification and good separation. A perfect coding system would include all of the instances with no equivocation. The codes would neither overlap nor have spaces into which instances would fall as noncoded. (The common "Other" code is a device used to clean up any otherwise noncoded instances.) The codes are adequate to the instances (cover them all), but the articles themselves contain more than one argument. We see that in the articles that start out as property claims and end up as arguments about consequences.

In my coding, I assigned the article according to its methodology, not its claim. Survey methodologies provide direct evidence for properties and at best indirect evidence for consequences. If an article reported on a survey, it was coded as a property argument regardless of its subsequent consequences claims. There are a couple of other ways I could handle this problem. I could use primary and secondary coding, basing the primary code on method and the secondary codes on other claims. An article like Billings et al. (2008) would be coded as property for its primary code and as consequences and value for its secondary codes. Or I could have coded the articles for all combinations (24 codes in all). Both of these methods provide me with more information about the articles, but they also complicate the analysis. For my purposes, I wanted to start with a clean count and then deal with the complications in the discussion.

The step where I assign the articles to their code membership is the most problematic, and shows a growing distinction between metric, interpretive, and hybrid approaches. Like most interpretive approaches, I used myself as the coder with no confirmation by another. This approach would not be appropriate for traditional metric analysis. In the center of that method, I would need at least two coders, neither of whom could be me. My job would be to develop a coding procedure—a set of instructions for my coders—and training in those procedures until my coders reached an agreement criterion, usually greater than 80%.

Methodologists would agree that the metric approach is more systematic and that it provides measures of the reliability (degree of agreement) of the coding. They do not agree that it is better, particularly when an expert is available to do the coding. No matter how complete the coding instructions are, the expert will always have greater knowledge and greater ability to deal with unanticipated conditions. What we don't know is whether she or he will use that knowledge on every case. The value of a second set of eyes is as a safeguard against those moments of inadequate reading, fatigue, and other personal conditions that lead to errors.

Hybrid scholars might appear quite cavalier in their approach. Rodino-Colocino (2006) basically tells us that she took a bunch of PR and advertising texts to capture the selling approach and characterization of women—no codes, no coding, but an immersion through close reading of an appropriate set of texts. The reason why so little attention is paid to method in these approaches is that the method does not justify the argument as it does in metric analysis; the argument justifies the method. It is the coherence of the argument (its rhetorical force), not the systematicity of the method, that counts.

It is important to keep these distinctions in mind. It would be foolish and futile for me to argue that Rodino-Colocino should have used codes and a coding procedure or that she should be an expert in advertising. That's like arguing that apples should have an orange peel. What I can address is the quality and coherence of the argument. Has she made the case? I don't think she has, but that is a different issue and one in which I have an equal responsibility to justify my criticism—inside the hybrid framework—as she had in making the claim.

The last thing I would like to point out in this review of the method of this chapter is the argument itself, which is contained in the presentation of the 15 examples. As an analyst (of any sort), I have a responsibility for the entire data set. I have not discharged that responsibility. What I have done is cherry-pick the best examples (and the low-hanging fruit at that) to achieve my pedagogical goals. Cherry-picking and poaching (e.g., stealing examples out of context) are serious problems in any textual analysis (content analysis, critical analysis, analysis of field notes, etc.). If this chapter had been aiming at a research report rather than a teaching tool, I would have been responsible for not only what worked but also what did not, not only what I could explain but also what I could not—in short, the good, the contradictory, and the unexplainable.

MOVING ON

This chapter has finished the foundation for the next several chapters as they in turn take up each of the methodological domains. The very next chapter takes up the methods of constructing a literature and accessing databases within the problem development process. Regardless of the methodological domain to which you ultimately gravitate, you will have to know these skills. So, let's get this party started. We're off to the library or, if we're lucky, the nearest keyboard.

REFLECTIONS

What Are Some Points to Remember?

- Properly formed research hypotheses in metric empiricism are the conclusion of a train of reasoning that uses theory and prior research as the general premise, the protocol of the study as the minor premise, and the hypothesis as the consequence if the major and minor premises are true.

- Interpretive research questions involve the recognition of coherence in action or in the meaningfulness of discourse. The question poses the possibility and directs the research to see if the evidence for that coherence can be found. Oftentimes the proper question does not emerge until after the analyst gains an understanding of what can be asked.
- Questions and hypotheses are further divided by topic across properties, processes, consequences, and character.

Why Does It Matter?

Good research problems have to be transformed into good research practices before any contribution can be realized.

What Else Could We Talk About?

It seems awfully easy to criticize research. No study ever seems smart enough, sophisticated enough, or sufficiently well designed to withstand scrutiny. Most criticism is advanced from some state of ignorance, however. The critic may well have never done a study of the kind under review or never studied the concepts and constructs in play. At all levels of expertise, we reject the research we don't like or that does not support our beliefs.

What Else Might Be Interesting to Read?

Voss, G. B. (2003). Formulating interesting research questions. *Journal of the Academy of Marketing Science, 31*, 356–359.

CHAPTER 7

Literatures and Databases

CHAPTER PREVIEW

What's It All About?

In this chapter, we take up the principles and practices of literature searches and reviews. The different roles for the literature in metric, interpretive, and hybrid research are considered. Simplified practices of database searches are presented, followed by a more complex set of strategies for the beginning professional. The chapter ends with a discussion of the ethics of literature searches and reviews.

What Are the Major Topics?

Metric research follows a deductive line that starts in the literature and ends with study hypotheses. The literature is very much at the front end of such studies.

Interpretive research follows a propagation model in which the current study adds to the body of narrative possible. This form of research uses the literature review to demonstrate that the current study both fits inside the domain and is distinctive from other elements within the set. The literature is used to understand the study rather than to direct it. It is very much at the back end of such studies.

Hybrid studies use the literature to establish the rhetorical force of the study as a front-end review and then show the connections and implications with the literature in the concluding part of the argument.

The beginning researcher can make use of issue-based databases that aggregate entries across the topics of their targeted disciplines. Issue-based databases provide a level of prescreening and organization that is often helpful to the entering analyst.

Professional researchers and those who aspire to be professionals need to develop a set of search strategies that direct the process of the search and a set of tactics that will be appropriate to the topic at hand. These strategies include writing to read, understanding disciplinary literatures, database selection, journal sets, and a competence in the rules and codes of the search engines.

The ethics of the search and literature review start with the protection from colonization and inadvertent plagiarism. Writing to read helps with both. Ethical considerations extend to fairly representing the work of another in citations and quotations and establishing an authentic connection to the literature.

What Special Terms Are Used?

Boolean search operators

Inadvertent plagiarism

Reductionism

Rhizomatic

Serendipity

INTRODUCTION

A central responsibility for any professional is to remain current on the developments in her or his field. For the academic and professional researcher, that means reading extensively and intensively, attending conferences, and conversing with colleagues about issues that have to do with the substantive claims within a topic area and those that have to do with the methods of gathering and constituting the evidence for those claims. To use a down-home example, the substantive issues are what's on the menu; methods are the recipes and implements (you can't eat what's in a can without a can opener).

To stick with the cooking analogy for a line or two, professional researchers create their mise-en-scène (or "miz" as it's known in the kitchen and theater) that contains all of the tools and utilities for conducting research. For nearly all of us, that starts with a personal library of books and journals, includes memberships in professional organizations, and then extends to online resources and the software to effectively use them. This chapter is about online resources and the tools and techniques of their use. The chapter is written in two parts, each attached to a different level of expertise. The first presumes a reader whose needs are limited to those of the classroom, and the second is for a reader who aspires to professional practice. We begin, however, with an overview of the demands for a competent review from each of our three research perspectives.

METRIC, INTERPRETIVE, AND HYBRID LITERATURE REVIEWS

The first topic of this chapter is a comparison of the literature review as it is used in metric, interpretive, and hybrid research. Some of these differences are fairly simple, but others reach to the epistemological foundations. We will conduct this discussion by focusing on the strong programs in each of these domains.

Reviews in Metric Research

Metric research uses a deductive logic that starts with a general premise that is developed out of the theory that directs the current understanding of the area of interest. The major premise gives rise to the minor premise, which is a particular instance of the theory. In research, the minor premise forms the protocol of the study. An analysis of the minor premise in relation to the major produces the conclusion, which, in the research process, is the research hypothesis. The research hypothesis is, of course, what is tested in the protocol, and if it is supported, there is evidence that the reasoning from theory to protocol to test was appropriate and supportable (we never say the *P*[roved] word).

The literature review is very much in the front end of this approach. It is required to establish the theory in play and its principles in regard to the protocol. It is necessary to justify the protocol of the study as an appropriate method of investigation. And it establishes the research hypothesis as a useful test of the theory.

Reviews in Interpretive Research

Interpretive studies are built on a logic of coherence. The first requirement is that the narrative of the social process under observation must meet the standards of good narrative structure. It's not simply that one can make up a good story. It is that a good story can be constructed that will accommodate all the facts of the case. It is true that more than one story might meet those requirements (just as it is true that more than one research protocol and hypothesis can be drawn from the same set of theoretical principles). Once the story is in place (my story for homelessness for men is the loss of masculinity), the task shifts to its critical evaluation. That evaluation will include the other narratives and explanations that have been produced and will read them against the research in production.

The literature review, then, comes in after the observations and site and field notes have been completed and the coherent narrative of the experience has been achieved. The review is used to further explicate and to critically evaluate that narrative. Extensive review of the literature prior to the entry into the field would be suspect, especially for the inexperienced researcher (the opposite of the handling of inexperience in metric studies).[1] The whole point of interpretive studies is to carefully read your own experience, not someone else's. If you address the literature too early, your own experience will be lost in the multitude of voices.

---

[1]Not to put too fine a point on it, when you recognize that you don't know very much, everybody else can seem like an expert (even me). The whole point of interpretive studies is to carefully read your own experience, not someone else's. Jump in the pool. If you don't drown, you can then make good judgments about coaching advice.

There is a second major difference: Metric research is reductionistic; it aims at a final explanation—a covering law that holds for all cases within its scope. Interpretive research is rhizomatic; it aims at the propagation of a new explanation—an ever-expanding body of understanding.

A major purpose of the metric search, then, is to find an unresolved issue, a hole in the theoretical fabric, a missing link, all of which your study will help to reduce. The result of the study in progress will be a clearer understanding of the final answer. The metric literature review intends to point to these problems and to position the proposed study as a resolution of those problems.

The interpretive search is not searching to produce the final answer, because another narrative can always be written. It is similar to doing a search for all the plays that involve political power and the destruction of the soul. You are not looking for the single play that says it all. Rather you are celebrating the great variety of ways that relationship can be expressed. You could certainly describe homelessness as a weakness of personal character—an inability to overcome dissoluteness and addiction. The description is actually a very useful narrative, because it allows us—the domesticated—to demonstrate our superiority.[2] Different narratives do different work. The literature search helps in understanding what each narrative achieves.

Metric and interpretive literature searches do share a common purpose when it comes to methodology—to provide a justification for the methodological choices one makes. The difference between them is that metric methodologies are more conventionalized, more settled if you will. Interpretive methods, by the very demand that they be exquisitely responsive to the context and the performance, resist conventionalization. Metric justifications, then, end up using other experts that support the choices made, whereas interpretive justifications use other experts to justify the need to do it differently.

Hybrid Reviews

In Chapter 6, we noted that hybrid studies develop out of the rhetorical force of some set of conditions. That rhetorical force was demonstrated in an analysis of the necessity for the rhetorical action of the study. Hybrid reviews, then, are front-end reviews in much the same way metric reviews are. They are necessary to support the analysis of the rhetorical force that justifies the study.

At the same time, the character of the review is more like that of interpretive studies (perhaps, that is why they are a hybrid). There is a greater need to show the interplay of ideas. There may be more quotations in play. The argument is more likely to follow a narrative line. Whereas metric reviews justify one's problem and interpretive reviews make after-the-fact sense of the interpreted observations, hybrids have to provide both justification for the study and the understanding of what it all means. Given that understanding of the different needs of different kinds of reviews, let's start at the beginning for the beginner.

---

[2]So, why is my story more trustworthy? Because it is based on systematic and publicly reviewable data, and it does not pander to my own interests as a member of the domesticated.

IN THE BEGINNING, FOR THE BEGINNER

Good research of any sort starts with a problem. In professional practice, whether academic or corporate, problems fill our conversations. Consequently, the professional has a fulsome resource for starting a research project. If you are new to a topic area, like mediated communication, you might not have access to that resource. The problem of picking a problem becomes a problem of its own. You know that good writing always stems from your own interests. The trick is to associate your interests with topics of public interest—topics of sufficient importance that they can be seen as addressing serious issues. There are at least three databases that help you make that connection: *CQ Researcher, Issues & Controversies,* and EBSCO's *Research Starters.*

Issue-Based Indexes

CQ Researcher claims excellence for "in-depth, unbiased coverage of health, social trends, criminal justice, international affairs, education, the environment, technology, and the economy."[3] It publishes weekly reports 44 times per year and archives all previous reports. For example, I entered *media effects on violence* in a quick search. The search returned 208 issues that connected in some way to those search terms. The database organizes the results based on a relevance score. The issue that scored 100% relevance was titled "TV Violence." Relevance drops off pretty quickly in this search. The 30th listing scored only 10% and was titled "Emerging India."

You can also let serendipity work for you on these kinds of searches to get to something that might be more interesting. Coming in at 27th on the relevance scale was an issue titled "Television's Future." The issue gave a respectable overview of what is going on in that medium as YouTube, TiVo®, and personal video players change the traditional mass market.[4] In a sidebar to the issue, CQ also listed all the other issues in the archive that related to this one. There were 32 reports in the years 1944 to 2008. There was more than enough information to lay out a brief review of the literature and to develop a respectable set of research questions.

Issues & Controversies claims its excellence "in politics, government, business, education, and popular culture."[5] It offers weekly updates and a 13-year archive on over 800 "hot topics." My library does not subscribe to Facts On File online services, the vendor for the *Issues & Controversies* database. Facts On File, however, does provide a trial subscription.[6] Using my trial subscription, I tried to search on the same key words *media effects on violence.* The database returned an error message. My work-around was to go to the complete

---

[3]http://www.cqpress.com/product/Researcher-Online.htm. Accessed April 20, 2011.

[4]CQ even provides the reference for you (Greenblatt, A. [2007, February 16]. Television's future. *CQ Researcher, 17,* 145–168. Retrieved September 29, 2008, from http://library.cqpress.com/cqresearcher/cqresrre2007021600); just copy and paste.

[5]http://factsonfile.infobasepublishing.com/Database Home.asp?page ID = 3&ISBN = 1578520274. Accessed September 29, 2008.

[6]Trial subscriptions are available to those individuals who might influence the sale of the service to an organization. If you are a student in a class, your instructor or librarian would have to arrange the trial.

article listing and navigate down to television. There was an October 5, 2007, update on television violence. The article gives much of the history of the controversy and some current facts (as of 2007). At the end of the article were some discussion questions that could easily be turned into research problems.

Sidebars listed additional information, related articles, key news events connected to the topic, and overviews. Again letting serendipity work, I went to the key issue on censorship. There I found an interesting complexity surrounding paternal protectionist impulses, First Amendment rights, legislation, and court review.

When the search feature returned to service, the search terms generated a list of 37 articles. The article I selected, "Television Violence," was number 33 on the relevance list, although it would be number 1 on my needs list. "Women in U.S. Politics" was number 2 (an interesting article in its own right, but overrun by current events). That result reminds us that databases are affected by the instructions you give them but are not working on your agenda or necessarily on your understanding of what the search terms entail. The terms *media*, *effect*, and *violence* do occur in the article on women in U.S. politics but only separately and never in a common context. The conventions of searching allow me to put quotation marks around words that I want read as a unit. When I do put quotation marks around "media effects" and conduct the search, no documents are returned, even though I know that there are several documents in the database that would be of interest. We'll spend a good deal of time on search strategies, but none of them will work to give you exactly what you need every time you search.

Research Starters from EBSCO Publishing (communication's central database) has recently initiated a service intended to "provide students with authoritative, discipline-specific articles offering comprehensive overviews of important academic subject areas and topics."[7] As of this writing, essays are available only within business and education with little value outside those fields. As with all three of these services, the user needs to be at a library that subscribes (a problem called the digital enclosure or digital divide in the scholarship of this area).

There is a fourth option available for the beginner—databases' browse feature that allows a reader to virtually page through a journal. This feature involves going to the list of publications, selecting a publication, and then meandering through the contents until something strikes up a response. Let's work an example from EBSCO's *Communication and Mass Media Complete* database. By whatever method available to you, log on to the EBSCO site and select the *Communication and Mass Media Complete* database. You will get a page something like Screenshot 7.1.[8]

The second menu item in the blue banner is "Publications." The menu returns an alphabetized listing of all the publications catalogued as in Screenshot 7.2. I navigated down to the *C*s to find *Columbia Journalism Review*. I checked the box next to the journal (1), clicked on "ADD" (2), and then clicked on "SEARCH" (3). That action returned all of the indexed content of the journal. I could then select articles with interesting titles to find what

---

[7]http://www2.ebsco.com/en-us/NewsCenter/Pages/ViewArticle.aspx?QSID = 246. Accessed October 1, 2008.

[8]EBSCO has been changing its layout fairly regularly. Consequently, you can expect to see some differences between the current version of its site and these screenshots. The basic structure remains the same, however.

Screenshot 7.1 Menu Bar for "Publications"

Source: http://www.ebsco.com/

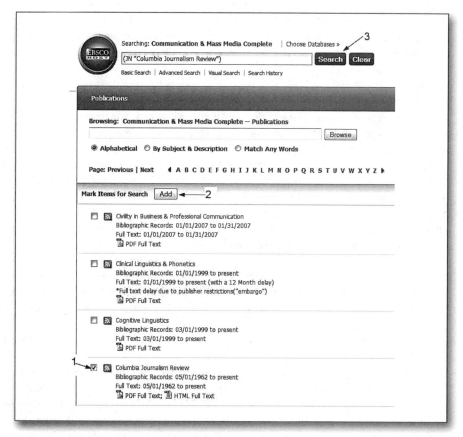

Screenshot 7.2 Steps to Select a Particular Journal

Source: http://www.ebsco.com/

might be a problem worth further research. The article you select will also provide you with additional key words for further searching and with references to build the literature review. Whichever of these methods that you use to select your initial topic, retrieve the overview or article as that will serve as a foundation for your next steps in searching the literature.

Archives and Databases in Mediated Communication

There are several online databases that a professional scholar or consultant would routinely use. Each one has its advantages and limitations that have to be taken into account when developing a review of the literature. In the sections that follow, I have developed a short description of each of these databases, offer some comments on advantages and limitations, and indicate at least one primary use.

Communication and Mass Media Complete (EBSCO). C&MMC may be the one-stop shop for academic articles in mediated communication. It covers all of the association journals and is aggressively up-to-date. Its primary limitation is that its historical record reaches back only to the mid-1970s. Default thinking might suggest that we need little from the past, but one misses the trajectory and the repetitiveness of ideas by neglecting the early work.

CommunicationAbstracts (CIOS). ComAbstracts covers most of the association journals and was the first of the online databases dedicated to communication. It is slower than C&MMC in updating its entries, but it has a deeper historical record. For example, a search for *talk radio* reaches to 1971 on ComAbstracts but only 1988 in C&MMC. The two databases do not conduct their searches in the same way—a fact that is generally true across different companies or organizations. C&MMC machine-searches the entire content of the article; ComAbstract searches a human-constructed entry. The search for *talk radio* returned 65 items from C&MMC and 48 items from ComAbstracts. C&MMC searched more journals, but ComAbstracts widened the content that it retrieved, perhaps showing the effect of the human judgment that would appear in the constructed entry. For the professional, it is always a good idea to search both of these databases.

Academic Search Premier (EBSCO). If the intent is to go wide, Academic Search Premier covers over 8,000 serials including some 3,500 peer-reviewed journals, representing a compilation of most of the EBSCO indexed journals. Most bibliographic records, however, are only a decade deep. A search for *talk radio* returns almost 1,200 entries. Not my recommended way to do searches, it nevertheless has utility when looking across a variety of literatures.

LexisNexis Academic and Congressional. Another way of going wide is with any of the LexisNexis databases (Academic and Congressional are very useful). LexisNexis Academic searches "major U.S. and world publications" both English and non-English, wire services, TV and radio transcripts, blogs, web publications, and corporate and legal documents. Clicking on the entry retrieves the entire document. The terms of service by individual libraries typically limit the number of items returned in any search. At my library, the magic number is somewhere around 1,000. For example, if one searches for *talk radio* across the past decade, one gets 994 entries, 86 of which appeared in 1999. But if one searches across just that year (1999), one gets 1,000 entries. LexisNexis is not very forthcoming on how the search engine selects the 86, but it appears to be a relevance criterion. If you really want everything in the database, you need to find out or figure out the terms of service and search across successive time spans that generate returns within those terms.

JSTOR. JSTOR is probably the premier source for full-text academic scholarship with the deepest historical reach. It is an archive rather than a simple index and includes "over one thousand leading academic journals across the humanities, social sciences, and sciences, as well as select monographs and other materials valuable for academic work."[9] If you are an academic wonk, JSTOR is as seductive a database as you can get. You will need all of your tools of discipline and focus to get in and get out in a timely fashion. Our search term *talk radio* returned 28,301 full-text entries. You could spend a career reading all of them and never have to write a thing.

ProQuest Newspapers. This archive returns full-text articles of over 300 U.S. and international news sources, including *The New York Times* and *The [London] Times.* Very often, these newspapers are the only sources available for government documents from agencies like the Federal Communications Commission (FCC), the Surgeon General's office, and the national institutes. In our continuing example of talk radio, I searched for *talk radio* and *Federal Communications Commission* and found a report on an FCC-proposed rule emphasizing local needs over syndicated programs (like Rush Limbaugh's talk show). I was then able to use that information to access the document.[10]

SIRS Researcher, Government Reporter, and Renaissance (ProQuest). These databases were originally developed for public school use. Their recent purchase by ProQuest has found them marketing to higher education as well. SIRS Researcher offers a service similar to *CQ Researcher* with timelines and overviews developed by ProQuest staff. Government Reporter provides information on and by government agencies, and Renaissance covers arts and humanities. The historical reach is very short. I use it mostly for recent and obscure government sources such as a Department of State press release saying that talk radio has little effect on election choices.

Other useful databases. There are several other databases that are routinely useful.[11] They include *AccuNet/AP MultiMedia Archive*—images from the Associated Press; *International Encyclopedia of Communication Online*—theories, methods, and concepts across the field;

---

[9]http://about.jstor.org/content-collections. Accessed April 20, 2011.

[10]To retrieve a government document, one needs to search the appropriate Government Printing Office database—in this case, the Federal Register at www.gpoaccess.gov. In our example, I searched for *localism,* as that is what the proposed rule was about across the last five years of the register. That search returned *fr13fe08P Report on Broadcast Localism and Notice of Proposed Rulemaking* as the top selection.

[11]As compiled by Ceres Birkhead, the communication area librarian at the University of Utah, from services available at the university. Consult your local area librarian for choices available at your library. Librarians are mostly wonderful people who are very helpful.

Film & Television Literature Index—entries on the applications, processes, definitions, and use of electronic media equipment; *Global NewsBank*—a repository of news articles and broadcast transcriptions from international sources around the globe; and *Journalism and Mass Communications Abstracts*—abstracts of dissertations and theses in mediated communication.

CONDUCTING PROFESSIONAL, PROBLEM-BASED LITERATURE SEARCHES

Shopping for topics is a mark of and perhaps a necessary process for the beginner. The search activity need not be highly tuned; it simply has to return something of interest. For the more advanced scholar or practitioner, searches have to be focused and efficient. I would argue that the best way to focus one's search is to write before reading. On the face of it, this advice may appear to be counterintuitive. It is certainly counter to the usual advice given for the classroom paper.

Writing to Read

Writing to read is an iterative process in which the researcher writes increasingly detailed descriptions of the problem in order to identify his or her knowledge and ignorance. It allows the researcher to be in charge of the problem, resists colonization of one's thinking by others, and helps to avoid the inadvertent plagiarism where the ideas of others seem to become one's own. Writing to read is a preliminary activity that establishes the boundaries of the research activity and of the final argument that will result, but it is neither the research nor the argument.

Our work in Chapter 3 where we explored the development of a study on talk radio provides a good example of how writing to read works. At the end of that analysis, we knew the concepts and components of the research and the methodological requirements for the evidence needed. In that example, I went to my colleagues for advice and counsel. Here, we will use the search engines to provide that input.

Let's take an example from the new-media side of mediated communication and investigate the relationship between online and mainstream journalism. This example is both personal and professional. It is personal because a study I did on the relationship between the amount of desktop real estate that one has (number and size of computer monitors) and one's productivity was picked up by a *Wall Street Journal* (WSJ) blog and went viral (by academic standards).[12] It is professional because anyone in media has to be aware of this relationship.

There are any number of questions that one could raise within this example: How does the flow of news move between blogs and print? What is the relationship between independent bloggers (amateur and advertising-supported), media bloggers (like Ben Worthen

---

[12]*The Wall Street Journal* online (http://blogs.wsj.com/biztech/2008/03/10/bigger-computer-monitors-more-productivity/; accessed March 30, 2008) published a report of the research following its website release by the funding source and its promotion by a PR firm. That resulted in published reports in technical journals and newspapers around the world, ending with a 15-minute interview on NPR.

of WSJ), and print? My own interests tend to move toward audience communities and interpretive praxis rather than industry practices, so I will be formulating some questions about the relationship between the blog and the comments attached to it. This issue seems to be similar to the question about talk radio and its callers. Screenshot 7.3 shows the WSJ comments.

The comments are funny, salacious, confirming, and incredulous. They show interaction (and some social network marketing), with posters directing comments to one another. Here is a data set that is already digitized and can be moved into computer-based analysis with ease. Further, there is an almost unlimited supply of pages like this one. A descriptive study comes to mind in examining the expression of community

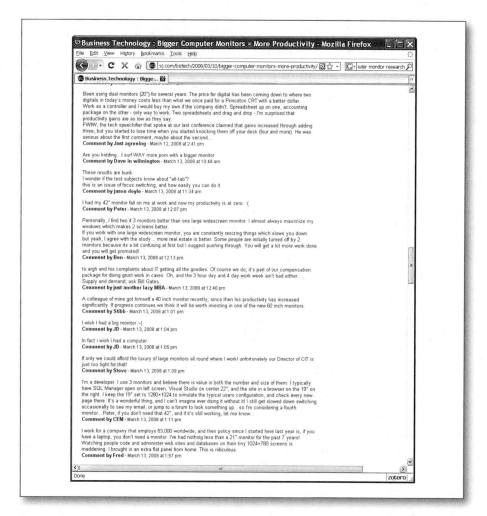

Screenshot 7.3 Reader Comments on Multi-monitor Study

Source: http://blogs.wsj.com/

among comments posted on a media blog. Where does community happen? How is it expressed? Where is community absent?

An experimental study also comes to mind: What is the relationship of the comments to the credibility of the original post? Most of the comments attached to the WSJ blog are confirming (the claim really isn't neural science), but a few are dismissive. What if we manipulated that ratio? Would that change the overall believability of the reported findings or of the online report or both?

At this point, I have a couple of emerging studies, one a survey investigating community formation in comments and the other an experimental study looking at the effect of comments on the credibility of the content, the story, and the reporter. My next step would be to write out a one-page description of the selected study. An interesting thing will happen in that writing. I will begin to see additional components of the study. For example, this is a business technology page, presumably visited by techno-savvy readers who are well experienced in computer postings. Clearly, I will have to investigate other kinds of content.

As this writing continues, I will develop not only a list of topics that I will want to search the literature for but also a set of criteria by which I can evaluate the relevance of what I find there. It will also direct me to the literature that I should search. The next section takes up the concept of research literatures and their relationship to online databases. Our literature is not singular; it is multiple. We need to first understand that multiplicity in order to focus our search methods.

Research Literatures

A discipline creates its own sets of literature—that body of work that is under the supervision of the discipline's membership and through set membership defines its internal divisions. As we saw in Chapter 1, how a person or an argument is identified professionally makes a difference. The literature of a discipline presents evidence and claims that meet the disciplinary criteria of what counts as evidence and claims and produces arguments that resonate with the membership. Disciplinary writers tend to use language in similar ways and use the same terms to reference concepts and ideas. Consequently, there will be clearer distinctions between productive and nonproductive key words, and productive key words will carry a richer and more useful set of results. An effective search may well cover a wide area, but it will also privilege the sources privileged by the discipline. Remember that the goal of a search is not to identify everything published in an area, but to generate the resources that you need to advance your own argument.[13]

Our communication databases list more than 1,000 communication-related journals. Within those many journals are several different literatures. The most common literatures would be critical-cultural studies (the location of most hybrid studies), communication theory, empirical studies (metric and interpretive), journalism, and rhetoric. Within each of those broad areas would be topical subheadings such as

---

[13]There are a few forms of writing where an exhaustive search is needed. Those include some theses, most dissertations, and certain meta-analyses.

"Postcolonial" under *Critical-Cultural Studies* or "Intercultural" under *Empirical*. The consequence of this mixture is that any search using broad key words is going to return a very large number of entries, the great majority of which will not be useful. For example, if one types in *media effects* as key words in the EBSCO communication database, one gets nearly 5,000 entries. If one is shopping for a topic, this return is a rich resource. If one is working to develop a specific idea about effects, this return is a very difficult way to enter the conversation. My experience suggests that fewer than 10% of those 5,000 results will be useful, but I will have to read all 5,000 entries (not articles) to find that out.

One way to manage the excess is to limit the journals to a central core that publishes broadly across communication, plus a set of journals that are likely to have a specific interest in one's topic. The *Iowa Guide* is an excellent place to investigate the journals that publish the literature in mediated and mass communication.[14] The guide provides a list of over 125 journals, providing the focus, publication schedule, publisher, and submission requirements for each. I have gone through the guide to select the journals that have *mediated* or *mass communication* listed in their key word descriptors and that publish empirical (metric, interpretive, and hybrid) studies (as of this writing). I have also added in journals that regularly appear in my own work and the work of my colleagues, using the same criteria. The additions are mostly from the fields of psychology and sociology, with a sprinkling of new media and film studies. They are listed in blue just to indicate their source. See Table 7.1.

The list of 104 journals is impressive, even daunting, and I would make no claim that it is exhaustive. It does, however, give a good range of possibility. Nonetheless, it certainly omits somebody's favorite journal (marketing and advertising journals have been proposed by reviewers). The list is a heuristic; the reader should adjust to fit the need.

Literatures and Databases

Unfortunately, there is not a one-to-one correspondence between a discipline's literature and the available databases. Consequently, one needs to create a screening device to quickly access the journals one wants and to ignore those that are unlikely to return anything of value. One does that using database search code. If, for example, you wanted to limit a search on articles with *media effects* in the title to the core association journals that publish empirical research (the core associations are the American Communication Association, the Association for Education in Journalism and Mass Communication, the Broadcast Education Association, the International Communication Association, and the National Communication Association and its regionals),[15] you

---

[14]http://www.eric.ed.gov:80/ERICWebPortal/search/detailmini.jsp?_nfpb = true&_&ERICExtSearch_SearchValue_0 = ED434359&ERICExtSearch_SearchType_0 = no&accno = ED434359. Accessed April 20, 2011.

[15]*Journalism Studies* is associated with but not owned by the International Communication Association. Although it is not an association-sponsored journal, I also added *Communication Research* to this list because of its long history in the field, and *Media Psychology* because its principal objective is media effects research.

Table 7.1 Selected Journals in Mediated/Mass Communication

1. *American Behavioral Scientist*
2. *American Communication Journal*
3. *American Journal of Psychology*
4. *American Journal of Sociology*
5. *American Political Science Review*
6. *American Psychologist*
7. *American Sociological Review*
8. *Annual Review of Sociology*
9. *Asian Journal of Communication*
10. *Australian Journal of Communication*
11. *Child Development*
12. *Chinese Journal of Communication*
13. *Columbia Journalism Review*
14. *Communication, Culture & Critique*
15. *Communication Monographs*
16. *Communication Quarterly*
17. *Communication Reports*
18. *Communication Research*
19. *Contemporary Sociology*
20. *Convergence*
21. *Critical Inquiry*
22. *Critical Studies in Media Communication*
23. *Cultural Science*
24. *Cultural Studies*
25. *Developmental Psychology*
26. *Discourse & Society*
27. *Discourse Processes*
28. *Discourse Studies*
29. *European Journal of Communication*
30. *European Journal of Cultural Studies*
31. *Feminist Studies*
32. *Game Studies*
33. *Human Communication Research*
34. *Images*
35. *Information, Communication & Society*
36. *International Journal of Cultural Studies*
37. *International Journal of Public Opinion Research*
38. *Journal of Advertising*
39. *Journal of Advertising Research*
40. *Journal of Applied Communication Research*
41. *Journal of Applied Social Psychology*
42. *Journal of Black Studies*
43. *Journal of Broadcasting and Electronic Media*
44. *Journal of Communication*
45. *Journal of Communication Inquiry*
46. *Journal of Computer-Mediated Communication*
47. *Journal of Consumer Research*
48. *Journal of Contemporary Ethnography*
49. *Journal of Educational Media*
50. *Journal of Educational Research*
51. *Journal of Family Communication*
52. *Journal of International Communication*
53. *Journal of Media Practice*
54. *Journal of New Media & Culture*
55. *Journal of Personality*
56. *Journal of Personality and Social Psychology*
57. *Journal of Popular Culture*
58. *Journal of Popular Film and Television*
59. *Journal of Public Relations Research*
60. *Journal of Radio Studies*
61. *Journal of Social History*
62. *Journal of Social Issues*
63. *Journal of Social Psychology*
64. *Journal of Visual Culture*
65. *Journal of Visual Literacy*
66. *Journalism*
67. *Journalism and Communication Monographs*
68. *Journalism and Mass Communication Quarterly*
69. *Journalism Studies*
70. *Jump Cut*
71. *Keio Communication Review*
72. *Language & Communication*
73. *Media Psychology*
74. *New Media & Society*
75. *New Review of Film and Television Studies*
76. *Newspaper Research Journal*
77. *Nordicom Review*
78. *Oral History Review*
79. *Particip@tions*
80. *Pediatrics*
81. *Personality and Social Psychology Bulletin*
82. *Political Communication*
83. *Psychological Bulletin*
84. *Psychological Reports*
85. *Psychological Science in the Public Interest*
86. *Public Opinion Quarterly*
87. *Public Relations Review*
88. *Qualitative Inquiry*
89. *Science Communication*
90. *Sex Roles*
91. *Social Psychology Quarterly*
92. *Social Science History*
93. *Social Science Quarterly*
94. *Sociological Inquiry*
95. *Southern Communication Journal*
96. *Technical Communication*
97. *Television & New Media*
98. *Theory & Psychology*
99. *Visible Language*
100. *Visual Anthropology*
101. *Visual Communication*
102. *Visual Communication Quarterly*
103. *Western Journal of Communication*
104. *Youth & Society*

would insert the following code (note the opening and closing double parentheses on the journal list):

((JN "American Communication Journal") OR (JN "Communication, Culture & Critique") OR (JN "Communication Monographs") OR (JN "Communication Quarterly") OR (JN "Communication Research") OR (JN "Communication Research Reports") OR (JN "Communication Studies") OR (JN "Communication Theory (10503293)") OR (JN "Conference Papers—International Communication Association") OR (JN "Conference Papers—National Communication Association") OR (JN "Human Communication Research") OR (JN "Journal of Applied Communications Research") OR (JN "Journal of Broadcasting & Electronic Media") OR (JN "Journal of Computer-Mediated Communication") OR (JN "Journal of Radio Studies") OR (JN "Journalism & Communication Monographs") OR (JN "Journalism Monographs") OR (JN "Journalism Quarterly") OR (JN "Journalism Studies") OR (JN "Media Psychology") OR (JN "Review of Communication") OR (JN "Southern Communication Journal") OR (JN "Western Journal of Communication")) AND TI media effects

With this code, the search engine (in effect) assembles the list of journals and then searches the list for articles that have *media effects* in the title. It returns a respectable and manageable 108 entries (see Screenshot 7.4)—much more efficient than going through the 5,000 that searching all of the publications returns.

A word about the conventions in the code. Parentheses order the work of the search. By putting parentheses around the journals, that selection gets done first before the titles are examined. If we wanted to expand the search terms on the title side of the condition, we would put that action inside parentheses. For example, media violence studies are a common form of media effects studies. To be sure that they are included in the search, you would include the parenthetical expression AND ((TI media effects) OR (TI media violence)). You could add other terms to find other forms of effects such as *sex*, *gender*, *race*, *age*, and the like as well as variants of the search terms (such as *effects of media*). All of these will increase your reach, though not necessarily the return. They all need to be inside the parentheses; otherwise the search engine will search *all* the journals in the database for the second and all subsequent terms, not just the selected core.

The Boolean search operators OR and AND (using all caps is simply a convention; lowercase works as well) serve to expand the search (the role of OR) or to narrow the search (what AND does). The search operator OR directs the search to each of the items in the OR list. The search item AND tells the search to select only those items that meet both conditions of the AND operator. In our case, a selected list of journals is on one side, and the title search term *media effects* is on the other. The resultant selection has to meet both conditions (hence it limits the search to both conditions). Note that the Boolean effect is the opposite of the grammatical effect.

The remaining Boolean search operator is NOT. In our original example, some of the items returned could be book reviews. Let's say we are not interested in book reviews; we are interested only in original research. One way to control that selection is to add the term NOT "book review." The quotation marks are also part of the search instructions. They direct the search to treat the two words *book* and *review* as a single term. Otherwise the

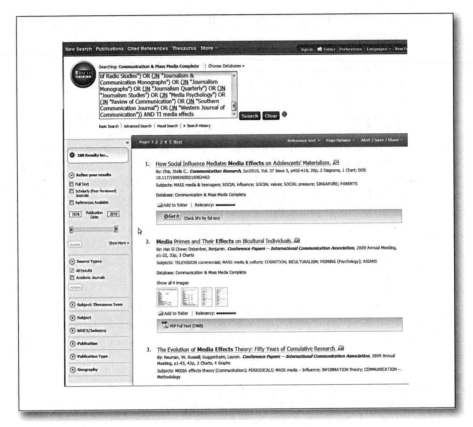

Screenshot 7.4 Search on "Media Effects" Across Selected Journals

Source: http://www.ebsco.com/

search considers *book review* as if it were *book* OR *review* and would reject any item with either term.

One last comment on Booleans: AND and NOT have priority over OR. They will be executed first. If you write TI media effects OR TI media violence NOT AB "book review," the search will find all entries with *media violence* in the title but no "book review" in the abstract and then go find all entries with *media effects* in the title whether or not the entry has *book review* in the abstract. It is the same as writing the search as TI media effects OR (TI media violence NOT AB "book review"). The way to solve the problem is to put the parentheses around the OR expression—(TI media effects OR TI media violence) NOT AB "book review." (And you thought your algebra days were over.)

The initials JN and TI direct the search to certain fields in the entry—journal name and title, respectively. The other common fields are TX for all text, AU for author, SU for subject terms, AB for abstract, and KW for author-supplied key words. *All text* is the default term, so if no field is marked, all the text is searched. In our book review example, we simply entered NOT "book review," which means that all the text was searched for those two words as a single term. It might have been safer for us to limit the term to the abstract. We might still get a few reviews that did not identify themselves as such in the abstract, but we would not lose entries because the author refers to a book review somewhere in the text.

Professional Practices in Search Strategies

In watching people conduct searches, I've noticed that most people use some form of a linear opportunistic search strategy. They will begin with some general term (like *media effects*), pull the four or five most relevant listings to check their key words and reference lists, and continue this practice through half a dozen search terms. This is an adequate strategy if one is writing a one-off paper. If, however, you intend to develop and sustain professional expertise in an area (or write more than one paper in your college career), this is a very poor strategy. Its poverty lies in its lack of reproducibility, knowledge durability, and complexity. You can increase the worth of a search in terms of reproducibility and durability (but not of complexity) by making a record of your search terms and the results. Some databases will make this record for you. If you use the advanced search feature in any EBSCO database (I'm not really shilling for EBSCO—though its people are very nice; it just happens to be central to media communication), each search will be saved, and the code that reproduces all of the searches in a single pass will be created. The value of this code is that the next time you search on this topic, you will have the benefit of what you learned before, and the algorithm will continue to "learn" in future searches. Unfortunately, not every database does this for the user, which means that one must keep good records of search terms and results to achieve reproducibility and durability as well as to learn how to do it better.

You can increase complexity by searching incrementally in focused searches rather than broadly. Do your groundwork first by writing a refined description of the problem. That description will specify the concepts and relationships in play, which will allow you to evaluate the materials returned and provide focused search terms. In our talk radio example, our search terms might look like these: talk radio AND (politic* OR beliefs OR ideology OR value? OR identity OR self image OR community).[16] I would then start with the core communication journals. That search returns 23 citations, a very manageable number.

Clicking on the preview icon (see Screenshot 7.5) allows me to make a decision on whether to download the article for further reading.

The example in the screenshot shows an article discussing the concept of "value equivalence," an idea I might want to pursue further. I will certainly want to download this article.

Another article in the list clarifies the value of a focused search. The title "Macho Media: Unapologetic Hypermasculinity in Vancouver's 'Talk Radio for Guys'" might ordinarily be skipped in a shotgun review. Because I know that it has to have something to do with politics, identity, and/or community, however, I check out the citation page (see Screenshot 7.6).

---

[16]The asterisk is a truncation symbol that instructs the search to use any form of the word (*politic, politics, political*, etc.). The question mark is a wildcard character that allows the searching for *value* or *values*. The parentheses cause the search to test for each of the combinations of *talk radio*. If the parentheses were deleted, the search would be over *talk radio* and *politic** but then the other terms would be searched without the limiter of *talk radio*.

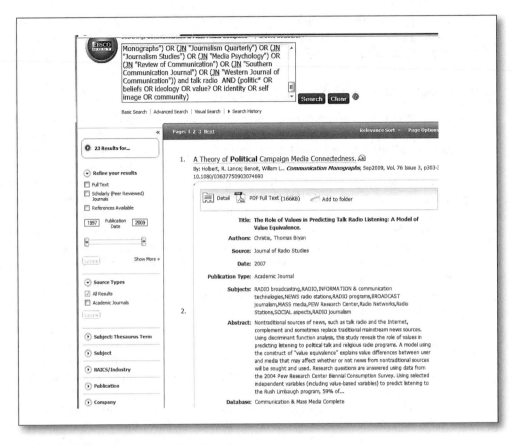

Screenshot 7.5 Accessing a Search Entry

Source: http://www.ebsco.com/

The words in bold in the abstract correspond to my search terms. They point me to the phrase "to construct a representational space for 'guys' to assert their gendered *identities*." A couple of things are suggested here: first that talk radio is a performative space in which I can enact a particular identity rather than a formative agent that produces an identity and, second, that talk radio may intersect with gender in other ways as well. It may be useful to add *gender* to my list of search terms. This article is a keeper as well.

Once I download an article, I go to the reference list to see if I should enlarge the journal list in search or if there are particular references that I should pursue. In the value equivalence article, I note the entry, Davis, R. (1997). Understanding broadcast political talk. *Political Communication, 14*, 323–332. That entry appears to be worth a look. It also seems that the journal *Political Communication* might be list worthy. The journal is in the database, albeit with a 12-month delay on full-text retrieval (a nasty bit of commercialism). Adding the journal gives me 10 new entries. The fourth of these new entries (Barker & Lawrence,

Macho Media: Unapologetic Hypermasculinity in Vancouver's "**Talk Radio** for Guys."

Authors:	Darnell, Simon C.[1]
	Wilson, Brian[2]
Source:	Journal of Broadcasting & Electronic Media; Sep2006, Vol. 50 Issue 3, p444-466, 23p
Document Type:	Article
Subject Terms:	*PRIMARY audience
	*RADIO broadcasting
	MASCULINITY
	GENDER identity
	SOCIAL aspects
Company/Entity:	MOJO Radio (Company)
	CANADIAN Radio-Television & Telecommunications Commission
Abstract:	In this article, the researchers report findings from a study that investigated the social construction of masculinity in programming offered by "MOJO **Radio—Talk Radio** for Guys," a station launched on August 6, 2002, in Vancouver, British Columbia, Canada. These results support the notion that commercial media targeted toward certain male demographics employ traditional concepts of hypermasculinity to construct a representational space for "guys" to assert their gendered **identities.** The research also sheds light on the decisions that guided MOJO programming in relation to the shifting **political** and regulatory economy of commercial broadcasting in Canada. [ABSTRACT FROM AUTHOR]

Screenshot 7.6   Entry for "Macho Media"

Source: http://www.ebsco.com/

2006) crafts an argument for the direct effects of talk radio as an active agent in forming political beliefs. Aha, conflict in the archive, an unresolved issue that creates the space for a contribution with the talk radio study. It's a great find.

I use a standard convention in downloading any article. Clicking on "PDF Full Text" downloads the article as an Adobe PDF file that opens within the browser window. Click on "Save a Copy" (see Screenshot 7.7) and use the authors' names, the date, and a shortened title as the file name (e.g., "Barker & Lawrence 2006 Media Favoritism").

The reason for this convention is that the American Psychological Association style sheet uses authors' last names and the date of publication as the citation. Everything stays connected in this manner.

Managing Citations

There is one last task in this process, and that is to extract the citation and prepare it for the reference list. Screenshot 7.7 shows the citation icon (in the background layer between the two menu bars). The citation page provides access to the "Bibliographic Export Manager," which will allow the user to download the citation directly to a reference software application as an RIS file (see Screenshot 7.8).

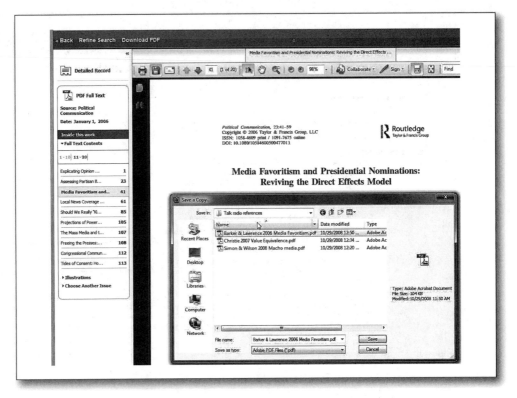

Screenshot 7.7 Saving the Full Text of an Article

Source: http://www.ebsco.com/

The reference software that I use is EndNote, but there are others as well, online and off. EndNote will manage the whole citation process for you from inserting the proper citation form in the text to creating a reference list and ensuring that the citations and the reference list correspond.

The reference software will store the citation information and then format it according to the style manual that you are using. Most journals that publish empirical work use the style manual of the American Psychological Association, but not all. Different style manuals require different sorts of publication information. EBSCO provides all the information for all styles (at least the ones I tested). I presume that other databases do as well, but some may not. If you are in doubt, download the citation in MLA (Modern Language Association) or Chicago style. That will store the greatest amount of information.

Preparing a manuscript for presentation or publication is an important and time-consuming part of the process. Estimates suggest that better than 50% of the readability and credibility of a paper is held in mechanics and formatting of the text in comparison to the content. In professional publication, about one third of the total preparation time is spent on these issues.

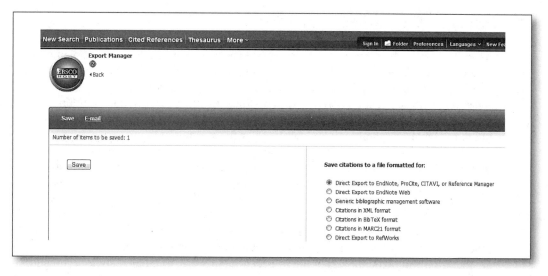

Screenshot 7.8   Exporting Bibliographic Information to a Local Reference Application

Source: http://www.ebsco.com/

A lot of this time can be saved, and the task can be made immeasurably easier, with some simple organizational practices. (a) Save your searches. Either establish an account on the database or keep track of the search terms in a separate document. If you misplace a reference, you can retrace your steps to find it again. And you can reuse a successful search algorithm as the starting point for the next paper on the same issue. (b) Use a file folder system to organize your reference library—perhaps a master folder for the research topic, a subfolder for drafts, a subfolder for reference materials, and inside that folder a subfolder for downloaded manuscripts. Create this structure before you start to write. I have almost 2 million files and thousands of references on my computer. Probably 10% of those are lost to me because I didn't follow this advice every time. (c) Always create a reference library whether you use reference software or a simple spreadsheet. The advantage of the software is that it is automatic, but you can usually copy and paste an entry into a spreadsheet. (d) Attach the manuscript file to the reference entry in your reference software or spreadsheet. This action places a shortcut to the file in the reference entry. If there is a problem in the citation—the incorrect page number in a quotation, for example—you can quickly retrieve the document and correct the error. (e) And last, if you are pointing toward a profession in research, create a master reference library that contains all the references of all the topical libraries you created. Some graduate students will spend 4–5 years writing papers and then 40 years writing articles but still approach each paper as if the reference requirement were a surprise (faculty do this too).

THE ETHICS OF LITERATURE REVIEWS

As with all research practices, there are ethical considerations in the conduct of and in the application of literature reviews. The first issue has to do with ensuring the originality of your contribution. To begin, I am far too much of a postmodernist to hold to the notion of "discovery." All of us depend on the work of others to make our own contribution, and the history of scholarship, from calculus to evolution to the double helix to the AIDS virus, is full of examples of simultaneous "discovery" with attribution being the real race. We are nodes in a memetic cultural network. Nonetheless, we need to protect ourselves from inadvertent plagiarism and to ensure that we give proper due to those from whom we take ideas. As we have seen, writing to read is both an effective and an ethical practice that sets one's own ideas in place before the colonization that will occur as one reads the works of others. It helps us to clearly delineate what is ours and what is not. Increasing the specificity of our citations will help give proper credit. If your argument is essentially derived from others, then cite early and cite often. Use page numbers to point to specific passages that are in play. It will no doubt lessen the impact of your work, but that is an honest result.

Quotation is another place where great care has to be taken to ensure that no damage is done to the meaning of the original author. Writers do deliberately take things out of context to establish a position not held by the originator. Writers will use fragments or careful editing to create opposition or support where none exists. With digitized records, we can now quickly search an entire manuscript, folder, or hard disk for certain key words, plucking juicy quotations from files we've never opened before. Searchability is an invaluable characteristic of digitized files, but it is also a great temptation to shortcut the process of connecting. It can play a large part in the unethical representation of the other. I am writing this in the last days of a major U.S. political campaign. Much of that campaign has been filled with words taken out of context to deliberately misrepresent the other. Researchers are usually not out to damage the other person. Rather, they seek to advance their own arguments by whatever means available. The result can be the same.

A particularly noxious practice is "salting the review." This description refers to an Old West practice of putting gold flecks in a shotgun load and blasting the side of an outcropping to make a claim look more profitable than it was. Writers, all too often, sparkle up their literature reviews on the basis of title alone. But just as one has to listen to be an authentic member of an interpersonal conversation, so too does one have to read to be part of the research conversation. A citation is a writer's bond that there is a connection between the concept being presented in the paper and the argument being cited. As a reader, I should be able to pick up the cited work and readily find a similar argument. Using specific page numbers in a citation increases the credibility of that expectation.

In the days before digitization, a reviewer had to take extraordinary effort or be personally knowledgeable about the references used by an author. This requirement gave the less-than-honorable author some protection. That protection is gone. As a reviewer for multiple communication journals, if I am the least bit suspicious of an author's practice, I can easily download (or find in my own library) a citation or two to see how they are being used. If the article is to earn my recommendation for publication, the connection will be evident, and the argument will be appropriate to the claim.

The major ethical issues, then, have to do with adequate attribution, appropriate representation, and authentic connection. Good practices in these issues don't happen by chance. In fact, in the absence of a recognition of the issues, specific safeguards, and the continuous oversight of one's own work, it is most likely that the work will fail the ethical test. The pressures to produce, whether for a grade in a class, a publication for tenure, or a research report for upper management, will almost surely lead us down the wrong path.

MOVING ON

The mark of the professional is a well-described problem that provides the direction and evaluative criteria for a focused search of the literature. Reviews are best conducted by building outward from a core set of sources, references, and search terms. Focus is achieved first of all by identifying the primary sources in which that literature appears. That focus, in turn, requires us to recognize that *literature* and *database* are not synonymous terms and that, consequently, databases have to be refined through selection processes to represent a literature. I recommend starting a search from your disciplinary home to identify a few key references that connect directly to your problem statement. From those references, you can enlarge the set of sources and further refine the search terms in use. In this way, you can construct a review of the literature that does the work that you want done, instead of being misdirected by every shiny thing in the literature. That literature review should locate you squarely in the ongoing conversation and open up the space for your contribution.

One of the hallmarks of a scholar or researcher is the constant asking of questions: What is this? How does that get done? Why did that happen? What is the value of this action? We are inquisitive about our world. That is what leads us into this business. And we look to find answers by devising effective protocols that produce information in various forms. Such is our next step.

REFLECTIONS

What Are Some Points to Remember?

- The professional practice of research requires an ongoing connection to the conversation that appears in the literature and in the communities of the discipline. Students may have to use a literature review to make that connection.
- Literature reviews should be strategic and directed by the demands of the argument. A good tactic is to write what one knows first and then read to support and to fill in the blanks.
- Effective and efficient searches are supported by the selection of the appropriate publications, databases that index those publications, and search terms that access the most useful articles. The goal is to return 50 citations, half of which are spot-on, rather than 4,000 citations, of which fewer than 1% are useful.

- In order to avoid reinventing the wheel, successful literature searches should be saved. Citations should be recorded in bibliographic software. Articles should be downloaded, classified, metatagged, and archived. It should be no surprise that there will be another paper to write.
- There is an ethical responsibility to acknowledge the contribution of others and to use that contribution in a way that honors the work rather than exploits it.

Why Does It Matter?

All research—academic, professional, and proprietary—has to connect to the conversation that is in progress in the literature. Failure to make that connection can result in banal claims, wasted resources, and a lack of sophistication and complexity in argument.

What Else Could We Talk About?

Communities of research and scholarly practice tend to "silo" up, building walls that limit the time frame and subject matter of engagement. Strategic literature searches participate in that narrow view. In some manner, the professional has managed the tensions between reading broadly across subject matter and historical purview and the specific demands of an argument in writing. One should never confuse a literature review with an overview of a topic.

What Else Might Be Interesting to Read?

Literatures, databases, and search engines change rapidly. Librarians deal with these issues on a daily basis and share their information with the world. Just search for *literature reviews* to return a trove of resources.

Section III

Designing Protocols in
Metric Research

$\mathbf{A}$ question is a challenge to find an answer. We meet this challenge by designing study protocols that provide the information that will allow us to formulate an answer. This section focuses on those protocol types that answer questions through metric methodologies. There are four major topics that define metric research: quantification, sampling, the research protocol, and statistical analysis. Chapter 5 took up the issues of quantification in measurement. This section will cover the remaining three topics.

As we start this major investigation of metric research, it may be useful to remind ourselves of the epistemological foundations of this type of research. Metric research is built on the epistemological foundation of an individual with material, durable, and stable characteristics and attributes that are themselves consistent in operation given unchanged conditions and are commonly but differentially distributed. These characteristics or attributes can be independent, structurally related, and/or connected in causal or catalytic associations. Consequently, an individual can be considered as the sum of these attributes and their relationships. Allowing for individual differences, any given characteristic or attribute carries its terms and relationships across individuals. Knowing those terms for one set of individuals provides information on all individuals with those characteristics. Finally, because an individual's behavior is considered the product of these characteristics and attributes, knowing the values of the characteristics can indicate what the behavior will be.

When we take these assumptions together, they produce an assumptive field of transcendent, material properties that are independent of any individual and are separate from any action they might produce. They persist through time, location, and context and are consistent within knowable limits in their relationships to other properties and in their operation on behavior. This persistence and consistency allows for reliable measurement. The materiality and independence support validity of measurement as well as levels of accuracy and precision in measurement. In this set of assumptions, the transcendent properties of the individual (e.g., height, weight, gender, age, race, personality attributes, cognitive structures) take on the role of building block elements that together produce the individual. In effect, there is a large but presumably finite set of attributes that will provide a complete description of any one of us. In sampling and measurement, these attributes are treated as having the same quality as objects, space, time, or, say, the electrical charge of a capacitor. This set of assumptions and the epistemological foundation they produce will help us understand the standards of good metric research and why metric analysts do what they do.

CHAPTER 8

Sampling

CHAPTER PREVIEW

What's It All About?

It is the tradition of metric research to develop claims that generalize across populations of people, media industries, media texts, and the like. Most metric research, therefore, involves some sort of sampling process that enters a subset of the population into the research. There are two primary forms: probability sampling, in which each member of the population has an equal or known chance of selection, and nonprobability sampling, which systematically includes and excludes members.

What Are the Major Topics?

The simple random sample is the benchmark of sampling and requires that every member of the population be included in the sampling process on equal terms. These requirements are rarely met. Stratified random sampling divides the population along some category, such as age groupings, and then samples with each category. Other probability sampling forms include cluster sampling, multistage sampling, multiphase sampling, and proportional sampling.

Nonprobability sampling systematically excludes some members of the population in the sampling process.

All sampling procedures produce error. The extent of error is essentially unknown, although it can be estimated in probability sampling, but not properly in nonprobability sampling.

The sampling process starts with the identification of the appropriate population; moves to the sampling frame, which is the device (list or process) that makes the members of the population available for sampling; and then successively progresses through selection and data collection. The sampling process ends with the in-tab (in-hand) data set.

The power of a sample is its ability to distinguish an effect from error. It is formed in the ratio of the size of the effect to the size of the sample in an inverse relationship. Samples can be too small and miss an effect or too large and create a significant effect out of something trivial. A power analysis, considered a best practice, starts with determining the size of the effect that would be considered important and ends with developing a sample that will be responsive to that effect.

What Special Terms Are Used?

Inferential testing

Random-digit dialing

Random error

Sampling error

Systematic error

INTRODUCTION

My morning newspaper quoted Time Warner Cable Executive Vice President and Chief Strategy Officer Peter Stern as saying, "The primacy of the TV platform is clear." The article went on to say that "97 percent of viewing is still on TV; the average person consumes 4 to 5 hours of TV a day but only 2 to 6 minutes of online video a day. The average American home has many more TVs than people" (*Salt Lake Tribune*, Monday, November 30, 2009, p. C6).[1] The article was a pretty standard job of reporting: Numbers are just thrown out without attribution, and with no critical evaluation. The first sentence looks like it might be saying something important, but upon reflection it simply means that most of us would rather watch our entertainment on a large screen (with a cable or satellite connection, I would guess) than a wireless handheld device.

The claim that an average person "consumes" (I'd like to see the operational definition of that word) 4–5 hours of TV but only 2–6 minutes of online video daily leaves me with a lot of questions. The U.S. Census clock tells me that we are a population of 308 million people of rapidly increasing diversity. Does it make sense to talk about an average person in a population of that size and diversity? Would I see myself in the face of that average person? Would any one of us? We see this sort of information with increasing frequency. How do we get it?

I'm glad I asked that question. Information on all but the smallest of populations comes from a process called sampling. Sampling is a method by which a set of individuals or other elements is selected for study. The information collected from the sample is used to

---

[1]This wire story has disappeared from the *Tribune*'s archive but, as of April 24, 2011, was still available at http://www.denverpost.com/entertainment/ci_13867269.

describe the population as a whole. Whether the information has any utility at all depends on the information collection (measurement) process. Whether the information from the sample can be used to stand for the population depends on the representivity[2] of the sample. These are two different issues, but they end in the same two-ended result for our population inference. Both the measurement and the sampling processes have to be good for the information about the population to be useful.

What about Peter Stern's average person? I was not able to track down either the source of his data or even his original remarks on his organization's website, but the TV viewing average is what A. C. Nielsen (the TV ratings people) has reported for a number of years. To cross-check, I went to the American Time Use Survey (ATUS) website, where I found the interesting graphic reported in Figure 8.1.[3]

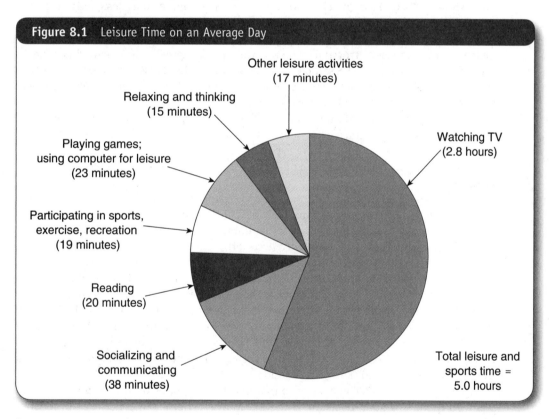

Figure 8.1 Leisure Time on an Average Day

Other leisure activities
(17 minutes)

Relaxing and thinking
(15 minutes)

Playing games;
using computer for leisure
(23 minutes)

Participating in sports,
exercise, recreation
(19 minutes)

Reading
(20 minutes)

Socializing and
communicating
(38 minutes)

Watching TV
(2.8 hours)

Total leisure and
sports time =
5.0 hours

Source: U.S. Department of Labor, Bureau of Labor Statistics. (2011). *American Time Use Survey: Charts by topic: Leisure and sports activities*. Retrieved April 21, 2011, from http://www.bls.gov/tus/charts/leisure.htm

Note: Annual averages for 2009. Data include all days of the week for all persons 15 years of age and older.

---

[2]*Representivity* is a word in common usage but not in any dictionary I could find. It is easier to write than *representativeness*. Be part of the movement to make *representivity* a bona fide word.

[3]http://www.bls.gov/tus/ charts/leisure.htm. Accessed April 21, 2011.

The ATUS data report 2.8 hours of television watching per day—a big difference that can be accounted for by the different measurement processes. A. C. Nielsen uses a "tuning metric" that records when the set is on, to what channel it is tuned, and, for those households with people meters, who is logged in as watching. ATUS asks respondents to provide the number of hours per day that they watched. The actual data probably lie between these two estimates, as reported values typically underestimate viewing but metered estimates can be based on "empty room" viewing.

A. C. Nielsen uses a national panel sample of 9,000 households, involving some 18,000 individuals, all of whom agreed to participate. ATUS uses over 85,000 interviews (one per person) collected from 2003 to 2008. The ATUS sample is drawn from the respondent panel for the Current Population Survey, which is based on a "multistage stratified sample of approximately 72,000 assigned housing units from 824 sample areas designed to measure demographic and labor force characteristics of the civilian non-institutionalized population 16 years of age and older" (U.S. Census Bureau, 2006, p. 3-1). ATUS is a sample of a sample, increasing the chance of error and involving two separate agreements to participate. Nonetheless, I would trust the ATUS sample more than I would the Nielsen sample because of its size and full public disclosure of its methodology, but I would trust Nielsen's metered measurements more than I would ATUS's self-reports.

We see that the information on viewing times is pretty soft and probably closer to 3–4 hours per day than 4–5—still a lot of time and apparently the most used leisure time activity. But what about the notion of an average person? We can get a good idea of both the limitations of averages and the importance of the representativeness of the sample by looking at Figure 8.2.

The graph is taken from an A. C. Nielsen white paper on teen media use.[4] The reported overall average of 29 hours and 15 minutes most closely matches the over-65 age group—not the face of the average Internet user that immediately pops into my mind. You might be surprised by the values of your own age cohort.

We can go a little bit further in this investigation. We can examine the Nielsen sample by taking each age group's proportion of the total population and multiplying it by the time estimates provided (converted to minutes). The proportion of U.S. adults aged 65 or older in the total U.S. population is .13. Therefore, 13% of our composite person should represent the time values for that group (1,714 minutes). When one adds the weighted values up for all eight age groups, they total 26 hours and 41 minutes, 2.5 hours less than the Nielsen average, almost a 10% error. This difference suggests that the Nielsen sample is somewhat overpopulated on the old (25 and older) side.

What does it matter? The answer to that question depends on the level of precision we need to make a good decision. If the question is whether Internet use approaches television use, the data are more than adequate (less than 1 hour per day versus something like 3). But if the question addresses some tipping point (such as ad buys) that happens at 1 hour of Internet use per day, then the difference has material effects. On the

---

[4]http://en-us.nielsen.com/main/insights/consumer_insight/August2009/breaking_teen_myths. Accessed September 15, 2010.

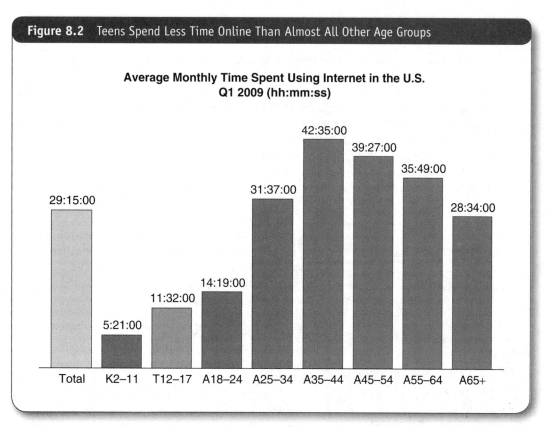

Figure 8.2 Teens Spend Less Time Online Than Almost All Other Age Groups

**Average Monthly Time Spent Using Internet in the U.S.
Q1 2009 (hh:mm:ss)**

Source: The Nielsen Company (http://www.nielsen.com).

Note: Graph shows the average monthly time persons used the Internet in the United States during the first quarter of 2009. Numbers at the tops of the bars indicate hours:minutes:seconds.

other hand, consider the results if the sample had been based on the typical academic convenience sample of college students. Presuming the Nielsen age-cohort results transfer (but consider the reasons that they might not), Internet use would have been substantially underestimated.

There are a number of lessons available from this excursion into usage times. First, values reported out of their location in method are not trustworthy. They may be just fine, but if you don't know where they came from, remain skeptical. (It's a good general rule.) The quality of a metric value is determined by both its measurement and the sample on which the measurement is taken. Bad measurement produces low-quality information no matter how good the sample. Poor sampling procedures limit the value of even excellent measurements. One needs both bits of information to make good judgments. Finally, the practical worth of information depends on the decisions to be based on it. Archival quality claims, however, should aspire to the highest quality of measurement and sampling.

UNDERSTANDING SAMPLING

We are required to sample anytime the population or set in which we have an interest is too large or conditions are too impractical to take a census (which is almost always the case). The best possible sample is a smaller reproduction of the population with all of its characteristics in their proper proportions. That requirement is far more stringent than what we need, however. Our sample need be representative of the population only on the parameter(s) of interest and, as we saw, only at the level of precision needed by our decision requirements. For example, if the analyst is sampling a population of voters to predict the outcome, it is not necessary to represent the population on any other parameter. That sample would certainly limit our ability to draw any inferences about how the vote was distributed and would provide no evidence of its representativeness. The only way we can validate a sample against this criterion, however, is to know the population, which, of course, negates the need for a sample. As a result, research professionals practice a good deal of self-deception in analyzing and evaluating samples. We will try to take the sheen off some of that gloss (see box, left).

The benchmark of sampling is probability-based sampling. The best of probability-based sampling assigns every member of a population either an equal chance, as in simple random sampling, or a known chance, as in stratified random sampling. The remaining forms of probability sampling (cluster, multistage, multiphase, proportional to size, etc.) give every member of the population some unknown chance of being selected, although that chance may be very small.

Nonprobability sampling includes all the other forms of sampling and is the most common form we see in our communication literature. Nonprobability sampling would include convenience samples of enrolled college students—for example, volunteer respondents, respondents purposefully selected to meet some criteria (judgment or quota sampling), respondent-directed sampling, and the research panel.

Anatomy of a Sample

Population or Universe: The totality of people or elements to be represented in the sample.

Sampling Frame: The list or method by which the members of the population can be selected.

The Gap: The difference between the membership of the population and the membership included in the sampling frame.

Procedural Losses: The reduction of the sample by contact failures, refusals to participate, and other collection and response errors.

In-Tab Sample: The final "cleaned and corrected" data set that is submitted to analysis.

Probability Sampling

Simple Random Sample

A simple random sample is one in which every member of the population has an equal chance of being selected into the sample. It requires the analyst to be able to access every member of the population or set. No general population sample can meet these requirements. The reason for this failure is that there is no sampling frame that encompasses all the members of the general population. A sampling frame is the means of access to a population's members. It might be a list of all the people who belong, the boundaries of a neighborhood, or some technique that puts the membership in access.

For example, everyone (students, faculty, administrators, and staff) at the University of Utah has an eight-digit ID number, and we all have an e-mail address based on that number. It would be fairly simple to use a random-number generator to develop a sample of, say, 500 ID numbers and e-mail out a survey to those 500 numbers. (Note that it is a sample of 500 ID numbers, not a sample of members of the university.) Many organizations have this sort of sampling frame available to them. Nearly any population of interest from the general public does not. We do have large lists or procedures that would put many people in access, such as telephone directories or random-digit dialing or city directories of addresses. Each of these, however, systematically excludes certain segments of the population, thereby failing to meet the requirements of a simple random sample.

Stratified Random Sample

A stratified random sample can be used when the population divides into mutually exclusive groups that are at least more homogeneous than the general population. To return to the university example, there are four more or less mutually exclusive groups (students, faculty, administrators, and staff). A simple random approach should return a sample having all four types in approximately the same relative proportion as the university population. That's good and a problem at the same time, because students outnumber everyone else and students and staff greatly outnumber faculty and administrators. The proportions are such that a sample of 500 would return fewer than 10 administrators, a number too small to be of much use. The solution is to take a random sample inside each population type, which is the stratified random sample approach. To use this approach in our Utah example, the analyst would have to have four complete sampling frames, one for each of the member groups. The size of each sample drawn would be set by the requirements for good information from that group.

Other Probability Samples

The remaining probability-based sampling procedures are all basically workarounds—that is, procedures that work around the costs and problems posed by an individual-based sampling frame. Cluster sampling (aka unit sampling) identifies geographical subsections, political units, membership groups, or other subdivisions of a target population and then randomly selects from that sampling frame. For example, each state is divided into counties (or county-like entities, e.g., parishes). A national sample of cable franchise fees could be based on a random sample of counties. Because I would expect such fees to vary across terrain and population density, I would probably use a stratified approach, sampling by dividing the United States into mutually exclusive areas (Northeast, Southeast, Midwest, etc.) and then randomly selecting counties within each area.

A multistage sample is one in which there is an initial random selection and then a following random selection from within each element in the first sample. In our county example, the analyst might want to sample townships (or similar political entities) from within each selected county. The American Time Use Survey is a multistage sample based on the larger sample that collects employment data and then samples within that sample.

A multiphase sample is basically a multistep (usually two-step) questionnaire. Let's say our interest is in the experience of cable TV subscribers in a particular franchise area. We also want to know the proportion of cable versus satellite versus off-air users. Because we want to know about the universe of service options, we need to take a random sample of the population within the franchise area. We might use a telephone survey with a random-digit dialing technique limited to the local exchanges. The first question would be about which service option is in use. In this example, no further questions would be asked of satellite or off-air users. The second phase of the survey would be directed only toward cable subscribers. This technique is also known as "qualifying respondents."

Proportional to size sampling is cluster sampling, where each cluster is the same size but the population is not evenly distributed. Larger population sites are assigned more clusters. Consider a household survey of a rural area, using a cluster size of 10 households. Many more clusters will be assigned to the population density of the small towns than in the open farming areas. A random sample of clusters is then drawn. The clusters selected should distribute according to the proportion of in-town/out-on-the-farm households in the area. This approach better represents the living conditions of the people than, say, a sample based on an area grid.

Nonprobability Sampling

Nonprobability sampling is any sampling process that does not depend on the random selection of elements from a sampling frame that reasonably matches the boundaries of the target population. The problem with nonprobability samples is that they are not trustworthy representatives of the population, because the process of selection increases the probability of certain kinds of people or elements over others. We would say that the sample is biased toward those selections. That condition of bias, in turn, violates the theoretical basis for calculating a measure of sampling error, which is the foundation of inferential testing.

How can we accept a sample from a biased procedure that by definition fails representativeness and does not meet the requirements for inferential testing? We go about this acceptance in a couple of ways. The first is based on the principle of functional equivalence. This principle holds when we are studying some aspect that is universal in application or operation. Nearly all studies that use convenience samples such as research conducted in a classroom or from a research course respondent pool make use of some form of this assumption. Effects studies often work this way. It is enough to show that people can be affected by some message or content type without having to demonstrate the extent of the effect within some population or the likelihood of the effect in the everyday communication ecology. Medical studies are frequently based on recruited or self-presenting volunteers made acceptable on the premise that a given group of healthy or afflicted people will be much like any other group of healthy or similarly afflicted people.

In a similar fashion, nonprobability sampling can be used to demonstrate what could be true of some segment of the population. Consider this actual example: An organization that delivers services to clients via the Internet used survey data with a response rate of 11% to show that 95% of its client base has a high-speed Internet connection. The survey was based on a random sample of the client list and was delivered via the Internet. As a potential user of this service in a way that requires both a substantial investment on your part and a high-speed Internet connection on the client's part, do you accept the organization's findings?

If all you know is that a survey has shown that 95% of the client base has an Internet connection, why wouldn't you get on board? The potential user group in this study wanted additional assurance that a high-speed Internet connection was as common as claimed among a diversity population that was an important target group. The potential user group arranged for a paper-and-pencil administration of the survey to a self-selected assembly of diversity clients. The paper-and-pencil data reported a significantly lower percentage of high-speed Internet connections. Additional study showed that the diversity group was not necessarily different from the general population, but the respondent group in the original survey was. That group had greater connection requirements for its style of Internet use.

Would we want to claim that our serendipitous sample would represent a diversity population or even the diversity clients of the company? Of course not, but the sample provides powerful evidence that the respondent sample itself is not representative of the client base. The potential user can make better decisions as a result of that information.

Quota or judgment sampling seeks to build a sample that corresponds to some known population characteristics or to the analyst's judgment of what constitutes an appropriate sample. Such sampling approaches often use a variety of sampling frames, contact methods, and/or measurement instruments to identify, reach, and collect information from the various elements comprising the sample. Up to this point, quota and judgment sampling look much like stratified sampling. The difference appears in the final stage when the respondents are selected on some principle of convenience rather than randomization.

For example, a local survey of 1,000 respondents might want to be sure to have 13% of the sample be bilingual in Spanish and English to correspond to local estimates. There is no available sampling frame for this population. Consequently, interviewers might be stationed at stores catering to Spanish speakers until 130 bilingual respondents have been entered into the sample. So, why is this not a random sample? Because we assume that an individual's presence at a particular store is purposeful and not a random event. The individual went to the store to buy something. That alone makes that person different from all those who didn't go to the store. Is that difference important? Only if that difference is systematically related to the criterion measures. We are once again in the fog of doing our best but not knowing the consequences. Nonetheless, the sample is vulnerable to critique because it is biased from random.

Respondent-driven sampling (RDS), also known as snowball sampling or chain sampling, is an "each one brings one" approach that is best used in socially linked groups. Initial contact with group members is made at some point of access. Each respondent from that point forward is asked to identify other individuals who meet the inclusion criteria.

RDS is often aimed at the members of so-called hidden groups—groups without membership lists, meetings, or hierarchical structure—whose members, nonetheless, maintain personal contact. These informal groups may form around a common work life, profession, interest, or social status. Each individual may know only a portion of the membership but can be connected to all members through others.

In the best practices of RDS, the initial contacts chain off geometrically to a number approaching the membership size. That list of contacts can then form a sampling frame from which the actual respondents are drawn. In the typical practice of snowball sampling, a predetermined sample size sets the limits of the sampling effort. If the desired sample is 25 members, once that number is reached, sampling stops. The danger is, of course, that the researcher ends up with "Joe and his 24 friends" who themselves are a unique cell in the membership.

The research panel is often a randomly selected sample from a target population whose members participate in the research activity over some extended period. The panel study is the only approach that can measure change both across a population and within individual members of that population. Simple trends research that uses multiple random samples can measure only population change. The Nielsen media reports that we engaged at the top of this chapter are generally built on research panels in order to track the ebb and flow of media use, for example. Although the sample may have been drawn initially as a probability sample, it is considered as a nonprobability sample because of the inevitable erosion of membership and because the research experience itself is presumed to participate in the response.

Critique and the Question of Representativeness

Let me state at the onset that the question of the representativeness of a sample is empirically unanswerable because the answer always involves knowing the population values across the criterion measures. (If the analyst already knows these, there is no reason to sample.) The question, then, needs to be reworded to examine the capability of a sample to represent a population across the criteria. The ability of a sample to represent a population depends first of all on the quality of the sampling frame, regardless of the method used. Absent a perfected list of every individual, any other sampling frame systematically excludes all those individuals not contained in the frame.

Telephone samples, for example, exclude those without telephone service (including those with their cell phones turned off), even with random-digit dialing. The unanswerable question is what difference does it make? It can make a difference if those outside the frame are also systematically different over the criterion measurement of the study. If they are not systematically different on the criterion measures, then their exclusion may have no effect on the result. And here's the kicker: Even if they are different on other measures, the excluded ones may still be similar to the included ones on the criterion measures.[5]

Any reasonable sample is, then, both vulnerable and defensible. It is vulnerable because the exclusions could make a difference and defensible because they may not. Further, the potential error of a systematic exclusion is not estimable; it is not part of the sampling error, which is calculated on the obtained sample. The sample in question can be compared to other samples drawn using different methods (which one is right?) or with previous results. None of those comparisons definitively resolves the question. In the end, the decision to accept the results from a sample is a judgment call, not an empirical one.

---

[5]For an example, see http://people-press.org/report/276/. Accessed April 21, 2011.

Unfortunately, there are additional issues that erode our confidence in a sample. Samples of individuals are always those of persons who agree to participate. Participation rates vary according to method of contact and the communicative and interpersonal strategies that are used in that contact. Mail and Internet surveys generally return a 10%–15% response rate (yes, that means that 85%–90% of the sample does not participate). Using postcard follow-ups or monetary incentives (say, a drawing) can increase that rate by another 5%. The response rates for telephone surveys might run as high as 40%–50% of the net sample (actual working, nonbusiness, nonfax numbers). And face-to-face interviews might garner as high as a 70% response rate in highly cooperative areas (it varies by locale and by technique).

It gets a little harder to dismiss the possibility of error when 30%–90% of the sample goes missing because of nonparticipation, but it is still possible. Let me show you a Monte Carlo example. We'll take two 100-element samples of random numbers, ranging from 1 to 7. From the first, we will extract every other number to represent a very successful telephone survey and to create a sample of 50 responders and 50 nonresponders (oh, if only we actually could). This comparison mimics a condition where there is no systematic relationship between nonresponse and a 7-point scale criterion measure. The means for the two samples are exactly the same: 3.98 with standard deviations of 1.89 and 1.97, respectively. Clearly, under this condition, it does not matter that 50% of the sample did not participate. We get the same results, although we lose some statistical power because of the smaller in-tab sample size.

Now let's construct two samples in which participation is systematically associated with the criterion. The scenario could be a situation of collecting data over a hot topic in which the spiral of silence[6] was functioning. I take the second sample of 100 and split it into two columns. With no intervention on my part, the mean of one column is 4.46; the other is 3.5 (honest). Both of these means are just inside the confidence interval for a mean of 4.00, which indicates that the difference can be attributed to chance. We'll call the first column *responders* and the second *nonresponders*.

In our scenario, people who disagree on this issue are inside the spiral of silence, meaning that those who score 1 or 2 on this scale are less likely to participate and those who score 5 or above are more likely to participate. To mimic that effect, I moved three "people" with a response of 5 or above from the nonresponder column to the responder column and three "people" who score either a 1 or a 2 from responder to nonresponder. Changing just 6% of the total, the means are now 4.68 and 3.28, a significant and substantial difference. The mean of the entire sample of 100, however, is 3.98. With this sample of responders, everything we would conclude about the population would be wrong.

If the best of our sampling methods present problems for interpretation of the results, what about the lesser, nonprobability sampling methods? From one view, the blatant convenience sample of the classroom is a more honest approach than claiming a random sample from a procedure that puts less than 15% of the selection into data analysis. At least we do not have to adopt some pretense of representativeness.

---

[6]The spiral of silence is a probability theory that holds that people who consider themselves at odds with the majority are less likely to express their opinions (Noelle-Neumann, 1974).

The way we typically handle this problem is to report the response rate without further comment. Surprisingly, that seems entirely appropriate because the problem is intractable. In actual practice, I know nothing about the nonresponders. I have to presume that their nonresponse is not systematically associated with any of the criterion measures of interest (we tested only one criterion measure in our Monte Carlo example, but there could be several). Or, ethically, I have to throw the sample out and not report any findings. Clearly, the evidence of a sampling failure has to be overwhelming before that happens. There is no practical solution except to keep working on developing data collection methods in which more people will participate.

As readers, we are under no such pressure to accept the findings, however. Nearly none of the reports we hear in the boardroom or read in the press and on the Internet or often in our journals provide the fundamental information about the sample that will allow us to make good judgments. At most, a margin of error will be reported—something like "This survey is accurate within plus or minus 4 percentage points." A claim of that nature is always false, because it is based on a perfectly executed sampling process. It does not account for the error that is introduced by the exclusions inherent in the sampling frame; the errors that are included in the sampling frame itself; the individuals who cannot participate because of absence, language, disability, or another issue; the individuals who refuse to participate; and those who fail to competently participate. There is no protection from those sorts of problems, and they may or may not affect the accuracy of the results.

The realities of sampling may appear quite grim, but only in comparison to the sunny silence that we usually encounter in proprietary reports and academic journals. A better comparison is to the knowledge we would gain by not collecting any information. Even Joe and his 24 friends give us information we did not previously have. The issue is the confidence we are willing to accede to the sample for inferential purposes. I am not talking here of statistical inference and confidence intervals that we will encounter later. Those are calculations that are taken entirely inside the sample. I am talking about the confidence we are willing to grant to, say, that sample of Joe and his 24 friends to stand for the population of their membership.

First of all, let's summarily limit all data from reality programs, talk shows, sportscasts, and other call-in surveys to their own boundaries. These are not samples of anything, but rather collections of responses. Second, let's retain a high degree of skepticism of any report that does not provide the details of its sampling methodology. That directs a jaundiced eye toward most of what we see in the popular press, online blogs, and many websites. Third, let's remember that nonprobability samples work best when the research question involves some universal condition. They are not appropriate for representing heterogeneous populations or populations differentiated across culture, experience, or realm of practice. Finally, let's keep in mind that there is error involved in even the best sampling methodologies that remains unknown and unestimated. Any confidence we grant to a sample should recognize the potential cost of that unknown error and should, therefore, be temporary, held in place for only as long as the costs of being wrong are manageable.

SAMPLING METHODS

This short section provides some techniques for collecting limited probability and non-probability samples using readily available sampling frames or other collection methods.

Probability Sampling

It is somewhat facetious to say that successful probability sampling involves the selection of an accessible population. Nonetheless, more than one research study has failed because it was impossible to contact the members of the targeted universe. The best possible situation is where there is a reasonably up-to-date list of the membership. Many organizations and institutions maintain such lists of members, registered owners, contacts, and the like, but they are usually proprietary. Access might be granted if the research had value to the organization and its management.

Public and Proprietary Documents

There are public documents such as voter registration rolls that are available in many states upon request. In Utah, live access to the voter registration file is available for a fee of about $1,000. The best source for identifying available rolls is the government documents section of your library. There are also a number of library websites[7] that provide guides to public documents. Finally, there are multiple online databases[8] that provide free and fee-based lists as well as those that will create a random sample from their proprietary data (see box, right).

Random-Digit Dialing

Random-digit dialing is a rather straightforward approach to reach the telephone subscribers in an area. Once the targeted population is defined, the telephone area codes that cover the geographical area of that population can be identified, and the landline and cell phone exchanges can be determined from online databases. The last four digits of the number can be selected

Randomizing a List

- Number the items in the list consecutively. Determine the sample size needed. Go to Random.org and generate a random sequence, ranging from the smallest value to the largest in the list. Starting at the top of the list, count down to the number needed. Pull the elements with the selected ID numbers into the sample.
- Alternatively, divide the number in the list by the number needed in the sample to get an interval value. Take the first value in the random sequence as the starting point. Take that element and every element that falls on the interval value into the sample.

---

[7]For example, http://ucblibraries.colorado.edu/govpubs/gd/publicrecords.htm. Accessed April 21, 2011.

[8]For example, http://www.virtualgumshoe.com. Accessed April 21, 2011.

using a random-number generator. There will still be considerable work to be done, as this procedure will generate numbers that are not in use, disconnected, or attached to a business, as well as out-of-area cell phone users. (You will also need some strategies for handling the irate who think you are violating the "Do-Not-Call Registry." Telephone surveys are exempt.)

Area Code	Prefix	City	Latitude & Longitude	Zip Codes			County	LATA	Type
801	201	S SALT LAKE, UT	40.7578N, 111.8818W	84105	84115	84106	SALT LAKE	660	Mobile Phone
801	202	S SALT LAKE, UT	40.7578N, 111.8818W	84105	84115	84106	SALT LAKE	660	Mobile Phone
801	203	S SALT LAKE, UT	40.7681N, 111.9159W	84105	84115	84106	SALT LAKE	660	Landline
801	204	S SALT LAKE, UT	40.7677N, 111.8851W	84105	84115	84106	SALT LAKE	660	Landline
801	205	S SALT LAKE, UT	40.7578N, 111.8818W	84105	84115	84106	SALT LAKE	660	Mobile Phone
801	206	PARK CITY, UT	40.5903N, 111.6397W	84060	84121	84092	SUMMIT	660	Landline
801	207	S SALT LAKE, UT	40.7677N, 111.8851W	84105	84115	84106	SALT LAKE	660	Landline
801	208	MIDVALE, UT	40.6166N, 111.9099W	84047			SALT LAKE	660	Landline

Screenshot 8.1   Telephone Number Prefixes and Type of Service (Salt Lake City)

Source: Virtual Gumshoe (http://www.virtualgumshoe.com/about/).

Landlines and cell phones represent different sampling units. A landline is generally considered to be a household unit, whereas a cell phone is considered to be an individual unit. Landline numbers, therefore, will need an additional step to randomly select an available individual in the household. Techniques that are used include asking for any adult over 18. Cell phones pose their own problems. Volume 71, Issue 5, of *Public Opinion Quarterly* (2007) is a special issue on telephone sampling worth reading.[9] Paul Lavrakas and his coauthors (Lavrakas, Shuttles, Steeh, & Fienberg, 2007) point out a number of issues involving cell phones, including whether to continue an interview when the respondent is apparently driving. (Don't.) The Pew Research Center website is a very good place to find the latest on telephone sampling and other polling (sampling) issues.[10]

Living Units

Google Earth has provided an outstanding tool for conducting household interviews by providing the pictorial location of each building in an area. Presume a research problem that centers on social networking by 12- to 17-year-olds living in small towns. Because our fabled researcher works at Indiana University, she determines to set the population boundaries as in Indiana. This is a decision based on convenience in that she has no basis for excluding small towns in other states except time and money.

---

[9]The entire issue is available at http://poq.oxfordjournals.org/content/vol71/issue5/#ARTICLES. Accessed April 21, 2011.

[10]http://people-press.org. Accessed April 21, 2011.

Nonetheless, within those boundaries she can conduct a probability sample. She defines a small town as one having a population of fewer than 1,000 residents and located at least 15 miles from a major population area. Those are fairly stringent requirements that would require a couple of tools. She can get a list of small towns from a site like CityTownInfo. com, which will also give her some location information, but the requirement of distance will have to be verified on a map. She might also stratify her sample by county to ensure that the whole state is covered, accounting for the population and geographic diversity of the state.

Once the list of qualified towns is established, a random selection from the list can be made. The selected towns can be accessed on the street-view feature of Google Earth. The first thing we might want to do is to confirm the rural small town character of each selection. The map shows one of the ostensibly selected towns, Atlanta, Indiana, population 761, located 15 miles west of Anderson and 31 miles north of Indianapolis.

The question is whether it would meet the standard of rural. The analyst would have to establish criteria, but there appears to be a lot of face validity in the picture.

Google Earth can also be used to conduct the selection of households within each town. Raising the magnification level on the map, Google Earth will render each building in the town in quite a bit of detail as shown in the detail from the previous map.

At this level of magnification, it is a relatively simple task to overlay a numbered grid or even to number the actual buildings and then to randomly select the required number of households for the sample. The visual map gives good indication of the difficulties that can arise in this sample. Though not shown in the photo, there is a high-density trailer court at the south of town and a low-density, high-end subdivision running along the creek (replete with SUVs, RVs, boats, and horse barns). Location is clearly associated with social class.

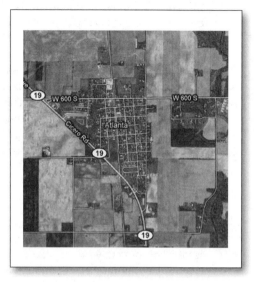

Screenshot 8.2   Google Map of Atlanta, Indiana

Source: http://maps.google.com/

Screenshot 8.3   A Neighborhood of Atlanta, Indiana

Source: http://maps.google.com/

Nonprobability Sampling

Nonprobability sampling requires as much thought and care as probability sampling. While technically biased, a nonprobability sample can still represent a population on the criterion measures, although at unknown risk. Every effort has to be made to control the sources of likely errors. For example, a convenience sample of students in a journalism class is an unlikely stand-in for a population of experienced newspaper professionals. On the other hand, a convenience sample of experienced newspaper professionals from two metropolitan newspaper organizations may show the same cross-industry characteristics as a random sample of professionals, based on the premise that all are similarly enculturated. Note that the ostensible sample makes use of two metropolitan newspapers rather than just one, and they are metropolitan rather than rural on the assumptions that local eccentricities will wash out across major organizations and that professionals at large newspapers are more likely to have greater industry experience.

Convenience Samples

In selecting a convenience sample, the analyst attempts to anticipate the arguments against its acceptance. The motivation is high because if the claim is denied entrance into the public or organizational discourse due to the dismissibility of the sample, the value of the work is lost. This preanalysis also allows the analyst the opportunity to collect information about the sample that may answer potential doubts about the sample itself during the measurement process.

The analyst can also build in protections by collecting deliberate samples of potentially troublesome groups. For example, presume an analyst to save time and money conducts a voter preference study using a telephone sample based on a published directory. The Business Research Lab website gives a national estimate of 28% unlisted numbers with cities ranging up to more than half.[11] Additionally, Pew Research puts cell-phone-only subscribers at 20% and rising every day. Even a fully randomized sample from a published directory will miss both those sets of individuals. To reduce its vulnerability, the analyst can supplement the larger directory sample with a smaller random-digit sample that includes cell phone exchanges and provide the reassurances that can be gained across the comparison.

Quota and Judgment Samples

Quota and judgment sampling need to ensure that the evidence for the quota values and the judgments made is strong enough to justify their use. Census data and other government reports are the most secure foundation for demographic quotas. But many quota values (e.g., the percentage of undocumented residents in a regional population) are guesstimates at best. Quotas and judgments should be based on multiple, well-documented sources. Beyond the quotas and judgments, the sampling process will come in for the same scrutiny as any other. The fact that the sample is balanced across gender may have little import if the sample does not make sense for the criterion measures in play.

---

[11]http://www.busreslab.com/articles/article3.htm#phone. Accessed April 21, 2011.

Snowball Samples

The quality of a respondent-driven sample is greatly affected by the initial point of access—the person that starts the snowball. That selection, in turn, requires advanced knowledge of the shadow population being sampled. There is an ethnographic element in gaining this knowledge. The analyst needs multiple informants who can provide the insight into the structure of the membership and how communication works within that structure. For example, members of the technological elite within any organization form a membership that is local, cosmopolitan, and global. They serve on common organizational committees and share memberships across organizations and agencies. They are the members necessary for any discussion on standards, application, and evaluation. The group fractures across technologies and topics within technologies. The access points along these technologies and topics result in quite different samples. The methodological advice here is to first know the population ethnographically—be secure in your knowledge of the boundaries and communicative practices of the population before initiating a respondent-driven, snowball, or chain sampling process.

Panel Studies

Whenever possible, the research panel should start out as a random sample drawn according to best practices. Because the sample will constitute an extended time frame of data, the limitations of an inadequate sampling frame and even simple sampling errors will be magnified across time. In my reading of the research literature, age, gender, and language ethnicity play significant roles in media use and message interpretation. Research panels should be formed using stratified random sampling or even quota sampling to ensure the appropriate representation of these important groups.

The major problems in panel studies are member dropout, response fatigue, and measurement obsolescence. Some member dropout is inevitable, and it grows with the time required and the complexity of the response process. Response fatigue is a form of dropout in which repetitive items generate refusal to answer or the even more troubling auto-responses—responses that generate data with no connection to an actual state of mind. Measurement obsolescence is a factor when the environment being measured changes in unanticipated ways, thereby rendering the instrument unreliable or invalid. There are no tried-and-true solutions to these problems, although shorter questionnaires, regular redesign, and incentives to continue are good practices.

Sampling Things, Texts, Processes, and Episodes

Not all of what we sample are people. We also sample across things such as technologies, products, and even electronic files; we sample across texts such as newspaper stories, commercials, programs, webpages, gaming narratives, and events; we sample across processes such as news and entertainment programming and experiences; and we sample across episodes of participation and usage. Whether the items are people or not, the requirements of sampling are the same. The goal is to randomize a selection from a population. And the problems are similar: What is the population of interest? It is not always easy to conceptualize or to put boundaries around the population of interest, however. What is a unit of process and the population of such units, for example? What is an adequate sampling frame? How does the analyst make selections from that frame? The one advantage with inanimate elements is that the elements sampled do not have to participate voluntarily, but they often have to be volunteered or made accessible.

The typical solution to sampling issues is to operationally define the population, the sampling frame, and the unit through the sampling method used. For example, experience sampling uses some form of randomized scheduling of response requests through cell phone contact or programmed handheld devices. Programming is similarly cross-sectioned into weeks or days with the constructed week being the most preferred (Hester & Dougall, 2007). A newspaper story is usually defined as a content unit of a newspaper, but the newspaper coverage of a story changes the goal of the sampling into all content units with the same central topic.

Nonprobability sampling is widely practiced in nonhuman sampling. Researchers use whatever they can find or whatever their library holds as the basis of a sample of texts. They use a judgment sample of games to sample narratives. And they sample episodes of participation across a usually very limited number of people. All of these samples return information to us, but all of them entail bias and pose the substantial risk of costly error just as nonprobability samples of individuals do.

Best Practices

Whether the sample is of individuals or units, there is a set of best practices that can be put into play. These practices start with the careful specification of the population as considered without regard to its availability. That specification starts with the clear description of and justification for the boundaries of exclusion and inclusion—who or what belongs, who or what does not. The description and justification have to match up with the demands of the research problem. What is required to answer the questions the problem generates? Just as I suggest that the analyst spend a good deal of time writing out the terms of the problem, so I suggest that a good deal of time be spent in writing out the specifications of the population. These two documents will work to qualify one another. The problem sets the requirements for the population, but if the population doesn't exist or is unobtainable, the problem has to be revised.

The next step is the identification of the sampling frame. The sampling frame is the device or practice that delivers the individuals or elements of the universe into the sample. The best sampling frame is an overlay, a perfect match to the population. A good sampling frame is an unbiased reduction. Most sampling frames involve systematic exclusions (all sampling frames in voluntary human research involve systematic exclusions). It is important to conduct a careful analysis of the sampling frame, listing all the potential errors that are encoded in it. This process runs completely against the pressures of doing research, which are always pushing the analyst to move forward with as few doubts as possible. Here, instead, the analyst is writing down all the things that are wrong with the research before it has even begun. Nonetheless, this work is the best protection against drawing strong conclusions based on risky evidence.

There is an interaction between the sampling frame that identifies the elements for selection and the selection process itself. Sampling frames that have their own internal structure need to be carefully assessed for the proper selection method. That structure can be surprising. Any list of surnames also encodes race and ethnicity and, perhaps not surprisingly, geo-location encodes it as well. Taking the first page of entries for every letter of the alphabet will result in ethnic bias as will selecting only from a restricted number of neighborhoods. Even probability sampling can run into difficulties with internal list structures. A quick estimate of the number of entries in the Salt Lake City directory gives 106,000 entries. A sample of 25 drawn systematically, starting with a random entry point and taking every 4,248th entry, could easily miss entire alphabetical sections and gravely undersample the ethnicities involved (more on this issue under "Power or Size Counts").

The sampling process is not over until the data are delivered into analysis. The first step in this phase are the strategies for controlling the gap that is made up of frame errors, refusals, nonresponders, not-availables, and associated measurement problems. These strategies include refining the frame, designing the contact process, pretesting all contact scripts, training interviewers, developing a schedule of repeat contacts, providing incentives, and the like. In the second step, the analyst has to account for the possible differences that exist in the gap between the sample drawn and the sample delivered to tabulation. This accounting might include special efforts to reach a small sample of refusals and nonresponders to provide, if not comparison data, then at least some indication of the circumstances of each. Careful follow-up might show that the high nonresponse rate was due to a fatally flawed sampling frame, for example.

Best practices impose a heavy burden and require a high level of discipline. A good sample is difficult to achieve, and the literature shows we are far more likely to take whatever we can get. The result, however, is data that simply are not trustworthy no matter how hard we wish they were.

Power or Size Counts

The power of a sample is its ability to distinguish an actual effect from spurious sampling noise or error. In simple terms, larger samples are better at distinguishing effects from errors. Larger samples also cost more, and they can produce reports of significant effects that are, in fact, trivial.

Let's take up the good part first. In the Salt Lake telephone directory example of a few paragraphs ago, I took a sample of 25 entries from a list of 106,000. The list was not random; it was organized alphabetically by surname, thereby structuring it across ethnicity. The sequence value of 4,248 was large enough that entire alphabetical sections could be skipped. Although ostensibly every entry has a known chance of selection, different starting points would result in samples with ethnic configurations different from each other and the population. This result is sampling error. The sample does not match the population. The estimate of this sampling error that we would calculate from a sample of 25 would also be relatively large, indicating the risks involved in reading supposed effects.

If we increase the sample to 100, we now take every 1,060th entry (or 1 for every 5 pages). Much better: Any starting point above the 600th entry would still miss all the Zs, but that is only 40% of the samples rather than 86% of the samples of 25. With a sample of 1,000, the sequence is every 106 entries, which ensures getting at least 5 entries from last names beginning with Z.

Here is another way of looking at the relationship between size and error: Take samples of 25, 100, and 1,000 numbers ranging from 1 to 5 from Random.org. Sort each sample. If the sample represents the population of such numbers, there should be an equal number of each value. In my test of this exercise, the sample of 25 returned 8 entries for the value of 1, a 60% oversample of that value. The sample of 100 returned 23 entries for 1, or 15% oversampling error. The sample of 1,000 returned 207 entries for 1, a little over 2% error. In every sample, there is error (there is always error), but the effect of the error diminishes as the sample gets larger. (Remember, though, this is random error, not systematic error, which is our major difficulty in sampling.)

We can also see this same effect in the mean scores and estimates of sampling error. The mean of each of these samples is 2.36, 2.73, and 2.93, and the estimates of sampling error (standard error of the mean) are 0.25, 0.14, and 0.04, respectively. If we look at the progression, we see that the mean gets closer to the expected value of 3.00 (the middle of a numeric string from 1 to 5) and the error estimate gets smaller as the sample gets larger. There is substantial error in the small sample (actually significant error). There is still error in the sample of 1,000, but it is now trivial.

It may seem that the moral of this exercise is to get the largest sample possible. Not so, because sample size is a balancing act. The balance is in getting a sample size that is large enough to be responsive to the hypothesized effect and at the same time both cost-effective and unlikely to report spurious effects. The cost-effective point is pretty straightforward. Every sampling point above what is needed adds unnecessary costs in time and money. The spurious effect point is a bit more tricky. The easiest place to see it is in correlational studies. Because most of our measurement uses language-based scales and because language has an inherent internal relationship among its elements, it is very difficult (I would say theoretically impossible) to achieve independence between language-based scales. There is always some small positive or negative residual relationship. With a large enough sample, that residual relationship becomes significant even though it is not theoretically meaningful in the analysis. We also see this problem in experimental effects studies (an example is given in the experimental protocols chapter) where change in fewer than 10% of the respondents can result in significant differences that are reported as occurring across all respondents.

Because of the likelihood of spurious effects, there is a contemporary move away from reporting all significant differences as important and instead starting with an analysis that attempts to determine the size of an effect that would be considered substantively or clinically important and then designing the sample to be responsive to the hypothesized effect. This analysis is called a power analysis, and it is conducted before the study. A similar analysis, conducted after the data are collected and the sample size and variability are known, is called an effect size analysis. Effect size analysis is supposed to give us some protection against trivial significance. I suspect that if we were to be completely honest, we would agree that not much has changed, but the promise is there.

There are a number of software applications that provide power analyses and effect size analyses[12] that are simple enough to use, given estimates of the assumed difference and the variability of the data for power and the actual means and standard deviations for effect size. More interesting, however, is the idea of determining what effect is substantively or clinically important—not just statistically significant. The discussion of effects that have authentic social impact has been nearly absent in academic media research, although it is commonplace in proprietary research (where different economic incentives are in play).

MOVING ON

The success of any metric study begins in the quality of its measurement and the quality of the sample or set of respondents, texts, processes, etc., that are involved. Once the quality of those two elements is secured, the analyst can move to protocol design and statistical analysis in confidence. Those, dear reader, are the topics of the next three chapters.

REFLECTIONS

What Are Some Points to Remember?

- There are two kinds of samples—probability and nonprobability samples. Probability samples can be unbiased; all nonprobability samples are presumed to be biased. Most probability samples are samples of things—telephone numbers, addresses, voter registrations, or locations, for example. Samples of people are most likely nonprobability samples because people have to agree to be included.
- Bias and representativeness are not the same thing. Bias occurs across selection; representativeness occurs across the criterion measures. A biased selection can properly represent a particular criterion measure. Representativeness, however, is always unknown.
- Sampling moves from the specification of the target population to the sampling frame that provides access to that population, to the processes of selection from that frame, to the protocols of access and data collection to produce the final in-tab data set. There can be a 90% loss between the sample selected and the in-tab data.
- Few samples that appear in our literature are professional-grade probability samples because of their high demand on resources. Most samples are convenience samples.
- Sample size needs to fit the requirements of evidence. A sample can be either too large or too small to generate the proper evidence of effect.

---

[12]www.clintools.com. Accessed April 21, 2011.

Why Does It Matter?

Nearly all metric research starts with some sampling process. The quality of the sample, along with the quality of the measurement, forms the foundation for the value of the findings and the trustworthiness of the conclusions. The analyst's ability to project to a population depends entirely on the sample.

What Else Could We Talk About?

The problem with any study based on sampling is how much credibility we want to invest in the results that claim to represent a population. The question of representativeness is unanswerable no matter how well the sample is conducted. Most sampling is less than well done, and authors are stakeholders in readers' credibility. Nonetheless, every study tells us something.

What Else Might Be Interesting to Read?

Connolly-Ahern, C., Ahern, L. A., & Bortree, D. S. (2009). The effectiveness of stratified constructed week sampling for content analysis of electronic news source archives: AP Newswire, Business Wire, and PR Newswire. *Journalism & Mass Communication Quarterly, 86*(4), 862–883.

CHAPTER 9

Statistics and Statistical Analysis

CHAPTER PREVIEW

What's It All About?

This chapter explores statistics, which are characteristics of data sets, and statistical analysis, which is the analysis of those characteristics for what they can tell us descriptively about the data set or inferentially about the population from which they were drawn. The discussion is organized around the characteristics of dispersion, convergence, distribution, association, and composition and across research questions relating to description, difference, relationship, and structure. The chapter ends with a discussion of the ethics of data handling.

What Are the Major Topics?

A statistic is a property of a numerical data set. Statistics are multiple properties, and *statistics* is a term for the study of those properties. Statistical analysis examines properties for what they can tell us descriptively about the data set and inferentially about the population from which they are drawn.

The common descriptive measures of dispersion are the variance, standard deviation, standard error of the mean, and range; for convergence, we focus on the averages—the mean (arithmetic average), the mode (most common value), and the median (value that cuts the set in half); for distribution, we use relative frequency and its graphic counterpart, the histogram; for relationship and composition, we look to the correlation matrix as a descriptive form.

Questions of difference, relationship, and structure are all related. A test for one also includes information about the other two. The common inferential statistics are chi-square (for nominal data), the *t* test, ANOVA, and the Pearson Product Moment Correlation.

Monte Carlo analysis uses constructed data sets as a method for learning statistics and statistical analysis. This chapter uses a Monte Carlo approach to demonstrate descriptive and inferential statistical analysis over dispersion, convergence, distribution, association, and composition.

Tests of statistical significance and rules for public decision making account for but do not control for the possibility of error in that decision making.

The chapter ends with a discussion of the ethics of analysis and claim.

What Special Terms Are Used?

Binomial data	Hypothesis testing	Q-matrix
Centrality	Linear relationship	R-matrix
Contrasts	Matrix data set	Scalar data set
Correlation matrix	Normal distribution	Type I error
Data set	Null hypothesis	Type II error
Histogram	Pair-wise data	

INTRODUCTION

A statistic is a characteristic of a numerical data set. Statistics (the plural form) are both the characteristics of a numerical data set and the general approach to the study of those characteristics (generating a confusion similar to method, methods, and methodology). Statistical analysis is the analysis of the characteristics for what they can tell us about the data set in hand and about the population from which they were drawn.

There are two types of statistical analysis: descriptive and inferential. Descriptive statistical analysis provides information about the data set in hand with no reference to an actual or theoretical population. There are no tests of significance in these analyses, because the data are what they are. No sampling error is involved. Inferential statistics treat the data set as a sample from a population and consider the characteristics to be estimates of population values. Sampling error is presumed to be present and has to be accounted for. Analysis proceeds in reference to actual or theoretical populations, and tests of significance are routine. Most of what we read in the literature concerns inferential statistics and their related tests of significance—a regrettable circumstance, as we shall see, that results in the loss of vast amounts of information.

Data sets are generated in the measurement process. In metric analysis, measurements translate some material or virtual property into a numerical value. That numerical value can belong to one of four families of numerical scales (covered in Chapter 5): nominal, ordinal, interval, or ratio (mostly we work with nominal and interval data). The property being measured is attached to some entity. The entity is called the unit of analysis. It is a singular construct over which the value of the property can vary. In many studies, the property is an item on a questionnaire and the unit of analysis is a person, such as TV viewing choices and the child. But, the property could also be topics, and the entity could be the newspaper story or cable subscription and the household or graphic elements and the webpage. Generally, we measure a number of properties across multiple instances of the entity or unit of analysis (i.e., we ask a lot of questions of each respondent over a group of respondents).

There are two types of data sets: scalar and matrix. A scalar data set is a single column (or row), as when several respondents answer a single item. A matrix data set is most typical. It is generated when there are several items (properties) on the questionnaire and multiple respondents (units of analysis). When we array matrix data on a spreadsheet or a data entry form, we most often arrange the measurement items across the top as columns of the matrix and the entities down the side as rows. This is sometimes known as an *R-matrix*, or response/respondent matrix, and is used to analyze the measured characteristics of the entities (respondents). The other form is a *Q-matrix*, which has the questions as rows and is used to analyze the respondents (entities).

All ordinal and above scalar data sets have three major characteristics: dispersion, convergence, and distribution. For nominal data, only the characteristics of distribution (frequencies, relative frequencies, and percentages) are appropriate as the values represent independent conditions.

Dispersion is a measure of the differences across the units of analysis on the properties measured. Convergence is a measure of the commonality of the units over a given property or properties. Distribution shows the relative weight of each measured property and, in ordinal and above data sets, describes the relationship between dispersion and convergence by showing the relative strengths of these two characteristics.

Matrix data sets allow us to investigate two additional characteristics: the amount of association between properties and the relational or causal composition that might appear in that association. All of our statistics and statistical analyses relate to one or more of these five characteristics: dispersion, convergence, distribution, association, and composition.

With this overview in hand, we will spend the rest of the chapter working through the specifics of each of these elements. I will do that by using a technique called a Monte Carlo analysis (see box, next page). In this technique, the analyst creates data sets with known characteristics to see how different statistical procedures respond to those characteristics. Let's begin an example by presuming that we are interested in social networking sites (SNSs). Following good practices, we spend some time exploring different sites, maybe join a few, and make some detailed observations. We start looking into the literature, which points to differences across groups that use SNSs and across SNSs themselves. As a result, we begin a research study that focuses on age and gender and the relationship among gender, age, and the approval ratings for three types of social networking sites. We will use three measures of gender: sex of the respondent, a femininity measure, and a masculinity measure.[1] Age will be self-reported chronological age. (We really don't believe that the number of years is the important value, but chronological age is a shorthand for the combination of multidimensional development and sociocultural status.) The three SNSs will be Myspace, Facebook, and (you read about it here

[1]Despite considerable theoretical work on the social construction of gender, an actual gender index apparently awaits development (but see Hofstede, 1983, and Lee, 2005, for some ideas). The methodological and ideological issues are many. The index itself would reify some social construction of gender. For example, what descriptors does one use to anchor the endpoints? Whose cultural values of womanliness and manliness would be featured? In this virtual study, we can easily solve all those problems, however.

Monte Carlo Analyses

Monte Carlo analyses build data sets with known characteristics to see how analytical procedures respond to those characteristics.

Here's how: Open up a blank spreadsheet. Go to www.random .org; click on the Random Integer Generator in the first column, second set. You can generate a data set of your choosing, but most social science analyses use data that range from 1 to 5, 1 to 7, or 1 to 10 as I do in these examples. Get 3 to 5 columns of 25 to 50 integers. Copy and paste into the spreadsheet (in Excel, right-click on row 1, column 1; select paste special and then text).

Don't know what a variance is? Calculate one; then change the numbers so there are fewer extremes and calculate it again.

Want to see how distribution changes as you manipulate convergence and dispersion? Create a table of frequencies, graph it, and find out.

Excel (IMHO) is a clunky spreadsheet for data analysis and benefits from one of the statistical add-ins such as SigmaXL or Analyse-it. Generally, these add-ins have a free trial period.

first) Forte.[2] The three SNSs have different histories, images, and ostensible appeal to different clientele.

Let's say that we have asked a group of 50 high school students to rate three social networking sites. We had them rate each site on a 10-point interval scale ranging from 1 (*really hate it*) to 10 (*absolutely love it*). We collected the demographic information on sex, gender, and age. Our imaginary (but desperately needed) gender scales are also 10-point interval scales. Sex of the respondent is a nominal scale, following the accepted fiction of two types; age of the respondent is a ratio scale (there is a real zero point). In addition, we calculated a total SNS approval value by summing across the three SNS values. The R-matrix data (truncated to the first 10 respondents) would look like Table 9.1. Each row contains the measurement values for a single unit of analysis, here an individual high school student.

The columns correspond to some property held by the unit of analysis. Respondent ID in this table is simply a sequential numbering of answer sheets or electronic entries; it is an important connection to the original data (which also have to be so numbered) in case of error in data entry. Sex of the respondent is coded as 0 for males and 1 for female, and age is in months (to be more responsive to rapid social development changes). The next five are 10-point scales, and the last is the sum across the approval values for the three sites ($15 = 4 + 9 + 2$).

In all of the examples in this chapter,[3] I want to encourage you toward best practices, the goal of which is that you can come back to this data set or any analysis of it six months from now and still be able to make sense of it. That means lots of labeling and tracking of the manipulations that are done. It's tedious and boring, but oh so important (and usually painfully learned).

DESCRIPTIVE STATISTICS

One of the unfortunate unintended consequences of hypothesis testing—the locus of publication—is that researchers have lost interest and motivation to carefully study the

---

[2]Forte is an invented site where members have to qualify to belong by demonstrating some passion of consequence (other than sex). By connecting people of like passion, Forte can build a critical mass of people who make a difference. Myspace may have disappeared as an SNS by the time you read this example.

[3]Most of the examples have been calculated in Excel because it is widely available and can be adopted in the classroom. Typically, the analyst would work with a dedicated statistical package such as SPSS or SAS.

Table 9.1   R-Matrix Data for Social Networking Site Ratings

	A	B	C	D	E	F	G	H	I
1	Respondent ID	Sex of Respondent	Age of Respondent	Femininity	Masculinity	SNS Facebook	SNS Myspace	SNS Forte	Total Approval
2	1	0	174	6	4	4	9	2	15
3	2	0	212	8	4	8	6	10	24
4	3	1	213	6	2	5	3	9	17
5	4	1	171	7	3	7	9	3	19
6	5	0	177	3	8	5	7	2	14
7	6	0	221	6	5	7	4	9	20
8	7	1	184	8	3	6	7	4	17
9	8	0	198	5	9	5	5	5	15
10	9	1	176	6	1	8	9	3	20
11	10	1	187	8	6	7	7	3	17

characteristics of their data sets. They learn only what the testing of the hypothesis can reveal. Generally speaking, the data have much more information that can be extracted. Consequently, I recommend making two passes in the descriptive analysis, one before testing the hypotheses and one after. The prior analysis is to ensure the trustworthiness of the data and to create benchmarks for the subsequent inferential analysis. The postanalysis assists the investigation in determining why things turned out the way they did.

There are three scalar classes of descriptive statistics: convergence, dispersion, and distribution (ordinal and above data, remember). Convergence is shown in the measures of centrality—the mean, which is the arithmetic average; the mode, which the most frequent value; and the median, which is that value that cuts the distribution in half. All of these measures point to the commonality among units (respondents). Dispersion is measured in the variability and spread of the values. The most common statistics are the variance, the standard deviation, the standard error of the mean, and the range. The first three of those statistics are based on the difference between the raw scores (a unit's value on a given property) and the mean of that set of scores. The range is the difference between the highest and lowest raw scores. Distribution is concerned with the shape the data fall into across the possible values of measurement in response to the relative strengths of convergence and dispersion. Many of the inferential tests—called parametric statistics—are theoretically based on the raw scores falling into a particular distribution, often the normal density distribution—the familiar normal or bell-shaped curve. We will see that the graphic display of distributions can be a powerful diagnostic tool.

Analytical software routinely provides descriptive packages that generate the common measures on each of the three classes of scalar statistics. Table 9.2 presents the output from Excel, although I have rearranged the rows to put like measures together.

The preliminary analysis would take us to some common checkpoints: The minimum and maximum values have to be inside the boundaries of the scale; the number of respondents has to match; a notation of the means and standard deviations should be made as a check for all subsequent analyses. It is surprisingly easy in even moderately complex studies to select the wrong variable or the wrong column for analysis. The checkpoints keep everything straight.

The problem for the beginning analyst in the investigative analysis is what the numbers and distributions mean; how can they be interpreted? In order to answer those questions without a strong mathematical background, the analyst has to build some models. What would the values look like if the data were more or less normally distributed around the midpoint of the scale? What would the numbers look like if the data were simply random numbers? Both of these questions can be quickly answered by creating data sets that match those characteristics. Figures 9.1 and 9.2 show the histogram for a normalized distribution and for a random distribution, respectively. And Table 9.3 presents the descriptive statistics.

Table 9.2 Excel Output for Scalar Statistics

I	J	K	L	M	N
SNS Facebook		SNS Myspace		SNS Forte	
Mean	6.10	Mean	5.58	Mean	5.04
Median	6.00	Median	6.00	Median	4.50
Mode	7.00	Mode	6.00	Mode	2.00
Standard Deviation	1.39	Standard Deviation	2.48	Standard Deviation	2.92
Sample Variance	1.93	Sample Variance	6.17	Sample Variance	8.53
Standard Error	0.20	Standard Error	0.35	Standard Error	0.41
Confidence Level (95.0%)	0.39	Confidence Level (95.0%)	0.71	Confidence Level (95.0%)	0.83
Range	6.00	Range	9.00	Range	9.00
Minimum	3.00	Minimum	1.00	Minimum	1.00
Maximum	9.00	Maximum	10.00	Maximum	10.00
Sum	305.00	Sum	279.00	Sum	252.00
Count	50.00	Count	50.00	Count	50.00
Kurtosis	−0.74	Kurtosis	−0.97	Kurtosis	−1.38
Skewness	−0.14	Skewness	−0.12	Skewness	0.27

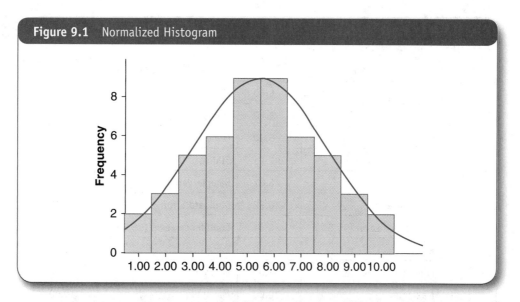

Figure 9.1   Normalized Histogram

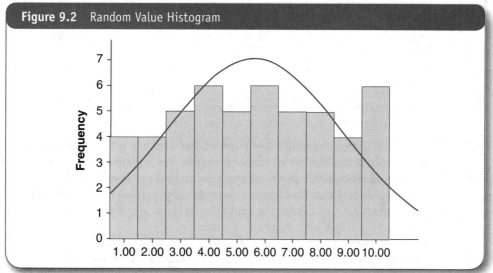

Figure 9.2   Random Value Histogram

My recommendation is that the analyst create a set of these models for each type of interval scale in use. It has to be done only once in a career.

In a normalized distribution, all three measures of centrality will be approximately the same. The first clue that something more complex is going on in the data is when those measures differ as they do in the Forte data set. Our normalized data set shows a sample variance of 5.07. Variances smaller than that on this scale will signal greater convergence around a common value. Larger variances suggest a lack of consensus or even multiple populations in the sample. The variances for Facebook, Myspace, and Forte in this constructed example are 1.93, 6.17, and 8.53, respectively. Those values tell the analyst that there is a good deal of agreement about Facebook, substantial disagreement about

Table 9.3 Descriptive Statistics for Random and Normalized Data

Normalized		Random Value	
Mean	5.50	Mean	5.66
Median	5.50	Median	6.00
Mode	5.00	Mode	4.00
Standard Deviation	2.25	Standard Deviation	2.82
Sample Variance	5.07	Sample Variance	7.94
Standard Error	0.32	Standard Error	0.40
Confidence Level (95.0%)	0.64	Confidence Level (95.0%)	0.80
Range	9.00	Range	9.00
Minimum	1.00	Minimum	1.00
Maximum	10.00	Maximum	10.00
Sum	275.00	Sum	283.00
Count	50.00	Count	50.00
Kurtosis	−0.51	Kurtosis	−1.11
Skewness	0.00	Skewness	−0.01

Myspace, and something unusual in Forte as that variance is higher than what would be expected from a random set of numbers. When the variance rises above what can be expected from random values—something the analyst can know only by constructing the models—it indicates that something systematic is going on. The largest variances occur when all the scores are clustered at either end of the scale, indicating a systematic failure of the scale or multiple populations in the sample.

While I like looking at the sample variance because it emphasizes differences, the most commonly reported measure of dispersion is the standard deviation, which is the variance expressed in scale values by taking its square root. (The standard deviation is the square root of the sample variance.) The standard deviation can be reported only for interval scales; the range must be used for ordinal data.

Interpreting the standard deviation (SD) can be a bit tricky for a reader. Let's try another example, this time shifting to a commonly used 7-point scale. How would you interpret a data set of 100 scores from a 7-point scale with a mean of 2.71 and an SD of 1.53? Is this data set normally distributed around a mean of 2.71? What if I tell you the range is 6 units? You're waiting for me to answer the question, aren't you?

Rather than answer, let me just show you in two histograms. Figure 9.3 presents the histogram (or frequency of each score value) for a data set that is approximately normally distributed around the center point of the 7-point scale. It has a mean of 4.00 and the same valued SD of 1.53. Figure 9.4 presents the histogram for the data set with the mean of 2.71.

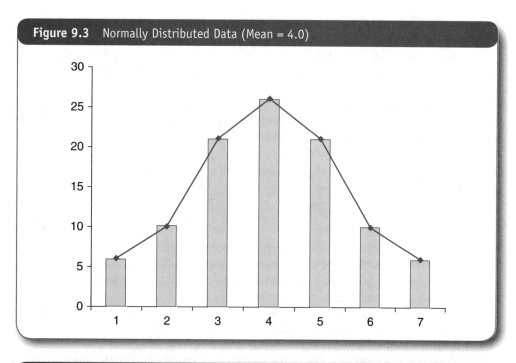

Figure 9.3   Normally Distributed Data (Mean = 4.0)

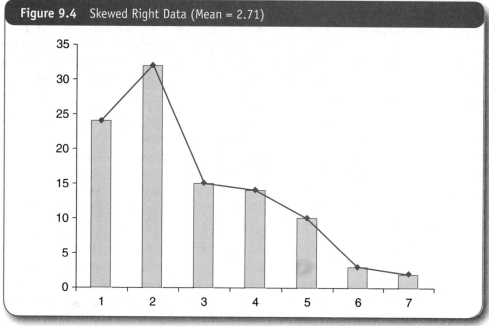

Figure 9.4   Skewed Right Data (Mean = 2.71)

One glance, and the reader knows exactly what is going on. It's not a normally distributed set of scores around a mean of 2.71. (It never could be, could it?) The distribution is skewed right (the tail extends positively). And the reason the SD is slightly larger than one might expect is because of those outliers, scoring from 5 to 7.

Measures of centrality and dispersion are independent of one another. We saw that the 10-point-scale, normalized data set in Table 9.3 generated a mean of 5.5 with a standard deviation of 2.25. A set of 25 values of 1 and 25 values of 10 will also generate a mean of 5.5, but it will have a standard deviation of 4.55. Finally, random data sets using a 10-point scale will float around a mean of 5.5 with standard deviations in the 2.8+ range. Consequently, even though the means remain the same, the dispersion of the scores differs substantially. The independence of centrality and dispersion is the basis for much of what we do in inferential statistics that are often based on some ratio of a difference between means over the variability of the raw scores.

Because centrality and dispersion are independent, just looking at the values will not give the analyst much insight as to what is going on in the data set. In order to get a better idea of what is going on in the data set, the analyst has to explore the distribution of values. Most descriptive packages will return two values that describe the shape of the distribution: skewness and kurtosis.

Skewness refers to the symmetry of the distribution. The skewness value is zero for symmetrical distributions, negative when the distribution is skewed left, and positive when the distribution is skewed right. The direction refers to the side with the long tail. Because of the fixed boundaries of most measurement scales, it is not unusual for raw scores to be skewed. On a 10-point scale with 10 being *most positive*, positive objects of judgment will be skewed left and negative objects will be skewed right, because of the upper and lower boundaries (see Facebook and Forte above).

Kurtosis evaluates the rise of the distribution. Positive kurtosis scores indicate a peaked distribution, and negative scores indicate a flat to sagging middle. Most software packages calculate kurtosis as excess kurtosis—excess being beyond that expected in a normal curve, which returns a kurtosis value of 3. You can astound your friends with the terms *platykurtotic* for a peaked distribution (positive kurtosis values); *leptokurtotic* for a flat distribution (negative kurtosis values); and *mesokurtotic* for a normal distribution (value of zero). Nearly all measurements using interval values will show some kurtosis. Even our normalized curve is negatively kurtotic (leptokurtotic) because the design of the scale restricts the distribution of the data. Kurtosis values above ±1.00 are clues to follow, however. Try working those terms into your next conversation.

The best way to follow those clues is to plot the histogram. In fact, it is excellent practice to always graph every data set. A histogram is a frequency chart for the number of occurrences for each possible value. The graph often gives clear visual evidence of out-of-boundary data points, unusual groupings of data, and outliers that would distort subsequent calculations, as well as systematic effects to be explored. Figures 9.5 to 9.7 present the histograms for the three social networking sites in the same order as the table. The visual evidence presented in the graphs confirms the consensus on Facebook and shows that subsets of the respondents have strong negative and strong positive opinions about Myspace and that there are two subgroups in the evaluation of Forte.

We have been looking at descriptive statistics for scalar arrays (one column at a time). Data matrices that report the values for the same set of properties over all entities of analysis allow us to consider additional information across relationship and composition. The quickest way to get to that information is to run a correlation matrix. Again most software will let you select the data fields and run the matrix with a few clicks. The matrix across all of the SNS data is presented in Table 9.4. You may

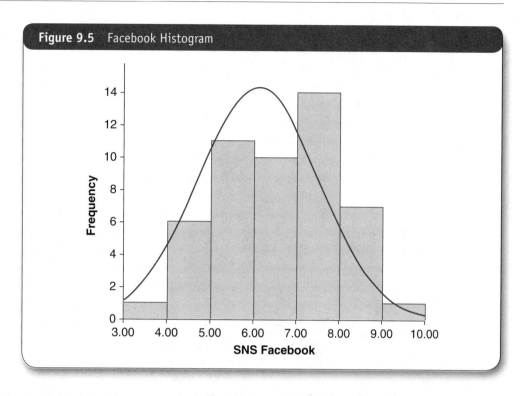

Figure 9.5   Facebook Histogram

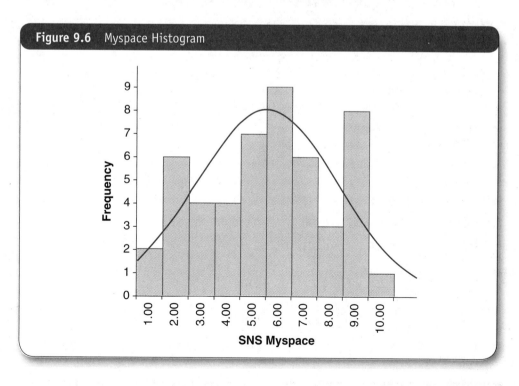

Figure 9.6   Myspace Histogram

Figure 9.7   Forte Histogram

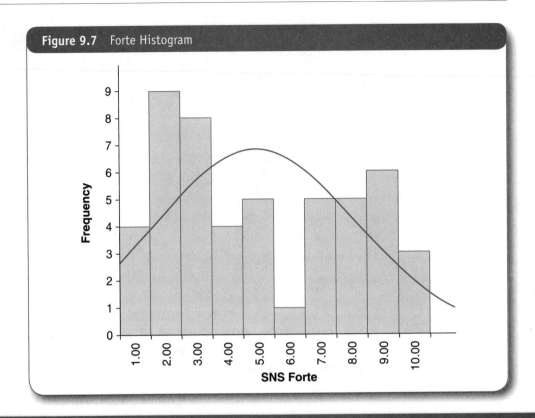

Table 9.4   SNS Correlation Matrix for SNS Variables

	A	B	C	D	E	F	G	H	I
1		Sex of Respondent	Age of Respondent	Femininity	Masculinity	SNS Facebook	SNS Myspace	SNS Forte	Total Approval
2	Sex of Respondent	1.000							
3	Age of Respondent	−0.014	1.000						
4	Femininity	0.615	−0.018	1.000					
5	Masculinity	−0.735	−0.050	−0.556	1.000				
6	SNS Facebook	0.538	−0.003	0.459	−0.454	1.000			
7	SNS Myspace	0.252	−0.682	0.431	−0.300	0.273	1.000		
8	SNS Forte	0.097	0.835	0.182	−0.244	−0.016	−0.541	1.000	
9	Total Approval	0.510	0.228	0.690	−0.644	0.622	0.395	0.479	1.000

remember that the Pearson Product Moment Correlation is a value that runs from −1.00 to +1.00; the former indicates that high values on one property are associated with low values on the other, whereas a positive correlation shows high values on each. (This is a cross-sectional study; language implying change is not appropriate.) So, in the table, higher scores on masculinity are associated with lower scores on all social networking sites. We can get additional clues about Myspace and Forte as well in the correlations between the approval values for those sites and age of the respondent. How would you interpret those values?

Here is the point of doing this sort of analysis: A test of a simple null hypothesis that there is no difference in approval scores across the three social networking sites would be rejected, and the alternative that Facebook rates significantly higher than the other two would be accepted. Happy news for Facebook (if the data were real); bad news for our understanding of what is going on. Even the best formal analysis during the hypothesis development stage of the research cannot anticipate what the data will actually show. It is not fair play to go back and change one's hypotheses (or to finally develop them) once the data are in. It is, however, the mark of a sophisticated analyst to be able to offer a more complex explanation for what went on.

INFERENTIAL STATISTICS

Inferential statistics are used to test inferences about a population from data collected from a sample. Inferential statistics are used to test hypotheses of difference, relationship, or structure. These classifications—difference, relationship, and structure—are overlapping categories. Difference is a relationship between the respondent groups (unit-of-analysis sets) and the criterion measure (property); a relationship occurs between properties over units of analysis, and structure is a complex of relationships and differences among properties measured over units of analysis.

The statistic is a derived (calculated) property of the sample—a t value, an F value, a correlation, a chi-square value—that can be used to test the trustworthiness of a difference, relationship, or structure found in a sample as an estimate of a similar difference, relationship, or structure existing in a population. Inferential statistics first give us information about the sample. That information is then used in public decision rules that govern how sample characteristics are used in knowledge claims about the population.

Significance and Public Decision Making

The inferential part of inferential statistics has to do with testing the sample as an estimate of the population from which it is drawn. The test accounts for sampling error in properly drawn probability samples. Under those conditions, the test provides us with an estimate of the probability that the sample we have in hand approximates the population. The test accounts for no other source of error than the random error that occurs with perfectly drawn probability samples. It does not account for the error introduced by biased samples, poor measurement, inadequate protocol design, respondent refusal, nonavailability, incompetence, analytic error, and other sources. There is no protection in tests of significance from those sources of error. As a professor, critic, journal reviewer, and institutional review board member, I review about 500 studies per year (the majority are medical studies). Most studies fail long before they get to the tests of significance (publication is no safeguard either).[4]

In the main, however, the other sources of error are the result of people doing their best given limited resources, nascent theory development, outdated and inadequately developed measurement practices, and a recalcitrant respondent pool. We push forward (the desired direction, at least) in the hopes that, someday, we will finally figure it out. In the meantime, we will use tests of significance and a faulty peer review process to determine what should rise to the level of a knowledge claim, but don't believe everything you read.

In testing the significance of a property, we compare the obtained value of the statistic with its formal distribution. All of the statistics we will explore have a formal (theoretical) distribution attached to them. In making the comparison, the analyst is seeking to determine the likelihood of the obtained value presenting itself under the conditions of the null hypothesis (no difference, no relationship, no structure). Let me take one and show how it works.

I'll use the *t* statistic (which we will visit again in its own section). The *t* value is generated in the ratio of a difference across means and a measure of variability (remember that centrality measures and dispersion measures are independent of one another). The *t* distribution is a family of distributions whose members are leptokurtotic symmetrical curves (flattened normal curves) that approach a normal density distribution as the sample size gets larger. At some point (50 is often used), the approximation is close enough that the normal distribution can be used. I will use the normal distribution in these examples.

The *t* test is used to compare the difference between a sample mean and a population mean (obtained vs. expected) or between two sample means. The expected value or population mean can come from the measurement design (what is the expected value of the mean of a 7-point scale?) or from some formal analysis or other studies—census data, for example. The sample mean is the mean of the raw scores as calculated by

$$\Sigma X / N.$$

where Σ is the symbol for summation, X is a raw score, and N is the number of scores.

The formula for a *t* test for sample mean and population mean looks like

$$t = \frac{\bar{X} - \mu}{s / \sqrt{N}}$$

where $\bar{X}$ is the sample mean, μ is the population mean, s is the standard deviation of the sample, and N is the number of items in the sample.

Formulas can be daunting, but they are just elements and operations.[5] Let's divide them into those above the line and those below. The numerator (above the line) is the deviation of the sample mean from the expected value. All things being equal, the larger that

---

[4]I've been on a number of faculty panels, and the consensus is that the state of our research is awful.

[5]No, we won't do much with formulas, but if you go into the business, you will need to know them. Computer algorithms are not error free, board members can ask embarrassing questions, and legal depositions can require you to recite them from memory, as I discovered during one panic-stricken answer. I was either right, or the opposing attorney didn't know if I was wrong.

difference, the larger the t value. The denominator is a value called the standard error of the mean (SE). It is one of those signpost values that we use all the time. We calculate it by dividing the sample standard deviation by the square root of the number of items. The standard deviation tells us how much the raw scores vary; the SE tells us how much repeated sample means will vary.

Let's calculate the t value for the comparison of the Facebook mean with the expected value of a 10-point measurement scale (5.5). The descriptive data set gives us all the information we need; we don't even have to figure the square root. The calculation is $t = (6.10 - 5.5) \div .20$. And $t = ?$

Well, that was fun, but so what? The "So what?" answer comes when we compare the t value with its distribution to see how rare it would be to get that value from a sample that was actually drawn from a population with a mean of 5.5. Let me diagram the example. Figure 9.8 shows two barely overlapping normal curves. The curve on the left represents the theoretical distribution of sample means drawn repeatedly from a population having a mean of 5.5 and a standard error of .20; the one on the right represents the theoretical distribution of sample means drawn repeatedly from a population having a mean of 6.10 and a standard error of .20. Neither of these distributions are empirical distributions. They are both based on the formula for a normal density distribution with a sigma (variance measure) of .20.

The test of significance poses this question about the obtained value of 6.10: Is it likely to belong to the population with a mean of 5.5, or is it likely to belong to the population with a mean of 6.10? It could come from either. The height of the curve represents the frequency of samples with means of 6.10 in both populations. There are nearly none in the dark blue curve (but some), while that value is the most common value in the light blue curve. I don't know about you, but I would go with the light blue. Could I be wrong? Sure, and in this single event, I am either right or wrong; there is nothing in between. If I made this decision over a large number of such choices, I would be right 99.99% of the time, but I could still be wrong here. We risk our lives driving in conditions with lower probabilities than that.

All tests of significance work in this fashion by comparing an obtained value with what could be expected under the conditions of no difference, no relationship, and no structure. Each statistic has its own distribution, so the test will not graph out as in Figure 9.8, but the principle is the same. Instead of graphing the results, we use conventionalized probability values to govern the decision as to which population to choose. In choosing what probability values to use as the cut points, the analyst has to balance the two types of error that can occur in the decision. We can err by rejecting the null hypothesis when it is true, which is equivalent to assigning the value to the light blue curve when it really belongs under the dark blue curve. Or we can err by accepting the null hypothesis when it is false, which is equivalent to assigning the value to the dark blue curve when it really belongs under the light blue curve. In the poetic of statistics, these are called Type I and Type II error, respectively. In science, Type I error is the most costly because it makes a false knowledge claim. Type II error continues our ignorance but does not confound it with false information. But do notice that we are balancing the probability of each error against the probability of the other. We are not controlling error or providing evidence of the presence or absence of error, just reporting the relative likelihood of each error. We never know if we have made an error.

The choices in this balance are not always that simple in the decisions researchers have to make. If a finding suggests some positive change in a very difficult situation, then a Type II error prevents the appearance of a possible solution, and it would be more costly. This is

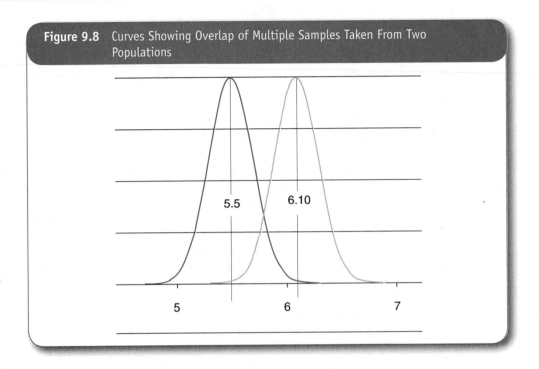

Figure 9.8 Curves Showing Overlap of Multiple Samples Taken From Two Populations

the balance that has to be addressed in testing some new chemical cocktail for cancer treatments, for example. This is also the position taken by some effects scholars on the issue of violence in the media. If the studies are correct, even if considered implausible, could implementing regulation save lives? (My analysis says no—see Anderson & Colvin, 2008a; another analysis says yes—see Comstock, 2008. Which would you choose?)

Most academic research is governed by the concerns of science for the competence of the archive of claims and, therefore, sets the bar against Type I error high by using alpha values of .05 and .01 in tests of significance. These values mean that if the obtained value is within 95% or 99% of all the values in the population of the null hypothesis, the null hypothesis will be retained. In proprietary research or in exploratory academic research, larger alpha levels might be selected such as .10 or .20 when Type II error is more costly or the risks imposed by a Type I error are minimal. In every case, the alpha value or the point of significance is set before the test is run, and it is a go/no-go gauge. There are no degrees of significance despite continuing efforts of authors and editors to write them in.

In testing the difference between sample means or between a sample mean and a population mean, there is one more issue to consider in tests of significance. Difference between means can be positive or negative. Our finding with the fictional Facebook data showed a positive difference. If we were to plan a test of the difference, in the absence of any basis for holding otherwise, we would have to allow that difference to be either positive or negative. That means that we would have to divide the risk of a Type I error between both ends of the curve. This is called a two-tailed test, and it effectively sets the alpha level at each end at .025 rather than .05, thereby requiring a slightly greater difference between the means for significance. In our Facebook example, that translates into a 0.1 larger difference. The moral might be to always write directional hypotheses to be most efficient, but if the analyst guesses wrong, there is no chance of a significant finding. Directional hypotheses and the number of tails in a test is an issue only with directional data. It is not an issue with chi-square or the F ratio, whose distributions start at zero and get larger, or with correlation (even though that is a t test) because the test is always against zero. One can get a negative correlation, as we shall see, but a negative chi-square or F value is not possible.

Common Tests of Difference

There are three common tests of difference across samples or properties: chi-square, which tests the difference between obtained and expected frequencies and between or among samples on categorical properties (see box, right); the t test, which tests differences between a sample mean and a population mean or between two sample means (see box, next page); and analysis of variance (ANOVA), which tests differences between two or more sample means (see box, p. 200).

Chi-Square

Chi-square is used to test the frequency distribution of categorical values between the obtained values from a sample and the expected values established in formal analysis or other studies or between or among samples. Let's say that we wanted to test the first choice of a social networking site across the male and female high school students. These are both categorical variables: Each person is either male or female; each SNS is either first-choice or not. The data generate a two-by-three cross-tabulation table (see Table 9.5).

Inspection of the table shows us that there are differences, but are those differences large enough that they would justify claiming a systematic relationship between sex of the respondent and first choices? A chi-square test returns a chi-square of 2.29 with 2 degrees of freedom and a p value of .32.

Disappointing—there is not enough evidence for the analyst to conclude anything about the relationship between sex of the respondent and SNS choice. The problem is not that there is not a systematic relationship (these data were contrived to produce an effect). The problem is that the sample is not robust enough for the effect to be

Chi-Square

- Tests nominal data (frequencies).
- Measures mutually exclusive categories within some common domain.
- Rows are usually categories of units, and columns are categories of a property.
- In measures of association, columns are considered the independent variable.
- Can handle any number of rows and columns, but:
  - Large cross-tab tables are difficult to interpret.
  - The more rows and columns, the bigger the sample needed (rule of thumb: minimum of 5 per cell).
  - A significant χ^2 refers to the whole table, not individual pairs or sets of cells.
  - Separate analyses have to be run to determine the significance of individual pairs or sets of cells.
- Is a nonparametric test (requires no assumption about the population).
- Value is always positive.

Table 9.5 Cross-Tabulation Table

	Facebook	*Myspace*	*Forte*
Males	9	6	10
Females	6	11	8

t test

- Tests interval or ratio data (scores).
- Compares sample mean to population mean, two independent sample means, or two pair-wise means (repeated measures design).
- Is a ratio of the mean difference over a standard error for that difference (centrality over variability).
- Makes use of a family of curves (the *t* distribution), each identified by the degrees of freedom in the test.
- Degree of freedom equals the sample size minus one ($N - 1$) for one sample and pairwise tests and $N1 + N2 - 2$ for independent samples.
- Approaches the normal distribution with large samples.
- Is a directional test; can be positive or negative.
- Requires directional (one-tailed test) or nondirectional (two-tailed test) hypothesis.
- Multiple comparisons require ANOVA.

significant. Chi-square is a relatively inefficient statistical test. If these proportions held across a larger sample (meaning that a real effect exists), it would take a sample almost three times larger (or 138 in round numbers) in order to return a significant chi-square. That corresponds to the general rule of thumb that nominal data require sample sizes about three times larger than interval data.

t tests

The *t* test is used to compare pairs of means: population to sample, two independent samples, or pairwise measures (two measures on the same sample). We have seen the use of the *t* test in comparing an obtained mean with a population mean in the example used in discussing significance. Our SNS data set also allows us to demonstrate the other two uses of the *t* test. We could consider the data set as two independent samples of males and females. If the overall sample was a probability sample, each subgroup would also be a probability sample. We could then compare males with females over each of the other measures. While possible, this approach is not a particularly good analytical design because it limits the information to one variable at a time and because running multiple tests increases the likelihood that at least one of them will be significant by chance. Nonetheless, a good use of the *t* test in this data set is to compare males with females over total approval—the sum of the approval ratings for the three SNSs. In the two-sample case, the *t* test is the ratio of the difference between the means and the standard error of the difference, still a measure of centrality over a measure of variability.

Table 9.6 shows the means and standard deviations for total approval for the two groups. Inspection of the table shows that females are more positive about SNSs in general than are males. The *t* test returns a *t* value of

−4.113 with 48 degrees of freedom and a two-tailed p value of .0002. The difference is significant (and note that even though the probability of a Type I error is considerably less than the conventional value of .05, it does not make this finding *more* significant).

Table 9.6   Means and Standard Deviations

Sex of Respondent	Males	Females
Count	25	25
Mean	15.080	18.360
Standard Deviation	3.054	2.564

The third use of the t test is with pairwise measures. Any two properties in our data set would provide a pairwise comparison. They would not all make sense, mind you, but they could be analyzed. Pairwise comparisons appear in what are called repeated measures designs. A repeated measures design is simply one where more than one measurement is taken on each respondent. The appropriate use of the t test occurs when the two measures are conceptually in the same domain and the measurement scales are in the same dimension—in short, comparing apples to apples and inches to inches.

In our data set, there are two sets of properties that meet those requirements: the two measures over gender and the three measures over SNSs. We would have very different expectations for these two sets. In the gender comparison, we would expect no significant differences to appear because we expect that males will tend to score higher on masculinity and lower on femininity, and females will tend to score higher on femininity and lower on masculinity based on the cultural expectations between gender and sex. Because we have 25 of each sex, we would expect the differences to wash. In fact, a significant difference would be something of a concern for the measurement instruments. The t value is less than 1.00 in the analysis.

With the social networking site measures, we would expect a difference. Facebook is more popular than Myspace (and Myspace is in the process of repositioning itself at this writing), and Forte is largely unknown (particularly as it is fictitious). Table 9.7 shows what the results table would look like. We would interpret this table as Facebook rating significantly higher in approval than either Myspace or Forte with no significant difference between Myspace and Forte. We get that information from the title of the comparison (which can be read as "Facebook minus Myspace"), the positive mean difference (which means that Facebook was the higher value), the t value, and the level of significance. A sharp-eyed reviewer would probably wonder why the more appropriate analysis of variance was not run but, as this is a very low-level claim—it has no transcendental implications—would probably also let it pass.

Analysis of Variance (ANOVA)

Analysis of variance supports a large group of statistical designs from simple one-way tests to complex interactions among respondents and properties. The test of significance is called the F test or F ratio (after Ronald Fisher, who devised it). It is used in any comparison of three

Table 9.7   Tests of the Difference Between SNS Pairs

		Mean Diff.	Std. Deviat.	Std. Error	t	df	Sig. (2-tailed)
Pair 1	Facebook - Myspace	0.7	2.44323	0.34553	2.026	49	0.048
Pair 2	Facebook - Forte	1.02	3.37149	0.4768	2.139	49	0.037
Pair 3	Myspace - Forte	0.32	4.70536	0.66544	0.481	49	0.633

Analysis of Variance

- Tests interval or ratio data.
- Compares three or more means.
- Determines the ratio of two estimates of variance: one based on means, the other on raw scores.
- Value is always positive.
- Uses independent groups, repeated measures, or mixed designs.
- Is an overall test; must break significant finding down into component comparisons.
- Based on family of curves, each identified by numerator and denominator degrees of freedom.
- In multifactor designs, analysis moves from highest interaction to main effects.
- Significant interactions confound the results for main effects.

or more means.[6] The F test is the ratio between two estimates of variability—one that changes with the addition of a treatment effect over one that does not. The logic behind analysis of variance is based on the independence between the mean of a data set and the variance of that same set. If one adds a constant to all members of a set of raw scores, the mean will change by the value of the constant, but the variance of the raw scores will not. The principle is used in ANOVA in that a treatment or a condition is considered as adding a constant value to each raw score of the group receiving the treatment or exposed to the condition. That produces a change in that group's mean score but not its variability. The change of value in the one mean score changes the estimate of the variability based on the means because only one (and not all) of the mean scores has changed value. It does not change in the estimate of variability based on the raw scores of the groups.

The F test always returns a positive value (the numerator and denominator are the sums of squared values), and like chi-square it is an overall test. Finding a significant F value means that somewhere in the analysis there is a significant contrast (comparison) or set of contrasts (comparisons) between weighted or unweighted means in the data set. (The F ratio is not all that informative.) The significant contrast or contrast set has to be determined by additional analysis, and it may not be one of the contrasts of interest to the analyst.

Like the t test, the F test depends on a family of curves to determine its probability of occurrence by chance effects. Each particular curve is established by the degrees of freedom for both the numerator based on the number of groups involved and the denominator based on the sample size (generally groups-1 and N-groups, respectively). Determining degrees of freedom can be complex, but thankfully the software programs do the calculation.

---

[6]It can be used to compare two means as well (F is the square of t), but it returns a nondirectional value as F is always positive.

ANOVA designs can have a number of components, but the primary issue revolves around whether the data are collected in individual measures from independent groups, in repeated measures from the same group, or in some combination of both. In our SNS example, we have two group variables—age and sex—and five repeated measures—masculinity, femininity, and approval ratings for each of Facebook, Myspace, and Forte. The Total Approval variable is a constructed variable. The presence of those variables allows us to ask several different questions that would require different sorts of ANOVA designs. We will explore three of those designs: single-factor and two-factor independent groups and a mixed design.

Independent Groups

To demonstrate an independent groups design, we could divide the sample into three approximately equal age subgroupings—young, middle-aged, and old (for high schoolers)—and test the level of overall approval across these age groups. We might hypothesize that older students will be more positive toward SNSs in general (though I don't have any theoretical basis for doing so). The data set would look like Table 9.8. The design is a one-factor design and would be called unbalanced because there is not an equal number in each group. You might read about it in older stat books, but it is no longer an issue in contemporary general linear solutions.

The ANOVA table that would be returned from this analysis is in Table 9.9. The means are 16.47 for young, 15.56 for middle-aged, and 18.06 for old high school students. Despite these differences, the F ratio of 2.688 (degrees of freedom = 2, 47) is not significant. A t test would show the old group to be significantly higher than the middle-aged

Table 9.8   SNS Total Approval by Age Groups

Young	Middle-Aged	Old
15	17	21
19	13	24
19	12	15
11	15	17
15	14	15
15	20	14
18	19	13
20	16	21
14	15	15
17	11	22
14	16	20
18	15	15
20	14	23
17	19	20
15	18	23
12	15	15
21		14

Table 9.9   ANOVA Analysis Across Age Groups for Total Approval

ANOVA Table					
Source	SS	DF	MS	F	p-value
Between	52.966	2	26.483	2.688	0.0785
Within	463.11	47	9.853		
Total	516.08	49			

Table 9.10 Data Format for Test of Total Approval Over Age and Sex of the Respondent

SOR	Age Group	Total Approval
1	1	15
1	1	11
1	1	15
1	1	15
1	1	14
1	1	14
1	1	18
1	1	12
1	2	13
1	2	12
1	2	15
1	2	14
1	2	15
1	2	11
1	2	14
1	2	18
1	3	15
1	3	14
1	3	13
1	3	21
1	3	15
1	3	20
1	3	15
1	3	14
2	1	19
2	1	19
2	1	18
2	1	20
2	1	17
2	1	20
2	1	17
2	1	15

(Continued)

group, but it is not legitimate at this point to move forward to comparisons of pairs of means—the simple contrasts. As you might expect, this is "worst luck" if your tenure or next consultancy depends on the finding, which explains all the "write-arounds" that we see in the literature. The temptation is real; it would take a change in just three values (the 20 and two 19s) in the middle-aged group to produce a significant F test.

While we are looking at independent group designs, we could also consider our finding about sex of the respondent and total approval. Males were less approving of social network sites than females. Perhaps, that would help us better understand what is going on with age. It is possible that controlling for sex of the respondent (SOR) will reduce the within-groups variance and give us more sensitivity to the differences between the means. The data set would look like Table 9.10. I randomly discarded two scores to give us equal N across the groups. I now have 6 independent groups of 8 respondents each in a two-factor, 2 (SOR) $\times$ 3 (age) design. There are three components in this analysis: There is the main effect of age that we just examined, there is the main effect of SOR that we looked at in the t tests, and there is the interaction effect between age and SOR that is unique to this two-factor design. An interaction effect indicates that the group means in one main effect are not in a consistent relationship across some other effect. In our case, it would mean that SOR approval means are not consistent across age, that age approval means are not consistent across SOR, or both.

It is easier to show you what our case is than it is to write it out because the interaction effect appears when the lines graphing the group means are not parallel. The first figure (9.9) shows a condition where the group means are different from one another but there is no interaction. The figure shows the difference between males (blue) and females (black) across the three age groups. While there are differences between sexes and between age groups, the pattern is consistent. But when we look at data configured to produce an interaction,[7] we see a much different picture. In the second figure (9.10), the graphing lines are clearly not parallel, and the third figure (9.11) graphs the values with SOR, as in the x-axis the lines actually cross.

---

[7]What? I made them up in the first place.

The results table for this analysis is presented in Table 9.11. Note the two main effects and the interaction effect. All three effects are significant, but the interaction effect directs us to an analysis of the six SORs by age means rather than the main effect means (SOR combined over age, and age combined over SOR). Publication practices vary, and in some articles, the reader may see main effects being analyzed even with a significant interaction. It can be done but at a substantial loss of information. One wonders why the multifactor ANOVA was run at all.

Mixed Designs

Mixed designs make use of grouping or categorical data that create independent groups and repeated measures that all members of all groups have completed. For example, we might be interested in how males and females completed the two gender scales. SOR is the grouping variable, and the gender scales are the two repeated measures. To do these analyses, I have to shift over to SPSS because Excel will not support repeated-measure ANOVA analyses as of yet.

Table 9.10 (Continued)

SOR	Age Group	Total Approval
2	2	15
2	2	17
2	2	20
2	2	19
2	2	16
2	2	16
2	2	15
2	2	19
2	3	21
2	3	15
2	3	17
2	3	22
2	3	20
2	3	15
2	3	23
2	3	23

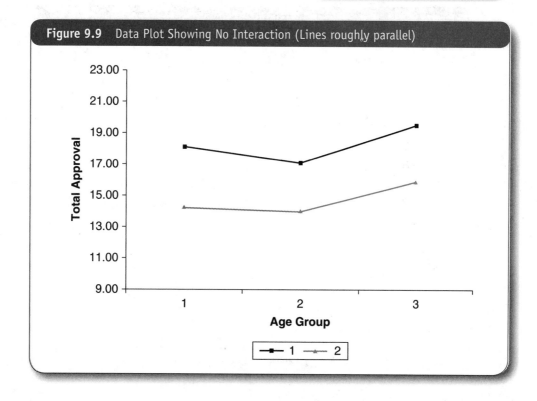

Figure 9.9   Data Plot Showing No Interaction (Lines roughly parallel)

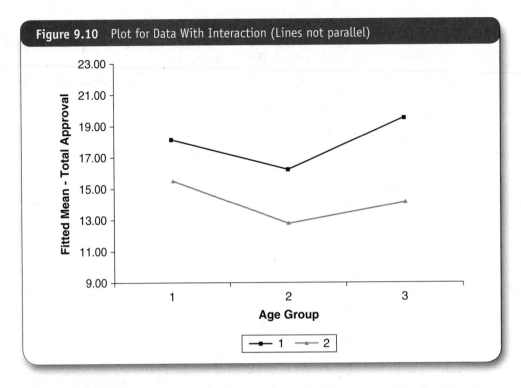

Figure 9.10 Plot for Data With Interaction (Lines not parallel)

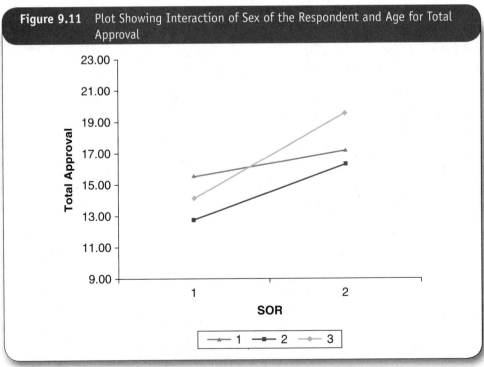

Figure 9.11 Plot Showing Interaction of Sex of the Respondent and Age for Total Approval

Table 9.11   Results Table for Test of Total Approval Over Age and Sex of the Respondent

Analysis of Variance:					
Source	DF	SS	MS	F	P
SOR	1	147	147	43.250	0.0000
Age Group	2	47.375	23.688	6.969	0.0024
Interaction	2	23.125	14.063	4.137	0.0229
Error	42	142.75	3.399		
Total	47	365.25	7.771		

Mixed designs return two sets of results tables: one for the within-groups factor(s), which in this case is the main effect across the two gender scales and the interaction between SOR and the gender scales, and the other for the between-groups factor(s), which in this case is SOR. They are presented together in Table 9.12. As might be expected, there is a significant interaction between SOR and the gender scales. As something of a provocation, I designed the data so that they would reflect what the literature suggests is a greater diversity in gender definition for girls and women in U.S. culture as opposed to boys and men. The graph in Figure 9.12 clearly shows the interaction. The black line for high school girls is longer, indicating a greater range of values than the blue line for high school boys. It would be very interesting to actually investigate this phenomenon and to have the instrumentation to do it.

Table 9.12   Mixed Design Tables for Test of Gender Over Sex of the Respondent

Tests of Within-Subjects Effects Gender					
Source	Sum of Squares	df	Mean Square	F	Sig.
Gender	2.560	1	2.560	.666	.418
Gender * Sex	268.960	1	268.960	69.981	.000
Error(Gender)	184.480	48	3.843		

Tests of Between-Subjects Effects					
Source	Sum of Squares	df	Mean Square	F	Sig.
Sex	7.840	1	7.840	3.027	.088
Error	124.320	48	2.590		

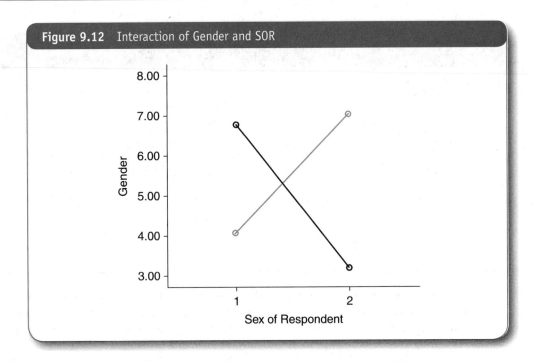

Figure 9.12 Interaction of Gender and SOR

What Are Degrees of Freedom?

The mathematical concept of degrees of freedom refers to the number of components that have to be known before all the components are known. In a completely free system, all the components have to be known. Most systems are not completely free—for example, a matrix display of data, where the row and column totals are known. An analyst would need to know only $N - 1$ entries in a column, because the last entry could be determined by subtraction, and would need to know only $C - 1$ columns, because all the data in the last column could be calculated. Consequently, the degree of freedom in an analysis is the number of "free variables," which in turn establishes the parameters of the statistical distribution and identifies the best-fitting curve. The truth of the matter is that the field makes little use of the concept—although perhaps it should—and modern statistical software obviates the need for knowing the geometry behind it. It is necessary to report degrees of freedom correctly, however, as reviewers check that sort of information.

Common Measures of Relationship

Measures of relationship or association can be taken on all forms of data—nominal, ordinal, interval, and ratio (see box, next page). The most common form is the Pearson Product Moment Correlation (hereafter, correlation), and that will be the measure we will focus on. But first a bit of explanation about difference and association.

The Connection Between Relationship and Difference

Measures of relationship are closely related to measures of difference. In chi-square, for example, as the differences in row values for each column increase, knowing the column value increase one's ability to predict the row value. Again, it might be easier to show how this works rather than describe it. Figure 9.13 shows the relative distribution of males and females across three social networking sites. These data produce a significant χ^2, which means that the groups are different from one another. Another way of understanding that difference is that it matters whether one is a male or a female in the choice of social networking site. If I told you John and Mary just joined social networking sites, assuming cultural naming practices, would your best guess be that they joined the same sites or different sites? (A good student would have said different sites.) We have a significant difference across SOR on group membership, because SOR is associated with the choice of membership. The relationship between difference and association is strong enough that it is good practice in χ^2 analysis to always report a measure of association (usually Cramer's V) along with the χ^2 value.

In interval data and independent groups, difference can be seen as the relationship between the treatment effect or property and the criterion measure. Consequently, in our analysis of the Total Approval score and SOR, the difference can be attributed to the relationship between Total Approval and SOR. In repeated measures, a significant t test is often coupled with a significant correlation between the two measures. If the effect of the second measure or treatment is to add a constant value to the first, the means will be significantly different, but the scores will be correlated. You have the tools to demonstrate this result for yourself to your own satisfaction. Reporting the correlation matrix in the analysis of repeated measures is also good practice.

Measures of Association

- Can be run on all numerical scales.
- Most common measures are Cramer's V for nominal data and Pearson's Product Moment Correlation for interval data.
- Cramer's V is a measure of the association between the column and the row values; it is symmetrical and positive.
- Correlation is the measure of the shared variance between two measures taken on a common unit (data collected in a repeated-measures design).
- Correlation varies from 0.0 to ±1.00; positive correlations indicate match pairs, negative correlations indicate inverse pairs.
- Correlation is a measure of the shared variance of the two measures.
- The best interpretation of a correlation is the coefficient of determination (r^2), which returns the proportion of shared variance.

Pearson Product Moment Correlation

Karl Pearson was one of the most prolific scholars in mathematical statistics. His work, along with that of Ronald Fisher and William Gosset (of Student's distribution fame), is the

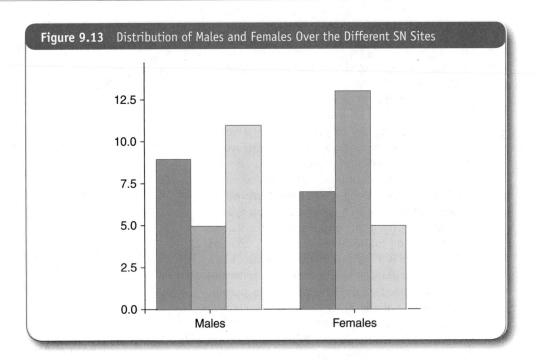

Figure 9.13   Distribution of Males and Females Over the Different SN Sites

foundation of much of contemporary statistics as well as the methodologies of the modern social sciences. A singular contribution from Pearson was the development of linear regression and correlation. Linear regression is an analysis of the structure of a data set, and we will spend time with it in the next section. Here we are concerned with correlation as a measure of the relationship between two properties across a unit of analysis. This measure varies from 0.0 to ±1.00 with a positive value indicating that small values on one property are matched with small values on the other across the units of analysis, and large with large. A negative value would indicate an inverse relationship (large values on one property associated with small values on the other).

The requirements for a correlational analysis start with interval-level data collected in a repeated-measures design. The unit of analysis provides the common linkage between two properties and justifies examining the properties for a relationship. To understand how correlation works, we will start with two columns of 25 random numbers. The ones I generated are in Table 9.13. Enter these numbers into a spreadsheet and run the "correl" function in order to generate a live measure that changes when the data change. My number set generates a correlation of −.008, about as close to no relationship as one could get. How many numbers would I have to change to get a perfect direct (positive) relationship? As I look at the data set, there are only two matched pairs—pairs 9 and 11. Consequently, I would have to change 23 numbers to get a correlation of +1.00. To put a little icing on the effect, copy the data set and correlation over to an open set of columns or on a new sheet and graph the two columns in a scatter plot graph. It will look like Figure 9.14. Note that only the two matched pairs (1,1 and 4,4) are on the diagonal. Change the values in one column to create matched pairs. When you reach the 13th pair, the correlation will be +.416, and the scatter plot in Figure 9.15 (a single dot can represent multiple pairs) will begin to show something of a linear figure. As you complete matching the pairs, all of the dots will be on the diagonal, and the correlation will be +1.00.

Calculating the inverse relationship is a bit more difficult but also more instructive (funny how it works that way). Make another copy of the original data set with the correlation value. Now, what does the number in column 1, row 1, have to be to create the inverse of 7? Yes, it has to be 1, but what is the inverse of 4 in this situation? Actually, it is another 4. The brilliance of the correlation coefficient is that it is built on the match-up between the relative deviations from their respective means of each element in the pair. In a perfect correlation inverse or not, each element in a pair makes the same relative contribution to the variability of its own set. In a positive correlation, all one has to do is match the numbers to meet that criterion. In an inverse relationship, the matching number has to be the same relative distance from its mean as the criterion is from its own mean. A set of random integers varying from 1 to 7 will have a mean of 4 in whole values. Consequently, the inverse has to be the same distance from 4 as its match. Use the data to demonstrate this rule for yourself.

One way to think about correlations is that they are an index of the shared variability between two sets of scores. As the index approaches 1.00 from either direction, more of the variance is held in common. In fact, if one squares the correlation, the resultant value, called the coefficient of determination (r^2) is the proportion of variance held in common. The coefficient of determination is the best single interpretation of a significant correlation, because it helps to understand just how much knowledge has been gained. With large samples, it is not unusual to see correlations as small as .10 turning up significant. A correlation of .10 returns an r^2 of .01, or 1% of the variance explained and 99% unknown. Given that our language-based measures are inherently correlated, I don't get too excited until the correlations are above .40.

Table 9.13	Correlation Data Set
3	7
6	4
4	3
5	4
7	4
7	4
4	7
1	4
1	1
5	6
4	4
4	1
1	4
4	1
5	4
2	7
2	5
1	4
3	4
5	4
3	7
6	3
7	6
3	4
5	2

Finally, correlation gives us information about the joint variability of two measures taken on a single unit; it gives us no information about the joint means. (Remember the independence between variability and centrality.) Just as it is good practice to run correlations with *t* tests on repeated measures, so, too, is it good practice to run *t* tests on correlations.

Multiple Correlation

The simple binomial correlation can be extended into multiple correlation designs that have multiple independent (predictor) variables and one (most common) or more (rare)

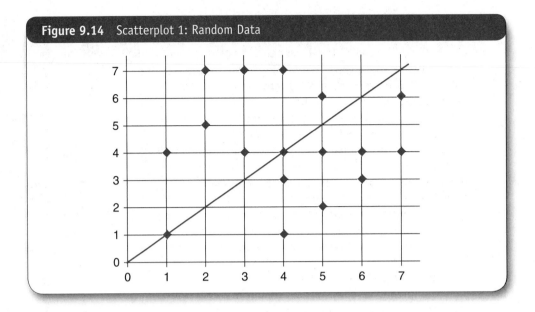

Figure 9.14   Scatterplot 1: Random Data

dependent variables. Multiple regression is better suited to model building, but I am seeing an increasing use of it as a more complex correlation, where the interest is not in predicting the dependent values but simply in showing that there is a relationship. In model building, the presumption is that a model can be built from the independent variables (*X* variables) that will predict the values of the dependent (*Y*) variable, such as knowing certain traits might predict media use. That model is then tested using new data. Relationship testing

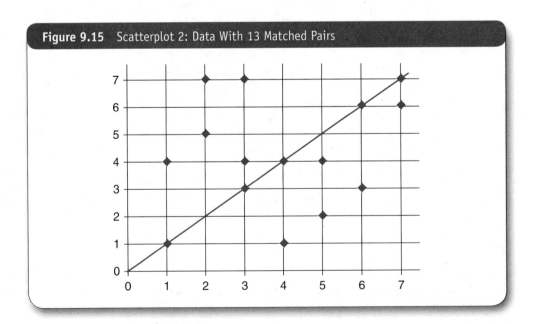

Figure 9.15   Scatterplot 2: Data With 13 Matched Pairs

uses a lower standard in that certain traits only have to be associated with different forms of media use. The multiple R is the correlation across the actual Y-variable value for each respondent and the predicted Y-variable value that would be generated by the independent variables. Again, R^2 (note the capitalization), or the coefficient of multiple determination, is the best single interpretation of the relationship indicating the percentage of variance in the dependent variables explained by the joint information of the independent variables. There is a lot more information in multiple regression than in a significant relationship as we shall see in the next section.

A Peek Into Structure and Modeling

All data matrices contain structure ranging from complete independence to complete inter-relationship. That structure can be marginally planned as it is in most data collections, or it can be hypothesized as is done in structural modeling. This section is a very modest introduction to the methods of investigating and using structure in data matrices. The first subsection looks at investigative and data manipulation procedures, and the second considers the concepts and difficulties of modeling.

Investigation and Manipulation

Data matrices develop when the researcher has multiple observations on each unit of analysis. The standard survey with multiple questions for each respondent produces a data matrix that can be investigated for the structural relationships between and among items. We will very briefly consider two approaches here: the correlation matrix and factor analysis.

Correlation Matrix

The most common approach is the intercorrelation matrix that can display the correlations of every measure with every other measure. Clearly correlation is for interval or higher data, but for investigative purposes, it is not unusual to dump it all in and sort it out later. The intercorrelation matrix for the SNS data was presented in Table 9.4.

The investigation of structure by running the correlation matrix is not a hunting license to find significant results to present. It is rather a means of generating a more sophisticated understanding and explanation of the results of hypothesis testing, an examination of the underlying assumptions of the data, the recommendations for future research, and a recognition of the limits of the research itself.

Factor Analysis

Factor analysis is a structural analysis that is commonly used to collapse multi-item scales into smaller, more robust measurements. Factor analysis is based on the correlation matrix, and it essentially attempts to identify clusters of items that relate to one another but are relatively independent of other clusters. In this manner, a scale of 10 or more items might be reduced to two or three dimensions. Although there are general rules of thumb, factor analysis is not a highly conventionalized procedure and always involves a researcher's judgment in assigning items to a factor, determining the number of factors to extract, and identifying what the factor actually measures. Even such esoteric questions about whether to use orthogonal or oblique rotation are left to the researcher's discretion (always use oblique).

Modeling

Tests of difference and relationship are widely used within our field, but they do not represent the highest level of analysis. For example, the typical effects study shows that certain cognitive states exist after media exposure that did not exist prior to the exposure. Such simple studies provide little information that models how influence works in the nexus of conditions that produce the freedoms and constraints of everyday life. A model providing that information would require a large number of measures collected over a lengthy span of time. The closest we've come to that approach is in experience sampling where respondents are queried via cell phone or PDA to provide a few data points several times throughout the day.

In the absence of adequate theory, sophisticated measures, the technology of continuous data collection, and systems-based statistical procedures, modeling the management of influence remains a goal of the future. Most of the current modeling work makes use of cross-sectional surveys whose measures are entered into either regression analysis or its somewhat more sophisticated sibling, path analysis. Regression analysis considers a linear model connecting independent predictors of a dependent variable. Path analysis is a regression approach that looks at the explanatory effectiveness of a model composed of independent, intermediary, and dependent variables.

Regression Analysis

Regression analysis is the modeling form of binomial and multiple correlation. Linear regression analysis attempts to find the best-fitting straight line that describes the relationship between the independent variable and the dependent variable in binominal regression and between the set of independent variables and the dependent variable in multiple regression. The model is built on the data in hand, but its purpose is not to predict what is already known. The purpose of modeling is to predict the consequences of the presence of certain conditions (the independent variable(s)) on some other condition (the dependent variable).

Whether binomial or multiple, the regression equation is composed of the same three parts: the constant—the value of Y when X is 0 or, in graphing terms, the point where the line intercepts the Y (vertical) axis, the weighted contribution of the independent variable(s), and the resultant predicted Y value. In formula form, the binomial relationship looks like this: $Y = bX + a$, where Y is the predicted Y value; b is the regression or beta weight, also known as the slope (as it determines the angle of the line); and a is the intercept or constant. In multiple regression, the formula just expands to accommodate the additional independent variables. In generalized form, it would look like this: $Y = b_1X_1 + b_2X_2 + b_3X_3 + \ldots + b_nX_n + a$.

The additional analysis in multiple regression involves the extraction and allocation of the information about Y that is shared by the X variables. When the independent variables are correlated both with the dependent variable and with each other, it is likely that some of the information that is provided about Y will be duplicated among the independents. The beta weight in multiple regression analysis reports the unique contribution that each X value makes, assigning the common information to the first X variable encountered. This encounter can be governed by the strategic choice or happenstance of order in the analysis or in a more sophisticated approach by using stepwise analysis that evaluates each independent variable for the strength of its contribution starting with the independent having the greatest simple association (correlation) with the dependent.

Model building is not an end in itself, although it is often treated as such in our literature. A model proves itself valuable by what can be done with it. It would be a very unusual data set that did not show some interrelatedness. Consequently, the formulation of a model in a post hoc analysis is not a highly valued contribution. The statistical support for a model that was hypothesized is a substantial step-up, increasingly so with the increasing specificity of the hypothesis. A supported hypothesized model that demonstrates its predictive value in subsequent data analysis makes the highest contribution.

Path Analysis

The appropriate use of path analysis starts with a model of the relationships among independent, intermediary, and dependent variables. One hopes for a model based on the careful investigation of theory rather than the kitchen sink approach that would assemble whatever variables seem likely. Oftentimes, it is a combination of careful theory with insurance variables added just in case.

For example, Johnson, Bichard, and Zhang (2009) were interested in the selective exposure practices of blog users. They sent an e-mail invitation to 5,000 members of a 20,000-member opt-in consumer panel "operated by a media research lab at a major university in the southwestern United States" (pp. 67–68).[8] They had a 15.4% response rate. The model they used is reproduced in Figure 9.16. In this model, the set of demographics and political variables are the independent variables (there are no arrows of influence pointing to either set), online and offline discussion variables are the first intermediary sets, reliance on political websites is the second-level intermediary set, and selective exposure is the dependent variable. This model is a one-directional model, with no correlation predicted between variable sets (usually shown with double-headed arrows) and no feedback loops: "Should selective exposure affect the political variables?" might be a reasonable question.

The researchers found that respondents who rely on blogs are liberal and highly partisan and "are more likely to seek out blogs that support their pre-established views" (p. 76). The word *liberal* jumped out at me. I wondered if the location of that major university might have some consequence for the findings. Texas Tech is located in Lubbock County, which went 68% Republican in the 2008 presidential election (presumably close to the time of the data collection). Consequently, my question would be "Is selective exposure a function of being politically liberal or a function of being in a clear minority position?" Would the result have been different if conducted at the University of Massachusetts, whose voters

---

[8]Because the researchers are all from Texas Tech, we can probably guess the university.

Figure 9.16   Model Predicting Selective Exposure to Political Blog Sites

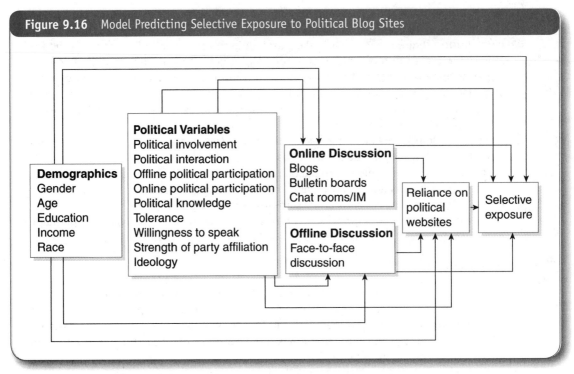

Source: Johnson, Bichard, and Zhang (2009).

went overwhelmingly Democrat? To their credit (and this is a good study), the authors in their discussion of the limitations of the study say, "Future researchers may wish to acquire a larger sample with a more diverse demographic and psychographic profile in order to examine the degree to which people seek out supportive information online and avoid information that challenges their views" (pp. 76–77).

The point of my question is not to second-guess the researchers but to point out that any modeling activity is highly vulnerable to the limitations of variable selection. Had the researchers in this case used a political distance variable (see the box immediately below for one idea), the findings might have been quite different. In fact, any changes in the set of variables would have produced different outcomes. Modeling through path analysis is most effective theoretically when the design compares alternative models to determine which one produces the strongest effects and the clearest explanations.

Please locate your position relative to local opinion:

More liberal								Prevailing				More conservative					
10	9	8	7	6	5	4	3	2	1	0	1	2	3	4	5	6	7	8	9	10

Modeling in any form presents additional problems. It is extremely rare that a proposed model will be supported in all its predicted relationships; it did not happen in the Johnson et al. (2009) study. What does a partially supported model mean? Testing a single model is logically the same as testing a series of hypotheses. A set of hypotheses, taken together, forms an understanding of how things work in the domain of the problem, just as a model does. When only some of the hypotheses are supported, it means that something is wrong—with any or all of the initial understanding, the design, the sample, or the measurement, for example. Although researchers would like to argue that partial support means that they are on the right track, partial support can also mean that the model is fatally flawed or that only some small part of what is happening has been captured. The problem is exacerbated by the fact that in testing a large number of hypotheses, we would expect some to fail—or to be significant—just by chance circumstances. Consequently, it is not the presence of a failure (although I would never accept a model with multiple failed components) but the centrality of the failed hypothesis(es) to the argument that is more important. The issue of partial support has to be resolved on the basis of judgment rather than statistical analysis.

THE ETHICS OF ANALYSIS

The ethical consideration of metric analysis starts with the handling of the data themselves and then ends with them properly meeting the requirements for the analysis. The researcher has a responsibility to preserve all data, record them accurately, prepare them properly for analysis, effectively use the information provided by the respondent, and match data to analysis. The issues surrounding the preservation of data usually concern missing or faulty data as entered by the respondent or as recorded by the researcher. Losing a sheaf of questionnaires is clearly a breach, however. Decision rules for dealing with missing data—blank items on a questionnaire—or faulty data—out-of-range, impossible answers; sabotage; and the like—need to be put in place before the data collection begins in order that the outcome might not sway the decision. It is good practice to test the rules in Monte Carlo analysis to be sure one can live with them.

Transferring data from paper-and-pencil measures to data entry forms always involves some level of error. Quality control checks need to be designed to both correct as much as possible and estimate the remaining error. When possible, data should be collected electronically. Although that eliminates the keyboard error, the process can introduce its own error in the respondent interface or in the transmission of information.

I would hate to have to own up to the number of times, over my career, that I have entered the wrong column of numbers, started on the wrong row, set up a matrix incorrectly, or misread the way an analysis proceeded. Because we know that these errors happen, we are ethically enjoined to set up stringent controls that will identify these errors. Mostly, that involves having secure benchmarks at the descriptive level that are used to certify the more complex analyses.

Researchers need to respect the contribution of the respondent. They do that best when they account for all the data in the reports that emanate from the study. It is a waste of respondent time to collect data that have no value or for which there is no intention to analyze. There is an inherent contract in the data collection that the respondent's work is necessary and valuable.

Last, it is unethical to deliberately mismatch the characteristics of the data with requirements of the analysis. This mismatch most often happens when nominal or ordinal data are entered into analyses that require interval forms. As there is a good deal of latitude in that rule, it becomes a problem when it is not clearly identified to the reader or when the conclusions entirely ignore the mismatch.

MOVING ON

Statistical analysis is the last step before the formal write-up of the findings begins in earnest. The statistical analysis of a study should consider all four of the analytical domains—description, difference, relationship, and structure—as they relate to the five characteristics—dispersion, convergence, distribution, association, and composition—that constitute the analysis of scalar and matrix data. In this chapter, I have argued for a more expansive course than simple hypothesis testing, which often inflicts the analyst with tunnel vision, eliminating further opportunities for insight. I have also argued for a Monte Carlo approach to learning statistical analysis. Many media students do not have the background to intuitively understand the implications of formulas, but most have good computer skills that would allow them to build data sets for testing and learning how an analytical framework operates.

Finally, let me share my enthusiasm for the detective work that all research entails. One of my colleagues remarked that she knew each of her respondents in her large multiple-regression analysis. She did not know them personally; rather, she knew the characteristics of those who fit the model and of those who did not. She could describe the variations of attributes that marked the people in her study. That should be our goal: to extract the greatest amount of information possible.

The next two chapters show the work of developing metric research protocols. A protocol describes the entire research activity from measurement and sampling to data collection and analysis. The next chapter explores survey protocols.

REFLECTIONS

What Are Some Points to Remember?

- A statistic is a characteristic of a data set; statistics are a set of characteristics or the field of study of such characteristics. An inferential statistic is a characteristic of a population inferred from a sample; inferential statistics are a set of characteristics or the field of study of such characteristics.
- Scalar data sets have three major characteristics: dispersion, convergence, and distribution; matrix data sets add association and composition.

- Analysis of these characteristics considers description, difference, relationship, and structure. There are statistical procedures to describe a data set as well as indicate the degree of difference, the strength of relationships, and the structural composition within that data set. These procedures are separate from tests of significance.
- Tests of significance are a method of public decision making concerning the trustworthiness of a population inference that rests on the probability of error in the sample. They do not reveal error or protect the analyst or reader from error.
- Data have to be safeguarded, and when adjustments or corrections have to be made, they must be made by publicly reviewable rules.

Why Does It Matter?

Statistical analysis is the heart of any claim that is supported by metric research. The level of sophistication and trustworthiness of that claim depends on the analyst's understanding, proper application, and full utilization of the tools of analysis.

What Else Could We Talk About?

Statistics in a box, whether as simple as Excel or as complex as SPSS, has allowed the mathematically challenged access to procedures they may not understand. Standard publication practices allow little or no access to the data themselves, even for those who review the manuscripts prior to acceptance. There is an enormous demand for trust and little protection if that trust is not warranted.

What Else Might Be Interesting to Read?

Gonick, L., & Smith, W. (1994). *Cartoon guide to statistics*. New York: HarperCollins. (A serious treatment of the concepts, presented with a humorous touch of cartoons)

C H A P T E R   1 0

Designing Surveys

CHAPTER PREVIEW

What's It All About?

The survey is the most common form of metric protocol. Its primary use is to determine what's "out there" in terms of properties and attributes. This chapter examines the principles of design, the types of survey items, and the formatting of the survey questionnaire. It then considers the components of data collection.

What Are the Major Topics?

Remembering that communication variables are often synthetic composites, this chapter begins by dividing variables into those that infer cognitive states (called behind-the-eyes variables) and those that have a material presence (in-front-of-the-eyes variables).

Three kinds of questionnaire items—statement scales, bipolar scales, and adjectival checklists—are discussed.

Questionnaire items can have different work to do. Items can qualify respondents, provide evidence for hypotheses, collect exploratory information, or provide the data for analyzing different components of the sample. Additional items are often used to describe the sample along demographic and psychographic characteristics.

The format of a questionnaire has to be appealing to the respondent and support accurate and efficient data handling.

The survey instrument has to be connected to some data collection process. The choice of data collection process involves consideration for the accessibility of the respondent, the means of contact, participation, and quality of the response.

The ethics of survey design turn on voluntary participation, informed consent, deception, privacy, confidentiality, anonymity, and honoring the respondent effort.

What Special Terms Are Used?

Categorical data

Co-orientation

Operational definition

Operationalism

INTRODUCTION

Surveys are designed to generate numerical data or discursive information in response to a research problem that requires the description of the properties of some entity or entities.[1] That entity might be a cohort of individuals, a class of activities, types of objects, an influx of technology, and the like. There are two components in survey design—the means of measurement and the methods of data collection.

Because surveys are typically intended to be representational of a larger population, their design is also closely tied to sampling design. Data collection itself can be considered as the last step of sampling, and the first few questions on a survey may be the final qualification of a respondent.

Sampling, data collection, and measurement all interrelate in survey design. It is, however, the measurement of the properties of interest that is actually the most important. Measurement takes precedence because without good measurement, the best sample and the best collection of data have no value. Good measurement, on the other hand, creates value from even the worst sample.

That said, we should note that the level of difficulty is inversely related to the level of importance, because our greatest failure in surveys appears in the return rate—the proportion of the chosen that actually become respondents. Problems in measurement are common but can be approached with careful work. The problems of sampling and data collection are persistent and generally intractable. This chapter starts with the important and works its way to the difficult.

One caveat: What you will not find in this chapter is any reference to SurveyMonkey, eSurveysPro, Zoomerang, SurveyBuilder, or similar free survey design services. These are wonderful services to use once you know what you are doing and why you are doing it. The free side of these services offers prepackaged solutions that may be just

---

[1]Is it a survey, or is it a questionnaire, or is it a survey questionnaire? These devices have some interchangeability. For me, a survey is the protocol marked by the intent to represent, a questionnaire is a data collection instrument, and the survey questionnaire is the data collection instrument in the survey. Questionnaires can be used in different sorts of protocols.

what is needed, but too often the analyst is tempted to substitute what is easy for the work to do it right.

MEASURING PROPERTIES: DEVELOPING CONTENT

The first step in developing survey protocols has to do with what we want to know—what are we going to measure in our survey? Traditional survey methodology starts with the assumption that what we wish to measure has definable boundaries and generalized properties. The purpose of the survey is to discover the edges of the boundaries and the specific values of those properties. I know that the desk at which I write has height, width, and depth (as well as mass and kinetic energy). If I wanted to measure it, I would find the edges and determine how many standardized units (inches or centimeters) would fit between them. In doing so, I would follow the conventions for measuring rectangular objects like a desk.

Understanding Communication Variables

Designing a survey follows much the same process. Our first task is to define the properties we wish to measure and to locate their boundaries. Communication variables often do not have the convenient edges by which to identify where they begin and end. Consequently, we have to define those into existence. We start understanding this process by making a division of whether the variable exists "behind the eyes" (BTE) or in front of the eyes (FTE). BTE variables are all of the postulated cognitive structures of the mind such as attitudes, values, aptitudes, attraction, and the like. These variables are more metaphysical than empirical and can be measured only indirectly, but they are important and practically necessary for the conduct of much of our research. In fact, most surveys are made up of primarily BTE variables.

FTE variables are physical or physiological responses, acts or behaviors, and actions that we can see or are directly measurable at least in some major component. I've ordered that list according to its "empiricalness." The empirical clarity of a reflex, for example, is much higher than the action of reading a textbook. I can connect the tap of the hammer to the movement of the foot with little difficulty and can measure the speed of response, its force, or its range as I could any material movement. The action of reading a textbook is much more difficult. I have to infer intent and define reading, and the action has to be sufficiently competent in its performance to be recognized as such among other tasks. There are, nonetheless, independent, measureable physical acts that constitute the action, which is not the case with BTE variables.

The appeal of BTE variables is unmistakable. They allow us to conduct studies that would otherwise be impossible. For example, in preparation for a journal review, I am reading in an area that concerns the effectiveness of public service announcements (PSAs) promoting safe-sex practices (something I'll never see in Utah—the PSAs, that is). The premise of some of the authors in this field is that there are high and low sensation seekers. High sensation seekers are believed to be more at risk for unsafe sex (and drug) activity.

They should, the argument goes, be targeted by the PSAs. One targets this portion of the audience, according to the researchers, by creating media messages that have a high perceived message sensation value (PMSV; see Palmgreen, Donohew, et al., 1991; Palmgreen, Stephenson, Everett, Baseheart, & Francies, 2002).

This is a standard message effectiveness study. In this study, I count three BTE variables that will manifest their existence only in their measurement: degree of sensation seeking, perceived message sensation value, and message effectiveness. This analysis is not to say that people cannot (or should not) be divided by sensation seeking or that messages are not divisible into more or less sensational and effective. We would generally agree that such divisions are reasonable.

The problem is that we don't know what sensation seeking (or PMSV or effectiveness) is other than in the way we measure it. We are in danger of operationalism that has no empirical content. We have to assume that the scale connects to a constellation of behaviors that have some underlying physiological or cognitive cause. But the "thing" here is not the constellation of behaviors; it is the underlying cognitive source of those behaviors, which under our present abilities is undiscoverable.

The common practical solution is to develop a scale that returns some consistency in item-marking behavior. We then use that consistency to infer that there must be something that generates the consistent response.[2] The payoff comes when we can use the differences the scale generates to explain something else—the something else here being sensation seeking, PMSV, or message effectiveness.

We can certainly develop a scale about any concept we can imagine and put into words. This capability is worrisome to an epistemologist because there are no limits on the number of attitudes, opinions, values, or similar BTE concepts that can be held by people. It is reminiscent of earlier science use of instincts—also unseen—to explain any behavioral sequence. Thousands of such scales have already been developed. It is very good form to use someone else's (with attribution, of course), but it is not difficult to develop one's own. A scale is simply a statement or descriptor—or, much better, a set of statements or descriptors—coupled with a scoring system.

Statement-Based Scales

Historically, there have been three types of statement-based scales, each named after its developer, Louis Leon Thurstone, Louis Guttman, or Rensis Likert. Both Thurstone and Guttman scales require the researcher to develop a very large number of items (up to several hundred) and then have those items evaluated by a panel of judges to sort the items into equal appearing intervals (Thurstone) or into a hierarchical order of increasing or decreasing intensity (Guttman). Likert's process requires a few statements (20 would be unusually high) that can be evaluated as to which should be retained after the data have been collected. I suspect we don't need a scale to determine which is the most popular of the three.

---

[2]The consistency could also be automatically generated based on the requirements of completing the scale. If you check "I like to go to wild parties," you are also likely to check "I like to drive fast," simply because it makes sense that someone would do that.

Yes, you are right; it is the Likert scale, with its familiar agree-disagree scoring system. For example,

I like to go to wild parties.						
Disagree strongly	Disagree	Disagree slightly	Neutral	Agree slightly	Agree	Agree strongly

would be called a 7-point Likert scale.

If we were interested in developing a scale—say, a sensation-seeking scale—what would we do? The first thing, of course, is to do a literature search on "sensation-seeking scale" to see if one has already been developed. My search returned 1,576 entries with scales available in four different languages and tested over multiple topics and respondent groups. At this point, all I have to do is pick one that is a good fit to my study. (The one that has been used with PSAs was adapted from Zuckerman, 1979, 1994, as reported in Hoyle, Stephenson, Palmgreen, Lorch, and Donohew, 2002. It is the basis of the example.)

If a scale is not available, one searches for what others have done in the analysis of the construct. Zuckerman (1979, 1994), for example, considers sensation seeking as composed of thrill and adventure seeking, experience seeking, disinhibition, and boredom susceptibility. Given that analysis as a foundation, it would not be hard to write items that connect to each of the dimensions. Once the items were written, they would have to be pretested to demonstrate their internal consistency and offer some evidence that they are valid measures of sensation seeking. This is a substantial step that is necessary for good research but is often missing in classroom work. Our discussion of reliability and validity in Chapter 5 gives some insight into how that work gets done.[3]

Descriptor-Based Scales

There are two common forms of descriptor-based scales: bipolar adjectival scales popularized in *The Measurement of Meaning* (Osgood, Suci, & Tannenbaum, 1957) and the adjectival checklist (e.g., Merrill & Heathers, 1954). Both of these methods have been more popular than they are now, but they remain in use in interpersonal studies. They still have utility for work in media.

Bipolar scales are paired adjectives that intend to be polar opposites (e.g., *hot* and *cold*). They can be displayed dichotomously (respondents must circle one or the other) or with an interval scale (usually seven steps) in between. The interval scale is preferred as it generates additional information and can be used in more types of statistical analysis.

Adjectival checklists are lists of adjectives that connect to some dimension. For example, the adjectives *noble, strong, alert, active, useful, serious, heroic,* and *honorable* have been considered favorable personality traits in the literature. Adjectival checklists are usually

---

[3]A very quick overview can be had at http://www.statisticssolutions.com/methods-chapter/statistical-tests/reliability-analysis/. Accessed October 25, 2010.

scored as a ratio of adjectives selected from a dimension over the total number of adjectives in the list.

Adjectival scales are most often used to classify external variables (such as a set of television shows) rather than to measure internal cognitive structures, but clearly they work both ways. People who would attach *adventuresome, exciting, experiential*, and similar adjectives to their favorite activities would probably score high on the sensation-seeking scale.

There are some advantages of descriptor-based scales over statement-based scales. They offer fewer interpretive constraints simply because they work with less of a language burden. They are usually faster and easier to complete for the respondent. They do require panel evaluation prior to use, however.

Qualifying, Exploratory, Analytical, and Focal Measures

Surveys routinely ask for information about the respondents, their activities, their environment, and the like—anything from whether they subscribe to a newspaper, to how many television sets they have, to questions about Internet access. These questions can have widely different purposes, however. Qualifying items are the last step in identifying the respondents in a survey, exploratory items anticipate future work, analytical items look to composition and structure in a data set, and focal items are the stuff of the research question or hypothesis. We take them up in that order.

Qualifying Items

Let's start with an example. Let's say you wanted to examine the television viewing habits of cable and satellite subscribers and off-air viewers. There might be some interesting differences among those who pay over $100 per month for television, those who pay half that amount, and those who don't pay at all. There is not a lot in the literature on this question (see Yim, 2003, for an example of what does appear). This absence follows the trend that we know little about actual audiences except as provided by the commercial interests. Getting a baseline on this issue now might help us understand future changes in video such as a projected change to a music model where one buys programs instead of "watching television."[4] That change has substantial implications for content development, effects research, and family dynamics, not to mention the changes in the industry.

It seems fairly easy to come up with definitions of these classes of viewers (even with certain anomalies like cable service piracy). The method of incorporation might take more effort. Lists of cable and/or satellite subscribers are not ordinarily available. One could certainly go cable drop, dish, and antenna hunting, but it is probably easier to sort respondents as part of the contact process, which itself might include telephone, door-to-door, or Internet methods. To be included in the survey, respondents would have to "qualify" by meeting the definition of one of the classes.

Interestingly, a few days after writing those comments, I was contacted by the A. C. Nielsen Company of TV ratings fame for a telephone interview on my television choices. The caller

---

[4]This is already the model in my household in that we watch almost exclusively what we record, can download, or have available on DVD (see Wolf, 2007).

had a soft, mid-South drawl; was very engaging; and fully identified himself and the company. After collecting information on the types of shows household members were likely to watch, the interview was terminated because there was no one of "Latino or Hispanic" origin in the household. The company was "qualifying" respondents, and we didn't fit.

Exploratory Items

Exploratory items are those that anticipate another study. Their purpose is to gather the necessary information for the construction of another protocol that will move to some conclusion. Exploratory items are not designed to do the heavy work of supporting a claim. The researcher has a slightly lessened responsibility. But even these simple questions have to be carefully crafted. For example, if you were to ask me, "How many television sets do you have?" I would wonder what you were really asking, because I would assume you were not actually interested in the couple of CRTs I've got out in the storage shed. You might be interested in how many television sets I regularly use, which is a much smaller number than the number I have. If you are interested specifically in ownership, then technically I don't own any, as it is all joint ownership.

You might be confusing ownership with control. In my household, certain programs get recorded on certain DVR-set combinations because of conflicts of interest and program times. In the television pragmatics of this household, one set is "hers," and the other is "mine." In other households, individuals may have purchased their own set or watch television on their computer, cell phone, or player. That simple question—"How many television sets do you have?"—is fraught with multiple possibility and might be better asked in a series of questions that drill down through the alternatives.

The moral is that the researcher has to be quite knowledgeable about what is possibly out there to design even simple-appearing questions. Certainly, as a respondent, I will figure out an answer appropriate to the question. But my solution may not be another respondent's solution, and neither may correspond to the information the researcher actually wants.[5] These differences generate a significant source of error that most often goes undetected. Developing competent survey instruments requires careful work.

Analytical Items

Analytical items are used to search or to test for differences or relationships across different conditions. In our qualifying-item example of subscription television versus off-air television, the measure of how one gets the television signal could also be an analytical item. The power of the protocol (its ability to detect relationships or differences) and the validity of the conclusions depend on the quality of the analytical items. Analytical items that don't make clear distinctions or do not clearly distinguish the way the researcher thinks they do lead to the failure of significance or to faulty conclusions. Analytical items call for a sophisticated analysis because there can be complex issues attached to seemingly simple

---

[5]To complete the story, the number of sets I have (as a representative of the household) is 9; the number that are hooked up for use is 7; the number we normally use over a week's time is 3; the number in daily use is 1.

differences.[6] In our subscription television example, the researcher may consider that increasing levels of service means an increasing level of interest in or of the centrality of television. That analysis is insufficient on at least two dimensions: It does not account for the costs of subscription, so a basic subscription might not mean low interest; and it assumes that both off-air and subscription services are available to all. Neither assumption is true. Consequently, asking simply if one subscribes and then concluding about interest would be a vulnerable protocol because of inadequate care in design.

Focal Items

Focal items are those that are the criterion measure for a research question or hypothesis. They are the result of a line of argument that starts in the researcher's interests, moves through the literature, and arrives on the survey as the defensible operational definition that will support the major claim of the research. Focal items demand our highest level of work. They have to map the world (or at least the analyst's part of it) in a manner that validates one's claim. If one's argument is that subscribers to a television service use television in ways that are different from those of off-air viewers, the first task is to conceptualize the ways in which that difference will and will not appear. That conceptualization has to match initial interests, be supported by the literature, and be advanced and verified through pretesting. I don't think I can overemphasize the importance of quality work when designing focal items. If they fail or are dismissible in argument, then the researcher has wasted his or her time and resources as well as the time and effort of the respondents.

Demo- and Psychographics

Demographic and psychographic items take the measure of our respondents. Demography is the study of the characteristics of a population. In surveys, demographics generally refer to the material properties of the individual such as age, sex, race, ethnicity, and location. Demographic survey items attempt to gather the characteristics of the set of respondents (perhaps to draw inferences about a population they might represent).

Psychography is the writing about the inner self (as when I share my inner feelings with you, dear reader). Psychographic items attempt to measure the attitudes, opinions, values, and similar inner characteristics of those respondents (and the population they represent). (The sensation-seeking scale can be considered a psychographic measure.) The term *demographics* is often used to cover both inner and outer characteristics.

It is rare to be equally interested in all members of a population. The careful specification of *who* we want and *who* we can get helps us to be efficient in our data collection and analysis, on the one hand, and reminds us of our limitations, on the other. Our interests in who we want are directed toward understanding the qualifications of people who can give us useful answers. Useful answers are ones that are under the governance of the research problem. The principal way we specify *who* is in demographic and psychographic questions.

---

[6]Does the researcher know, for example, that cable Internet subscribers are also required to carry a basic cable subscription and yet may never use it?

There seem to be two polar approaches to these items in research practice: Ask everything one can think of because one never knows what might be useful, or ask only those things for which there is good reason to believe they make a difference. I'm not a big fan of fishing expeditions mainly because the analyst will find differences and then will be required to give an explanation for the difference. If the analyst didn't have a reason for asking the question in the first place, where will the reason for the difference be found?

There is a larger ethical issue than just speculation-standing-for-information because, when we do attribute found differences across age, sex, race, ethnicity, and similar items to an extrinsic condition of age, sex, race, ethnicity, and similar items, without the needed justification, we participate in the stereotyping of individuals in those categories. Our research becomes ageist, sexist, racist, and otherwise problematic as a result. And no, we are not just reporting objective findings because we are in charge of the attribution (see Anderson, 1996, Chapter 8, for this argument).

At the other pole, if the analyst hasn't done adequate prestudy, then some important difference is likely to be missed. The analyst won't know what it is that is missed, of course, except in the curious variability that will appear in the data. It's this fear that pushes folks to the other side, but I still hold to the stronger ethical position.

In a similar practice, researchers often have a set of demographics items that they routinely append to the survey. There is some value to this approach because over multiple surveys the researcher learns how these classifications interact with different criterion measures. That deliberate approach leads to meta-analyses that can make valuable contributions. The mindless cutting and pasting of demographics from the last survey, however, is a poor practice that can lead to worse practices. The worst of these is taking a found difference and promoting it as theoretically substantive.

The point of putting the demographics in the survey is that we hope to find differences across the categories, but when we do so without any basis for understanding the mechanism that creates the differences, we quickly fall into post hoc reasoning. This is the sort of Monday-morning prognosticating that explains elections after they have been held. Anybody can create an explanation after the fact. Good metric research establishes the reasons for what happens before it happens.

We usually find the demographic and exploratory items at the end of the survey. Demographic items often represent information of personal identity that evokes a refusal to participate. Exploratory items may seem needlessly lengthy or irrelevant. We stick them at the end to keep the respondent engaged as long as possible. The one study I found on this question (Giles & Feild, 1978) found no significant effect on return rate, so this rule may be unsupported wisdom, but like many such rules, one is reluctant to take the risk of violating it. If you have good reason, stick the items where they make sense.

Giles and Feild (1978) did find that the way the researcher asks the question on sensitive issues did make a difference on response bias—the likelihood that the answer given represented the true value. Requesting continuous values (one's actual age, for example) resulted in higher levels of response bias (giving a false answer) than asking for categorical values (18–24, 25–30, etc.). Constructing the categories has to be thoughtfully done, however. A category cannot span a suspected break point in the data. If the researcher is interested in the effects of PSAs on alcohol use, for example, an age category of 18–24 would appear to mask important information in an age-21 requirement state.

Format

Format deals with the way one asks the question. Good formats reduce respondent error, frustration, and bias (that euphemism for deceptive responses) and collect the information in a way that is appropriate to and simplifies the process of analysis. Items are often classified as open or closed format, which corresponds to short-answer or multiple-choice items. Format is much more, however. It refers to layout, typography, font size and emphasis, use of color, symbols, and other graphics. It manages the distinctions among instructions, questions or items, and responses. It anticipates any necessary scoring and the process of entering the data into analysis. There is a lot to think of, and there is no one-size-fits-all answer. The goal is a format that is easy to engage, maintains the respondent's attention, provides all the necessary information for a response when and where it is needed, minimizes reading and registration (lineup) errors, uses space well, provides adequate space for answers, and supports data handling and entry (see next heading).

Although I can give you no hard-and-fast rules, I can recommend that you use the list above as a checklist to specify each design requirement and approach taken in the instrument. Then go look at the hundreds of examples of formatted items and questionnaires that are available on the Internet.[7] There is a lot of good work out there, but know what you need before you search, and pretest, pretest, pretest the draft design.

Anticipating Analysis and Data Handling

Throughout the drafting process, the researcher should be considering how the data are going to be prepared for analysis and the analytical framework the data will support. In thinking about the relationship between the items and the analysis, one starts with the research questions (RQs) and hypotheses. RQs and hypotheses, while allowing some latitude, will generally have a best fit across categorical, ordinal, or interval data. The researcher needs to check that the focal and analytical items that are to be used in testing these questions and hypotheses meet the requirements of those research questions and hypotheses. It's not uncommon that they don't. It's a mistake made by beginning and experienced researchers alike that can be avoided by matching the hypothesis to the items to check their correspondence. I do recommend that the survey designer mark each item as to its type (qualifying, exploratory, analytical, or focal), the RQ or hypothesis to which it is connected, and the analytical method in which it will be placed. I would put that last sentence in flashing neon if I could.

Any data that are collected on paper—whether a mail, door-to-door, or group collection survey—will have to be entered into the computer for analysis. Simple techniques like using a layout that tracks easily so that your eye moves directly to the next item, leaving wide margins for scoring (transferring the scale value to a number), grouping the items by content and then by scoring system, using a layout and construction that simplifies paper handling, providing sufficient space for actually writing a response to an open-ended

---

[7]A couple at random are http://www.customerthink.com/blog/guidelines_writing_effective_questionnaire and http://www.questionpro.com/images/Online-Research-Handbook.pdf. Both accessed April 23, 2011.

Figure 10.1 Usability Questionnaire

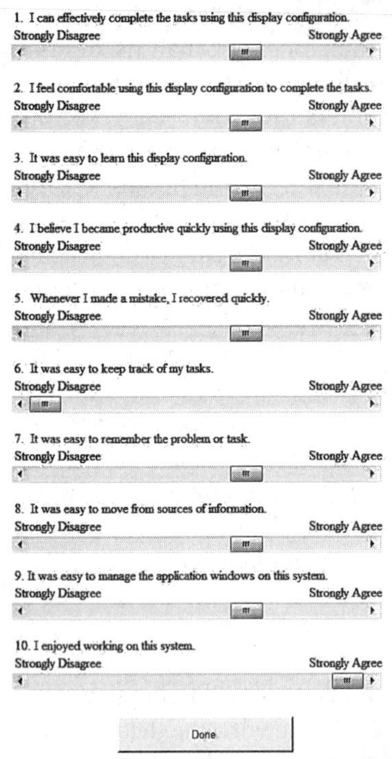

question that can be read (if you want to save trees, don't use paper), using definitive response collectors (circles, boxes, brackets), and pretesting the process will save a great deal of time and frustration as well as reduce errors.

Data entry can be automated by collecting responses on machine-scored response forms, through some midlevel programming in Excel (see Figure 10.1), and/or handheld devices (Palm Pilots, some smartphones, and dedicated devices) that will enter the data directly into a computer format.

These are more costly but certainly preferable to doing it by hand. That is not to say that direct computer entry is without error. In fact, computer entry creates untraceable and often undetectable errors because they happen at the point of entry (mistakenly selecting the wrong response, for example) or because the program does something unexpected by the researcher (treating blanks and zeros as the same, for example). Again the best recourse is to pretest the process, attempting to mimic the common conditions such as skipping an item, selecting the wrong response (can you change it?), and the like.

METHODS OF DATA COLLECTION

We turn now to the second component of survey design, the methods of data collection. Data collection is one of the many steps of a survey, but it is also the last step of the sampling procedure. In sampling design, the analyst specifies the target population, the sampling frame by which potential respondents will be identified, and the particular targets from that frame. Data collection manages the actual contact with the respondent (or other entity of interest). The success of data collection is measured across the accessibility of the respondent, the means of contact, gaining and sustaining participation, and assessing the quality of that participation. Guess what? Our discussion of each follows.

Accessibility

Good sampling procedures and the careful design of demographic and psychographic measures go a long way toward establishing who is included in the survey. Who is not there is often not a research decision but one determined by the accessibility of the individual. Accessibility is established by four factors: the skills and resources of the researcher, the availability and willingness of the respondent, the relationship between researcher and respondent, and the technology of contact.

It may seem strange to start a discussion on respondent accessibility by considering the researcher, but if one wishes to explore the media habits of first-generation Tongan immigrants in Salt Lake City, that researcher had better be able to speak Tongan or pay for interpreters. Language skills, funds for door-to-door contact or long-distance calling, and even the ability to utilize technology all affect the researcher's ability to access a respondent group.

Respondent availability functions at both the group level and the individual level. There are many respondent groups from vulnerable populations to proprietary memberships that pose high barriers to access. While overselection coupled with qualifying items can overcome some barriers, others remain impenetrable.

At the individual level, most research participation has to be enacted on a voluntary basis. People cannot be coerced into participating (certain exceptions apply, especially in proprietary research). The failure to participate may run as high as 90% in mail surveys, and returns of 40% on the initial attempt would be considered high with any method of contact.

The relationship between the researcher and the respondent can greatly alter accessibility. In my household, we screen all calls and do not answer the phone unless we recognize the caller. If an analyst wants to use our time and our resources to advance his or her goals, we better know something about them. It approaches naïve arrogance to believe that others would be interested in something just because the analyst is interested. If the time and resources of others are needed, those others need to be invested in the project. The researcher accomplishes this relationship by building the relationship through adequate publicity about the study and what it will accomplish. In short, avoid cold contacts; build the relationship first.

Finally, accessibility is governed by the availability of the technology of contact. As short as 10 years ago, we could assume that 90% of the households would be accessible by a landline telephone. With the percentage of cell phone–only households increasing, that number has dropped another 15%–20%, standing at 70%–75% of households (including the 10% without any service), and my expectation is that it will continue to decline. Why does this matter? For the present, landline phones are considered the household phone—anyone in the household can be reached at that number. Cell phones are considered individual phones. Yes, they can be passed, but then you are using my minutes to contact someone else. Cell phone-only households are on a steep growth trajectory, which will only make it more difficult to use telephonic means of contact.

Internet access is currently reported at 75% of all U.S. households, which for its part greatly increases the value of that means of contact. Three cautions: First, not everybody who has Internet access uses it. Extrapolating from National Telecommunications and Information Administration data, about 60% of the 75% do use it and about 85% of the 60% make use of e-mail.[8] Second, access to the Internet is not equally distributed. It breaks across race (do you really think the genetic constellations we call race are the source of this difference?), income, age, and, perhaps surprisingly, number of parents in the home. And, third, about 85% of all e-mail can be considered spam. Nonetheless, the Internet is rapidly

---

[8]Starting with a population of 300 million individuals living in households, 225 million have Internet access in the household, 135 million use it, and about 115 million use e-mail. The total population would include 21 million children under 5 and 38 million persons over 65 years of age; both groups are least likely to use the Internet. All of these numbers will undoubtedly increase. You should update them with an Internet search.

becoming the technology of choice. The percentage of spam, however, puts a premium on the relationship with the respondent.

Accessibility and the question of who is not included is not just an issue in design. It has real consequences for our science. First, the research we read in our journals is very ethnocentric. A very slight fraction involves other nationalities, different language groups, different economic systems, different media systems, and different political systems from the United States. Nearly all we know about media is U.S. bound, with some small additional portion from English-speaking, Western cultures. All too rarely do we acknowledge that limitation. The exclusions, however, don't stop there. People without phones, Internet service, and/or household addresses are routinely excluded. People who cannot speak English or who speak English and Spanish are excluded because the researcher cannot speak the language of the respondent. People who refuse to participate never show up. One's research will be located in some subset of U.S. culture. It is important to understand who is not there and why.

Gaining and Sustaining Participation

As vice chair of the institutional review board that approves all University of Utah research that involves human subjects, I see a substantial proportion of the research done there. As the annual renewals come in, the reason for the failure to complete a study in the expected time is more often than not the underaccrual of respondents. Getting people to participate is a very big problem. We see it directly in the return rates of surveys, which, if they top 40%, is cause for celebration. But it is also hidden in the necessity of research classes to require participation in a study in order to gain credit for the course (considered coercive by many) and in the difficulty in filling the ranks of subjects in experiments, even where payments in the hundreds of dollars would be offered.

A related problem is the dropout rate where the respondent fails to complete the survey, leaves the experiment in progress (no, you can't lock the door), or leaves responses blank (all responses are voluntary, remember)—also called missing data. As researchers, it is easy to blame our respondents for this problem, but it is probably more useful to consider our protocol design as the source of these difficulties. Really, we can't do anything about the choices our respondents make, but we can do a lot to make our surveys more inviting, more intelligent, and less frustrating. In print-based or web-based surveys, pay attention to the basic principles of design, typography, and the use of color. In telephone and door-to-door surveys, be careful of items that have long-response forms—a seven-step agree-disagree response, for example. Researchers usually require each step to be read for each item. By the fifth time you have intoned in that singsong voice of standardization, "Do you strongly agree, agree, agree slightly, neither agree nor disagree, slightly disagree, disagree, or strongly disagree with this statement?" many have hung up or closed the door.

Provide escape choices when there is any chance of a legitimate alternative to the elements you have provided. Unless you are sure you have covered every alternative, provide a "Not Applicable" or "Other" escape. Researchers usually prefer "Other" followed by a probe for what the other is as the escape because it can generate useful information.

Justify the request for what is considered to be private or sensitive information (age, income, etc.). Telling the respondent that it is "just for classification purposes" or that "all information is confidential" indicates that it is either not very important (so, why should he or she tell you?) or very important (so, why should he or she tell you?). A more useful approach might be "People in different walks of life prefer different kinds of services. We would like to provide the services that you want. Please take a moment to complete these categorical items." Be sure to ask only for information for which you have some theoretical or action justification. Don't be a voyeur.

Before going to the field with any survey instrument, pretest, pretest, and pretest the instrument again using the same conditions that you will use in the field. It is advice given by all the texts and too often ignored. It is true that it adds time and expense to the process, but it is far less expensive than a failed set of items.

Ensuring and Testing Quality Responses

Our convenient research myths include the beliefs that respondents understand every item as we do, are as committed to the study agenda as we are, and always tell the truth (except when we catch them in a lie). I suspect that such beliefs are not justified and can be quite harmful to the quality of our research. The defense against the harm comes in good communication practices. These practices require adequate framing, repeated co-orientation, and a sustained relationship.

Framing

It is not unusual in survey development to just start writing items. The writer has done some preliminary thinking and is ready to go. One item leads to another, and without much notice the writer is deep inside some conceptualization of the problem. Unfortunately, the respondent often has none of that framework available for understanding what is written. My reading of practices is that there are two misconceptions in play. The first misconception is that it is possible to write items that read themselves (are literally referential) and need no contextual support. The second is that providing the contextual support will necessarily bias the respondent. The first is patently false, and the second is not necessarily so.

The tighter we can frame our research questions, the more closely can we specify the information that we need to collect. In our "subscription versus off-air audience" example, our research question is vague—we expect differences to occur across viewing, which in turn may have consequences for the uses that viewing has. We can speculate what those differences might be and design a questionnaire based on that speculation. It is an efficient way to collect information but not a good way to gain knowledge.

The reason it is not a particularly good way to gain knowledge is that we are practically assured of getting differences. The groups are different at the start. Our basis for understanding the additional differences we reveal, however, is only our initial speculation. Research like this is fairly common, but it would be much better to approach the question incrementally from an increasing base of information by using methods initially that are more grounded in the conditions rather than our speculations. Before designing a survey to be administered to a large number of respondents, the researcher should be systematically talking to a sizeable number of representatives from the study groups either in long-form interviews or in focus groups. Both of those methods (described more fully below) are conversations targeted on the topics of interest but open to the directions the respondents want to go. These conversations will provide much better specifications for the information that should be collected in the survey. They might allow us to develop hypotheses to add to our theoretical knowledge as well.

You might wonder why that is not the standard procedure for developing survey instruments. Its absence has a little to do with the impatience of the researcher, but more to do with all the nonscience reasons research entails—time, money, resources. It is quicker, cheaper, and easier to just speculate on what the measurements ought to be. Unfortunately, it is much more expensive in terms of time, money, and resources in the long run when the data are not particularly useful. For example, in an examination of the differences between service subscribers and off-air viewers, we discovered in our prestudy that the visible presence of the dish was an issue in the way that it marked the inhabitants of the house as a "certain kind of people" for a "certain kind of people." We never would have anticipated that moral dimension of difference without an adequate prestudy.

Framing has its counterpart on the respondent's side of the survey as well. The respondent's task in answering a questionnaire is to create the fit between what she or he does, feels, thinks, or opines and the items designed to measure those conditions. Cognitivists call this the creation of a pragmatic meaning, and social action theorists say it is embedding the sign in the action. The more information the researcher can provide the respondent about the intent of the items, the more consistently that meaning can be formed across respondents. Good practice is to group the items by content and to provide an introduction to each section—something like "The next five items measure how secure you feel about your children's use of the Internet as it affects their potential for exposure to harmful content and overall moral lifestyle. Each item has a 10-point security scale ranging from 0 (*not at all secure*) to 10 (*very secure*)." Framing sets of questions in this manner forces the analyst to commit to the meaning of the questions and to interpret the answers received in accordance with that meaning. It also allows the respondent some context by which to understand how these items are intended to be read.

Co-orientation

Framing creates a common border of understanding or the contextual domain of communication. Co-orientation directs our attention to the elements, topics, or other issues that are addressed within that context and works to specify the element that the item intends to measure for both the researcher and the respondent. For example, co-orientation in the item on Internet safety might read something like "Thinking now about your child's Internet practices and excluding schoolwork." By specifically framing and co-orienting items, we, as researchers, reach a deeper understanding of what we are measuring and explicitly accept the level of ambiguity we cannot or choose not to resolve. We also hope that we put a greater percentage of the respondents on the same page.

Sustained Relationship

Barbara Johnstone (1991), in her analysis of in-person surveys, points out that the standard advice of textbooks is to work for relational neutrality, but the actual practice of those charged with collecting the information is full of relational tactics and strategies. (Research advice has many of these disconnections.) Clearly, all communication has to occur inside some sort of relationship, and it is probably also true that the character of that relationship is going to affect the quality of the information that one receives. Finally, it is also true that the relationship is a coconstruction—no one party controls what that relationship will be. The result of these factors is that it is not possible to produce a nonvalenced relationship— that is, one that has no effect on the outcomes.

That argument, plus the very small amount of research we have on this issue, suggests to me that we ought to be going into the field with the knowledge that in-field interpretations will be called for by respondents and should be given. We should also go with the presumption that we are asking a favor of our respondents when we ask them to participate and should treat them in that manner. The design of our text- or web-delivered surveys should attempt strategies to achieve similar goodwill.

To some extent, this is contrarian advice, but it runs contrary to practices that often see respondents as marks to be manipulated through compliance gaining and resistance reduction strategies or through forms of deception rather than treating them as collaborators in the research process. Remember that, as we are academic researchers, our respondents are volunteers who have full rights to informed consent. The informed part of that consent is not what the analyst can get away with or the means for lulling the respondent into submission. Proprietary research, while not under the threat of government action, is nonetheless equally bound by this ethical principle.

It is also contrary to the "I know best, and I know what's best for you" attitude that sometimes infects researchers who get angry with or dismissive of respondents who apparently don't understand some item despite its clarity and brilliance. That attitude prevents us from learning from the problems that our respondents have with our survey instruments. Researchers who do not collect information on the data collection process put their heads in the sand.

Let's go from sermonizing to summarizing this section on ensuring the quality of our respondents' efforts. Data collection is not iron mongering; it is a communication process. As such, it involves the moment-by-moment effort to maintain a common frame of understanding in which the communicant can co-orient to some common element. That co-orientation is not the independent focus of the individuals but occurs within a relationship. It is not until the frame, co-orientation, and relationship are in place that the final piece—the content—makes sense. The whole thing looks something like Figure 10.2.

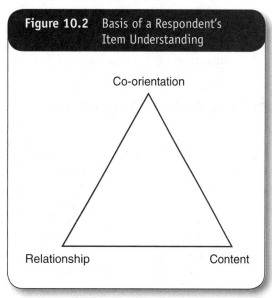

Figure 10.2   Basis of a Respondent's Item Understanding

Co-orientation

Relationship

Content

Our efforts to produce quality responses have to begin with the work required to produce good communication practices.

Testing Quality

The question then arises as to how we know if we have done our job in producing the conditions that allow that quality to appear. A simple way is to ask. I usually include a few open-ended questions at the end of the survey that inquire about the process itself—something like "At any time during this survey did you feel that you could not give the answer that best described your situation?" "Were there any issues that you felt were missed?" "Do you have any recommendations for making this survey better?" (Positive responses evoke follow-ups, of course.) If you immediately get consensus on a problem in the survey, you can fix it. You will have to treat that group of respondents as part of the pretest and perhaps increase your respondent pool, but that is better than having an unknown problem in all the responses.

Researchers will sometimes include more than one question that ostensibly measures the same thing for the purpose of checking to see if the respondent is telling the truth (a different practice from using multiple questions to cover an issue). There are some difficulties with this approach. First, there has to be considerable pretesting to ensure that indeed the items are measuring the same thing. Even if the analyst repeats the same question, the context of the second question is different from the first, which does change its meaning. Second, what does the analyst do if the answers are different?

The practice of using multiple questions to cover an issue, however, seems to have real value for the quality of the response. Most of the things that we ask questions about have multiple components or facets. By having several items that take slightly different orientations on the issue, the analyst clarifies the topic for the respondent (and the researcher) and generates additional information as well. If the respondent is actually giving random responses, the errors will cancel each other out. If the respondent is deliberately lying and sustains the lie over the several items, the pattern is quite noticeable. (Of course, then there is the question as to what to do about it.) Incorporating multiple items is a very useful technique. The research is at risk if only one item is used.

THE ETHICS OF SURVEY DESIGN

Even seemingly neutral activities such as survey design immerse the researcher in ethical considerations. There are at least four issues to consider: voluntary response; informed consent and deception; anonymity, privacy, and confidentiality; and honoring the respondent's effort.

Most academic research is under the supervision of a local institutional review board, mandated by federal regulation but with a great deal of local autonomy as we have seen. It is common practice among these boards to require that all participation in research be on a voluntary, uncoerced basis. Generally, that is translated to mean that a respondent is free to end his or her participation at any time and may also refuse any part of the study, including answering specific questions. Collecting data under conditions that reduce that freedom—such as the classroom—comes in for special scrutiny, a topic we will consider at some length in a later chapter. For now, we meet this issue in forced-choice questions in online surveys that do not allow for skipped questions.

In online, forced-choice questions that have no escape alternative, the respondent whose real answer does not appear has two choices: abandon the survey or produce a fake answer. The respondent who does not wish to provide an answer has those two choices and the choice of providing the actual answer despite an unwillingness to do so. The situation becomes coercive when there is some heightened value to completing the survey. That value reduces the voluntary character of the participation. An oft-heard response to this concern is "So what? It's just a questionnaire." True—no animals will be harmed—but if the researcher is that cavalier about his or her respondents, why should we trust the data and the analysis?

The failure to provide an escape alternative (e.g., *not sure, no answer, not applicable*) is difficult to justify from a respondent's perspective. It can be read as the researcher elevating his or her goals over the rights of the respondent. I don't want to push the issue too hard here because there is relatively little harm, but the principle is worth remembering.

We meet a similar principle in the issue of informed consent and deception. Most survey deception is of the purposeful-omission sort where the researcher fails to disclose what the survey is really about or in some way fails to provide the information needed to make a decision appropriate to the respondent's circumstances. I recently participated in a telephone survey that promised just a few questions on my Internet use. The caller had the right credentials, so I agreed. Thirty questions later, I hung up, just as he was getting to the good stuff. Thirty is not a few; he completely lost my trust through his deceptive approach.

Anonymity, privacy, and confidentiality are three different elements in a constellation of a respondent's rights to his or her personal information. Anonymity means that no one, not even the researcher, can connect the information with the person. Anonymity is not the same as de-identified data, where the person and the data are connected initially but then the identity information is discarded, or as identity-protected data that has the survey information in one location and personal identity information in another; the connection, however, remains in place. Respondents cannot ethically be promised anonymity if de-identified or identity-protected designs are used. Anonymity can be breached in other ways as well: Computers have signatures, and if that information is collected (or returned), it is possible to trace a respondent. Increasingly detailed information about respondents can permit identification of the individual, particularly in small samples. And, of course, there are all the deliberate techniques of identity snatching as well.

Privacy involves the respondent's right to keep personal information personal and to be free from unwarranted intrusions into privacy. Privacy deals with whether the researcher is justified in asking the personal question in the first place. What is personal depends on the individual's sense of privacy, the cultural values in play, the relationship between the respondent and the researcher, and the benefit or harm that may accrue to the respondent. Clearly, the researcher cannot always know what will be considered private (another reason for escape alternatives), which does not discharge the deliberate evaluation of the issue.

Researchers sometimes confuse privacy and confidentiality, claiming that they will keep the information private and not tell anyone else. If the researcher knows, then the information is no longer private, but it may be held in confidence. Confidentiality has to do with access to and use of the data, not its privacy, which is lost when the identifiable respondent answers the question. Confidentiality guarantees that access to and use of the data will be limited by some set of rules. In practice, confidentiality means that those with access to the data, from collection to analysis to reporting the results, will make no additional use of the data beyond their research responsibilities. The data are not the source of lunchtime stories, and the recorded questionnaires are not just tossed in a trash can.

The final ethical issue in this list is honoring the respondent's effort. This rather virtuous language points to a responsibility of the researcher to meet both the explicit and the implied expectations of the respondent that the answers have value and will be used in the research toward some good end. It assumes that each item has a purpose that advances the research; every item has a place in the analytical framework and plays some role in the conclusions—in short, the survey has been competently designed. When we as researchers stray from that expectation by junking up the survey with extraneous items, we're susceptible to some well-deserved criticism.

There is another side, however, and that is to use the information that has been provided in competent ways. The "Other" alternative provides a good example. "Other" calls for the respondent to produce a written alternative to the ones provided. Sometimes it is used as an escape alternative by the researcher and gets coded as simply "Other," but at the same time the respondent thinks he or she is actually telling the researcher something. That is a minor disconnect. More serious is when the researcher either does not want or does not have the ability to analyze language-based responses (or whatever the form).

There is one last consideration here: What happens when the respondent's effort does not appear to be worth honoring? Instances that appear to be deliberate sabotage—contradictory answers, answers that form a graphic pattern, or impossible answers, for example—are not uncommon, particularly in paper-and-pencil collections. Can we throw those questionnaires out? My answer is "Yes, we can." We can do that, however, only by a prior set of rules that governs our acceptance of the response set. Those rules will vary according to the data collection, they need to be put in place prior to data analysis, and one cannot capriciously decide when an answer counts and when it does not.

MOVING ON

In this chapter, we looked at protocol design for generating numerical information about the properties of entities. In the next chapter, we look at how to design experiments to test questions of cause and consequence.

REFLECTIONS

What Are Some Points to Remember?

- Survey protocols are developed in response to a research problem that requires the analyst to represent the properties of some population, predominantly through the use of numerical data.
- The design of surveys starts with the specification of who (or what) is to be represented. This specification aims at achieving clear, distinct boundaries of membership with good separation from others.
- Our methods of contact (in-person, telephone, Internet, mail) almost always involve some compromise between what we want and want we can get. Further compromises occur in our efforts to get and to sustain participation. All of these compromises make some sort of difference, of course, but the differences are unknown and uncontrollable.
- Even the best methods of contact and strategies for participation will come to naught without the careful design of the data collection instrument (survey questionnaire). Again this process starts with the research problem, moves to the good specification of what we want to measure, and then moves to exploring the tools we have for its measurement and even developing them if necessary.
- Good measurement requires us to anticipate the circumstances of the variables to be measured and to specify the rules of measurement in order to return consistent values. Some of those rules are encoded in the way we format the questionnaire. Formatting helps the respondent return good information to the researcher and helps the researcher preserve the data as given by the respondent.
- Resist the temptations of the free survey design services until you have done the analysis, measurement design, layout, and pretesting on your own.
- The analyst is ethically required to provide for voluntary participation; to eliminate coercive methods; to achieve and preserve informed consent in surveys; to consider the issues of anonymity, privacy, and confidentiality; and to honor the effort of the respondent by attending to all the information provided in a careful and thorough manner.

Why Does It Matter?

Surveys are the most widely used protocol in both academic and industry research. It is the most likely form of research that a beginning analyst would conduct. Doing it well counts.

What Else Could We Talk About?

The typical newspaper report of a survey will include a line about the accuracy of the survey—something like "This survey has an error range of ±4%." What is being reported is the confidence interval that describes the likely range of the population characteristic given a perfectly executed random sample of the population of respondents. Of course, we know there is no such thing. We know that some portion of the individuals to be sampled were unreachable, some refused to participate, some were incompetent, and some gave false responses. Some analysts claim that the accuracy of a widely reported survey lies in its ability to create the conditions it reports as existing.

What Else Might Be Interesting to Read?

Babbie, E. R. (2010). *The practice of social research* (12th ed.). Belmont, CA: Wadsworth.

Dillman, D. A., Smyth, J. D., & Christian, L. M. (2009). *Internet, mail and mixed-mode surveys: The tailored design method.* New York: Wiley.

Rennekamp, R. A. (n.d.). *Documenting practice change with mailed questionnaires.* Retrieved April 23, 2011, from http://www.ca.uky.edu/agpsd/toolbox4.pdf

Sudman, S., & Bradburn, N. M. (1982). *Asking questions: A practical guide to questionnaire design.* San Francisco: Jossey-Bass.

CHAPTER 11

Protocols for Experiments

CHAPTER PREVIEW

What's It All About?

Experiments are the method of choice when testing questions or hypotheses that involve causation—the effect of one variable on another. Experimental design attempts to isolate the relationship between the variable that is thought to be the cause and the variable that will show the effect so that only those two variables are in play.

What Are the Major Topics?

For experiments to make sense, there has to be a foundation of a causal relationship. In classical terms, if you touch a hot enough stove with an unprotected finger, you will get a burnt finger. In communication, causal relationships are considerably more mushy with both multiple causes and absent effects.

Well-designed experiments follow a deductive model in which theory forms the major premise, the experimental protocol forms the minor premise, and the hypothesis to be tested is the conclusion.

Without an adequate theoretical foundation, the analyst cannot anticipate the needs for control in the experimental design.

There are four kinds of variables that can be in use in an experimental design—the experimental or independent variable that is thought to be the agent of the effect, the criterion or dependent variable that is the effect to be measured, covariate variables that may affect the relationship between the independent and dependent variables, and control variables that serve to isolate contaminants.

An experimental treatment is a set of conditions determined by the analyst based on his or her examination of theory and previous research that will produce the desired effect.

An experimental protocol involves the management of variables, their presentation, the assignment of respondents, and the statistical procedures of analysis.

Statistical analysis should always begin with an examination of the characteristics of the data set called the descriptive statistics.

The ethics of statistical design include the requirements for a meaningful test, the care of respondents, and the appropriateness of the test's conclusions.

What Special Terms Are Used?

Central tendency	Necessity clause	Simple means
Composite variable	Pattern recognition	Sufficiency clause
Cross-respondent effects	Pre-post design	Surrogate measure
Interrespondent effects	Research hypothesis	Telegraphing
Intrarespondent effects	Response demand	

INTRODUCTION

Within the scientific method, experiments are the gold standard for demonstrating causation. A perfectly designed protocol for an experiment tests potentially alternative routes to the same outcome, holding all other conditions constant. The alternative that initiates the projected outcome is determined to be the cause of that outcome. The argument follows Mill's classic canon for A being the cause of B: Whenever A, then B (the sufficiency clause); and no A, no B (the necessity clause). We demonstrate Mill's canons every time we flip a light switch: When the electricity flows (A), the lamp glows (B); no flow, no glow.

Mill's canons are wonderful standards for designing electrical circuits. They are much less useful for studying communication variables. The reasoning here requires me to locate you into some prior assumptions about why these limitations in classical causation occur. Let me begin with the least controversial. Let's presume that A is some message and B is some behavioral response. Few communication scholars would argue that A can exist as a consistent force or motive for action regardless of its context and conditions of presentation and reception, and few would argue that B can be an automatic and fully encoded action routine independent of its context and conditions of performance. The result is that both A and B are not elemental variables but are composite variables with many different manifestations.

These multiple manifestations of either A or B share at least something in common but over the range of manifestations may show more differences than commonalities. An A is never just an A. Nor is a B ever just a B. The result is that an A in an experimental protocol cannot be the A that appears on your living room television set. And similarly the B of the laboratory is not the *B* of the streets. Big problem; bigger still, we don't know what the differences might be or what differences those differences might make. We don't deal with Mill's certainties; we deal with the shadows of possibilities and implications. Some will immediately argue that it's not all that bad, but, yeah, it really is.

The controversial part of this problem comes when we add agency to the equation. Agency, remember, is some ability to do otherwise. In simple terms, this ability means that no cause occurs unless the individual allows it to occur, whatever the term *allows* entails. Experimentalists and all the other shades of determinists don't like and usually don't accept the concept of agency.

Agency is an axiomatic belief; it is irreducible to evidence. Hold it or don't, but interrogate the requirements of what you hold and be consistent in its application. I believe in a restricted form of agency that comes into play only with effort. It's a supple position.

What, then, is the role of experiments in a composite variable world? Experiments can clearly demonstrate the change in the probabilities of outcomes. I can, in fact, design an experiment in which *B* is a more likely outcome than Not *B* (almost Shakespearean). This is a contingency outcome. It occurs when the cause is necessary but not sufficient for the outcome or neither necessary nor sufficient for the outcome. In the first of these two conditions, the outcome *B* does not occur without *A*, but also occurs not always with *A* as some other condition is also required. In the second, *B* can occur without *A*, but occurs at a higher rate with *A*. Of these two conditions, the first gives us a lot more information. We know we can eliminate *B* by eliminating the appearance of *A*. And we know that to produce *B*, we need something to work in concert with *A*, although we may be uncertain as to what that something is.

The second condition is what we usually get. We can set up conditions in which *A* increases the likelihood of *B*, but *A* alone will not produce this increase, because there are other conditions in which the likelihood of *B* does not increase when *A* is present. Further, *A* can be absent and *B* will still appear. This contingency relationship typifies most effects experiments.

Consider the example of the public health announcements concerning the use of condoms for safe-sex practices. That condom use is the *B* of this example. The basic message of those announcements is "every partner; every time." That is the *A* of this example. The *B* of this example is widely practiced and for many is the standard of practice. Those people do not need *A* for *B*.

Clearly, if I set up an experiment varying the appearance of *A* (the message) to see the effect on *B* (condom use), I will have to collect indirect measures on that effect, most likely some paper-and-pencil measure on respondent intentions. In that experiment, *A* will most likely increase the probability of surrogate *B*. A well-designed message in a well-designed experiment will almost always produce the effect on a surrogate *B*. Does that mean that engaging the public service announcement will eliminate this unsafe-sex practice from among the announcement viewers? Eliminate all those "What the hell?" moments? I think not. But individuals might indeed be more likely to be prepared or at least to feel some concern (or—dare I say it?—guilt) about the risk.

What do we learn from an experiment like this one? First of all, if the research hypothesis fails and the message does not produce the expected change in the surrogate measure, the information gained is confounded in that we cannot distinguish between a failed message and an inadequate experiment. That said, if I were responsible for the distribution of the message, it wouldn't be going out.

If the research hypothesis is supported and the measures show gains in the expected direction, then I have reason to believe that the message will be effective for some people under some conditions (called the some-some conclusion). That some-of-the-people-some-of-the-time conclusion is the fundamental limit of information gained from composite variables (and their surrogates) within contingent outcomes. The remaining issue is "How much trust can one invest in the effectiveness of the message?" or, in other words, "How broad is the application of the some-some conclusion?" The answer to that question lies in the topic of this chapter—the quality of the protocol of the experiment.

COMPONENTS OF EXPERIMENTAL DESIGN

There are four overarching components of experimental design: causality, theory, control, and ecological validity.

Causality

Experimental design is built on a causal model. It is a test of the possibility that one condition or set of conditions is the result of another condition or set of conditions. The first requirement of a competent experimental design, then, is the reasonable basis to hold the possibility of a causal relationship between two variables or variable sets.

Cause in the social and discursive sciences is not the same sort of thing as cause in Newtonian science. That latter sort of cause works like the presence or absence of an electrical current on a functioning incandescent lightbulb. Flip the light switch on to connect the circuit, and the filament glows. In a working system, there is no equivocation. If the light does not go on, one changes the bulb and does not suspect that for this lightbulb the character of electricity is different or that the tungsten filament has decided not to glow.

In an experiment, then, what we would like to happen is that a consistent, perhaps slightly variable but nonetheless robust, contribution to the criterion variable be made by the experimental condition to each respondent's score. We do not have that sort of certainty in our field of study. In our field of study and with a very strong relationship, it is quite likely that one flips the message switch on 100 audience circuits and 20 of the lightbulbs glow more brightly, 75 register no measurable change, and 5 return even less light. Fair example? I compared the means of a random set of numbers from 1 to 7 with that same set where the first 20 numbers of 5 or less had 2 units added to them and the last 5 numbers of 2 or more had 1 unit subtracted from them. The respective means were 3.96 and 4.31. The t value was 4.083; $p < 0.000$. That result would have brought on dancing in the hallway.

This Monte Carlo example emulates a pre-post experimental design and demonstrates the some-some conclusion of composite contingencies. Of the respondents (circuits in the example), 75% were unchanged by the message (light switch); 20% changed in the direction hypothesized; and 5% changed in the opposite direction. The outcome, however, was significant and in the direction predicted. The conclusion would have read something like "The evidence showed that the message created more positive attitudes toward. . . ." or some similar statement based on the global effect on the means. What actually happened was that *some* respondents (the 20 and the 5) under *some* circumstances (the experimental conditions) exhibited *some* change (both positive and negative).

Is this outcome typical? I believe I have some—albeit slight—basis to claim that it is typical. I do not have access to the raw data of others, and our theory development is so preliminary and data collection so limited that few researchers approach an analysis of the contrary cases in their respondent set. I can tell you that those contrary cases exist in every data set I have collected, and my theory in use has never been strong enough to explain the some-some effect. In short, I cannot tell you why some change (in any direction) and some don't.

Like others, I use a Las Vegas economy; I can make my contribution on the 20% who support my hypothesis, the 5% who run opposite do little damage, and the other 75% provide the mass I need for statistical power and acceptable numbers. Recognize that I am being crass here, but realistic as well. (I also sleep well at night.) This is the nature of cause in a world of composite contingencies.

The epistemological requirements for causality establish the ontological characteristics of all elements in an experimental protocol. On the face of it, one could run experiments using interpretive methods. An ethnographic technique called Garfinkeling (named after Harold Garfinkel, 1967) makes use of breaching experiments where social conventions are deliberately broached. The data collection is by field notes. There is almost no contemporary use of this approach in communication studies. I found but two entries in our core set of references in which breaching experiments or Garfinkeling appeared. Both were convention papers that used the term in the literature review. Clearly, breaching experiments are not much in use, and actually are not experiments as understood in this chapter. There are clear epistemological reasons why they are not that involve the researcher-respondent relationship, the standards of ecological validity, the concept of variables, the relationship among variables, the researcher as instrument, the use of field notes as a criterion of difference, and the like.

We deal with many of these issues in the chapter on ethnography. For our purpose here, we will talk about the required assumptions that apply to the nature of the variables in use. You will recall that metric research is based in part on the principle of atomism, which, as a philosophical concept, holds that the world is made up of independent elements that act upon one another in a more or less consistent fashion. There is a transcendent order that is the sum of its parts and that can be revealed through empirical analysis. In media research, this principle translates into a number of practical axioms that in turn direct experimental design (messages are independent of one another; messages are independent of the audience; audience members are independent of one another; the message is independent of its technology, etc.). These axioms allow us to design experiments that study message effects across audiences and technologies, as we will see in the examples presented in subsequent sections.

At the same time, these axioms are quite a challenge both to our experimental designs and to the conclusions we draw from them because they assume an ontological character for our variables that we (or at least a good portion of us[1]) are pretty sure is not the case. More and more media scholars hold, for example, that a message is not the same as the material text and that the message of a material text is created in the interaction among the text, the audience, the technology, and the provenance of action. We will see the tension in the opposing experimental requirements and philosophical understandings of how communication works in all of the discussions that follow, as we have seen it here in our discussion of causation.

Theory

In the best practices of research, an experiment is the test of a hypothesis that has been drawn up to test a theoretical proposition. As we saw in Chapter 6, theory provides the major and minor premises, and the hypothesis is the conclusion that is necessary if the major and minor premises are logically true. An excellent example of this process is provided in a study by Smith and Boster (2009). This study begins with the premise that individuals attend to mediated messages in the copresence and under the extended influence of others. That presence and influence creates some part of the context in which messages are interpreted. This concept has a long history in social psychology (e.g., Sherif, 1936). In that history, however, the meaning of the message was fixed and knowable (at least to the researchers); it was the individual perceptions of the message that changed.

Smith and Boster (2009) do not reference that literature, but rather take a more cultural studies approach that holds the meaning of any text to be fundamentally uncertain or unfinished (*ambiguous* would be their term) until it is actualized in some interpretation. The research problem that is the driving energy behind this experiment is whether the context of reception creates different perceptions of the same text or actualizes different texts. A "different perceptions" perspective poses the research question as one of accuracy of interpretation; a "different texts" perspective poses the question as one of identifying the message being processed. The experiment reported in Smith and Boster adds support to the latter.

Smith and Boster provide a methodical argument from theory to hypotheses that is unusual to see in the literature, but they have an advantage of working in an area where the theory has reached a fairly high level of development (even if they think it is wrong). In the much more common case, the analyst starts with a set of empirical studies that are more or less tangential to the problem at hand and creates a mash-up of theoretical propositions to justify a set of research questions and subsequent hypotheses. (No criticism of the analyst is meant here, just a recognition of the state of our theory development.)

Haumer and Donsbach (2009) were also concerned with contextual influence on judgments, but, in their case, not on texts but on the image of integrity, personal qualities, leadership, and competence projected by a political figure. They investigated the effects of nonverbal reactions to shots of the audience, the talk show host, and the nonverbal behaviors of the political figure in an experiment simulating a talk show interview of a political candidate.

Their study is a mixture of theory-driven research and opportunistic empiricism. We are not given, for example, a solid theoretical foundation for the choice of the four image

---

[1]Even "hardened" effects scholars like James Potter (Potter & Tomasello, 2003) have begun to incorporate interpretation in their research.

measures, but they are certainly reasonable. There is also no theoretical formulation of why a reaction shot, per se, should affect judgments on, say, leadership, but, then again, why not? The major problem, however, is the absence of any theory on the quality and influencing force of nonverbal behaviors and reaction shots and of any theory on the narrative structure of the talk show as text.

The findings from Haumer and Donsbach (2009) are mixed and, as is the typical result in experiments without strong theoretical foundations, subject to multiple interpretations. They, subsequently, bring us no closer to an understanding of how all this stuff works but do provide one more contribution to the theoretical bricolage on social influence.

Finally, theory is nearly absent in most proprietary research, which typically focuses on narrow empirical questions. Because this research is not ordinarily entered into the public domain, let me use one of my own examples. Researchers at the University of Utah and at Utah Valley University have conducted studies looking at the relative efficacy of multiple-screen and different-format computer displays. They compared one-screen, two-screen, three-screen, and wide-format screens across typical office editing tasks (spreadsheets, Word documents, and PowerPoint presentations). Respondents were faster and more accurate in multiscreen displays and gained advantages in wider-screen formats.

These studies are typical of industry-driven experiments. They offer no contribution to a body of theory but do aid in the decision making of IT officers and in justifying requests to budget managers. They even provide an aphorism to guide these decisions: "The real estate of the desktop should match the footprint of the work." The findings, however, are completely dependent on "how things are right now." Changes in the technology of displays, in how operating systems handle displays, in how applications display their information, and even in the cultural definition of an accounting sheet or a page of text will render their findings obsolete.[2] This circumstance, by the way, is also common in any research that chases the development curve of technology.

Managerial practices have become increasingly data-based, substituting atheoretical empiricism for managerial expertise, authority, or intuition. That may be a good thing (particularly for consultants) except that the substitution is too often characterized by a blind faith in the truth-telling qualities of empirical data. In our monitor studies, we used criterion tasks that were common in office work but that would also benefit from multiple or larger displays (and reported the relationship). The translation we hear back from managers is that multiple screens increase productivity. The fact of the matter is that they don't but they can. The work has to be appropriate, and the worker has to use them appropriately. The same is true with experiments.

Control

The purpose of experimental control is to establish conditions such that the hypothesis provides a complete explanation for the outcome. If the hypothesis fails to be supported,

---

[2]That said, if you go into the business of research or scholarship, given present conditions, you should use multiple monitors with at least one in portrait orientation. If you use them to play more solitaire, your productivity will not increase, however.

it can be declared falsified. If it is supported, it can be certified as supported. (Note the absence of true-or-false designations.) Well-designed experiments do not readily admit alternative explanations for either success or failure.

Control, consequently, is a part of every aspect of protocol design. We want the specifics of the test to line up with the generalized knowledge claims we want to advance. This goal means that (a) testing conditions apply to actual conditions, (b) treatments break across intrinsic differences and eliminate extrinsic ones, (c) participating respondents correspond to the designated population, and (d) measurements have a secure connection from operational definition to variables, to constructs, to the theoretical concepts that are the basis of the initiating premises.

Proper experimental protocols are designed to control the influence of unmeasured variables and to allow the full expression of the measured ones. Controls are put into place either to eliminate the possibility of an effect by an untested variable or to permit the extraction of its effect through analysis. It is a harsh criterion because it demands both perfect anticipation and flawless execution. Time and again, the actual experimental protocol achieves something substantially less.

Experimental studies are meant to be works in progress with an aim toward the steady improvement both of the theory the experiments are testing and of the design of the experiments itself. Most of the experimental work in mediated communication has been concerned with the social implications of the findings rather than the steady improvement of the theory or experimental design. The actual result has been an amazing proliferation of theory and an equally amazing repetition of the same experimental design.

The same would hold true for much of the "Six Sigma" movement (no more than four errors in a million events) that is part of the data-based management initiative. If academic work trumpets overreaching social disaster, business research focuses on narrow empirical issues of the here and now (even as the here and now is so quickly there and gone) using prepackaged designs (the expertise is in the box) that provide little basis for the careful analysis of needed controls. The outcomes do solve the problem of what to decide today, given whatever assumptions are in play, but offer little insight into the quality of the decision or of what to decide tomorrow.

The consequence for both spheres of experimental work is that we have a lot of results but little understanding. The opposing tension, of course, is the multiple instances of the Edison myth where advances and fortunes are made by persistence, atheoretical empiricism, or the serendipity of messing around. "Demonstrate utility, and theory will follow" is the apparent dictum. Most of our actual experimental work falls somewhere between the best practices of deductive logic and the worst practices of plugging variables into design software.

Ecological Validity

We have probably all read or seen the news reports of some new food additive (usually a sweetener) causing cancer in rats when ingested at rates 800 times the normal amount. The story will usually go to underscore the problem in applying the results across species and at those dosage rates. The National Cancer Institute concludes simply that the studies "have not provided clear evidence of an association with cancer in humans."[3] The issue for reader, reporter, and scientist alike is the ecological validity of the experiments.

Ecological validity refers to the transferability of the results found under the conditions of the experiment to the ordinary conditions under which the constructs under study might present themselves. Unfortunately, the issue of transferability is fundamentally irresolvable. The conundrum resides in the relationship between normality and control. The closer one moves toward controlling all of the possible nonexperimental influences on the effect, the farther one moves from the normal conditions of that influence. And, similarly, the closer one moves toward normal conditions, the less control over those nonexperimental influences one can exercise. The simple story is that the better the experiment, the less probable its ecological validity, given the composite variables and semiotically dynamic conditions of communication studies.

Life is hard, but not unlivable. Good design works to hit the sweet spot that balances the issues of control and ecological validity. Bringing a mixed-sex group of 18- to 24-year-old college students into a classroom, showing them sexually charged video materials, and then comparing their scores on a sexual behavior measure with the scores from a control group that read a chapter on relationships probably does not achieve that balance (see Taylor, 2005). But every decision will be case-by-case as the analyst deals with the conflicting critiques that can be anticipated while trying to satisfy the motivating belief that there is something there to be revealed.

One of the major problems we have in achieving that balance is that the ecology of mediated communication varies widely across age, gender, socioeconomic class, and other demographic variables, and it has been in a state of rapid change for the past two decades. It would take a particularly dedicated researcher to be knowledgeable, for example, about the current media ecology of, say, junior high–aged respondents, the over-70s, or any group substantially distant from him- or herself. Even within those groups there are substantial differences. My friends and colleagues—all in the same age cohort—who do not have a time-shifting DVR, watch television in substantially different ways than I do.

In a similar vein, there is the issue of the differences between researcher and respondent literacies and sensibilities. I have already confessed to you that I am not a gamer. Now, I will reveal that I rarely carry a cell phone. These are deliberate choices that I have made that suit me, but they do close me out from the skills and understandings that gamers and texters possess. Quite frankly, the biggest threat to ecological validity is researcher ignorance and the passive acceptance of this ignorance by reviewers and readers.

The first step in working toward an acceptable level of ecological validity is to recognize that in working with composite variables, we cannot rule out the possibility that everything can make a difference. The thought that one can design a study that will control all conditions does not seem to be realistic. Given that assumption, the analyst will have to carefully specify the scope of the study by answering questions as to the conditions to which the study can generalize. What are the conditions of reception and common usage? What are

---

[3]http://www.cancer.gov/cancertopics/factsheet/Risk/artificial-sweeteners. Accessed April 28, 2011.

the characteristics of the audience practitioners?[4] How does the content vary in activation across those practitioners? What are the ordinary action routines of the class of individuals envisioned? What cultural, social, or societal challenges or privileges are in play? What is the typical technological environment, usage skill level, literacy? What are the interactive elements, shared experience, collaboration, intertextuality, social and cultural extensions? And, perhaps most important, does the analyst have a firm empirical basis for providing the answers?

To provide that basis, the analyst should consider starting the design process with an extended effort at observation of "behavior in the wild"; plan interviews with the target group(s); let focus groups reflect on the proposed design; and, finally, run a test group with full debriefing of the participants individually and together. This degree of careful work, I am sorry to say, is far more than what we typically see in the literature. I think we would be the better for it, nonetheless.

CREATING THE PROTOCOL

Creating experimental protocols is a lot like building custom furniture or sewing designer clothes. We all use a set of common tools and design elements, but the finished work is unique. The common tools in experimental design are the variables, the treatments or contrasts, the testing conditions, the selection and assignment of respondents, and the analysis—usually statistical. The experimental variables are the ones the analyst thinks have some causative effect, the criterion measure or measures are those that are suspected of being affected by the experimental variables, the treatments are the contrasting experimental-control comparisons that provide the test of the hypothesis, the testing conditions are the circumstances under which the respondents participate in the study, the respondents in experiments are almost always recruited rather than randomly selected but are then randomly assigned to one of the protocol groups, and the statistical analysis is usually analysis of variance (ANOVA), with one criterion measure; multiple analysis of variance (MANOVA), with two or more criterion measures; or analysis of covariance (ANCOVA), when one can test the effect of mitigating variables on the causal relationship or their (ANOVA/MANOVA/ANCOVA) general regression equivalents (whew). Let's walk our way through this list.

Variables

We start with variables in this discussion because the impetus for an experiment usually comes from an analysis of theoretical concepts or, perhaps more likely, the variable elements in an observed problem. In experimental design, we talk about variables that serve functional roles in the design and variables that serve as evidence for a claim (see below).

---

[4]Even our ordinary language for describing the relationship between media and user is stuck in early-20th-century conceptualizations of the audience as a passive receiver of media content. More and more, the end user is also the final moment of content production. One does not simply "receive" it anymore but also cocreates it.

There are four functional types of variables that can be brought into play in experimental design: experimental variables (the agent of the effect), the criterion measure (the measured effect), covariates (variables that presumably moderate the relationship between the experimental and the criterion), and control variables (potential contaminants of the criterion). Of these, the first two appear in every experimental design.

It is sometimes difficult to identify what variable serves what purpose in a complex design, as any variable could presumably serve any of the four purposes. Here are some rules of thumb to help in identifying a variable's role in a design. The experimental variable is the one that is manipulated by the analyst. If there is no manipulation, then the protocol is likely not a true experiment, but rather a correlational analysis. Sorting respondents by some preexisting condition (like education) is generally not considered a manipulation. Criterion variables are the ones that are tested for differences across the treatment conditions. There may be more than one criterion in a study, but mostly each criterion has its own analytical frame. (We don't see much MANOVA, but we do see replications of the same design using different criterion measures.)

Covariates and controls can look much alike. We have different kinds of interests in these two, however. We hold a theoretical interest in the consequences of covariate variables. We hope to demonstrate that X kinds of people or Y kinds of texts have consequences on the relationship between the experimental and criterion variables. We hold a cautionary interest in control variables. Our concern is that Z kinds of conditions (people, texts, circumstances, etc.) might contaminate the criterion such that we get a false reading of the relationship between the experimental and criterion variables. Analysts are an opportunistic lot. Disappointing covariates can become controls, and interesting controls can become covariates as the results begin to appear. (Squishy ethics? You bet.)

In media studies, there are six common evidentiary classes of variables: message (text), mode (medium or technology), audience (characteristics), reception (including issues of interpretation), interaction (Web 2.0),[5] and outcomes (cognitions, behaviors, etc.). Specific variables from these six classes can be used in any of the four locations (experimental, criterion, covariate, control) of the experiment, although clearly there are affinities between class and experimental location (e.g., outcomes are often the criterion).

How variables are used in what locations depends on the problem under investigation and on the theory in use. The analyst might be interested in the relationship between certain kinds of messages and the decision behaviors of the audience. In an effects model, the design would likely locate the message as the experimental variable, designating it as the agent of a decision, but a uses and gratifications model would likely locate the decision behaviors as the demand factor (agent) for certain kinds of messages, and a social action model would look at audience lifestyles as the experimental factor with both message selection and decisions as the criterion measures or in some combination of covariate-criterion configuration (e.g., certain lifestyles lead to different decision-making patterns given the availability of different technologies).

---

[5]Consider the common practice of real-time polling, for example, in which part of the media text is created by the audience texting responses to an on-air poll.

Let's look at a couple of examples from the literature: McKinney and Rill (2009),[6] working from the principle that the simple act of engaging campaign communication raises the level of civic engagement, set up a quasi–field experiment to test the effect of exposure to two kinds of debates during the 2008 primary and presidential campaigns. They used two outcome measures, an 8-item political cynicism scale and a 5-item political knowledge confidence scale in a preexposure-postexposure design.

Their experimental variables were exposure to a real-time debate and to the type of debate to which respondents were exposed. The exposure variable had only one value in that everyone saw a debate, but the nonexposed condition was inferred from the preexposure test scores. This design adequately isolates the effect of exposure, but is weak in supporting the importance of the content. What if control group members had watched a lively discussion of the importance of civic engagement? Would their political cynicism scores decline and their knowledge confidence scores increase as well?

The study also used a covariate variable of sorts. Respondents self-identified as committed to or leaning toward one party or another. They were then assigned to watch either the Democratic candidate debate or the Republican candidate debate according to the party of their self-identification. Here, too, one might wonder if there would have been more information gained concerning the initiating question if the groups had been split with half of each group randomly assigned to watch the opposite party debate. If participation is the basis of the effect, it might not matter if one is for or against the content. In that sort of design, party identity becomes a true (potential) covariate.

Grabe, Kamhawi, and Yegiyan (2009) designed a study to examine memory for news stories presented on television, in the newspaper, and on a news website by respondents with different levels of education and over different time periods. In this study, the criterion was a complex of three memory measures—encoding, storage, and retrieval—based on some form of written recall (recognition, cued, or free). The experimental variable was the presentation of topically equivalent messages across the three media. The covariates were education (no more than high school vs. postgraduate degree) and time of recall (immediate and two-day delay).

The researchers also added some control variables. To control for the possibility that there might be a content-medium interaction, they replicated the comparison over four different news stories. They also instituted a control for the order of the media the participant engaged, randomly assigning respondents to one of the possible sequences. And, finally, they collected information on the respondent's interest level for each topic in case interest affected recall. Although not fully reported, the authors apparently found no topic, sequence, or interest effects. Note that the authors had no expectation of a topic, sequence, or interest effect. They were checking for the possible contamination of the criterion by one or more of these effects. I would have preferred a full report of the finding, nonetheless.

Measurement Controls

Up to this point, we've been engaging the variables at the construct level. The empirical evidence for the operation of these variables will, of course, come from the measurement

---

[6]Read the full results available online at participating libraries everywhere.

process. We discussed the technical aspects of measurement in Chapter 5. Here we want to look at how the choices of measurement affect the design and possible outcome. Just to remind ourselves: The measurements we take are the variables we study. The whole enterprise hangs on the quality of those measurements, which in turn is dependent on the measurement process. Measurement controls, then, intercept that process in order to suppress the appearance of extraneous effects. Those effects would include fatigue, boredom, frustration—even sabotage, practice, telegraphing, pattern recognition, response demand,[7] the testing environment both physical and social, skill and literacy requirements of the measurement, and motivation of the respondent.

Further, measurement almost always involves some performance of its own that in turn demands its own skills and competence of enactment. Elements within the measurement set can interact with one another, setting up expectations for "what the experiment is actually trying to do" or for "what the right or desired answers are." As with the development of survey instrumentation, the best insurance is to carefully pretest the entire protocol, with special attention to the measurement process.

All of these effects are in play to some extent in every measurement situation. They are part of the noise in the system—the error component of measurement. What we control for is the systematic appearance of these effects. If nearly everyone hits a wall of fatigue at approximately the same place in the measurement process, then the measurements that follow are systematically affected by that fatigue. Further, if this effect is associated with one treatment group and not another, then the results of the comparison will be false—perhaps not fatally so, but false nonetheless.

In addition to these extrinsic and spurious effects, there are the intrinsic effects that are part of the measurement device itself. These are the standard test issues of item discrimination, reliability of the instrument, and the ever-elusive questions of validity. Generally speaking, these issues are dealt with prior to the experiment. But it probably doesn't hurt to remind ourselves of them here.

In even a cursory exploration of the literature, the first thing we notice is the heavy dependence on paper-and-pencil (P&P) measurements. Historically, this dependence developed because of the message effects orientation of mass communications and its confluence with the development of cognitivism, but it continues out of some practical considerations of the difficulties of measuring the actual behavior for which these P&P measures stand as surrogates. Nonetheless, they remain as Plato's shadows on the cave wall, mere indicants of possible material performance. And it is, of course, material performance that matters. (I consider the fact that we have not been able to advance our typical measurement devices in the past century our greatest failure.)

Paper-and-pencil measures do, however, allow us to conduct experiments over topics that would otherwise be difficult or ethically impossible to conduct. One cannot, for example, ethically conduct an experiment in which the criterion measure is actual physical harm inflicted upon another; even inducing a firm belief that one is harming another is

---

[7]These three effects have to do with test construction where a prior response telegraphs the answer to a following item, questions on different dimensions are in a recognizable pattern, or the items reveal the interests of the research in such a way as to "ask" for certain answers.

considered ethically suspect, as the response to the Yale studies showed.[8] And we cannot physically document that a condom was used following exposure to a message on safe-sex practices. (Despite their necessity, I would not trust the paper-and-pencil measures in either case, because violent and sexual behaviors are not under the governance of messages or even under the reliable control of language-based cognitive processes.)

The point is to use paper-and-pencil measures where we must but also to examine our protocols closely for measurement processes that allow the actual performance to be the criterion. For example, in Kelly Schmitt and Daniel Anderson's (2002) study comparing young children's behavioral learning from direct observation and from watching the behavior on television, the criterion measure was the actual performance of the activities to be learned (placing or finding a toy in another room).

Lee (2005) demonstrates that you don't have to lose any of the convenience of P&P measures with his study of gender roles in which he used a computer adaptation of a *Jeopardy* game (see Figure 11.1). This sort of computerized data collection has the added advantage of controlling for respondent and clerical input errors.

Whatever the instrumentation, measurement is not a neutral process. It often calls on the respondent to adopt an "as if" state of mind to render judgments as if the object or person were there; as if a single, global rating could stand for all the variations of conditions that an object or a person might encounter; as if the reality of the testing situation could

Figure 11.1 Computer Adaptation of *Jeopardy*

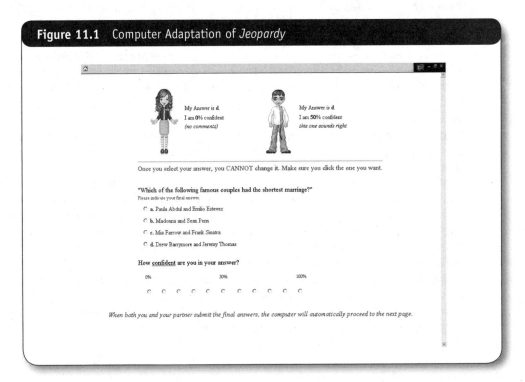

be ignored. Consider how measurement participates in our understanding of the focal object. Presume that you are a researcher studying the online presentation of a research class. You are interested in getting some baseline information concerning the respondents' prior experience with online courses. You ask the "How many?" and "How often?" questions and then ask, "Overall, has your experience with online courses been very positive, positive, somewhat positive, neutral, somewhat negative, negative, or very negative?" There is a likelihood that you are causing the respondent to evaluate online courses in a way he or she has not done before. "Huh," the respondent thinks, "I never realized that I really like online courses. This really changes everything." And so it does.

Treatments and Equivalence

A treatment in an experiment is any set of researcher-determined conditions that is measured. Every experiment compares one condition with another. One cannot have an experiment without some manipulated comparison, which dismisses all those correlational studies from the realm of experimental evidence—parsing variance is not the same thing as comparing different conditions. In the next section, we will discuss the controls the comparison has to exercise; in this section, we are talking about the equivalency the comparison has to achieve. The basic form of the comparison is to set up identical conditions, both of which allow for the appearance of or change in the criterion event. In one set of these conditions, the experimenter introduces the variable thought to act on the appearance of or change in the criterion. Simple to write; hard to read; very difficult to achieve.

The design problem is complicated by the composite nature of our variables (here we go again). For example, let's say the analyst wanted to compare the effect of engaging a message, being exposed to that message, and the absence of that message on the perceived likelihood of some subsequent action, say wearing sunscreen while skiing (water or snow—your choice—and OK, snowboarding or skateboarding too). This question is a standard message effects question with the added dimension of an engagement-exposure comparison. The question of engagement versus exposure deals with the common criticism of message effects in that the laboratory setting encourages a heightened level of attention that does not occur in normal viewing.

In the engaged conditions, respondents are told that they will be eligible for a $20 drawing if they are able to correctly answer 5 questions about the message in order to simulate a prior interest in the topic and heightened attention during its presentation. In the exposure condition, respondents are periodically given a simple arithmetic problem to solve on an "at-hand" computer during the presentation of the message. This device allows for continuous aural attention but diverts visual attention to simulate a typical multitask viewing condition. In the absence-of-the-message conditions, one set of respondents (the engaged comparison) is told of the drawing but then not given the message (the screen remains blank because of technical problems), and another set (the exposed comparison) is given the periodic arithmetic problems but again technical problems with the television set prevent the showing of the message.

The design, then, has four independent groups with random assignment of respondents to group membership. It would be seen as a 2×2 design with *engaged-exposed* as one dimension and *message-no message* as the other. We could draw it up as Figure 11.2.

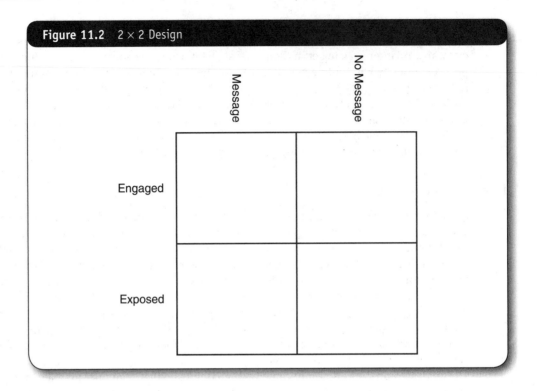

Figure 11.2 2 × 2 Design

The question we are engaging is whether these are equivalent conditions varying only across the engaged-exposed difference and the message-no message difference. Notice that we are not asking if they are the same. We know they are not the same. Equivalence, on the other hand, occurs within some framework. The framework for us is always the criterion measure. Our framework, then, is the reported likelihood of wearing sunscreen while skiing or boarding. Is there anything in the design that suggests that something other than the experimental variables will affect the outcome on this measure?

Beats me. I'd be a little concerned about the effect of frustration on the engaged-no message group, but that could work to motivate existing strategies for test success (what, you've never been unprepared for a test and still survived?) or to sit back and give up. So, maybe that's a wash. (Seizing a teachable moment here: In what order would the analyst administer the criterion measure and the content test? What would be the rationale for the order selected?) So this is it? This is the level of technical accuracy I can achieve in the design process? Initially, yes, technically we would say that it achieves face validity on equivalence or, in less technical parlance, "It looks good." The analyst doesn't have to settle for just face validity, and if one's job, degree, tenure, or funding were riding on the outcomes, it would certainly be worth the effort to pretest the design, using a small sample.

The results from the test run can be used to conduct a power analysis to determine the number of respondents needed to distinguish the effects. It can also be used to explore effective covariates (third variables that modify the relationship between the cause and the effect) and to improve on both the theoretical contribution and the sophistication of the hypotheses. Unfortunately, even a small sample of 10 per group results in a requirement of 40 respondents in this fully randomized design.

Comparisons and Contrasts

The design of the *contrasts*, which is the term used for the comparisons across groups we intend to make, provides the first level of control by comparing results across groups that are presumably under the same influences with the exception of the experimental variables. In our engaged-exposed example, the contrast between the engaged message-presented group and the engaged no-message group provides a control for the effect of the message; the contrast between the engaged and exposed message-presented groups controls for the engagement motivation; the contrast between the exposed message group and the exposed no-message group controls for the effect of the message when no engagement motivation is present; the final contrast between the two no-message groups would allow the analyst to explore the incitement effect (possibly confounded with a frustration effect) of the monetary reward.

What might be added to this set of controls would be a typical message-presentation group (no motivation or distraction) with a typical no-message control group. In this addition, the analyst would be anticipating concerns that the original design would not permit the "clean" extraction of either the engagement or the distraction conditions. The addition would, however, raise the costs of the study by nearly one third.

In considering treatments, we generally talk about experimental and control conditions. An experimental condition is one in which the variable under study is present at some value. A single variable can produce more than one treatment. Weaver and Wilson (2009), for example, posed three levels for their experimental variable, quality of depicted violence—none, sanitized, and graphic—to determine the consequences for three criterion measures, enjoyment of the program, emotional reactions to the program, and judgments on the content (violence, graphic quality, level of action). The variations were produced by editing a set of five programs to remove all depictions of violence (action without violence conditions) and retain only scenes with no blood or gore (action and sanitized violence), and by no editing of violent scenes (action and graphic violence).[9]

The five programs are also a variable in this study, a control variable in this case. They serve as a control for the possibility that the effect of the graphic quality of violence will be changed by the story line or characters in a given program. The combination of three levels of violence and five programs actually produces 15 different treatment conditions. Respondents were randomly assigned to one of these conditions.[10]

---

[9]Action is preserved in each of these conditions because of Zillmann's (1991) arguments about the effect of arousal in television viewing.

[10]Weaver and Wilson also tested the effects of sensation seeking, trait aggression, and prior exposure to violent programs. These are not treatments, because respondents come to the study with these conditions; they are not varied by the researchers, only measured.

The development of treatments is a substantive part of experimental design. Weaver and Wilson used selections from *24, The Sopranos, The Shield, Oz*, and *Kingpin*, which all follow the same basic story line of tarnished good versus burnished evil presented in gritty, screen noir. This choice is a deliberate one to contain the effect of the program on the criteria, which at this stage of investigation is perfectly appropriate. Thoughtless choices can set one up for failure, and as long as one's conclusions recognize the scope chosen, a reduction of risk to the hypothesis can still produce a fair test. On the other hand, a narrow set of conditions cannot be matched to a broad set of conclusions.

Respondents

To meet the requirements of a fully randomized design of either the Weaver and Wilson example or our sunscreen example, respondents have to be randomly entered into one of the independent groups. We know that true random samples of human respondents are very difficult to obtain. The usual solution is random assignment. Respondents are recruited from a common pool (say, the research requirement of an introductory communication course) and are then randomly assigned to one of the treatment or control groups. In both of our examples, a given respondent would participate in only one of the possible treatment or control groups. Random assignment of this sort is a technique that eliminates cross-group, intrarespondent effects as respondents appear only once. It also limits the influence of interrespondent differences by distributing those differences more or less equally across the treatment or control groups. Usually, this assignment is done by randomly selecting a starting group for the first respondent and then following a standard assignment sequence for all subsequent respondents.

Random assignment, of course, does not guarantee equal distribution of unknown covariates, but it does provide the strongest argument against the presence of some systematic effect. I consider it stronger than balancing treatment groups across selected demographic variables such as sex (not gender in this case) and age. Balance in the absence of evidence of some interaction is only for show.

Random assignment can offer no control over the differences the respondent pool may show in relation to the general population. Major areas of academic study are chosen by students for some reason, and fewer than half of U.S. citizens attend college, so differences clearly exist both between different groups of college students and between college students and the general population. I have no evidence, however, that those differences affect the outcome of the experiment. (If I did, I would also know the outcome of the experiment.) We saw in Chapter 8 that a random sample from the general population is mostly out of reach except for the well-funded few. Typically, the analyst would have no access to a general population pool, which renders the question (but not the criticism) moot at any rate.

Other experimental designs allow for other methods of controlling respondent effects. Repeated measures designs where respondents participate in more than one treatment group eliminate interrespondent effects but raise the likelihood of intrarespondent effects (covariates, practice effects, boredom, sabotage, etc.). Our sunscreen example has no control for topic. Perhaps some substantial portion of the pool disconnects from skiing of any sort. We could add two other safe-practices topics (automobile seat belts and bicycle helmets; we already did condoms). Each respondent would be randomly assigned to one of the message, no-message, engaged, or exposed treatment groups (one of the six combinations, that is) as before but would now complete the tasks across the three topics. Cross-respondent effects would be controlled over topics, but an order effect would be introduced. That effect could be controlled by randomly selecting the starting topic and then following a standard sequence so that each topic has an equal number of respondents who took it in the first, second, and third order position.

As we can read, respondent controls get complex quite quickly. Table 11.1 offers some order. We ought to offer a word on the "college sample." The purpose of conducting experiments is to create a generalizable claim about some part of the world in which we live. The more narrow the variables, measurements, and treatments, the less generalizable the information. This relationship also holds true for the issues that surround our respondents. Academic research has long been subject to the complaint that it relies upon a respondent pool that is demonstrably different from other subgroups of the general population, and yet offers conclusions that entail all of us. The simple answer to the complaint is "Yes, that is true—caveat lector." Any attempt to justify a college student sample as representative of the general population that does not use an authentic general population sample for comparison is just smoke and mirrors. The current college graduation rate in the United States is 25.6%, ranging from 45.2% in Washington, DC, to 17.0% in West Virginia.[11] Is Washington, DC, different from West Virginia? You draw your own conclusions.

Table 11.1   Respondent Designs and Effects Controls

Respondent Design	Controls for:	Has No Effect On:	Additional Control
Random sample	Pool effects	• Sampling error • Unequal distribution of unknown covariates	Random assignment to treatment groups
Random assignment from respondent pool	• Cross-group intrarespondent effects • Reduces probability of interrespondent effects	• Pool effects • Chance group inequalities	None
Repeated measures (with random assignment)	Cross-group interrespondent effects	• Sampling error or pool effects • Order effects • Chance group inequalities	Random assignment of order

[11]http://www.census.gov/acs/www/Products/Ranking/2003/R02T040.htm Accessed January 6, 2010.

Well, so what? The end user of the research has to exercise care in determining the amount of risk that is involved in applying a conclusion drawn from a limited sample to his or her particular situation. But that does not mean that academics should stop doing research or that all academic research is suspect. Total ignorance is not better than some information. You do have to think about it, however. Is an 18- to 24-year-old age group, regardless of education level, the same as a 45- to 64-year-old age group? I have never known these two groups to coidentify. Further, only 7% of the males in the younger group have a bachelor's degree, but slightly over 30% of the older-group males do. The rate for females is 11% and 27%, respectively.[12] What do these different educational attainment levels over sex and the reversal over age tell you? They tell me that the 18- to 24-year-old cohort is not the same as other age cohorts and not even the same through time. If my job depended on either extrapolating information from a college sample or collecting a sample of 45- to 64-year-olds, I'd get the new sample.

Finally, most experimental protocols present the need for methods in managing respondents from first contact to completed data set. These are not trivial issues; not only does the experiment depend on the respondents being there in a timely fashion, but also getting them there can be a major expense, being sure that they respect the work can determine outcomes, and their negative word of mouth can bring recruitment to an abrupt end. The entire process should be scripted or flowcharted. Entries should include timing of the elements in recruitment; method and message of first contact; scheduling and reminders; the informed consent process; dealing with people who are early or late; the step-by-step movement of individuals through the protocol, including the timing and location of these steps; debriefing; payment (money, course credit, eternal gratitude); and dismissal. There is a great deal of preplanning as well as disaster preparation that is needed.

Analysis

Nearly all analysis of experiments involves metric measurements and, therefore, statistical analysis. Remember that statistical analysis is both a way of displaying information about the characteristics of a data set and a way of providing a public decision making process for determining how we are to act toward some finding. We should find both analytical frameworks in any experimental study. The responsibility of the analyst is to provide sufficient descriptive information that the inferential tests can be placed in proper perspective and to conduct a sufficient number of the appropriate inferential tests such that the reader can be confident in the sources of the data events.

Descriptives

You know from the chapter on statistical analysis that I am a great fan of descriptive statistics. Let's take a specific example by using the report by Weaver and Wilson (2009) to show you why. They reported on the relative enjoyment of television programs edited

---

[12]Surprised? Check it out at http://factfinder.census.gov/servlet/DTTable?_bm = y&context = dt&ds_name = ACS_2007_3YR_G00_&CONTEXT = dt &mt_name = ACS_2007_3YR_G2000_C15001&tree_id = 3307&redoLog = true&_caller = geoselect&-geo_id = 01000U.S.&-search_results = ALL&-format = &_lang = en. Accessed April 28, 2011.

to display no violence, sanitized violence, and graphic violence. Let me just take one of their major results:

> An ANOVA on the two-item enjoyment measure revealed a significant main effect for treatment condition, $F(2, 8) = 10.24$, $p < .01$, $\eta^2 = .03$. Both the graphic version ($M = 2.29a$, 95% CI = 2.21, 2.38) and the sanitized version ($M = 2.29a$, 95% CI = 2.20, 2.38) were enjoyed significantly *less* than the no-violence version was ($M = 2.54b$, 95% CI = 2.45, 2.63). Thus, to answer research question 1, violence had a negative effect on enjoyment when action was controlled. (p. 454)

To begin our critical analysis of these three sentences, we would probably note that they are nearly unreadable with a great deal of information compacted into codes and abbreviations. Nonetheless, they follow the standard pattern of presentation. The first sentence reports the test of significance and tells us that under conventional rules we are justified in considering the difference among the levels of depicted violence across the criterion of enjoyment to be of import. The next sentence reports the descriptive data. It provides the three mean scores (2.29, 2.29, 2.54) and a measure of dispersion. The measure of dispersion is not the standard deviation or the standard error of the mean but rather a confidence interval (95% CI) that is based on an error term that comes out of the ANOVA. The 95% confidence interval is the range in which 95% of the scores can be expected to fall. The endpoints of 2.21 and 2.38 are reported for the first mean. What counts here is that the high end of the confidence interval is smaller than the mean for the no-violence condition, indicating that we are looking at two different sets of values. The last sentence is the implication of the result or the finding.

What work does the reader have to do to get an understanding of what is being said and what is very much missing? The first thing we have to do is to understand the criterion measure. On pages 451–452 we are told that the criterion measure is composed of two questions: "How much did you enjoy this program?" and "How entertaining was this program?" The two items were averaged on a 5-point scale that was anchored at 0 instead of the more conventional value of 1. That indicates that the expected mean would be 2.00 and not 3.00 as might be expected, a point easy to forget while reading.

Much further down (p. 456), we discover that the reported means are summed across the five programs. Consequently, the average reported is an average of an average of an average. The law of central tendency tells us that each of these consolidations will reduce the dispersion of the scores. The error term reported (about a .048 standard error of the mean) is very small but tells us little about the dispersion of the actual data.

In order to discover what a data set for a particular program might look like, I created a dummy set of data of 50 scores based on the average of a two-item 5-point scale with an averaged mean of 2.29 and a correlation of .82 between the two items to duplicate those two findings of Weaver and Wilson. I started with a set of random numbers from 0 to 4 in two columns of 50 each. I shifted a few numbers up in the first column to get a mean of 2.28. I then adjusted the numbers in the second column to get a correlation of .82. Figure 11.3 shows the distribution of scores.

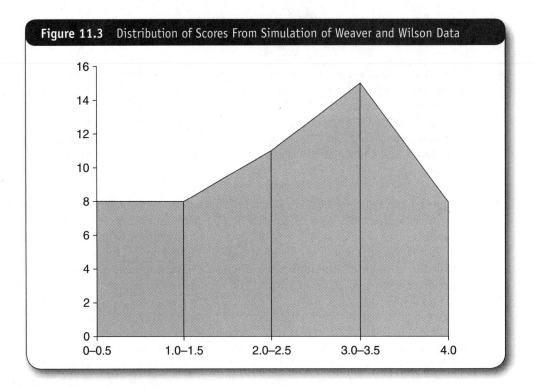

Figure 11.3   Distribution of Scores From Simulation of Weaver and Wilson Data

Remember that these are manufactured data, not data from Weaver and Wilson. The first thing we see is that the numbers are skewed left (longer negative tail) and that the mode is between 3 and 4. Even though this mean score is for the lesser-liked depictions, most people could like it "a lot." The standard deviation for this data set was 1.33.[13]

To continue this analysis, I adjusted the values of the two columns to get an averaged mean of 2.54 (the equivalent of the "no violence" condition) while maintaining the correlation of .82. Figure 11.4 shows that distribution.

The slope of skew gets sharper as I decrease the low-end values and increase the number of high-end values. The standard deviation of this data set is 1.22. It drops because the data have to become more compact as the respondents like the program more (ceiling effect), thereby increasing the likelihood of significant differences.

If Weaver and Wilson had given us this level of information, would we have reached a different conclusion than they did? I think we would have from the more relevant measures of dispersion but particularly from the histograms. The quoted data report a difference between the no-violence and two depicted-violence program sets as .25 or one fourth of one step on their enjoyment scale. Their conclusion was that violence had a generalized negative effect on enjoyment. That conclusion implies that there was a

---

[13]The value is similar to the standard deviations reported on p. 453. The standard deviation was for the first column 1.29 and for the second 1.49. The effect of averaging is to approach the lower value.

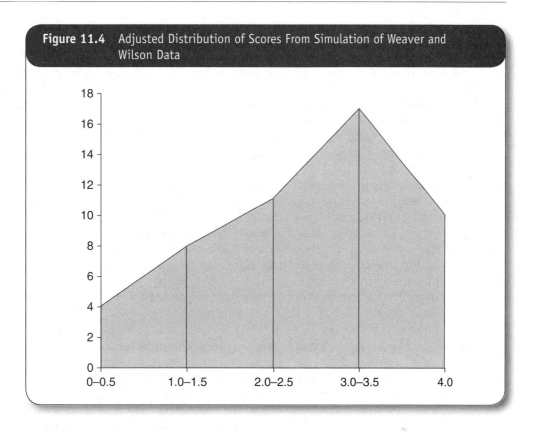

Figure 11.4   Adjusted Distribution of Scores From Simulation of Weaver and Wilson Data

lowered probability of low scores and/or a higher probability of high scores producing a global effect. In fact, no score can shift by one fourth, so the actual effect has to occur in relatively few data points. In the manufactured data set, it took about eight changes to adjust the mean and another four to recapture the correlation. More than three times the number of values remained the same as had to be changed. The Monte Carlo findings suggest that the entire effect may be the result of a few respondents holding particular attitudes about portrayed violence. We are back to the some-some conclusion with no evidence of a global effect.

If the means are significantly different, does it matter why they are significantly different? This Monte Carlo work gives us a resounding "Yes!" for the answer. But no reader can discover the actual facts unless the analyst provides the basis for them. Unfortunately, editors of carbon-based journals have a limited resource of space. They are often misguidedly ruthless in cutting the most valuable information and focusing on the inferential statistics instead. My recommendation, therefore, is to write a complete report, if for no one else than yourself, in which you provide both the inferential tests of the hypotheses and the complete set of descriptives. It is important to write it up, not just look at the results. Demonstrating the results and their implications in writing forces the writer to pay attention to the details so often missed but that lead to greater insight and, I think, more realistic conclusions.

Inferential Statistics

When the term *experimental design* is used, it most often refers to the design of the statistical analysis, not to the design of the protocol (which includes the statistical analysis). The complexities of statistical design have to do with the isolation of the treatment effect(s) and the calculation of the proper error terms and their conditional corrections. For nearly all of us who use statistics, these issues have been resolved in whichever statistical software package we use. Statistical design in a practical sense mostly means fitting our respondents, the criterion measure, and the experimental and control variables into one of these preexisting models.

Respondents in these models are categorized in one of two ways: in independent groups or as participating in repeated measures. An independent groups design such as that used by Weaver and Wilson employs a separate group of respondents for every treatment. Independent groups are called for when there is the possibility of contamination of responses by some previous activity in the experiment. Weaver and Wilson may have been concerned that watching several programs of that genre would lead to emotional or enjoyment fatigue for the later programs viewed.

Nonetheless, Weaver and Wilson could have respondents view one graphic, one sanitized, and one no-violence segment, randomizing the order and using different programs for each edit type. That design would employ a repeated measures factor. The supposed advantage of repeated measures is that they control for differences across subject groups that might contaminate the treatment effect. The repeated measures design suggests that the same set of respondent values is in play during each presentation type because the same respondents are involved. The choice between independent groups and repeated measures should be all about controlling the most likely sources of contamination. But, repeated measure designs are also ordinarily less costly to run as they require fewer respondents.

The criterion measure is the variable that is measured across all respondents regardless of conditions. The criterion in the Weaver and Wilson example we used was the two-item enjoyment-entertainment scale. Everyone completed those two items, no matter which of the edited versions each respondent saw. It is the criterion measure because the differences that occur across it are the basis of the claims of an effect by an experimental treatment and/or control variable(s).

Experimental variables are the ones controlled by the experimenter and are the center of the hypotheses to be tested. Control and covariate variables are typically characteristics, conditions, or states that the respondents walk into the experiment with. The terminology can be a bit confusing as we also talk about control groups or control conditions, which are actually one of the contrasts in a treatment set. A control group is often one where the manipulation of some treatment is absent; its value, however, is still manipulated by the experimenter (just set to zero).

Control and covariate variables can be exactly the same variable, and both function in the same way in an ANOVA design, but they differ in the role they play in the research argument. Analysts are not very consistent in the use of the terms *control* and *covariate*, but generally we use the term *control variable* when we expect the effect to be the same across the different values of the variable but of different magnitudes or at different starting places. The variable serves to "control" the variability of the scores (which would reduce power) by separating out the variance due to differences across the control variable. The control variable does not have (at least initially) theoretic implications.

We use the term *covariate* when the variable is expected to play some part in the hypothesis. In these cases, we have some theoretical basis for our expectation of difference. In the safe-sex message study, sensation seeking was theoretically linked to the likelihood of unsafe sexual behavior and to receptivity to more sensational messages. The more sensational message was hypothesized to be more effective for those with higher levels of sensation seeking.

Both control and covariate variables can be introduced to the design in a serendipitous, "just in case" sort of thinking. Weaver and Wilson add an inventory of shows watched "to control for prior exposure to violent media." They offer no justification for doing so or any prediction as to effect, but they also don't need to, unless, of course, it turns out it makes a difference. In that case, they would be caught in post hoc, catch-up reasoning. It was not significant. They also collect a fairly large number of other demographic and psychographic variables that were not reported in the study, but were undoubtedly examined.

Weaver and Wilson used sex of the respondent as a fully preplanned covariate. They hypothesized that males and females would enjoy violent and nonviolent content differently based on some preliminary findings from previous research. It too was not significant. I suspect that here was a case where gender and not sex is the operating variable. A measure based on masculinity or femininity rather than physiology might have been more effective.

An Invented Example

Let's see how it all gets put together by going back to our engaged-exposed example where we were considering the effect of sunscreen-use messages on those participating in outdoor activities with high sun exposure such as those based on snow, water, and other full-sun environments and/or at higher altitudes with less atmospheric protection.[14]

We would want to identify our respondents based on their participation level using some measure that would divide the group into high, moderate, and low participation segments. The criterion measure would be a measure of effectiveness, perhaps a combination of a P&P intent-to-use measure with the actual purchase of a sunscreen product from a kiosk outside the experimental setting. We would want to develop three to five public service announcements (PSAs), all based on the same content elements but with different production values. (Why?) We could also use different types of messages—fear or a threat, humor, social responsibility—but each would have to have multiple examples. And, we would need four treatment conditions—engaged, exposed, and two no-message conditions for every message variation we used. The study gets very big, very fast.

We are now faced with some decisions. The first has to do with how to use our respondents. Can we control for intergroup differences and gain some efficiency in cost and time by using repeated measures? Perhaps respondents could randomly cycle through engaged, exposed, and no-message treatments. That approach would cut the number of respondents

---

[14]I really wanted to write something here about the difference between the skilled grace of skiers and the knuckle-dragging character of boarders, but my reviewers wouldn't let me.

for each control group in half, but, unfortunately, the subterfuge of a technical failure might influence the two other treatment performances when the no-message condition is encountered first in the sequence. The danger of contamination seems too high to me.

I would recommend using different types of messages as there is a strong theoretical base to support it. It would give the study more appeal to editors and potential sponsors. Again, however, I don't think that respondents can evaluate more than one form because of the attenuation effect of message repetition.

Where we can use repeated measures is with the criterion variables. We have three criteria: content acquisition, intention to use, and a likely-to-purchase measure collected at the sunscreen kiosk. Everyone would complete all three criterion measures, but independent groups would be used for every other treatment, control, or covariate condition.

Let's say we decide on three message types, each with three examples. We then have three respondent groups sorted by level of participation, by three message types, by three examples, and by two engaged conditions (message and no message) and two exposed conditions (message and no message) with the three criterion measures (content acquisition, intent to use, and subsequent purchase likelihood). Consequently, we have three instances (one for each criterion) of a $3 \times 3 \times 3 \times 2 \times 2$ for a total of 108 groups. If we put 15 respondents in each group, we would need 1,620 individuals, each of whom would have to sort nicely into one of the 108 participation groups. Good thing we have a big grant.

This is an enormously complex design,[15] but we can begin to reduce the complexity if we combine the three examples of each message type. In order to do that, we have to show that the effects of message type are stable across the three examples. Unfortunately, that puts us on the "wrong" side of the way inferential tests work. You may remember that tests are typically designed to make it difficult to show differences in order to protect from Type I error (accepting the research hypothesis when it is false). Consequently, the ordinary tests are set up to show no difference, which is what we would want in this case. It follows the old rule of thumb: "Don't ask questions you might not like the answer to." Even though this is a standard way of dealing with issues like these, we have to do better. The least we can do is to set our alpha level at something like .10 or .20. Much better would be to establish the specific conditions under which we declare the set of individual PSAs within each type to be consistent prior to testing to reduce our dependence on "wrong-sided" statistical testing.

The practical pressure to use the easiest test for "sameness" is quite strong, because the cost of finding difference is quite high. Weaver and Wilson used five different exemplars in each of their three violence edits. They found no significant interactions over the message factor (p. 456). But the significance level used was appropriate to the control of Type I error and not the Type II error they would be in danger of committing. They provide no graphs and indeed report no means. It is a typical approach. As readers, we can usually depend on the combined effort of analysts, reviewers, and editors to ensure that the right inferential tests are run, but only if the right questions are asked and asked in the right way.

The task of any protocol design is to answer the questions posed by the problem at hand and to generate additional information so that new problem statements can be formed. The task of any analysis is to definitively extract the answers and to mine the data for all that might

---

[15]And, frankly, very slow reading. The best way to work through this section is to run the Monte Carlo experiment yourself.

be of value. To demonstrate how one goes about these tasks, I built a data set for one portion of the engaged-exposed experiment, setting terms for what I would expect to be the intent outcomes for the engaged conditions. These terms can be considered hypotheses, which themselves would ordinarily be built on the careful review of previous research. I was working from what I know about the literature, personal observation in working with outdoor participants, and the goals of this section—a mixture of literature, plausible guesses, and pedagogical intent.

The requirements for the data set were as follows:

1. High participation levels would be associated with low intent for sunscreen use, and low participation levels would be associated with high intent.

2. All message types would show higher intent to use scores than the no-message condition.

3. Humor would be the most effective message type, personal safety the least, and fear intermediate.

In order to meet these requirements, I changed the permissible range for the random numbers to be generated. For example, in the no-message data, I truncated the upper values to ensure a lower mean score. Even with this manipulation, the data set could still show plenty of surprises. Let me remind you (as I remind myself) that none of our data or findings is real. The purpose is to show the techniques of analysis.

The data set produces a 3 (levels of participation) by 4 (message types—fear, humor, personal safety, none). The requirements do not specify an interaction between participation levels and message type, although the method of data generation allows one to appear. I use SPSS as my statistical application. As in all SPSS analyses, each row in a data set represents one respondent. Nominal values identify the participation group (1, 2, or 3) and message type the respondent was assigned. Table 11.2 shows the transition point from participation group 1 to participation group 2 with the message type resetting to the first type. With this data set, I would go to the "Analyze" menu and would select a univariate analysis under the General Linear Model (Figure 11.5). That selection generates a sorting table that allows me to enter the data into the analysis, according to its participation by message type source (Figure 11.6).

Intent is entered as the dependent variable as it is our criterion measure. Participation level and message type are entered as fixed factors because they have been manipulated

Table 11.2 Data Set Showing Transition Point

Part_Level	Messge_Type	Intent
1	4	2.00
1	4	5.00
2	1	3.00
2	1	6.00

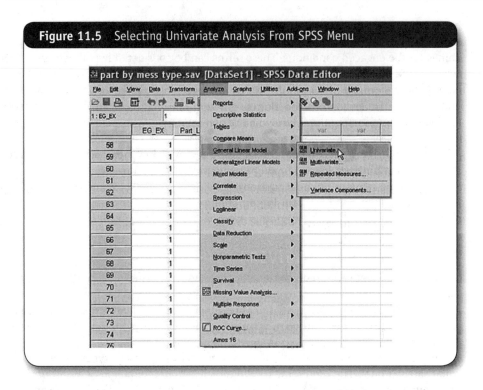

Figure 11.5 Selecting Univariate Analysis From SPSS Menu

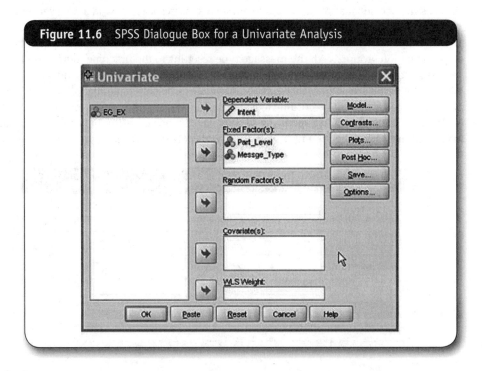

Figure 11.6 SPSS Dialogue Box for a Univariate Analysis

by the analyst (random factors are not manipulated). The table allows a number of options, which are beyond our scope here except to say that I always collect descriptive statistics and plot the simplest (lowest-level) means.

After I have confirmed that the data were entered correctly (using the methods described in Chapter 9), I then go to the inferential tests to check significance. The arguments that I can create for the results are different depending on how those tests turn out. If nothing is significant (and I still believe in the hypotheses), then the lesson to be learned is about the design of the protocol that led to the failure. The requirements for this data set establish two main effects hypotheses—there will be differences across participation levels and message types—and specify certain differences among levels and types. Consequently, if the results show a significant level effect and a significant message effect, and no interaction, I have the first level of support for the hypotheses and would move to an investigation of the main effect means to see if the specifics hold up as well.

In our case we have a significant interaction that indicates that the effect of level varies across different message types and that the effect of message types varies across participation levels. It is not legitimate (but also not unheard of) to discuss main effect means given this outcome. In short, my hypotheses failed, but in an exciting and informative way. These results suggest that I will be able to refine, not simply support, existing theory. Table 11.3 shows what the ANOVA table would look like. The far-right column indicates the significance level (some value beyond .000).

At this point, I go to the plots of the simple means as presented in Figure 11.7. The lines are participation levels, and the points are message types. The interaction is shown at the points where the lines cross or substantially deflect from parallel.

Table 11.3 ANOVA Results for Message Type by Participation Level Over Message Effectiveness

Dependent Variable: Intent					
Source	Type III Sum of Squares	df	Mean Square	F	Significance
Corrected model	178.420	11	16.220	7.903	.000
Intercept	9134.891	1	9134.891	4450.744	.000
Part_Level	59.959	2	29.980	14.607	.000
Messge_Type	64.850	3	21.617	10.532	.000
Part_Level by Messge_Type Interaction	53.611	6	8.935	4.353	.000
Error	1083.699	528	2.052		
Total	10397.000	540			
Corrected total	1269.109	539			

The analyst is charged with explaining this complexity with an appropriate set of mean scores and inferential tests. The initial explanation has to account for each point and each line on the plot. For example, early questions might include "Is the control group significantly lower than any message group for each of the participation levels?" "How does each message type vary significantly across participation levels?" But there are also mysteries to be sorted out such as "Why does the intermediate group not act like an intermediate group?" "Why are fear appeals so effective and humor appeals relatively ineffective for high-participation respondents?" (Remember these data and findings appear more realistic than they are.)

The analyst has to throw off the limitations of the hypotheses to conduct this exploration. The hypotheses have failed. The effort, now, is to develop better hypotheses, not to defend the failed ones as is ordinarily done in the literature. In the end, the analyst will have something to say about every meaningful combination of lines and points. How much of it ends up in a particular report will depend on the purposes and audiences for the report. Regardless, the analyst has to be secure in the totality of the analysis—that every valuable question has been asked and explored—even if uncertain as to the answers.

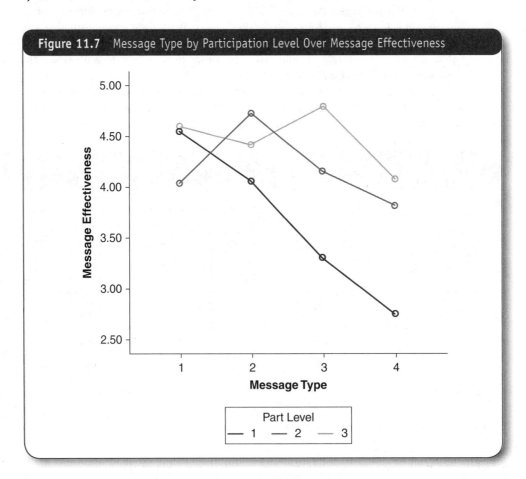

Figure 11.7 Message Type by Participation Level Over Message Effectiveness

THE ETHICS OF EXPERIMENTS

The ethical principles governing the design of experiments are threefold: The design must allow the research hypothesis to both meaningfully fail and adequately succeed; treatment and controls must not pose nonconsensual or inappropriate risk to respondents; and the design must engage the contexts of its conclusions.

The research hypothesis can meaningfully fail when the treatments and controls create a fair test. Weak or meaningless controls give the appearance of a test without actually challenging the treatment. Or a control might produce its own effect as the potential frustration induced by the no-message condition in our example above.

In most cases, communication experiments involve little more than everyday risks, but there are some interesting issues. What about exposure to content that is presumed to have negative consequences for the viewer? Researchers have testified that every exposure to violent content has a negative effect in the same vein as secondhand smoke. How do they justify another experiment? Physiological measures such as eye-marker cameras can cause damage in combination with underlying conditions that the researcher may not be qualified to evaluate. Deception that is not adequately debriefed may leave the respondents with a false assumption about a class of people or about themselves.

Finally, experiments must achieve a minimal level of ecological validity to permit the transfer of findings from the laboratory to naturally occurring contexts. The production of the evidence for that level of ecological validity has to be part of the overall design. Speculation that it might transfer is no conclusion. We can all speculate without running an experiment.

CONCLUSION

The design of experimental protocols represents some of the most demanding work in research. The researcher has to create the conditions under which we can have confidence not only in the testing of a causal relationship, but in that the relationship will generalize to the conditions found normally in society. It is work that requires a great deal of technical skill in measurement and metric analysis as well as creative solutions to the problems of ecological validity. Ofttimes they involve managing large numbers of people in protocols that allow respondents to return good information, that make efficient use of participants' time, and that in themselves do no harm.

The work starts with a problem that somehow implicates a causal relationship between an agent or agents and the context in which the agent is located that might include moderating conditions, preexisting states, and/or concurrent cognitive and actional requirements. The protocol sorts all these out into the components of theoretical concepts and constructs, variables and their measurement, treatments, controls, respondent requirements and assignments, statistical analysis, and, to close the circle, the implications for theory.

MOVING ON

This concludes the center of our engagement with metric methods. The next two chapters begin the transition to interpretive methods by taking up the analysis of content and texts.

REFLECTIONS

What Are Some Points to Remember?

- Experiments are based on a deductive approach based on theory and previous research. The stronger that theory and previous research, the better the experimental design.
- The experimental protocol has to isolate the relationship between the independent and dependent variables. The more complete that isolation, the more secure the conclusion. The greater the isolation, however, the greater the likelihood that the conclusions will fail to show ecological validity and will not translate to actual conditions.
- Good statistical analysis is not simply a report of the tests of significance. It involves the use of all available statistical tools to achieve a thorough understanding of how the treatment works.

Why Does It Matter?

Experimental designs are intended to draw instrumental conclusions. Instrumental conclusions are those that are intended to provide guidance for or to direct the actions of significant social actors such as parents, teachers, and policy makers.

What Else Could We Talk About?

A survey of high school students from 20 Cleveland-area high schools reported in late 2010 that hyper-texting—sending more than 120 text messages per day—was associated with increased likelihoods of smoking, drinking, and sexual activity. Hyper-texting was also associated with increased likelihoods of being female, a member of a minority, of lower socioeconomic status, and in a single-parent household with a missing father. The lead researcher concluded in a Case Western Reserve University School of Medicine press release, "The startling results of this study suggest that when left unchecked texting and other widely popular methods of staying connected can have dangerous health effects on teenagers."[16] This study poses significant issues both to a methodological critic (surveys posing as experimental evidence) and to a social advocate (ethnic, racial, class, and gender typifications).

What Else Might Be Interesting to Read?

Slater, M. D. (1991). Use of message stimuli in mass communication experiments: A methodological assessment and discussion. *Journalism Quarterly, 68*, 412–421.

---

[16]http://case.edu/medicus/breakingnews/scottfrankhypertextingandteenrisks.html. Accessed December 12, 2010.

Section IV

Conducting Research in the Interpretive Paradigm

In this section, we transition from metric research to interpretive research. We do so by looking at the requirements for studies that investigate texts, first from the metric framework and then from the interpretive framework. The purpose of this transition is to show the basic commonalities that are part of both of these frameworks. From there, Geoff Baym leads us through the intricacies of the critical interpretive analysis. Finally, we return to the action of ethnographic studies.

As I did in the introduction to Section III, let me remind you of the assumptions that form the borders of the epistemological domain you will reach at the end of this section. We will be walking away from causality, certainty, and closure and into agency, multiplicity, and indeterminacy; away from objectivity, measurement, and the individual and into epistemological standpoints, interpretive frameworks, and the community; away from well-conventionalized method and into emergent forms; away from the dominant and into the disruptive. It will be a slow but steady transition, and in the end, we will be in a very different place.

Interpretive research focuses on the meaningfulness that arises not from some intrinsic set of characteristics, but from cultural, societal, and membership practices. Meaning is a joint production of human actors. The purpose of interpretive methods is to document the practices and to craft the narrative of the multiplicity of this socially constructed meaningfulness. The research narrative itself is multiple. Instead of reaching closure, there is always another story to be told that will enlarge our understanding of the social world in which our lives emerge. The analyst is center stage, not as the skill technician of metric research and not as the discoverer or great explorer, but as a cultural agent, an instrument of interpretation. I hope you enjoy the tour.

C H A P T E R 1 2

Coding Text

CHAPTER PREVIEW

What's It All About?

Coding is a process that seeks to reach below the surface manifestations of symbolic and discursive texts for the purpose of identifying the underlying characteristics, structures, social meanings, and cultural work that such texts have, produce, or enact. Coding is done in both metric and interpretive research. In metric research, one typically has a template that guides the investigation; in interpretive research, that template emerges from the engagement of the texts.

What Are the Major Topics?

Texts are not the production of some innocent author. Rather, they appear at the intersection of the author, the industry, the media, the audience, the act of interpretation, and the demands of the text itself.

Metric coding starts with an investigation of theory and prior research; continues to the development of the sample of text, the classifications that will be used to code the texts, the instructions for the independent coders, the quantification of those codes, and their statistical analysis; and ends in their contribution to theory.

Interpretive coding starts with the selection of texts; continues to the close reading of those texts, during which codes will begin to emerge, and the iterative processes of coding and recoding; and ends in their contribution to theory development.

Whether metric or interpretive, all coding begins with a thorough understanding of the facts to texts. Gathering these facts can be greatly aided by computer analysis.

Texts can be coded in word processing programs, spreadsheets, database applications, and dedicated programs.

What Special Terms Are Used?

Database program	Live text	Reflexivity
Digitized text	Meta-communication	Window of text

INTRODUCTION TO CODING TEXTS

A text is any symbolic or discursive form. A symbolic form might be a framework of dance, a set of photographs, or a visual narrative as well as a genre of music or natural sound recordings. Discourse is any extended language and symbolic use that is under some common governance. A classroom lecture, a magazine article, a strategic communication campaign, a newspaper story, and even a tweet (although not very extended) are all discursive forms, because there are implicit rules that govern topic, construction, word choice, and performance that are recognizable in their performance and in their violation. The analysis of texts is the bridge between metric and hermeneutic epistemologies and methodologies. The analysis must be both factual and interpretive in order to be complete. Theorists and methodologists, naturally, disagree on the relative balance between these two. One of the reasons for this disagreement is that the balance changes according to the purposes of the analysis.

For an example of how this balance works, we could think of a study that examines the effect of contemporary newspaper layout design on the amount of news content. Many newspapers have gone from a 54-inch broadsheet to a more "reader-friendly" 48-inch width.[1] Modern designs make a heavy use of "white space"; use large-font callouts, "refers," and promos; and put a strong emphasis on visual elements (number and size). All of these elements would appear to reduce the amount of unique story content. In taking this approach, newspapers appear to be following the trend of many manufacturers of reducing the standard "container size" (a half-gallon of ice cream is now 1.75 quarts) in order to charge the same for less product. For newspapers, reducing the "news hole" (or making a graphic element larger to fill it) means that less story product is needed with the attendant savings in reporting costs.

A study of this sort is heavy on the factual side of the balance beam. We have limited interest in the meaning or meaningfulness of the content; we are mostly interested in the factual characteristics of that content. Certainly, we have to put into place some definitions and reliable procedures to identify white space, nonstory print components, visual

---

[1]See http://www.observer.com/node/32911 (accessed April 29, 2011) for an insider's analysis of this movement.

elements, and the dependent variable of unique story content. These requirements do not appear to be high in difficulty, however.

They also don't tell us very much, simply increasing the precision by which we can describe what is a fairly obvious set of consequences—newspapers print all the news that fits. Let's change the question to investigate the quality of the news that is printed. The loss of capacity may not be as important if the quality of the reportage has increased in equivalent measure. A very recent survey taken by the Associated Press Managing Editors (APME) indicates that "seventy-one percent of the survey participants said cutbacks have 'somewhat affected' or 'greatly affected' the quality of their newspapers' coverage."[2] More than 100,000 jobs have been lost in the industry over an 18-month period.

This clearly is a much more difficult question than that of measuring column inches of white space. I will need some set of criteria that define the quality of a story. Those criteria would appear to be both intrinsic to the construction and writing of the story itself and extrinsic to the event that is being reported. To build the first set of criteria, I would probably go to the style manuals that provide the conventions of good reporting—the inverted pyramid; *who, what, when, where, why,* and *how;* local angle; multiple sides; good sources; and other norms. (Notice that these criteria have no connection to the quality judgments of an actual reader. The analyst cannot directly conclude about readers or audiences from content data.)

The second set of criteria—the extrinsic set—is much more difficult to specify. I would need to have some standard of the event or circumstances of the story. That standard does not exist. Consequently, I might use a set of experts to evaluate the story for both its factual content and its utility for understanding the implications of the event (why it is news).

Quite clearly, none of these criteria is simply factual. The conventions of "good" journalistic writing are in part arbitrary, in part practical (the inverted pyramid is said to have developed to preserve the meat of the story should most of it be lost in telegraphic transmission), and none guarantee good writing, which itself is a judgment. The value of the criteria is that they are not idiosyncratic to the analyst and can be justified to others. A modernist scholar would call them objective; a postmodernist would call them culturally embedded. All of them appear in an act of judgment exercised by the analysts. Our confidence in those judgments vary. The presence or absence of white space is nearly unequivocal; whether the *who, what, when, where, why,* and *how* of something has been adequately presented is not.

Metric scholars manage these equivocal conditions by developing a set of rules—a coding manual—that directs the activities of the coders toward the theoretically determined properties of interest. The coding manual itself is developed in iterative pretesting, in which codes are added, divided, eliminated, or combined as needed until the code set creates a good fit between theory that directs the study and the properties of the content. Metric

---

[2]http://www.editorsweblog.org/newsrooms_and_journalism/2009/05/apme_survey_75_of_us_editors_confirm_tha .php. Accessed April 30, 2011.

coding reports on the degree of agreement among coders as evidence of its nonidiosyncrasy or objectivity with 100% being desired and 60% to 70% considered publishable. Disagreements are resolved by adjusting the coding rules or, if irresolvable in that manner, by a third party, usually the principal investigator.

Hermeneutic scholars (and hybrids who do coding) typically use a grounded approach that eschews theoretical direction but builds the coding scheme in interaction with the texts. When a unit of text doesn't appear to fit any available code, a new code is provided. Subsequent analysis might divide, eliminate, or combine codes. When multiple coders are used, disagreements are expected, considered a valuable insight, and usually negotiated to a new code conclusion (if the disagreement is intractable, the senior author wins). In the end, the primary differences between the two approaches are the starting point—metric in theory and interpretive in the discourse—and the final form of the argument. In the middle of things, there are not many differences between the best coding practices of each approach, though those differences are hotly defended.

SYMBOLIC AND DISCURSIVE PROTOCOLS

Symbolic and discursive protocols most often address questions of the properties of content, but they can also participate in the analysis of processes, consequences, and quality. Our introductory example of the newspaper is primarily a study of properties, but if conducted as part of a pre- and postlayout changes protocol, it becomes a consequences analysis. And, clearly, the second half of the example is intended to speak to the quality of current reporting. Finally, the whole of the analysis might be a good explanation for what appears to be the death spiral of newspapers as we currently know them and begins to speak to economic and information theory.[3]

Four Intentions

Symbolic and discursive protocols can also be understood by the intentionality or intentionalities they serve. There are four sets of these intentions: the intention of the author (industry), the intention of the text, the intention of the auditor (audience), and the intention of the interpretation (auditor and analyst). These four sets work both extrinsically on the object of study and intrinsically on the research argument (research is discourse too).

For example, as I write this section, my intention (authorial intention to the extent that I can know it) is to enlarge the discussion of metric approaches to content analysis in order that a more inclusive view can be obtained. My "handlers" at Sage Publications (industry intentions) will advise and edit based on their own set of goals for the writing. The fact that I am writing a textbook imposes pedagogical requirements on the writing (intentions of the text) but also allows for a more personal "teaching" style.

---

[3]Rasmussen Reports concludes from its polling data that 65% of U.S. respondents believe that newspapers will be gone in 10 years. But, as it was for Mark Twain, the notice of their demise might be premature. I hope they hang on long enough to make this example useful. I know; it's all about me. (See http://www.rasmussenreports.com/public_content/lifestyle/general_lifestyle/65_say_daily_papers_will_be_gone_in_ten_years. Accessed April 29, 2011.)

For most textbooks, the intention of the auditor reflects the primacy of the instructor as she or he adopts the book. It is these adoptions that create the audience. Both author and industry intentions have to account for this set of auditor intentions. Both author and industry presume that the instructor wishes to produce a competent course. The question for all three—author, industry, instructor/auditor—is the extent to which this section of writing helps achieve that goal.[4]

And what of the intentions of the audience created in the course adoptions? Is there a model reader here? Can we assume any global characteristics of the members of the reading class? I think it is fair to presume that most are not here because of their choice, or, at least, the choice was not of the book but of the course. Are the majority motivated to learn, get credit, or do something of both? If it is just for credit, then my burden is less, because in creating a list of intentions, I have created an excellent short-answer question for an exam for which the reader can get credit. If it is to learn, my burden is greater, because I have to be sure that I demonstrate the value of this heuristic for analyzing discourse. We'll see.

Finally, we arrive at the intention of the interpretation. Consideration of this intention is probably the most contentious and has the least presence in the literature. It is contentious because of the lack of agreement as to where this event (the interpretation) occurs. For some, it is behind the eyes in some cognitive process that has behavioral consequences. For others, it is in front of the eyes in some action—the interpretation is not fully formed until one does something that entails the text. It has the least presence in the literature because of the methodological obstacles to its investigation.

How that behavior or action entailment is conceptualized is also problematic. Is it behavior that can be independently addressed without reference to the context of its performance or to the regularized practices of the individual? Or is it action that is embedded in an ecology of performance and further informed by the sociocultural protocols of competent enactment?

Finally, there is the question of the relationship between the interpretation as performed by an auditor (audience) and the interpretation as performed by an analyst (discipline). Can the analyst speak for the auditor? In metric research, do the marked properties of the content reliably direct the interpretation of the audience? In hermeneutic studies, does the interpretation generated in analysis resonate in the multiple contexts of reception?

The four (plus the parenthetical three) intentionalities provide us with the justification for careful analysis of content. That analysis allows us to draw conclusions about the approaches of an author, the standards and conventions of an industry, the appeals directed toward and the resources made available to an auditor or audience, and the potentials for action based on the materials of the text both in everyday life and in the context of research. In its best light, the analysis reveals what is hidden in the flow of the narrative just as a strobe light can reveal the elements of a continuous flow of movement.

---

[4]A competent course may also have to account for nonreading. The percentage of students not buying a text is on the increase, with estimates of between 10% and 50% not having a book. Instructors are advised to speak approvingly of buying the book and to have course activities that depend specifically on reading the book. (See, for example, http://www.psychologicalscience.org/teaching/tips/tips_0603.cfm. Accessed April 29, 2011.)

Analysis of Intentionalities

Any media text will show all of these intentionalities—author (industry), text, auditor (audience), interpretation (auditor/analyst)—either encoded in material fact or latent in its potential for actualization. We can extract a particular component of these intentionalities by means of the protocol design and the focus of the analysis. (Additional discussion of these issues can be found in Fürisch, 2009.)

Author (Industry)

The usual method is to hold the source of the effect of interest constant or common and let the other sources vary. For example, if an analyst was interested in the contributions of an author (actor/artist/auteur/etc.), the analyst would look at a body of work by that author. We could examine the films of Quentin Tarantino from *Reservoir Dogs* to *Inglourious Basterds* (sic)—given evidence that producers, film crews, cinematographers, and actors vary across these films—to illuminate the devices and structural components that regularly occur. Identifying the evidence of these regularities would give us some confidence in describing a Tarantino signature. (For an analysis based on a single film, see Weinberger, 2004.)

If the concern was more for industry practice, the analyst would examine a collection of texts produced under particular industry conditions or compare sets of texts from different conditions. Think of a study comparing stories on common subject matter from Fox News with those from, say, CBS. Haigh et al. (2006) studied the content differences between Iraq War coverage by embedded versus nonembedded journalists. They found that embedded journalists were more positive about the military and were judged by coders to be more authoritative (p. 150). If I were in charge of military press relations, I might conclude that the risks of having embedded journalists were worth taking.

(Media) Text

We come now to the intention of the (media) text.[5] Of course, a text cannot have an intention in the sense of a foresight as to what the author should write next or how the reader should make sense of it. But, clearly, both writer and reader have a set of expectations as to what will come next based on what has preceded. Once even the first few words are written or read, only certain subsequent elements can be competently elaborated while others will necessarily be excluded and suppressed. I write to a model reader; you read based on a model author. Consequently, the intention of the text is that I should be able to write as you should be able to read.

The extra-authorial intention of the text is expressed in metacommunicative concepts like master narratives, master contracts, genres, forms and conventions, and framing. These similar concepts all share the central notion of a "set of rules" that direct author and reader in the construction and reading of the media text. These concepts have a long history in literary theory (e.g., Propp, 1928/1968), although they are fairly recent in metric analysis.

---

[5]The concept of this intention is attributed to Umberto Eco (Eco, 1992, pp. 64–66).

One reason for their late arrival is the difficulty in establishing the factual basis of, say, a frame. The evidence for a frame cannot be found in a particular text or even across multiple texts. It has to be found in both (see Matthes & Kohring, 2008). The evidence has to point to the factual traces of the frame in each text and to its structural force across the texts in what appears and what is omitted. It is easy to leave solid ground. Esser (2009), for example, in his study of German newspaper coverage of the Iraq War, found it necessary "to determine whether the framing devices were salient enough to create a specific frame—by means of frequency, prominence, homogeneity, and semantic meaning" (p. 721).

Auditor (Audience)

The remaining intentionalities have to do with the audience and individual audience members (in psychological approaches, one is concerned with auditors—the effects on individuals; in sociological and cultural approaches, the concern is with audiences). Content analysis has a conflicted relationship with audiences. On the one side, the reason we study content is because we presume there is an audience for it and that the content characteristics interact with or have effects on that audience. On the other side, content analysis, per se, cannot demonstrate either of those presumptions.

As a result, the content analyst has to rely on either propositions holding the literal transmission of meaning and the global nature of meaning—propositions mostly rejected by communication theorists—or more indirect arguments based on the potential for some interpretation, which would then have the possibility of a set of effects. It is admittedly not very satisfying.

Content analysis can play an important (and often neglected) part in audience effects studies, however. Most effects studies are rather cavalier in the selection of content with the researcher selecting the content with an "of course it's true" approach that this content is violent, sexy, gender based, or whatever the issue. It would be much better if we adopted a more sophisticated analysis of the content and could point to the properties by which the genre claim is made. Researchers could then vary the appearance of those properties to better test their consequences.

As you remember from our discussion on experiments, we have been able to demonstrate certain consequences for some auditors in media effects studies. Unfortunately, we have no idea how those laboratory effects scale up in audiences once released into the wild. There is the implicit assumption in such studies that a relative handful of people encountering artificial content under extraordinary conditions can stand for 30 million or so encountering content in an ecology that generates context, comment, competition, distraction, fragmentation, intertexuality (e.g., my quoting someone else), textual interpenetration (e.g., reading while listening to music), and multiple other conditions all in some action that includes the text of interest. If we know little about auditors, we know almost nothing about audiences beyond the aggregated values of attendance provided by commercial research services.

The hermeneutic concept of interpretive communities more deeply inscribes the intentionality of the audience. The concept ranges from the culturally broad (e.g., all U.S. conservatives) as suggested by Fish (1980) to the locally enacted (Radway, 1984). Our now long-ago political talk radio example constituted a market-wide interpretive community in the regular callers, and our dance club, *Dancing with the Stars* congregation that we will meet in Chapter 15 shows us a very local interpretive community. It is likely that audiences are made up of multiple interpretive communities (as well as the disconnected) and those interpretive communities exercise different levels of interactivity and rhetorical force.

Interpretation (Auditor/Analyst)

The intentionality of an auditor's interpretation—the action initiated or behavior produced—or the governance of an interpretive community is even more distant from the content analysis itself. Again, however, it is part of the justification for the analysis. The real consequences of one's engagement with content occur in how the individual lives her or his life in interaction with that content. We are a long way from being able to conduct that sort of study, but it does start with a thorough understanding of the content.

Despite postmodernism's callout for reflexivity—that self-conscious analysis of one's research practice—the analyst remains something of the wizard behind the curtain in both metric and interpretive research. Whether directed by theory or grounded in the discourse, coding is, in the end, a set of judgments that themselves are beyond the reach of the research. Attempts to explain those judgments typically achieve nothing more than a false sense of rationality.

ELEMENTS OF CONTENT PROTOCOLS

Content analysis is a set of systematic technical procedures intending to reveal the properties, not otherwise observable, of a class of content. At its most surface level, the focus is on the facts of the text—the words, sentences, paragraphs or shots, transitions, angles, exposure or vocal pitch, rate of speaking, or whatever are the factual components of the class of media texts involved—and their rates of occurrence—the number of unique words, the ratio of close-ups to establishing shots, the correspondence between framing and angle, and other measures. Computer algorithms are the most effective, error-free method of collecting the facts of the text.

The analysis moves beneath the factual surface when it is focused on the meaningfulness of the text—everything from topic to frame to narrative to intertextual allusions is a claim about the meaningfulness of the text. Meaningfulness involves the relationship between the text and a "meaning maker" and is, therefore, not inherent in the text itself. The meaningful properties of a text are revealed in processes that involve analytic judgment. There are four steps in this process: developing codes, selection and coding of the cases, selection and coding of the units of analysis, and coding of the content within the unit.

Metric and interpretive content protocols show their primary differences on the front end of the process: in the conceptual differences between content and text, in the formulation of the problem under study, in the manner in which the coding is conducted, and in the purposes held for the coding. Once past that not-insignificant list, the procedures are much the same. Here let me spend just a few lines highlighting the differences, again selecting centroid positions and recognizing the multiple positions in between.

For the metric scholar, content is static with its meaning more or less fixed in durable and stable processes of engagement. One can speak of being exposed to content and have expectations for an effect. It is the same language we would use for the consequence of being in the presence of some agent. No action on the part of the person exposed is required.

For the hermeneutic scholar, text is dynamic; its meaning depends on the action in progress and the actors who will engage the text in that action. Meaning is never contained or fixed; new meaning can be produced from old texts. Meaning emerges from the interaction.

The import of the difference is that the metric scholar is justified in addressing content with an a priori set of codes because the content either will or will not support that code set. The hermeneutic scholar would not be justified because the text will always respond to any code set, even if in unpredictable ways.

Given the different understandings for content and text, the problems in play would necessarily be different. The center of that difference rests on the difference between the questions of what meaning is there and what meaning can emerge. For the metric scholar, meaning is there to be measured; for the hermeneut, it is a set of potentials that can be differentially actualized. Further, the metric scholar sees content as more or less rationally produced, purposefully guided by the author. For the hermeneutic scholar, the author is continually subverted by cultural, societal, and other critical influences. Authorial intent is often the least interesting part of the text. The cultural work of this textbook would be more interesting to the interpretive scholar than the informational intent of this paragraph.

Metric coding is a top-down process using preestablished codes, a codebook of rules for applying them, and research-naïve coders who can be tested for their reliable performance working independently of the researcher and one another. Interpretive coding is a grounded, emergent approach with the text initiating and justifying each addition to the code set. Coders are immersed in the research problem and work together to resolve differences and exchange insights.

Finally, metric coding is used to declare what is there and to show the relative rates and differences within and between content sets. Interpretive coding is used to show the work that can be done with a text, the interpretations that can be produced, the cultural consequences, and the like. Again, I take no stand on these differences other than to note them. It is enough to know that they are different, intend to be different, and will not be dissuaded from being different. There is a need not to resolve these differences, only to honor them.

METRIC CODING

This and the next two sections will look at the practices that define metric coding, those that define interpretive coding, and those that are common to both. We start with metric coding.

The process of metric coding starts with a clear problem statement. Deductive processes presume the analyst knows what she or he is looking for. The clarity of that search is established in the clarity of the problem. (If the analyst is on a fishing expedition, exploratory methods should be used.) Given a good problem, the analyst then makes a list of the theoretical concepts that are the foundation of the study. For example, if interested in the question of the representation of the gendered body in music videos, the analyst has to start with concepts dealing with gender, body image, representation of the body, male and female gaze, musical forms, and conventions of music videos as a partial list. There is a good deal of work involved and a real competence that has to be achieved.

This list of concepts has to be transformed into a list of constructs—the concepts as rendered in the content. In order to achieve this construct list, the analyst has to systematically and deeply engage the content to identify the content elements that fill the requirements of the theoretical concepts in play. It remains for the analyst to take a bunch of cases (but something less than, say, a third of a sample in hand) and search for the exemplars that fill the concepts with actual content, all the while ensuring that the codes connect to the research questions and particularly to the hypotheses. The analyst should be able to specify the coding outcomes that will support or falsify the hypotheses. There should be no confusion as to the value of the work once it's done.

Cases

The analytical process starts by the aggregation of the cases that will contain the units of analysis and, in turn, the content that will be coded. Cases are the articles, editorials, letters, advertisements, programs, commercials, films, videos, blogs, tweets, e-mails, or whatever collectable content form is the focus of the study. The case has to be appropriate to the research question of the study, and the collection has to provide a fair (unbiased) representation of the type of case involved. For example, if the analyst is studying major market newspaper reporting, then the articles selected have to come from newspapers in major markets and be written by local reporters. This necessity seems obvious, but it doesn't always work out in obvious ways.

Sampling Frame

Cases are generally selected within some form of a sampling frame. A sampling frame, as we have seen, is simply a set of rules and resources that identifies all the cases that could be selected into the study. That set is usually smaller than all the extant cases. A study of regional reporting, for example, ostensibly targets all newspaper articles that focus on the market's region. That target generates far too many articles to be practicable. A sampling frame that limits the markets, newspapers, and articles to a reasonable and reasonably fair set has to be defined. Particular articles would then be selected from that frame according to a set of sampling rules.

Reasonableness usually requires some compromises between what is wanted and what can be done. In his study of the moral panic surrounding the resurgence of heroin use in the mid-1990s, Denham (2008) selected 1,770 articles as his cases using the sampling frame of all such articles published in one of three "national" newspapers (*Los Angeles Times, The New York Times, The Washington Post*) between 1990 and 1999. For me, that sampling frame is not wide enough to justify an argument for a national moral panic. That claim depends on some sort of here-undemonstrated reverberation effect that multiplies the effect of material published in these highly recognized newspapers. On the other hand, it certainly is deep enough to be representative of the various treatments the topic received, and moral panic was clearly one of them.

In evaluating sampling frames, what the critic looks for is evidence that the cases identified can do the representational work that is desired and that the cases to be selected will permit a fair test of the research question. Denham's work presents a mixed bag. The combined circulation for the three newspapers in the '90s was something fewer than 3 million in a population of 250 million. But the big problem is that Denham is claiming an effect in the audience "creating a moral panic" (p. 945). He has no evidence of that panic at all because he samples no readers.

On the positive side, he has a very large number of articles from three newspapers known to give a diversity of coverage to a topic. We can probably be confident that if "moral panic" is the dominant treatment across these articles, it represents the way news—given the incestuous nature of the business—was treating the resurgence of heroin use. In that manner, the set of cases allows for a fair test (the researcher's position can fail) of the study.

Case Coding

At the descriptive level, cases are coded to document their *provenance*—a term that speaks to the circumstances of the cases such as source, ownership, and authorship; classifications dealing with content type (news, feature, commercial, etc.); and characteristics such as audiences, medium of presentation, dates, and history. In their study of music videos, Conrad, Dixon, and Zhang (2009) coded the videos (their cases) by the "video name, the name of the main artist, whether or not there was a supporting artist, and the name of the supporting artist if there was one" (p. 141). Case coding allows the analyst to describe the characteristics of the collection for the reader, document its components, and test for differences and relationship across and between these components.

Cases can also be coded according to global judgments made about the content. Topic, voice (authoritative, comedic, ironic, ingenuous, etc.), and frame are the types of code that is used across cases. Whether the analyst codes the case by its predominant characteristic on a given code (say, topic) or by multiple characteristics (topics) depends on the research question once again.

Case coding can be used in conjunction with unit coding (see below), or it can also be the end game of the analysis. The analyst codes the case and makes no further division of the content. For example, Molyneaux, O'Donnell, Gibson, and Singer (2008) were interested in the ways men and women communicated through vlogs.[6] They coded the vlog cases by posting date, posting type, number of hits, and viewer response. (In a nice turn, they had collected audience response data from 60 respondents recruited from a North Atlantic university.[7]) They coded the content over five topic categories (personal, public,

---

[6]http://ac-journal.org/journal/2008/Spring/3GenderandYoutube.pdf. Accessed April 30, 2011. This study of the critical issue type is not theoretically complex or methodologically sophisticated, but it does what it sets out to do. It also demonstrates one of the limitations of content analysis: No one should expect that the findings will have much staying power. Both the technology and the culture surrounding the technology are changing too quickly.

[7]It was most likely the University of New Brunswick where the researchers work and play. Again, I'm not sure why we persist in using this mysterious language.

entertainment, YouTube, and technology), image quality, and gender (actually gender expression[8]) of the producer.

Looking at the videos,[9] however, it's clear that much more content diversity could have been illuminated had the researchers broken the content down into smaller units. These were three-minute videos, and there is considerably more complexity than the global judgments allow us to see. The combination of case coding and unit coding can provide for some powerful analytical approaches.

Unit of Analysis

Unit content coding brings together two separate tasks: parsing out the unit of content and then applying the appropriate codes or completing the prepared checklist. Developing units of analysis smaller than the case such as a thought unit,[10] sentence, paragraph, scene, shot, or passage is not without attendant difficulties. Some of these units can be defined unproblematically such as a sentence or a paragraph in a professionally produced text. Others require sets of rules that approach the arbitrary—what is a sentence in conversational speech? How do you classify a camera shot that has camera movement or lens zoom? What is the beginning or end of a scene? What is an episode of action? What is a thought unit? All of these units have to be operationally defined, according to a set of instructions that will direct the identification of the unit. These instructions have to be appropriate to the material being unitized, but one can learn from the work of others.

For example, Taylor and Donald (2004) had a reasonably good conceptual definition of a thought unit ("a complete idea," p. 458), but a perfectly awful operational definition ("two coders . . . experienced in parsing dialogue," p. 458). But perhaps they were the same two coders used in the study (Taylor, 2002) where coders were "briefly trained using example dialogues," practiced on "approximately 10 percent of the data," and then addressed "all disagreements" (p. 21).

McMillan, Hoy, Kim, and McMahan (2008) faced a different problem in their study on web-based interactivity. The researchers were interested in developing a method of assessing interactivity that would transcend the problem of a rapidly changing technology outdating the methodology. Their cases were health-related websites. Their units of analysis were the interactive features within the websites. Coding identified the unit, classified it according to three forms of interactivity plus additional criteria (unreported), and then developed a description of the interactive feature. The interesting part of this coding approach is that it is an open system of coding. It starts with a known set of interactive features (the unit of analysis) and of classifications but allows the coders to add features

---

[8]Gender expression refers to the manifestation of sociocultural gender distinctions in clothing, hairstyle, body decoration, and the like. Coding was a judgment based on appearance. Apparently, the researchers couldn't tell in nine cases.

[9]The following links were accessed on April 30, 2011: http://www.youtube.com/watch?v = 7htGWybRzLo&feature = PlayList&p = 99E36BBA7E7CC17D&index = 1, http://www.youtube.com/watch?v = vH2oHbOVe8Y&feature = PlayList&p = 6411FB47197D38CB&index = 0, and http://www.youtube.com/watch?v = iTGgA61UxJY&feature = PlayList&p = E0A06E6C2EC42C81&index = 1

[10]This sentence could be coded into three thought units: coding process, content segment, and global judgment.

and codes not anticipated in the known set. This open-system approach keeps the definition of a unit and the code set current and appropriate to an emerging technology.

Both of these studies were making use of difficult units of analysis, and both of them opened up the coding process to allow that process to be responsive to unanticipated conditions in the texts without abandoning the code sets developed to be appropriate to their research problem. I would generally recommend this approach as the foundation for all metric coding. It appears to combine the best of an a priori theoretical analysis with a grounded connection with the data to develop the best fit.

Finally, as with case coding, units can be coded in their own right independent of their content. This coding can include anything that can be known about the unit without making judgments about the content of the unit. This coding has the same purposes as descriptive case coding. The question of provenance here has to do with the relationship of the unit to its case. A sentence taken from an introductory paragraph, for example, has different work to do than that same sentence offered in conclusion.

Codes

Remembering that metric studies are most often directed by a deductive approach, it should not be surprising to learn that the development of a set of codes is a very early step in the process. Metric codes are in the service of the hypotheses or sometimes even serve the role of hypotheses. The starting point for metric coding, then, is not the content, per se, but rather the demands of the theory in play. For example, Holly Semetko and Peter Valkenburg (2000) investigated 2,601 newspaper stories and 1,522 television news stories for the use of five frames: responsibility, conflict, human interest, economic consequences, and morality. They drew the five frames they used to code the stories from an extensive literature on framing. They found that it was not the medium of presentation that made a difference in what framing approach was used but rather the character of the outlet (sober vs. sensationalist) that mattered.

Semetko and Valkenburg point out both the benefits and the difficulties of this approach (pp. 94–95). They note that this approach can be readily replicated and advanced to other comparisons, providing a consistent base to examine topics and media, and because the task involves sorting cases into a relatively few codes, it can handle large samples such as theirs. The primary danger, of course, is that the initial work to identify the frames will be inadequate and will produce a set of codes that are inadequate to the task of discriminating actual effects.

Because of that clear and present danger, many researchers use a mixed approach to the development of codes (see Matthes & Kohring, 2008, for a review). A preliminary set of codes is developed according to the theory in play for the problem. That set is tested against some subset of cases to ensure its effectiveness with corrections, substitutions, and additions being practiced. Those cases are often discarded from the research sample, though there is no need for that as long as the coders themselves have not dealt with them.

Once the code set has been formulated, a codebook is developed. The codebook is composed of the codes and a set of rules for sorting content into the code categories. Those rules work well if the analyst can use a decision chain (if *a, b, c,* and *e,* then *x*) as Semetko and Valkenburg did, rather than lengthy instructions that are easily forgotten. If an analyst can't get to a decision chain description, there may not be an adequate foundation for deductive methods, and again exploratory or more grounded work should be done.

The code list should include codes that provide descriptive information about both cases (*this is a rap video*) and units of analysis (*two-person, mixed-gender scene*), as well as sort the content within the unit (*seduction narrative*). Multiple-level coding allows for multiple-level conclusions such as X percent of the scenes in rap videos are two-person, mixed-gender and Y percent of such scenes represent a seduction narrative.

The codebook is then handed off to a set of coders (usually teams of two). The use of independent coders—who are typically naïve vis-à-vis the research problem (or "blinded to the hypotheses")—is typical of metric studies. The intent is to neutralize the effect of the researcher so that the coding does not become self-fulfilling. In metric studies, the combination of the codes, codebook, and coders forms the measurement instrument that will be applied to the content. This approach sees the content as effectively stable in response to the measurement process.[11]

The set of codes and the instructions that guide their application is usually the mystery activity of content analysis. As readers, we rarely see the entire set of codes that were in use, and we are never privy to a peak inside the codebook. Even major works on content analysis (e.g., Krippendorff, 2004) tell us little about codes and codebooks, per se. Semetko and Valkenburg, however, handled this issue quite well. They prepared a checklist of 20 items that each coder completed for each news story, and were able to provide examples in the article.

Nonetheless, we rarely see in media research the sort of systematic development of codes and coding represented by Rogers's relational work (e.g., Rogers & Escudero, 2004), or the ongoing work of the Child Language Data Exchange System.[12] Perhaps the Annenberg studies in cultivation analysis of the '70s and '80s are our closest examples (see Newcomb, 1978).

Issues in Reliability and Validity

Because most metric approaches make use of a priori codes, there are requirements for demonstrating the reliability and providing the indications of validity for the code set. Reliability in content analysis is usually defined as agreement among observers, and validity is defined as what is claimed to be there is indeed there. There is relatively little difficulty on these two issues when dealing with the facts of the text: Does this word appear or not? How many individuals are in the picture? What colors are used in a graphic? There will not be perfect agreement among observers on some of the cases, but it will be high enough that the issue will be trivial.

The issues of reliability and validity become much more prominent when researchers are dealing with the meaningfulness of the text—its topics, structures, themes, advocacies, affective valences, allusions, references, frames, intertextuality, and cultural location. The

---

[11]Interpretive coding is more likely to celebrate the effect of the researcher and ofttimes presumes that different passes and certainly different coders will produce different results.

[12]http://childes.psy.cmu.edu/. Accessed April 29, 2011.

evidence for these elements is not simply in the text but involves some judgments. In metric research, these judgments are managed by a set of rules that are inscribed in a codebook. Dealing with how to identify the topic of a paragraph, the analyst might offer these directions: "Topic is the essential concept or concepts of the paragraph." Effective coding directions or well-developed checklists will reduce the possibilities to a single "right" answer.

In metric research, then, reliability is initially a measure of our ability to write good coding directions and of the coders' ability to play by those rules. But, of course, we want it to be more than that. We want our disciplinary community to feel secure that the content is properly coded. We want the content to be validly represented by the codes. If the coding directions lead the coder to consistently miscode a unit of text, the result is code work that is reliably wrong. There can be little argument that this outcome can happen and probably little question that it has happened in some studies. We don't know which studies, of course, because as readers of research we rarely have access to the rules of coding, yet it is in those rules that the validity issue is met.

As a critic of research, I treat reliability measures as an entrance requirement. If you want to get the work into the conversation, you have to meet this requirement. I mean, really, if an analyst can't develop coding instructions and training methods that have the coders in agreement at least 70% of the time, maybe the analyst doesn't know enough about the fundamentals of the content to conduct the study. At the same time, I'm not willing to grant such measures any greater credence. The question of the validity of the claims will await the competence, and consequences, of the argument.

INTERPRETIVE CODING

Interpretive coding starts at the same place that all research starts: with an engaging problem. In interpretive research, the problem is generally found in some issue that resides on the surface of the text and appears to be a fertile location for the generation of theory. Instead of testing the implications of a preconstituted theoretical framework, interpretive research seeks to add to the body of theory that is explanatory of texts. Instead of demonstrating theory, it generates theory. It does this work through the identification and selection of a set of texts, the close reading of that set, and, finally, the coding of the units of analysis within the text using a grounded or emergent approach.

Selection of Texts

The selection of texts takes on a heightened importance given the principle of dynamic, interactive texts. Clearly, the texts selected are going to closely participate in the conclusions drawn. The task here is to select texts that meet the requirements of the problem without merely confirming predrawn conclusions. The selection has to meet some sense of fair play in a process that is open to review. Hard-core qualitative researchers might shudder at the notion of a sampling process, because it implies the rejected argument about representation, but the principles of carefully specifying the domain of texts to be addressed, considering their accessibility, and determining the reasonable effort to be expended in collecting them still have value. Many times, the problem itself will sufficiently specify the texts to be used. Jennifer Peterson (2009), for example, used two months of online message exchange for an HIV support group to investigate the themes of support that were evidenced within the messages.

Close Reading

Before the first code is assigned, interpretive researchers routinely address a close reading of the entire set of texts.[13] A search of the communication core journals with the term "close reading" in quotes returned 168 entries.[14] Unfortunately, the reader of these 168 will not learn much about the method called "close reading." The study of weathercasts by Doherty and Barnhurst (2009) offers a typical explanation. They say that their study is "based on a close reading" (p. 212) for the entire reference to the method. Richard Doherty and Kevin Barnhurst are fine scholars (and Kevin a longtime acquaintance). The fact that they feel no need to explain the method would indicate that the discipline does not require that description either because what is done is so obvious or, perhaps, because there is no conventionalized method.

The concept of close reading, if not its conventions, has been with us for a long time in literary theory as well as in ethnography. A quick search on JSTOR generates almost 19,000 entries, taking us back to the earliest literary reference in 1866 in the *North American Review* and to ethnography in 1884 in *The American Naturalist*. Geoff Baym, my guide in such matters, points to the beginnings of contemporary usage in communication studies in Stuart Hall's introduction to *Paper Voices* (Smith, Immirzi, & Blackwell, 1975). In that piece, Hall is writing against content analysis with its focus on manifest content and writing in favor of the literary or linguistic focus on latent content. He calls for a "long preliminary soak, a submission by the analyst to the mass of . . . material" (Smith et al., 1975, p. 15).

Close reading is, then, at least, the reading of, viewing of, or listening to the set of texts multiple times (at least three) with the goal of understanding the range and quality of content. Even closer reading involves the identification of embedded values, internal and external references, and symbolic resonances—all of the components of a text that give it a richness of meaning beyond its material facts. It is unlikely that the beginning researcher is going to get to this level of analysis, but she or he can start the systematic effort to get there by careful note taking and an unslackening curiosity about the cultural work the facts are intended to do. Close reading should not be just an exercise in reading. The analyst should construct the written analysis of the insights gained, refining it on each subsequent pass.

Many studies, as we have seen, stop at close reading with the author then reporting what he or she found. Speaking for myself, I believe that approach opens the door to self-fulfilling outcomes and requires far too high a level of trust from the reader. Coding

---

[13]The reader might want to review the "Interpretive (and Hybrid) Evidence" section in Chapter 5.

[14]No, I did not read all 168 entries. What I did do was go to a table of random numbers with a preselected entry point and take the first 10 numbers from 1 to 168 with no repetition. I then searched the PDF files of those entries for the term "close reading" (enclosed in quotation marks) and recorded any description of the method.

demonstrates the systematic engagement of the work and prevents both the rush to judgment and the self-fulfilling conclusion. It is a discipline of practice and of argument. Nonetheless, I have to admit that apparently good work gets done without it.

Cases and Units of Analysis

Hermeneutic research does not necessarily adopt a case-and-unit approach. Close reading addresses the whole of the archive of texts, and coding may do the same. If the set of texts is seen as a common cultural agent, it doesn't matter much about the specific conditions of authorship or presentation. There are research problems that would lead the analyst to conduct coding over the whole of the text set. This was the approach used by Peterson (2009) in her HIV support study.

Texts can be preserved in their case-by-case presentation and may be further parsed into units of analysis, however. Thompson (2008), in his study of teacher and parent interviews, maintained each interview as a case along with its case identifiers and adopted a line-by-line unit of analysis (thus, interestingly advancing the importance of margins). In his study, this requirement meant that he considered each line for possible coding but did not maintain the unit in subsequent analysis (pp. 206–207).

The moral here is a cautionary tale: The interpretive analyst wants to get deep enough and systematically enough into the text to understand the specifics of how the text does its work. At the same time, the force of the text is not simply in its parts. If the analyst only looks at the elements of the text, the action of the whole of the text is lost. Thompson's apparent solution is not a bad one, because in his subsequent coding, he reviewed the entire document once again.

The cautionary note notwithstanding, the analyst needs to set some rules as to how the text will be addressed. It is simply too easy to read without understanding or evaluation. Setting expectations for the appearance of codes is a good check. In my work, I routinely code at the paragraph or paragraph-equivalent level. My quality control check is to ensure that each paragraph or its equivalent has a code attached to it. If that code is the same as the previous one, I reread both passages to ensure against the easy solution, fatigue, or boredom. It is a good plan to choose some window of text, whether it is a unit of analysis or not, as the basis of systematic engagement.

Coding

Coding in interpretive research is typically done by the research authorship rather than the anonymous coders of metric research. This dual role is based on the interpretive principle that the analyst is the instrument. Unlike the anonymous coders of metric analysis, the "interpreter" matters here and is personally responsible for the interpretation. I like to promote the practice of multiple coders auditing the work of one another. An auditor asks the obvious pointed question—why this and not that?—to ensure that the coding is systematically done and can be reasonably justified. Differences in coding are negotiated. That negotiation has to be conducted on the premise that both codings are culturally possible but point to different shadings of understanding. The result of the negotiation might

The Axial Coding Controversy

Grounded theory is an extension of the intellectual thought associated with the Chicago School of Sociology, with the development of symbolic interactionist theory, and, most recently, with a group of social action theorists. The basic principle is that meaning is a social practice discoverable through interaction.

Grounded theory was introduced by Barney Glaser and Anselm Strauss (1967) working separately and together in the '60s and '70s. They split over the issue of axial coding that uses predetermined theoretical categories and a coding paradigm (Glaser, 1992; Strauss & Corbin, 1990).

Axial coding involves the "intense analysis" of a category of codes that uses the paradigm of conditions, interactions among the actors, strategies and tactics, and consequences to plot the connections among the codes that make up that theoretical category (see Strauss, 1987, p. 27).

For Glaser, the use of the predetermined categories and the paradigm breaks the connection with the data. For Strauss and Corbin, the indeterminacy of open coding leads to weak theory (Kendall, 1999). Neither claim has been demonstrated (and probably cannot be demonstrated).

Most practitioners agree that axial coding simplifies the task of

(Continued)

be the development of a new code (and a review of all previous coding) or a deeper understanding of the code retained.

The interpretive scholar's code building is never finished, but it does come to an end. The interpretive code is an open system. There is always one more way to look at the texts. A typical interpretive code set is the product of multiple cycles through the texts. The coding itself starts with a preliminary and tentative set of codes that have come from the problem definition and from the close reading analysis. As each window of text is engaged, the analyst evaluates both the text and the code set. The initial set becomes grounded in the texts as the analyst comes across units that can be understood as representing a given code. New codes are added; old codes are refined, divided, and discarded. (The metric scholar will have done the same thing in pretesting his or her code set on a preliminary chunk of the texts.) The final code set will not be in hand, however, until the last unit is coded for the last time.

An initial pass at coding is often followed by a subsequent recoding in which the commonly coded units of text are reviewed as a set for (a) additional distinctions that might have value and/or (b) connections among the codes.

Subcodes can always be found because there is always more complexity in the text than can be coded. At some point, nonetheless, the value of the additional distinctions is judged as minimal—an exhaustion of interpretation sets in. Lindlof and Taylor (2002) describe this circumstance as the text being thoroughly saturated with theory as if it were a sponge that could hold no more. Their phrase is probably a more discipline-acceptable explanation for when to stop than exhaustion or just being sick of reading, as the text is never depleted of additional meaning.

Coding across connections and relationship is a form of metacoding as these codes are once removed from the data and are based on the properties of initial, emergent, or open codes rather than the textual units. There is benefit and significant danger in this sort of recoding. The benefit comes out of seeing the interrelationships and recognizing that codes like texts are not independent elements but form a matrix of meaning. The danger lies in the fact that the analyst is coding the codes and whatever misunderstandings are encoded there are multiplied in the recoding. As you might expect, the tension between benefit and danger has generated a debate over the method. The sidebar on axial coding presents some of this debate.

Issues in Trustworthiness

Measures of reliability make little sense in the typical hermeneutic approach. Nearly all such work uses some form of a grounded approach rather than an a priori approach. Codes are developed in response to the analyst's interaction with the text. The code set remains open until the coding is done; the set can change at any time. The pretense would be a bit much to then go back to calculate some degree of agreement, albeit the possibility that such scholars are a schizophrenic lot.

Nonetheless, we can ask for and expect markers of quality work. Those markers start at the selection of the texts, include the quality of the close reading and its evidence, and need to show the character of the engagement of the text as well as the coding effort. The reader deserves some assurance that the final argument treats the body of texts with respect and fairly represents the complexity, contradictions, and glosses that it surely contains in the claims the argument advances. The reader should be skeptical of any analysis that works out wonderfully well for the analyst.

COMMON ELEMENTS IN CODING

This section takes up the activities that anyone coding content or texts faces in that task. To start, there is a significant overburden of effort that is encountered in handling the large number of textual elements that one usually encounters in these studies. It is not unusual to be dealing with thousands of cases that might be further broken into units of analysis. The result can be research archives that run hundreds of pages long. As short as a dozen years ago, the researcher might have had several file boxes of materials for a single project. Now we can begin to approach less paper-intensive and more electronic-based methods. Some discussion of these methods follows.

(Continued)

moving from data to claim, because it provides the theoretical language and a set of conventional practices to achieve that goal. At the same time, critics worry that the approach is more reproductive than insightful.

Corbin and Strauss retitled their enterprise Qualitative Data Analysis (QDA), and Corbin (Strauss is deceased) has moved away from the basic principles of classic grounded theory (Corbin & Strauss, 2008, p. viii).

For Glaser, QDA has appropriated the terminology but not the method or intention of grounded theory. He rails against QDA practitioners "acting like an expert when they really have no notion of classical [grounded theory]" (http://www.grounded theory.com/booksjournals .aspx. Accessed April 30, 2011).

As a postmodernist, I have no basis to claim epistemological superiority for either method. The goal of each is a more thorough understanding of the text as both a product and constitutive of a culture, not some empirically verifiable causal relationship. As a coherence scholar, I see QDA as a move toward the hypothetic-deductive and away from the emergent. As a methodologist, my expectation is that QDA will continue its rise in popularity even while calling itself grounded theory. The history of methodology is always toward simplification and normalization regardless of epistemological consequences.

Computer-Aided Analysis

The task of analyzing content can be greatly simplified through the use of computer analysis. Getting the data prepared for computer analysis, however, can be difficult and very time consuming. To conduct computer analysis, the case data have to be digitized. Paper-based photographs, graphics, and text have to be scanned or digitally photographed, and video and sound have to be captured or converted into digital files. The process can require a good deal of equipment and multiple computer programs.

We are, nevertheless, moving ever so slowly toward a fully digitized world. Most contemporary newspaper and magazine content is now online; libraries are working constantly to digitize their collections; all contemporary film is digitized, and more and more of the classic archive is appearing on DVDs; inexpensive computer software allows successive screen shots to be taken with a stroke of a hot key to capture video game sequences. It all can be done now, and it will get easier—and cheaper—in the future.

Digitizing Carbon-Based Print

To show the whole scope of the work, let's start with one of the more difficult forms: the paper-based print article. The article as an object of research comes in four common types—in the original format, in that format within a bound library volume, as a microform, or as a PDF file.[15] Microforms are of two kinds—microfilm (on a roll) and microfiche (on a sheet). Most microform readers will produce either a paper copy or an electronic picture-of-the-text file. PDF files are also of two types—a picture of the article or a digital text file. If you can copy and paste a word from the file, it is a digital text file. If you are lucky enough to have a digital text PDF file, the digitizing work is nearly done.

If the article is in its original, carbon-based format, it will have to be scanned or digitally photographed to create a digital picture file.[16] That file is a picture of the page and not a "live text" (editable text). In order to create the necessary live text file, the picture file will have to be run through an optical character recognition (OCR) program. The OCR program changes each character in the text from its set of pixels in the picture to its ASCII code in live text (every letter or symbol has its own code, which is rendered into what you see on the screen). There are very expensive OCR programs, and there is freeware as well. I use a very expensive program, because, over time, the cost of fixing recognition errors has shown itself to be higher than the initial cost of the software.

Our goal is to produce an RTF (rich text format) file that can be used in a coding process. Just look for that option in the output formats or "Save As" choices. The rich text format can be used in any of the coding choices we will discuss. A couple of cautions: No OCR program produces output that is entirely without error. Errors increase according to the quality of the original and of the initial digitizing effort. If the original is in poor shape or has been underlined or otherwise marked up (there has to be a special place in Hell for those who write on library copies), the results will be poor. If the picture file shows speckling, broken characters, or skewed lines, it may be impossible to perform OCR at all. One

---

[15]*PDF* refers to Adobe's portable document format, which was developed early on as a cross-platform readable file.

[16]A low-resolution picture is actually better. Many cell phone cameras (2 MP) will suffice.

last word of caution: Errors not only are introduced in the OCR process but also preexist in the text. Those latter errors should be preserved.

If the unit of analysis is anything but the entire case, attention has to be given to preserving the formatting of the original. Paragraphing can be lost, and punctuation can be misread. Headings and footnotes pose special problems. In a large database of articles, just preparing the cases for analysis can take weeks. It can make the old-school technique of writing codes on paper copies seem attractive (until the analysis phase begins).

Once the texts are digitized, the ease with which complex analyses can be conducted will quickly extinguish any nostalgia for old-school methods. But first, good practices call for saving a copy of all of the data files in a separate file folder (I name mine "Data Vault") and placing a copy on a flash drive or an external disk. That way, if any of the analyses require disassembling the text or if something untoward should happen, the analyst can always retrieve the original data.

The Facts of the Text

Analysis starts by getting the facts of the text. I recommend getting word counts, word frequencies, and key word analysis on all data even if the research questions or hypotheses do not call for them. The more one knows about the texts under analysis, the more informed one can be in drawing out the implications of the main findings.

Word counts are available from most word processors' "Tools" menu. Word counts are particularly important when comparing sets of texts. For the comparisons to be balanced, the word counts have to be more or less equivalent. Word counts across files have to be generated by the same algorithm as there are different methods for determining what counts as a word.

Frequency counts provide the number of occurrences for each word that appears in the text. That analysis provides two kinds of information: information about the vocabulary in use and, through the analysis of nouns and verbs, the topics and action of the narrative.

A handy single-value measure of vocabulary is the type-token ratio where *type* is a unique word and *token* is an occurrence of that word. The type-token ratio is the number of unique words compared to the total number of words. Word counts are necessary for any comparisons across the type-token ratio because this ratio typically returns a smaller value for larger texts. Many words are used over and over (*the, a, as, in, to, is*) in any text, so the ratio usually declines as the text gets longer.

As noted, inspection of the frequency table will quickly identify the topics and the action of the text. Table 12.1 provides an example using a 1949 text on comic books and juvenile delinquency. The topic of the article is obvious from the list that is mostly nouns. The verbs in this article (as is typical of academic reports) were mostly of existence (*is, are, was*). This is not an action narrative. The relatively high occurrence of *not* and *no* signals that this article takes a contrarian position (holding that comics and motion pictures have little effect on juvenile delinquency—that era's video game violence issue).

Finally, key word analysis is a method for comparing a given text against a large corpus of work. The *key words* of a text are those words that are unique to the given text or words that are common in the given text but rare in the corpus. Most available key word analyses use a large sample of texts taken from common forms such as newspapers, books,

Table 12.1 Word Frequencies for 1949 Text in Comic Books

Word	Frequency
Is	54
Are	38
Comics	38
Delinquency	38
Not	23
Comic	18
Crime	18
Was	18
Behavior	16
Delinquent	15
Children	14
Research	14
Social	14
Wertham	14
Books	13
No	13
Studies	13
Criminal	11
Delinquents	11
Juvenile	11
Movies	10
Wertham's	10
Cause	9
Motion [picture]	9
Sociology	9

magazines, and the like. It allows for a determination of the quality of writing or uniqueness of style in comparison to common usage. A more sophisticated approach would use a corpus of texts taken from the discipline. For example, the 100 contemporary articles reviewed for Chapter 7 would provide an excellent base for the analysis of a recent article.

A second use of key word analysis allows the analyst to compare one set of texts against another. For example, if Denham wished to extend his study on the coverage of heroin use in the 1990s, he could select a sample of news articles on heroin from the first decade of this century (or even from the 1950s when France and the United States were supporting the Southeast Asian drug warlords) and run a key word analysis comparing one set to the other. In this manner, key word analysis quickly expands the horizon of analysis from the one-off content analysis we typically see.

Professor Tom Cobb in the Department of Linguistics and Languages at the University of Quebec has made it easy to conduct these types of descriptive analysis at his website.[17] You will find online frequency and key word routines among a host of other handy tools for text analysis (including a sentence extractor for coding at the sentence level)—all "dedicated to the free dissemination of knowledge on the Web." If you prefer offline work, http://www.lexically.net/wordsmith/ will sell you a text analysis program for around $100. There are undoubtedly other options available as well.

Coding Digitized Texts

Coding can be done in a word processing program, a spreadsheet, a database program, or a specialized (and costly) program. Note that these more or less technical procedures are the same whether one is doing metric, hermeneutic, or hybrid research.

Coding in a Word Processing Program

With a small database of a hundred pages or so and coding at the case or paragraph level, it is quite easy to set up a word processing table of two columns. The left-hand column should be about 25 characters wide for the codes. The remainder of the page is reserved for the

---

[17]http://www.lextutor.ca/. Accessed April 29, 2011.

right-hand column, which contains the text to be coded. Copy and paste the text from the first case into the right-hand column (never code the original file); then double click in the left-hand bottom corner of the left-hand column to insert a line return on the left for every line on the right. This method keeps the codes in alignment with their attached text. Insert a row into the table. Put in the text from the next case on the right and a set of returns on the left. Repeat for the entire set of cases. The setup should look like Figure 12.1, which shows a three-paragraph example for a text to be coded at the paragraph level.

The tedious part of this setup is the insertion of the rows for each case. One could certainly just dump all the text in the right-hand column for all the cases, but it is quite easy for the codes and the text to get out of alignment, as both columns are dynamic in their formatting. A mistake at the beginning—where most mistakes are made—would have alignment consequences throughout the remainder of the data. So, do it right and do it once, or hope to be lucky. Figure 12.2 shows what the coded outcome might look like.

Coding in a Spreadsheet

There are some advantages to coding in a spreadsheet application rather than a word processor. The primary advantage is the ability to sort units or cases that have the same set of

Figure 12.1   Text to Be Coded

	Themes come both from the data (an inductive approach) and from the investigator's prior theoretical understanding of the phenomenon under study (an a priori approach). A priori themes come from the characteristics of the phenomenon being studied; from already agreed on professional definitions found in literature reviews; from local, commonsense constructs; and from researchers' values, theoretical orientations, and personal experiences (Bulmer 1979; Strauss 1987; Maxwell 1996). Strauss and Corbin (1990:41–47) called this theoretical sensitivity. Investigators' decisions about what topics to cover and how best to query informants about those topics are a rich source of a priori themes (Dey 1993:98). In fact, the first pass at generating themes often comes from the questions in an interview protocol (Coffey and Atkinson 1996:34). Unlike pure literature reviews, these themes are partly empirical.
	Mostly, though, themes are induced from empirical data—from texts, images, and sounds. Even with a fixed set of open-ended questions, one cannot anticipate all the themes that arise before analyzing the data (Dey 1993:97–98). The act of discovering themes is what grounded theorists call open coding and what classic content analysts call qualitative analysis (Berelson 1952) or latent coding (Shapiro and Markoff 1997).
	There are many variations on these methods, and individual researchers have different recipes for arriving at the preliminary set of themes (Tesch 1990:91). We next describe eight observational techniques—things to look for in texts— and four manipulative techniques—ways of processing texts. These twelve techniques are not exhaustive and are often combined in practice.

Figure 12.2 Coded Outcome

Description Recommendation Claim	Themes come both from the data (an inductive approach) and from the investigator's prior theoretical understanding of the phenomenon under study (an a priori approach). A priori themes come from the characteristics of the phenomenon being studied; from already agreed on professional definitions found in literature reviews; from local, commonsense constructs; and from researchers' values, theoretical orientations, and personal experiences (Bulmer 1979; Strauss 1987; Maxwell 1996). Strauss and Corbin (1990:41–47) called this theoretical sensitivity. Investigators' decisions about what topics to cover and how best to query informants about those topics are a rich source of a priori themes (Dey 1993:98). In fact, the first pass at generating themes often comes from the questions in an interview protocol (Coffey and Atkinson 1996:34). Unlike pure literature reviews, these themes are partly empirical.
Claim Description	Mostly, though, themes are induced from empirical data—from texts, images, and sounds. Even with a fixed set of open-ended questions, one cannot anticipate all the themes that arise before analyzing the data (Dey 1993:97–98). The act of discovering themes is what grounded theorists call open coding and what classic content analysts call qualitative analysis (Berelson 1952) or latent coding (Shapiro and Markoff 1997).
Claim Transition	There are many variations on these methods, and individual researchers have different recipes for arriving at the preliminary set of themes (Tesch 1990:91). We next describe eight observational techniques—things to look for in texts—and four manipulative techniques—ways of processing texts. These twelve techniques are not exhaustive and are often combined in practice.

codes attached to them. By bringing all the commonly coded units together, the analyst can move on to recoding, which is either adding additional distinctions to materials already differentiated or coding the relationships among the initial set (or both). Note that any subsequent recoding poses some challenges to a priori approaches, as new coding rules would have to be developed.

The disadvantages of spreadsheet coding have to do with the handling of text. Spreadsheets seem to have awkward formatting requirements for placing chunks of text in cells. There is an outside character limitation that figures out to be about 20 pages of double-spaced text that can be placed in a single cell.

In using a spreadsheet, place the text to be coded in the first column and then use as many columns on the right as there are codes for the unit or case. It is good practice to use the same column for a given code (neatness counts), although that can be ungainly with a large number of codes. Figure 12.3 shows an example.

Figure 12.3   Coding in a Spreadsheet

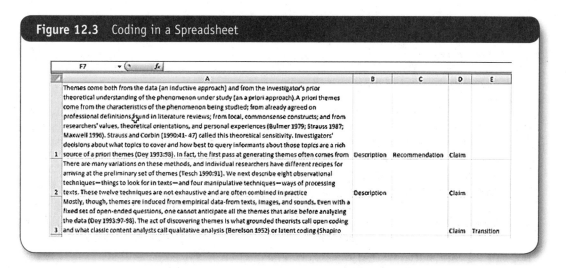

	A	B	C	D	E
1	Themes come both from the data (an inductive approach) and from the investigator's prior theoretical understanding of the phenomenon under study (an a priori approach).A priori themes come from the characteristics of the phenomenon being studied; from already agreed on professional definitions found in literature reviews; from local, commonsense constructs; and from researchers' values, theoretical orientations, and personal experiences (Bulmer 1979; Strauss 1987; Maxwell 1996). Strauss and Corbin (1990:41- 47) called this theoretical sensitivity. Investigators' decisions about what topics to cover and how best to query informants about those topics are a rich source of a priori themes (Dey 1993:98). In fact, the first pass at generating themes often comes from	Description	Recommendation	Claim	
2	There are many variations on these methods, and individual researchers have different recipes for arriving at the preliminary set of themes (Tesch 1990:91). We next describe eight observational techniques—things to look for in texts—and four manipulative techniques—ways of processing texts. These twelve techniques are not exhaustive and are often combined in practice	Description		Claim	
3	Mostly, though, themes are induced from empirical data-from texts, images, and sounds. Even with a fixed set of open-ended questions, one cannot anticipate all the themes that arise before analyzing the data (Dey 1993:97-98). The act of discovering themes is what grounded theorists call open coding and what classic content analysts call qualitative analysis (Berelson 1952) or latent coding (Shapiro			Claim	Transition

Coding in Database Applications

A database application is an electronic filing system, and like filing systems, there are simple and complex ones. Both Microsoft Office and OpenOffice.org provide database applications (Access and Base, respectively). These applications are particularly useful when coding is being done on the basis of a list of attributes or a set of questions. The database form can be set up to automatically present the unit-of-analysis ID and each of the attributes or questions and their fixed-choice responses. It might take the tyro three to four hours to figure out how to design the form. That investment can be easily offset by the amount of time saved in data entry. Figure 12.4 shows an example of one I use to code media violence studies.

File applications can also be used to build a database of cases that can be used in a variety of research activities. The analyst can then specify the type of cases needed for a specific analysis and "pull" them into coding frame. Most researchers approach a study as if it were the only study they were ever going to do. Consequently, they build their data

Figure 12.4   Coding Using a Database Application

met	medi	televis	prin	film	intern	rad	video	author	date	title	
☑	☐	☐	☐	☐	☐	☐	☐	Alessi, N.	1992	Debate: effects of watching violence	J Am Acad Child
☐	☑	☑	☐	☐	☐	☐	☐	McIlwraith, Robert D	1994	Marshall McLuhan and the Psycholoç	Canadian Psych
☑	☐	☐	☐	☐	☐	☐	☐	Charren, P., A. Gelber, et al.	1994	Media, children, and violence: a publi	Pediatrics 94(4 F
☐	☑	☐	☐	☑	☐	☐	☐	Johnston,-Deirdre-D	1995	Adolescents' motivations for viewing ç	Human-Commun
☐	☑	☑	☐	☐	☐	☐	☐	Davie, William R; Lee, Jung-؟	1995	Sex, Violence, and Consonance/Diffe	Journalism & Ma
☐	☐	☑	☐	☐	☐	☐	☐	Bushman, B. J.	1995	Moderating role of trait aggressivenes	J Pers Soc Psyc
☐	☑	☑	☐	☐	☐	☐	☐	Gerbner, George	1995	Marketing Global Mayhem	Javnost/The Pub
☑	☐	☑	☐	☐	☐	☐	☐	Potter, W. James, Vaughan,	1995	How real is the portrayal of aggressiv	Journal of Broadc
☐	☑	☐	☑	☐	☐	☐	☐	Jones, Suzanne W	1995	Reconstructing Manhood: Race, Mas	Masculinities, 19
☐	☑	☑	☐	☐	☐	☐	☐	Linne, Olga	1995	Media Violence Research in Scandin	Nordicom Review
☑	☐	☑	☐	☐	☐	☐	☐	Lometti, Guy E	1995	The Measurement of Televised Violer	Journal of Broadc
☐	☑	☐	☐	☑	☐	☐	☐	Rondeli, L D	1995	"Movie Menu" of School Children	Sotsiologicheski
☐	☑	☑	☐	☐	☐	☐	☐	Signorielli, Nancy; Gerbner, (	1995	Violence on Television: The Cultural I	Journal of Broadc
☑	☑	☑	☐	☐	☐	☐	☐	Sorensen, Birgitte Holm	1995	Media Violence-Young People	Nordicom Review

analyses specifically for each study, ofttimes repeating the same work over and over (just like creating bibliographies for papers over and over). With databases, content is entered once, forever.

Coding in Dedicated Programs

There are at least three major programs that are dedicated to the task of coding text: QSR's NVivo package, ATLAS.ti, and the newer Framework. All three require a substantial investment in money and training. All three provide trial versions (and other student assistance). NVivo and Framework are 30-day full versions (you have to request one from Framework), whereas ATLAS.ti is a limited-ability demo without a time limit. While often associated with qualitative coding, they are useful regardless of approach.

Data handling is really quite spectacular in these programs. NVivo and ATLAS.ti can handle video, sound, and graphic files in ways that allow for nearly complete control over the types of cases and the elements within those cases that can serve as units of analysis. If coding is going to be a part of your professional career, an investment in a dedicated program would be quite worthwhile.

MOVING ON

Content coding is both reductionistic and revelatory. It is reductionistic because it tries to extract some set of fundamental characteristics that describe the text. In doing so, it reveals the structure, framing, themes, and intentions encoded in the text. Content analysis may be a lesser god in the pantheon of research, but it is a necessary one. Those who claim to be media scholars and yet do not systematically study the content of the media put themselves at some risk of being irrelevant. And, similarly, those practitioners who are not systematically aware of the text and messages produced by their organizations—and their competition—are equally at risk.

In the next chapter, we investigate texts that are produced by the research process and provide a grand overview and checklist for evaluating metric and interpretive research, whether your own or that of others.

REFLECTIONS

What Are Some Points to Remember?

- Metric coding moves from theory to codes to cases and units. Interpretive coding moves from cases and units to codes to theory.
- Much is made of the differences between metric and interpretive coding, and at the extremes, those differences can be substantial. Most of the coding that we see in our publications, however, happened in the more mellow middle, where differences are less significant though still hotly contested.

- Axial coding is an example of the development of conventionalizing practices within interpretive coding and the resultant movement toward the middle.
- The outcomes of coding of any sort depend in no small measure on the cases selected and the unit of analysis to which a code is attached. Case selection establishes the trustworthiness of the study, and the unit of analysis sets the gradient of discrimination from coarse to fine.
- Close reading is at the heart of interpretive coding and is an inevitable part of metric coding. It is a nonconventionalized practice, however, with little assurance of quality.
- Coding is labor intensive. Computer-assisted approaches should be used to ease the labor. Quality controls should be established.

Why Does It Matter?

Coding is a central activity in media research. It is the fundamental method by which we come to understand both the content and the cultural activity of our media.

What Else Could We Talk About?

Whether metric or interpretive, the critical moment in coding is the engagement of the unit of analysis by the coding agent. In metric coding, the agent is developing the coding instructions for assigning codes to units of analysis; in interpretive coding, the agent is making sense of a unit of analysis by assigning a code to it. In both cases, the act is an unprotected decision that the specifics of this unit fit the general category represented by the coding term. The agent in both cases is not some independent intellect assessing the objective characteristics of meaning, but rather a cultural subject located in history and social space.

What Else Might Be Interesting to Read?

Glaser, B. G., & Strauss, A. L. (1967). *The discovery of grounded theory: Strategies for qualitative research*. Chicago: Aldine.

Krippendorff, K. (2004). *Content analysis: An introduction to its methodology*. Thousand Oaks, CA: Sage.

Strauss, A. L., & Corbin, J. (1990). *Basics of qualitative research: Grounded theory procedures and techniques*. Newbury Park, CA: Sage.

Discursive Protocols

Creating Texts

CHAPTER PREVIEW

What's It All About?

This chapter furthers our understanding of coding text by looking at the texts that are produced in the research process itself. From long-form interviews to field notes, certain research methods produce narrative texts, often of great length, that require coding in their own right. This coding places a special burden on the analyst who may be considered a "coauthor" of such texts. The second half of this chapter pulls together all that we have learned across both coding chapters.

What Are the Major Topics?

Interview formats range from the highly directed long-form interview, in which each response is generated by a question, to the conversation that is directed by topic choices.

All interviews produce data in the facts of the text, the framing of the answer, the narrative structure, the language in use, and the discursive performance itself. Few analytical procedures make use of all of this information with metric approaches focusing on facts and framing and interpretive approaches looking at narrative structure, language, and discourse.

Focus groups and protocol analysis are little-used methods that, nonetheless, serve specific purposes well.

Humans have been depicted as storytelling animals. Narrative methods—"tell me the story of your first breakup"—gives access to this ability. It is the method least under the control of the analyst and most open to social and cultural influences.

Noninteractive observation done well produces texts of recordings and field notes.

Coding starts with the selection or production of texts that are appropriate to the problem under study. Each text is a case. Cases are generated across topics—such as the question in a long-form interview—and sources—such as a given newspaper—or both. The first level of coding occurs across cases.

The second level of coding occurs across a unit of analysis. A unit of analysis is some component of a text—a paragraph, sentence, thought, or topic, for example.

Codes are generated from theory in metric coding and from the texts in interpretive coding. Checklists for metric and interpretive coding procedures are provided.

What Special Terms Are Used?

Paradigm

Syntagm

INTRODUCTION

In the previous chapter, we looked at the coding of texts that were produced by the media industry (journalism, entertainment, gaming) or by the user (blogs, tweets, e-mails). In the first half of this chapter, we look at the coding of texts directed and often coproduced by the researcher. These texts include long-form interviews, focus groups, protocol analyses, narratives, and noninteractive observation. Each of these methods produces a text—field notes, sound recording, transcription, videography—for analysis and, typically, subsequent coding. Each of these methods is designed to produce a text of specified content and amenable to particular analytical techniques. This is caged (or at least fenced-in), not free-range, discourse. The intent of the analysis is paramount. We will walk through the text production methods of each of these techniques and then turn to the process of coding the outcomes.

PRODUCING AND CODING RESEARCH TEXTS

Whether it is a list of responses to an "Other" response alternative or a set of stories told by respondents, researcher-initiated or -produced texts need to be examined for both the conditions under which the texts are produced and the analytical framework that is applied to the subsequent texts themselves. We will start with the most directed forms and then move to the least.

Long-Form Interviews

This form of text ranges from the open-ended interview to the directed conversation in order of decreasing control. The open-ended interview is a series of questions that require short answers—usually one or two sentences. Each question may have additional probes or follow-up questions attached to it. In the least systematic approach to developing the research text, the interviewer simply makes notes on the answers and archives no other information; best practices would require digitally recording the answers, making notes on the process, and creating a transcription of the recording.

Creating the Text

The value of the open-ended interview approach is that all of the topics of interest to the researcher are explicitly covered. Further, they are covered in a format that allows for a ready comparison across respondents. Every answer to each question is presumed to be under the control of the question with each respondent attempting to give a meaningful response to the question.

The limitations of the open-ended interview stem from the same condition—the answers are only as good as the questions. If the researcher has failed to anticipate the significant issues of the topic, the respondent has little avenue for raising them. Occasionally, a respondent will force a path through to other issues, but there is no way to incorporate them in the interview without starting the whole process over or at least splitting the sample.

The directed conversation is at the other end of the control spectrum in interviews. A typical approach sets up a premise for a conversation. For example, "I'd like to talk to you about your feelings when you play *Grand Theft Auto*. What goes on emotionally when you play?" The respondent might ask for additional clarification, but at some point the premise is set and the conversation begun. The interviewer will have a set of "must-cover topics" ("Are you ever tempted to live one of the episodes in real life?") and will practice active listening.

Figure 13.1 shows an exemplar of instructions that might be given to an interviewer in a study on family screen-use rules. A fair question upon looking at those instructions is "Why not just write questions for each of the topics?" What the conversations approach attempts to take advantage of is (a) the framing of the issue by the respondent, (b) the narrative structure that is produced by the respondent, (c) the language in use by the respondent, and (d) the discursive performance itself.

Framing establishes the social location of the issue and the requirements of the narrative that is produced within that frame. For example, *Grand Theft Auto* can be framed as a morality play in which the paradigmatic roles of good and evil are fundamentally blurred. The narrative that would be developed would be substantially different from that developed if the frame were about responsible parenting.

Narrative structure connects concepts and actions, generates motive and justification, poses tensions and resolutions, and attempts to preserve coherence from the beginning to the end. The vocabulary in use can identify resources through intertextuality, demonstrate emotional valence, indicate significance, and the like. And, finally, the discursive performance demonstrates the uncertainties and contradictions of one's understanding in the glosses, elisions, thought fragments, and apparent conflicts that are present in the performance. All of this information generated by the respondent can be lost in question

Figure 13.1   Example of Instructions for Interviewers

Instructions for Conducting Interviews

We will be using the directed conversation method of interviewing. This method sets up a premise for a conversation and then follows the lead of the respondent. Our conversation is about the rules (or the lack of them) and the actual practices for the use of media by the children in the household. Be sure to get coverage over the following topics:

Parents (caregivers)	Children (and friends)
Importance of rules	Family rules
Existence of rules	Self-governance
Requirements and purpose	Importance of rules
Supervision enforcement and punishment	Existence of rules
Conflicts	Requirements and purpose
Work in actual practice	Supervision enforcement and punishment
No explicit rules but active supervision	Conflicts
Justification for no rules	Work in actual practice
	Issues with friends

formats that substitute the researchers' constructions for the respondents'. (All of this information is also lost, of course, without specific analysis to extract it.)

Active listening involves taking notes on interesting points that deserve follow-up, jotting down unknown vocabulary and distinctive phrases, letting the respondent complete a full turn of talk without interruption, and, in general, following the respondent's lead, even while nudging toward given topics. It is unlike many conversations where the participants spend most of the time preparing for their turn of talk rather than actually listening to what the other is saying. You will be able to tell your own conversational listening practices by the level of fatigue that active listening usually produces.

The art form in active listening involves discerning and pursuing the particular topical insights that can be provided by the respondent. Success in doing so requires a suspension of sense-making closure and an elongation of wonderment that allow for holding the narrative of each respondent as a fresh contribution. The hundredth conversation should be as new and enlightening as the first, but quite often the interviewer tunes out or shifts to the classification task rather than maintaining focus on the task at hand.

A comparison of the open-ended interview approach and the directed conversation shows two important shifts between them. In the interview, we note that the locus of control lies with the researcher. The researcher establishes the topics, framing, and vocabulary, as well as the terms of performing an answer in the interview approach. Even the duration of the interview is set by number of questions; it all ends with the last question. The directed conversation is initiated by the researcher, but control is (should be) quickly deeded to the respondent. The conversation ends when the respondent has nothing more to say.

The second shift concerns the location of the workload. The primary workload for the open-ended interview comes in the creation of the question list. That list is the instrument by which the information critical to the success of the study can be generated. If the questions are inadequate, so too is the study. In the directed conversation, the text production work is primarily in the conversational practice. The a priori list of topics is directive but not exhaustive—more of an assurance of communality across conversations. The conversation should be much more than the list. The burden of work is carried in the real-time performance of the conversation. The researcher as conversant has to be sure the necessary work gets done.

Coding the Text

The a priori structure of the open-ended interview lends itself to an a priori approach to coding. Mostly, a researcher who would use this approach has specific information requirements. If the analyst has asked a set of questions, then the answers have already been anticipated even if they are yet unknown. Coding would be designed to meet those needs. For example, given a researcher's interest in media access in adolescents' bedroom (see Jackson, Brown, & Pardun, 2009, for one such study), the answers to the question "What media (television, players, computers) do you have access to in your bedroom?" pretty well code themselves. An open-ended approach of this sort extends some flexibility to the respondent but generates few surprises in the responses, although if someone had an antique wind-up Victrola, coding it as an MP3 player would lose something.

The further the researcher moves from clear expectations and specific information needs, the more some form of open-system coding is needed. Open-system coding simply means that new codes can be added to a set of codes already in place as justified by differences in the answers. At the point of the directed conversation, the analyst has given up so much control that coding involves an authentic investigation of the text. Nonetheless, the conversation is under the guidance of the initiating premise and the steering topics. A response that has no connection to these would be considered a failed attempt at turn taking. The result is that the analyst starts with a tentative set of codes and works through an iterative process of coding and recoding.

The central question in this process is "For what will the coding be responsible?" Most analyses use a very small proportion of the information that is available in the conversational text. Rarely do we find all four of framing, narrative structure, language, and performance as well as the facts of the case being discussed. Most coding does not stray very far from factual information. This narrowness is due partly to the narrowness of our research questions and partly to the paper-and-ink traditions of our publication venues. One study that does show the potential of more complex coding is Domingo's (2008) study of online newsrooms. But even there the carbon-based journal format greatly contracts the contribution that could be made.

In contrast to the hyper-processes of media text coding, current practice on the coding of research-produced texts is pretty loose. Davis's (2009) simple "Interview responses were . . . analyzed at a qualitative, interpretive level" (p. 208) is a common gloss of the methods in use. I can only speculate as to the source of this difference, but I suspect it has to do with the personal connection to the texts themselves. My recommendation is that the analyst proceed as if the texts were of unknown origin and code them with as much systematic care as one would with media texts. Without such systematic controls in play, the rush to judgment can be overwhelming.

Focus Groups

Focus groups involve the collection of information from members of an affected or targeted group about their responses to or experiences with, for example, messages, texts, or circumstances. It is a well-known but little-used methodology—a search of the communication set returned only 38 entries, the most common of which were conference papers. There was resistance to its introduction at the height of metric hegemony, and it has the somewhat sullied reputation of a marketing tool. Nonetheless, it is a legitimate method that is, at the same time, substantively undertheorized (Zorn, Roper, Broadfoot, & Weaver, 2006).

Creating the Text

As the name suggests, the method attempts to leverage group dynamics to produce an interactive discussion that has more depth and complexity than what could be achieved by interviewing individuals separately. Groups are small (usually between 5 and 15 members), homogenized over some target criterion (such as experienced game players), but otherwise diverse. Just as with interviews and conversations, the discussion can be controlled through specific questions or flow quite freely over some initial premise. The focus of the group is directed by this initial premise and can be augmented by materials distributed for review, programs screened, or other presentations made. In any case, the researcher sets the agenda and guides the discussion toward certain research goals. Good practice calls for a recording and transcription of the recording along with observational notes by either the focus group facilitator, a dedicated observer, or both.

The text is most often the transcription, which means that the nonverbal and aural information is discarded. The transcription is considered group-authored and is generally presented in snippets of individual voices.

Coding the Text

Alice Hall's (2006) study of reality programming and college-aged audiences gives a short (two paragraphs, pp. 195–196) but adequate description of her method of coding, which is more advanced than most. She reports reading the entire transcripts several times, doing initial coding in an iterative process, and then returning to "identify and clarify" features of the themes (p. 196). To apply what we developed in the preceding chapter, her cases were the individual transcripts of the four focus groups she conducted, and her unit of analysis was (effectively) an individual's turn (interruptions ignored).

Hall's work is commendable, but she apparently throws away more information than she keeps. Her cases could have been coded with her observational notes and then used to distinguish events within cases. Without that coding, her notes become submerged background material of unknown influence. Her units could have been coded by source and provenance. She talks of the diversity of her respondent group. Being able to compare comments across that diversity would demonstrate its value.

She makes a very low-level use of information on the interaction between respondents, noting only that the ideas "that were greeted enthusiastically by the group and that triggered concurring comments were seen as having been supported by the other participants" (p. 196). Certainly, there were disagreements, contradictions, marshalling of support, and other typical group activities that may have been valuable as well (see Lunt & Livingstone, 1996, for more on this argument).

Protocol Analyses

Protocol analysis (aka the think-aloud method; see Van Someren, Barnard, & Sandberg, 1994) involves asking respondents to vocalize the cognitive processes that are supporting some ongoing activity. It has roots in the early history of cognitive study and returned to the research scene in the early '80s. My search of the communication database turned up no current studies, although it has an extensive appearance in studies on decision making, critical thinking, design processes, writing, and reading.

A related methodology called the experience sampling method (Kubey, Larson, & Csikszentmihalyi, 1996), which calls on respondents to report their current experiences and their quality, had some play in the literature in the 1990s. (Today it might be called the Twitter analysis as the respondent repeatedly answers the equivalent of the question "What are you doing now?")

I report on protocol analysis here because it would seem to have such obvious value in investigating the use of technology in business, education, and entertainment. It would be a powerful addition to the effects literature.[1] It is, however, a demanding, time-consuming, and usually expensive methodology.

Creating the Texts

There are two texts involved: the action text, which is the actual performance of the process, and the oral text, which is the report of the action and its sequencing, motivation, and justification. Presume that the analyst was studying the cognitive processes that occur during the development or maintenance of a personal social networking site page. It might be quite interesting to investigate the design intentions and user strategies in the process of this application.

The requirement of the performance text is to capture both the content of the page and the actions of the page owner as he or she moves through the site and manipulates content. The requirement of the oral text is to capture the oral report of the cognitive activity, corresponding to each significant action. Finally, the two texts have to be synchronized, if they are collected separately.

In our example, the performance text might well be a set of observer notes. A common execution of protocol analysis is an observer sitting side-by-side with the respondent as the respondent goes through the task. The observer takes notes on the action and prompts the

---

[1]It could also be that because I like it, so you ought to use it.

respondent when necessary and appropriate. A digital recorder can be used for the oral text, but a one-camera AV recording that collects the oral text and additional information on the action would be better. Very sophisticated action texts can be created for computer-based performances using dedicated software (such as Morae) that collect keystrokes, mouse work, page content, and an AV recording of the user all synchronized on a common timeline.

Coding the Texts

In protocol analysis, the episode is the case. The two texts of the case can be coded separately or together. The unit of analysis for the action text is marked by change in what is being done. The unit, then, is the inclusive action between transitions. In the comment text, the thought unit is often the unit of analysis. Coding both usually means simply marking the thought unit by its location in the action, but the analyst might also code the interaction between the two. Either the thought unit or the action unit can be the base unit of analysis.

As always, coding is driven by the purposes of the research. It makes the most sense to use protocol analysis when considering questions of praxis that call for connections between past, present, and future activities. So purposed, coding not only has to deal with the characteristics and content of the individual unit; it also has to attend to the unit's connections to other units in the process.

The simplest way to make these connections is to code the unit's place in the sequence, using a timeline value or sequence ID. The analyst then codes the content of the individual unit, paying special attention to references to other points in the action. Coding is then conducted over the referenced unit sets. If the process coding stops at this point, it accounts only for those instances where the respondent provides the connection. A more sophisticated method is to add a form of coding that employs a sliding window of sequence blocks (three to five units wide) that moves across changes in the action text. This method provides a systematic search for connections.

Narratives

It is not by coincidence that all forms of journalism tell their news in stories. Humans tell stories to make sense of events, the unconnected, and the unknown. Even science tells its stories of the universe, time, the shaping of the planet, and life's evolution upon it. Walter Fisher (1987) has popularized the notion of *Homo narrans,* or the human as storyteller. Asking respondents to "tell the story of. . . ." offers them a well-practiced way of providing information.

Stories, however, are more than a container to be filled with whatever words are at hand. Stories carry requirements for their competent performance. A good story makes cultural sense. Its people, action, motives, outcomes, and values connect to the cultural paradigms (characters), syntagms (action lines), morality (motives and outcomes), and truths (values). Further, stories are told at the intersection of gender, race, ethnicity, and memberships—all of the locators that fix the storytelling self. Consequently, a story is a local performance of a culturally embedded text.

Creating the Text

The analyst engages the respondent in much the same way as when using the extended conversation approach—a premise is set, the story gets told, and the analyst follows up with questions that are based on the story itself, although certain topics may also be preselected.

A competent story has a beginning, a middle, and an end. It has a main character and a narrator (who may be the same individual). The character expresses a relationship with itself, others, nature, and fate. The character acts on this relationship with intention, motive, and purpose, in knowledgeable or unwitting ways. There are consequences to this action that are just or unjust.

The text of the story is created out of these elements, which can be explicit in their presence, implied in the narrative, or notable in their absence. In addition, there are the facts of the case—what the story is about. The content of the story reveals itself in layers: There are the surface-layer facts—this person did these things with those results—and the underlying foundation of our cultural understandings of how things work.

Coding the Text

The coding of these two texts (surface facts and cultural understanding) usually requires two very different approaches. Because the factual content of the story is under the direct control of the respondent, it is fairly difficult to come up with an a priori coding scheme that will cover the widespread variation expected across respondents. That circumstance would recommend a grounded approach.

On the other hand, because so much of our cultural understanding is of the "of course it's true" variety, it is very difficult for most of us to see the "cultural moments" in the text. But cultural influence moves across respondents to exercise a constant and consistent influence. (That is the point of culture—to give us a common foundation from which to interact.) Those circumstances recommend an a priori approach with codes and their exemplars taken from the literature of narratology and cultural studies.[2]

The story gets more complicated if it reaches across cultures. Then the analyst becomes responsible for addressing the appropriate literatures and most likely securing the help of a cultural guide. In a multicultural society such as the United States, one crosses culture boundaries relatively quickly, especially when leaving the academy where 12 years and more (often much more) of prior institutionalization has produced our own dominant discourse and homogenized speech patterns.

Storytelling is an oral form. Although transcriptions[3] are a valuable assist, it is often necessary to code the recording (rather than the transcription) in order to be responsive to the meaningful variations across intonation, stress, emphasis, elongation, elision, and the other oral techniques of expression. The recording will also preserve dialect and underline

---

[2]Brandice Palmer's (2005) master's thesis on the folktale in journalism provides a serviceable bibliographic review. See http://scholarcommons.usf.edu/etd/805/. Accessed April 30, 2011.

[3]The transcription will be much more useful if it follows a "conversation analysis" coding scheme. Such a scheme is well beyond the scope of this book, but see http://www.sscnet.ucla.edu/soc/faculty/schegloff/TranscriptionProject/index.html (accessed April 30, 2011).

the occurrence of specialized vocabulary as well as the tonal variations that change the meaning of words (e.g., "yeah, right").

Coding a recording has the same responsibilities as coding a written text. The analyst has to be able to connect the codes to the textual units and to review commonly coded units for consistency and for subsequent coding. The unit of analysis in a story might be a scene, an action segment, a thought unit, or the text between orally signaled endings (sentences are unreliable in oral texts). Best practices require the use of dedicated software, but adequate (if very tedious) work can be done by using a computerized playback that provides a continuous timeline. Units are marked and manipulated by their time values.

Finally, all discursive protocols are under the jurisdiction of the form-in-use, whether it is question-and-answer, conversation, or narrative. The narrative, however, would appear to exert a special influence. The story form often takes precedence over the facts of the case. In telling a story, the narrator often supplies or subtracts whatever is necessary to make the story "work." If the analyst's goal is strictly factual information, the story form (or the conversation) may not be the best means of collection. If the goal is to gather insights on how things are understood, however, the story form is outstanding.

Noninteractive Observation

Noninteractive observation (NI-O) is conducted by "the fly on the wall," the person behind the one-way mirror, the spy in public places, the camera and microphone in the corner. Its title distinguishes it from participant observation, which is the mainstay of ethnography. NI-O is very useful for analyzing anonymous public behavior and for studying site-based practices such as family viewing or arcade game playing where relational or practical barriers preclude true participant observation. NI-O is also a returned product of computer-mediated communication in which the communication process is conducted using the computer. The computer retains the text of the exchanges. Observations also can be made on specific behaviors such as keystrokes on a computer or channel selections on a television set. These are automated collection devices that collect this information and function entirely in the background.

Creating the Text

Noninteractive observation of behavior in static locations lends itself to audiovisual recording. The observer in the corner or behind a one-way mirrored window is not nearly as good as a properly placed camera and sound setup. Cameras don't get tired, distracted, busy writing, and all the other disconnections that observers suffer. Trained observers—even highly trained observers—provide no factual basis for the claims to be advanced other than having been there. (Showing up is important, but it is not enough.) Further, there is no opportunity for review or subsequent analysis. Current technology, from its low cost to its high capability, has eliminated most of the reason why recordings were not made in the past. That said, there are certainly times when a recording is not an option (e.g., action across multiple locations). In those cases, second best may be better than none. Observation without recording creates a written record either in field notes or in some coding scheme.

Observation, whether in person or by device, will often raise the question of an intrusive influence changing the "normal" behavior of the observed. The question is essentially meaningless, as whatever normal behavior may be, it cannot be known without observation. The question becomes a method for dismissing observation-based analysis. On the other hand, observation techniques that radically change the environment of the activity have to be suspect. So the proper question is not whether the subjects changed their behavior in the presence of observation, but rather whether the researchers conducted the observation in the least intrusive manner. No one can answer the first question, but we can all analyze the second.

Coding the Text

There is little new to be added to the coding process with these sorts of recorded texts. Coding a recording would follow the procedures recommended elsewhere and reviewed in the following section. A unit of analysis would have to be determined. Codes would be developed in either a priori or grounded fashion, and evaluation of the quality of the coding process would have to be made. The fact that the text is not an industrial product makes little difference.

Coding "on the fly" using some preset coding sheet on "live" action provides no further options but to proceed to the analysis as no review or subsequent coding can be made. Observations recorded in field notes should be coded and do require some additional techniques. These issues will be discussed in the ethnographic chapter.

One final note: Observation is remarkably absent from the contemporary mediated communication–media studies–mass communication literature as referenced by our communication core.[4] Various forms of the term *behavior observation* yielded fewer than a dozen studies. Even the term *ethnography* returned fewer than 100 (76 to be exact), the overwhelming majority of which were conference papers (and many of those were interviews and not ethnographies). That a method is being reported in conferences but not showing up in the journals suggests either that the methodology is riding a wave of the future as much of the conference work is by graduate students or that the methodology is not being accepted by the discipline's journals. My sense of it from talking to reviewers and editors is that it is not moving forward.

CODING TEXTS: PULLING IT ALL TOGETHER

Let me use this final section to pull the two chapters on text coding together, as whether the text is produced independent of the researcher or codependent with the researcher, the process is much the same. The current fashion in media analysis is to use the term *text* to refer to any semiotic (meaningful) object or performance around which the analyst can place plausible boundaries. Consequently, radio and television programs, magazine articles, the front page, blogs, tweets, social networking site pages, the family performing "watching television," interviews, stories, recorded observations, and even field notes are all considered texts. Any text can be coded.

---

[4]Observation is much more likely to be found in older, interpersonal communication studies.

The Texts of the Problem

The process starts, then, by identifying the texts that are of interest. These texts have to have a demonstrable connection to the research question, and the more direct that connection, the better. The most common error in this regard is to use content to infer consequences in the audience, but anytime the conclusions reach beyond the text, the argument is on shaky ground.

The analytic boundary of the texts has to be coherent. This is the standard apples-and-oranges problem or any circumstance where the coding breaks down or radically changes because the class of content changes. For example, if the analyst is comparing television news coverage, newspaper news coverage, and online coverage, the coding used has to make sense for use across all three forms. One can code only across an expectation of commonality; otherwise, the differences found will be banal (green is different from red, or TV news has more pictures).

Approach to Analysis

An approach to building the code set has to be chosen. In most cases, this is a moot issue because the analyst has already connected to a particular community of researchers. If your membership is metric, the approach will import a coding structure from the literature and refine it in the data. If your membership is interpretive, the approach will build a code set from the texts and refine it in the literature. (Large ideological differences can be reflected in small practical differences.) Critical issue theorists and cultural studies scholars generally behave more like metric analysts than like interpretive ones in that there is an imported overlay of concepts that directs any grounded approach.

Where the approach matters is not so much in the coding (all good coding accounts for preexisting concepts and is thoroughly connected to the material), but rather in the argument constructed from the evidence generated in the approach. Each research community values certain characteristics of evidence (and teaches its new members its truths). As members of a research community, we trust the evidence that meets those values and discount that which does not. Consequently, the answer to an approach lies in the audience for the claim and the site of publication.

Unit of Analysis

A unit of analysis or window of engagement has to be chosen. This is the level at which the coding will be conducted. It can range from the entire text to any meaningful component that has reasonably separate boundaries, such as paragraphs, sentences, thought units, chapters, scenes, shots, bars of music, or vocalized transitions. The unit chosen has to correspond to the level of commonality across the texts. In our example across three forms of news coverage, it would be difficult to argue for a commonality that sorted much finer than the global level. On the other hand, broadcast stories on the same topic from stations competing in the same market can be addressed in great detail because we have a much greater common foundation.

The texts have to be prepared for coding by the unit of analysis. This preparation involves an increasing amount of work the finer the screen of the unit of analysis. It would be fairly easy to code this page by paragraphs as the conventions of layout provide strong visual markers. It would be much more difficult to code it by sentences and more difficult still to code it by thought units. Visual and aural texts are a real challenge and usually require specialized computer applications to mark off the units (see Audacity for sound; DVDStyler is a possibility for video; NVivo 9 works for either).

Ofttimes the analyst will mark off the units and code in the same pass. Generally, this is a good approach when the unit is to be coded in its context (as is most often the case). The units do have to be durably identified—not just marked in the analyst's mind, however—in order to check agreement between coders or to do subsequent coding.

Coding

Coding is both reductionistic and extractive. It is reductive in that it reduces the surface manifestations to an occurrence of a category of content. It is extractive because it reaches below the surface to reveal the cultural concepts, societal values, and social practices that provide for the meaningfulness of the text.

Coding can go beyond organizing and revealing what is "there." It can reconstitute the text by adopting a particular frame of understanding that will allow a purposeful interpretation to be supported. It is somewhat controversial to say that such coding initiates rather than reveals meaning by providing for a hitherto unused interpretation, but certainly critical issue theories have given us new insights to old texts. Recognizing this inventive property is not to say that anything goes. There are facts in every text—this word and not that; this image, this sound, this action—that have to be accounted and maintained as sensible. The interpretation has to be warranted in the facts of the text. The absence of this accountability, in fact, should raise questions of fairness in the reader's mind.

Building the Code Set

Regardless of approach, the components of code building are quite consistent. Codes are developed from a theoretical framework, the work of others, and the characteristics of the text. The proportion and emphasis of these components change across approach, of course. The metric and critical issue scholar will be heavily invested in a theoretical framework and the literature and will use the texts as a proving ground for final adjustments to the set. Interpretive scholars will tend to work this relationship in reverse. But the interpretive scholar does not go to the texts in ignorance or without expectation or without an extensive history of reading the scholarship of others.

Doing the Coding

It is not possible to overemphasize the importance of the coding effort. The whole study stands or falls on its quality. Despite its importance, the typical research report tells us little about the codes in use, the process of developing them, or the means of application. Beyond simple intercoder reliability estimates, there is little discussion in metric studies of the validity of the coding scheme or of its evidentiary base. Interpretive coding suffers from its own defects in the sometimes magical appearance of codes that do just the right work or the failure to adequately deal with glosses, contradictions, and contrary evidence.

Each approach will have its own set of practices for conducting the actual coding and dealing with its limitations. We spent a great deal of time addressing those in the previous chapter. What remains for comment here is the physical and mental costs that coding involves. As a matter of fact, whether metric or hermeneutic, coders do get tired of reading, viewing, listening to, or engaging their set of texts. Coding is a somatic (whole-body) effort, and, despite our effort to sanitize it, the quality of the work affects the quality of the results. Material procedures have to be put into place to keep the effort fresh, limit fatigue, and prevent destination fever when the end is somewhere in sight. On the other hand, one cannot code forever. At some point, it will have to be declared at an end. Try to get there in a reasonable fashion.

Analysis

The end of coding is the start of analysis. Analysis in metric and interpretive research follows the divisions noted in Chapter 4. It breaks on the importance of the relative rates of events (metric choice) or the critical instance of events (interpretive choice). Rates are amenable to statistical analysis; critical instances are amenable to the interpretive eye.

Metric analyses generally fall into four kinds: the analysis of characteristics, generating a report of what's there; an examination of differences, comparing different classes of cases; the testing of relationships, looking at the way one characteristic affects another; and the search for structure, leading to predictive models of interaction. The statistical approaches that would be attached to those analytic frames are descriptive statistics, analysis of means and variances, correlation and regression, and structural modeling such as path analysis, factor analysis, and multiple regression.

The sort of arguments that are developed from these analyses can be shown in this quotation from the Johnson, Haigh, Becker, Craig, and Wigley (2008) study on e-mail and relationships:

> The first research question asked how email is used to enact maintenance behaviors with family members, friends, and romantic partners. To explore how email is used to enact maintenance behaviors with family members, 71 individuals who exchanged email with their long-distance family member and 34 individuals who exchanged email with their geographically close family member during this week were examined. The top five categories of maintenance behaviors for family members were openness (26% of email units), social networks (24%), positivity (16%), assurances (13%), and discussion of joint activities (7%). (p. 390)

In this quotation, Johnson et al. are describing the characteristics of the selected e-mails. Later they offer this comparison:

> Emails with family members were most likely to exhibit the maintenance behaviors of openness, social networks, and positivity. Emails with friends illustrated the same top three categories of maintenance behaviors. However, romantic partners were most likely to report assurances, openness, and positivity. (p. 394)

The implication is clearly that there is something different about romantic relationships from relationships with family or friends that leads to different maintenance strategies and results in the different rates of appearance in the categories.

Interpretive analysis is directed toward the practical meanings and cultural significances of the texts, particularly in the ways in which the texts serve to formulate and preserve the "of course it's true" understandings upon which we all act and to distribute and maintain power relationships among the disparate groups of society. Baym's (2005) analysis of *The Daily Show* gives us a good example:

> Drawing on live broadcast coverage of public statements and government proceedings, the content of *The Daily Show* resembles much of the mainstream news media. Empowered by the title of "fake news," however, *The Daily Show* routinely violates journalistic conventions in important ways. For one, while it covers the same raw material as does the mainstream news, its choices of soundbites turn contemporary conventions on their head. The unwritten rules of journalism define a good quote as a coherent statement of policy or attitude, ideally containing emotion or character and completed neatly in about 8 to 12 seconds. Professional journalists are trained to ignore long, rambling verbal presentations; quotes with poor grammar or misstatements; and soundbites with long pauses or any significant absence of verbal content. In the effort to package 8 seconds of speech, that which does not conform to conventional expectations is left on the proverbial cutting room floor. *The Daily Show*, however, mines those outtakes for a wealth of informative content. (p. 264)

In this argument, Baym is serving in the critical role of the professional guide, illuminating the characteristics of the text that create its cultural significance and practical importance.

Implications and Conclusions

Discursive protocols are not journalistic reviews of particular programs, articles, or other texts. Their purpose is to draw some conclusion about larger issues. Johnson et al. are concerned not (just) with content of selected e-mails but with the manner in which mediated communication can provide the support resources for individuals who find themselves away from home and in unfamiliar circumstances. They write in their conclusions (with perhaps a little cheerleading for the mediated communication team):

> The cheap, convenient channel of email may provide students with more opportunities to receive support from family and friends who live far away. Considering only face-to-face proximal contact may severely underestimate the social support that college students are receiving. It also ignores an important channel for the maintenance of many college student interpersonal relationships. (p. 397)

Baym, too, reaches beyond his targeted text (although he clearly enjoys the task of engaging *The Daily Show* and Jon Stewart). He writes:

> The suggestion here is not that *The Daily Show* itself should become *the* news of record, the 21st-century, discursively integrated version of Walter Cronkite's *CBS Evening News*. The program is a product of a specific historical moment, fueled both by the post–September 11 dissuasion of open inquiry and the particular talents of its current host. Whether its specific approach can withstand the test of time certainly remains to be seen. The greater significance of *The Daily Show*, however, lies in its willingness to experiment, in its opening of a door to a world of discursive possibilities. *The Daily Show* thus offers a lesson in the possible to which all students of journalism, political communication, and public discourse would be wise to pay attention. (p. 274)

An apparent lesson for us all.

Objectivity and Vraisemblance

Objectivity and vraisemblance are the metric and interpretive sides of the same coin. They are the indicants of competent work that preserves and is grounded in the facts of the case. The connection to the empirical is traceable. The empirical does not disappear behind some ideological screen to reappear recostumed to match the conclusions. Whether by arguments for reliability and validity or by arguments for trustworthiness and vraisemblance, the connection to the facts of the case is maintained.

In the end, reader and researcher alike evaluate the sensibility of the conclusions drawn. We are all more or less active and effective communicators and users of media. Conclusions that make little sense when *carefully* examined in the life-world or that appear only in the lives of "those people"—whoever the "Other" is—or that seem to require an unusually insightfully blessed researcher or interpreter lack the evidence of sensibility. As researchers, we need to reach for this sensibility in our arguments. As readers, we need to demand it of the research we engage.

As researchers, we all struggle to do the job well, even while recognizing our inability to do the job perfectly. There are markers along the way that will allow us to check our progress. The next section organizes those markers across approaches.

CRITICAL QUESTION CHECKLIST

Table 13.1 gives a list of critical questions that can serve as a checklist for analysts and readers alike. Analysts can use the list to be sure that adequate preparations have been made for the study and that the subsequent write-up provides sufficient information. Readers can use the checklist for evaluating the final work. One caveat: The questions are particular to the approach. One cannot honorably poach from the columns to poke irrelevancies at the other (even if it is fun).

Table 13.1 Critical Questions

Metric Approaches	Interpretive Approaches
• What evidence was provided of a systematic engagement of the content prior to code development?	• What evidence was provided of a systematic engagement of the content in a close reading?
• What evidence was provided that the analyst has an understanding of the audience?	• What evidence was provided that the analyst has an understanding of the audience?
• How were the media texts selected? What were the sampling frame, case, and unit of analysis?	• What was the literature that provides a foundation for the analysis?
• If codes were drawn from the literature, what was the diversity and quality of the sources?	• What evidence was provided for the analyst's competence for coding this content?
• How contemporaneous were the sources with the content?	• How were the media texts selected? What were the sampling frame, case, and unit of analysis?
• Were the facts of the texts provided?	• Were the facts of the texts provided?
• What access was or is provided to the codebook?	• What were the a priori expectations for codes?
• Were the coding instructions for the critical codes provided and explained?	• What were the safeguards against idiosyncratic coding?
• Were the codes pretested against a sample?	• As codes were developed, were written descriptions of each code recorded?
• How many iterations of pretesting were conducted?	• As new codes were added to the list, was the previous content recoded according to the new list?
• What were the results and resolutions of any pretesting?	• What was the iteration cycle of recoding?
• What training and instructions were provided to the coders?	• Was axial coding conducted?
• How was the burden of engagement handled?	• How was the burden of engagement handled?
• What quality control checks were conducted to guard against oversight, fatigue, distraction, time pressures, and the like?	• What quality control checks were conducted to guard against oversight, fatigue, distraction, time pressures, and the like?
• What proportion of the content was coded?	• What proportion of the content was coded?
• What proportion was uncoded because it was irrelevant to the study?	• What proportion was uncoded because it was irrelevant to the study?
• What proportion was coded as "Other" (a nonspecific code)?	• What proportion was coded as "one-off" or as otherwise disconnected material?
• Were measures of assignment certainty provided by coders?	• Was a discussion of the difficult or unresolved cases provided?
• Was the coding output verified that it met standards?	• What "performance review" procedures were in place?
• Were the reliability requirements established and justified prior to the start of coding?	• What was the evidence against a self-fulfilling process?
	• Were the instances of contrarian cases and exceptions presented?

Critical Answers for Metric Studies

Systematic Engagement. Regardless of approach, the analyst has to know—have intimate familiarity with—the content in order for the reader to have confidence in his or her selection of codes. The analyst is not an automaton driven by the literature, but someone exercising professional judgment.

Knowledge of Audience. Nearly every review of content is somehow justified—however indirectly—by some audience. Despite our egalitarian impulses, we are not all alike. Less than 30% of the U.S. population graduates from college; less than 1% holds an advanced degree. Researchers write from some distance from the audiences of our media unless they have a program of study that includes the audience.

Text Selection. Sampling frames make studies possible by limiting the universe of content into something addressable. The sampling frame is the key to the representational quality of the work. Case selection occurs within the sampling frame. What constitutes a case and what constitutes a noncase are equally important. Esser (2009), in his study on the framing of Iraq War stories, indicates that his research team evaluated 3,705 newspaper reports. If Iraq coverage represented 10% of the newspaper content, then something close to 30,000 other stories had to somehow be discarded. Esser is silent on how that was done. Unfortunately, it is not a trivial issue as the story selection is central to the study outcomes. Finally, the unit of analysis establishes the fineness of the sifting of content. If the unit is the entire three-minute video as in Molyneaux et al. (2008), the engagement is much coarser than that of Conrad, Dixon, and Zhang (2009) in their use of scenes to study music videos.

Source of Codes. Metric approaches place a strong emphasis on building theory incrementally. Consequently, the quality and reach of the literature review can be a good indicator of the quality and reach of the analysis. The majority of the readers of research can readily test the quality of the literature review through the availability of online databases.

Cotemporality. One of the questions to ask of that review is whether the literature is cotemporal with the content. Content changes rapidly in response to creative innovations, technology, and audience demands. The relationship between the content and the literature can be anachronistic, as in, say, taking a theory from the 1970s and applying it to contemporary media.

Facts of the Text. Computer-assisted analysis can provide the facts of the text with little effort. There is no longer any reason why this information should not be routinely provided, particularly with written texts.

Access to Codebook and Codes. Publication restrictions usually preclude any extensive presentation of a codebook. But that does not mean that it cannot be made available in an institutional repository or on a personal webpage. The codebook is the validity argument. Even with publication limitations, descriptions of the critical codes—the ones that are the basis for the tests of the hypotheses or research questions—need to be presented. There is no valid reason to accept the study without them. Otherwise, it's "Trust me; I'm a scientist."

Pretesting. Pretesting ensures that the codes are not simply arbitrary identifiers. Validating the pretesting by demonstrating the effectiveness of the coding procedure on a separate subsample completes the effort. Reporting the results and resolutions is a part of the contribution of the study. Finally, the reader needs to know how all of this effort was translated into the training of the coders.

Managing Engagement. Reading, watching, listening, and otherwise engaging content all has to be done through some method and often with the support of some technology. Coding is physically and mentally fatiguing work. The urge to push through to get it done can be strong. Prior limits have to be established and kept. Some portion of the work has to be reviewed to ensure that quality is maintained. Errors here can be controlled.

The Coded and Uncoded. Responsibility for the representation of the content will vary according to the purposes of the study. If, like Hetsroni (2008), one is simply interested in the frequency of occurrence of a particular topic, there is little responsibility for the rest of the content (other than defining why it is the "rest"). If one is trying to document "news coverage," as Esser (2009) did, then the proportion of content coded, the proportion deemed irrelevant, and the use of nonspecific "Other" codes in metric coding and single-instance codes in interpretive coding become important. The goal is to have most of the content coded with little deemed irrelevant and the minor appearance of disconnected codes. Results that don't meet this standard can represent either a lack of coherence in the content or a failure of the coding theory and design.

Coding Certainty. Measures of assignment certainty are a little-used but valuable bit of information that can be collected from metric coders, particularly in the pretesting of the coding scheme. The measures simply ask the coders to rate their certainty of code assignment on a numerical scale. They are very helpful in pinpointing difficulties in the code design.

Quality Control. The literature is amazingly quiet about quality control, routinely accepting an error rate in excess of 30%. How much of this error rate is intractable, and how much of it is just sloppy work? In the absence of evidence to the contrary, I think it should all be judged as poor efforts at quality control.

A Priori Reliability. Finally, metric authors often treat reliability analysis as if it were a roll of the dice. Reliability outcomes should not be unanticipated but should be predictable given a thorough understanding of the equivocation and ambiguity levels of the content and the quality of the coding scheme. If the analyst can describe the limits of each, then the explanation for the outcome sounds much less like self-serving excuses.

Critical Answers for Hermeneutic and Hybrid Studies

Systematic Engagement. We might excuse a metric scholar for not documenting a systematic engagement of the content because "close reading" is not a talisman of that approach, but there can be little excuse for interpretive approaches. It is not enough to declare that a close reading was done; it has to be documented.

Knowledge of Audience. Interpretive scholars are equally at risk as metric scholars in making claims for an audience they do not systematically know. Most 30- or 40-something professors are long removed from the junior high age group (and would be trampled in the hallway of any high school).

Literature Review. In the early days of interpretive work, there was a big deal made out of going "presuppositionless" into the analysis, as if one could erase the mind with one of those "flashy" things from *Men in Black*. The purpose of the argument was to exaggerate the distinction between metric and interpretive approaches, but it led to some degree of silliness. The literature review still serves to locate the analyst in the conversation, and its quality is important.

Selection of Texts. Both the process of selection and the quality of the selection—its reach across time, topic, medium, and genre, for example—are important elements that speak to the value of the scholarship. Otherwise, it's "I looked at a bunch of stuff; trust me."

Facts of the Text. A presentation of the facts of the text is strong (and often the only) evidence of a close reading.

Analyst Competence. Interpretive coding depends on the competence of the analyst to be responsive to the distinctive qualities of the text. The competence needed depends on the research question, of course, but, in any case, it cannot be taken for granted. (I would not trust my coding of digital games, for example, because I am inexperienced.)

Prior Expectations. That prior competence of the analyst produces a priori expectations for the content, but so does the analyst's motivations, research questions, and theories. If I code music videos, I would expect sexuality issues to be a major element in the coding. How they get coded, however, will depend on the stance I take in relation to the content. Grounded coding engages the content but is not determined by it. The analyst is an integral part of the process.

Safeguards From the Idiosyncratic. The analyst is an integral part but cannot be uniquely so. The coding has to make sense to someone else lest it be judged mostly idiosyncratic.

The evidence here is easy to present by using a "coding auditor" who checks all and questions when necessary. If the coding is divided among a team, team members can serve as a check on one another, recognizing the inherent pressure for a rush to consensus.

A Record of Understanding. A code is shorthand for some deeper understanding of the content. An analyst might be able to keep the descriptions of five or six codes in mind without recording them, beyond that, information gets lost. Codes will also often be enlarged in their purview, so what was initially the basis gets changed. Writing down what the code is coding is an immense help in conducting subsequent recoding and in drawing conclusions.

Recoding. There is an interesting tension in grounded coding (which also appears in metric coding). New codes are added as different content is encountered or when some subtlety in the content is finally recognized by the analyst. If the new code is of the "I haven't seen this before" kind, the study can go forward without recoding. But if it is an "aha" moment, there is a responsibility to go back through all of the content previously coded. Analysts who finally discover something near the end of the coding may be severely tempted to skip this step. Recoding can also involve the disaggregation of major codes into subcodes. This recoding requires the analyst to identify the distinctions that occur within a given code, thus furthering the sophistication of the engagement.

Recoding Method. The recoding iteration cycle (returning to the content with new codes) is mildly interesting as it can be done after each new code or after the first pass of coding has been completed. There are arguments for each.

Axial Coding. Axial coding (applying a template to theoretical categories) is an additional safeguard against superficiality, but can also lead to conventionalism.

Evidence of Quality Work. This and the next four questions raise the same issues as in metric coding. The fact that the coding is interpretive cannot mean that it is not methodical and carefully analyzed for its quality. A report that in essence says, "We read a bunch of stuff, and here's what we found" is simply unacceptable.

Disagreements. If an auditor doesn't disagree with the coding at some point, one suspects the auditor. The auditor should force a deeper understanding of the content and coding. That's worth reporting.

Performance Review. The auditor is an important part of the performance review, but only the primary coder can fully understand the impediments to quality work. In my experience, I come to recognize where I make errors (but who knows how many are unrecognized). I then recheck the entire work for those errors. The analyst has to commit to this performance review and keep a written log of problems.

Protections Against Self-Fulfillment. Without adequate methods of text selection, engagement, and regular performance review, the whole process is in danger of finding out what we knew all along to be true.

Contrarian Cases. "Cherry-picking" is a common temptation in interpretive research. It refers to the practice of selecting the examples that best represent the argument being constructed. The practice is aided by completely ignoring the contrarian cases and those that just don't fit. The researcher is responsible for all of the information, not just the good stuff.

MOVING ON

For the postmodernist, coding represents something of a challenge because it invests the analyst—whether metric or interpretive—with "special powers of insight and sensibility." One has to wonder where those powers come from. Who owns the insight? Whose sensibility is empowered? Those are central questions of the critical-cultural approach that Geoffrey Baym so masterfully outlines for us in the next chapter.

REFLECTIONS

What Are Some Points to Remember?

- Particular research methods produce their own texts. Best practices call on the analyst to systematically code these texts.
- The content of a text is but a single element among many sources of information that texts contain. Facts, framing, structure, language, and discourse are among the other sources.
- Coding of any sort proceeds through the following steps: selection and production of texts; determination of the case and the unit of analysis; development and refinement of the code set, either as an a priori effort in metric or as an emergent process in interpretive; analysis of the coding data for their quantities and rates in metric and for what they reveal about the social and cultural influences and activities of the texts in interpretive; and drawing the implications and conclusions from that analysis to the initiating problem.
- There are specific criteria of good practice that guide both the analyst and the reader for each of these steps.

Why Does It Matter?

Coding of texts that are the coproduction of the analyst provides good protection against the superficial analysis that can occur when one assumes knowledge not rightly earned.

What Else Could We Talk About?

All coding appears to rest on the sophistication and interpretive ability of the principal investigator. In metric coding, those abilities come into play in the engagement of a body of theory and prior research from which the appropriate code set will be extracted. That dependence continues in the refinement of the code set as it is tested against the texts. In interpretive coding, the code set emerges and is refined through the engagement of the texts. The metric scholar who has a superficial understanding of theory and research can produce a reliable but inadequate code set. The interpretive scholar who reads superficially produces a superficial analysis. The questions relating to the qualifications of the analyst and the depth of effort are rarely addressed.

What Else Might Be Interesting to Read?

De Fina, A. (2009). Narratives in interview—the case of accounts: For an interactional approach to narrative genres. *Narrative Inquiry, 19*, 233–258.

Glaser, B. G. (1992). *Basics of grounded theory analysis: Emergence versus forcing*. Mill Valley, CA: Sociology Press.

C H A P T E R 1 4

Critical Interpretive Methods

Social Meanings and Media Texts

Geoffrey Baym

CHAPTER PREVIEW

What's It All About?

This chapter delves into strategies for reading media texts, in search of their social, cultural, and/or political significance. Unlike the empirical methods covered in the previous chapters, here we develop an interpretive approach to textual analysis, one that exchanges breadth of generalizability for depth of insight. Successful interpretive analysis, however, also must be systematic and rigorous. This chapter offers a series of steps that can structure the interpretive process.

What Are the Major Topics?

Interpretive analysis is always a form of social criticism. It seeks to *read* media content of all kinds and draw from it the particular sociocultural meanings the content potentially creates and circulates.

Although interpretive analysis shares some similarities with quantitative content analysis, a number of important distinctions between the two approaches are discussed.

Interpretive analysis can proceed from the general to the specific—from a sociocultural issue that needs study to specific media texts that speak or contribute to that issue—or from the specific to the general—from a particular text that seems to be doing something unique, interesting, or troubling, to a general issue the text invokes.

The interpretive analyst must be able to justify the specific texts selected for analysis and have guaranteed, repeated access to those texts.

The analyst then must develop "intimate familiarity" with the texts, identifying the regularities of content and form, as well as their idiosyncrasies. Constructing a content log is valuable here.

Interpretive analysis also needs a sophisticated theoretical framework. The study must draw on and fit into wider thinking about that issue or those kinds of texts.

Interpretation is largely the examination of signs and signifying systems—the multiple ways a text constructs meaning. These include visual, verbal, and aural signs that exist in both synchronic and diachronic relationships. The analysis also looks for wider patterns of organization, or underlying grammar, that give a text coherence.

Texts always exist in relationship with other texts, and to contexts—cultural, political, historical—of production, distribution, and reception.

The end result of the process is an argument about a text or a series of texts. That argument must be insightful, valid, and valuable.

What Special Terms Are Used?

Connotation	Intertextuality	Representation
Context	Narrative structure	Signification
Interpretation		

INTRODUCTION

In this chapter, we turn to the family of media research methods that can be considered under the rubric of *interpretive analysis*. Speaking in broad terms, methods of interpretive analysis seek to *read* media content of all kinds and draw from it the particular socio-cultural meanings the content potentially creates and circulates. That is to say, we can think of media content as a *text* (perhaps as a *textbook*) that offers lessons in how to understand the social, cultural, and political worlds within which we live our daily lives.

So, for example, you may have seen the "reality" show that the FX television network produced in the spring of 2006 titled *Black. White.* For that program, a White family (a man, a woman, and her teenage daughter) and a Black family (a father, a mother, and a teenage boy) agreed to participate in a remarkable project designed to explore the question of race in America (and, of course, to get ratings, sell advertising, and earn money for Fox and its parent company News Corporation). Using state-of-the-art Hollywood makeup techniques, show producers transformed the two families, turning the White family Black and the Black family White (at least in appearance). Not only did the two families live together (both in and out of makeup), but for each episode, all six people took part in various exercises designed to expose them to life as the other. They also spoke at length to the camera and with each other about their experiences.

For our purposes here, the program *Black. White.* is interesting on two levels. On one, the program explicitly was grappling with the serious questions of racial identity and race relations in the United States. It forced the participants and encouraged the audience to confront their assumptions about race—what it is, where it comes from, and, indeed, what it means. At various points, the White daughter realized that race has much more to do with the cultural experience of a people than it does with the color of one's skin, the Black father argued with his son about whether or not race is still a relevant concept, and the White father insisted that racism is just a figment of Black people's imagination (even as he spouted one racial stereotype after another). The program thus opens avenues, at times rather uncomfortable ones, to think about issues of culture, identity, and racial politics (the term *politics* is used here not to mean voting and elections, but to mean the relationships of power that profoundly shape our daily lives).

At the same time, however, *Black. White.* itself is contributing to our understandings about the meaning of race. In other words, the program is participating in the *social construction of* race. Methods of interpretive analysis rest on the fundamental assumption that reality is socially constructed, which is to suggest that things *are* what they mean. It is clear that the significance of skin color lies less (and likely not at all) in biology, and more in the meaning it holds for those within a given society, culture, or community. Indeed, many would argue that communities, cultures, and societies can only come to exist through the process of sharing, and often arguing about, meaning. To put the point differently, communities come into being through communication—which we can understand here as the circulation of meaning. The media scholar James Carey (1988) has argued that it is through communication that reality—or at least the sets of meanings, values, and assumptions we hold about ourselves and the world—is constructed, maintained, and at times transformed. Thus, the interpretive analyst would argue that by circulating meanings about racial identity, *Black. White.* is participating in maintaining or potentially transforming the socially constructed concept of race.

If one were to pursue an interpretive analysis of *Black. White.*, one goal could be to examine how the program defines racial identity, how it allocates value to the concept of race, and how it either perpetuates or complicates common understandings and assumptions about the nature of race relations. From this perspective, *Black. White.*, or any assemblage of media content for that matter, can be understood as a text: something that contains meanings, which in turn can be *read*. The challenge of interpretive analysis is to offer an insightful reading of the text, one that helps us to better understand both the text itself and the issues of social, cultural, and political significance of which the text speaks.

The interpretive analyst is always, by definition, also a social critic—media texts provide us with critical windows into an endless range of social, cultural, and political phenomena,

phenomena that are continuously in flux and often the sites of contestation. In his work on media and the representation of race, the media scholar and social theorist Stuart Hall (1982) suggested that media texts are often a location of *struggle*, an argument in words, images, sound, and story over meaning and value. If media texts are sites of struggle, then they equally are products of, or exercises in, power. To read a media text is also to confront the play of power in shaping the meanings and assumptions that delimit the boundaries of communities, cultures, and societies.

GOALS

Interpretive analysis is the search for the meaning circulated by media texts. Scholars of the semiotic often disagree where one can find meaning. Some insist meaning is created at the moment of creation, through the production processes—industrial, organizational, sociological, and personal—that bring media texts into being. Others maintain that meaning exists in the act of reading, that only by studying the audience and its moment of reception can one begin to understand what a text means. The method articulated in this chapter, however, focuses on the text itself. We don't deny that media producers have intentions and that the production process shapes the nature of the text; nor do we argue that everyone must decipher a given text in the same way or extract from it the exact same meanings. At this point, however, we leave the study of media production to the organizational sociologists and the ethnographers, and the study of reception to the audience analyst. Here we see the text as existing somewhere between those two ends of the production-reception circuit, and we seek to delimit a method for unpacking the content itself.

At this point, the astute reader might begin to wonder if we are simply describing *content analysis* by a different name. Thus, before we can proceed, we need to tackle the distinctions between the interpretive textual approach being developed here and the methods of quantitative content analysis that a different family of researchers has long employed. In their helpful exploration of content analysis, Riffe, Lacy, and Fico (1998) define content analysis as "the systematic assignment of communication content to categories according to rules, and the analysis of relationships involving those categories using statistical methods" (p. 18). Thus defined, content analysis is the attempt to break media content apart into discrete units, each of which can be positively identified, sorted, categorized, and then assigned a numerical value. By converting content into numerical data, the analyst can then employ statistical methods to explore the relationships among content categories and, by extrapolation, lay the groundwork for experiments to measure how those variables might affect an audience. Indeed, quantitative content analysis has its roots in the social-psychological study of media effects—its ultimate goal is to try to determine (and here *determine* is the correct word) what the content *does* to the people who consume it.

Content analysis depends on the fundamental premise that the content, and by inference its *significance*, is divisible into discrete units, the sum of which renders the whole. By contrast, the approach to interpretive analysis developed here begins from the assumption that while the analyst certainly can (and must) identify different aspects or elements of the text, the content is always something more than the sum of its parts. Meaning is holistic, ultimately indivisible into clearly cut and neatly described categories. Both content and interpretive analysis agree that to grapple with media content one must penetrate the surface, but where content analysis sees discernible building blocks, interpretive analysis finds interwoven webs of significance, some strands of which may be measurable, and others of which defy quantification.

Interpretive analysis further differs from content analysis in other ways. Again, although both claim media content as the object of study, content analysis only can consider the manifest content—that which the text explicitly presents. Obviously, manifest content is a good place to start, but it seems equally clear that analysis that remains at the level of the manifest will be unlikely to reach the point of significance. As the theorist Roland Barthes (1964) reminds us, meaning hardly ever exists at the denotative level—the manifest and the literal—but rather is produced at the fundamentally more complex and perhaps less generalizable level of the connotative. Similarly, content analysis offers no tools to deal with nonliteral systems of meaning such as irony, sarcasm, or any other textual moment that requires the audience to "read between the lines." Interpretive analysis allows the researcher to explore connotation and inference, the unspoken level at which texts so often construct meaning. Likewise, interpretive analysis allows the researcher to consider the *contextual* factors upon which any given text depends, and without which it would be rendered meaningless. The interpretive analyst also can explore the text's silence—that which it omits. Absence is as much a factor in meaning as is presence, but content analysis offers no tools to confront that which the text elides or ignores. Finally, the content analyst's concern for categorizing the manifest content can too easily conflate recurrence with significance, two concepts that are by no means synonymous. That which the text most repeats is not necessarily its most important element. For example, two of the most repeated words in any news story are *said* and *and*, but one would be hard pressed to suggest that the significance of the news lies therein. At the same time, the most significant moments of media texts—a particularly powerful image, phrase, or turn in a narrative—are often those that occur only once. Interpretive analysis can explore the moments that otherwise would escape the quantitative net.

At this point, however, the proponent of content analysis would be quick to counter that interpretive analysis, with its concern for the momentary, the connotative, and the contextual, can too easily degenerate into unsystematic and idiosyncratic readings that offer us little more than one individual's reactions to the text. A similar argument is often made by those who are sympathetic to the holistic and qualitative underpinnings of interpretive analysis. Those who advocate notions of the active audience or of postmodern indeterminacy would suggest that the text can mean anything to anyone—that it is fundamentally polysemic—and no one reading can capture "what the text means," because it will mean something different to each person and at each time it is read. To take the argument to the extreme, the claim would be that texts ultimately mean nothing, because they can mean anything. Interpretive textual analysis thus is assailed on both sides, by the quantitative researcher who demands replicability and the radical postmodernist who denies the text coherence.

In response, we suggest that the text does indeed mean something. Its meaning, as we will discuss in much greater depth shortly, may not exist in the neatly divisible categories of its manifest content, but neither is the content meaningless. If interpretation is always a process of engagement between an audience and a text, the text plays a privileged role in the exchange. It provides the semiotic resources—the words, images, sounds, and stories—with which the audience can construct meaning. To borrow from the novelist and semiotician Umberto Eco (1992), we suggest that there is an "intention of the text"—the text is always trying to say something, something that might differ from what its producers intended or what any given person extracts, but that nonetheless can be identified and opened for examination. The intention of the text, Eco argues, is a *semiotic strategy*, a mechanism of making meaning. Thus, the goal of interpretive analysis is to lay bare the particular set of sociocultural meanings contained within a text and, perhaps more important, to uncover the textual mechanisms by which those meanings are constructed and circulated.

IDENTIFYING ISSUES AND TEXTS

As we turn to some of the specific strategies that can guide the process of interpretive analysis, we need first to briefly consider one more important distinction between content analysis and interpretive reading. If the former seeks to generate generalizable proofs that offer predictive value about the nature of particular kinds of media content, the latter instead aims to construct reasonable arguments that deepen our understanding of specific media texts: the way they work, the meanings they construct, and, perhaps most important, the lessons they have to teach us about issues of wider social, cultural, and political significance. We need to remember that the interpretive analyst is equally a social critic, and the study of media texts is as much the study of the sociocultural landscape as it is the study of media content, and perhaps more so.

Thus, the initial challenge facing the interpretive researcher is to both define an issue that warrants scholarly attention and identify specific media texts that deserve exploration. The researcher can proceed by one of two directions here. In one approach, the first step is to define a problematic—an issue of emerging or continued sociocultural importance about which the existing scholarly literature is incomplete. In an ever-changing world, there are no limits to the number or range of issues that can fit under this heading, but it remains the interpretive scholar's burden to articulate the sociocultural issue in question and to justify it as a realm of study. The second step here is to identify the *textual manifestation* of the issue in question. In other words, what media texts illustrate or contribute to the problematic? What media texts offer us critical windows through which to grapple with the issue? For example, a current topic of interest in the editorial pages of one of your author's local newspapers is the changing nature of gender roles and, specifically, conceptualizations of "manliness." One can identify a number of textual manifestations of this issue, including the now-defunct reality show *Queer Eye for the Straight Guy*, the new wave of "men's" magazines and their portrayal of the ideal man, or even the letters to the editor that address the question of what a man should be. Again, there are few limits to the kinds of media texts that could be tackled under the heading of "changing representations of masculinity," but the researcher's initial task is to justify the text as worthy of study.

If one approach begins with the sociocultural problematic and then identifies specific textual manifestations that warrant study, the opposite approach begins with a particular text that seems on its surface to be making a unique, interesting, or troubling contribution to the world of meaning in which we live. For example, this chapter began with a brief discussion of the program *Black. White.* Judging both from an informal viewing of the show and from the conversations about the show that appeared in the popular press and in interpersonal circles, it seems clear that it was doing something interesting and perhaps important. That seems as good a place as any to begin the interpretive process. From there, however, the researcher must take the next step and *justify* the text. That is to say, it is not enough to study a particular text simply because the researcher personally finds it interesting. We have to be able to argue that by studying the text, we can gain insight into an important issue. So, for example, someone may find the reality program *Survivor* to be compelling, but the case must be made that studying the program will help us understand something that deserves to be understood. In and of itself, a study of *Survivor* may not be worth anyone's time. If one could argue that *Survivor* provides a critical window into contemporary attitudes toward interpersonal relationships, ethics, and ideals of success, *then* it becomes an object worthy of study.

SELECTION

Whether the interpretive process begins with an issue of sociocultural significance or with an intriguing text, the next step is to determine the *specific texts* that will be studied. Every scholarly project, be it in biology, physics, literature, or media studies, must have a clearly defined *object of study*. The media stream provides us with a continuous flow of content. In a digital age of 24-hour on-demand media, there appear to be few clear boundaries among programs, genres, and content forms. Good media scholarship, however, must be about something—it cannot be about everything. The successful researcher thus must be able to identify, in precise terms, the object of attention; one must carve out the domain of study, to impose boundaries of inclusion and exclusion. For example, if one wanted to study *Black. White.*, one would have to consider exactly what that meant. Would the researcher look at all six episodes or just one? If only one, then which one? The first? The last? Would the study include the television promotions for the show? Would it include the companion website from FX or the show's own Myspace site? Would it include the streaming version provided by the MSN website and the complementary elements that appeared on the computer screen? Would it include the advertisements that ran during the individual shows? What about the music video for the rapper Ice Cube's theme song? Would it include news coverage of the show or the wide-ranging discussions about the show that appeared on the Internet? Any of these elements could contribute to a fascinating study, but in today's infinitely complex media stream, the interpretive researcher must make careful and deliberate choices to define the object of study.

In quantitative content analysis, the "sample"—the specific pieces of content selected for study—ideally is designed to be a random collection that offers any variation of the content an equal chance of appearing in the data set. Because the intention of *interpretive* analysis is not to produce generalizable findings but to better understand specific texts, the selection of a sample is governed by a different logic. The challenge is not to generate a statistically representative sample designed to capture all possible textual manifestations, but instead to come up with a strategically defined window into a specific phenomenon. The content analyst might call this a "purposive" sample, one selected for specific reasons and that allows the researcher to ask a particular set of questions and tackle a particular range of issues. Thus, the next challenge in the interpretive process is to define a sampling rationale—a justification for selecting a particular set of texts (and thus not others) for analysis. Although there are no "rules" for the selection of texts, we offer here a brief discussion of some of the more common strategies one finds in the scholarly literature.

Single Text

Here the interpretive analysis delves deeply into one single media text. Examples can include a study of an individual film; a particular episode of a dramatic program; one website; a single newscast, magazine, or paper; or even a single news story. The selection of one text is easily justifiable when the intention is to make sense of a film that appears to make a unique contribution to both media and the social environment (say, for example, Hitchcock's *Psycho*, Tarantino's *Pulp Fiction*, or perhaps the 1980s made-for-television nuclear holocaust drama *The Day After*). Such an analysis is limited only by the creativity and value of the *critical questions* one can ask of or about the film.

An analysis of a single program, newscast, news story, or other media text—that is to say a study that looks at one example of a recurrent type—becomes harder (although by no means impossible) to justify. The content analyst shivers at the thought of a sample size of one, and indeed, it is impossible to generalize from one to the whole. However, a close reading of one—what the scholar of cultural studies might call "thick description"—can at times offer a fascinating window into a moment of media content, a study that results not in a generalizable statement of *what is* (or what usually will be), but rather in a reading of the very conditions of the possible. In other words, an individual newscast certainly can't tell us what all newscasts look like, but it can provide a rich resource to investigate a single example of what is possible, what any given newscast *may* look like. The emphasis in such a study must fall on *depth* of analysis. In exchange, the researcher cedes claims to *breadth*.

Time-Based

Perhaps more common than an analysis of a single text is a study that explores a number of similar media texts drawn from a particular time frame. Examples could include a full week of newscasts, one full season of a dramatic program, or perhaps every episode of *The Daily Show* for the six months leading up to Election Day. Here the key is that there is some significance in the time frame selected for analysis. For the study of news, we can think in terms of "critical event research"—an approach that seeks to explore how the news media performed during a specific and important moment in history (say, during the impeachment of President Clinton in 1998 or the invasion of Iraq in the spring of 2003). Again, the effort is not to determine how the news always covers (or is likely to cover) impeachments or wars, but rather is to determine how, in specific terms, particular media did cover a particular event. It remains the analyst's responsibility to articulate the justification for studying the exact time frame in question.

Comparative Within Time

This approach mirrors a time-based strategy, but adds the comparative component. Rather than just looking at one group of texts (e.g., a number of episodes of *Friends*, *The Daily Show*, or *CBS News*), the researcher looks at similar types of media from the same time frame (e.g., *The Daily Show* and *CBS News*). Here the key point is that the various groupings of texts have similar, yet identifiably (and significantly) differing, approaches. Thus, it makes sense to compare how *The Daily Show* and *CBS News* covered the presidential election, or how *The Daily Show* and *Late Show with David Letterman* differ in their approaches to interviewing politicians. Likewise, one could make an argument that it would be worthwhile to compare a number of reality programs (say, *Survivor*, *American Idol*, and *The Apprentice*) in any given year. It would be harder, however, to justify a study of *American Idol* and *CBS News*, even if the programs were drawn from the same week. The analyst must be able to offer compelling reasons both for selecting texts from a particular time frame and for comparing the specific texts in question.

Comparative Across Time

This is the interpretive scholar's counterpart to the social scientist's "longitudinal analysis." The effort here is to examine related media texts as they appear at different historical-cultural moments. So, for example, one could compare network news coverage of the Clinton impeachment with network news coverage of the Watergate scandal 25 years earlier, as Baym (2003, 2004) did. Or one could examine letters written to the president from the 1860s to the 1960s, as Alexander (2005) did. Likewise, one could explore how women were portrayed in the top-rated sitcoms from the 1950s up to today. How different or similar were Lucy, Mary, and Grace? For any such analysis, the focus falls on *change*. The critical questions here tackle issues such as how the particular kind of media text evolves over time, reflecting developments in the landscape of media production. At the same time, this approach can help reveal how particular kinds of media might be contributing to changes in the wider environment of sociocultural meaning. Thus, the above studies should tell us something about how network news has changed over the years, about how our understandings of what (or who) the president is continues to evolve, or about how our assumptions about gender identity have developed during a particular time frame.

Comparative Across Media

In this approach, the analyst selects a set of texts drawn from different media that have a similar agenda or deal with similar topics. The effort here is to examine how similar but different kinds of media compare with each other. If McLuhan was right, and the medium is the message, such an approach can reveal much about the interconnections between media types and the construction of sociocultural meanings. So, for example, one could study the differences in how traditional newspaper reports and blogs approach the work of journalism and public information. Similarly, one could examine the emerging genre of web-based political documentaries, and compare that with traditional documentary films or perhaps television news.

Thematic

Finally, a common approach to interpretive analysis can be labeled "thematic." Here the analyst selects a number of texts that illustrate a common theme or textual approach of sociocultural significance. Texts here can be drawn from within the same media type (i.e., prime-time drama) or across media types (drama, films, news, and any other combination that makes sense). So, for example, Shugart (2003) identified the pairing of a straight woman and a gay man as an increasingly popular narrative device. To explore the significance of that issue, she looked at both the sitcom *Will & Grace* and a number of films, including *My Best Friend's Wedding* and *The Next Best Thing*, that featured friendships between a straight woman and a gay man. (Although she didn't include it in her study, one sees a similar theme emerging in *The Mexican* between characters played by Julia Roberts and James Gandolfini.) Likewise, one could explore how images and understandings of "the president" are being constructed across a variety of media, both factual and fictive. Here one could look at network news and comedy shows such as *The Daily Show*, and also prime-time dramas such as *The West Wing* and *Commander in Chief*, and any number of Hollywood films. Again, the motivating factor for these kinds of studies is an interest in the theme (gay man–straight woman) or the topic (presidentiality) as it is constructed in various media locales.

The above are just a few common approaches to selecting specific texts for analysis. Defining the object of study remains one of the primary arenas for creativity in interpretive analysis. There are, however, two rules one must keep in mind. First, the sample of texts—what the social science researcher would call the data set—must give us insight into an issue of sociocultural or political significance. Second, the researcher always must be able to articulate a compelling rationale for the choices she or he makes about which media texts to include, and which to ignore.

TEXTUAL CAPTURE

After one has defined the specific texts that will compose the object of study, the interpretive effort necessarily must turn to a decidedly more mundane yet equally important task—obtaining copies of the selected material. It is mandatory that the researcher be able to collect or at least have guaranteed access to the texts, ideally in their original form. Interpretive analysis demands that the researcher be able to return continually to the texts under consideration and be confident, especially in the case of websites, that they won't change their form or content or simply disappear before the analysis is completed.

This labor is governed by practical, logistical realities that can be as simple as saving the newspaper or remembering to press *record* on the DVR or as tricky as tracking down a copy of a long-forgotten program or off-line storing websites and all of their linked content. Regardless, the analyst must be prepared to work out the details of textual capture.

Obviously, some media are more easily available than others. It is a simple matter to program a DVR to record a prime-time drama once a week or to buy a film on DVD. Recording multiple programs from a variety of sources poses a slightly more difficult challenge (thus your authors' love for their DVRs!). Thanks to databases such as LexisNexis, the collection of printed articles and even transcripts from several television news outlets is relatively easy. For archived television news stories, many researchers turn to the Vanderbilt Television News Archive, a remarkable collection of network newscasts that dates back to 1968, assembled and maintained by Vanderbilt University. On the Internet, the Vanderbilt Television News Archive makes available written abstracts of stories from CBS, NBC, ABC, and CNN newscasts. For a fee, the archive will provide videotape copies of requested stories. The archive only contains the nightly newscasts, however, and thus the analyst interested in network morning news, news magazine programs, local news, or 24-hour cable other than CNN's flagship evening programs must look elsewhere.

The Internet offers an entirely different set of possibilities and challenges in textual capture. A wealth of audiovisual material is available online, and of course downloading and saving much of it for later viewing is a simple task. Streaming video, however, is a different animal. At the time of this writing, convenient software for saving streaming content on one's computer was not readily available. Capturing an image of the entire computer screen is certainly possible, but such "screenshots" cannot include active links. Therefore, the researcher must devise a supplemental plan for capturing linked content. There are an increasing number of web-based archives of Internet material. See, for example, the collections available at WebArchivist.org and the Internet Archive "Wayback Machine" (http://www.archive.org). Even more so than the Vanderbilt Television News Archive, web archives are infinitely incomplete. With the sheer number of websites and their fundamentally transitory nature, no archive can hope to contain everything.

Likewise, the researcher dealing with current web-based materials faces similar difficulties. The web is inherently vast and unbounded. Although some websites are relatively simple, many provide access to layers upon layers of content—content that at times is altered or updated literally on a minute-by-minute basis. The boundaries between sites are also difficult to discern. The hypertextuality of the web makes it a remarkable communication phenomenon, but it challenges any attempt to pin down the content, to define clear borders and convert the amorphous nature of the web into an identifiable object of study. None of this is to say that the web cannot be studied—indeed its omnipresence in contemporary life demands that we pay it close attention. Rather, the point here is that the web raises specific hurdles—both conceptual and logistical—that must be confronted as one considers assembling a textual collection for study (see Markham & Baym, 2009; Mitra & Cohen, 1999).

Finally, the question of textual capture raises issues of *ecological validity*. Inevitably, interpretive analysis is conducted at a distance from the original context in which a particular media text is read, viewed, and/or heard. As discussed earlier, our goal here is not to study the audience or the moment of reception. But we must remain sensitive to the ways in which the text was likely received—after all, our goal is to reach some conclusions about the contribution the text makes to the landscape of sociocultural and political meanings outside the walls of one's office or study. Thus we must take steps to ensure that, at the least, the texts we examine have some relationship to the texts that actually circulate in the world around us. So, for example, we cannot study written transcripts of television news and then assume we have learned something about televisual content. Rather, if our goal is to better understand television, then we must watch (and listen to!) television—words, images, sounds, and all. Likewise, it may be difficult to extrapolate from streaming video provided on the web (with its compressed image that never quite looks like the real thing) to television content. It would also be a mistake to equate the online version of a newspaper (say, http://www.nytimes.com) with the printed version (*The New York Times*). Many of the words may be the same, but ultimately, those are two different animals and need to be considered as such.

INTERPRETIVE READING

Finally, with texts in hand, we can at last turn to the specific labor of interpretation. Ultimately, interpretive analysis is more art than science, and thus what follows here is not a precisely defined step-by-step protocol but rather a strategic approach that can help structure the interpretive process.

Gaining Intimate Familiarity

A wise teacher of communication once suggested that in order to study the media, one must first be "seduced by the text." Her point was a good one: that interpretive analysis will always be a struggle if it is not a labor of love. The analyst must spend a great deal of time with the text, and no more so than during the first stage of the process, when one develops an *intimate familiarity* with the texts in question. The initial goal simply is to learn what— at least on the surface—is there. Stuart Hall (1975) suggested that the interpretive process begins with a "long preliminary soak" in which the analyst saturates him- or herself in the text. The primary tools at work here are observation—reading, watching, listening. As with several of the methodologies discussed in this book, the analyst functions as an empirical scholar during this first stage, letting the text speak for itself.

Textual Regularities

The challenge is to gain a handle on the basic composition of the text. For the study of a television program, this can include the general structure of the individual show (for example, most half-hour local news programs begin with two segments of news, followed by weather, then sports, and conclude with a light story at the end), the people or characters who regularly appear and the standard locations in which they do (*Seinfeld* focused on four characters—Jerry, George, Elaine, and Kramer—who usually gathered at

Jerry's apartment or the coffee shop supposedly down the street), and the general kinds of topics or subject matter the show deals with (most plotlines on *Star Trek* involved encounters with aliens and other unexpected obstacles to the crew's mission of peaceably exploring the universe). For the study of a website, one could pay attention to the layout of the screen (including what elements appear—headlines, graphics, photographs, text, etc.— and where on the screen they are usually positioned), the kinds of links the site provides (the categories the site uses to organize its domain), and the general kinds of topics with which the site deals. For the study of a film, this could include the setting (time and place), the main characters, and the major plot points (the events that punctuate and advance the narrative).

This list is not intended to be comprehensive; any kind of media will contain certain regularities of form. It is the task of the interpretive researcher in this initial stage simply to identify those regularities. We don't need to be concerned (yet) with the specific properties of each individual text in our sample; on the initial pass, we are looking for the elements, structure, and general topics that help to define the text as a recognizable if not entirely predictable entity. So even though we might not be able to predict exactly whom Jon Stewart will interview on tomorrow's *Daily Show*, any regular viewer knows that the show undoubtedly will have an interview. We may not be able to predict what the headline or picture will be on the front page of tomorrow's local newspaper, but we can be confident that the paper *will* have a headline and a photograph. Likewise, we know that the crew on the Starship *Enterprise* will encounter some kind of problem in outer space, but we can't know in advance just what each of those problems will be (unless, like some people out there, you know all the episodes of *Star Trek* by heart).

Developing a Content Log

Once the analyst has developed a measure of familiarity with the text's regularities, the next step is to construct the template for what we can call a content log. The goal here is to return to the text for (at least) a second time, working through all of the material selected for study and recording the specific instances of each of those regularities. For example, if we've discovered that *The Daily Show* is always structured in three segments that roughly divide into satirical news, parody reports from the show's staff of comedian-reporters, and in-studio interviews, a content log could note what topics were covered in the first segment, which reporter appears in the second segment (and what story he or she is covering), and who appears as the guest for the interview segment. A content log should also note the more mundane aspects of each specific text, such as (to continue with the example of *The Daily Show*) the date the show was aired, the length of each segment, the specific audiovisual materials used (news footage from a cable channel, sound bites from the president, silly graphics produced on Photoshop, etc.), the particular people who are quoted, and the "real" news sources from which Jon Stewart gets his information. Although there is flexibility in what details one chooses to record in a content log, the analyst would be wise to make the effort to be as comprehensive as possible. In the case of audiovisual media, we do not suggest engaging in the time-consuming labor of transcribing spoken content at this point. However, the more information that is noted at this stage, the more useful the content log will be in the interpretive labor that still awaits. Finally, in addition to textual regularities, the analyst should be sensitive to the text's irregularities—to anything that seems out of the ordinary, especially interesting, compelling, or potentially significant.

A Theoretical Starting Point

At this point, the initial engagement with the text must be driven by a theoretical understanding of both the critical problematic and the relationship between the media text and the social landscape. Here the interpretive process deviates from that of a purely empirical approach. If the true empirical scholar would insist that research begins from neutral or atheoretical observation of the object of study, the interpretive analyst holds that no research is or could be theory free. Rather, some methodologies refuse to acknowledge or articulate the set of theoretical assumptions upon which they rest, and which they inevitably reenact. The interpretive process, by contrast, begins from a theoretical standpoint. Thus, the initial stage of analysis is as much a period of theoretical study as it is a period of textual observation—the researcher must be actively developing the theoretical frame that will guide the interpretation. This is not to say that interpretive reading is the search for a set of predetermined theoretical precepts—the effort to identify within the text that which the theory says should be there—but rather is to say that interpretive analysis must proceed hand-in-hand with a theoretical understanding. Theory provides the ground from which the interpretive process develops, and in turn the interpretive process (as we will discuss in more detail later) must inform, and ideally clarify or complicate, the prevailing theoretical understanding of the sociocultural issues in play and their textual manifestations.

SYSTEMATIC ANALYSIS OF MEANING CONSTRUCTION

Having developed a measure of intimate familiarity with the text, one is ready to move to the next stage, a systematic analysis of the textual construction of meaning. In the sections that follow, we discuss a methodology for unpacking what Stuart Hall (1982) has called the "work of signification" (p. 77), the multiple levels in and through which the text comes to have meaning. We conceptualize this process here in three stages that move from the local to the global. We begin by considering the *play of signs and signifying systems* within the text. We move then to a discussion of the *organizational patterns* that give the text its coherence. Finally, we conclude by turning to the linkages between text and context that shape how we understand the world around us.

The Play of Signs

We suggest that any attempt to read textual meaning must begin from the perspective of semiotics. For the semiotician and the interpretive critic alike, a media text can best be understood as a complex *assemblage of signs* (e.g., de Saussure, 1986). Our challenge at this stage of the analysis is to begin exploring the nature of and relations between the specific signs that compose a given media text. So what is a sign? Although a full discussion of semiotic theory lies beyond the scope of this chapter, we can start with the basic semiotic understanding that a sign is something that stands for something else. A *sign* is that which signifies—*to signify* is to convey meaning (and, thus, to have *significance* is to have meaning). Anything (and perhaps everything) within a given text can function as a sign. That includes the words the newscaster speaks, the graphic image in the corner of the website, the music soundtrack, or even the tattoo on the character's arm. Our concern here lies with anything (any word, image, or sound) we can identify in the text that may convey meaning.

At this stage, one begins the (admittedly) laborious work of identifying the signs that make up the texts. For most media, a good place (but by no means the only place) to start is with the words, either spoken or written. Verbal language is one of our primary signifying systems and perhaps the most obvious means by which a text conveys meaning. As we revisit the texts we've selected for analysis, we can pay close attention to the use of words—which words the text includes, the textual situations in which particular words are used, and also which words the text excludes. So, for example, while we were writing this book, U.S. forces occupied both Iraq and Afghanistan and struggled to overcome insurgencies in both places. When the semiotician reads news coverage of these wars, she or he may notice the particular choice of words used to describe the enemy that U.S. troops are facing. (Notice even the choice of words here. The word *enemy* clearly is negative; it carries with it an orientating point. To speak in terms of enemies is by default to declare what side one is on.) Are the people planting roadside bombs "insurgents"? Are they "terrorists"? Are they "the resistance"? Could they be "freedom fighters"? For that matter, how are U.S. forces described? Are they "occupiers"? "Liberators"? "Our sons and daughters"? Each choice of label carries with it a drastically different connotation (*connotation* is a key word we will think more about shortly); each label *defines* the situation in markedly different terms.

Verbal language, however, is just one of the signifying systems that make up a media text. Even newspapers, which remain the bastion of the printed word, usually contain photographs. For the semiotician, photographs (or visual imagery) are another signifying system, and the visual clues contained within the picture—the elements within the frame—are the individual signs. Thus, if one were analyzing newspaper coverage of the occupation of Iraq, one would need to pay close attention to photographs that depict the situation. For example, we've all seen the familiar photographs that show Arab men firing guns into the air, and their counterparts, Arab women, grieving over the deaths of their loved ones. These photographs, although certainly traces of things that have actually happened (what we could call "indexical signs"), are at the same time functioning on a more symbolic level. Taken as a whole, they paint for us a picture of a people—they offer a *representation* of a culture (see Hall, 1997). At the same time, one could examine the photographs of U.S. troops in Iraq. Are they depicted with guns blazing? Handing out school supplies to smiling Iraqi children? Again, such images—these visual signs—construct a set of meanings, in this case about the nature of U.S. troops and their role in Iraq. Finally, here one can consider the relationship between photographs and verbal language. A picture may be worth a thousand words, but usually, newspaper photographs are accompanied by a particular set of words—the caption. Captions may "anchor" the meaning of the image—directing the audience's attention toward certain aspects of the visual signs and providing further clues as to how we are expected to understand the visual meanings (Barthes, 1977).

When we begin to consider the *moving* images that make up the vast majority of television and film content, we must broaden the interpretive net and take into account a number of other signifying systems. If the *word* is the "basic unit of analysis" for the examination of verbal language, and the *frame* is the basic unit for analysis of the photograph, scholars of film and television generally agree that the *shot* provides the starting point for consideration of the moving image (see Metz, 1990). Thus, at this stage of the analysis, one must carefully examine each shot that makes up the televisual or filmic text. Like every object of study, the shot is demarcated by identifiable borders. We can think of the shot as being defined as that which is visible within the frame (or on the screen) between edits. As the pace of editing (itself a signifying system) has increased over the years, the number of shots has increased as well. Alfred Hitchcock shot his remarkable film *Rope* without any edits. Thus, each shot runs for 12 minutes (the length of the reel of film). By contrast, individual shots in some contemporary music videos may last less than a second. The conventional rule of thumb in television production is that shots should last somewhere between three and five seconds each.

Like the still image, the moving picture can be analyzed in terms of its content—the objects, people, and places that appear within the frame. Both still and moving imagery also can be analyzed in terms of the camera techniques. Camera angles, for example, can add meaning to a shot. An object shot from below can appear large, powerful, and perhaps menacing. The same object when shot from above may seem small and meek. So too does field of view—how wide or tight the camera frames the image—impact the meaning of the shot (see Zettl, 2010). The same person shot in extra close-up or in a wide shot may appear to have different characteristics. Wide shots (or the standard "head-and-shoulders" shot one sees in news) can emphasize a person's *official* identity, while a close-up may stress the subject's humanity. Indeed, widely accepted conventions used to forbid news photographers from framing the president any closer than from a medium distance, because he was to be respected as the holder of a grand office. By the time Bill Clinton was impeached for lying about a sexual relationship, however, he regularly was framed in extra close-up, with his face filling the frame and neither his hairline nor the bottom of his chin visible (Baym, 2003).

For moving pictures, camera motion also can contribute meaning to the image. Zooms, pans, and tilts can emphasize certain physical attributes (height, for example), draw linkages between otherwise unrelated objects, and direct the audience's attention. So too is editing a signifying system—a language of its own. The nature of the transitions *between* shots—dissolves, wipes, and the standard "hard cut"—suggest different kinds of relationships between the subjects of consecutive shots. Likewise, the use of special effects can change the meaning of the image (Zettl, 2010).

We can identify two other sign systems common to moving imagery, and many websites as well. Graphics—hand-drawn or computer-generated images and words—often convey meaning and demand close attention (especially as graphics software becomes more and more ubiquitous, and animated graphics play a larger and larger role on the web). Finally, music is also an important signifying system that can create powerful sets of meaning. Consider, for example, the use of music in *Psycho* or *Jaws*, which added an undisputable element of fear to what were otherwise nonthreatening visual moments. We "read" music as much as we do verbal language—not only do we often rely on it to know how we are supposed to feel during any given moment of film or television, but music also can help define that which we are seeing. Here the introduction to *The Daily Show* provides an excellent example. The show begins with traditional "news" music—the heavy and serious sounding beats we associate with news programming—but that quickly gives way to upbeat guitar-driven rock-and-roll. In just a few seconds of sound, the program clearly tells us that it conflates the genres of news and entertainment (Baym, 2005).

Signs, therefore—be they words, images, camera motions, or music—are the building blocks of meaning. The interpretive labor here is to identify the individual signs that make up any given moment of media content and to consider what they may mean. It is useful, then, to consider the semiotic distinction between *denotative* and *connotative* meaning (Barthes, 1964). "Denotative" has to do with the literal objects the pictures reveal or to which the words refer. Thus, to return to a previous example, the news footage may show us a U.S. soldier in Iraq or perhaps an American flag. The flag is the official symbol of the United States, Iraq is a country in the Middle East, and a soldier is a person who serves in the armed forces. That is all the denotative level—and recognizing it is a necessary initial analytical step. If we are interested, though, in what the flag *means*, then we must enter the realm of *connotation*. Connotation speaks to the conceptual associations we draw with a word, an image, or a sound. Thus, for some the flag may connote "the land of the free and the home of the brave"; the soldier may connote "the brave." Of course, here we have to confront the fact that to others, the flag may connote "the great Satan" and the soldier "the occupier." Although specific connotations may differ among various individuals, we suggest that they largely are culturally drawn. That is to say connotations are rarely purely individual, but instead are socially constructed. In fact, the boundaries of a particular community, culture, or society may be forged as much through shared connotations as through geography, law, and other administrative arrangements.

From a semiotic perspective, connotation is always guided by the relations among individual signs within a given text. Thus, if an image of a soldier is followed by a shot of a close-up of a waving American flag, all while "The Star-Spangled Banner" plays, a particular set of meanings is invoked that is something different from the connotation of any individual sign. It is helpful, therefore, to draw the distinction between relations among signs that are *synchronic* and those that are *diachronic* (de Saussure, 1986). When we look at the synchronic aspect of a text, our attention falls on all the signs (and sign systems) that occur together at any single moment. So, if television or film can be understood as a series of shots, the synchronic refers to all the signs present within a given shot. These, of course, can include any combination of verbal, visual, and aural signs. The same is true for all the signs that appear on a single screen of a website or (minus the aural signs) that which appears on a single page in a magazine. Here it becomes clear that rarely do individual sign systems exist in isolation. Rather, they are almost always multiple and overlapping. Verbal, visual, and aural signs exist in combinations and, as such, may complement or contradict and, at the least, complicate the meaning of one another.

When we turn to the diachronic, however, our attention falls on the flow of signs—their appearance through time, shot after shot, screen after screen, page after page. Diachronic relations are a question of progression, how one set of signs is replaced by or changes into another. Indeed, the great Russian filmmaker Sergei Eisenstein (1992) insisted the power of film lay not in the individual shot but in the ability to *combine* shots, to juxtapose sometimes radically different shots to achieve startling new meanings. Thus, if, in our earlier example, a sequence of shots of a U.S. soldier, an American flag, and "The Star-Spangled Banner" is immediately followed by a sequence of exploding bombs and crying children, the meaning of the text changes drastically.

A consideration of the diachronic flow of signs moves us from our starting point—an explication of the signs that make up a text and their likely connotations—to the next point in our interpretive strategy: attention to the *assemblage* of signs, to the *patterns of organization* that we can identify and that always serve to shape the text's labor of signification.

Patterns of Organization

In verbal language, one can arrange words in infinite combinations to make meaningful sentences. It is obvious, though, that not all arrangements of words are meaningful. To be sensible—that is, to make sense in the first instance—the arrangement of words must conform to the grammar of language, the underlying rules by which meaning can be produced. The same is true for the assemblage of any kind of signs. If a text can be read as an arrangement of signs, it equally is governed by an underlying grammar, by an implicit set of conventions, traditions, and social expectations about how signs can be combined in meaningful ways. As deep in the media stream as most of us are, the conventions of textual assemblage largely have become *naturalized*, which is to say we have come over time to take them for granted, to assume they are transparent reflections of the way the world is and not arbitrary conventions of textual practice (Barthes, 1972).

Here a quick example may suffice. One of the most common conventions in television editing is to follow a shot of the exterior of a building with a shot of an inside room (think *Seinfeld*, for example). As audiences, we have come to assume that there is a connection between the shots of exterior and interior, that the interior room is *necessarily* inside the building we have just seen from the exterior. Of course, that is hardly ever the case in actuality. Seinfeld's "apartment" was a sound set in a production studio, not a real room in a New York apartment building. However, the linkage from outside to inside appears seamless and, for most, is never noticed as the result of conventions of editing. The philosopher Wittgenstein once suggested that the grammar that structures our language is like a pair of glasses through which we see the world—a pair of glasses it never occurs to us to take off. The challenge at this stage of the interpretive process is indeed to take off the glasses, to see the patterns of assemblage that link one sign to another, and to lay bare the particular set of sociocultural meanings those patterns construct.

Although at this point the analysis can move in many different directions, we will focus here on what may be the most prevalent pattern of assemblage in the contemporary media stream: *narrative*. Many people have argued that narrative—the telling of stories— is the primary method through which human beings construct meaning and make sense of the world. Similarly, scholars of media generally agree that the media have become the preeminent storytellers in contemporary culture. This is as true for the Hollywood film industry as it is for network television and even the daily news ("our top story today. . . ."). The social critic Michel de Certeau (1984) once wrote that we walk all day in a "forest of narrativities" (p. 186). Thus, through an analysis of how a given text functions as a narrative, one can profitably uncover a set of meanings constructed in the text.

Like all assemblages of signs, narratives are built around a few core elements: plot, character, narrator, and audience. A profitable interpretive strategy, therefore, can be to examine each of those and their implications. The *plot* can be defined as the sequence of events that give shape to the narrative. The Russian formalist Todorov (1969) suggested that most narratives move through a "dramatic triangle," beginning in a state of equilibrium—a picture of someone's world as it usually is. From there, an event occurs to disrupt the status quo and move the narrative world into a state of disequilibrium. From there, the problem, conflict, or crisis is in some way resolved, and the narrative ends with either a return to the original state of equilibrium or the creation of a new point of balance, a new status quo. This dramatic triangle—beginning, middle, and end—provides the backbone of the familiar three-act structure that shapes nearly all film and television. Within the three-act structure, most screenwriters think in terms of plot points—the key moments that move the narrative forward. These usually include the *inciting action*, the initial event that disrupts the status quo; *complication*, in which the characters find the problem is greater than originally thought; *crisis*, when the problem builds to its most threatening point; *climax*, when the effort to solve the problem or resolve the crisis comes to a head; *resolution*, when the crisis is averted or the problem is solved; and *denouement*, the return to equilibrium. It is possible, therefore, to identify these plot points—in both fictional and nonfictional stories.

Perhaps the most important point here is that plots almost always enact some form of problem and solution or crisis and resolution. A critical issue, therefore, becomes the nature of the problems or crises and their resolutions. Thus, from a critical standpoint, for the film *Die Hard* starring Bruce Willis, the problem is an attempt to steal private property or, more specifically, a raid on corporate wealth. The solution, as in many films and television programs, lies in the heroic actions of the macho individual (the cowboy?), who single-handedly, and rather violently, takes on the bad guys until he has killed them all, restoring law and order, eliminating the threat to corporate wealth, and (not coincidentally) winning back the love of his estranged wife. Similarly, one can think of the prevailing narrative constructed in the American news media following the terrorist attacks of September 11. The crisis was said to be an unprovoked attack by a group of people who "hate America"; its resolution was to lie in the unleashing of largely unilateral military force. In what was undoubtedly an overly simplified (but nonetheless significant) narrative, the cowboy once again was to take to his guns and shoot his way out of the problem.

Of equal importance to the plot itself are the characters who enact it (see Propp, 1968). Every story must have its hero—its protagonist—who often, like the "America" of the post–September 11 narrative, is reluctantly forced into action. The hero, of course, is in conflict with the villain—the antagonist. (Indeed, semiotics suggests that *binaries* are a primary method of meaning making—a hero necessitates a villain and vice versa.) Hero and villain must fight over something or someone, perhaps a princess—the object of the hero's desire. So too does the hero often have an assistant—a sidekick or a partner in the fight (think Robin to Batman, Han Solo to Luke Skywalker, or maybe Tony Blair to September 11's George Bush). In narrative, there is a fine line between character and characterization. We can think carefully about the nature of the characters in any given narrative (who is the hero, the villain, the princess?), and so too can we assess the construction of character types—the roles in which various types of people are placed and the aspects of identity that the narrative imagines, emphasizes, or elides. Through their characters and characterizations, narratives offer representations of group and cultural identities. Indeed, it largely may be through mediated stories that we learn about *others*, those cultural groups with which we have no firsthand experience or knowledge.

Much critical study is interested in the representation of identity and of difference, the ways in which media texts define (and too often stereotype) cultures and group identities. Consider, for example, the portrayal of the "Muslim man" in the stories of both fiction and news over the past several years. Through media representation, he has been characterized as "our" enemy—the villain to the American hero. This may have begun with the Ayatollah Khomeini in the early 1980s, who was replaced by Moammar Khadafi, who in turn was replaced by Saddam Hussein, who gave way to Osama bin Laden, who then was replaced in the narrative by Saddam Hussein. The individual continues to change, but the character type remains remarkably constant. The cultural critic would go on to argue that media characterizations not only define "the other"—them, the out-group—but, in so doing, define us. That is to say media representations simultaneously teach us who "they" are *and* who "we" are.

We can also assess mediated narratives in terms of their narrators. Every story has a narrator, whether explicit or implicit, and stories are always told from a certain perspective and network of values. The narrator is in a position of power—to tell a story is to have the power to shape the nature of the plot, its problems and solutions, and the characters. This becomes of considerable importance in the realm of documentary and news, the narrative types that claim to represent the world *as it is*. The power to narrate is the power to define places, people, and events. Narration is a form of authorship, and there is a fine line between authorship and authority. Thus, it is profitable to consider who is authorized to tell a story, who claims the credentials to speak in terms of "what is."

Finally, we can consider how a given narrative speaks to its audience. It may seem counterintuitive to look for the audience *in* the text itself. Obviously, the audience comprises real people. Scholars of narrative, however, suggest that all stories (and, indeed, all media texts) invoke an "ideal" audience, an imaginary type of person toward whom the text and its meanings are directed (Chatman, 1978). Novels from the 19th century would often speak directly to "you, dear reader," but then again, so too did Ferris Bueller talk to the audience (a textual move mimicked more recently by John Cusack's character in *High Fidelity*). Television newscasters regularly speak of "you," the audience, and in so doing construct an elaborate and subtle understanding of who the ideal audience might be. The French scholar Althusser (1969) argued that media texts position their audience, that they carve out a conceptual space which the audience is expected to inhabit. Thus, one can read a narrative in terms of how it speaks to the audience, the value system, or subjectivities a media text encourages the audience to adopt.

Linkages to Context

The approach to the study of media texts laid out so far is not without its critics. Both semiotics and narrative analysis suggest that meaning primarily is constructed and contained *within the text*. To put it differently, these approaches can be considered *structuralist*, because they look to the structure of the text to find meaning. The *poststructuralist* complaint is that these analytic methods tend to see the text as existing in a vacuum, independent of any *context* within which the text is created and received. While we agree with the semiotician that the construction meaning always begins from the assemblage of signs in a text, the interpretive effort will be fundamentally incomplete if it does not take into account the linkages between text and context—the positioning of the text within a historical (that is, located-in-time) landscape of other texts, wider economic and political social structures, and broader patterns of sociocultural discourse. Therefore, we now turn to an explication of those factors of meaning.

One of the defining features of the contemporary media stream is the overlap among various texts. Some theorists envision a "conversation" of sorts, in which each individual text is in part a response to a previous text—a borrowing from, a reference to, or a commentary on that which has come before (Bakhtin, 1981). The technical word for this is *intertextuality*. Intertextuality can appear in a number of guises, from the obvious to the subtle. When *The Simpsons* parodies a scene from a well-known movie, that is a clear example. It is difficult to understand *The Simpsons* without a well-rounded knowledge of popular culture. Likewise, when *The Daily Show* parodies the news, the meanings in play depend on recognition of the texts to which the show refers. Parody, however, is just one example of intertextuality. Any textual borrowing (*poaching* is another word used here), whether it's the use of a verbal phrase popularized through another text, the re-creation of a production technique used elsewhere, or an imitation of (or innovation on) the style and form of previous texts (i.e., Tarantino's *Kill Bill*), can be considered intertextuality.

One can also find intertextuality at work in the real world. Ronald Reagan (who, of course, was an actor long before he was president) borrowed from *Dirty Harry* when he told the Soviet Union to "go ahead, make my day." Similarly, when George W. Bush made his infamous landing on the aircraft carrier to declare "mission accomplished" in Iraq, the scene was reminiscent of *Top Gun*—the president dressed in a flight suit, swaggering with his helmet and goggles under one arm. If life imitates art, then intertextuality has become a primary meaning-making vehicle. Any text—a presidential speech, a Hollywood film, a television comedy, a popular website—exists now as a node within a network and to some extent is indecipherable without illuminating its intertextual linkages.

At the same time, we can look for a text's "extratextual" meanings—in other words, ones that refer outward to some aspect of the wider historical, sociocultural, political, and economic environment within which the text cannot help but exist. The literary critic Terry Eagleton (2008) once complained that the semiotic approach is "hair-raisingly unhistorical" (p. 95). We must, therefore, consider the text's positioning in a moment of history, be it the moment of its production or the moment of its interpretation. The film *Rambo*, for example, is difficult to understand apart from the historical context in which it came to be—the Reagan presidency and desire among many to reaffirm American strength in the shadows of the Vietnam War. The same can be said for Sylvester Stallone's other mid-1980s tribute to American machismo—*Rocky IV*—in which Rocky battles the Soviet man-machine Ivan Drago. Located in a moment in history, both films address a particular set of concerns and speak to the construction of a particular version of American identity. We don't mean to suggest, however, that the moment of production (or the author's intention, for that matter) *determines* the meaning of a media text. One of the fascinating aspects of texts is their innate ability to be *reread* in ever-changing historical circumstances. Thus, another challenge is to recognize the historical context of one's own act of interpretation.

Other scholars insist that textual meaning is inseparable from the *political-economic context* in which a text is produced, distributed, and received (e.g., Garnham, 1995). The critical concept of political economy here refers to the nexus of economic and administrative power that undoubtedly shapes the nature at least of textual production and distribution. So, for example, the political-economic media critic would suggest that one cannot understand the meanings produced by the NBC *Nightly News* (which at the time of this writing was the most attended-to news outlet in the country with a nightly audience of some 11 million people) without first recognizing that NBC is owned by the corporate behemoth General Electric. GE, of course, produces many things other than television programming, including the aircraft engines used in military fighter jets. When one draws that connection, the particular stories NBC news tells about—say, the war in Iraq—as well as its use and arrangement of particular signs, may take on a rather different reading.

The significance of political economy has become a topic of major dispute among scholars of media studies. One camp would argue that political-economic context *is* the bottom line—that any effort to read a media text ultimately boils down to an exploration of its economic implications. Such a perspective clearly privileges the moments of production and distribution as the key points in the construction of meaning. The other camp insists that the moment of reception—the space of interpretation—is the privileged spot in the circuit of meaning. That perspective views interpretation as a relatively unconstrainable process that can never be reduced simply to the economics of cultural production (for example, see the exchange among Garnham, 1995; Grossberg, 1995; and Murdock, 1995). We suggest, as with so many things, that the truth may lie somewhere in between. The arguments on both sides have merit. In a media age dominated by corporate capitalism, specific media texts are rarely produced or distributed that do not, in some way, advance the interests of the corporate masters (the Internet, of course, has the potential to stand outside of this dynamic). At the same time, however, political-economic context can never determine specific meanings (we're a long way from media effects here). An interpretive reading that neglects political-economic context is liable to miss critical aspects of a text; but a reading that reduces textual meaning to economic intent is equally lacking.

Finally, the interpretive analyst can (and certainly should) look for the linkages between a given text and the wider context of *discourse* that surrounds both the text and the sociocultural issues it addresses. Indeed, the ultimate goal of interpretive analysis may be to examine how the text contributes to or complicates wider discursive patterns. Here we are drawing on Foucault's (1972) understanding of discourse as cultural structures of talk that define or construct particular domains of the world. In his own work, Foucault examined discourses of sexuality, of madness, and of discipline, exploring how a society comes to understand those domains of the world through a multiplicity of "discursive artifacts"—or what we have been referring to as texts. No one text can define a discursive object ("presidentiality," for example), but when taken as a whole, mediated texts help shape popular understandings (and thus we cannot understand a concept such as "the president" apart from the wider discourse of presidentiality that inform our assumptions). For Foucault, discourse provided the link between specific texts, cultural knowledge, and social power. A profitable interpretive reading, therefore, must turn a careful eye toward the connections between the ways in which a particular text speaks of its domain of the world and the wider patterns of sociocultural discourse that help to construct the boundaries of that domain and define the objects within it.

EMERGENCE AND CONFRONTATION

At this point, we have reached the core of the interpretive effort. From a position of intimate familiarity, supported by detailed content logs and a sophisticated theoretical understanding of the issues at hand, we are ready to engage in the *close reading* of the play of signs, the patterns of organization, and the textual linkages to context. This is a time of extensive note taking, of transcribing verbal content and writing detailed descriptions of the visual and aural elements. It is also the point in the process when the unique shape of the text and its critical features are called into relief—when the analyst can begin categorizing and arranging textual elements, envisioning connections among them, their context, and the theory that guides the study.

The media scholar David Altheide (1996), whose name for this kind of work is "ethnographic content analysis," has suggested that this is a process of *emergence*, a gradual shaping of meaning through repeated engagement with the text. With each viewing, the analyst may *see* the text slightly differently; with each viewing a different aspect of the text may call attention to itself. We also suggest, however, that this equally is a process of *confrontation*—between text and theory. In part, the analyst's job is to confront the text with theory, to see how the discipline's theoretical knowledge of media and the sociocultural problematic under consideration can illuminate the text. At the same time, it is also the analyst's job to confront the theory with the text, to consider how the theory holds up in light of the text. Just as media texts are always changing, so too is theory always a work in progress. Each new kind, genre, or generation of media text demands that we reconsider the theory that precedes it.

FINELY GRAINED EXAMINATION

If this work is done well, the analyst should at this stage of the process be able to begin constructing a relatively clear reading of the meanings articulated in the text and developing an argument about their sociocultural significance. To put it differently, the analyst should be able to start crafting a framework of understanding—a set of potential answers to the critical questions that drive the study. Thus, the interpretive labor begins to shift, away from a broad-based exploration of textual signification and toward a finely grained analysis that elucidates and supports the emerging understanding.

We suggest the analyst should return to the text once again, first with the goal of *tightening the interpretive net*. The metaphor of a net is appropriate here. With each pass through the text, some features and linkages become more readily discernible. Undoubtedly, earlier stages of analysis may have skimmed over individual textual instances of importance—the use of a given word or phrase, a particular shot or visual image, a connection between what once seemed to be disparate moments that in light of the emerging framework of understanding begin to take on significance. By returning to the text with a more tightly woven interpretive net, the intention becomes to catch every one of those moments of signification, however subtle, in which the underlying work of meaning making is evident.

At the same time, the analyst equally should be searching for the *representative examples* that will provide the meat of the written analysis. If quantitative studies of media content sacrifice detailed analysis in exchange for identifying broad-based statistical patterns, interpretive reading instead delves deeply into individual textual moments of particular interest. The bread and butter, so to speak, of interpretive analysis—its unique contribution—lies in the "thick description" of representative examples, the careful working through of textual moments—either extraordinary or apparently benign—that illustrate the critical argument. Undoubtedly, particular examples emerged during the stage of analysis discussed above. Now it is time to relocate those examples (and identify others) and to carefully compile accurate transcripts, descriptions of the visual imagery, and other notations that help to place the example within the framework of understanding and to develop the critical argument.

CRAFTING THE ARGUMENT

Having worked through the text multiple times—each time honing in on a different aspect or level of meaning making—we have reached the ultimate stage of the interpretive process. It is worthwhile to remember here that the end result of interpretive analysis is not generalizable proofs, but compelling arguments about media, meaning, and sociocultural significance. A successful interpretive project should answer the critical questions with which it began in ways that blend text, theory, and interpretive insight. Although there are few rules, and indeed much dispute, among qualitative scholars about what any particular argument should look (or read) like, we do suggest that there are three questions that should always guide the process of crafting a compelling argument. The analyst must always ask her- or himself if the analysis is insightful, if it is valid, and if it is valuable. We now briefly take up each of those three questions in turn.

Is the Analysis Insightful?

The first thing the analyst must ask is if he or she has learned something from the interpretive process. The goal, of course, is to advance our understanding of a particular sociocultural phenomenon and its mediated manifestations. The study of textual significa-tion, therefore, must land us in a place somewhere different from where we began. The strength of interpretation lies in its ability to reveal—sometimes deeply—the construction of meaning and in turn to tease out the implications therein. To be worth a reader's time (or a journal editor's pages, for that matter), the analysis must offer an original contribution that moves us beyond the obvious or the easily predictable. So too must the successful analysis do more than simply find the theory in the text or, perhaps even worse, impose the theory on the text. Such "cookie-cutter" analyses that apply a particular set of meth-odological precepts to a convenient text may be easy to complete but are of limited value. Ultimately, insight is the coin of the realm.

Is the Analysis Valid?

The test of insight, however, is a question of validity. Validity refers to the "truth-value" of a statement; for the empirical study, it is found in the correspondence between a claim and the "true" nature of the reality to which it refers. For the interpretive analysis, however, valid-ity is less a matter of correspondence to reality than it is a product of the well-reasoned argument. An argument is a claim—in this case about the nature of a media text, a sociocul-tural phenomenon, or the relationship between the two. To be considered valid, such claims must meet a number of basic conditions. First, claims must be grounded in evidence. Inter-pretive scholarship may lean more toward art than science, but it still remains beholden to the basic rule of argumentation that claims must be *supported by grounds*. Here, however, the evidence upon which our claims rest is rarely raw facts or empirical measurements, but instead thick description of representative examples—detailed examination of textual moments that reveal the construction of meaning and illustrate the analyst's critical claims. At the same time, claims and the marshalling of evidence in their support must be *warranted by theory*. That is to say an interpretive analysis lacks validity if it is incoherent with or, even worse, ignorant of the theoretical tradition that informs study of the problematic in ques-tion. We never want to simply reproduce the theoretical claims that others have made, but it remains our responsibility to locate our claims within a credible body of theory.

Third, to be considered valid, a claim must fit in, or *be coherent with other available evidence and argument*. Claims must recognize the interpretive findings advanced by other scholarship on the subject and, if need be, explicitly confront any contradictions raised therein. So too are our claims beholden to contextual evidence, to the available body of fact and argument about the context—historical, social, cultural, political, and economic—within which the particular problematic under consideration unfolds. Finally, and per-haps most important, interpretive claims must not be easily contradicted by other pieces of evidence drawn from the same text. Inevitably, even the most thorough of interpre-tive readings will leave out more of the text than they include. Texts are remarkably com-plex, and no analysis could possibly include every textual example or address every potential moment of meaning making. The interpretive critic is always handpicking, so to speak, examples that help to build the most compelling argument. What is absolutely critical, though, is that the analysis not overlook significant counterexamples. If the text can contradict its own analysis, then the analysis necessarily lacks validity.

Fourth, because texts are complex, the valid analysis must *preserve the complexity of the text*. Often texts themselves are inherently contradictory. Rarely does a text produce an air-tight system of meaning making reducible to a neat taxonomy of key points. Instead, texts may lack internal coherence, they may construct opposing meanings, or, as the post-structuralist may argue, they may provide avenues for their own deconstruction. So too can texts contain moments of meaning making that simply do not fit within the whole, that resist allocation within an otherwise sound interpretive framework. As the semiotician would say, *excess* is always unavoidable. Although some might argue that this is the Achilles' heel of the interpretive project, we see the problem in less fatalistic terms. Simply, it becomes the analyst's responsibility to acknowledge the limits of the analysis and to not offer an overly reductionist argument that claims to represent the entirety of the text with absolute certainty.

Fifth, the interpretive claim must avoid the pitfalls of what Umberto Eco (1992) has called "overinterpretation," or concluding the maximum from a minimum of evidence. To word the point differently, *the claim must not overreach its evidence*. The real danger to interpretive validity may lie in what Eco calls an "excess of wonder," a desire on the part of the analyst to leap to grand conclusions. For example, a student once read the green background in a magazine advertisement as commentary on global capitalism—green, of course, being the color of money. Green certainly is the color of money, but the text offered no other evidence of a critique of capitalism, and indeed, it seems fundamentally unlikely that, to return to Eco's phrase, the *intention of the text* (in this case an advertisement in a fashion magazine) would be to critique its own raison d'être. In this case, the critique of capitalism was the student's invention and not a logical interpretive step beginning from the color green. The interpretive critic must keep in mind that sometimes the color green is just the color green, or, as Freud may have put it, a cigar is just a cigar.

Finally, the interpretive critic must *be careful not to overextend the argument*, to make claims that textual analysis itself is not equipped to address. By this point, it should be clear that textual analysis can offer great insight into the workings of media texts and draw linkages between text and context. What it *cannot* do, however, is tell us anything about the audience, about the real people who encounter the text in a multitude of ways. An all-too-common mistake is to leap from the play of signs to a statement about media effects—from an analysis of textual properties to a claim about how real people will think, feel, and behave because of the text. It is one thing to explore textual meaning but quite a different thing to make claims about audiences. The latter is an entirely different object of study that requires a completely different set of methods. One can never access the audience, however, through the text. Likewise, one can never read authorial intention—what the author or creator meant to say or do—from the text. Again, such questions require us to look elsewhere for answers.

Is the Analysis Valuable?

The last question to which the analysis is beholden is one of value. The argument may be insightful and it may be valid, but the question remains: Is it valuable? Empirical science has long struggled with the (some would say) artificial or arbitrary split between fact and value. (For example, the hydrogen bomb presented a remarkable scientific challenge to a generation of physicists, but the moral challenge implicit in creating such a powerful weapon of mass destruction remained largely undiscussed.) Interpretive analysis, however, is necessarily value laden. Remember, the textual critic is always also a social critic, and criticism itself must be motivated by a desire for what could be.

This point may become clearer when one realizes that the end result of interpretive analysis is itself a text—an essay, an article, perhaps a book—that is engaged in its own process of meaning making. Every text makes a contribution (although some larger than others) to the wider play of discourse. The interpretive analysis enters the struggle in signification, and therefore the critic is always a semiotic agent. Interpretive analysis thus demands a measure of reflexivity, an awareness of one's own standpoint, perspective, and agenda. Although different camps of interpretive scholarship disagree on how explicit the analyst qua author must be in this process of reflexivity, we suggest simply that the interpretive scholar must consider the value of the analysis, the contribution it makes to the sociocultural landscape of which it speaks.

MOVING ON

This is the last of the three chapters that focus on text. In this trilogy, we have moved from the objective approaches of content analysis to the culturally embedded approaches engaged in this chapter. In the next chapter, we leave text to immerse ourselves in the action of ethnography.

REFLECTIONS

What Are Some Points to Remember?

- Interpretive research methods explore the connections between media texts and wider social, cultural, and political issues. The fundamental premise is that media texts help to construct meaning—that they influence the ways in which we think and talk about any number of sociocultural or political phenomena.
- Unlike content analysis, which seeks to break media content into discrete units, interpretive analysis takes a holistic approach, looking at the internal relationships between textual elements and the external relationships between media texts, other media texts, and political, economic, historical, and cultural contexts.
- The selection of texts for analysis must be justified—not all media texts are equally interesting, important, or worth the reader's time. The interpretive process also must be systematic and rigorous, avoiding the twin temptations of superficial analysis that remains largely on the level of description and "overanalysis" that concludes too much from too little evidence. Finally, the analysis itself must be valuable, adding to our understanding of the media text and of the wider set of issues it considers.

Why Does It Matter?

Interpretive methods offer tools to make sense of the social construction of meaning and to better understand media as critical pieces of our wider cultural discourses.

What Else Could We Talk About?

Interpretive analysis never enables us to make claims about media effects. We can examine, with great sophistication, the meanings articulated within a given text, but that never tells us anything about how any individual person makes sense of, or reacts to, that text. Similarly, textual analysis can never reveal the intention of the text's creators. Their intentions never entirely determine the meanings contained within a text, nor does authorial intent exist within the text. When done well, however, textual analysis can tell us a great deal about the nature of media content and its relationship to the world around us.

What Else Might Be Interesting to Read?

Altheide, D. L. (1996). *Qualitative media analysis*. Thousand Oaks, CA: Sage.

Barthes, R. (1977). *Image, music, text* (S. Heath, Trans.). New York: Hill and Wang.

Eco, U. (1992). *Interpretation and overinterpretation* (S. Collini, Ed.). Cambridge, UK: Cambridge University Press.

CHAPTER 15

Ethnographic Methods

CHAPTER PREVIEW

What's It All About?

Ethnography means the writing of culture. Traditionally, it has meant members of one culture observing and participating in the culture of another. In its appropriation by communication, it has come to mean any outsider's analysis of any membership that organizes itself across discourse and performance.

What Are the Major Topics?

Ethnography is a term loosely applied to a variety of methods ranging from noninteractive observation to interviews to participant observation. This chapter limits the term to the method of participant observation.

Participant observation is deemed the best way to achieve a member's understanding of what and how things are done in the membership as well as the values attached to those practices.

Questions of what, how, and of what value constitute the ethnographic problem. Questions of why, so prominent in other methods, recede in ethnography.

Ethnography starts with the identification of an appropriate membership to which the analyst can gain access and achieve some member recognition. It proceeds through a series of participant engagements and field-note writings in the field and at the desk. It collects artifacts, creates maps and genealogy charts, and captures images and speech. Field notes and all materials are considered texts, which must themselves be analyzed. Ethnography ends with a contribution to the theory of membership, organizing, social action, and/or cultural studies.

Reflexivity—the analyst's self-awareness—is an integral component of the ethnographic argument.

Ethnography carries a heavy ethical burden because of the inherent exploitive relationship between the ethnographer and the membership. The ethnographer enters the membership as a guest, extracts value from that membership in potentially disruptive methods, and writes the results for her or his own value. We often cover this exploitive relationship with glossy visions of doing good, giving voice, or reframing society's view, but the evidence for these outcomes is most often missing.

What Special Terms Are Used?

Emblematic

Holistic

Methodological holism

Methodological individualism

Structurations

INTRODUCTION

As we leave texts and turn the corner into ethnographic methods, we leave behind many of the epistemological foundations of metric research. Ethnographic research is not based on metric's deductive, hypothetical, reductionistic, atomistic, causal, or variable analytic foundations. Rather the strong, cultural formulation of ethnography is semiotic, emergent, holistic, rhizomatic, and centered in the coherent narrative. It sees human behavior as sensible and sense-making action that is directed by holistic and dynamic understandings about what has been done, is being done, and will be done. These understandings are made sensible by the very practices they support in an intertwined relationship between knowing and acting.[1] The goal of the ethnographer is to grasp and subsequently to provide the narrative of the underlying understandings that make action sensible through the careful observation of and very often participation in the practices the understandings advance.

Two methodological criteria naturally flow from the epistemological foundation we have just drawn up. The first is the explanatory goal of the narrative of member understanding, and the second is the signature practice of participant observation. These two work hand in hand. To abandon one is to fail at the other. We may have left behind metrics, but we have not left careful, systematic, well-documented, experientially based methods that produce reviewable evidence for the claims they justify.

---

[1]This language is quite dense. For most readers, it is enough to know that I am claiming that metric and ethnographic research are *really* different. If one aspires to the business, then she or he should unpack the language over time and at her or his convenience. A glutton for punishment might read Anderson (1996).

Member Understanding

Member understanding is a theoretical concept that moves across both modern and post-modern, structuralist and poststructuralist formulations. On the modernist-structuralist side of epistemology, member knowledge is the particular expression of universals. In the high modernist-structuralist period of the 1940s, psychologist Abraham Maslow formulated the concept of a hierarchy of needs that all humans must in some way satisfy or actualize, and sociologist Claude Levi-Strauss held that cultural forms and social structures all stem from the common physiology of the human brain. Both positions are universalist. Human needs, cultural forms, and social structures might show surface differences, but the underlying foundation and structure would be the same for all needs, forms, and structures. The ethnographic goal was to move through the surface distractions of the particular to demonstrate the universal character.

Postmodernist and poststructuralist theorists abandoned universals in principle but constituted some explanations that do much the same work. The major difference is that there can be no presumption of an underlying foundation that is beyond local practice. In the poststructuralist world, it is sociocultural practice (praxis) that gives meaning to foundations, not foundations that make practices meaningful.

A modernist approaches member knowledge in order to discover the underlying foundations; a postmodernist approaches member knowledge for the foundations (think structurations) it justifies. For example, a modernist—say, a genetic anthropologist—might argue that the whole purpose of cultural and societal sexual functions is to ensure that the strongest gene pool moves forward into the future. The capabilities of the media are in some part converted to this goal by keeping us in a state of continual sexual tension and by providing models of the preferred genetic characteristics. Government regulation, moral complaint, family rules, safe-sex public service announcements (by raising the value of unsafe sex), and even methodology textbook examples simply serve to heighten the effectiveness of media in this regard. The role of the ethnographer (in what is sometimes called material ethnography) is to document the practices that achieve the effect.

A postmodernist would start with less writing on his or her slate, but it would not be blank. Certainly, no postmodernist would deny sexuality or desire, but the sexual content of the media may or may not be connected to the fate of the future gene pool. It may be connected to power through concepts like carnival, consumption, resistance or to gender or to the construction of race and the like. Further, individual cultural groups may use it for different purposes. Multiple explanations are possible.

What is unlikely in this constitution of member knowledge is a cognitivist approach. Cognitivism works from the epistemological standpoint of methodological individualism (the individual is the criterion) whereas ethnography is usually founded on methodological holism (the group is the criterion). Frankly, there is little justification to take on the difficult methodology of ethnography if one works from a cognitivist viewpoint. There are simpler methodologies that produce acceptable evidence appropriate to that theory.

Member understanding is not the same thing as *a* member's understanding, and it is also not the sum of all the individual understandings. (If it were, we could just take a survey.) Member understanding is a jointly enacted mindfulness that produces the "of course it's true" certainty of the narratives of how things are. That language is metaphysical and nonempirical, but it is no more so, and no less, than the foundational language of psychological individualism. These are the axioms, the irreducible propositions of the research approach.

Member knowledge is the basis for understanding the emblematic practices of a membership. Emblematic practices are those practices that make the group recognizable as something different (which is what probably generates our interest in the group). Member knowledge answers the question of how those practices are made sensible to the members as ways of being in the world. Member knowledge exists in the intersection of the how and why of membership. Practices (how) demand justification (why), which in turn produces justified practices or member knowledge. The starting point in both constituting and analyzing a membership is a set of shared practices. We have a history of enactment, and from that history, we understand the local rules of performance. That knowledge appears in the presence of others and is partially constituted in the performances given.

Participant Observation

That last sentence—that knowledge appears in the presence of others and is partially constituted in the performances given—is the engine for ethnographic research based on participant observation. As the name suggests, participant observation is two activities. It is the interplay between a participation that approaches member competence and a systematic process of observation that starts with an onsite awareness and concludes with carefully documented field notes.

The participation of participant observation connects to member knowledge. Without a commitment to the explication of member knowledge, ethnography loses its *ethno*-prefix and becomes a descriptive case study. Such case studies are useful in the way that any descriptive study is useful in that they provide a detailed description of what was done. They also have the same limitations: Because action is always some combination of the spontaneous and the reliable, a description without a foundation of understanding cannot readily distinguish between the substantial and the trivial. It simply is what it is until the next case study is done. Case studies have their contribution to make; it is just not an ethnographic one.

The demands of participant observation are the reasons why ethnographic studies based on a recalled personal narrative (autoethnography), simple observation with no participation, in-depth interviews, and swarm/blitzkrieg approaches, as well as the abbreviated forms of ethnography—while popular—are considered problematic by interpretive methodologists. None of those alternatives both systematically studies the constituting action and achieves a location in member knowledge. (I hold to the necessity of both.) These forms are more under the rubric of biography or journalism rather than interpretive scholarship, their obvious value notwithstanding.

Researchers get into even more epistemological hot water (if that is possible) when they use a process that is strictly descriptive and extend it into an interpretation of why the action appears as it does. Strictly descriptive methods are any noninteractive observation—one-way mirrors, videotaping, keystroke capture, eye marker cameras, and the like. The strong ethnographic position would claim that any interpretation of the significance of the action based on these sorts of research texts would shift the primacy of understanding from that of the group to that of the researcher. Again, those methods have contributions to make; it just makes no sense to call them ethnographic.

Hybrid Forms

At the same time, we have to recognize that ethnography has been invoked in the hermeneutic rebellion against formalism and conventional notions of methodological rigor. If Denzin and Lincoln (2000) are right, and we are somewhere in the seventh moment of the hermeneutic, then at least some of what calls itself ethnography has one foot firmly on the rhetorical and the other quite lightly on the systematic empirical (see Patton, 2002, for further discussion). In this book, we have designated those approaches as hybrid methodologies, and we wish them well. They help us understand our own assumptive frameworks, the strength and weaknesses of our methods, and particularly the tenuous connections between evidence and claim. In this chapter, however, we will retain a dedication to understanding the "Other" according to the discipline of practice by which the Other understands itself.

With that "we're not in Kansas anymore" introduction, we can address ethnographic methods from a consistent viewpoint, while at the same time realizing that many folks who claim ethnographic methods never left Kansas at all. Research, too, is a messy, improvisational, human practice, despite our textbook efforts to contain it.

ADAPTIVE STRATEGIES IN ETHNOGRAPHIC RESEARCH

With those preliminaries aside, we can start the discussion about the methods of ethnography. Because of the emergent nature of ethnography, methods cannot be recipes. The methods have to be formed around adaptive strategies that work to complete the ethnographic task. There are five components in this work: the ethnographic problem, the membership, gaining access, fieldwork, and making sense of it all. Because this is a textbook, you know what comes next based on your member knowledge.

Understanding an Ethnographic Problem

Ethnographic problems tend to migrate toward *how*, *what*, and increasingly *quality* questions. They are somewhat less dedicated to *why* questions because of the presumptions of global-order social construction and local-order framing that serve to create temporary *why* conditions that have little extended reach. There may indeed be immediate and even midterm causes of an individual's behavior, but the more powerful ethnographic question is *how* those causes get constituted in local social action and put in place by the performance of that action. The greater contribution to knowledge is not the transitory "whyness" of behavior but the much more long-lived "howness" of social action. If, for example, the analyst wants to find out why individuals use Twitter, the problem gets formulated in the practice of tweeting within the social processes in which the individuals are engaged.

What and *quality* questions are similarly formulated. We live in a socially implicated reality populated with semiotic objects that are constituted in the practices by which we engage them. That green piece of paper has material properties but no intrinsic value until we treat it like money. Things come into their practical existence and achieve value for us in the ways we behave toward them. Consequently, ontological and axiological questions are also located in problems that deal with practices—in these cases, the practices of constitution and valuation.

Let's take a look at some published examples to better understand what an ethnographic research problem looks like. To select these examples, I ran a search over the terms *ethnography* in the abstract and *media* in all text using Academic Search Premier, PsycINFO, Sociological Abstracts, and Communication and Mass Media Complete databases. The two searches generated about 1,000 entries. From those entries, I was able to identify about 70 articles that appeared to be actual ethnographies using some variation of participant observation. As I worked my way through those articles, the real number turned out to be considerably smaller. The point is that over a very large number of mainline and marginal journals and a span of 45 years, the body of ethnographic work in media is slim at best. There are good reasons for this scarcity. We will illuminate them as we go along, but for now, we'll look at four studies that give us a good range of the type of studies that are conducted. I have ordered their presentation from the ethnographically marginal to the ethnographically centered.

Dylan Tutt's two publications (Tutt, 2008a, 2008b) were based on a yearlong video ethnography (the most distant from participant observation) of six households that he terms "Nuclear Family, Single-Parent household, Student House, Bachelors' Pad, Young Couple, and Retired Couple" (Tutt, 2008b, p. 1177). The problem that he is interested in (we will get to his methodology later on) focuses on the household practices by which individuals both separately and in relationships negotiate both the interface with "living room" media[2] and the interactions with other members of the household. Tutt notes that the virtual and the mediated are merged into the face-to-face and situated action "by household members in unique and individual ways through their everyday living room life" (p. 1157). The principle is that media and their texts are engaged and made meaningful in the social action of the everyday or every-night; the question for Tutt is how that gets done in different social action settings of close and intimate living.

Vicki Mayer has investigated the intersection of practices of identity and practices of media use at several field sites. One of her earliest sites (1997–1999) was a cultural arts center on the west side of San Antonio, Texas. There, she began a study on the means by which young people manage both a Mexican and an American (U.S.) identity with a focus on the part that telenovelas might play in that process. She notes that "all of the young people saw telenovela consumption as an important part of their heritage and as a way to travel to Mexico without leaving home. At the same time, they distinguished their own viewing patterns as particularly 'American'" (Mayer, 2005, p. 485).

---

[2]Tutt's study occurred nearly a decade ago (though the publications are recent) and in Great Britain. In the United States, there has been a great diaspora of media from a central location to the bedrooms and pockets of family members. For example, in a survey conducted by the author (me), fewer than 30% of University of Utah students had to share access to a computer. Computers are no longer living room media for many of us; they are personal media.

Mary Ann Moser took advantage of a government-sponsored project (2000–2003) to introduce "information technology to transform social services delivery to individuals 'at risk'" at three homeless shelters in Calgary, Alberta, to conduct research that "attempted to find out what was going on in everyday lives with this new technology" (Moser, 2009, p. 708). She documented the ongoing outcomes of the project (both intended and unintended) by attending to the practices of the clients and staffs of the three centers for nearly a year.

Moser makes a particularly interesting connection in her narratives to Anthony Giddens's concept of structuration (Moser references Giddens & Pierson, 1998) and to Dorothy Smith's (1990) focus on "what we can actually see and talk about in concrete terms" (Moser, 2009, p. 711) that constitute the practices of institutional structurations.[3] Smith focuses on text, and Moser focuses on technology as "powerful text-producing tools" (p. 711).

David Ryfe's question involved the "adapt or die" necessity of transforming the newspaper and "the culture of professionalism in the newsroom" (Ryfe, 2009, p. 198). His 18-month participant observation study documented one attempt at this transformation in the effort at changing a particular newspaper from a source of breaking news to a resource of "news you can use" (p. 201). This transformation required, in the estimation of the newly installed editor, a complete change in "the way that reporters gathered and reported the news" (p. 200). The practitioners of the newsroom, for their part, adopted the language of the transformation but not the practices. The front page showed little change. Ryfe attributed this stability to the resilience and durability of professional practices.

Let's try to reconstitute the initiating problem for each of these four studies. For Tutt, the problem has to do with the integration of what he calls "living room media" (think lower-middle-class British homes, not U.S. McMansions) into ordinary household practices and the relationships they foster. For Mayer, the larger issue had to do with how Mexican Americans both produce and consume media (see Mayer, 2003). The specifics of telenovelas and her young informants were a result of a provisioned but serendipitous realization of being in the right place at the right time and being responsive to the opportunity.

Mary Ann Moser reported in our e-mail exchange that she is a science communication practitioner who cares about science, technology, and society and now conducts project-based action research. In doing her dissertation research, she was a volunteer at the shelters, valued for her communication and tech skills. It was a deliberate selection, given that a government-funded program had just recently installed computer terminals. David Ryfe is a journalism professor charged with understanding professional journalism practices. It would be nearly unthinkable for anyone in newspapers not to be interested in their future. At the time of his ethnographic study, he wrote in an e-mail that he was onsite, working to update the literature on professional practices. I can imagine his excitement when he learned of the impending editorial changes. Change situations are an ethnographer's Valhalla, because institutional practices get revealed as they are discussed.

What is common about these four problems is that they all start with some abiding interest on the part of the researcher and then bring together an observational site with

---

[3]Structuration theory holds that institutional member practices produce the terms that govern member practices. Part of what members do is to make certain activity possible and other activity unlikely. Our connection to this theory is that much of that work is done through texts and technology.

rich potential as well as a membership that is jointly involved in some set of common practices. The specific problem that we see in the article in the literature emerges from this combination of an overarching interest in issues that appear in very local conditions of performance that itself extends over many months. Each article represents only some smaller part of what was studied and learned. Given how this works, one can see that it would be difficult to walk in the door with a set of hypotheses. The analyst could not be responsive to the conditions at hand.

The Membership

Ethnography, to be "ethno-graphy"—the writing of culture—has to be located in some membership that creates the cultural understandings of and for action. While they obviously vary in significance, memberships are formed in any social grouping that provides the resources of action. Memberships are families, friends, social clubs, social networking sites, political groups, religious congregations, corporate organizations—any interactive set of relationships in which there is both a claim to membership by the individual and a grant of membership by the group.

The research claim for a membership is based on the documentation of the relational practices among the members. It is these practices that establish, rehearse, and sustain the common understanding that in turn justifies the action and its character and establishes the utility of the ethnographic approach. Communities are defined by their interactions and not by size or location. In metric research, we most often use aggregations of individuals—people who have no necessary relationship to one another. The reason for this choice is that the underlying theory that supports the research holds that all the needed information is contained within the individual. In interpretive research, we most often use what might be called congregations of individuals—people who are interconnected through common practices of understanding, recognized activities, and mutual obligations.

The degree of congregation in membership varies widely across memberships. The density and the complexity of relational practices define the density and complexity of the communal understanding that explains those practices. Note the circular relationship between practices and understanding. They develop together, and they are mutually reinforcing. As analysts, we step into the middle of this process, and it just looks like reason precedes action. Note also the implications of density and complexity. Congregant memberships sustained by shallow and limited practices are themselves shallow and limited in their effects on membership.

Consider three different audiences for a national television dance program—say, *Dancing with the Stars*: One audience group is a dance club that records the program and gathers together for a viewing and critique. The group carefully dissects each routine, noting choreography, costuming, and performance. Members will perform a routine, demonstrate steps, show errors, and demonstrate the correct performance. The total activity can last three hours or more. The second group is a fan club (e.g., http://www.fanpop.com) with 935 registered fans and about 1,500 interactive posts per month. The 10 most active members have posted an average of 3,400-plus posts over the several seasons of the program (facts are a composite from more than one site in this example). The third group is an assemblage of randomly selected viewers who claim to regularly watch the program.

Taking the groups in reverse order, we can see that members of the viewer-only group have nothing necessarily more in common than they turn on the television set to watch a particular program. This group is much more an aggregation than a congregation as, among the individuals, there is no interaction, no relationship, and no investment in one another. This group would not be a proper subject for an ethnography because there can be no common understanding (no *ethno-* of ethnography) performed among the individual viewers.[4] The analyst can certainly sit in, say, 25 living rooms and document the viewing practices of individuals in those rooms, but there can be no legitimate subsequent claim that the practices documented are the practices of *the audience,* because none of these practices governs the practices of anyone else who views the program.

The fan community, however, crosses the threshold for ethnography, at least for those members who regularly participate or even just regularly lurk. The fan club practices introduce a set of communication routines by which members can influence the actions of others and work to establish a value system for the character of those actions. For example, Figure 15.1 is a screenshot from BuddyTV.[5]

It shows a discussion of the ethics of choice. The exchange does not appear to be particularly powerful rhetoric, but this set of turns is typical of how organizational members influence one another (see Taylor & Van Every, 2000, for an explication of the theory). The exchange is documented evidence of material practices of membership that in turn influence viewing.

The third group shows the extraordinary power of membership to organize lives. This group[6] gathers every Wednesday evening to critique the previous Monday's show.

Figure 15.1 Online Fan Community

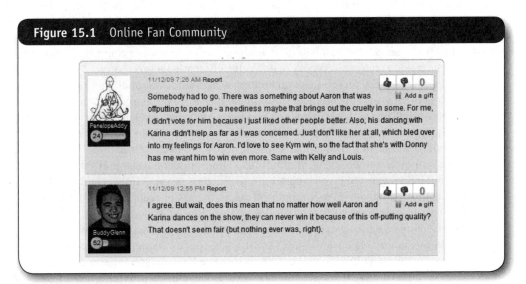

---

[4]Unless, of course, the analyst breaks the epistemic paradigm and adopts an effects model where the common governance of viewing behavior would be supplied by the program instead of the actions of members.

[5]http://www.buddytv.com/dancing-with-the-stars.aspx. Accessed May 4, 2011.

[6]This is a fictionalized example loosely based on a local dance club.

Every member will have watched or be full of apologies. The critique, talk, and demonstrations are full-on. People are tired when they leave. And the program? It is a resource for all this action but not the source of it. The source of the action is the commonly held and enacted set of understandings. That set is the proper object of ethnography of this group.

The insightful contribution of an ethnography is not the careful documentation of behavior just as the facts of a text are not its meaningfulness. That factual documentation is a requirement, but the contribution is the illumination of the understandings that provide for the action documented in behavior. Any of the interpretive approaches that connect to ethnography will have the social realities of membership as a central claim. Coding behavior in the absence of a membership or in absence of access may be valuable research, but it is not ethnography. A governing membership is part of the standard.

Of our four exemplar studies, Ryfe's analysis most closely meets that standard. He is working in an organization with a high threshold for membership and clear boundaries of membership. One cannot just sign in; one has to be admitted, serve something of an apprenticeship, and then continue to perform to a stringent set of criteria that are supervised, with infractions noted and adjudicated. Ryfe gains access because he is qualified to be a member by his own professional training and experience. For others to achieve his insight, they would have to achieve his level of member competence.

Tutt, on the other hand, has little to no chance of gaining membership in any of his family or roommate groups and makes no effort to do so. He is limited to what the camera and microphone can record from a single camera placement. His video recordings create a set of texts that he carefully transcribes and analyzes. His reports are the sense he makes of these texts, providing the story he wishes to tell. This process closely follows the typical analysis of constructed texts—texts purposively created as research texts. The difference is that Tutt's texts are created in their analysis, not by an independent cultural agent deliberately making choices to meet the demands of creating a text.

The raw material for the text Tutt creates is the improvisational lines of action that enter and leave the voyeur coverage of the camera, but the text entered into the analysis is composed of the scenes that Tutt selects to craft a narrative, much like a director's cut. As a result, Tutt both creates the text and critically analyzes the text, giving him nearly complete control of the results. Those results are founded on what Tutt knows before he sees the tapes and demonstrate the strength of his cultural understanding. They are not the result of what he has learned by participating in the action. In fact, the researcher is in control of the entire argument—"it makes sense to me, so it must be true." His claim has to be that all familial groupings are sufficiently alike that an outsider, based on her or his own familial experience and existing cultural narratives, can determine "what is going on."

The studies by Mayer and Moser occupy the space between these two endpoints. The centered membership of Mayer's study is teenage girls engaged in the cultural process of identity construction. It is a membership that Mayer cannot join but in which she can participate in some identifiable role (visitor, counselor, sounding board, etc.). She has also had to complete the same cultural task in her own life. Mayer has access because of her role in the community center, but she also has value to the girls as a confidante. There is a demonstrable interactive process between her and the membership. The membership, however, is much more loosely formed than either the relationships in Tutt or the newspaper in Ryfe.

Individuals can sign in and sign out of this membership with little cost. Consequently, the governance, obligation, and explanatory power of membership is slight.

Moser addresses two classifications of participants. One group is the staff memberships of three homeless shelters; the other is the individual clients of those shelters. The staff memberships are coherent, clear, and separate. Moser gains access to each because of her skills with technology. She holds a position of a volunteer "who can actually do stuff" as local staff members might describe her. She participates as a stakeholder in their accomplishments. Working with three staffs over the course of the study allows her to use a compare-and-contrast approach, but it does limit the depth of membership she can attain.

Moser's second group comprises the clients of the homeless shelters. Moser addresses these individuals serially as they come in to use the computer work stations. Consequently, she never directly connects to any of the communities of the homeless (there would be several different communities involved). In this case, she is using a demographic classification (no address) to sort respondents and then collecting interviews. This is not an ethnographic approach, but it is a common technique.

In the fantasy world of textbook research, an ethnographic community would have clearly defined boundaries, established procedures for gaining membership, open processes of socialization, a coherent set of structurational practices, organizational texts that codify those practices, and compliant members who follow those codes (and who, of course, are immediately forthcoming to the ethnographer). In real life, communities have sketchily drawn boundaries that are permeable and poorly policed; memberships are negotiated; socialization is competitive among the organizational stakeholders; practices are often incoherent, marked by resistance and sabotage; much of official policy has little to do with practice; and members are self-serving in the way they present themselves to the organization and to the ethnographer. Ethnographers will usually find themselves in something in between those two extremes. It's usually not all bad, but it is never all good, in my experience. It matters because the complexity of membership is the baseline for the quality of the insight.

Whatever its character, for ethnography to make sense, there has to be some kind of membership that imposes and supervises some discipline of practice that in turn generates a framework of understanding that justifies the action. We spend most of our lives in memberships and relationships that help form our world. What we learn in ethnography is how other people make sense of the world in which they live and that they help create. It's not about cataloguing behaviors; it's about achieving insight into the lives of others. But the community, organization, membership, or relationship has to have a material presence and consequence. There has to be a "there" there, not just a classification or some form of aggregated communality.

Gaining Access

Once a community, an organization, or a membership that has a useful relationship to one's problem has been discovered, the issue becomes how to gain access to the membership and how to become accomplished at some level of a member's knowledge. The degree of access establishes the base level of member knowledge that can be attained. Not everything is possible. Some groups have high barriers to entry, requiring qualifications that may be impossible for the analyst to meet. Groups that are defined by sex, age, race, ethnicity, or social standing; groups that have high training requirements, rely on one another for personal safety, or are defined by law; and groups that are family or based on an extensive personal history or a unique common history are examples of groups to which an analyst might be denied or granted only limited access.

That is a pretty lengthy list, but the issue of access is more extensive than a list of the impossible. Even when the analyst is granted full access to an organization, that access is likely to be different from that granted to a member. That difference may be positive, as in "I tell the analyst things I would never share with the group," or negative, as in "I'm not showing the analyst how we get around policy," and is likely to be mixed across the membership. Just as there is no solution to the sampling problem in metric research, there is no solution to the problem of access in ethnography. Access is as the analyst gets it, and there is no control group for comparison.

The terms of access establish the vantage point from which the group is engaged. Common terms are contained in titles such as *college professor, visiting researcher, student, intern, volunteer,* and *consultant* that reference an "outside" position. The analyst can hold an inside position with a membership title and an overt or covert research presence. It might seem that an inside position with a hidden (covert) research identity would be the most effective. But it can also mean that the analyst is permitted access to only those elements of the organization that pertain to, say, a job. Spending eight hours a day in a cubicle or holding a light stand on a movie set doesn't allow for much insight, whereas a visiting researcher might be given unprecedented access if limited participation.

For the analyst, the terms and quality of access have to be a continuing part of the observation and analytical writing. It is not enough to say, "I was there as a student" and not carefully detail what it meant to be there as a student (or any other access position). For the critic (or user of the findings), it is not enough to accept or dismiss a study based on the terms of the access ("Oh, the author was there only as a student") without any evidentiary basis. The critic simply cannot know, except perhaps through some process of divination or plain guessing, what the terms of access meant. On the other hand, if the analyst does not detail the terms and character of access, then the critic is certainly justified in advising caution in accepting any findings. As always, it is best for the analyst to err on the side of modesty—don't claim more than what can be supported—and for the critic to err on the side of caution—don't accept more than what was supported.

Access starts with some sort of entrance, but it does not remain static. It can increase with trust, competence, returned value, and good practices of social networking. All of these elements of access are part of one's member knowledge—knowing how to be trustworthy and competent, what is valuable to the membership, whom one should know and connect with, what are the good practices of relationships, and the like. As the ethnographer becomes more competent in member knowledge, access generally increases with that competence. The analyst can fail in this competence as well, and access can diminish or be revoked.

Fieldwork I: Achieving Member Knowledge

Two reasonable questions remain for this section to answer: How does the analyst get this member knowledge? And, how does one know when she or he knows it? This is the point where tidy theory devolves into messy practice. There are four components in this practice: informants, guides, and mentors; within the membership, texts, artifacts, and dynamic and static space; supervised performance; and reflexive writing.

Informants, Guides, and Mentors

One mark of the achievement of member understanding is the recognizable support from informants, guides, and mentors. Their absence in the study would be a strong caution to the reader. Fortunately, almost any reasonable conditions of access will generate informants or members who are willing to talk to the analyst about local conditions. These conversations tend to become less frequent as time progresses and are less likely the more significant and closely held is the information being sought. Guides do more than talk; they volunteer to show where things are and how things are done. A guide offers much more investment of personal time than an informant. At the top of this hierarchy is the mentor. Mentors do all the work of informants and guides and then add an active effort in assisting the analyst to succeed and supervising his or her performance. Mentors anticipate the needs of the analyst and ensure correct enactment. They are rare, but then it only takes one.

Whether informant, guide, or mentor, almost all of this support work is on the margins of what the members have to accomplish just to maintain their membership. Because helping the researcher is not centered, efforts and information will be partial, incomplete, contradictory, and most likely confusing, not unlike any other initiation. The analyst's field notes (which are written off-site) need to mark those conditions and pose strategies to fill in the blanks during the next participant session.

Patience plays two very important parts in this process. One is knowing how much demand for clarity can be placed on the membership. When people start ducking into the closet upon approach, the analyst has pushed too hard and needs to slow the process down. The larger requirement for patience is in the need to keep an open mind and to keep examining what one presumes to know. The natural work of the mind is to fill in the blanks, to make sense of things. It is difficult but necessary to suspend that gestalt impulse.

Texts, Artifacts, and Space

Memberships make the jump into organizations as they codify their practices into durable texts such as mission statements, codes of values and conduct, business plans, goals, markers and mileposts, policies and procedures, and rules of governance and conduct, as well as the more common but ordinarily short-lived communiqués, memos, and e-mails. These are the texts of membership. Most texts are in some way the product of talk—talk in the hallways, committee meetings, task forces. Talk works its way up through some process of vetting, consensus building, and approval until it is cemented into durable text. Durable text is often dead (or at least latent) in the everyday. A common rule of organizational life is that policy is there to punish behavior that had a bad outcome. It is not capable of giving good guidance in the fast-moving everyday circumstance.

The relationship between talk and text is such that the ethnographer who carefully reads through the policy and procedures handbook may be the only person, besides a few organizational wonks, to ever do it. Nonetheless, the relationship between talk and text is important to explore. Texts archive past disputes and problems that still appear in veiled references in talk and provide a source for the metaphors and allusions that give texture to organizational action. Current talk may well become the durable texts of the future.

Finally, there is the increasingly familiar virtual organization that is a membership held together entirely by text, such as fan clubs, activist organizations (see Figure 15.2), political campaigns, social networking sites, and the like. These are pretty much unexplored areas for communication and mediated communication in particular.[7]

An artifact is an object held in meaningfulness by the membership. Artifacts are common even among the most loosely coupled memberships. A now defunct women's faculty group had a special apron (indescribable in this family text) that any male who would join them at the poker table (yes, there is card playing in Utah) had to wear. It was good fun but with a serious purpose. It marked the male as female, but also as the Other. That is precisely the sort of artifact the ethnographer seeks—objects that have meaning greater than their ostensible purpose. Such artifacts denote membership in the organization and its subgroups, longevity, hierarchical position, authority, speaking rights, and the like.

I carry a small digital camera (a cell phone camera works wonderfully) and take pictures of desktops both physical and virtual, walls, furniture, fashion, bulletin boards, and

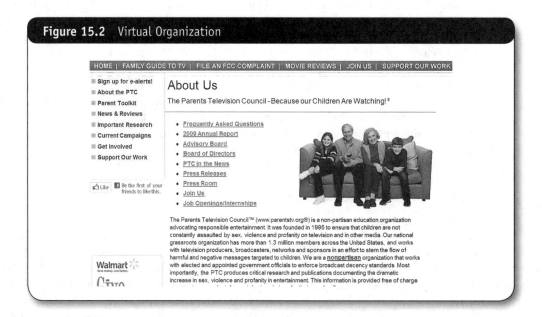

Figure 15.2 Virtual Organization

---

[7]A search on *Communication and Mass Media Complete* yielded only 6 hits on "virtual organizations" and 100 hits on "social networking sites." These low numbers indicate that academic research is a bit behind the curve. These sites of text (and all of web interactivity) have the potential of restructuring mediated communication research. It would represent a huge shift to move from the typical message effects model to a model that puts the interactive community at the explanatory center (see Booth, 2008). It would be such a large shift that at this writing, we do not have adequate protocols fully developed. (Marketing is making the first moves here; see Kozinets, 2002, 2006, or Cova & Pace, 2006, for an approach).

entrances, capturing all the evidence of local signification that I can.[8] When some pattern or something curious appears in those pictures, I can go to an informant for an explanation.

Space has both dynamic and static characteristics. Walk about any college campus; the purposes of space are immediately apparent in their static arrangements—classrooms, meeting rooms, offices, departmental work space, front receptions, and janitorial closets—all clearly indicate their uses. Space can often be radically changed, however, as it is put to use. Classroom theater arrangements (rows of chairs facing front) indicate a hierarchical teaching style with its sacred (front desk or podium) and profane (student desks) areas. The instructor who walks in and announces, "Let's put the chairs in a circle" dynamically changes both the space and the social arrangements.

The dynamic use of even unchanged space both large and small (don't sit in my chair even if you are my dinner guest) speaks to all the elements of membership from belonging to position to authority and power. But the analyst has to know the rules of practice. In cartoon parlance, the most important individual in a boardroom sits at the head of the long table. In typical organizational practice, media have changed that favored location. The head of the table is where lesser folks make presentations. If one sits at the head, she or he is likely to be blinded by the data projector. This is a discovery of participation, not observation.

The laptop computer and Wi-Fi are making major changes in household space delegated to video media use. Less than five years ago, space had to be dedicated to large, heavy devices that were tethered to multiple cords. Those circumstances meant that individuals had to be in particular places to watch or have devices all over the house (as was our solution). The wireless high-definition, (relatively) large-screen laptop or the wireless distribution center changes that. Let me hasten to write that most U.S. households that I visit still have large heavy devices (now larger and flatter) tethered to even more cords than five years ago. But it is changing. We are but a technology moment away from wired or satellite delivery to an effective wireless distribution point that delivers the AV signal to any point in the house. The scale of savings in copper alone will drive this change.

Changes in space and spatial arrangements change relationships and the framing of messages. The household with a single display monitor (or highly favored one) creates a necessary location for negotiation and community viewing. The message is delivered into what can be a cauldron of comment. Multiple viewing locations mean that when household members view together, they do so for relational or multitasking purposes. (It does not have to be positive: Families can turn the set on to prevent conversation at the dinner table.) All of that has consequences for how we understand media and their messages.

Dynamic patterns in the use of space emerge over the time and events of participation. Careful observation lays the foundation for these analytical insights. Consider a family viewing setting: How many seats are in the common viewing location? What is the angle of view of each of those seats? What are the pathways, as well as protected and isolated areas? What are the available resources in technology, furniture, appliances, food, drink, and personal comfort? This is the stage of action, and it helps explain why the action follows certain lines. Important as they are, it is very difficult for the beginning ethnographer

---

[8]Yes, taking photographs is risky. Be willing to delete any picture taken and to stop the practice if challenged.

to make and record these observations. We already know what a family room looks like. It looks like a waste of time to detail this one, but it's not.

Member knowledge and performance activate texts, artifacts, and space. When the analyst knows the story behind the text, the value of the artifact, and the meaning of the use of space, not from the material properties of each but from multiple explanations and performances in which they are involved, the evidence for member understanding mounts.

Fieldwork II: Supervised Performance and Reflexive Writing

Supervised performance is the highest level of participation. The supervision of this performance can be close or quite distant, but it means that someone else cares—and cares in a membership-relevant way—about what and how something actually gets done. The key is that the membership has a stake in the analyst's performance. The performance itself is not necessarily something that a member would actually do. The analyst might never be a teenage girl again. The membership, however, becomes invested in the research and directs the analyst to get it right. (OK, I can feel the modernists among you circling the wagons here. Let it rest for a moment, and I promise we will take up researcher independence and going native in a later section.) I'm not a big fan of taking the final written product back to the membership for "correction." That strategy simply deflects responsibility for the argument and gives a false veneer of validity. I am very much in favor of being shown by the membership how to get it right before I touch the keyboard for the final argument.

Writing is the third pillar of ethnography along with observation and participation. Writing is there at the beginning with the unobtrusive scribbling of site notes recording players, places, conversations, reminders, and all the rest. One cannot be walking around with a clipboard or an obvious notebook; a multifolded sheet of paper works well. Digital recorders are small enough to slip into a shirt pocket, and they will record continuously for 50 hours or more. Ethical practice would require that the presence of the recorder be made known, but if accepted, the analyst can simply dictate notes. (Just get a Bluetooth device, and it's indistinguishable from cell phone practice.)

Writing gets intensive back at the office as the analyst crafts field notes following each participant observation session. The discipline of writing field notes is at the center of the quality of the research contribution. It is limited by the quality of participation, but the effort of participation is lost without adequate field notes. Field note writing calls on the analyst to gather all the resources for understanding what went on and then to bring that understanding into a textual form: This is not journal or diary writing. It is a systematic exploration of one's experience taken under observation in the writing. To personalize it: You, the writer, become the observer of you, the participant.

The first purpose of field note writing is to catalogue the resources gained during the last period of observation. This work involves the pictures, artifacts, texts, measurements, new vocabulary, ways of speaking and acting, and other observations that were noteworthy during the session. The physical and conceptual provenance of each piece should be recorded—what it is inside member reality and why it was noted inside the ethnographic reality; what it means to the members and what it means to the ethnographer. The goal is that even after much time has passed, the item is still recognizable and has utility for further analysis.

The second purpose of field note writing is to detail the narrative of what happened. This is not plain empirical writing. There is a firm foundation of "just the facts" writing, but then, the ethnographer typically adds motive, intention, purpose, outcomes, goals, emotional response, and all other elements that have to be inferred from our common humanity. If conclusions are offered, they are tentative, and alternatives are given.

The narrative is often incomplete because the action itself was incomplete or, equally likely, the writer's understanding of the action is incomplete. The recognition of those breaks, however, become the directions for improvement in the participatory process, which is why it is important to write soon after each participation episode. It is also why it is important not to push the narrative to completion—to fill in the blanks, so to speak. That completion is not justified from the analyst's experience and is akin to making up data. If after some number of iterations, the action pattern still cannot be completed, the analyst should find it useful to question the narrative as the wrong story or the perspective taken on the action as incorrectly located.

All of the technical aspects of this advice would push this paragraph into another book, but the short take states this: Field notes are narratives; narratives have structural qualities (just as numbers do); the task is to fit the structural qualities of the narrative to the characteristics of observations (as we do in metric research). And for the action: Competent action itself is an improvisational narrative line of behavior with a beginning, a middle, and an end; if the action does not cohere, it may be incompetent, per se, or the observation may be of a fragment (seeing only the end of a larger action line) or a misattributed segment (seeing the middle as the beginning).

This analysis is all pretty orderly. My more radical colleagues see all this reasoning as an expression of my vestigial modernism, especially the part about the relationship between narrative and action. Point well taken. On the other hand, if there is no correspondence between what we do and what we write, and if there is no discipline or containment of the narrative by the experience of participation, why bother to go to the field at all? My argument makes the field note open to critique (otherwise it is wholly owned by the analyst, and you know I do not like that). There have to be empirical warrants for the narrative claims. The field note is an evidentiary argument.

That fact allows another player to come into this process: the auditor. The field note auditor is someone who will critically evaluate the writing for the strength of its evidence. A personal example might clarify: I was doing family media-use ethnographies focusing on early-afternoon viewing by the children in the house. I wrote of an incident where a younger child had control of the remote and would tease an older child by switching to a program his older brother wanted to watch, staying on it for a while, and then going back to the program that he claimed to have wanted to watch. This action invoked loud complaints from the older brother with pleas for the younger brother to go back. My initial write-up was about technology and power. My auditor asked if there was a parent at home. There was. "Sounds like something else is in play," she said. On my next visit, I found out that there was a household rule that gave control of the set to the younger brother during that time period. The rule worked when there was an enforcer present.

Auditors cannot correct the ethnographer's field note, but they can recognize when a note does not pass the "sniff test." An experienced ethnographer is an excellent auditor as she or he knows all the tricks we play on ourselves to reach the end of the writing. It takes as long, and sometimes much longer, to write field notes as it does to participate in the field. It can be very frustrating when things don't make sense. Staring at a cursor for an hour is not much fun. At those times, the analyst has to be encouraged to write the sequence narrative ("I drove into the parking lot at 8:10 in the morning") and to write about not being able to write.[9] The cycle of participation and field note writing may go on for an extended period of time. We saw in our examples that a year or more is not uncommon. At some point, however, it has to end to move on to the last phase of the method—the construction of the ethnographic argument.

Making Sense of It All: The Ethnographic Argument

The resources for this construction include the collected texts, artifacts, photographs, sketches, maps, e-mail exchanges, pages of field notes, and the wealth of experience from the field. It also would not be surprising if the problem that motivated the field experience had now morphed into a half-dozen or more ideas.[10] The problem is to corral this surfeit of resources into a set of contributions. This process requires a systematic effort in its own right. That effort begins by considering the whole set of resources as a text that is available for coding and then to adopt the methods we have for analyzing such texts as developed in Chapters 12 and 13. Again, I would suggest a heavy-duty piece of software such as NVivo or ATLAS.ti.

It may seem odd to code one's own field notes. After a year or more in the field, however, it is unlikely that the ethnographer remembers much about the first half of the writing. Equally important, the first step of close reading of the entire set of field notes should allow for the discovery of the advancement of understanding gained by the analyst as the field-work progressed, open up the insights that we gain from the juxtaposition of experience, and provide the opportunity for a critical review of one's field writing technique—nothing like finding out that the analyst as writer doesn't make sense to the analyst as reader.

Systematic coding also lessens the temptations of opportunistic poaching. Poaching occurs when the analyst starts with a claim and then goes hunting for the best quotes or episodes to support the claim. Ignored in this process, of course, is the evidence that contradicts or modifies the claim as well as that evidence that supports an alternative. Competent coding will require the analyst to account for all the data before the writing of a claim begins.

Coding will lay out all the pieces of the puzzle. It will be an interpretive process to fit them together into the framework of the arguments they support. The interpretive insight composes the elements into coherent explanations. Because I have direct knowledge of the process, let me use two examples from my own research: My primary argument in the homeless studies is that homelessness has different beginnings for men than for women.

---

[9]Ethnography is a difficult methodology. I love it (as I do all methods), but I don't often recommend it.

[10]Admittedly, most people reading this paragraph will not be in these circumstances. If the nonprofessional does ethnography at all, it usually comprises a few weeks in the field, more interviews than participation, field notes of uncertain quality, and little in the range of other resources. Nonetheless, it's useful to see what the method entails.

For homeless men, who outnumber homeless women by a factor of 5, the common beginning is some circumstance that results in the loss of masculine identity (Anderson, 2008c). This claim arose out of the stories the men told of the loss of the home connection, my observations of and participation in a system that disempowers and emasculates, and the vision the hopefuls have for their return to a "normal life." It takes all three of these pieces for the argument to adequately cohere.

In the media violence textual analysis, one of our most startling conclusions (Anderson & Colvin, 2008a) was the claim that the persistence of the concern over media violence was motivated by fear of the Other, particularly in the form of the delinquent, Unknown Child. That claim came together out of the early direct and later veiled references to the race and ethnicity (or immigrant status) of "those people" who were at risk, the repeated references to "those parents" who failed to properly supervise their children, the "fine child" exception to immutable cognitive laws, the absence of any self-awareness on the part of the researchers, and the near total absence of a concern for the violence-infected child whose life would be spent outside the law and in prison.[11] It this case, it was both what was there and what was not there that made the argument work.

The interpretive insight that puts it all together may appear to be something of a miracle, but it comes after the systematic extraction and cataloguing of the information that the ethnographic process provides. The discipline of the mind is in avoiding the premature conclusion, the rush to closure, while the systematic close reading and coding is in progress. That process can extend over weeks of frightening uncertainty with the analyst wondering if all of the work will ever make sense. It usually does. We do hear the stories, and I have had the experience, of when it doesn't, however. When conception fails or insight is weak in my work, I blame the foundation of effort in the field—better to blame me, the worker, than me, the perspicacious one. That ego protection aside, the cure is typically a return to the field with the clearer focus that the failed analysis provides.[12]

The interpretive insight provides the "name of the narrative"—loss of masculine identity (Anderson), White middle-class fear of the delinquent child (Anderson & Colvin), negotiating access (Tutt), managing cross-cultural identity (Mayer), technology as stabilizing a homeless life and threatening the identity of a homeless shelter (Moser), persistence of professional standards (Ryfe). The analyst knows the story to be told by the name, but it still has to be written. We'll take that task up in Chapter 16.

Reflexivity is part of all these writing tasks—site notes, field notes, close reading notes, coding, and the ethnographic argument. Reflexivity is simply one's self-awareness in the writing that acknowledges one's complicity in any claim made. There is no nondelusional position in interpretive research (and, as a postmodernist, I would say metric research as well) that would allow the analyst to claim that results "presented" themselves or that an

---

[11]The "aha" of this last piece came from working with George Comstock's manuscript as coeditor of the special issue on media violence for the *American Behavioral Scientist*. While Professor Comstock and I disagree on the issue of media as a substantial source of social violence, his argument was the first I had seen to show compassion to the "other victims"—the children whose lives were ruined by being "turned by the media."

[12]We use the same procedure with a failed hypothesis. We examine the protocol to get it right. Rarely do we give up on our theory in metric research or on our belief in the coherence of action in ethnography.

explanation was "discovered." Both results and explanations are firmly grounded in empirical evidence that resides outside the mind of the analyst, but the insight that puts it together into an argument is clearly the product of the analyst as situated in an episteme, zeitgeist, culture, society, field of study, and academic practice. Because there is not much left of the idiosyncratic, rugged individual after all those modifiers, there is not a lot of concern about the analyst-as-instrument requirement of interpretive research expressed in the articles we read. We trust, however, that the thoughtful analyst has considered the role that his or her self-interest might have played in the claim and worked to contain it.

Reflexivity, then, is generally a backstage activity for the writer, a guardian task for the auditor as well as the editor and associated reviewers, and a skeptic's eye for the reader. For the writer, the activity is a recognition of one's likelihoods and limitations of interpretation. The attempt is not to write someone else's experience or substitute one's voice for the voice of the other without adequate basis. I could not write Vicki Mayer's article because I do not have her language skills, I did not experience teenage girlhood, and my relationship with the respondents would have been quite different. I might have been able to reach Mayer's conclusions, however, from my own analysis.

For the auditor, the task is to flag those instances in the writing prior to the ethnographic argument that appear to exhibit arrogance, condescension, projection, or us-them constitutions; that do more to present the ethnographer (in perhaps a favored role); or that fail to show the evidence for some conclusion. We expect the ethnographic argument to be vetted by the journal reviewers and editors.

Alas, for us readers, both auditing and editing are of uneven quality and sometimes absent. In the end, it remains for us to judge the trustworthiness of the effort. The following questions might guide the skeptic's eye: What was the level of insertion into the membership? What was the level of engagement? How complex and extensive was the participation? What other resources were collected or developed? What was the practice of field notes? Was an auditor used? What methods were used to analyze the field notes and other resources? How did the analyst guard against poaching and self-fulfillment? If most of the answers are unknown, I would be reluctant to put much trust in the study, even if I enjoyed the reading.

Finally, for my own moment of reflexivity, not everyone agrees with me that ethnography need be this complex, lengthy, and intensive or that it needs such a solid empirical foundation. I have been in more than one pointed but loving conversation with my fellow researchers (to read a systematic analysis of some of these complaints, see Shank & Villella, 2004). There are clearly events worthy of study that cannot support that effort, the argument goes. For example, the annual Burning Man event held in the Nevada desert creates an entire community for a few days in September and draws together thousands of free spirits and counterculturists. The time is so short that one can do little more than be in the moment and then come back and write about it. I agree, and that is what a journalist does, not an ethnographer. To do ethnographic work, consider the Burning Man leadership group that works year-round to make the event happen or the extended membership that returns year after year. The single event is exactly that—an event unique in its particularity—and so must we assume is its description. The focus of ethnography is not the moments of serendipity or spontaneity but the cultural under-standings that provide them.[13]

Emerging Forms of Argument

New media forms are just beginning to have an impact on old forms of research. Nowhere is this impact shown more dramatically than in ethnographic research. Substantial change is appearing in the handful of hypertext ethnographies or ethnographic data that can be accessed on the web.[14] The most complete example of these is Wood's Congo Project.[15] This ethnography is a re-creation of Belgian colonial sensibilities that shaped the cultural under-standings of the Belgian Congo through the use of the constituting exhibits of the Royal Museum for Central Africa and the memory work captured in the narratives of colonial veterans. The study poses a number of interesting issues in its own right as the time and place of the culture it attempts to understand has disappeared.

Our interest in it here, however, has to do with its presentational form in which Wood not only lays out a particular ethnographic argument but also supplies the resources for that argu-ment, which could then be used for such other arguments that might be created, all in hyper-text linkages that allow the auditor to move from argument to resource with but a mouse click. In this repository of field data and the linkages to those data, hypertext expands the capacity of ethnography to present the Other. It allows us to hear the voices and see the people that Wood heard and saw and to apparently judge for ourselves as to the probity of the argument.

There is one missing resource, however: Wood cannot supply the experience of his participation. No matter how often I access the information on this site, something I have done many times,[16] I cannot access it as an ethnographer. I am always an observer.

Hypertext, therefore, both gives and takes away. It gives us access to the written, oral, and visual texts, but it also strips those texts from their provenance in experience. In doing so, it releases us from the discipline that experience would impose on the argument and exposes those texts and the voices and persons behind them to uses inappropriate to the context of their collection.

Consider this similarity: Hiking in southern Utah, I hunt for pottery shards in the dry creek beds and washes. Holding up one of these (to be replaced as I found it), I can wax

---

[13]Note to the reader (sotto voce): Don't be distracted by the argument in this paragraph. It is telling you about me and the extent to which I will maintain a position. Now, whether that is steadfast or stubborn is for you to decide. The paragraph also shows the problems with reflexive writing. How is this writing the voice of objective reason? A text-book writer is supposed to be above the rough-and-tumble, casually resolving the disputes with "on the one hand this" and "on the other hand that." So, I have violated the traditional reader expectation, but that's my point, isn't it?

[14]For some examples, see http://www.anth.ucsb.edu/projects/axfight/index2.html (accessed May 5, 2011); http://ctwsearch.wesleyan.edu/conncoll/Record/t911615 (accessed May 5, 2011); and http://www.youtube.com/watch?v=tYcS_VpoWJk (accessed May 5, 2011).

[15]http://www.woodcollab.com/congo/index.html. Accessed May 5, 2011.

[16]Full disclosure here: Professor Wood used this project in his dissertation (Wood, 2011). I served as his supervising chair. I, of course, consider it to be an outstanding study, creative and innovative, even as I am conflicted as to what it may portend.

eloquently about the hands that formed it and the hands that used it. Washed downstream from its site of use, I know nothing about the people or about the pot itself. It could be that hypertext will turn out to be our virtual creek bed, turning digital ethnography into a YouTube of research. Wood (2011) addresses many of these issues in the written text of his dissertation and provides a robust set of sources to pursue as well.

THE ETHICS OF ETHNOGRAPHY

The scientific practice of ethnography was born during an aggressive period of European colonization. It was the known addressing the unknown, the centered looking on to the exotic. Ethnography was often put into the service of the subjugation of the Other using traditional antipathies and enemies to subdue resistance. The impulse that sees the ethnographer as centered and the focal membership as the unknown and exotic still courses through ethnographic study. It appears in the justification for the study and in what the ethnographer considers worthy of comment. The focal membership is, of course, neither unknown nor exotic; the ethnographer is simply ignorant and different.

Self-centeredness of the ethnographer can lead to a false sense of doing good, helping, or correcting, so certain is the ethnographer of her or his better understanding of how to be in the world. Researchers working with the "disadvantaged" start out with the assumption of being "advantaged." Similarly, researchers working with children can bring adult models to bear on the practices of the child, showing the inappropriateness of childlike behavior.

There is also the danger of contracting ethnographer arrogance when the inevitable contradictions and glosses are discovered between policy and practice within a membership. That danger extends across any other discovery about the membership that an outsider might consider foolish. All human organizations are replete with breaches, glosses, and contradictions, including all the ones the ethnographer belongs to. The very idea of ethnography itself seems a bit strange to those who do not practice it.

The key to resisting these misdirections is the subjugation of the self to the other. This submersion involves the recognition that one is a guest in a membership, a novice in search of enlightenment and training. If the ethnographer is there to fix things, to gather information for the police, to assist social services, or to demonstrate the superiority of one's own culture, he or she is not there as an ethnographer. Given those intentions, I would not trust the analyst's conclusions concerning the membership because they are directed not toward the membership but toward the other purposes in hand. The relationship of the ethnographer to the membership is essentially exploitive, depending on the generosity of the membership for the gift of information. The analyst will take advantage but should not also be disrespectful, condescending, essentializing, or self-righteous.

MOVING ON

It is the Saturday after Thanksgiving as I come to the end of this chapter. While I am thankful to be at the end (no cheap shots, please), I am also fearful of the limited view I can provide. My friends at Sage have sent me their 500-plus-page handbook on ethnography and their 1,100-plus-page handbook on qualitative research. The variations on what is called ethnography and on its practice will support that much text and more as the dozen or so other books on my shelf attest. In the 11,000-plus words of this chapter, I have tried to provide insight into what I consider to be the best practice. You should not turn the page thinking you know ethnography. Ethnography is not something you read about and then know how to do. Ethnography is something you do and then know how to write about. I have tried to give you the standards, but it will be your job to achieve them. We move on to the final chapter where we take up a look at a career of research and writing.

REFLECTIONS

What Are Some Points to Remember?

- Ethnography is a difficult, time-consuming, emotionally demanding method that offers no shortcuts to excellence. In poker parlance, the ethnographer is all in on every bet.
- The quality of the ethnographic argument depends on the coherence of the membership, the level of access that can be gained, the amount of time spent in participation as well as the complexity of its performance, the sophistication and completeness of the field notes and other texts, the ethnographer's intimate familiarity with and systematic analysis of those texts, and the insightful capacity of the interpretation.

Why Does It Matter?

Cultures develop over centuries; coherent membership can span decades; ethnography has to be more than a weekend in the field.

What Else Could We Talk About?

Ethnography can fail as well as succeed. The marks of failure are insufficient time in the field; no evidence of systematic writing and analysis; the appearance of obvious prepackaged narratives that are too coherent, too clever; a dismissive tone; a lack of reflexivity or reflexivity that is sympathetic to the ethnographer; and conclusions that reaffirm what we already know to be true.

I've been musing over the consequences of using a Twitter account open to the members of the focal community as a repository for all site notes and a similar blog site as the repository for all field notes. It is, of course, quite possible that members wouldn't care, but if they did, I believe the ethnographic process would be radically changed by the continued oversight and comment that might be produced. The authority of the ethnographer to speak the truth of the community recedes.

What Else Might Be Interesting to Read?

Rose, D. (1990). *Living the ethnographic life*. Thousand Oaks, CA: Sage.

CHAPTER 16

An Excursion Into Writing

CHAPTER PREVIEW

What's It All About?

This chapter has two half-chapter essays that pertain to a career in research and scholarship. The first takes up the logistics and practices of professional writing. It is applicable to anyone whose professional activity is marked by writing at its center. The second takes up the personal mastery that can be gained through the practice of foundational reviews. It is applicable to anyone whose career depends on having a command of both historical and contemporary literature.

What Are the Major Topics?

Professional writing, whether it is for scholarship, proprietary research, or even creative fiction, is all about joining and making a regular contribution to an ongoing conversation.

Writing generally requires dedicated time and space. In that time and that space, the task is writing.

Professional writing is rewriting. The first draft is a thinking draft. The second draft prepares one's thoughts for the reader. The third draft is directed by an outside review process. Subsequent drafts are refinements and copy edit work.

Contemporary publication makes technical demands on the author. One must be competent across a variety of software applications dealing with graphics, photographs, and desktop publishing. The delivery draft must be style perfect.

Few manuscripts are ever published without further revision after submission. Be prepared to deal with less-than-friendly and less-than-brilliant reviews. Even the worst review has some contribution to make.

Unlike literature reviews, foundational reviews are encyclopedic in their scope of venues and historical reach and are an ongoing practice rather than a one-off effort.

Historical reach is important because scholarship recycles more than it innovates.

In order to be fully functional, a foundational review is completely digitized, metatagged, and coded.

What Special Terms Are Used?

Consilience

Meta-analysis

INTRODUCTION

This chapter is divided into two distinct sections: The first finishes the task of research by taking up the practices of writing across a career. The second introduces a background practice that can support a lifetime of work. I write the first section as someone who has been a recognized professional author, reviewer, and editor for several decades and the second as someone who is filled with the proselytizing zeal of recent conversion. This will be very much a practical rather than theoretical review.

PROFESSIONAL WRITING

There are a good number of texts and articles that introduce the craft of writing. Alexander and Potter (2001) offer a good enough one (and full disclosure: I have a chapter in it). But I don't want to reprise any of that. Rather, I want to introduce you to the career of writing. There is a substantial difference between the sort of one-off episodic writing that marks the student as well as much of the professoriate and the continuous writing activity of the highly productive scholar. Despite the myths of scholarship, almost 40% of the communication professoriate does not publish in our journals; the lower 25% of those who do produce about one article per 10 years. The upper 5%, however, show a continuous production of about two articles per year (adapted from Stephen & Geel, 2007). Writing at the level of the highly productive scholar is a dedicated activity that assembles specific resources and durable conditions, develops particular skills, and establishes ongoing practices.

Get Connected

Writing starts with a program of active reading, listening, and participating. It is important to be connected to one's discipline by reading its books and journals, listening to presentations (live and recorded), and participating in the informal discussions that arise at gatherings and conventions. All it takes is one good idea—or one idea that you can make good—to make the effort worthwhile.

The active part of this program indicates that it is focused on the goals of the author. With several hundred discipline-related journals, three major and at least four regional conventions hosting several hundred presentations, hundreds of websites, and catalogues of books, there is far too much material available to effectively engage. I have colleagues who read to the point that they cannot write because there is no time left. Focused participation is the key. Build a small library of key books. Read selectively across the journals. I use my graduate seminars to stay current with the latest and greatest, remembering that what is now passé once held that position.

Media scholars have an additional burden, for they must also stay current with the technology, industry, and content of the media as well as audience practices. It is a fatal elitism to consider oneself automatically knowledgeable about the common media. It is very apparent when an author designs a study or writes out of ignorance on these matters. A common reason for studies failing in ecological validity is that the analyst just did not know enough about how things actually get done.

When at conventions, pay as much attention to the performance as to the content (the paper will be available online). It is a good way to learn the culture of the discipline. What ideas capture the audience? What are people discussing and arguing about? Do there appear to be trends or new directions? Convention presentations are mostly the work of the newly minted. They are the harbingers of the discipline.

Finally, it is always a good idea to connect with others. If asked, reviewing and commenting on someone else's work is a great gift that returns as much to the giver. Assisting on a research project or coauthoring helps one to better understand the research and authoring process. Seek out the opportunities to review for conventions or journals. All of these activities make writing present instead of automatic and build a cohort of scholars at the same time. All of this advice would hold true for anyone in any industry.

Develop Skills

There are a number of basic skills that an author has to have (or be able to pay for). They start with keyboarding skills. It sounds absolutely elemental, but the typescript for this text ran over 200,000 words. Typing at 150 words per minute versus 25 words per minute saves over 100 hours or more than two weeks of working time. Keyboarding also connects to composing. If typing is slower than thinking, ideas get lost, foreshortened, or glossed. The sophisticated keyboardist knows the keyboard shortcuts that increase typing speed. Reaching for the mouse slows the process down. If increasing keyboard competence is not an option, the author might consider a voice recognition program such as Dragon Naturally-Speaking. It types about as fast as one can speak, although it is excruciatingly slow over citations and references.

Other more technical skills include professional competence in applications for word processing, spreadsheets, and metric and interpretive data handling; in the techniques for formatting pictures, objects, tables, graphs, and other figures in manuscripts; in managing search strategies for databases and the Internet; and in working with drawing programs and digital photographs. More specialized—but often needed—skills consist of desktop publishing applications, editing sound and video files, producing audio and video streams, and even writing in hypertext.

I believe that the academy will be forced into the 21st century by escalating book and journal costs. When that happens, we may each become not only author but also publisher or at least be responsible for the entire digital layout according to some set of publication rules governing our submissions. The association conventions, and several online journals, have reached that point. As a result, authors already need to know how to follow required style sheets (buy the manual), as well as how to lay out a manuscript; incorporate graphs, statistical tables, photographs, and figures; and convert it to a PDF file for inclusion in a database. The demands on these skills and abilities will only grow as more journals go online. Many universities provide free short courses, and there are web-based courses from major software publishers that will help in attaining these skills.

Assemble Technology

The computer and its attendant word processing software have literally revolutionized publication and authoring. It is a revolution akin to the printing press and the typewriter. It is still up to each author to find the best configuration of that technology to efficiently accomplish the task of writing. If the author puts in one or two writing stints per year, the issues are not too important, but if the career is daily writing sessions of four to six hours per day, everything counts.

The issues start with the physical configuration of an ergonomically correct working arrangement. Fellow authors report that having a dedicated location is the first step, whether a separate room or an appropriated corner where a more or less permanent setup can be established. Seated or stand-up desk is a choice to be made. There are established standards for the angle of attack on the keyboard, location of the mouse, distance from the viewer to the monitor, and multimonitor configurations, and all are readily available on the Internet. Writing on a laptop curled up on a couch might seem appealing until the attendant difficulties of back pain and repetitive motion syndrome begin to appear. These difficulties have done in more than one career.

It will likely be necessary to purchase and learn the needed software and devices. I research and write on both sides of the metric-interpretive divide. The applications and devices I find useful include those for document handling: high-speed adjustable-resolution flatbed and duplex scanners, an optical character recognition application, and JPEG and PDF file applications; for document production: word processing, desktop publishing, and HTML applications, a duplex printer, and a high-quality photo printer; for fieldwork: a digital camera (5 MP is plenty, although one that will record a raw image format is helpful), a digital sound recorder, a digital video recorder, sound, video, and photo editing applications, and a document filing application; and for metric analysis: a spreadsheet application with a statistical add-in, a full-service statistical package, and a data collection design application. It's quite a shopping list (and, to all you techies, you're welcome; your purchases are now fully justified and typically tax-deductible). Authors working across media production would want devices and applications appropriate to that form of scholarship as well.

Develop Good Practices

Discover your own rhythms for your best writing. Writing is a somatic (whole-body) activity. The author needs to attend to and care for the body and be cognizant of the ebb and flow of energy and focus.

Write on a regular time schedule—every day if possible. One's writing skills decline from peak performance (one loses vocabulary, grammatical structure, and language facility) in a few short weeks of layoff. The writer can become disconnected from the field of ideas. Time is wasted recapturing those skills and connections.

Privilege the task of writing. One advantage of a dedicated location is that it signals the work. Sitting down at the desk is a commitment to the effort. It is a sign of what is being done to all in the household or office. If your life's career is in the academy, you will find that scholarship is the road to advancement, but it garners little respect for the demands of its practice. Give your writing time a course title and number; no one asks a colleague to skip class for a committee meeting. Employed elsewhere one can use a committee name or the name of a fictional colleague.

Read good writing carefully for its strategies and techniques and evaluate everything read for its writing quality. It is important that the author regularly study the practice of writing in order to effectively review one's own practices. Most nonprofessional writing is very personal and unexamined (I'm a good person/student; I must write well). If the author cannot articulate the strategy of the piece, then the writing is an unknown practice. The author should know what she or he is doing by making the writing effort present as an object of evaluation.

Doing the Writing

Career writing is not a destination but rather a continuing practice. In career writing, one does not sit down to write a paper or an article; one sits down to write. The destinations are simply markers along the journey. This difference implies a practice that is regular, steady, and consistent, not frantic and pressured. Of course, the author is writing something, which means making good time estimates in relation to deadlines and then having a regular schedule in which the author arrives on time and ends on time and in between is dedicated to and focused on the task.

Career writing is never done. Consequently, the effort also has to be contained and reasonable. It is good to go with the flow, but important to end on time as tomorrow will come. One strategy that works for me is to end in the middle of a sentence. It is a good discipline of control of destination fever, and I am comforted that I am prepared for the next day. Finally, find ways to reward yourself. It's a lonely business. Be nice to yourself; you may be the only one who is.

Professional writing moves in four distinct steps: The first two occur in the drafting phase and the last two in the manuscript preparation stage. The two steps of the drafting stage are the development of the thinking draft and its revision into a "reader's" draft. The two steps of manuscript preparation and revision are the preparation of the delivery draft and its subsequent revision into the publication draft.

Writing the Thinking Draft

The first step works to establish a thought structure. Some authors do this in outline form; some work a first draft. Whatever the strategy, the task is to lay out the requirements of the argument and begin to fill in the blanks. As the writing begins, the author writes what she or he knows and then researches what she or he doesn't, building the initial literature search along the way. It is important for the author to put down her or his foundation first to establish the unique contribution of the writing. Otherwise the writing is simply derivative, and the author is in danger of inadvertent plagiarism. Once the first draft is completed, the literature review can be fleshed out with the relevant (and read!) sources.

This first step is relatively unreflective writing. One's natural voice appears and limited care need be taken to "get it right." The focus is on getting it down. Release the writing; follow every interesting idea; write out the distraction. Take advantage of the serendipity that occurs in the actual writing that produces new ways of considering old issues. The time for review, reflection, and the cruelties of editing will come in the second step; don't anticipate them.

Revision Into a Reader's Draft

Professional writing is rewriting. (It has little in common with classroom assignments.) These pages have multiple fingerprints (here, spreading the blame). In the first step of writing, the author is writing a thought structure. The focus is on ideas and concepts that will populate an argument. In the second step of writing, the focus shifts to the reader, and the draft is rewritten to find the effective ways to present the ideas and concepts to the reader— to fill in the holes, develop additional ideas, eliminate the distractions, and cut the merely useless. This step can take up to half the time of the original writing.

There are a number of strategies for conducting this redrafting. I outline the draft to find out where the thought structure drifts, jumps, elides, or is broken. Again, for me, this outline is most effective when done at the paragraph level. It is the best way for me to find that odd idea that crept into a different topic. It also forces me to read everything written with an unfamiliar eye. In the process, I reparagraph so that each paragraph presents a single idea where possible.

A few other techniques guide the redrafting. A copy is kept of every draft and of all outtakes. The reference list is begun. The rereading will usually reveal any repeated strategy of conceptualization, style, sentence construction, or that favorite phrase that appears to distraction. (A search technique should be used to discover each instance, cutting all but the best appearance.) The author should make sure that the parts cohere. The introduction and the conclusion should correspond; lists that note five things should clearly contain five things, not four or six; requirements in one section should be the same requirements in another section; and the like.

If the author is at the beginning of a career, then she or he should be alert to the four marks of student writing[1]: The first mark is an overdeveloped literature review. Students use reviews

---

[1] These characteristics speak to power relations between the student author and the instructor evaluator.

to establish credibility; professionals use them to advance the argument. Literature reviews should connect the dots from the ongoing conversation to the writer's contribution with precision, not bulk. The second mark is an unwillingness to take responsibility for the argument. No idea is advanced without a citation. This strategy is fairly common in academic writing, and is often unmindfully supported by copy and journal editors (not any I know, of course). At some point, however, authors need to own up—others may have said the same, but I am saying it here. The third follows from the second in an excessive use of quotations. As an editor, my rule of thumb for an article is no more than two blocked quotes; none is best. Capture the idea in the flow of the argument. Readers don't read quotes. The last (four of four) is the heavy use of content notes where the argument is continued or enlarged (the error for senior authors is the content aside—how wonderfully complex my thinking is). Again, as an editor, I recommend no more than four content notes per article. The rest belong either in the text or in the cut file. (I mourn every bon mot I've cut from here.)

Dealing With Writer's Block

The last two steps of writing follow the completion of a reader's draft, and we will get to them. For the moment, let's consider when the author cannot get to that draft. There is nothing quite so discouraging as staring at the blank page and a blinking cursor waiting for inspiration to come, watching the hours and sometimes days of a carefully timed schedule slip by. The pressure builds, making it even harder to write. My first strategy is to recognize the block, forgive myself, and walk away.

In talking with members of our local author's support group (a great idea for those of you writing dissertations), many cases of writer's block come from a premature attempt to write. The author has the data and results or the field notes and analysis, and yet the argument will not come together. The problem seems to be the time needed to process the information. The mind has to catch up. The group's advice? Break away, go for a walk, pull weeds, or get a night's sleep; it'll be there after a bit. Staying glued to the page only increases anxiety. In difficult cases, shift media; make a model; do something focused on the work that is productive; perhaps, shift the focus to the block itself to understand the problem; write out this analysis just to start the writing process once more.

Other cases of writer's block are caused by a conflict in the writing. The author has something that presumably has to be written, and at the same time there is something that the author wants to write. The advice? Write what you have, not what you have to. That writing may never end up in the finished piece, but it also might form the basis of another text. At any rate, writing it out releases its hold on what has to be done.

In the worst case, the block is not a block but an absence of having something to say. Abandon the work and start again.

Manuscript Preparation

The next steps in professional writing start with the preparation of the manuscript for delivery into an extensive review process. Remember that the draft first has to be taken to the author's best effort at a reader's draft—an effort that usually takes three or more revisions.

Developing the Delivery Draft

That reader's draft is then released for local review by trusted colleagues or your writer's support group for the purpose of gathering the feedback that will direct the development of the content for the delivery draft. These reviews, when done right, can substantially increase the chances of publication, as nothing should be sent out that has not been professionally reviewed locally. But, reviews at this level have a couple of weaknesses: Good friends know how you think and talk and are often willing to fill in the holes in your argument. Such friends do not provide good reviews. Peers can react competitively or indifferently. Those peers do not provide good reviews. Evaluate the review and reviewer carefully. Once you have identified the people who do good work, keep them close. They are few.

Once the delivery draft content is secured, the manuscript has to be prepared for submission for outside review. It takes two to three days to properly prepare a journal manuscript for submission, and two weeks to a month for a book. The manuscript has to be made style perfect, following the journal or publisher requirements exactly. Editors often refuse to accept the manuscript otherwise. The task for most editors is to eliminate submissions; poorly prepared manuscripts simplify that task.

Some suggestions for the proper preparation of the manuscript include copyediting pages out of order and from the bottom up. Professional copy editors are talented and skilled people; we lesser souls have to disrupt ordinary reading to catch our own errors. Correlate citations with references—every citation has a corresponding reference and every reference a citation; make sure the dates agree. Check every reference. With a journal article, write the abstract and the key words. Finally, do a last rewrite on the introduction and conclusion, upload the draft, and click the submission button.

Revise and Resubmit

The author should be anticipating the revisions that will surely follow in the last phase of the writing process (four of four). Within the average revise-and-resubmit cycle, submissions undergo four to five revisions before acceptance. As an editor, I have never published a first draft because the reviews never supported that action. As a reviewer, I spend four to six hours on a review. I read the cited articles for their relevance to the argument, check all analyses, and work the argument for inconsistencies, faulty evidence, and unsupported conclusions. My job is to ensure that the work meets the high standards of quality of the journal. Authors appreciate the work but may not like the review.

For any author, the return of a review set that enters a finding of revise and resubmit is cause for celebration. That finding means that there were no fatal errors and that something of a path to publication has been established. The typical first reaction for the beginning author, however, is outrage at the ignorance or perfidy of the reviewers who obviously did not read what was clearly on the page. Let it all out; give voice to all that anger, recognizing that the revision will, nonetheless, follow.

My editor's advice to authors is to let the manuscript sit for a while to gather the necessary distance for a solid rewrite. Once a more objective view can be taken, the author should go back through each comment and consider what justifies it and whether the changes requested are appropriate. It is still the author's argument. The author has to decide whether to make the changes or to craft the argument for not making them. It has to be one or the other.

The cover letter for the resubmission will respond to each reviewer's note indicating the changes that have been made or the reasons why they have not. This letter is a device for educating the reviewers, who will review the manuscript again, and the editor, who will make the final decision.

This process is likely to cycle more than once. And, while it can fail, the typical outcome is a publication. When that acceptance letter arrives, it is likely that only the author will truly enjoy it; the bar has been raised for everyone else. The author should reread the work as a stranger noting strategies, successes, and failures; enter the publication data into her or his vita and bibliographic database; consider how the next manuscript can utilize the publication; and then get back to work. Tomorrow will be another day at the desk.

BACKGROUND PRACTICES: FOUNDATIONAL REVIEWS

In this last section, I would like to introduce a background practice that can provide a continuing foundation for a career of writing. This practice involves the construction of foundational reviews of the current and historical literature on a topic on which you wish to claim expert status. The term *foundational review* enters into a conversation already well versed in concepts of literature reviews and meta-analytic reviews. I hope to carve out space for a review of a third kind. In the following paragraphs, I will attempt to draw the distinctions among these three kinds of reviews and to begin to develop the unique value of the foundational sort.

The Garden-Variety Literature Reviews

The general consensus in the literature is that literature reviews are driven by and provide support for the problem at hand. In their analysis of 131 manuscript reviews for the *Journal of Business and Psychology*, Rogelberg, Adelman, and Askay (2009) note the primary complaint is the failure to integrate the literature review with the goals of the study. Rocco and Plakhotnik (2009) are equally definitive in declaring that "all empirical studies—qualitative, quantitative, or mixed methods—must be connected to literature or concepts that support the need for the study, be related to the study's purpose statement, and situate the study in terms of previous work" (p. 120). Kwan (2006), in her review of work on literature reviews, indicates that first and foremost the rhetorical purpose of the literature review is to justify one's research and to situate that research as a unique contribution to the field (pp. 31–32). Similar arguments can be found in Creswell (2003), Hart (2001), Landrum (2008), and Rudestam and Newton (2001), among others.

The typical literature review that we conduct, then, is focused, purposeful, and rhetorically charged within the limited scope of the task at hand. It is an efficient approach for writing a particular article, but it results in a view of the literature that is disconnected, disjointed, and denaturalized. It is analogous to attempting to understand a landscape through occasional glances out an airplane window or in the glamour shots of a calendar.

Meta-Analyses

More complex and historically deep reviews appear in the literature under the titles of *meta-analysis, meta-analytic review, longitudinal meta-analytic review, systematic literature review* (mostly outside of communication), *review article,* and *bibliographic analysis.* Meta-analysis enters the literature in the mid-'70s following the work of Gene Glass and Robert Rosenthal (Salwen, 2000), who independently developed the methods for combining separate statistical findings into a common conclusion. Meta-analysis has come to mean, for many, a test of the strength of the effect that has been found across multiple studies. Meta-analyses of these sorts take each finding at face value with no evaluation of method or design, presuming that those differences or errors will wash out in the mix (Franke, 1992).

As with most things in communication, the definition of meta-analysis has not stood still. In 1999, the then-titled *Critical Studies in Mass Communication* ran a review section on meta-analysis in critical work (e.g., Allen, 1999). In contemporary times, we find meta-analysis and meta-analytic review holding to the 1970s meaning but also referring to any review process that attempts to achieve a synthesis of knowledge (e.g., Josselson, 2006). The remaining terms apply to what algorithmic reviewers call *narrative meta-reviews.* While somewhat dismissive in use, it is a fair term in that discursive reviews' intent is to "tell the story" of what's out there in the literature. Much of what is told is about what's new and recent, and much is about the consilience of a claim.

Meta-analyses, although usually larger than the typical literature review, retain a topical and methodological focus. Size too is not all that impressive, ranging from a typical minimum of 25 to a typical maximum approaching 200. For example, Hetsroni's (2007a) review of 57 content analysis studies of prime-time network programming from 1962 to 2004 sets the boundary along topic (violence), method (content analysis), medium (television), and program type (prime-time). Boundary setting of this sort is considered good form for meta-analytic reviews (Kennedy, 2007). It is good form for a review journal article, but insufficient for the foundation of a career in scholarship.

Foundational Reviews

The proposed foundational reviews are different in breadth, historical depth, and, most certainly, scale from article and meta-analytic reviews. The differences in intent start right at the beginning with the scope of the project. As we have seen, most reviews—even large meta-analytic reviews—hone in on some topic-methodology combination. Foundational reviews take a more genre-based approach that greatly broadens the scope of the search. In taking a genre approach, foundational reviews allow the analyst to plot a much larger scholarly field of endeavor.

Breadth

When we couple Hetsroni's work on violence with his work on 25 content analyses of sexual content over three decades (Hetsroni, 2007b), we get to something closer to the approach I am espousing. In two studies, Hetsroni has assembled a resource that would allow him to be more knowledgeable about the genre of content analysis than most of us. We can presume that this foundation served him well in his own content analysis (Hetsroni, 2008), investigating the cultivation effect across topic (contrary to expectation, the effect varies).

The multiple researchers who produced the 82 content analysis studies reported by Hetsroni were not working in a professional vacuum. They were undoubtedly influenced by the entire stream of scholarly work on TV programming, its critical evaluation, and popular press comment that was appearing simultaneously with their work. Without any lessening of the importance of the meta-analytic review, such reviews must necessarily miss this larger picture. Foundational reviews are directed toward this larger view. They would be open to nearly anything connected to the constructs involved appearing in the scientific, scholarly, industry, and popular press as well as political action, congressional hearings, and governmental regulations. The sweep of the net is much wider.

Historical Depth

If breadth serves to distinguish the intentions of foundation reviews from those of most other reviews, its focus on historical depth serves to complete the separation. Anyone who regularly publishes is well aware of the so-called decade bias. The force of our scholarly culture is such that sources get old after 10 years, and with the exception of certain seminal works (e.g., Bandura, Ross, & Ross, 1963, for violence studies), a piece with all contemporary sources is rarely criticized on the grounds that the sources are too new, too untested. Meta-analytic reviews might reach back 25 years (e.g., Kinross, 2005), but 10 years is a favored span (e.g., Freimuth, Massett, & Meltzer, 2006; Trumbo, 2004).

There are good reasons in meta-analytic reviews for these limitations—technology changes, methodology changes—and there are bad ones as well: The work is too hard; nothing happened earlier anyway (see Petticrew & Gilbody, 2004). I would argue that going beyond the good reasons of meta-analytical reviews and reaching beyond changes in technology and methodology allow the character of the sustaining cultural argument to appear. My coauthor Janet Colvin and I (Anderson & Colvin, 2008a) would not have so clearly seen the sustaining argument of fear of the "Other" (including the child as Other) in media effects studies except that it is repeated over a dozen decades, multiple technologies, and different methodologies. Time, media, or method doesn't matter; the argument is sustained across all these changes (for the ancients' expression, see Plato's *Phaedrus*[2]).

Scale

The third distinguishing characteristic of foundational reviews is their scale—scale of the work and scale of the archive. In terms of the scale of the work, a foundational review can easily be a multiyear, multi-individual activity. Our effects team of five members has been at this work since 2002, and the work continues. It may well continue over a substantial portion of the careers of the team, even as members leave and come back to the effort.

The scale of the effects archive is impressive, at least to us. We are now approaching an archive of 1,500 items, with new additions coming in annually. As our historical work is

---

[2]http://classics.mit.edu/Plato/phaedrus.html. Accessed May 6, 2011.

mostly done, current additions happen with a few clicks of the mouse. The archive and its siblings are connected to an annual review of published works as demonstrated in Chapter 7. It is then simply a matter of sorting each article into its appropriate archive (mine are held as NVivo projects), coding the article, and making the bibliographic entry. I daresay that few approach the scale of material available in a moment's time.

Consequence of the Effort

Foundational reviews differ from literature and meta-analytic reviews in the intentions to accomplish a genre-based review that has substantial historical depth and reaches a notable scale of labor and size. These differences also produce differences in the complexity of analysis they make possible. As a postmodernist, I do not seek refuge in explanations based on the invisible hand of science or its progressive nature. Rather, I would hold that one cannot properly understand the course of, say, media effects research except that one sees it in light of the tensions of immigration that mark the first part of both the 20th and 21st centuries; the fear of totalitarian ideologies of the 1930s, the 1950s, the 1980s, and post-9/11; the collapse of behaviorism, suppression of critical theory, and subsequent rise of cognitivists protocols that greatly simplified the empirical analysis of media effects; the concentration of expertise directing the war effort of the 1940s; the subsequent federal funding and its hegemony of leadership; the paradigmatic change in the economy of scholarship with the explosions of new journals in the 1930s and again in the 2000s; the demonstrable, continuing, and outstanding political value of scapegoating the media; and on and on. Of course, all of this is more than you need to know to do the ordinary work of our journals, but it is inescapable learning that results from the practice of foundational reviews that adds incredible depth to problem analysis, study design, and one's conclusions.

DEVELOPING THE ARCHIVE

In mentoring graduate students and entering faculty, I have found that individuals carry over what might be gently called undergraduate habits of work, focused on the short term. Sources are collected but not archived; bibliographies are built, but the citations are not retained in an easily retrievable manner. The good practices of foundation literature reviews will support a successful career, as conducting foundation literature reviews is a career-directed rather than a project-directed activity. The current state of technology allows each scholar to appropriate libraries of source work that will support these long-term, career-developing activities. In the following sections, I list those practices and the techniques that I have found useful. I start with some preliminaries.

Electrons for Carbon

Without denying the pleasure of the physical text, carbon-based texts are not addressable or searchable and cannot be easily manipulated or metatagged. Addressability has to do with location of access. If the journal is in the office and the analyst is at home, the problem is obvious. Electronic copies can be placed on a restricted website (copyright provisions still prevail), which makes them available wherever one has Internet access. They can also be copied into an e-book or another player or kept on a flash memory drive, though these methods also require a physical presence. Searchability refers to the ability to search for strings of text in individual articles or whole archives. Most know how to search a PDF or Word document; some may not know that Windows allows the analyst to search sets of files in standard folders or the new Windows 7 "libraries" for particular text strings. The ability to manipulate texts is the key to effective coding, and the codes themselves become metatags that allow for rapid access to ideas and concepts in the literature.

The fullness of these advantages, however, is not realized unless the texts are in "live file" formats. Bitmapped or image files have addressability but nothing else. The work of building foundational archives makes the problem of image files real. The analyst gets caught in the current year embargo set by certain publishers, in the pre-1990 practice of storing image rather than live files of some journals and databases, and in the limited historical reach of online databases that forces one to the library, copy camera in hand. When presented with an image file, it is necessary to run the file through some process of character recognition. While there is free character recognition software available for downloading, I use what is touted as the industry standard, Nuance's OmniPage Pro.[3] This software has a very high success rate, offers multiple options for document formats and file types, and allows the analyst to retain graphics and to capture statistical tables in original format. My justification for its cost is that image files are often of poor quality, which increases the number of recognition errors that have to be hand corrected. That time sink is a motivation killer.

A Classification System

My archive contains over a couple of thousand source files representing journal articles, newspaper clippings, book chapters, and even entire books (out of copyright). Additions are made nearly every day. All of these sources have been catalogued in reference software (I use EndNote), which allows me to attach key words and to link the reference to the source file. A search for, say, *agenda setting* will pull up all the references that have those key words. The links will allow for ready access to the actual article. All of this work can be done in the time it takes to read the abstract.

That work, however, is not enough. I have found that one needs a systematic file naming protocol. I use three elements in every file name: first author, date of publication, and topical key word(s). A fourth element is used when the article presents some unique feature such as an unusual context, technology, or respondent group.

Those files are then further classified in a system of folders that have major headings— such as *theory*, *methodology*, *effects*, and *media literacy*—appropriate to the interests of the analyst. Those are further broken down by subtopic. It seems clear to me that I have reached the limits of this system. It has become too difficult to track files; too many

---

[3]It's expensive, but Nuance provides educational discounts and bundles. Call for the best price.

duplicate copies are required, and not enough information is available. I am now exploring file management software such as PowerDesk Pro 7, SuperCat, and M-Files. The goal is to do a small amount of work on the front end to save a lot of work at the project level.

Setting Domain Boundaries

What is the domain of media effects literature: violence, sex, body image, gender, campaigns, media literacy, agenda setting, or something else? What methodologies should it include? What manners of practice: science, criticism, journalism, or popular comment? I recommend casting a very wide net, at least in the beginning. As with qualitative analysis, the center will come into focus as the analyst gets experience with the texts. It is easy to pull the boundaries in but difficult to recognize when they are drawn too close.

I also recommend doing the historical work (described below) first. Early work has not differentiated itself into specialties. As new work comes in, it strives for legitimacy by making connections to existing work. Those connections are invaluable. In short, I recommend a grounded approach: Let the work define the archive.

Building the Archive

A foundational archive is composed of actual source material, not references to source material. The construction task is not advanced until the live file of the source resides in some addressable location. This requirement poses different challenges over the history of our scholarship. The contemporary challenge is that the field is held in over 200 different publications, which easily overwhelms the archivist unless a restricted search algorithm is used. The historical challenge is that there was no intact discipline of communication prior to the 1950s. Consequently, the work is held in education, English, speech, journalism, psychology, sociology, and now defunct offshoots like audiovisual instruction. Further, that work is held in physical copy, which itself is unevenly distributed across locales. The contemporary problem requires the archivist to determine which journals will form the basis of an electronic search. The historical problem requires the decision as to which institutional libraries one will be responsible for. The criterion in play is not the impossible dream of everything or the equally implausible dream of everything important; it is rather of simply enough—enough material that is accumulated in a realistic, consistent, and describably reliable manner.

At some point, the archive gets large enough that criticizing it for not having a particular journal or source appears more than foolish. At the same time, I hold to no purity of process and am opportunistic in adding sources outside these boundaries. The nice way to say this is that boundaries are in place, but they are permeable, though I promise no consistency in addressing other opportunities (and who said I was rigid?). Those boundaries are regularly reviewed, however, which is why I always consider the archive to be a work in progress. New journals come available; new editors change the character of old journals. Managing the archive keeps one exquisitely up to date.

Capturing the Wily Source

Perhaps it has something to do with my moral character, but historical rather than contemporary work has been much more fun. Part of the fun is in the discovery that disciplinary ideas that we hold so new and innovative have had long-standing precedents in a literature no longer addressed—the qualitative turn, for example, looks something like introspection; postmodernism is a lot like premodernism. The other part comes out of the tedious work of paging through dusty journals looking for traces and tracks of work in media. Finally finding something and then recognizing the source of some long-standing truism in media effects is an actual experience of Latour and Woolgar's (1986) construction of scientific facts in action.

But the fun comes at the expense of a lot of work, the first part of which is to investigate library holdings in the light of the most likely historical sources within the genre of choice. From there, it is a snowball process of using one source to find another. To manage this process, the archivist needs to negotiate with the library for a method that will allow physical access to the journals (paper and online indices are not much help in my experience), as well as allow the journals to be pulled and the articles to be copied. Articles should be copied by a camera in black-and-white mode and saved in a low-resolution file, using some form of a copy stand that will hold the text square to the camera frame.[4] A bit of investment in a squaring jig will save hours of optical character recognition (OCR) correction work later. An afternoon's work by two people might generate 20 to 30 sources. Preparing those JPEG image files for the OCR software led me to becoming a minor expert in Photoshop. Images had to be straightened and cropped, exposure had to be corrected, and the like. I found that it was faster to create an image for each page in Photoshop than to work around the spine in OCR or to reframe the camera shot each time (20 sources might be 400 pages). Fortunately, Photoshop can automate much of the work through action macros.

The tasks involved in capturing contemporary sources will depend on the subscriptions that a given library holds and how advanced its technology of delivery is as well as how accommodating the members of its interlibrary loan staff are. Again, involving library staff is an important part of the process. They are librarians: Finding stuff and making it available is what they do. The archivist just needs to be a priority in their work life.

CODING THE WORK

The creation of an extensive archive of original works has enduring value in and of itself. The greater payoff, however, comes from systematically addressing the aggregated content. It is one thing to serially read the literature but quite another to read that literature for the relationship among its elements. That sort of reading illuminates the lines of argument that constitute a domain of work and moves the practitioner to a higher level of expertise. The work also has very high publication value, but that is a secondary consideration here.

---

[4]Readily available, at the time of this writing, at about $170 plus shipping.

Approaches to Coding

Readers of this book should be overly familiar with coding. Suffice it to say at this point that I use a pragmatic approach that simply gets the job done. This approach begins with some a priori codes based on what the analyst knows of the literature and wishes to be able to document in the literature and couples that with a grounded approach that is open to what the literature holds. As I reported earlier, I code by paragraph and require that each paragraph have a code attached to it. One can also code by sentence or idea, but I found that sentence-level coding loses too much continuity and involves too much labor (just extracting the sentences takes enormous time), and the boundaries of an idea are too vague to provide a consistent coding entity. (Authors are also not consistent in holding to their own boundaries.) The paragraph seems to work well. It has clear textual markers (unlike sentences); it allows for continuity in reading; and requiring at least one code provides a check against coding while sleeping.

Software Support

As you know, I recommend one of the major qualitative data analysis (QDA) applications such as NVivo, ATLAS.ti, or Framework. Any will work about as well for text; they are all expensive, but it will amortize over a career.

The advantages to using a high-end QDA application are several: Each source can be entered into analysis as one unit of that analysis. The source can be globally coded with unit descriptors such as date of publication, genre, methodology, key words, and the like. It also maintains the original file identity (and link), thereby keeping the information provided by the naming protocol. All of that unit information is retained as the analyst parses the article into its components (introduction, problem, method, etc.) or codes. A unique advantage of the software is the ability to pull up all text fragments represented by a given code or component identifier (along with the unit information) to permit axial coding—the reduction of a fragment into subcodes—or to investigate the cultural or argument character of a particular textual component—the cultural work that a competent introduction accomplishes, for example. It also allows for comparison of common codes across the unit information such as by decade of appearance, genre of presentation, analytic methodology, or source of publication.

The analyst might also consider using one of the Internet-based concordance services. The particular value of using a computer-based concordancer is that the computer examines every word or phrase (using a sliding window) with none of the physical impairments or reading errors to which we humans are prone. Concordancers can also make their own contribution to a subsequent study, as Hakam (2009) has shown in her discourse and concordance analysis of the "cartoons controversy" in English-language Arab newspapers. When research is examined with a wider lens, the analyst can begin to ask the larger questions.

The Value of Coding

Coding extensively and repeatedly reviewing the coding process adds tremendous value to the archive, not to mention an advanced level of domain familiarity for the analyst.

For example, if I want to trace the moral justification for a concern with sexual content in the media, I can pull up all the sources in the archive that are coded by a key word denoting a sexual content focus and parse those sources into both introductions where the significance of the problem should be stated and implications and conclusions where the consequences for society should be located. (Note that I would have no interest in the findings or results, here.) I can then extract the lines of argument as they are presented over time, noting, for example, where arguments leave and enter the literature. "Science as Moralizing Agent" might be a provocative title for the resultant article. Let me show you what that might look like with just a couple of pages of work that I and my coauthors have extracted from the work of collecting, archiving, coding, and analyzing a foundational review of over 1,000 entries connected to media effects research.[5] This is a scholar's argument directed toward other scholars, but its purpose is to demonstrate the sort of argument that foundational reviews support.

AN EXAMPLE FROM THE MEDIA EFFECTS ARCHIVE

Whether you address the media effects literature from the first decade of the last century or the first decade of this century or, for that matter, any decade in between, you will find the same basic arguments being presented. There is always a smattering of positive articles, mostly touting the educational or instructional capabilities of the media, but some prosocial effects studies as well, often the product of a single author or small group of contributors. The great bulk of the literature, however, is negative. The authorship may be moralist, social activist, public intellectual, critic, or scientist, but the message of harm is the same.

The media can be theater, newspapers, gazettes, dime novels, nickelodeons, movies, radio, comic books, television, video or computer games, social networking sites, or whatever technology will next provide. The victims can be children, boys, girls, young men and women, immigrants, the masses, lower classes, the less educated, or of specified or hinted race and ethnicity but never, in our reading, the moralist, social activist, public intellectual, critic, or scientist (who all apparently are made of sterner stuff). The list is inclusive enough and historically deep enough that it is safe to say that every one of us has been seen as a potential victim and a person of concern at some time or station in our lives. The harm (in more or less historical order) can be an increase in crime (or more knowledgeable criminals); social, cultural, and economic exploitation; sustaining and expanding prejudice and stereotypes; moral decay of every sort; sexuality among young people; drinking; smoking; drugs; gambling; the critical impairments of class, race, and gender; and, of course, violence—in terrorist attacks, in school-ground massacres, on the streets, in their neighborhoods (and soon ours), on the playgrounds and sport fields, in school classrooms, in corridors, in lunchrooms, and in living rooms everywhere. In short, nearly every social and

---

[5]This section has been adapted from Anderson and Colvin (2010). The contribution of Janet Colvin to this section is greatly appreciated.

cultural disorder has been attributed, at least in some part, to the media, but the mainstay has been violence.

The attack on the media has been so broad, so persistent, and so diverse across approaches and lines of evidence that I and my coauthors have come to view it as an ideology in and of itself. It appears to be one that frames its own epistemological foundations and devises methodologies that produce the necessary outcomes (Grimes, Anderson, & Bergen, 2008). We have called the scientific approaches "symbolic science" (Anderson, Colvin, & Osmond, 2008), following Edelman's (1964, 1971) lead in his notion of symbolic politics. Just as symbolic politics gives the appearance of actual political redress, thereby calming social unrest, symbolic science provides an "answer" to some pressing social problem without requiring any actual social change or, equally important, making a terminal epistemological contribution. Symbolic politics allows each new generation of political operatives to proclaim its dedication to the people without threat to existing power structures. Symbolic science allows each new generation of social science practitioners a ready-made avenue of activity and recognition with little threat to those who will follow or to existing power structures.

Symbolic science is dismissible science as evidenced by the over 50 years of media violence research that has reached a consistent conclusion but resulted in no significant social policy either through legislation or regulation. It has worked hand in hand with symbolic politics, however, producing dozens of congressional hearings (Anderson et al., 2008). Dismissible science weakens a discipline. We need to discover the lines of argument that have fallen into symbolic science (or its larger cousin, symbolic scholarship) in order to strengthen the health of the discipline, its effectiveness with funding agencies, and its impact on society.

The presence of symbolic science is documented in historical work that reveals the repeated appearance of the same or similar arguments with only cosmetic changes in focal objects or methodologies. Our conclusions came out of a multiyear effort to build a historical and current document archive of effects research published in mainline scholarly and popular press. The archive, as it stands now, reaches back to the 1860s and ends with a system of automatic notifications as new entries are added to selected databases. The intent for this archive is not to have every publication but to have a sufficient and diverse number that the major themes of what is being written can be adequately characterized. A number of publications and papers have come out of this archive (Anderson, 2008a, 2008b; Anderson & Colvin, 2008a, 2008b), but we still consider it a work in progress.

The insights that were gained from this practice have led me to encourage any scholar—but particularly the entering scholar—who is developing a program of research to conduct this foundational historical work. This foundational work is quite different from the ordinary literature review that is rhetorically charged with advancing a particular position that will support a subsequent claim. A foundational review is a neutral, grounded approach that is directed toward illuminating the characteristics of scholarship's aggregated labor. Participation in the process allows the analyst to develop a depth and complexity of expertise within the genre of the review. The archive itself becomes the invaluable resource in the advancement of scholarship in the area.

CLOSING FOUNDATIONAL REVIEWS

I have positioned this discussion mostly on the practical side of foundational reviews, but there is also sound theory for advancing the practice coming from cultural studies and, most particularly, critical rhetorical theory and discourse analysis. Scholarly and scientific writing are both rhetorical structures and discursive forms that are located within cultural systems of power (for the philosophy of these lines of argument, see Fuller, 1997; Gross, 1990; Prelli, 1989; and Shapin, 1995). The cultural work accomplished and the value accrued are demonstrated across the breadth of examples of this sort of writing. One-off reading has its value when a particular problem has to be solved or an obvious hole in one's argument has to be patched, but it leads the reader to no sophistication as to why that problem exists or why the hole in one's own writing appears obvious. Reading and writing of that sort simply reproduces the cultural dynamics that allow us to believe we can safeguard the privileges of middle and upper America with no social disruption simply by changing the media.

A FINAL ETHICAL NOTE

The ethics of writing are the ethics of attribution and argument. Recognize what is yours and acknowledge all contributions from others. Be scrupulous in the use of evidence whether from the literature or from one's own data or scholarship. Maintain a modesty of claim that recognizes all of the temporizing and compromising that goes into this process of scholarship. Acknowledge the weaknesses and limitations of the evidence and the claim. Do not deceive yourself or others.

The science and scholarship of communication continues its fight for notice, legitimation, and a place at the table. I think that part of the strategy should be becoming better scholars and scientists and have offered much comment throughout the book on how we might accomplish those goals. It comes down to the slogan "Do good work." If we are to advance, that slogan has to mean "Do better work."

REFLECTIONS

What Are Some Points to Remember?

- Professional writing is an everyday activity that makes physical demands and requires material resources as well as protected time.
- Classroom writing ordinarily has little resemblance to professional writing practices.
- Professional writing requires careful attention to all aspects of the writing process.
- Foundational review is the regular practice of collecting, digitizing, cataloguing, and coding contemporary and historical materials on a common topic from a variety of literatures.
- The goal of the foundational review is to create a broad-spectrum resource for research and scholarship and to produce a command of the literature leading to personal mastery.

Why Does It Matter?

The transition from student to professional researcher or scholar is a major one. Student practices will not ordinarily support a career that demands a high level of writing and research skill.

What Else Could We Talk About?

From a postmodern point of view, research and scholarly writing is rhetorical rather than representational and more political than veridical. Literature reviews are a persuasive device intended to move the agenda of the researcher or scholar. There is no intention to consider all voices or all points of view in such reviews. Rather, they are the product of the intersection of the like-minded.

What Else Might Be Interesting to Read?

Garson, G. D. (2002). *Guide to writing empirical papers, theses, and dissertations*. New York: Marcel Dekker.
Wolcott, H. F. (2009). *Writing up qualitative research* (3rd ed.). Thousand Oaks, CA: Sage.

Appendix A

A Short History
of Media Innovations

INTRODUCTION

My work as an ethnographer often has me inside people's homes where I get to see first-hand how they live their lives (and to peek into the silverware drawer). One thing I have learned in that research is that there is a great deal of difference among us both in our media ecology and in our historical perspective toward media. I can assure you that your mediascape and your perspective is only one of many, just as mine is. It's easy to forget that and to presume that everyone has access to technology as we do (or don't). The next section is a 60-second media history in an attempt to bring us nearer to the same page. The history is important because we will study and draw conclusions about people whose own media environments and perspectives are scattered along this history. Not everyone has reached the 21st century.

This history was developed almost entirely by searching webpages. It is something any-one with a high-speed Internet connection could do over a long weekend. I have not included all of the sites I visited but offer references to some of the less obvious ones. I tend to order my use of sites by source, being more likely to use sites supported by universities, libraries, and museums, but there are some very dedicated professional and amateur his-torians out there whose passion is to make their knowledge available to us, and many of the corporations that appear in this history maintain a timeline of their activity. And, of course, there is always Wikipedia[1]—a self-organizing, self-correcting site in which all can participate.

Scholars don't trust the Internet much. It is so, well, unsupervised. So consider this an unauthorized or noncanonical history, but still one that does its appointed task very well. It is organized by time of first appearance of the medium. A particular entry may take us to the present. The next entry may take us back in history to pick up the next innovation. We start perhaps surprisingly with language.

---

[1]http://www.wikipedia.org/

LANGUAGE

Face-to-face, spoken language has been considered the foundational, nonmediated form of communication. It is contemporaneous, coconstructed, and mutually supervised. But, clearly, language is an intermediary between us and the material world and others, as well as a system of exchange of orientation and relationship. But language does far more in that, within discursive frameworks, it constitutes much of the social world in which we live as humans. Media studies cannot afford to ignore language or to consider it merely a translation problem.[2]

We are reasonably sure that language (an integrated system of signs and syntax as opposed to separate icons, symbols, and signals) was well established by 160,000 years ago, with the start of the migrations of *Homo sapiens* out of Africa,[3] although our material evidence of a language reaches back only 15,000 years at most. Recent estimates list 6,912 living languages residing in 94 language families.[4] About 40 of those languages constitute the majority of users with Mandarin, Spanish, and English being the top three in that order (yes, English is third). About 10% of the languages in use are nearing extinction. It is undoubtedly true that we have lost many languages and dialects (with the concomitant loss of the unique understanding that a language provides) through conquest (the U.S. government forbade the use of Native American languages in Indian schools out here in the West) and other forces of homogenization. We probably reached our maximum number some 8,000 years ago as human migration completed its epic journey throughout the planet.

TRANSPORTATION AND TRAVEL

We might not think of transportation and travel as communication media, but both move language, ideas, technology, and DNA back and forth along lines of migration, commerce, and conquest. Advanced methods of transportation (beyond bushwhacking and dragging your stuff behind you) developed about 75,000 years ago as hominid groups began their migrations across the continents. With the coalescence of migration groups into tribes and tribes into city-states, systems of roads developed in Egypt, Greece, Rome, and China starting about 6,000 years ago (and about 1,200 years ago in the southwestern United States). These roads were among the first network systems. Most of our networking ideas derive from transportation processes. For example, the current hot idea of convergence of digital technologies was equally hot in the 1890s, only authors were talking about the convergence of railways, highways, and farm-to-market roads into a single transportation system.

Six thousand years ago, telecommunication over any distance beyond the carry of sound and the line of sight depended on the ability to physically move the body of the person who would personally deliver a message (no writing and no paper existed as of yet). Every

---

[2]The problems of the Western alphabet and the hegemony of English on the Internet demonstrate this importance.

[3]http://www.bradshawfoundation.com/journey/timeline.swf (a very cool website).

[4]http://www.ethnologue.com. Accessed April 28, 2011.

empire's systems of roads moved messages. (Low speed was a runner; high speed a horseback rider.) The Great Wall of China was as much a communication device as a defensive work. Runners would relay between guard stations, passing the message between them. They memorized each step so that they could run the route—stairs and all—in total darkness. The last well-publicized system of relay was the Pony Express, which ended in 1861. Today, the U.S. postal system physically transports 177 billion pieces of mail annually. And we still communicate through travel; no medium delivers the message like being there.

VISUAL COMMUNICATION I

Pictographs (icons and symbols painted onto rock) and petrographs (the same incised into rock) appeared 50,000 years ago in Africa, Australia, and Europe. Visual communication is probably the start of all media as we typically use the term. The "message" was asynchronous, was separately produced and interpreted, could be delivered to many, and did not need the presence of the author or the author's delegate. The reader's relationship with the message could be unsupervised and simply between the symbol and the reader. It will be a number of centuries before major changes in visual communication technology appear.

FROM WRITING TO PRINT

Writing appeared as a developed craft 5,500 years ago in Pakistan, 5,200 years ago in Sumeria, 3,200 years ago in China, and 2,500 years ago in Mexico. The writing that survived from those times was inscribed on metal, rock, and clay tablets. It was not a very handy distribution system (consider a 10-pound grocery list) until the invention of paper 2,700 years ago as papyrus in Egypt, 2,200 years ago as parchment and vellum (animal skins) around Persia, and pulp paper 1,900 years ago in China. Books as we know them (rectangular with pages) depend on parchment and pulp paper (papyrus is too brittle to turn as a page and is used as a scroll) and so are about 2,100 years old.

With the inventions of writing and paper, messages could be written out and delivered accurately by courier or carrier pigeon, or even tied to an arrow. Libraries developed; knowledge could be preserved beyond its endless retelling around the campfire. But it was all copied by hand (a thriving industry for 4,500 years). The system of hand copying on parchment and vellum (both considered sacred media to paper's vulgarity) would continue in Europe well beyond paper's introduction in the 12th century. (The irony of this preservation is that the academy is now desperately hanging on to paper as sacred to digital's vulgarity.) Hand copying took months, even years, for a large book like the Christian Bible. A book was a rare commodity.

Print

Printed books would change all that. Printed books appeared in China in the 9th century with each page separately carved on a type plate of wood or clay. It was not the final innovation of movable type, but still it was the invention of mechanical reproduction (as well as the critical rejection of mechanical reproduction because it replaced artistic calligraphy) and the glimmer of mass media sparkles. The Chinese had figured out movable clay type by 1041, four hundred years before Gutenberg.[5] By 1450, Gutenberg, however, had put it all together in a system of printing (convergence again) with movable type, a press, and a process. His shop was able to produce 180 bibles between 1452 and 1455, less time than the typical hand inking of a single copy. In 25 years, the press had spread all throughout Europe and Great Britain, producing an estimated 35,000 titles and 20 million copies.[6] Curators at the Harry Ransom Center (which owns a Gutenberg Bible) state that "the rapid spread of knowledge made possible by Gutenberg's printing press contributed to the Renaissance, the Scientific Revolution, and the Protestant Reformation."[7] Now there is a media effect for you.

Print continued to evolve with better fonts, paper, and inks, and added illustrations in engraving, color, and lithography (the modern—1798—petrograph). Illustrated magazines were a great success in the 19th century with circulations that many contemporary magazines would envy (P. J. Anderson, 1991). The Linotype automated linecasting from setting each type piece in a line of type (hence *Linotype* machine) by hand to punching keys on a keyboard. Four-color rotary presses and the computer bring us to the present day.

Newspapers and Serials

The printing press made possible the distribution of local information in a timely fashion without having to shout it from a tower or tell it to every passing person. These early broadsides, pamphlets, and miscellanies slowly evolved into something recognizable as the newspapers, magazines, and newsletters of today.

The first daily newspaper, *The Daily Courant*, appeared in London in 1702. Newspapers created the fourth estate of the realm (following the clergy, nobility, and the people; the royal person owned all four estates) and a true political force. The rise of the middle class brought a market with time, means, and literacy. When the technology of the cylinder press appeared, a print entity could be produced that was profitable at the price of a penny—hence, the penny press. My colleague, Glen Feighery, tells me that it was Ben Day's creation of the news story that produced the fusion of technology, product, and market that exploded into the newspaper. There were an estimated 7,000 independent newspapers by 1880.[8] From that high point, the number of newspapers and their relative readership has gone into a long, slow decline under the relentless competition of first broadcasting and then the Internet. But still somewhere around 40 million people in the United States have a newspaper on their front porch every weekday morning, though that figure is declining at about 8% per year.

---

[5]Once again, this demonstrates that history belongs to the people who write it.

[6]http://communication.ucsd.edu/bjones/Books/printech.html. Accessed February 13, 2006.

[7]http://www.hrc.utexas.edu/exhibitions/permanent/gutenberg/html/5.html. Accessed February 13, 2006.

[8]http://www.nyu.edu/classes/stephens/Collier%27s%20page.htm. Accessed April 14, 2011.

Illustrated miscellanies and news joined together to form the popular magazine. Magazines were first known according to their editors, essayists, and engravers. It was nearly a personal archive. The industrial character of today's large-circulation (1 million or more) magazines (anonymous writing in a style set by the genre's voice) arrived a hundred years later in the mid-1800s with the technology and audience of the mass market. Mass-market magazines with titles like *Life, Look,* and *The Saturday Evening Post* grew until the end of World War II, reaching circulations in the 8 million–10 million range. Today's large-circulation magazines are half that, although *Reader's Digest* tops 11 million, with *TV Guide* close on its heels.[9]

VISUAL COMMUNICATION II

The history of the visual that started 50,000 years ago with pictographs takes us through painting, perspective, representation, narrative, engraving, and lithography to photography. Photography started its modern history in 1800, reached the Kodak camera that brought photography to nearly everyone in 1888, brought in Kodachrome color film in 1936 (which exited in 2010), and arrived at the first digital cameras in 1991. Ten years later, the camera cell phone was introduced in the United States, and now estimates set camera phone sales at 1.1 billion sets for 2011 alone.[10]

TELEPHONY

The prehistory of the camera cell phone started in 1830 when Joseph Henry rang a bell from over a mile away by sending an electrical current to activate an electromagnet that moved the bell's striker. His demonstration paved the way for the device that has governed the lives of schoolchildren ever since. Six years later, Samuel Morse had developed an entire telegraph system based on Henry's demonstration by which an operator at one end of a wire could activate an electromagnet at the other end of the wire to send a message letter by letter in his namesake code to be decoded by a listening operator.

Telegraph

The idea of a telegraph system had been around for several thousand years in the form of beacon fires and simple codes to increase their information capacity (remember in Paul Revere's ride, it was "one if by land, and two if by sea"). These systems were limited by line of sight, strength of the signal (light energy decreases by the square of the distance), and complexity of the message (what if they weren't coming until tomorrow?),

---

[9]*AARP Bulletin* is often listed as the largest-circulation magazine at 21 million recipients, but it is a benefit of membership rather than a direct purchase. Given the changing U.S. demographics, that number should grow.

[10]http://www.mobiledia.com/news/86251.html. Accessed April 12, 2011.

so Morse's invention should have been well received. It was not. It took eight years to get to the historic message of "what hath God wrought" that demonstrated its value. The transcontinental telegraph line was completed in 1861, playing its part in ending the Pony Express the same year. From 1861 to 1877, the telegraph was the only method of moving messages across the continent in less than a month (the Pony Express had averaged 10 days).

Telephone

The telegraph's sole ownership of telecommunication ended on March 10, 1876, when Alexander Graham Bell rang up his assistant, so to speak. Compared to the telegraph, the telephone was an instant hit with the construction of lines beginning the next year. In the first few years, subscribers leased two phones and strung their own wire between them—an advanced tin can system. But by the end of the 1890s, the system we know as the telephone was materially in place. Bell's invention became AT&T, *the* telephone company until his patents expired in 1894. By then, Bell systems were in place in every major city, and competitors were left with the much less profitable small towns. AT&T went on to become *the* long distance company—a government-regulated monopoly in 1913. Its slogan was "One System, One Policy, Universal Service." It held true to that slogan for another 71 years until the federal government forced the divestiture of the local telephone service and opened up long distance competition in 1984. AT&T's principle of universal service created a telephone system like no other in the world. Seventy percent of U.S. households were reached by 1955, a remarkable interlacing of copper wire. It established the idea that one could reach anyone from anywhere. No other country had that amount of infrastructure or that level of service.

Cellular Service

AT&T proposed a commercial cellular telephone service for the United States in the late 1940s. It took the Federal Communications Commission another 35 years before it would authorize that use of the radio spectrum in 1982. But the installed copper infrastructure that provided such high service also slowed the advance of the cell phone. It would be another 12 years before the cell phone system as we know it today was in place. Lagging far behind Europe (where in some countries one had to go to the post office to make a long distance call over landlines), U.S. cell phone penetration did not top 50% until 2001, and then only in major cities. Cell phone service now is available to the majority of the U.S. population but not to its landmass. In the cities, however, the cell phone has brought us the concept of universal (and constant) connectivity. It is also the most successful example of convergence as smart phones bring together text, photography, music, the web, digital gaming, video programming, GPS, and the computer all in one candy-bar format. The cell is the last thing off as we board the plane and the first thing on when we land. It also generates the wonderful sounds of a $4 billion business in ringtones. How we got to those ringtones starts below.

SOUND RECORDINGS

Sound recording began with Thomas Edison's invention of the phonograph in 1877. He recorded on cylinders, not the disks that were invented by Emile Berliner for his own gramophone. Edison and Berliner fought for supremacy of recording format until Edison conceded in 1913. Recording times were short—under 10 minutes—so "albums" of recorded disks were produced to record longer works. These early works were all acoustic recordings using sound energy to drive the recording stylus. Electronic recordings could have started with the telephone. The telephone demonstrated that sound energy could be changed into an analogue of electrical energy, which then could be distributed by wire. But it was 50 years after Bell's invention when electronic sound recordings were first introduced by Bell Laboratories (1925). Elevator music debuted in 1931.

We march on through the long-playing (LP) record, which changed the concept of an album to a single record with multiple tracks, to the rebirth of the single in the 45, to eight-track and cassette tapes, to the CD and MP3 players. It is the last of that list that radically changed the mediascape of recorded music. Music is now available in huge quantity and is entirely portable, and its presentation is completely under the user's control. Apple's iPod sold its billionth download in the first quarter of 2006.

BROADCASTING

Radio first developed as a wireless telegraph capable of one-way transmission of Morse code. A patent was granted to Guglielmo Marconi in 1897. In 1906, Reginald Fessenden brought us AM (amplitude-modulated) radio (appropriately, the current haven of talk radio) that could carry all forms of sound wirelessly and laid the foundation for the mediascape of broadcasting. Fessenden's work made two-way voice transmission possible, thereby developing radio telephony. His work also laid the foundation for broadcasting—the one-to-many delivery of a radio signal. There was no business plan for such a process, however (technology advances when it can extract value from a market). Broadcasting started out with the very practical task of keeping contact with ships at sea. But there were innovators, tinkers, and even professors who were developing a different vision when World War I intervened. The Great War forced the merger of radio patents, which became the basis for the Radio Corporation of America—the equipment marketing arm of General Electric and Westinghouse. The period between 1919 (civilian broadcasting again permitted) and 1927 (passage of the Radio Act of 1927) is usually marked as chaotic by the history books as rogue broadcasters changed power, frequency, and location at will, thereby making the service uncertain for everyone.

But during this period, the business plan of commercial broadcasting developed. When the controlling corporations saw they could make money, stabilizing regulation soon followed. The growth of radio was phenomenal. From a nearly dead start in 1922 (400,000 sets), there were over 500 commercial stations and 33 million sets in use by 1933—in perhaps the deepest moments of the Great Depression. Local performers gave way to network programming, and the radio drama, comedy show, and music program all developed as entertainment formats. Radio became the premier mass medium in the home (or at least the urban, electrified home; only 10% of rural homes had electricity) and was beginning to challenge the motion picture as the supreme entertainment mass medium. It was not to last long.

VISUAL COMMUNICATION III

The systematic study of our perception of motion began in the early 1800s.[11] By 1830, Belgian physicist Joseph Plateau developed an instrument he called a "phenakistoscope" by which an illusion of continuous motion could be achieved by viewing revolving still pictures through a slit. A number of other devices followed (zoetrope, flip books, and peep show flip card devices, for example). (This led to experiments of filming motion through the use of multiple cameras as in the work of Eadweard Muybridge, ca.1888). Multiple cameras were used because early photography made use of glass plates as the backing for the photosensitive material—not the sort of material that one rapidly advances through a camera frame. Flexible celluloid film sheets and then roll film became widely available by 1890, which made possible the invention of the portable motion picture camera and the theatrical motion picture projector by Lumière (attributed as well to Edison and several others).

From the Motion Picture to Television

By 1896, the motion picture industry was firmly established. The 1920s brought us the Hays Office (industry self-censorship), early color films, and synchronized sound. The 1930s saw the start of animation, the success of Mae West, and the introduction of television. World War II slowed this march of technology, and the Federal Communications Commission preserved cinema's dominance until it got television color standards straight in the early 1950s.

From our place in the 21st century, it is a little difficult to understand the scope of the motion picture in American life during its two-decade span of supremacy (1928–1948). In 1940, the U.S. population was 132 million (Table A.1 presents the figures for the first five decades of the 20th century).

Table A.1 Total U.S. Population for the Decades 1910–1950

Year	1910	1920	1930	1940	1950
Total population	92,407,000	106,461,000	123,077,000	131,954,000	151,235,000

---

[11]This perception is commonly called the "persistence of vision," as if it were a retinal process. More likely, it is a perceptual process of making sense out of images that we continue to call the persistence of vision (J. Anderson & B. Anderson, 1993; neither of these authors is the author of this book).

During that time, more than 80 million tickets to a motion picture theater were being sold each week. More than 500 feature films were being produced each year, along with cartoons, Movietone News (movie theaters were the only source of this news form now common in our homes), and other short features. In many towns, Wednesday night was giveaway night when you could get free dishes or glassware with your 35- to 50-cent ticket. Going to the movies twice a week was common among the hip crowd, and for many, it was the dating scene.

As is the case each time a medium gains wide popularity (Grimes, Anderson, & Bergen, 2009), scholars and researchers were gravely concerned. Richard Fowler expressed those concerns in the 1938 *Journal of Applied Sociology*:

> Possessed of an overwhelming desire to substitute the fascinating world of make-believe for the detested school work in which she was failing because of refusing to apply herself to the task of mastering it, she left home each morning with money for her lunch, went down town and spent the day and her lunch money in the motion picture theaters, and returned home when school was out in the afternoon. An attendance officer found her in a theater on Main Street and she was taken to school where she remains only because she knows she has to.
>
> The unnatural excitement to which a girl who attends many motion picture shows is subjected, tends to make school seem an uninteresting place and studying an irksome task, and so leads to loss of interest in school and truancy. After a girl has received a wrong conception of life and love, it is but a step to where she is beyond the control of her parents, and unless someone intervenes the next turn in the path will almost inevitably lead her into immorality. (p. 83)

By the mid-1960s, the movie industry was broadly transformed through competition with television and federal antitrust actions. In sheer numbers, television asserted its primacy in the field of the visual narrative (and became the center of scholarly concern). Television moved forward with color surpassing monochrome sets by 1974 and two years later with the introduction of VHS tape recorders.

Beyond Television

In the last 20 years, we have seen the transition to cable and satellite delivery systems (to its current combined 87% of the market, a level that allows for specialized and commercial-free content), high-quality sound systems (video receivers), big-screen and then flat-screen television sets, the introduction of the DVD (both playback and recorders), digital video recorders with full-time shifting services, on-demand programming, and recently 3-D TV. At the 2006 Oscars, the president of the Academy of Motion Picture Arts and Sciences pleaded on television (ironically) for us to go back to watching movies in the theater.

Many of us are going to a theater of sorts, but not necessarily as audience members. We now go to websites such as YouTube.com as producers of original videos. YouTube.com, initiated in February 2005, now claims the availability of over 100 million videos (growing daily), the more popular of which play to audiences in the hundreds of thousands. At such sites, technology is moving to the final stages of media democratization in which the entire process is in the hands of those of even modest means who choose to use it. YouTube.com joins such sites as betarecords.com (for original music), wikipedia.org (conventionalized knowledge information), craigslist.org (local information and classifieds), and drudgereport .com (news and commentary) to bypass the high barriers of entry that have traditionally marked the production of and access to mediated content. The *Daily Mail* reported in 2006, that in Great Britain Internet use had surpassed television as the most used medium by adults and that in 2011 72% of British children under age 5 used the Internet daily.[12] It took less than 12 years from the start of the World Wide Web for the Internet to reach this level of presence in our lives.

COMPUTING

In 1981, IBM began delivering a device called the personal computer (PC).[13] It was the end of a remarkable history of innovation starting with the invention of the transistor at Bell Labs in 1947. In the intervening 34 years, all of the components of the personal computer from processing to memory to operating systems to disk storage and in/out devices were developed or adapted. It was also the beginning of a revolution in the workplace and in commerce that was accomplished in less than a decade. No company of any size does its business today without the computer.

The original IBM PC was a thousand times slower than the one I am keyboarding on, had a-thousand-times-a-thousand less memory and storage, and yet would type this page equally as well. The tremendous change in the capacity of the PC was driven increasingly by the requirement of the manipulation of graphics. From the graphical users interface of Windows 3.1 (1992) to the multicore multimedia machines of the mid-2000s, the modern computer has moved us closer and closer to the complete convergence of the media. At the present, for a moderate but growing number of households,[14] movies, video, music, games, media production, and personal communication can all be handled at one place and distributed to a home theater, desktop, laptop, PDA, iPod, or cell phone. This is the avant-garde technology of the present and may become the common place of the future, more likely now that Amazon. com, Google, and other major players have entered the convergence arena.

One cannot leave the history of computing without acknowledging the impact of the network. From the World Wide Web, to the proprietary networks of global corporations, to

---

[12]http://www.dailymail.co.uk/sciencetech/article-1361806/Majority-children-young-FIVE-use-internet-day.html. Accessed April 14, 2011.

[13]There were several other innovators in computing besides IBM, but the winner writes the history. And what about Apple? Apple could have held the market position in this history, but it made two significant errors: It overpriced its products, and it chose to keep its technology proprietary. IBM had a solid understanding of the business market, something Apple lacked, but under antitrust scrutiny from 1952 to 1982 had little choice but to opt for open architecture. Apple has less than 4% of the installed base, and IBM sold its PC business in 2005.

[14]This sort of convergence starts with a high-speed Internet connection available in about 65% of U.S. homes (about 30% have no Internet access). It then depends on advanced computer and distribution technologies that have current sales of fewer than a million units. These nested requirements suggest that, as of this writing, fewer than 10,000,000 homes would have the full reach of this capability. (See Digital Nation, 2010, www.ntia.doc.gov/reports/2010/NTIA_internet_use_report_Feb2010.pdf, and also the next footnote).

the university network upon which I teach my classes, to my very own home network, which distributes computing all through my house, the network changed nearly everything. And the liberation of the network from its copper tethers changed nearly everything again.

DENSITY AND DIVERSITY

Much of what we understand to be part of the current mediascape—that ecology of technology, content, and consumers—is less than 10 years old, and very little of it is more than 25 (see Table A.2).

Table A.2   Technology in 1984

- No fancy phones or cheap long distance. The effects of the Bell system divestiture (1982–1984) had not reached the consumer in most markets of 1984. It was still the good old telephone with long distance charges in dollars rather than pennies.
- No cell phones (service was approved in 1982 but took another 12 years to build).
- No home PC. The IBM PC was introduced in 1981, but it was almost entirely a business market. Very few homes would have one (I got mine in 1986; a Wang at that). The Mac came out in 1984, and Windows 3.01 (the first Windows system that actually worked—sort of) appeared in 1988. The IBM laptop would not come out until 1986. The laptop market awaited the color screen (c. 1991).
- No CD libraries. CDs in their current configuration were introduced in 1985 (only about 3 million sets sold). Only early adopters would have them; eight-track was still around.
- No BlackBerry. PDAs didn't appear as a market until 1992 (and would then be replaced by digital cell phones).
- No mega-cable (deregulation came in the 1984 cable act); high-end service would top out at 30 channels or so; most would have locals and 10 others.
- No fiber-optic cable (the first feed was in 1980, but the technical issues were not fully solved until the mid-'90s).
- No digital cable (the first feed was in 1994; fiber-optic and digital would converge in the mid-1990s).
- No small dish satellite service (this came online in 1990–1996).
- No MP3s (until 1989–1995) so no Napster, iPod, or peer-to-peer downloading.
- No video files either.
- No World Wide Web to do it with anyway (1992 start-up).
- No e-mail for the common folk (CompuServe started the first commercial e-mail service in 1989).
- No Google, AOL (1993), Hotmail, Netscape, Internet Explorer, or any other commercial interface (Mosaic debuted in 1993).
- No websites, social networking sites, or blogs, of course.
- No DVDs (until 1996).
- No digital cameras (until 1994) or camera cell phones (until 2001).
- No JPEG file protocol to pass the pictures around (until 1994). You would use CompuServe's GIF protocol if you were a power user.
- No digital cell phones (until 1991–1993).
- No LCD or plasma color screens (until 1991 and 1999, respectively).
- No GPS (in 1989 the final satellite went up).
- No DVRs (TiVo® and similar; until 2000).

Some of it may have the same name, but television today, for example, resembles little of television 30 years ago. It would be like comparing the original Pong game (1972) to the complex and online World of Warcraft game of today. The technology, content, and consumer have all changed.

Further, not all of us reside in the same place in the mediascape. We do not all have access to multiple channels of content—about 45 million are limited to broadcast signals only—and a very few of us (6 million or so) have no television at all. About a third of us do not have personal computers or cell phones (and many with cell phones are not active users). Most of us do not have PDAs or digital music players[15]; fewer than 2 million subscribe to TiVo® even though it is a highly recognizable name. A little more than half of us have DVD players, but most of us do not have a flat-screen television (as of this writing; CRTs will virtually disappear in 10 years or so) and fewer still have full HD television capability. Further, these differences cut across race, ethnicity, and economic class in surprising ways. White and rich are not always at the top of the list.

As a media scholar, I am charged with knowing as much as I can about the current mediascape. In practice, I am a power user in computers and their task-based applications, but a rank newbie in cell phone and text messaging communication as well as video and computer gaming (though a whiz at spider solitaire). The cautionary tale, then, is not to take your own situation as the basis for what is generally true. It is a common error for media scholars and students alike to extrapolate from themselves to the lives of others. The mediascape is multiple, and, across the world, people live all along the timeline of its history.

---

[15]Researchers have to be very careful not to confuse market buzz with market facts. For example, the iPod accounts for the majority of all digital music players (hard and flash drive), but fewer than 30 million had been sold worldwide by the end of 2005—an outstanding success no doubt, but not yet commonplace. In the first quarter of 2006, however, Apple shipped over 14 million iPods. Change can be very fast.

Appendix B
One Hundred Studies

Andersen, P. A., Buller, D. B., Voeks, J. H., Walkosz, B. J., Scott, M. D., Cutter, G. R., et al. (2008). Testing the long-term effects of the Go Sun Smart worksite health communication campaign: A group-randomized experimental study. *Journal of Communication, 58*, 447–471.

Andrejevic, M. (2006). The discipline of watching: Detection, risk, and lateral surveillance. *Critical Studies in Media Communication, 23*, 391–407.

Angelini, J. R. (2008). Television sports and athlete sex: Looking at the differences in watching male and female athletes. *Journal of Broadcasting & Electronic Media, 52*, 16–32.

Appel, M. (2008). Fictional narratives cultivate just-world beliefs. *Journal of Communication, 58*, 62–83.

Beaudoin, C. E. (2007). Media effects on public safety following a natural disaster: Testing lagged dependent variable models. *Journalism & Mass Communication Quarterly, 84*, 695–712.

Behm-Morawitz, E., & Mastro, D. E. (2008). Mean girls? The influence of gender portrayals in teen movies on emerging adults' gender-based attitudes and beliefs. *Journalism & Mass Communication Quarterly, 85*, 131–146.

Bennett, W. L. (2007). Relief in hard times: A defense of Jon Stewart's comedy in an age of cynicism. *Critical Studies in Media Communication, 24*(3), 278–283.

Besley, J. C. (2008). Media use and human values. *Journalism & Mass Communication Quarterly, 85*, 311–330.

Bilandzic, H., & Busselle, R. W. (2008). Transportation and transportability in the cultivation of genre-consistent attitudes and estimates. *Journal of Communication, 58*, 508–529.

Billings, A. C., Brown, C. L., Crout, J. H., McKenna, K. E., Rice, B. A., Timanus, M. E., et al. (2008). The games through the NBC lens: Gender, ethnic, and national equity in the 2006 Torino Winter Olympics. *Journal of Broadcasting & Electronic Media, 52*, 215–230.

Bucy, E. P., & Grabe, M. E. (2007). Taking television seriously: A sound and image bite analysis of presidential campaign coverage, 1992–2004. *Journal of Communication, 57*, 652–675.

Butterworth, M. L. (2007). Race in "The Race": Mark McGwire, Sammy Sosa, and heroic constructions of Whiteness. *Critical Studies in Media Communication, 24*, 228–244.

Carlyle, K. E., Slater, M. D., & Chakroff, J. L. (2008). Newspaper coverage of intimate partner violence: Skewing representations of risk. *Journal of Communication, 58*, 168–186.

Carter, E. L. (2008). Reclaiming copyright from privacy: Public interest in use of unpublished materials. *Journalism & Mass Communication Quarterly, 85*, 417–434.

Chia, S. C. (2007). Third-person perceptions about idealized body image and weight-loss behavior. *Journalism & Mass Communication Quarterly, 84*, 677–694.

Cho, H., & Boster, F. J. (2008). Effects of gain versus loss frame antidrug ads on adolescents. *Journal of Communication, 58,* 428–446.

Coe, K., Tewksbury, D., Bond, B. J., Drogos, K. L., Porter, R. W., Yahn, A., et al. (2008). Hostile news: Partisan use and perceptions of cable news programming. *Journal of Communication, 58,* 201–219.

Cohen, J. (2008). What I watch and who I am: National pride and the viewing of local and foreign television in Israel. *Journal of Communication, 58,* 149–167.

Coyne, S. M., & Whitehead, E. (2008). Indirect aggression in animated Disney films. *Journal of Communication, 58,* 382–395.

Cuklanz, L. M., & Moorti, S. (2006). Television's "new" feminism: Prime-time representations of women and victimization. *Critical Studies in Media Communication, 23,* 302–321.

Dillard, J. P., Weber, K. M., & Vail, R. G. (2007). The relationship between the perceived and actual effectiveness of persuasive messages: A meta-analysis with implications for formative campaign research. *Journal of Communication, 57,* 613–631.

Dixon, T. L. (2008a). Crime news and racialized beliefs: Understanding the relationship between local news viewing and perceptions of African Americans and crime. *Journal of Communication, 58,* 106–125.

Dixon, T. L. (2008b). Network news and racial beliefs: Exploring the connection between national television news exposure and stereotypical perceptions of African Americans. *Journal of Communication, 58,* 321–337.

Durham, F. D. (2007). Framing the state in globalization: The *Financial Times*' coverage of the 1997 Thai currency crisis. *Critical Studies in Media Communication, 24,* 57–76.

Elenbaas, M., & de Vreese, C. H. (2008). The effects of strategic news on political cynicism and vote choice among young voters. *Journal of Communication, 58,* 550–567.

Eyal, K., & Kunkel, D. (2008). The effects of sex in television drama shows on emerging adults' sexual attitudes and moral judgments. *Journal of Broadcasting & Electronic Media, 52,* 161–181.

Fahey, A. C. (2007). French and feminine: Hegemonic masculinity and the emasculation of John Kerry in the 2004 presidential race. *Critical Studies in Media Communication, 24,* 132–150.

Frosh, P. (2006). Telling presences: Witnessing, mass media, and the imagined lives of strangers. *Critical Studies in Media Communication, 23,* 265–284.

Gade, P. J. (2008). Journalism guardians in a time of great change: Newspaper editors' perceived influence in integrated news organizations. *Journalism & Mass Communication Quarterly, 85,* 371–392.

Glascock, J. (2008). Direct and indirect aggression on prime-time network television. *Journal of Broadcasting & Electronic Media, 52,* 268–281.

Goodman, J. R., Morris, J. D., & Sutherland, J. C. (2008). Is beauty a joy forever? Young women's emotional responses to varying types of beautiful advertising models. *Journalism & Mass Communication Quarterly, 85,* 147–168.

Graf, J., & Aday, S. (2008). Selective attention to online political information. *Journal of Broadcasting & Electronic Media, 52,* 86–100.

Groshek, J. (2008). Homogenous agendas, disparate frames: CNN and CNN international coverage online. *Journal of Broadcasting & Electronic Media, 52,* 52–68.

Hennessy, M., Bleakley, A., Busse, P., & Fishbein, M. (2008). What is the appropriate regulatory response to wardrobe malfunctions: Fining stations for television sex and violence. *Journal of Broadcasting & Electronic Media, 52,* 387–407.

Hess, A. (2007). "You don't play, you volunteer": Narrative public memory construction in *Medal of Honor: Rising Sun. Critical Studies in Media Communication, 24,* 339–356.

Hindman, D. B., & Wiegand, K. (2008). The Big Three's prime-time decline: A technological and social context. *Journal of Broadcasting & Electronic Media, 52,* 119–135.

Hoffner, C. A., Levine, K. J., & Toohey, R. A. (2008). Socialization to work in late adolescence: The role of television and family. *Journal of Broadcasting & Electronic Media, 52*, 282–302.

Hollander, B. A. (2008). Tuning out or tuning elsewhere? Partisanship, polarization, and media migration from 1998 to 2006. *Journalism & Mass Communication Quarterly, 85*, 23–40.

Housel, T. H. (2007). Australian nationalism and globalization: Narratives of the nation in the 2000 Sydney Olympics' Opening Ceremony. *Critical Studies in Media Communication, 24*, 446–461.

Jackson, C., Brown, J. D., & Pardun, C. J. (2008). A TV in the bedroom: Implications for viewing habits and risk behaviors during early adolescence. *Journal of Broadcasting & Electronic Media, 52*, 349–367.

Kalyanaraman, S., & Sundar, S. S. (2008). Portrait of the portal as a metaphor: Explicating Web portals for communication research. *Journalism & Mass Communication Quarterly, 85*, 239–256.

Kim, Y. M., & Vishak, J. (2008). Just laugh! You don't need to remember: The effects of entertainment media on political information acquisition and information processing in political judgment. *Journal of Communication, 58*, 338–360.

Kitch, C. (2007). Mourning "men joined in peril and purpose": Working-class heroism in news repair of the Sago miners' story. *Critical Studies in Media Communication, 24*, 115–131.

Ksiazek, T. B., & Webster, J. G. (2008). Cultural proximity and audience behavior: The role of language in patterns of polarization and multicultural fluency. *Journal of Broadcasting & Electronic Media, 52*, 485–503.

Lang, A., & Yegiyan, N. S. (2008). Understanding the interactive effects of emotional appeal and claim strength in health messages. *Journal of Broadcasting & Electronic Media, 52*, 432–447.

Lauzen, M. M., Dozier, D. M., & Horan, N. (2008). Constructing gender stereotypes through social roles in prime-time television. *Journal of Broadcasting & Electronic Media, 52*, 200–214.

Lee, E.-J. (2008). Gender stereotyping of computers: Resource depletion or reduced attention? *Journal of Communication, 58*, 301–320.

Lee, J. H. (2008). Effects of news deviance and personal involvement on audience story selection: A web-tracking analysis. *Journalism & Mass Communication Quarterly, 85*(1), 41–60.

Lee, J. K. (2007). The effect of the Internet on homogeneity of the media agenda: A test of the fragmentation thesis. *Journalism & Mass Communication Quarterly, 84*, 745–760.

Lewis, N. P. (2008). Plagiarism antecedents and situational influences. *Journalism & Mass Communication Quarterly, 85*, 353–370.

Li, X. (2008). Third-person effect, optimistic bias, and sufficiency resource in Internet use. *Journal of Communication, 58*, 568–587.

Lim, J. S., & Ki, E.-J. (2007). Resistance to ethically suspicious parody video on YouTube: A test of inoculation theory. *Journalism & Mass Communication Quarterly, 84*, 713–728.

Mastro, D. E., & Ortiz, M. (2008). A content analysis of social groups in prime-time Spanish-language television. *Journal of Broadcasting & Electronic Media, 52*, 101–118.

Matthes, J. R., & Kohring, M. (2008). The content analysis of media frames: Toward improving reliability and validity. *Journal of Communication, 58*, 258–279.

McCluskey, M. (2008). Reporter beat and content differences in environmental stories. *Journalism & Mass Communication Quarterly, 85*, 83–98.

Moriarty, C. M., & Harrison, K. (2008). Television exposure and disordered eating among children: A longitudinal panel study. *Journal of Communication, 58*, 361–381.

Nabi, R. L., & Clark, S. (2008). Exploring the limits of social cognitive theory: Why negatively reinforced behaviors on TV may be modeled anyway. *Journal of Communication, 58*, 407–427.

Nabi, R. L., & Riddle, K. (2008). Personality traits, television viewing, and the cultivation effect. *Journal of Broadcasting & Electronic Media, 52*, 327–348.

Neuman, W. R., Davidson, R., Joo, S.-H., Park, Y. J., & Williams, A. E. (2008). The seven deadly sins of communication research. *Journal of Communication, 58*, 220–237.

Oliver, M. B. (2008). Tender affective states as predictors of entertainment preference. *Journal of Communication, 58*, 40–61.

Ozmun, D. (2008). Opportunity deferred: A 1952 case study of a woman in network television news. *Journal of Broadcasting & Electronic Media, 52*, 1–15.

Paek, H.-J. (2008). Mechanisms through which adolescents attend and respond to antismoking media campaigns. *Journal of Communication, 58*, 84–105.

Paek, H.-J., Lambe, J. L., & McLeod, D. M. (2008). Antecedents to support for content restrictions. *Journalism & Mass Communication Quarterly, 85*, 273–290.

Pfau, M., Haigh, M. M., Shannon, T., Tones, T., Mercurio, D., Williams, R., et al. (2008). The influence of television news depictions of the images of war on viewers. *Journal of Broadcasting & Electronic Media, 52*, 303–322.

Pinchevski, A., & Brand, R. (2007). Holocaust perversions: The Stalags pulp fiction and the Eichmann trial. *Critical Studies in Media Communication, 24*, 387–407.

Pitcher, K. (2006). The staging of agency in Girls Gone Wild. *Critical Studies in Media Communication, 23*, 200–218.

Porto, M. P. (2007). Frame diversity and citizen competence: Towards a critical approach to news quality. *Critical Studies in Media Communication, 24*, 303–321.

Rodino-Colocino, M. (2006). Selling women on PDAs from "Simply Palm" to "Audrey": How Moore's law met Parkinson's law in the kitchen. *Critical Studies in Media Communication, 23*, 375–390.

Rolland, A. (2008). Norwegian media policy objectives and the theory of a paradigm shift. *Journal of Communication, 58*, 126–148.

Russell, A. (2007). Digital communication networks and the journalistic field: The 2005 French riots. *Critical Studies in Media Communication, 24*, 285–302.

Schaefer, P. D., & Durham, M. G. (2007). On the social implications of invisibility: The iMac G5 and the effacement of the technological object. *Critical Studies in Media Communication, 24*, 39–56.

Scharrer, E. (2008). Media exposure and sensitivity to violence in news reports: Evidence of desensitization? *Journalism & Mass Communication Quarterly, 85*, 291–310.

Schwalbe, C. B., Silcock, B. W., & Keith, S. (2008). Visual framing of the early weeks of the U.S.-led invasion of Iraq: Applying the master war narrative to electronic and print images. *Journal of Broadcasting & Electronic Media, 52*, 448–465.

Shiga, J. (2007). Copy-and-persist: The logic of mash-up culture. *Critical Studies in Media Communication, 24*, 93–114.

Slattery, K., & Garner, A. C. (2007). Mothers of soldiers in wartime: A national news narrative. *Critical Studies in Media Communication, 24*, 429–445.

Spohrer, E. (2007). Becoming extra-textual: Celebrity discourse and Paul Robeson's political transformation. *Critical Studies in Media Communication, 24*, 151–168.

Steiner, L. (2007). Editorial: Calling a halt to further proliferation of journals. *Critical Studies in Media Communication, 24*(5), 383–386.

Sun, S., Rubin, A. M., & Haridakis, P. M. (2008). The role of motivation and media involvement in explaining Internet dependency. *Journal of Broadcasting & Electronic Media, 52*, 408–431.

Sun, Y., Pan, Z., & Shen, L. (2008). Understanding the third-person perception: Evidence from a meta-analysis. *Journal of Communication, 58*, 280–300.

Sung, Y., & Hennink-Kaminski, H. I. (2008). The master settlement agreement and visual imagery of cigarette advertising in two popular youth magazines. *Journalism & Mass Communication Quarterly, 85*, 331–352.

Sweetser, K. D., Porter, L. V., Soun Chung, D., & Eunseong, K. (2008). Credibility and the use of blogs among professionals in the communication industry. *Journalism & Mass Communication Quarterly, 85*, 169–185.

Sylvie, G., & Huang, J. S. (2008). Value systems and decision-making styles of newspaper front-line editors. *Journalism & Mass Communication Quarterly, 85*(1), 61–82.

Tan, Y., & Weaver, D. H. (2007). Agenda-setting effects among the media, the public, and Congress, 1946–2004. *Journalism & Mass Communication Quarterly, 84*, 729–744.

Tewksbury, D., Hals, M. L., & Bibart, A. (2008). The efficacy of news browsing: The relationship of news consumption style to social and political efficacy. *Journalism & Mass Communication Quarterly, 85*, 257–272.

Tsfati, Y., & Livio, O. (2008). Exploring journalists' perceptions of media impact. *Journalism & Mass Communication Quarterly, 85*, 113–130.

Uhm, K. (2008). The founders and the revolutionary underpinning of the concept of the right to know. *Journalism & Mass Communication Quarterly, 85*, 393–416.

van Dijck, J. (2006). Record and hold: Popular music between personal and collective memory. *Critical Studies in Media Communication, 23*, 357–374.

van Zoonen, L., Muller, F., Alinejad, D., Dekker, M., Duits, L., van Romondt Vis, P., et al. (2007). Dr. Phil meets the candidates: How family life and personal experience produce political discussions. *Critical Studies in Media Communication, 24*, 322–338.

Vavrus, M. D. (2007). The politics of NASCAR dads: Branded media paternity. *Critical Studies in Media Communication, 24*, 245–261.

Vishwanath, A. (2008). The 360° news experience: Audience connections with the ubiquitous news organization. *Journalism & Mass Communication Quarterly, 85*, 7–22.

Volcic, Z. (2007). Yugo-nostalgia: Cultural memory and media in the former Yugoslavia. *Critical Studies in Media Communication, 24*, 21–38.

Wan, H.-H. (2008). Resonance as a mediating factor accounting for the message effect in tailored communication: Examining crisis communication in a tourism context. *Journal of Communication, 58*, 472–489.

Warren, R., Wicks, R. H., Wicks, J. L., Fosu, I., & Chung, D. (2008). Food and beverage advertising on U.S. television: A comparison of child-targeted versus general audience commercials. *Journal of Broadcasting & Electronic Media, 52*, 231–246.

Weibel, D., Wissmath, B., & Groner, R. (2008). How gender and age affect newscasters' credibility: An investigation in Switzerland. *Journal of Broadcasting & Electronic Media, 52*, 466–484.

Wise, K., Bolls, P. D., & Schaefer, S. R. (2008). Choosing and reading online news: How available choice affects cognitive processing. *Journal of Broadcasting & Electronic Media, 52*, 69–85.

Wise, K., Lee, S., Lang, A., Fox, J. R., & Grabe, M. E. (2008). Responding to change on TV: How viewer-controlled changes in content differ from programmed changes in content. *Journal of Broadcasting & Electronic Media, 52*, 182–199.

Wu, H. D., & Izard, R. (2008). Representing the total community: Relationships between Asian American staff and Asian American coverage in nine U.S. newspapers. *Journalism & Mass Communication Quarterly, 85*, 99–112.

Yang, H., Ramasubramanian, S., & Oliver, M. B. (2008). Cultivation effects on quality of life indicators: Exploring the effects of American television consumption on feelings of relative deprivation in South Korea and India. *Journal of Broadcasting & Electronic Media, 52*, 247–267.

Zelizer, B. (2007). On "having been there": "Eyewitnessing" as a journalistic key word. *Critical Studies in Media Communication, 24*, 408–428.

Zhang, Y., Miller, L. E., & Harrison, K. (2008). The relationship between exposure to sexual music videos and young adults' sexual attitudes. *Journal of Broadcasting & Electronic Media, 52*, 368–386.

Glossary

Agency: The ability to do otherwise. The principle that at least humans have the capacity to be the sole source of their actions without precondition.

Analytical methods: Methods for constructing arguments based on a set of rules governing the relationship among types of propositions such as logic, legal proceedings, rhetoric, and criticism.

Argument: A discursive form containing all or some of the components of an initiating problem, a proposed resolution, and warrants for evidence—often implied evidence in support of the resolution, analysis of the evidence and its implications, and the conclusions justified by that warranted evidence and its analysis.

Atomism: The principle that surface manifestation of the material and ideational can be reduced to a set of foundational elements.

Attribute: A trait or characteristic of an object or a person.

Axiology: The study of value and values.

Axiom: A proposition that is held to be true without specific evidence for its truth.

Binomial data: Data that can take one of two values.

Boolean search operators: Terms used to describe literature search operators such as AND (requires both conditions), OR (either condition suffices), and NOT (excludes a subset of conditions).

Categorical data: Data that fit into mutually exclusive categories; also called nominal data.

Centrality: Following the central tendency.

Central tendency: The characteristic of repeated measurements on the same characteristic to coalesce around a central value, usually considered to be the true value of the characteristic.

Certified claim: A claim that has passed a strong test and consequently can be acted upon as if true. The highest level of claim validity. The claim is still open to falsification, however.

Character: Referring to the quality, value, encoded values, or social-cultural utility of a concept, construct, variable, text, symbolic representation, or the like. One of the four major foci of research and scholarship (properties, processes, consequences, and character).

Cognitivism: A family of psychological theories that holds to the existence of mental states and operations that direct behavior.

Composite variable: A construct that when used as a variable obtains its measured value from more than one source.

Connotation: Meanings that arise from the association of concepts, emotions, or values with particular signs.

Consequences: Referring to the results of some prior condition or action. One of the four major foci of research and scholarship (properties, processes, consequences, and character).

Consilience: The unity of knowledge. A principle in argument logic that the preponderance evidence will ultimately point to the correct solution.

Context: The surrounding conditions of a text's production or reception.

Contrasts: A term used in statistical analysis to describe a test for difference, usually among simple mean scores.

Co-orientation: Term used to describe a precondition of communication, indicating the need of communicants to be located in the same ideational space.

Correlation matrix: The set of correlations among three or more variables presented in a rows-by-columns display.

Critical, The: Refers to a form of scholarship that addresses discursive and symbolic forms to reveal the underlying structures, meanings, utilities, and the like.

Critical issue theories: Theories that focus on usually one of the cultural practices of race, gender, class, ethnicity, and the like.

Critical rationalism: A philosophy of science attributed to Karl Popper whose foundation is upon the critical review of claim by the community of science.

Critical rhetorical theory: The redirection of rhetorical analysis (the means of direct and indirect suasion) to the discourses of power, according to Raymie McKerrow, a leading proponent.

Critical theory: A set of theories attributed to the Frankfurt School that seeks human emancipation; the expansion of this set to any theory that reveals power and domination and seeks social transformation.

Cross-respondent effects: A term used to describe a source of bias in experimental protocols that occurs when the results can be attributed to differences between respondent groups rather than the treatment manipulation.

Database program: A software application that works as an interactive filing system. The advantage of such a program in coding text is that it will retrieve all units coded by any particular code.

Data set: The totality of measures used in analysis from a study.

Deductive: A logical form of argument that moves from the general to the specific in a set of propositions called a syllogism. In deductive metric research, theory is the major premise, the research protocol is the minor premise, and the hypothesized result is the conclusion to be supported or falsified.

Dependent variable: The variable in an experimental protocol whose value (presumably) depends on the treatment manipulation. The criterion measure.

Determinism: A philosophy of the material world that all things and events have a cause. Determinism denies agency.

Digitized text: A computerized text that can be accessed symbol by symbol as opposed to a picture of the text.

Emblematic: A term used in cultural analysis to describe practices or conditions closely associated with a cultural grouping.

Emergent: The term used to describe the process of generalization appropriate to interpretive methods.

Epistemology: The study of knowledge and knowledge production.

Etiology: The study of cause and causal relationships.

Experimental controls: Elements in an experimental protocol that serve to limit the effects of variables other than the treatment manipulation on the criterion measure.

False consciousness: A term in critical theory that refers to the state of mind by which the oppressed accept their domination.

Falsified claim: A claim that has failed a strong test.

Frankfurt School: Term used to identify a group of theorists situated in German idealism who argue that theory must be explanatory of social disparities, ethically practical in resolving them, and normative in advancing solutions to social injustice.

Hermeneutics: The study of interpretation.

Histogram: A graphic display of the frequency of possible values in a data set.

Holistic: A philosophy that social action has to be understood as a unit rather than the separate actions of individual members.

Hypothesis: The conclusion of a line of reasoning from theory to protocol to hypothesis. The expected outcome of a test.

Hypothesis testing: The practice of conducting research using deductive logic.

Inadvertent plagiarism: Writing that naïvely does not recognize its sources.

Independent variable: The variable in an experimental protocol that is manipulated to produce an effect in a criterion measure. Also the predictor variable in a modeled relationship.

Inductive: A form of argument that moves from the specific to the general. Philosophy generally rejects the possibility of a competent inductive method. A term sometimes (wrongly) used to describe the interpretive approach (see *emergent*).

Inferential testing: The use of statistical analysis to justify claims about the population from which the study's sample was ostensibly drawn.

Interpretation: Culturally governed semiosis. The active work of making sense of a sign, symbol, or text.

Interpretive empiricism: The analysis of empirical events, texts, actions, and the like through narrative logic for the purpose of creating public knowledge.

Interrespondent effects: See *cross-respondent effects*.

Intertextuality: The links a given media text draws to other media texts.

Intrarespondent effects: A term used to describe a source of bias in repeated measures; experimental protocols that occur when the results can be attributed to changes in the respondent (e.g., fatigue, boredom, recognition of manipulation) rather than the treatment manipulation.

Linear relationship: A relationship between two variables whose graph forms a straight line and that can be described in a linear equation.

Live text: A digitized text that can be read symbol by symbol on a computer.

Matrix data set: Data that are arranged in rows and columns. Conventionally, the rows are respondents, and the columns are items.

Mediascape: Referring to the ecology of texts, audiences, technologies, industries, economies, regulation, and legislation, as well as scholarship and research that constitutes the agents and environments of mediated communication.

Meta-analysis: The analysis of a body of work appearing on a common topic, usually by independent researchers.

Meta-communication: Communication about communication.

Methodological holism: An epistemological principle that holds that understanding is gained in the consideration of complete systems rather than in their parts.

Methodological individualism: An epistemological principle in psychological sciences that all claim has to be located in the individual.

Metric empiricism: A form of public knowledge production that relies on the engagement of the material and ideational world through quantification and metric logic.

Narrative: A logical form involving paradigmatic agents, syntagmatic actions, motives, values, and consequences, which constitute an account of some sort.

Narrative structure: The underlying patterns of plot, character, setting, and theme that shape the construction of stories.

Necessity clause: One of Mill's two canons of causation (sufficiency). The agent is required for the consequent to appear.

Normal distribution: Normal density distribution; normal curve. A theoretical distribution with known properties that is used to model probabilities for many parametric statistics.

Null hypothesis: The hypothesis of no difference, relationship, or effect that is the default but usually unintended outcome of a test.

Objective: A contested term based on the epistemological principle that the material world can be engaged and represented without bias.

Ontology: The study of existence.

Operational definition: The practice of defining a variable by the means of its measurement.

Operationalism: The principle that knowledge of any entity is gained only through its measurement.

Pair-wise data: Measurements that are collected from the same respondent and considered in sets of twos.

Paradigm: A cultural concept of an acting agent (hero, villain, victim). A system of knowledge production.

Pattern recognition: The gestalt of interpretation when the relationship among ostensibly independent entities can be described.

Performative: Of or through performance.

Praxeology: The study of action, practice, and performance.

Pre-post design: An experimental protocol in which measurements are taken before some treatment manipulation and then again after the manipulation has taken place. Any form of analysis where the difference between two administrations of the same measure is attributed to what happened in the intervening interval.

Private knowledge: An epistemological principle that individuals have direct, experiential knowledge. A system of claim based on authority.

Processes: Referring to a connected skein of acts and activities that constitute a recognizable endeavor. An action system. One of the four major foci of research and scholarship (properties, processes, consequences, and character).

Properties: Referring to the recognizable and/or measurable attributes of a material or ideational entity. One of the four major foci of research and scholarship (properties, processes, consequences, and character).

Provisional claim: A claim that has standing in the public process of knowledge production but has not yet been certified.

Public knowledge: Knowledge and claim that is subject to systematic public review by those authorized to conduct such reviews.

Q-matrix: A data matrix in which the respondents occupy the columns. Used to analyze the items.

Random-digit dialing: A technique for sampling telephone numbers designed to account for numbers not otherwise listed.

Random error: Error that occurs without systematic pattern or cause.

Reductionism: An epistemological principle that all surface manifestations can be explained at some lower level.

Reflexivity: A criterion of poststructuralist interpretive work. The act of writing the interpreter into the interpretation.

Representation: The act or claim of standing in for, or taking the place of, something else.

Research hypothesis: The alternate to the null hypothesis. The predicted outcome of a test.

Research question: The guiding premise in the design and analysis of a research study.

Response demand: A biasing effect of a protocol design that elicits one response over another.

Rhizomatic: A poststructuralist term used to describe the growth of knowledge. A metaphor connecting to the action of plants to spread through rhizomes, a root-like structure.

R-matrix: A data matrix in which the questions occupy the columns. The typical data matrix.

Sampling error: Deviations of the characteristics of a sample from the parameters of the population that the sample is intended to represent. Can be random or systematic.

Scalar data set: Data in a single row or column.

Semiosis: Any sign process. The ability to produce meaning from a sign.

Semiotic: Of or pertaining to meaning production.

Serendipity: A chance set of circumstances that leads to an insight or a discovery.

Settled science: An area of knowledge production that has been highly conventionalized.

Signification: The sociocultural generation of meaning achieved through the connection of signs and referents.

Simple means: Referring to the means that appear in the cells of a multifactorial design. Generally, the means for the smallest constructs in the design.

Social construction: An epistemological philosophy that holds that knowledge is produced and sustained in human practice and has no validation independent of human practice.

Structurations: A term presented by social theorist Anthony Giddens to describe the effect of practices to produce the necessary resources and infrastructures for their reproduction.

Sufficiency clause: One of Mill's two canons of causation (necessity). The agent is all that is needed for the consequent to appear.

Surrogate measure: A measure used to "stand in" for some other behavior; for example, a paper-and-pencil measure for the use of condoms.

Syntagm: A cultural concept of an action line (hero's quest, seduction, betrayal).

Synthetic variable: A variable that is produced in the research process, not naturally occurring.

Systematic error: Error that can be explained by some element in the research design.

Technological determinism: The attribution of social and cultural conditions to the technology of the social system.

Telegraphing: The biasing effect of a protocol that provides indications of what is wanted or expected from the respondent.

Transcendental: Referring to claim that rises above history.

Triangulation: A principle of navigation that the location of a point can be precisely located by measuring from two other points. As used in metric and mixed-methods research, it holds that a property can be more accurately described when measured by two different methods. Presumes the independence of all three elements.

Type I error: The acceptance of the research hypothesis when the null hypothesis is true.

Type II error: The acceptance of the null hypothesis when the research hypothesis is true.

Universalism: The principle that certain social, cultural, ethical, and other human properties are universal to the species. The default position of modernism and the objection of postmodernism.

Variable: A construct that can be entered into measurement.

Window of text: A procedure used in coding that defines the unit of analysis as a segment of text.

References

Alexander, A. F., & Potter, W. J. (Eds.). (2001). *How to publish your communication research: An insider's guide*. Thousand Oaks, CA: Sage.

Alexander, M. S. (2005). Dear Mr. President: Changing media environments and the social construction of the president. *Communication Review, 8*, 1–2.

Allen, M. (1999, September). The role of meta-analysis for connecting critical and scientific approaches: The need to develop a sense of collaboration. *Review and Criticism, 373–379*.

Altheide, D. L. (1996). *Qualitative media analysis*. Thousand Oaks, CA: Sage.

Althusser, L. (1969). *For Marx*. New York: Pantheon Books.

Anderson, J., & Anderson, B. (1993). The myth of persistence of vision revisited. *Journal of Film and Video, 45*, 3–12.

Anderson, J. A. (1996). *Communication theory: Epistemological foundations*. New York: Guilford.

Anderson, J. A. (2008a). Media literacy, the first 100 years: A cultural analysis. In J. K. Asamen, M. L. Ellis, & G. I. Berry (Eds.), *Handbook of child development, multiculturalism, and media* (pp. 381–410). Thousand Oaks, CA: Sage.

Anderson, J. A. (2008b). The production of media violence and aggression research: A cultural analysis. *American Behavioral Scientist, 51*, 1260–1279.

Anderson, J. A. (2008c). Thinking qualitatively: Hermeneutics in science. In D. W. Stacks & M. B. Salwen (Eds.), *An integrated approach to communication theory and research* (pp. 45–65). New York: Routledge.

Anderson, J. A., & Colvin, J. W. (2008a). Is it just science? In T. Grimes, J. A. Anderson, & L. Bergen (Eds.), *Media violence and aggression: Science and ideology* (pp. 93–152). Thousand Oaks, CA: Sage.

Anderson, J. A., & Colvin, J. W. (2008b). Media research 1900–1945. In D. Park & J. Pooley (Eds.), *The history of media and communication research* (pp. 321–344). New York: Peter Lang.

Anderson, J. A., & Colvin, J. W. (2010, June). *The textual analytics of foundational literature reviews*. Paper presented at the International Communication Association, Singapore.

Anderson, J. A., Colvin, J. W., & Osmond, A. (2008). *Communication pragmatics and symbolic science*. Paper presented at the Congress of the Americas II.

Anderson, J. A., & Englehardt, E. (2001). *The organizational self and ethical conduct*. New York: Wadsworth.

Anderson, P. J. (1991). *The printed image and the transformation of popular culture, 1790–1860*. New York: Oxford University Press.

Bakhtin, M. (1981). *The dialogic imagination: Four essays* (C. Emmerson & M. Holquist, Trans.). Austin: University of Texas Press.

Bandura, A., Ross, D., & Ross, S. A. (1963). Vicarious reinforcement and imitative learning. *Journal of Abnormal and Social Psychology, 67*(6), 601–607.

Barker, D. C., & Lawrence, A. B. (2006). Media favoritism and presidential nominations: Reviving the direct effects model. *Political Communication, 23*, 41–59.

Barthes, R. (1964). *Elements of semiology* (A. Lavers & C. Smith, Trans.). New York: Hill and Wang.

Barthes, R. (1972). *Mythologies* (A. Lavers, Trans.). New York: Hill and Wang.

Barthes, R. (1977). *Image, music, text* (S. Heath, Trans.). New York: Hill and Wang.

Baym, G. (2000). Constructing moral authority: We in the discourse of television news. *Western Journal of Communication, 64*(1), 92–112.

Baym, G. (2003). Strategies of illumination: U.S. network news, Watergate, and the Clinton affair. *Rhetoric & Public Affairs, 6*, 633–656.

Baym, G. (2004). Packaging reality: Structures of form in U.S. network news coverage of Watergate and the Clinton impeachment. *Journalism, 5*, 279–299.

Baym, G. (2005). *The Daily Show:* Discursive integration and the reinvention of critical journalism. *Political Communication, 22*, 259–276.

Baym, G. (2007). Representation and the politics of play: Stephen Colbert's *Better Know a District. Political Communication, 24*, 359–376.

Belsey, J. C, (2008). Media use and human values. *Journalism & Mass Communication Quarterly, 85*(2), 311–330.

Benoit, W. L., & McHale, J. P. (2003). Presidential candidates' television spots and personal qualities. *Southern Communication Journal, 68*, 319–334.

Berger, P. L., & Luckmann, T. (1967). *The social construction of reality.* New York: Doubleday.

Billings, A. C., Brown, C. L., Crout, J. H., McKenna, K. E., Rice, B. A., Timanus, M. E., et al. (2008). The games through the NBC lens: Gender, ethnic, and national equity in the 2006 Torino Winter Olympics. *Journal of Broadcasting & Electronic Media, 52*, 215–230.

Booth, P. (2008). Rereading fandom: MySpace character personas and narrative identification. *Critical Studies in Media Communication, 25*(5), 514–536.

Boyer, E. L. (1990). *Scholarship reconsidered: Priorities of the professoriate.* Princeton, NJ: Princeton University Press.

Boyer, E. L. (1996). The scholarship of engagement. *Bulletin of the American Academy of Arts and Sciences, 49*(7), 18–33.

British Association for the Advancement of Science. (2007, September 14). *Is social networking changing the face of friendship?* Retrieved May 5, 2011, from http://www.sciencedaily.com/releases/2007/09/070912161147.htm

Caracelli, V. J., & Greene, J. C. (1993). Data analysis strategies for mixed-method evaluation designs. *Educational Evaluation and Policy Analysis, 15*(2), 195–207.

Carey, J. W. (1988). *Communication as culture: Essays on media and society.* New York: Routledge.

Chatman, S. (1978). *Story and discourse: Narrative structure in fiction and film.* Ithaca, NY: Cornell University Press.

Comstock, G. (2008). A sociological perspective on television violence and aggression. *American Behavioral Scientist, 51*(8), 1184–1211.

Conquergood, D. (1985). Performing as a moral act: Ethical dimensions of the ethnography of performance. *Literature in Performance, 5*(2), 1–13.

Conquergood, D. (1991). Rethinking ethnography: Towards a critical cultural politics. *Communication Monographs, 59*, 179–194.

Conquergood, D. (2002). Performance studies: Interventions and radical research. *The Drama Review, 46*(2), 145–156.

Conrad, K., Dixon, T., & Zhang, Y. (2009). Controversial rap themes, gender portrayals and skin tone distortion: A content analysis of rap music videos. *Journal of Broadcasting & Electronic Media, 53*(1), 134–156.

Corbin, J., & Strauss, A. C. (2008). *Basics of qualitative research: Techniques and procedures for developing grounded theory* (3rd ed.). Thousand Oaks, CA: Sage.

Cova, B., & Pace, S. (2006). Brand community of convenience products: New forms of customer empowerment—the case "my Nutella The Community." *European Journal of Marketing, 40*(9/10), 1087–1105.

Creswell, J. W. (2003). *Research design: Qualitative, quantitative, and mixed methods approaches.* Thousand Oaks, CA: Sage.

Csikszentmihalyi, M., & Kubey, R. (1981). Television and the rest of life: A systematic comparison of subjective experience. *Public Opinion Quarterly, 45,* 317–328.

Davis, A. (2009). Journalist-source relations, mediated reflexivity and the politics of politics. *Journalism Studies, 10*(2), 204–219.

de Certeau, M. (1984). *The practice of everyday life.* Berkeley: University of California Press.

de Saussure, F. (1986). *Course in general linguistics* (R. Harris, Trans.). Peru, IL: Open Court.

Denham, B. (2008). Folk devils, news icons and the construction of moral panics: Heroin chic and the amplification of drug threats in contemporary society. *Jounalism Studies, 9*(6), 945–961.

Denzin, N. K. (2003). *Performance ethnography: Critical pedagogy and the politics of culture.* Thousand Oaks, CA: Sage.

Denzin, N. K., & Lincoln, Y. (Eds.). (2000). *Handbook of qualitative research* (2nd ed.). London: Sage.

Doherty, R., & Barnhurst, K. G. (2009). Controlling nature: Weathercasts on local television news. *Journal of Broadcasting & Electronic Media, 53*(2), 211–226.

Domingo, D. (2008). Interactivity in the daily routines of online newsrooms: Dealing with an uncomfortable myth. *Journal of Computer-Mediated Communication, 13,* 680–704.

Dordick, G., & Rachlin, S. (1997). Television in the lives of the homeless. *Communicaton Review, 2*(2), 163–179.

Eadie, W. F. (1985). *Rhetorical force and the study of organizational communication.* Paper presented at the Western Speech Communication Association, Fresno, CA, February 16–19.

Eagleton, T. (2008). *Literary theory: An introduction.* Minneapolis: University of Minnesota Press.

Eco, U. (1992). *Interpretation and overinterpretation* (S. Collini, Ed.). Cambridge, UK: Cambridge University Press.

Edelman, M. (1964). *The symbolic uses of politics.* Urbana: University of Illinois Press.

Edelman, M. (1971). *Politics as symbolic action: Mass arousal and quiescence.* Chicago: Markham.

Edgar, A., & Sedgwick, P. (2005). *Cultural theory: The key concepts* (2nd ed.). New York: Routledge.

Eisenstein, S. (1992). A dialectic approach to film form. In G. Mast, M. Cohen, & L. Braudy (Eds.), *Film theory and criticism* (pp. 138–154). New York: Oxford University Press.

Esser, F. (2009). Metacoverage of mediated wars: How the press framed the role of the news media and of military news management in the Iraq wars of 1991 and 2003. *American Behavioral Scientist, 52*(5), 709–734.

Fish, S. (1980). *Is there a text in this class?* Cambridge, MA: Harvard University Press.

Fisher, W. (1987). *Human communication as narration: Toward a philosophy of reason, value, and action.* Columbia: University of South Carolina Press.

Foucault, M. (1972). *The archaeology of knowledge* (A.M. Sheridan Smith, Trans.). New York: Pantheon Books.

Fowers, B. J., & Richardson, F. C. (1993). A hermeneutic analysis of Huesmann and Eron's cognitive theory of aggression. *Theory & Psychology, 3*(3), 351–374.

Fowler, R. B. (1938). Motion picture shows and school girls. *Journal of Applied Sociology, 3*(1), 76–83.

Franke, G. R. (1992, May). Book review DSTAT: Software for the meta-analytic review of research literatures. *Journal of Marketing Research,* 276–279.

Freimuth, V. S., Massett, H. A., & Meltzer, W. (2006). A descriptive analysis of 10 years of research published in the *Journal of Health Communication. Journal of Health Communication, 11,* 11–20.

Fullagar, C. J., & Kelloway, E. K. (2009). "Flow" at work: An experience sampling approach. *Journal of Occupational and Organizational Psychology, 82,* 595–615.

Fuller, S. (1997). "Rhetoric of science": Double the trouble. In A. G. Gross & W. M. Keith (Eds.), *Rhetorical hermeneutics: Invention and interpretation in the age of science* (pp. 279–298). Albany: State University of New York Press.

Fürisch, E. (2009). In defense of textual analysis: Restoring a challenged method for journalism and media studies. *Journalism Studies, 10*(2), 238–252.

Garfinkel, H. (1967). *Studies in ethnomethodology.* Englewood Cliffs, NJ: Prentice-Hall.

Garnham, N. (1995). Political economy and cultural studies: Reconciliation or divorce? *Critical Studies in Mass Communication, 12,* 62–71.

Gerbner, G., & Gross, L. (1976). Living with television: The violence profile. *Journal of Communication, 26*(2), 172–199.

Giddens, A., & Pierson, C. (1998). *Conversation with Anthony Giddens: Making sense of modernity.* Cambridge, UK: Polity Press.

Giles, W. F., & Feild, H. S. (1978). Effects of amount, format, and location of demographic information on questionnaire return rate and response bias of sensitive and nonsensitive items. *Personnel Psychology, 31,* 549–559.

Glaser, B. G. (1992). *Basics of grounded theory analysis: Emergence vs. forcing.* Mill Valley, CA: Sociology Press.

Glaser, B. G., & Strauss, A. L. (1967). *The discovery of grounded theory: Strategies for qualitative research.* Chicago: Aldine.

Goffman, E. (1959). *The presentation of self in everyday life.* Garden City, NY: Doubleday.

Grabe, M. E., Kamhawi, R., & Yegiyan, N. (2009). Informing citizens: How people with different levels of education process television, newspaper and web news. *Journal of Broadcasting & Electronic Media, 53*(1), 90–111.

Greene, J. C., Caracelli, V. J., & Graham, W. F. (1989). Toward a conceptual framework for mixed-method evaluation designs. *Educational Evaluation and Policy Analysis, 11,* 255–274.

Grimes, J., Anderson, J. A., & Bergen, L. A. (2008). *Media violence and aggression: Science and ideology.* Thousand Oaks, CA: Sage.

Gross, A. G. (1990). *Rhetoric of science.* Cambridge, MA: Harvard University Press.

Grossberg, L. (1995). Cultural studies vs. political economy: Is anybody else bored with this debate? *Critical Studies in Mass Communication, 12,* 72–81.

Haigh, M. M., Pfau, M., Danesi, J., Talmon, R., Bunk, T., Nyberg, S., et al. (2006). A comparison of embedded and nonembedded print coverage of the U.S. invasion and occupation of Iraq. *The Harvard International Journal of Press/Politics, 11*(2), 139–153.

Hakam, J. (2009). The "cartoons controversy": A critical discourse analysis of English-language Arab newspaper discourse. *Discourse & Society, 20*(1), 33–57.

Hall, A. (2006). Viewer's perceptions or reality programs. *Communication Quarterly, 54*(2), 191–211.

Hall, S. (1975). Introduction. In A. C. H. Smith, E. Immirzi, & T. Blackwell (Eds.), *Paper voices: The popular press and social change, 1935–1965* (pp. 11–24). Totowa, NJ: Rowman & Littlefield.

Hall, S. (1982). The rediscovery of "ideology": Return of the repressed in media studies. In T. Bennett, J. Curran, M. Gurevitch, & J. Woollacott (Eds.), *Culture, society and the media* (pp. 56–90). London: Methuen.

Hall, S. (1997). *Representation: Cultural representations and signifying practices.* Thousand Oaks, CA: Sage.

Hart, C. (2001). *Doing a literature search: A comprehensive guide for the social sciences.* London: Sage.

Haumer, F., & Donsbach, W. (2009). The rivalry of nonverbal cues on the perception of politicians by television viewers. *Journal of Broadcasting & Electronic Media, 53*(2), 262–279.

Hester, J. B., & Dougall, E. (2007). The efficiency of constructed week sampling for content analysis of online news. *Journalism & Mass Communication Quarterly, 84*(4), 818–824.

Hetsroni, A. (2007a). Four decades of violent content on prime-time network programming: A longitudinal meta-analytic review. *Journal of Communication, 57,* 759–784.

Hetsroni, A. (2007b). Three decades of sexual content on prime-time network programming: A longitudinal meta-analytic review. *Journal of Communication, 57,* 318–348.

Hetsroni, A. (2008). Overrepresented topics, underrepresented topics, and the cultivation effect. *Communication Research Reports, 25*(3), 200–210.

Hofstede, G. (1983). National cultures revisited. *Behavior Science Research, 18*(4), 285–305.

Hoggart, R. (1970). *Speaking to each other: About literature* (Vol. 2). London: Chatto and Windus.

Hoyle, R. H., Stephenson, M. T., Palmgreen, P., Lorch, E., & Donohew, L. (2002). Reliability and validity of a brief measure of sensation seeking. *Personality and Individual Differences, 32,* 401–414.

Jackson, C., Brown, J. D., & Pardun, C. J. (2009). A TV in the bedroom: Implications for viewing habits and risk behaviors during early adolescence. *Journal of Broadcasting & Electronic Media, 52*(3), 349–367.

Johnson, A. J., Haigh, M. M., Becker, J. A. H., Craig, E. A., & Wigley, S. (2008). College students' use of relational management strategies in email in long-distance and geographically close relationships. *Journal of Computer-Mediated Communication, 13,* 381–404.

Johnson, B. J., & Onwuegbuzie, A. J. (2004). Mixed methods research: A research paradigm whose time has come. *Educational Researcher, 33*(7), 14–26.

Johnson, T. J., Bichard, S. L., & Zhang, W. (2009). Communication communities or "CyberGhettos"?: A path analysis model examining factors that explain selective exposure to blogs. *Journal of Computer-Mediated Communication, 15,* 60–82.

Johnstone, B. (1991). Individual style in an American public opinion survey: Personal performance and the ideology of referentiality. *Language in Society, 20,* 557–576.

Josselson, R. (2006). Narrative research and the challenge of accumulating knowledge. *Narrative Inquiry, 16*(1), 3–10.

Kendall, J. (1999). Axial coding and the grounded theory controversy. *Western Journal of Nursing Research, 21*(6), 743–757.

Kennedy, M. M. (2007). Defining a literature. *Educational Researcher, 36*(3), 139–147.

Keyton, J. (2006). *Communication research: Asking questions, finding answers* (2nd ed.). New York: McGraw-Hill.

Kinross, R. (2005). The claim of reason: A twenty-five year argument about information design. *Information Design Journal + Document Design, 13*(3), 211–215.

Kozinets, R. V. (2002). The field behind the screen: Using netnography for marketing research in online communities. *Journal of Marketing Research, 39,* 61–72.

Kozinets, R. W. (2006). Click to connect: Netnography and tribal advertising. *Journal of Advertising Research 46*(3), 279–288.

Krippendorff, K. (2004). *Content analysis: An introduction to its methodology* (2nd ed.). Thousand Oaks, CA: Sage.

Kubey, R., Larson, R., & Csikszentmihalyi, M. (1996). Experience sampling method applications to communication research questions. *Journal of Communication, 46*(23), 99–120.

Kwan, B. S. C. (2006). The schematic structure of literature reviews in doctoral theses of applied linguistics. *English for Specific Purposes, 25,* 30–55.

Landrum, R. E. (2008). Bringing the audience up to speed with literature reviews. *Undergraduate Writing in Psychology,* 89–104.

Latour, B., & Woolgar, S. (1986). *Laboratory life: The construction of scientific facts.* Princeton, NJ: Princeton University Press.

Lavrakas, P. J., Shuttles, C. D., Steeh, C., & Fienberg, H. (2007). The state of surveying cell phone numbers in the United States: 2007 and beyond. *Public Opinion Quarterly, 71*(5), 840–854.

Lee, E.-J. (2005).Wired for gender: Experientiality and gender-stereotyping in computer-mediated communication. *Media Psychology, 10,* 182–210.

Liebler, C. M., Schwartz, J., & Harper, T. (2009). Queer tales of morality: The press, same-sex marriage, and hegemonic framing. *Journal of Communication, 59*, 653–675.

Lindlof, T. R., & Taylor, B. C. (2002). *Qualitative communication research methods* (2nd ed.). Thousand Oaks, CA: Sage.

Lunt, P., & Livingstone, S. (1996). Rethinking the focus group in media and communications research. *Journal of Communication, 46*(2), 79–98.

Madison, D. S. (2005). *Critical ethnography: Methods, ethics, and performance.* Thousand Oaks, CA: Sage.

Markham, A., & Baym, N. (2009). *Internet inquiry: Conversations about method.* Thousand Oaks, CA: Sage.

Matthes, J., & Kohring, M. (2008). The content analysis of media frames: Toward improving reliability and validity. *Journal of Communication, 58*, 258–279.

Mayer, V. (2003). *Producing dreams, consuming youth: Mexican-Americans and mass media.* New Brunswick, NJ: Rutgers University Press.

Mayer, V. (2005). Living telenovelas/telenovelizing life: Mexican-American girls' identities and transnational telenovelas. *Journal of Communication, 53*(3), 479–495.

McKinney, M. S., & Rill, L. A. (2009). Not your parents' presidential debates: Examining the effects of the CNN/YouTube debates on young citizens' civic engagement. *Communication Studies, 60*(4), 392–406.

McMillan, S. J., Hoy, M. G., Kim, J., & McMahan, C. (2008). A multifaceted tool for a complex phenomenon: Coding web-based interactivity as technologies for interaction evolve. *Journal of Computer-Mediated Communication, 13*, 794–826.

Merrill, R. M., & Heathers, L. B. (1954). The adjective check list as a measure of adjustment. *Journal of Counseling Psychology, 1*, 137–143.

Metz, C. (1990). *Film language: A semiotics of the cinema* (M. Taylor, Trans.). Chicago: University of Chicago Press.

Meyer, M., & Zucker, L. G. (1989). *Permanently failing organizations.* Thousand Oaks, CA: Sage.

Middleton, M., Senda-Cook, S., & Endres, D. (in press). Articulating rhetorical field methods: Challenges and tensions. *Western Journal of Communication.*

Mitra, A., & Cohen, E. (1999). Analyzing the web: Directions and challenges. In S. Jones (Ed.), *Doing Internet research: Critical issues and methods for examining the net* (pp. 179–202). Thousand Oaks, CA: Sage.

Molyneaux, H., O'Donnell, S., Gibson, K., & Singer, J. (2008). Exploring the gender divide on YouTube: An analysis of the creation and reception of vlogs. *American Communication Journal, 10*(1). Retrieved April 30, 2011, from http://ac-journal.org/journal/2008/Spring/3GenderandYoutube.pdf

Moser, M. A. (2009). Text "superpowers": A study of computers in homeless shelters. *Science, Technology & Human Values, 34*(6), 705–740.

Murdock, G. (1995). Across the great divide: Cultural analysis and the condition of democracy. *Critical Studies in Mass Communication, 12*, 89–95.

Myin-Germeys, L., Oorschot, M., Collip, D., Lataster, J., Delespaul, P., & van Os, J. (2009). Experience sampling research in psychopathology: Opening the black box of daily life. *Psychological Medicine, 39*, 1533–1547.

Newcomb, H. (1978). Assessing the violence profile studies of Gerbner and Gross: A humanistic critique and suggestion. *Communication Research, 5*, 264–282.

Newell, A., & Simon, H. A. (1972). *Human problem solving.* Englewood Cliffs, NJ: Prentice-Hall.

Noblit, G. W., Flores, S. Y., & Murillo, E. G. J. (2004). *Postcritical ethnography: An introduction.* Cresskill, NJ: Hampton.

Noelle-Neumann, E. (1974). The spiral of silence: A theory of public opinion. *Journal of Communication, 24*, 43–51.

Osgood, C. E., Suci, G. J., & Tannenbaum, P. H. (1957). *The measurement of meaning.* Chicago: University of Illinois Press.

Palmgreen, P., Donohew, L., Lorch, E., Rogus, M., Helm, D., & Grant, N. (1991). Sensation seeking, message sensation value, and drug use as mediators of PSA effectiveness. *Health Communication, 3,* 217–234.

Palmgreen, P., Stephenson, M. T., Everett, M. S., Baseheart, J. R., & Francies, R. (2002). Perceived message sensation value (PMSV) and the dimensions and validation of a PMSV scale. *Health Communication, 14,* 403–428.

Patton, M. Q. (2002). Two decades of developments in qualitative inquiry: A personal, experiential perspective. *Qualitative Social Work, 1*(3), 261–283.

Peterson, J. L. (2009). "You have to be positive." Social support processes of an online support group for men living with HIV. *Communication Studies, 60*(5), 526–541.

Petticrew, M., & Gilbody, S. (2004). Planning and conducting systematic reviews. In S. Michie & C. Abraham (Eds.), *Health psychology in practice* (pp. 150–179). Oxford, UK: Wiley-Blackwell.

Pinter, S., & Nielsen, G. (1990). Intimacy and cultural crisis. *Candian Journal of Political and Social Theory, 14*(1), 69–86.

Potter, W. J., & Tomasello, T. K. (2003). Building upon the experimental design in media violence research: The importance of including receiver interpretations. *Journal of Communication, 53*(2), 315–329.

Prelli, L. J. (1989). *A rhetoric of science.* Columbia: University of South Carolina Press.

Propp, V. (1968). *The morphology of the folktale* (L. Scott, Trans.). Austin: University of Texas Press. (Original work published 1928)

Radway, J. (1984). *Reading the romance.* Chapel Hill: University of North Carolina Press.

Riffe, D., Lacy, S., & Fico, F. G. (1998). *Analyzing media messages: Using quantitative content analysis in research.* Mahwah, NJ: Lawrence Erlbaum Associates.

Rocco, T. S., & Plakhotnik, M. S. (2009). Literature reviews, conceptual frameworks, and theoretical frameworks: Terms, functions, and distinctions. *Human Resource Development Review, 8*(1), 120–130.

Rodino-Colocino, M. (2006). Selling women on PDAs from "Simply Palm" to "Audrey": How Moore's law met Parkinson's law in the kitchen. *Critical Studies in Media Communication, 23,* 375–390.

Rogelberg, S. G., Adelman, M., & Askay, D. (2009). Crafting a successful manuscript: Lessons from 131 reviews. *Journal of Business Psychology, 24,* 117–121.

Rogers, L. E., & Escudero, V. (2004). *Relational communication: An interaction perspective to the study of process and form.* Mahwah, NJ: Lawrence Erlbaum Associates.

Rudestam, K. E., & Newton, R. R. (2001). *Surviving your dissertation: A comprehensive guide to content and process* (2nd ed.). Thousand Oaks, CA: Sage.

Ryfe, D. M. (2009). Broader and deeper: A study of newsroom culture in a time of change. *Journalism, 10*(2), 197–216.

Said, E. L. (1983). *The world, the text, and the critic.* Cambridge, MA: Harvard University Press.

Salwen, M. (2000). Book review: Morton Hunt—*How science takes stock: The story of meta-analysis. World Communication,* 87–89.

Schmitt, K. L., & Anderson, D. R. (2002). Television and reality: Toddlers' use of visual information from video to guide behavior. *Media Psychology, 4,* 51–76.

Schultz, B., & Sheffer, M. L. (2008). Left behind: Local television and the community of sport. *Western Journal of Communication, 72*(2), 180–195.

Semetko, H. A., & Valkenburg, P. M. (2000). Framing European politics: A content analysis of press and television news. *Journal of Communication, 50,* 93–109.

Shadbolt, N., Motta, E., & Rouge, A. (1993, November). Constructing knowledge-based systems. *IEEE Software, 10,* 34–39.

Shank, G., & Villella, O. (2004). Building on new foundations: Core principles and new directions for qualitative research. *The Journal of Educational Research, 98*(1), 46–55.

Shapin, S. (1995). Here and everywhere: Sociology of scientific knowledge. *Annual Review of Sociology*, 289–321.

Sherif, M. (1936). *The psychology of social norms*. New York: Harper.

Shugart, H. A. (2003). Reinventing privilege: The new (gay) man in contemporary popular media. *Critical Studies in Media Communication, 20*, 67–91.

Simmel, G. (1949). The sociology of sociability (E. C. Hughes, Trans.). *The American Journal of Sociology, 55*(3), 254–261.

Smith, A. C. H., Immirzi, E., & Blackwell, T. (Eds.). (1975). *Paper voices: The popular press and social change 1935–1965*. Totowa, NJ: Rowman & Littlefield.

Smith, D. (1990). *Texts, facts and femininity: Exploring the relations of ruling*. London: Routledge.

Smith, R. A., & Boster, F. J. (2009). Understanding the influence of others on perceptions of a message's advocacy: Testing a two-step model. *Communication Monographs, 76*(3), 333–350.

Steinberg, M. W. (1993). Rethinking ideology: A dialogue with Fine and Sanstrom from a dialogic perspective. *Sociological Theory, 11*(3), 314–320.

Steinberg, M. W. (1999). The talk and back talk of collective action: A dialogic analysis of repertoires of discourse among nineteenth-century English cotton spinners. *The American Journal of Sociology, 105*(3), 736–780.

Steinberg, M. W. (2002). *Social movements*. New York: Oxford University Press.

Stephen, T., & Geel, R. (2007). Normative publication productivity of communication scholars at selected career milestones. *Human Communication Research, 33*, 103–118.

Strauss, A. C. (1987). *Qualitative analysis for social scientists*. Cambridge, UK: Cambridge University Press.

Strauss, A. C., & Corbin, J. (1990). *Basics of qualitative research: Grounded theory procedures and techniques*. Newbury Park, CA: Sage.

Tashakkori, A., & Teddlie, C. (Eds.). (2010). *Handbook of mixed methods in social & behavioral research* (2nd ed.). Thousand Oaks, CA: Sage.

Taylor, J. R., & Van Every, E. J. (2000). *The emergent organization: Communication as its site and surface*. Mahwah, NJ: Lawrence Erlbaum Associates.

Taylor, L. D. (2005). Effects of visual and verbal sexual television content and perceived realism on attitudes and beliefs. *Journal of Sex Research, 42*(2), 130–137.

Taylor, P. J. (2002). A cylindrical model of communication behavior in crisis negotiations. *Human Communication Research, 28*(1), 7–48.

Taylor, P. J., & Donald, I. (2004). The structure of communication behavior in simulated and actual crisis negotiations. *Human Communication Research, 30*(4), 443–478.

Thompson, B. (2008). Characteristics of parent-teacher e-mail communication. *Communication Education, 57*(2), 201–223.

Todorov, T. (1969). Structural analysis of narrative. *Novel: A Forum on Fiction, 3*, 70–76.

Toulmin, S. (1963, May). Science and our intellectual tradition. *Advancement of Science, 20*, 28–34.

Trumbo, C. W. (2004). Research methods in mass communication research: A census of eight journals 1990–2000. *Journalism & Mass Communication Quarterly, 81*(2), 417–436.

Tutt, D. (2008a). "Tactical" living: A situated study of teenagers' negotiations around and interactions with living room media. *Environment and Planning, 40*, 2330–2345.

Tutt, D. (2008b). Where the interaction is: Collisions of the situated and mediated in living room interactions. *Qualitative Inquiry, 14*(7), 1157–1179.

U.S. Census Bureau. (2006, October). *Current Population Survey: Design and methodology* (Technical paper 66). Washington, DC: Author.

Van Someren, M. W., Barnard, Y. F., & Sandberg, J. A. C. (1994). *The think aloud method*. London: Academic Press.

Weaver, A. J., & Wilson, B. J. (2009). The role of graphic and sanitized violence in the enjoyment of television dramas. *Human Communication Research, 35,* 442–463.

Weinberger, S. (2004). It's not easy being pink: Tarantino's ultimate professional. *Literature and Film Quarterly, 32*(1), 46–50.

Wolf, D. (2007, November 19). What is television these days. *Broadcasting & Cable,* p. 38.

Wood, R. (2011). *Hypertext and ethnographic representation: A case study.* Unpublished doctoral dissertation, University of Utah, Salt Lake City.

Yanovitzky, I., & Capella, J. N. (2001). Effect of call-in political talk radio shows on their audiences: Evidence from a multi-wave panel analysis. *International Journal of Public Opinion Research, 13*(4), 377–397.

Yim, J. (2003). Audience concentration in the media: Cross-media comparisons and the introduction of the uncertainty measure. *Communication Monographs, 70*(2), 114–128.

Yin, A. M. Y., & Tong, A. H. M. (2007). Text-messaging cultures of college girls in Hong Kong: SMS as resources for achieving intimacy and gift-exchange with multiple functions. *Continuum: Journal of Media & Cultural Studies, 21*(2), 303–315.

Zettl, H. (2010). *Sight, sound, motion: Applied media aesthetics.* Belmont, CA: Wadsworth.

Zillmann, D. (1991). Television viewing and physiological arousal. In J. Bryant & D. Zillmann (Eds.), *Responding to the screens: Reception and reaction processes* (pp. 103–133). Hillsdale, NJ: Erlbaum.

Zorn, T. E., Roper, J., Broadfoot, K., & Weaver, C. K. (2006). Focus groups as sites of influential interaction: Building communicative self-efficacy and effecting attitudinal change in discussing controversial topics. *Journal of Applied Communication Research, 34*(2), 115–140.

Zuckerman, M. (1979). *Sensation seeking beyond the optimal level of arousal.* Hillsdale, NJ: Lawrence Erlbaum Associates.

Zuckerman, M. (1994). *Behavioral expression and biosocial bases of sensation seeking.* New York: Cambridge University Press.

Index

About the Authors

James A. Anderson, PhD (University of Iowa), is a professor of communication and the director of the Center for Communication and Community in the Department of Communication at the University of Utah. He is the author, coauthor, or editor of 17 books. His more than 100 chapters, articles, and research monographs are in the areas of family studies, cultural studies, media literacy, organizational studies, communicative ethics, methodology, and epistemology. Professor Anderson has been recognized as a "Master Teacher" by the Western States Communication Association and was recently given the Distinguished Scholar Award by the Broadcast Education Association. He is a Fellow of the International Communication Association and an active consultant in university administration, distance learning, and applied technology.

Geoffrey Baym, PhD (University of Utah), the author of Chapter 14 in this book, is an associate professor of media studies at the University of North Carolina at Greensboro. He is the author of the award-winning *From Cronkite to Colbert: The Evolution of Broadcast News* (2010), which traces a trajectory from the dominance of the nightly news of the high-network era to the increasing influence of the satirical newsmen Jon Stewart and Stephen Colbert. His writings on the changing nature of news, public affairs media, and political discourse also have appeared in numerous scholarly journals and anthologies. Currently he is coediting the forthcoming collection *News Parody and Political Satire Across the Globe* (forthcoming 2012).

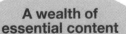